BEST CHOICES ALONG THE GREAT LAKES

Volume 1

Lake Erie, Lake Ontario, U.S.
Niagara, U.S. & Canada

by Alan Diede

Published in the U.S.A.

Best Choices Staff:

Alan Diede. . . Publisher
Maryann Huk. . . Managing Editor

Ohio, Pennsylvania, New York, and Ontario
Field Staff:

Suzan Glenn, Robert Villella. . . Production Managers
Suzan Glenn, Robert Villella, Peter Heavern,
Jane Kabai, Robin Caylor. . . Travel Writers

Editorial Staff:

Tracey M. Shank, Christina L. Fertig,
Linnea A. Jernstrom. . . Editors

Christina L. Fertig, Linnea A. Jernstrom,
Tracey M. Shank, Kathy Haskell, Jerry Haughey, Dawn Wonderling, Jerry Marshall. . . Staff Writers

Laura A. Petras, Patricia A. Dailey. . . Computer Design and Layout

Artwork:
Michael O. Cutruzzula. . . Graphics, Cover, and Maps

Cover Photo: Curtis Balog & State of Ohio
Travel and Tourism Division

Administration:

Julie Lynn Harris. . . Administration
Tracey M. Shank. . . Publicity, Public Relations

Library of Congress Catalog Number: 89-085288
ISBN 1-877912-02-6 First Edition: 1990

Best Choice Series:

Best Choices on the Oregon Coast (not in print)
Best Choices in Portland
Best Choices in Southern California / Bay Area Edition
Best Choices in Northern California
Best Choices in Western Washington
Best Choices in Orange County
Best Choices in Arizona
Best Choices in Colorado
Best Choices in San Diego
Best Choices in Sacramento
Best Choices in the Tampa Bay Area
Best Choices in Central and Southeast Texas
Best Choices in the Seattle-Tacoma Area
Best Choices in Eastern Washington
Best Choices in New Mexico
Best Choices in Alaska
Best Choices in Idaho
Best Choices in Los Angeles
Best Choices on the California Coast
Best Choices in St. Louis
Best Choices in Atlanta
Best Choices in Utah
Best Choices in Ohio
Best Choices in Pittsburgh and Western Pennsylvania
Best Choices Along the Great Lakes Vol. 1, Lake Erie and Lake Ontario

For additional copies, write or call:
Monongahela Publishing
541 Fifth Avenue
McKeesport, PA 15132
1-800-777-9930

This book is dedicated to my brother, Michael,whose help and generosity have been so very important to this publication. It is also dedicated to the good people of the Great Lakes, and to their abundant good will and to their pride in their wonderful region.

Acknowledgements

I wish to acknowledge the tremendous help of the entire "Great Lakes" staff, and especially from Suzan Glenn, Robert Villella, and, of course, Maryann Huk. All have contributed mightily to this publication, and all have my never-ending gratitude.

FOREWORD

Since their beginnings at the end of the last glacial age, these Great Fresh Water Seas have proven to be amongst the awesome phenomenons of the natural world. These two easternmost lakes were, by their very location, subjected to the excesses and ignorances of those of Old World heritage that settled on these shores. In this age when we are becoming fully aware of the folly of excess and the consequences of pollution, it is important to spotlight and applaud those places where the damage has been stopped and the healing hand of nature has reconstructed what was lost. Much more has yet to be done, and the threats to the Great Lakes have not yet completely ceased. However, if all those other places on the planet awaiting the constraint of reason and the end of pollution could enjoy these Great Lakes' refreshing revival, then the job of repairing this abused world would be a quick and happy one.

Therefore, please be our guests, and enjoy this rich, fascinating, and unique region, and all it has to offer.

Alan Diede

DISCLAIMER

Not all, but many of the businesses featured in "Best Choices" have subscribed to the project in advance of publication. Their participation in promoting this book includes acquiring copies of this publication for their own business purposes. This subscription was not mandatory for inclusion, and promotional consideration alone is not enough for selection as a "Best Choice." Most of these "Best Choices" were recommended by other "Best Choices," including those in the same category of business. All "Best Choices" were personally visited by one of our Travel Writers, and our report on each one is based on first-hand experience.

TABLE OF CONTENTS

SECTION THREE: LAKE ERIE N.Y.
NIAGARA U.S.A. - CANADA

SECTION FOUR: LAKE ONTARIO, N.Y.

LAKE ERIE

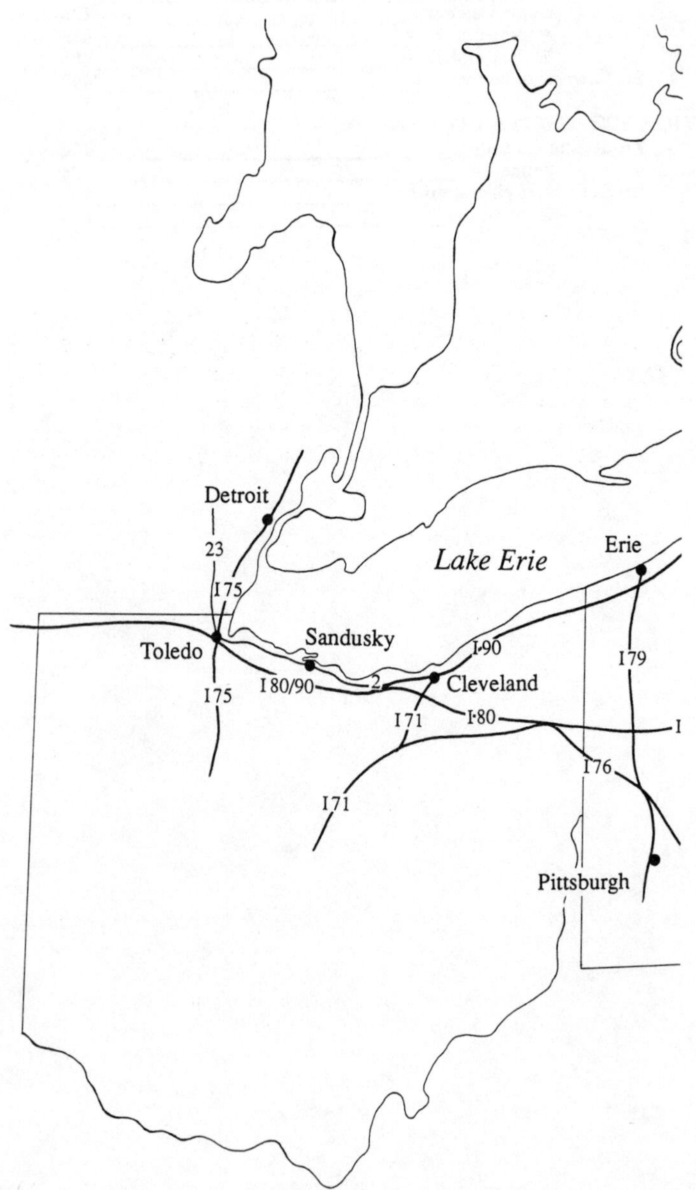

Detroit
23
I 75
Lake Erie
Erie
Toledo
Sandusky
I·90
I 79
I 75
I 80/90
2
Cleveland
I 71
I·80
I 76
I 71
Pittsburgh

LAKE ONTARIO

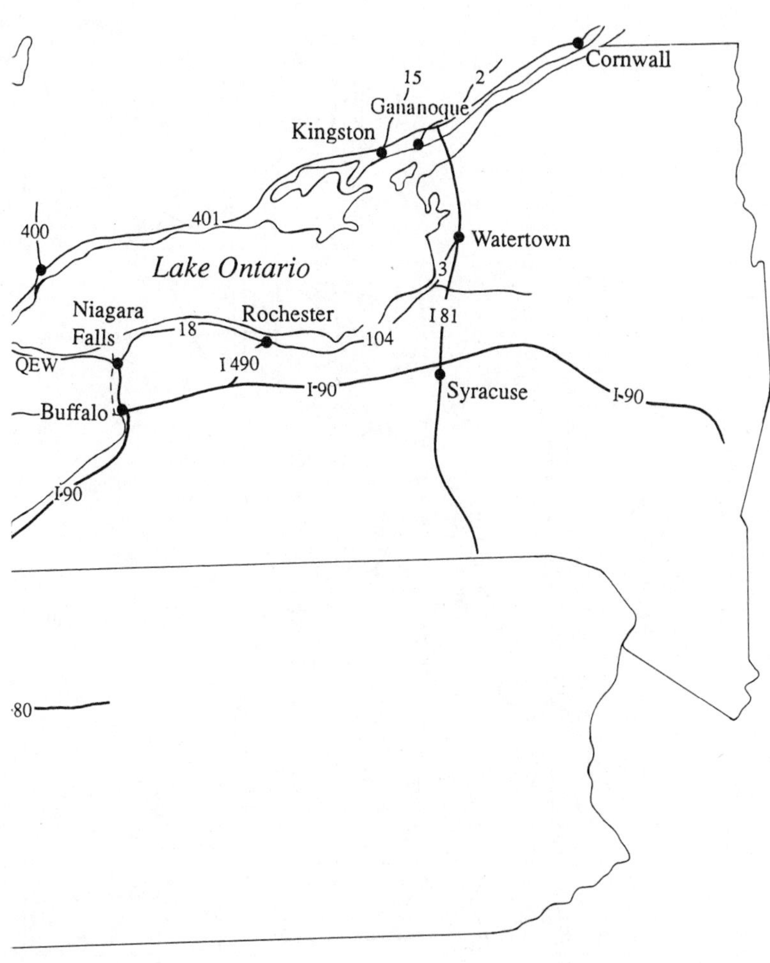

SECTION ONE: OHIO'S NORTH COAST

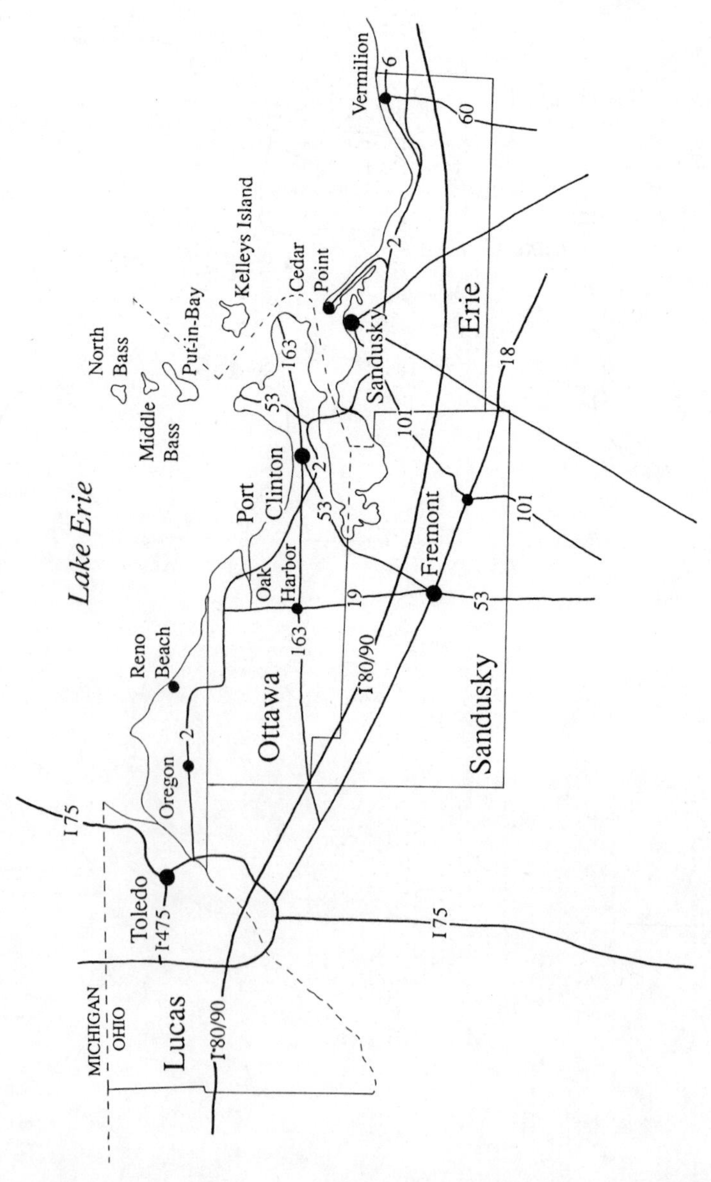

LUCAS COUNTY

Formed from sections of Henry, Sandusky and Wood Counties, Lucas County was established on June 20, 1835, and named after Robert Lucas, then governor of Ohio. The major physical features of this county are the Maumee River and Lake Erie, into which the former flows.

Throughout its early history, this area attracted attention from the French, English and American forces; each country in its turn building fortifications near the rapids of the river. During the War of 1812, a powerful Native American force attacked and overran the Kentucky troops sent to relieve Fort Meigs. At the end of the conflict with Great Britain, in the area secure from local raiding parties, settlement by Americans from the East began in earnest.

The coming of the Miami and Erie Canal, and later the railroads, brought ever-increasing industrial activity and new immigrants to work the factories. Today, Lucas County and its major city, Toledo, have endeavored to retain much of their history in buildings and museums, as well as much of the area's rugged lakeside beauty in parks and other recreational areas for generations to come.

attractions

Maumee Bay State Park in Oregon, Ohio: birdwatching is the watch word at this bird and wildlife haven. Activities include fishing and hiking, and the winter brings snowmobiling and cross-country skiing. The bird populations available for viewing include unusual and far afield species such as the Western meadowlark, dickcissels, bobolinks and the short-eared owl.

Irwin Prairie, located just five miles west of Toledo, is a wet prairie covering 172 acres. Via its boardwalk, the prairie offers many opportunities to observe the teeming variety of nature that inhabits this remnant of a habitat, once common in the area. Amongst the species in this marshy environment is the endangered spotted turtle.

Fort Meigs in Perrysburg is a reconstruction of a walled fort that was built in 1813. Visitors will find War of 1812 memorabilia, and, on occasion, military-living history demonstrations.

Over 3,000 acres, **Maumee State Forest** allows hunting and has miles of horseback riding trails. All-purpose and snowmobiling trails are also available.

Cedar Point National Wildlife Refuge is an important bird and wildlife sanctuary frequented by many migrating species of birds en route along the North American Flyway.

Metzger Marsh State Wildlife Area is also along Lake Erie. This state-run wildlife area is available for a variety of lakeside activities.

Isaac Ludwig Mill, open from May through October, is a 140-year-old, water-powered mill located in Providence Metropark.

events

The **Collector's Toy Fair**, at the Lucas County Recreation Center, is a large show held in July that features all types of old and new toys.

The **Lucas County Fair** is held in July each year at the fairgrounds in Maumee.

Children's Christmas Wonderland at the Lucas County Recreational Center is an annual, animated Christmas display that takes place around Christmastime and is a local favorite.

TOLEDO

Toledo is truly a city that has it all: a great museum of art; the internationally known Toledo Museum of Art; and those Triple-A baseball heroes with the one-of-a-kind team name, the Mudhens. Toledo also has one of the best zoos in the country, the Toledo Zoo, which includes a large mammal collection and an aquarium. And don't forget one of the best hot dog purveyors around: Max Klinger's favorite repast, Tony Packo's Hot Dogs. Any town that can boast this kind of excellent and eclectic range of choices is a town with a dynamic and interesting culture.

Toledo has realized its fascinating culture through a series of historic and economic occurrences that brought together varied and interesting people and cultures from around the world. Toledo's history begins with the obvious fact that Toledo's river, the Maumee, is among the largest physical features of the entire northwestern Ohio area. This natural transportation route was used by the early inhabitants to bring together the military forces of the British, French and Americans to battle for control of this strategic region. Toledo occupies the site where Fort Industry stood during the late 1700s. Not far from this site, off Jerome Road, is Fallen Timbers Monument, where a victory over the Native Americans was secured by General "Mad" Anthony Wayne and the forces he commanded.

Another conflict that ripped through this disputed area was the Toledo War of 1835, a rather spiteful boundary dispute between Michigan and Ohio over this highly desired area. Ohio gained the Toledo area, and in compensation, Michigan received its famous upper peninsula. In a way, both states won this battle.

During the beginning of the Industrial Revolution, Toledo gained a "premier" status in the railroad industry by being both the home of the first railroad system west of the Alleghenies, the Erie and Kalamazoo Railroad completed in 1836, and later as an important center of locomotive production. The advent of the Miami and Erie Canal had already ensured that this Great Lake port would be tied to the rising level of economic activity that spread across the Midwest.

With industrial growth came the immigrant populations that added so much of the flavor and charm to Toledo. These varied and proud ethnic populations today celebrate their grand heritages with folk festivals and celebrations that occur during every season of the year. Along with the diverse ethnic culture that infused Toledo came the industrial boom, and interest in culture and the fine arts that grew nearly as fast as the economy. The end result of this commitment to culture is a group of institutions and cultural organizations that in some cases rival the best in Chicago or New York. Foremost among these is the Toledo Museum of Art, which is considered one of the finest collections in North America.

In recent years, as the economy of the Great Lakes region has changed, Toledo has made a concerted effort to meet the new realities. The revitalized downtown features the Portside Festival Marketplace, a handsome riverside structure that houses a mixture of 80 different shops and also hosts special events and shows throughout the year. The marketplace is fast becoming the focus of the entire region's redevelopment. Recently built hotels and office buildings are creating a new and exciting skyline for Toledo.

Greater Toledo is a treasure trove of heritage and culture tied together by strong and active neighborhoods. A variety of outdoor activities are available here. The Toledo Area Metroparks system is the chain that links together many of these activities. These parks range from the historic canal locks built in the 19th century to the Wildwood Preserve, which maintains the river valley area the way it was before the coming of the settlers. The park system sponsors many diverse activities and events throughout the year such as jogging or walking the trails that criss-cross many of the parks.

Toledo offers a wide variety of sports for both fans and active enthusiasts. Lake Erie fishing tops the sportsperson's list; a large variety of freshwater fish take the bait nearly year-round in Lake Erie. Foremost among these species are Lake Erie perch, white and smallmouth bass, and the popular walleye. In fact, the moniker "Walleye Capital of the World" has been applied to Toledo because of the fantastic action. An active charter fleet caters to the dreams of many fishing enthusiasts. Hunting, hiking and camping are also among the outdoor activities available.

Golf is so popular and enjoyed at a wide range of fine golf courses, both public and private. Among the more famous courses are Inverness and the challenging Highland Meadows. Many semi-private courses are available to the public.

The Toledo Mudhens bring the excitement of Triple-A baseball to Ned Skeldon Stadium; the season begins in April. The University of Toledo Rockets bring NCAA basketball and football action to the Toledo area.

Raceway Park has excitement galore for those who appreciate the grace and beauty of harness racing. The season runs from March to December, and the glass-enclosed grandstand offers comfort and enjoyment regardless of the weather.

Along with the Toledo Museum of Art, Toledo boasts many other fine cultural organizations and activities. Performing arts include the Toledo Symphony, whose season runs from September to June. Most performances are at the Museum of Art's Peristyle Concert Hall.

The Toledo Repertoire Company performs in its own theater on 10th Street from September to June. The Toledo Ballet Association performs at various local festivals and events. Its version of the "Nutcracker" is a holiday favorite, while Ken Shaw Productions brings Broadway performances to Toledo's Masonic Auditorium each year. The Toledo Opera Association brings the excitement of opera to the stage. The University of Toledo Department of Theatre features several fine performances throughout the academic year as well as in the summer months.

attractions

The superb **Toledo Museum of Art** is located just off Interstate 75.

Crosby Gardens is a venerable Toledo institution. This fine collection includes gardens of herbs, roses, rhododendron, azalea and wildflowers. Artist studios and galleries are also a part of the gardens, and two excellent festivals are staged there annually. The Festival of the Arts is held in June, and the Fall Folk Festival takes place in October.

The **Ritter Planetarium** at the University of Toledo features presentations each weekend throughout the year. The planetarium brings the fascination of space to young and old alike.

The **Toledo Zoo**, located south of downtown off U.S. Highway 25, is among the best zoos in North America. With 560 species on exhibit, an aquarium, and the superb new African Savanna, the zoo makes for a family excursion par excellence. While at the savanna, do not miss the one-of-a-kind hippopotamus viewing area, featuring the incredible Hippoaquarium, a viewing site at which visitors see the underwater grace and beauty of these lumbering land giants. Along with the hippos, one can observe elephants, crocodiles, and other African animals as they enjoy this very special watering hole. Visitors will also enjoy the Diversity of Life exhibit. This award-winning display is a hands-on exhibit designed specifically for children. The zoo is open every day of the year except on major holidays.

The **Ohio Baseball Hall of Fame** is the place those die-hard Indians, Reds, Mudhens and Clippers fans can relive the glories and near-glories of the storied past. The hall is located at the Mudhens home in Maumee.

At **International Park**, along the Maumee across from downtown, is docked the venerable and historic Great Lake freighter **Willis B. Boyer**, which was first launched in 1911. Called the King of the Lake freighters, the Willis B. Boyer has been faithfully and carefully restored to preserve the memory and history of this important era in the ongoing story of the Great Lakes.

Along the southern bank of the Maumee, off Route 65 just west of Perrysburg, stands the original site of what was known as the largest walled fortification built in North America. **Fort Meigs** was built in 1813 by William Henry Harrison, who later became President of the United States.

At the **Historic Old West End**, visitors will find what is described as the largest concentration of fine Victorian architecture in all of Ohio. A self-guided tour brochure, available at the Chamber of Commerce office, will help guide newcomers through this outstanding neighborhood. Those in the area on the first weekend in June would do well to attend the annual Spring Festival.

The **Toledo Firefighters Museum** is located at the former #18 Fire Station at 918 Sylvania Avenue, near Lewis Avenue. This historic and interesting museum is dedicated to preserving the memory and the artifacts of the firefighters who have protected the city from fiery calamity over the decades.

Sauder Farm and Craft Village can be found in Archibold, Ohio. Authentic craftsmen and costumed guides re-create life and work as they were in those bygone days of self-sufficiency and self-reliance. Located in Fulton County, the village is about an hour south of Toledo.

ohio's north coast

Portside Festival Marketplace is leading the way of the waterfront development in a handsome and inviting urban environment. The marketplace features more than 80 different kinds of shops and restaurants.

Visitors can experience mid-19th century life at **Wollcott House Museum**, a restored landmark in Maumee.

The **Arawanna Star** and **Star of Toledo** operate daily beginning in May and September. These are the first paddlewheel excursion-dining boats to ply the waters of Toledo; they sail from Promenade Park Boat Basin.

On the **Baytowne Eagle**, a replica of the 1900s Great Lake passenger vessel of the same name, hourly sight-seeing cruises depart daily between May 30 and September 30 from International Park, behind the **Willis B. Boyer Maritime Museum.**

The **Sandpiper Canal Boat** is a replica of a Miami-Erie Canal boat that offers sightseeing tours every hour from May to September.

The **Shawnee Princess Steamboat** is a riverboat sternwheeler that leaves from Providence Metropark in Grand Rapids hourly from 1:00 p.m. to 6:00 p.m. on Saturdays, Sundays and holidays.

Centennial Carriage & Livery offers elegant horsedrawn carriage tours that can accommodate up to six people. Passengers board at the Boody House Restaurant in Fort Industry Square.

events

Each winter, the city of Toledo gathers together for its annual **Winterfest**-several days of indoor and outdoor activities and sports, including hot air balloons.

Holy Toledo, it's Spring! **Memorial Day Weekend** takes on a festive air as the city converges on the waterfront for the official opening of the port to recreational boating, and the unofficial start of the spring/summer outdoor season. Four days of fun, entertainment, children's events, and great food and drink are topped off by the exciting Toledo International Grand Prix Hydroplane Races.

Rallies by the River is the Midwest's biggest ongoing party and draws thousands of fun-seekers from Ohio and Michigan for sunshine, music, food and refreshment. The event is held every Friday between the hours of 4:30 p.m. and 7:30 p.m. from May 13 to September 16 in Promenade Park.

Held in early June, **Old West End Spring Festival** displays art, music and crafts in and among the outstanding collection of fine Victorian-era homes that dominate the area. Street boundaries for the event include Collingwood, Monroe, Detroit and Central.

Crosby Gardens Festival of the Arts hosts artists, craftspeople, entertainers and restaurateurs as city folk gather in early summer at this spectacular garden.

Fourth of July celebrations are special in this historic city. Along the waterfront a world class fireworks display is heightened by the dynamic reflections in the water.

Every Sunday evening from early to late August, if the weather permits, **Music Under The Stars** presents the Toledo Concert Band in a free performance at the zoo's amphitheater. Starting at 8:00 p.m., each concert has a different musical theme.

great lakes coast

It's August and time for the superbowl of barbecues, the **Northwest Ohio Riboff**-a competition with definite flavor! Toledo's top rib places meet head to head, and those who love ribs, great times and just plain fun come out the winners. This event is held downtown in Promenade Park.

Toledo Festival: A Celebration of the Arts, Toledo's number-one street fair, makes the Labor Day holiday a stay-at-home-and-enjoy holiday. Music, art, great food and super crowds top off the city's summer celebrations.

Ethnic Festivals that reflect the diversity and pride of Toledo's immigrants are featured throughout the year. These wonderful festivals share many things in common. In addition to the food, music and dancing, the friendly hospitality and pride that each group feels set a special mood that appeals to everyone.

accommodations

DAYS INN OF TOLEDO--PERRYSBURG
10667 Fremont Pike
Toledo, Ohio 43551
Tel: (419) 874-8771
(800) 325-2525 for reservations
Visa, MasterCard, American Express, Discover and Diners Club are accepted.

Days Inn of Toledo--Perrysburg offers 125 exceptionally comfortable rooms for smokers or non-smokers; modern meeting facilities; and a location convenient to many businesses, shopping, restaurants, and entertainment within walking distance to downtown Toledo. The modern building, fully refurbished in 1986 and 1988 with all new furnishings, is a further indication of outstanding attention to detail. Proving this point, Days Inn of Toledo--Perrysburg recently came through an unannounced 500-point inspection as one of the top 75 of 600 Days Inns nationwide.

A wide array of services and facilities further substantiates why Days Inn of Toledo--Perrysburg is a customer favorite. The rooms are comfortably furnished and include push-button, direct dial phones with free local calls. Guests enjoy HBO and ESPN, among other stations, on remote control color TV's in each room. Guests do not need to leave their rooms for much, since valet laundry and room service from a nearby restaurant are available. However, they may want to step out to use the theater-style conference room or the Fax and copier services. The outdoor pool, open Memorial Day to Labor Day, provides guests cool relaxation; or the lobby, with its fireplace and solarium is a great place to converse and relax with other guests. Stop in each morning for a continental breakfast of fresh fruit and pastries, toast, juices, coffee and tea.

A little over one mile from the Maumee River, the anglers flock in for the early Spring Walleye Run up the river each year. Less than 30 minutes from Port Clinton and Lake Erie, the Days Inn offers some unique three-day, two-night "Erie Island Hopping" packages to groups and tour planners.

Easy access from interstate highways and close proximity to nearby restaurants, shopping malls, downtown, and other attractions make Days Inn of Toledo--Perrysburg the choice of bus tour groups, families and business people. The intensively-trained staff excels at making people happy.

HAMPTON INN
1409 Reynolds Road
Maumee, Ohio 43537
Tel: (419) 893-1004
Hrs: Open 24 hours.
Visa, Mastercard, American Express, Diners Club and Carte Blanche are accepted.

The Hampton Inn in Ohio originally opened in 1987. In this short period of time, it has managed to be in the top five for service among all the Hampton Inns across the country. Hampton Inns are a nationwide chain of affordable and accommodating hotels. Guests will find a Hampton Inn in almost every major city in the United States. This Toledo-South branch is in a perfect location for vacationers as well as businessmen, just off exit 4 of the Ohio Turnpike. The convenient location is close to some of the area's finest restaurants, making the Hampton Inn an ideal spot for Toledo's visitors.

Hampton Inns are some of the most popular hotels in the country. This popularity is most easily recognized through the rate of repeat guests. Ninety-two percent of all guests return, and 98 percent go the extra distance to find and stay at a Hampton Inn. This success is due to a variety of reasons, beginning with the moderate rates. Unlike many hotel chains, these moderate rates are accompanied by surprisingly comfortable accommodations. Each room is furnished with either king size or double beds, oak finished furniture, separate climate controls and free Showtime. Hotel manager Susan Dunlap and her excellent staff guarantee that all rooms will be kept spotless. An outdoor pool, airport service, non-smoking rooms and a continental breakfast are among other special features offered. A valet (same day) service is provided for extended stays, and guests that stay often are given a "frequent guest" privilege that gives them their 10th night stay free of charge. Seniors also receive a special discount and children under 18 can stay with their parents for free.

Every guest of the Hampton Inn is received with open arms and treated with the best care and attention. The convenient location, high repeat rate, discount plans, affordable rates and wonderful accommodations are the reasons the Hampton Inn-Toledo South is a "Best Choice" along the Great Lakes.

RADISSON HOTEL TOLEDO
101 North Summit
Toledo, Ohio 43604
Tel: (419) 241-3000

Radisson Hotels are synonymous with superb service, attention to detail, and luxurious accommodations. Toledo is the site of one of the newer Radisson Hotels in the worldwide chain; Radisson Hotel Toledo opened in July 1987.

Located in the heart of downtown Toledo, the Radisson Hotel sits near the riverfront, providing a breathtaking view. The spacious, 400-room hotel features everything from deluxe suites to multi-level presidential accommodations. The contemporary, 15-story building combines modernity with Old World charm. When guests check into Radisson Hotel Toledo, they enter elegantly appointed rooms with marble and brass accents, beautiful floral arrangements, oriental rugs, and original art work. Amenities include fully-equipped recreation facilities featuring a health spa, sauna, Jacuzzi and exercise room. A business center with copy, typing, FAX, and secretarial services allows guests to combine pleasure and business within the same facility. In addition, the hotel offers a floor for non-smokers and a 32-room plaza club floor; conference and banquet facilities with more than 12,000 square feet of meeting and banquet space; and a grand ballroom with seating for up to 400 people.

Fine dining is a trademark of Radisson Hotels and Toledo's is no exception. Within the hotel are restaurants to suit any palate, from the Cafe Lounge for a light meal to the Toledo Cafe, a full-service restaurant offering breakfast, lunch and dinner. The Lobby Lounge offers an intimate atmosphere and a warm, late night meeting spot.

Radisson Hotel Toledo lists convenience among its many attractions with an attached garage that directly connects to Toledo Seagate Convention Center, the city's finest convention facility.

SECOR INN, 3540 Secor Road, Toledo Ohio 43606; Tel: (419) 531-2666. Under the same ownership as the next door Sheraton, this upscale economy hotel caters to both family and business travelers. Its 72 rooms offer color cable TV and computer phone lines; free continental breakfast is part of one's stay.

SHERATON WESTGATE
3536 Secor Road
Toledo, Ohio 43606
Tel: (419) 535-7070
(800) 325-3535
Hrs: Crystal Restaurant is open Monday - Sunday
Visa, MasterCard, American Express, Diners Club, Carte Blanche and Discover are accepted.

The Sheraton Westgate is Toledo's preferred accommodation and recreation spot. Both vacationers and business people love this hotel's contemporary style and posh facilities. Just stepping into the lobby, with its diamond-like chandeliers and tropical atrium, is a pleasant experience. What follows is even better: the rooms are magnificently decorated with plush cocoa-colored carpeting and beautifully bold, floral accents. All of the lavish rooms and executive suites offer cable color television and convenient work space.

The Sheraton Westgate offers a fabulous ballroom (for up to 500 people) that is easily transformed into a brilliantly designed boardroom for seminars and business meetings. Crystal's dining room offers fine continental cuisine, and The Brasserie, which overlooks the lush lobby, serves lighter fare. Crystal's Lounge, with its unique marble dance floor, offers wonderful cocktails and a cheerful atmosphere. The Atrium houses a heated swimming pool and two relaxing whirlpools. Toledo's Sheraton Westgate also has a quarter-mile outdoor fitness course with 32 workout stations.

The hotel is located just south of the I-475 interchange and is 20 minutes from the Toledo Express Airport, 10 minutes from downtown Toledo shops and theatres, and only five minutes from the University of Toledo. Whether a trip is business or pleasure, guests appreciate the Sheraton Westgate's commitment to excellence.

TOLEDO HILTON
3100 Glendale Avenue
Toledo, Ohio 43614
Tel: (419) 381-6800

Living up to its motto, "You'll come to expect everything," the new Toledo Hilton offers everything from state-of-the-art meeting and conference facilities and a banquet grand ballroom to a health spa, a comfortable lounge, and an award-winning restaurant. All this is complemented by luxurious hotel rooms and suites with parlors. The Hilton's contemporary decor showcases the art of Ohio artists. Each room has cable TV, pay movies, and Hilton hospitality--valet service, room service, and complimentary morning coffee.

The Hilton's conference facilities feature 17 meeting rooms, the largest of which will accommodate 350 people. Audiovisual and teleconferencing capabilities are provided in every meeting room. For business persons, there are work stations in every room complete with modems, and the hotel has secretarial, FAX and copy services. The hotel's fitness center, with its private club atmosphere, offers an indoor running track, whirlpool, sauna, racquetball, weight room, exercise equipment, a pool, and volleyball, tennis, and basketball courts.

A quiet haven for relaxing after the day's work or for meeting friends, Whisper's Lounge is multi-leveled and features a fireplace and comfortable, overstuffed chairs. Group areas for conversation as well as hideaway corners for intimate "small talk" are both available. The lounge features live entertainment on weekends, "Jazz to Top 40" and special theme nights on Wednesdays.

Iris' Restaurant features an appetite-stirring menu specializing not only in fresh seafood, but also in meat and fowl. Signature dishes such as black bean soup, Iris' salad and homemade bread make Iris' a popular spot among those who expect something special. Casual yet elegant, Iris' was noted among the top 20 restaurants in Toledo and first in its category for home-style cooking at affordable prices.

Guests may very well come to expect everything at the Toledo Hilton--it seems to offer it all.

TOLEDO MARRIOTT PORTSIDE
Two Seagate/Summit Street
Toledo, Ohio 43604
Tel: (419) 241-1411
Visa, MasterCard, American Express, Discover, Carte Blanche and Diners Club are accepted.

Discover a world of upscale accommodations at Toledo Marriott Portside. Dockside access, luxuriously appointed guest rooms with riverfront views, and fine restaurants and lounges are only a few of the hotel's many attractions. Guest services include use of a fully-equipped health club, a gift shop, and valet service. For the convenience of its guests, underground concourse walkways connect the hotel with a myriad of downtown shopping and cultural attractions. The hotel also offers a wide selection of function rooms for conventions, meetings and banquets.

Toledo Marriott Portside offers a choice of elegant or casual dining experiences. Ashley's sophisticated ambiance and panoramic view of the Maumee River makes the restaurant a popular eatery among locals. The a la carte menu features fresh seafood, steaks, lamb and duck-all prepared with a European flair. The Regatta Bar and Grille offers a more casual dining experience; the menu offers a choice of pastas, seafood, steak, lamb, pork, chicken and pizza.

For the perfect base from which to enjoy the sights of Toledo and the riverfront, stay at Toledo Marriott Portside, a "Best Choice" in fine accommodations.

antiques

KING STREET ANTIQUES
5633 North Main
Sylvania, Ohio 43560
Tel: (419)882-4136

Hrs:	Tuesday - Saturday	10:00 a.m. - 6:00 p.m.
	Sunday & Monday	Closed
	Extended holiday hours	

Visa and MasterCard are accepted.

King Street Antiques was opened in September of 1985 by Marty Druser. Marty has been interested in antiques since he was 12, when he purchased a carved glass china cabinet for $15, in which he stored his model planes. After collecting for many years, Marty finally turned his passion into a living and King Street came into being. He began traveling to England to import English antiques, which are still his specialty.

This unique shop is located 15 minutes from Toledo, in the heart of Sylvania, on Main Street, only minutes from I-475 via Route 23. The building itself dates back to 1890 and was originally built as a Masonic Temple. It is undergoing restoration to enhance the original architectural features.

Lynn Jacquot was an avid patron of King Street Antiques before becoming Marty's partner. Together, they also own and operate an antique mall in Perrysburg in South Toledo which features 20 dealers.

King Street Antiques carries a great deal of furniture including such pieces as an English Court cupboard from the early 1800s; a mahogany sideboard with beveled glass from Denmark; a walnut cylinder desk dating from 1875 made in America; or a German pine country cupboard circa 1850. The shop contains architectural pieces that will help restore any home such as turn-of-the-century brass lighting, stained glass windows, fireplace mantels, and antique hand-painted tiles, both English and American. Patrons will find a nice selection of general antiques at King Street too; including oil paintings, clocks, lamps, cut glass, china, Toledo memorabilia, collectibles, and wardrobes, some silver and English china, and many other accessory pieces. What isn't found in this 5,000 square-foot shop, Marty and Lynn will try to find. Appraisals, select estate sales, and free delivery in the local area are just a few of the other services offered at King Street Antiques.

Marty and Lynn are most proud of their ever-changing inventory of good quality antiques and collectibles which always make King Street Antiques an interesting place to shop. The changing inventory also keeps it fun and enjoyable for both the patrons and owners. So make a stop at King Street, for the "Best Choice" in antiques along the lakes.

MOODS AND MEMORIES

FINE ANTIQUES & GIFTS
3666 Rugby Avenue at South Detroit
Toledo, Ohio 43614
Tel: (419) 389-1160
Hrs: Monday - Saturday 11:00 a.m. - 6:00 p.m.
September - May only:
Sunday 1:00 p.m. - 5:00 p.m
Visa, MasterCard and American Express are accepted.

Moods and Memories is a total sensory experience, a shop designed from the ground up to appeal to sight, sound, smell, and color perception. The eclectic blend of antiques and contemporary gift items; the friendliness of the staff; and attention to customer service, all guarantee a one-of-a-kind shopping pleasure. Owners Gregg A Phenicie and R.F. "Sam" Simon began with a historic Deco design, which immediately presents a fitting portal to the store's unequaled interior. Elegant, classy, and colorful, Moods and Memories stocks a complete selection of antiques and fine art, including cut and pattern glass, perfume bottles, jewelry, sterling, china, advertising and toys. In addition to antique furnishings (18th century through Art Deco in both primitive and formal), the store carries contemporary giftware such as art glass, unique stationery and greeting cards, collectors' dolls and figurines, potpourri, candles, and collectibles of all descriptions. The selection of antique pottery, glassware, jewelry, and fine collectors' items is extensive, and much of the inventory has been obtained from exclusive estates and private collections.

A computerized request file ties the store into a network of other antique and collectible establishments and enables Moods and Memories to locate those especially hard-to-find pieces. If Sam and Gregg don't stock it, they will try their best to locate it. Browsers are always welcome at Moods and Memories--it is an antique and gift shop brimming with treasures.

apparel

MICHAEL DAVID LTD.
323 North Superior Street
Toledo, Ohio 43604
Tel: (419) 255-1039
Hrs: Monday - Friday 10:00 a.m. - 6:00 p.m.
Saturday 10:00 a.m. - 2:00 p.m.
Also by appointment
Visa and MasterCard are accepted.

Michael David Ltd. is a trend-setting men's clothing store owned by former golf pro, Michael David. The store carries a complete line of men's apparel ranging from stylish suits and sportcoats to colorful casual wear. Top-name designers include Freeman, Corbin, Robert Talbott, Trafalgar and Kenneth Gordon. Michael David Ltd. also features a variety of men's accessories that range from the avant-garde to the classic.

The quality of Michael's clothing line is first-rate, but the shop is best known for the happy, high energy service that Michael provides. Michael is always eager to share his impeccable taste with his customers, if they request it. His main concern is that each of his customers walks out with the most individually flattering apparel. Michael David Ltd. provides expert in-house tailoring and custom, made-to-measure clothing.

Located in downtown Toledo (within walking distance of several city hotels), Michael's shop immediately puts customers at ease with its cozy decor of natural woods and forest green accents. Michael has established such a terrific rapport with his manufacturers that he is able to provide his patrons with a degree of service that is unmatched by large department stores.

Michael David Ltd. offers a full line of stylish men's apparel that will update any wardrobe for any occasion.

THE SOPHIA LUSTIG SHOP
124 10th Street
Toledo, Ohio 43624
Tel: (419) 243-5131
Hrs: Monday - Friday 9:30 a.m. - 5:30 p.m.
Visa and MasterCard are accepted.

Toledo's Sophia Lustig Shop not only offers elegant ladies apparel in an exquisite shopping atmosphere, it also graciously caters to the classiest needs of all patrons.

Started in 1937 by Sophia Lustig herself, the shop remained a family business until she passed away in 1972. Paula Fall purchased the shop in 1981 in its original location on Toledo's Madison Avenue with the commitment of maintaining the superior standards which have served three generations. In 1987, the shop moved to its current location on 10th Street, where its unmistakable architecture including three bay windows and abundant natural lighting pay a perfect complement to the quality within the shop's confines.

It is a full-line shop with outfits appropriate from morning until evening and from formal to casual; included are a variety of choices for career women and many one-of-a-kind selections. Accessories range from leather goods to scarves, jewelry, fragrances and lingerie.

Emphasis is not only on the quality of construction and natural fibers, but also on affordable prices. Affordability in such lavish surroundings is not common; however, that seems to parallel Paula Fall's commitment to the customer. She is on the premises to listen to and accommodate the needs of everyone who visits. Further assistance is provided by an in-house tailor who renders aid by promptly responding to all requests. Complementary gift wrapping, delivery and UPS shipping give additional convenience to the ladies' apparel shopper.

The shop welcomes patrons with style and yet simultaneously relaxes them with a living room-like greeting area. The catering continues as guests are shown various garments rather than flipping through racks of clothes.

Dressing rooms have hand-painted floral designs, wrap-around mirrors and yet more natural lighting.

Elegance, style, and class in a friendly, relaxed atmosphere are reasons why no trip to Toledo is complete without a visit to the Sophia Lustig Shop, the city's most respected women's clothing shop.

catering

SOFO FOODS RETAIL & WHOLESALER OF ITALIAN FOODS, 5400 Monroe Street, Toledo, Ohio 43623; Tel: (419) 882-8555. For parties, holidays, or family gatherings Sofo's prepares party trays to one's specifications. Choose from deli meats, imported cheeses, fresh vegetables and salads, to create the perfect food selection. Sofo's provides "convenience with all the trimmings."

entertainment

THE TOLEDO BALLET, Masonic Auditorium on Heatherdowns Boulevard, Toledo, Ohio Tel: (419) 471-0049. With shows Friday, Saturday and Sunday evenings plus matinees, The Toledo Ballet is a "Best Choice" for classic and entertaining dance exhibits. Excellent performances of Sleeping Beauty, Midsummer Night's Dream and The Nutcracker should not be missed.

TOLEDO COMEDY CLUB
5319 HeatherDowns
Toledo, Ohio 43614
Tel: (419) 242-JOKE
Hrs: Tuesday - Thursday 9:00 p.m.
Friday - Saturday 8:00 p.m. and 10:30 p.m.
Visa, MasterCard, American Express, Diners Club and Carte Blanche are accepted.

Since the day it first opened late in 1986, the Toledo Comedy Club has been one of the hottest night spots in the city. Located on HeatherDowns just off Reynolds Road, this outstanding club features the finest in contemporary comedy found anywhere in the country. Owner Allen Seder's slogan says it all: "We are Serious about Comedy." The list of famous name entertainers who have played at the club is impressive. Visitors to Seder's establishment have laughed to the comedy antics of such greats as Pat Paulsen, Basile, "The Centerfold of Comedy", Joe DeLion, Mark Price, Skippy from Family Ties, Gilbert Gottfried, and Bill Kirchenbaur from The Ten of Us.

Many national touring companies consider the Toledo Comedy Club to be one of the most desirable stops on tour. The club is open and spacious, resulting in good visibility from every seat, and visitors encounter a warm and friendly atmosphere. Other factors responsible for the club's phenomenal success are good location, a welcoming ambiance, service and superb talent; but Allen says that the basic notion, "The Customer Always Comes First," is the main reason for the club's popularity.

A full-service bar and outstanding munchies round out the comic experience. As one of the city's lauded attractions, The Toledo Comedy Club is the place to come out and have a good laugh. Group reservations and discounts are available. The club's seating capacity is limited to 250 people, so reservations are recommended, especially on weekends. The Second Toledo Comedy Club opened in downtown Toledo in the fall of 1989.

TOLEDO SYMPHONY
1 Strahanan Square
Toledo, Ohio 43604
Tel: (419) 241-1272
Hrs: September - May:
Monday - Friday 9:00 a.m. - 5:00 p.m.

Performing everything from classical to jazz, traditional to new wave, pop to rock, the Toledo Symphony has become one of the nation's best regional music organizations. Since its founding in 1943, this outstanding symphony has delighted music lovers throughout the country with a wide range of musical styles.

The Toledo Symphony employs approximately 80 professional musicians under the direction of interim resident conductor James Meen and principal guest conductor Ole Schmidt. The orchestra's present schedule includes seven series with close to 40 concerts. Another 40 concerts and no less than 400 ensemble performances are given in Toledo neighborhoods and surrounding communities during the season. Besides the popular Classics Series, the symphony presents Mainly Mozart, the Pop Series, the Chamber

Series, Family Concerts, and the Music Today Series, which features premier performances and new works.

The Toledo Symphony has truly earned its reputation as one of the finest regional symphonies in America. During the season, the symphony's range of solo performers includes such internationally known celebrities as Peter Serkin, Christopher Parkening, Rudolph Buchbinder, Cecile Licad, and Aaron Rosand. Pops performers have included such greats as Judy Collins, Burt Bacharach, Lou Rawls, Chuck Mangione, John Dankworth, Pete Fountain, and Emmy Lou Harris. Other guest artists have included the Kronos Quartet, the Boys Choir of Harlem, and Bob McGrath from Sesame Street.

factory outlets

LIBBEY GLASS FACTORY OUTLET
1205 Buckeye Street
Toledo, Ohio 43611
Tel: (419) 727-2374
Hrs: Monday - Saturday 9:30 a.m. - 5:30 p.m.
November - December:
Sunday Noon - 5:00 p.m.
Visa and MasterCard are accepted.

The Libbey Glass Factory Outlet, which is connected to the Libbey Glass Factory, is somewhat unusual for a factory outlet in that even first-run merchandise is offered at discounts of up to 50 percent.

The Libbey Glass Company, formerly known as the New England Glass Company of East Cambridge, Massachusetts, moved to Toledo in 1888 to take advantage of the relatively inexpensive natural gas fuel. At that time, the company was in serious financial difficulty primarily because of its insistence upon producing fine lead glass, rather than the cheaper soda-lime glass. Its exhibit at the Columbian Exposition in Chicago in 1893, however, was seen by two million visitors and put the company's products before the public, thus ensuring its financial success.

Although the rich cut and engraved glassware is no longer available commercially, technical advancements have contributed to the economical production of truly fine glassware. Visitors to the Libbey Glass Factory Outlet find high-quality merchandise such as open stock tumblers and stemware, seasonal glassware, storage cannisters and L.E. Smith Handcrafted Glassware, as well as products with custom-designed logos or decorations at very reasonable prices.

gardens

TOLEDO BOTANICAL GARDEN
(Formerly Crosby Gardens)
5403 Elmer Drive
Toledo, Ohio 43615
Tel: (419) 536-8365
(419) 534-6006 Garden Hotline
Hrs: Monday - Saturday 10:00 a.m. - 5:00 p.m.
Sunday 1:00 p.m. - 5:00 p.m.
Closed during February.
Visa and MasterCard are accepted in the gift shop.

Cool, tranquil, and serene are adjectives that ideally describe Toledo Botanical Garden, a 56-acre wonderland of natural beauty that is home to 20 different arts, environmental, and horticultural groups. Toledo Botanical Garden has evolved into a nationally recognized formal gardens--it is a place where plants and people can interact in the same environment.

George P. Crosby originally bequeathed 20 acres of land to the city of Toledo in 1964. Farsighted civic officials expanded that gift, and Toledo Botanical Garden literally and figuratively blossomed. Today the garden has many goals: to establish and maintain botanical gardens for the public's enjoyment, and horticultural and environmental education; to collect and study plantlife; and to provide a setting for cultural activities.

Each June, Toledo Botanical Garden sponsors Festival of the Arts, the oldest juried outdoor arts festival in Ohio; it attracts artists and visitors from across the nation. Hundreds of paintings, sculpture, glasswork, weavings, and other crafts are on display. Late in October, the facility welcomes the annual Fall Folk Festival, a blending of traditional American crafts, arts, music, storytelling and 19th century food preparation. Although many of the educational programs and horticultural services at Toledo Botanical Garden are highly organized, visitors relish the chance to enter a serene, green world and wander over the criss-cross garden pathways.

Toledo Botanical Garden also provides a seasonal Garden Hotline for home gardeners and features a speaker's bureau, a conference center for educational meetings, group tours, volunteer opportunities, and a membership program.

hair design

C.H. DESIGNERS GLASS FORUM
4400 Heatherdowns
Toledo, Ohio 43614
Tel: (419) 381-0420
Hrs: Monday - Friday 9:00 a.m. - 6:30 p.m.
Saturday 9:00 a.m. - 3:00 p.m.

C.H. Designers Glass Forum is neither the typical beauty salon nor the average art gallery. It does offer, however, an outrageously unique medley of the latest hair design concepts and some of the most brilliant art work from Toledo Museum of Art students. As one can imagine, the decor is both bizarre and beautiful--it's so different that it almost defies description. C.H. Designers Glass Forum blends touches of Roman, Gothic, Neoclassic, and Postmodern designs to form a New York City or Los Angeles-style decor. There are pink cherubs over the mirrors; huge black and white checkerboard tiles with painted-on, multi-colored ribbons on the floor; concrete walls and columns throughout the salon; and dreamlike clouds painted on the ceiling.

The hair designs are done by co-owner Mike Janser, and the art gallery is run by co-owner Rebecca Bryant. Mike, an expert hair designer, and Rebecca, a glassblowing artist, transformed Mike's former beauty salon, California Hair Stylists, into this intriguing masterpiece, and the makeover is stunning. They really know how to mix it up. Even the salon/gallery's combination soft rock, trendy classical, and slightly toned-down new-age music adds to C.H. Designers' far from boring ambiance.

While Mike is busy with his makeover artistry, Rebecca is busy with her multimedia (glass, paintings, and sculptures) art exhibits, which are all for sale. The hair styling is incredibly reasonable (from about $9), and the original art work ranges from inexpensive on up (from about $10 to $5,000). C.H. Designers Glass Forum is one of the most creatively concocted and beautifully bizarre businesses along the Great Lakes. Stop in and see why it's a "Best Choice."

marinas

TOLEDO BEACH MARINA
11840 Toledo Beach Road
Toledo, Ohio
Tel: (313) 243-3800
Visa, MasterCard, American Express and Union 76 are accepted.

The largest marina on Lake Erie and one of the top 100 such facilities in the nation, the Toledo Beach Marina is known as "the most complete yachting service center" in the Midwest. For more than 25 years, this outstanding marine facility has been serving the needs of Midwest boaters by making available the finest quality merchandise and service at reasonable prices.

The Toledo Beach Marina is a deep water harbor that operates during both high and low tides. The marina's three boat hoists can handle yachts up to 80 feet in length and weighing 65 tons; a dry rack with storage for up to 400 boats and dockage for more than 500 boats is also available. The marina's service department features factory-trained personnel on duty seven days a week able to handle all repair and installation needs. The shop offers everything from custom molded fiberglass and aluminum fabrication to interior and exterior redesign and modification. The staff of expert carpenters can fabricate nearly anything for any boat. An extensive inventory of new and used boats is displayed, and a complete brokerage service is available.

The Dock-o-minimum, a condo for boats, supplies, water, electricity, telephone and cable TV hookups for guests are available. For the more transient boaters, the 700-foot gas dock features pump-out facilities, two shower houses, and a laundry. A ship store, deli and cocktail lounge round out the marina's extensive facilities.

museums

WOLCOTT HOUSE MUSEUM COMPLEX
1031 River Road
Maumee, Ohio 43537
Tel: (419) 893-9602
Hrs: Tours are by appointment only.
March - December:
Tuesday - Sunday 1:00 p.m. - 4:00 p.m.
Closed on holidays.

The beautiful and quaintly-named Maumee Valley, south of Toledo, is a green and fertile land that beckons visitors with a variety of historical and cultural attractions. The Wolcott House Museum Complex is one of the real gems in the area; the complex re-creates 19th century northwestern Ohio history in an impressive fashion.

Operated by the Maumee Valley Historical Society, the museum complex allows visitors a chance to experience how early Ohio settlers lived and worked through the years. Indian artifacts, antiques, toys, household goods, farm implements, and many other items from the 19th century are on permanent display. Lectures, educational classes, seminars and Early American art groups are but a few of the many interesting facets of the museum complex.

Six period buildings comprise the Wolcott House Museum Complex: the elegant Wolcott House, a sterling example of Federal-style architecture of the mid-1830s; an 1850s log home transplanted from the banks of the Miami River and Erie Canal; an 1840s saltbox-style farmhouse; the Toledo and Grand Rapids Railroad Depot from the 1880s; the Monclova United Brethren Church; and an 1840 Greek Revival-style home, which also houses the unique Talking Turtle Gift Shop. The gift shop is named for Miami Indian Chief Little Turtle, an ancestor of the Wolcott family.

Christmas By the River, a six-week display, is a special time for the Wolcott House Museum Complex. The buildings are festooned with handmade Christmas decorations, and the warm glow of candles and oil lanterns turns windows into golden beacons that invite visitors to come in out of the cold. The historical legacy of the American heartland comes alive at the Wolcott House Museum Complex; it is a fascinating journey through relics of a bygone era.

points of interest

FRANCISCAN LIFE CENTER
6832 Convent Boulevard
Sylvania, Ohio 43560
Tel: (419) 885-1547
Hrs: Performances year-round
Performances usually start at 7:30 p.m. or 8:00 p.m.
Visa and MasterCard are accepted.

The Franciscan Life Center is a not-for-profit cultural arts and conference center located on the 89-acre wooded campus of Lourdes College. Built by the Sisters of St. Francis in 1981 in the style of early California Missions, this structure includes a theater, gymnasium, conference rooms, serving kitchen, and a spacious Commons.

The theater features a large proscenium stage, unobstructed sightlines, excellent acoustics, and comfortable seating, making it the ideal place for drama and musical theater. The most talented performers in the area are proud to present their programs here; the Toledo Symphony, the Toledo Repertoire Theater, and the Cassandra Ballet are examples. The Center offers four professional performing arts series plus special events. One can experience exciting performances by The Lettermen, Banu Gibson and The New Orleans Hot Jazz Orchestra, and cellist Elsa Hilger. Equally entertaining are performances of A Chorus Line and Oklahoma.

The FLC is very flexible as a meeting place; one can bring a small group of 10-12 or a seminar-size group of 500-800. The Commons, a 9,000 square-foot area with natural brick walls, an earth tone floor, and skylights, can be used for luncheons, banquets, parties, art exhibits, and cabaret musical presentations. Conference rooms can be set up according to the needs of the group with round or rectangular seating available; rooms are equipped with a write-on board that also serves as a projection screen. The goal of the FLC is to be as accommodating as possible making sure that all scheduled meetings run smoothly.

Since its opening in 1981 "as a cultural, educational, and entertainment center for the general community," the Franciscan Life Center has been recognized for the quality of its programs and overall operation. For its ability to satisfy entertainment and conference needs in style, it is a "Best Choice" along the lakes.

ISAAC LUDWIG MILL/METROPARKS TOLEDO AREA
13827 U.S. 24 West
Grand Rapids, Ohio 43522
Tel: (419) 832-8934
Hrs: May - October:
Wednesday - Sunday Noon - 5:00 p.m.
Milling & Craft Demos:
Sunday 1:00 p.m. - 4:00 p.m
No admission charge

The Isaac Ludwig Mill, located in Providence Metropark, has outlived not only a fire, which destroyed its interior, but also the town it served and the canal era. The mill is a historically correct representation of a self-sufficient waterpower facility and accurately depicts the economic and social significance of settlement in the Maumee River Valley.

Settler Peter Manor built the sawmill in 1822, but it was demolished to make room for the Miami and Erie Canal. In 1846, the majority of the present-day mill was built. The mill produced meal, flour, and livestock feed until 1940 when a fire occurred. Afterward, the mill only produced livestock feed.

The mill was named after Isaac Ludwig, owner of the mill from 1865 to 1886. Ludwig's descendants, Mr. and Mrs. Cleo Ludwig, purchased the mill and donated it to the Metropark District in 1972. Since then, the mill has been restored and serves as a waterpower interpretive center. On Sundays, Metropark staff members provide working demonstrations of how water power was used by our ancestors. Park volunteers, likewise, demonstrate 19th century crafts, such as carpentry, baking and blacksmithing.

During the summer, over 3,000 pounds of whole wheat, cornmeal, and buckwheat flour are processed. Proceeds from public sale of the products go toward maintaining the mill. Visitors come from throughout the United States, England, Germany, Japan, Canada and China. The mill is located at U.S. Highway 24 and State Route 578, 25 miles southwest of downtown Toledo.

The Isaac Ludwig Mill in Providence Metropark is only one of the many features of Toledo's Metropark District. There are eight additional Metroparks, which are open every day from 7:00 a.m. until dark. The nine parks are housed on 6,400 acres of community-supported land. Activities in the parks include bird watching, bicycle/fitness trails, animal preserves, workshops, and sightseeing, to name a few.

The Metropark District of the Toledo Area was established in 1928. Independent of the State of Ohio, the district relies on community support.

Experience a trip to the past and present of milling in America at the Isaac Ludwig Mill in Providence Metropark.

restaurants

THE BOODY HOUSE
152 North Summit
Toledo, Ohio 43604
Tel: (419) 241-3322
Hrs: Lunch:
Monday - Friday 11:30 a.m. - 3:00 p.m.
Dinner:
Monday - Friday 5:30 p.m.-10:00 p.m.
Saturday 6:00 p.m. - 10:00 p.m.
Visa, MasterCard, American Express, Diners Club and Carte Blanche are accepted.

Built in 1872, the Boody House was designed as one of the most elegant hotels in the country. The hotel was named after Azariah Boody, president of the Toledo Wabash and Western Railroad. Established in 1982 and named for the famous hotel, the restaurant was brought forth to initiate the movement toward the new downtown and riverfront of Toledo.

The Boody House is considered to be one of Toledo's most elegant restaurants, and dining there is an extraordinary culinary experience. Exquisite food in a contemporary American style is carefully prepared and beautifully presented. The skilled chefs are proud to use only the finest ingredients in the preparation of their dishes. For lunch, choose from salads, hot sandwiches, full entrees, and special selections for the lighter appetite. The dinner menu features such entrees as Veal Porterhouse, Chateaubriand, and Rack of Lamb. Additionally, the restaurant's Cruvinet wine dispensing system offers 16 wines by the glass. All desserts, pastries, and chocolates are made in the "in house" confectioner's shop.

In addition to the main dining room, the Boody House offers Digby's Jazz Club, the perfect place for a casual meeting or quiet conversation. Digby's offers a light menu in which soups, salads, and sandwiches are complemented by live entertainment Tuesday through Saturday evenings. The Boody House also has five private dining rooms, which are available for business meetings, parties and other special occasions.

THE COLUMBIAN HOUSE
3 North River Road
Toledo, Ohio 43566
Tel: (419) 878-3006
Hrs: Lunch:
Tuesday - Friday 11:30 a.m. - 6:30 p.m.
Dinner:
Tuesday - Friday 6:00 p.m. - 9:00 p.m.
Saturday 5:30 p.m. - 9:00 p.m.
Visa, MasterCard, American Express, Diners Club and Discover are accepted.

Enjoy "A Unique Experience in Elegant Dining" at the world-famous Columbian House. Good food and history come together in this "eating and drinking museum." The three-story tavern was constructed in 1828 by John Pray, founder of Waterville. During the 1880s the tavern was the center of activity for the surrounding region, serving as hotel, tavern, trading post, post office and even jail. Just as it did for John Pray back in the early 1800s, the house serves as the residence for owners George and Jacqeline Arnold as well as their place of business.

The Columbian House features a superb menu of simple but elegant dishes. The lunch menu offers entrees such as Chicken Salad Cheesies, Chef's Salad with Garlic Toast, and Chicken A La King with vegetables and molded sal-corn sticks. The dinner menu lists excellent appetizers such as Soup Romaine and Escargot. For an entree, Chef Jacqueline recommends the Roast Chicken and Dressing, the Roast Prime Rib or the Baked Ham in Orange Sauce. All entrees are served with an outstanding tomato pudding and a full complement of side dishes.

The inn also features a fine full-service tavern with an excellent selection of wine, beer and cocktails. One of Ohio's best restaurants, The Columbian House is a historic and gastronomic landmark not to be missed. Oh yes, be sure to say hello to the inn's famous maitre'd, Toby the cat.

FIFI'S RESTAURANT
1423 Bernath Parkway
Toledo, Ohio 3615
Tel: (419) 866 - 6777
Hrs: Lunch:
Monday - Friday 11:00 a.m. - 3:00 p.m.
Dinner:
Monday - Thursday 5:00 p.m. - 11:00 p.m.
Friday - Saturday Until 11:00 p.m.
Visa, MasterCard and American Express are accepted.

Fifi's Restaurant opened its doors on October 1, 1980. Since then, Fifi's has become the proud recipient of both a three-star rating and a number-one rating by the food critic of the Toledo Blade. Fifi Berry, the owner, was striving for a certain ambiance from the start. She wanted her restaurant to combine romance, intimacy and elegance to create a truly memorable experience. Fifi fulfilled her goal by offering an interior that features subdued lighting, a romantic fireplace, a fresh rose on each spacious table, and a lounge boasting a baby grand piano and a remarkable wall painting of the owner.

Chef Mark Piaz, a native Californian, is proud to maintain a fabulous French cuisine. Tableside specialties include Steak Tartar, Steak Diane, Lobster Saute in saffron creme and Tournedos a la Bearnaise. A Caesar Salad is prepared at the table while awaiting an entree selection which may be Veal Oscar, Dover Sole Almondine, Breast of Pheasant or Poulet Emcee, consisting of tender strips of chicken breast in a mustard pepper creme. For an appetizer, choose a perennial favorite in the Clam Chowder or Fifi's Favorite Tidbits, stuffed mushroom caps, Oyster Rockefeller, shrimp, tomato bread and spare ribs. Finish the dining experience with a selection from the array of delicious desserts.

Fifi and her husband, Mike, are overwhelmed at their three-star rating, the best in Toledo. This is one of the reasons their business has grown over the years. Fifi makes an effort to treat every guest as if they were visiting her own home. This same attitude justifies the rewards of all of her accomplishments.

An upscale yet soothing atmosphere, great food, and personal touch from the owner herself helps make Fifi's Restaurant a charming place that must be visited in Toledo.

LOMA-LINDA
10400 Airport Highway
Toledo, Ohio 43558
Tel: (419) 865-5455
Hrs: Monday 11:00 a.m. - 11:00 p.m.
Tuesday - Saturday 11:00 a.m. - Midnight
Visa, MasterCard and American Express are accepted.

Loma-Linda has been a favorite Mexican eatery for Toledo residents since it opened its doors in 1955. Mother Ventura Cavazos and daughter Connie Barron opened the restaurant to demonstrate how Mexican cuisine could retain zest and flavor without being fiery hot. Mother and daughter started out simply, offering tacos with a sauce on the side; the rest is history. Today, Ventura's daughter, Adela, and four of Adela's sisters carry on the fine tradition. The family also owns and operates Carmel's Don Alejo, Casa Barron, Ventura's, and Concita's.

Loma-Linda's most popular entrees are beef enchiladas, beef and bean burritos, and guacamole salad. The menu features a sampling of tostadas, chimichangas, tacos, tamales, chili relleno, and flautas. Other combination and chicken dishes are also featured. Those with an adventuresome palate will enjoy sampling all the flavors of Mexican cuisine on the Mexican Plate Sampler: a complete dinner consisting of a taco, tostada, enchilada, tamale, frijoles refritos, Mexican rice and guacamole, followed by a dessert of broiled grapefruit with a surprise sauce. One of Loma-Linda's unequivocal delights is the restaurant's famous Margarita, a definite pleasure for tequila lovers.

Tapestries, stucco, and wrought iron blend to create an ambiance of Old World Spanish and New World Mexican charm. One need not be fluent in Spanish to enjoy the rich and varied flavors at Loma-Linda; a courteous food server will be happy to explain any selection. So, "Bien Venidos Amigos!" Good Eating!

MADISON'S STEAK & CHOP HOUSE
Spitzer Building on Madison Avenue, first floor
Toledo, Ohio 43604
Tel: (419) 241-3700
Hrs: Lunch:
Monday - Friday 11:00 a.m. - 2:00 p.m.
Dinner:
Tuesday - Saturday 5:00 p.m. - 11:00 p.m.
Reservations are recommended.
Free valet parking after 5:00 p.m.
Visa, MasterCard, American Express, Diners Club and Discover are accepted.

Those who enjoy a good steak should take the time to visit Toledo's newest downtown restaurant, Madison's. Located in the historic Spitzer Building only two blocks from the riverfront, this super steakhouse features superior certified angus beef, hand-cut to perfection right on the premises. Owner Allen Seder is an energetic gentleman with more than 15 years of experience in the food service industry who had always dreamed of owning an elegant steakhouse.

The menu reflects Allen's dream. Everything is made from scratch. No pre-processed foods are served at Madison's. The seafood is always fresh. For the customer's enjoyment, a bucket of peel-and-eat-shrimp is served as a complementary appetizer with each dinner. Pork, lamb, and veal dishes are cooked to order, and the prime rib is claimed to be the largest cut in the city. For those with a hearty appetite, try the 48-ounce porterhouse steak. Flavorful soups and a delightful array of salads become meals in themselves, and even the salad dressings are prepared in-house from scratch.

Madison's sumptuous collection of homemade desserts include chocolate-brandied mousse and fresh seasonal fruits as well as cheesecake, tortes, and flans. After dinner, guests can select from an extensive drink menu which includes Louis 13th Cognac and other fine Napoleon brandies, liqueurs, sherries, and imported champagne by the glass. For the quintessential steak served in a friendly, club-like atmosphere, the place to go in downtown Toledo is Madison's.

MAUMEE WINES CAFE
2556 Parkway Plaza
Toledo, Ohio 43537
Tel: (419)893-2525
Hrs: Restaurant:
Lunch:
Tuesday - Friday 11:30 a.m. - 2:30 p.m.
Dinner:
Tuesday - Thursday 5:30 p.m. - 9:30 p.m.
Friday - Saturday 6:00 p.m. - 10:00 p.m.
Visa, Mastercard and checks are accepted.

What once was simply a retail wine and beer store has been turned into one of the finest cafes in northwest Ohio. Maumee Wines Cafe offers the absolute finest in traditional French cuisine as well as an enormous selection of wines. Owner Bill Foster is very excited about the cafe he opened in 1985; it has quickly equaled the attention that his fine selection of wines has been receiving since 1977. Both visitors and residents of Toledo find Maumee Wines a truly unique dining experience.

The small exterior appearance of Maumee Wines is deceiving. Upon entering the cafe, visitors are surprised at the spacious accommodations. Maumee Wines also provides the opportunity to browse for the perfect bottle of wine to go along with the chosen meal. Over 4,000 labels are available, from the current releases to the older, vintage wines found in the cellar. Maumee Wines is second to none in quality and selection of fine wines.

Although the reputation for fine wines has existed since the late 1970s, Maumee Wine's French cuisine is quickly gaining a similarly high level of praise. The restaurant offers a unique open kitchen which features Grand Master Chef John Wesley. He invites guests to observe as their food is being prepared. John Wesley is one of America's finest chefs and specializes in traditional French food. Meals begin with appetizers such as Smoked Salmon, Pate and Cheese, and Steak Tartar. The delicious selection of entrees includes Fresh Pompano, Doversole Saute, Filet of Beef Tenderloin, and Fresh Norwegian Salmon. To finish this meal properly, a list of exquisite desserts includes Bananas Foster, Strawberries Romanoff, and White Chocolate Mousse Torte.

Maumee Wines Cafe is a fantastic wine and French cuisine experience. The selection of wines is so impressive that Maumee wines received the "award of excellence," one of only four given in the state of Ohio. Grand Master Chef John Wesey prepares his French specialties to perfection. The cafe also offers over 200 imported beers; provides gift boxes for fine wines; and carries a fine selection of gourmet food gifts. Bill Foster is most proud of the service provided by his staff and the vast selection of wines and food. All of these qualities make Maumee Wines Cafe the perfect choice for a wonderful dining experience.

MIDTOWN MUSIC CAFE
270 Superior Avenue
Toledo, Ohio 43604
Tel: (419) 243-6111
Hrs: Monday - Saturday 11:00 a.m. - 2:00 a.m.
Visa, MasterCard, American Express, Diners Club and Discover are accepted.

Although the Midtown Music Cafe just opened in late 1989, it is quickly becoming one of Toledo's hottest clubs. If fresh, crisp sound is a priority, the Cafe's live entertainment is perfect.

Owner Alan Seder features popular disc jockeys and uses music videos to complement live acts. The music memorabilia on display forms an impressive collection of curiosities from around the world. Autographed pictures of famous musicians, a sheet that the Beatles slept on, and a shirt once worn by Jimi Hendrix are among the multitudes of memorabilia housed in a music mini-museum comparable to music cafes found in major cities throughout the country. The cafe regularly seats 100 people but additional seating is often arranged closer to the performers.

In addition to the entertainment, a fine selection of seasonal and regional dishes are available. Some noted favorites include Grilled Breast of

Duck Salad, Crabmeat Cobb Salad, and Chicken Avocado Pasta. Appetizers such as artichokes and Brie with fresh fruit, and desserts are also available.

The interior of the building is done in exposed brick walls, brass and dark natural wood, along with the music memorabilia that is in abundant supply everywhere.

The Midtown Music Cafe is located in Toledo's Entertainment District at Frogtown Alley on Superior Avenue. It is within easy walking distance to the downtown hotels and the Portside Market. Toledo's Downtown Comedy Club is conveniently located next door.

The Midtown Music Cafe is an impressive blend of crisp sound, music memorabilia, and enticing entrees worth a trip to Toledo.

RICARDO'S
1 Seagate
Toledo, Ohio 43604
Tel: (419) 255-1116
Hrs: Monday - Saturday 11:00 a.m. - 2:00 a.m.
Visa, MasterCard, American Express, Diners Club and Discover are accepted.

Opened in July of 1982, Ricardo's is the culmination of owner Dick Skaff's 40 years in the restaurant business. Called Toledo's premier restaurant, Ricardo's is a crown jewel in the exciting redevelopment of the riverfront area. The restaurant's outstanding view of the river, superlative menu, and matchless service prompted local residents to name Ricardo's the number one restaurant in Toledo in a recent radio poll.

Located in Toledo's "underground" beneath the Owens-Illinois World Headquarters, the interior of Ricardo's has a predominantly nautical flavor, reminiscent of the great luxury ocean liners of the late 1930s. The subdued lighting and Art Deco decor add to the restaurant's romantic atmosphere. Under the careful eye of head chef Sam Zeilah, every meal is prepared to perfection using the freshest available ingredients. The appetizer menu features something for nearly every taste. Choose from such delights as Jumbo Shrimp Cocktail, Escargot Bourgogne, Stuffed Mushrooms Florentine topped with Hollandaise Sauce, Oysters Rockefeller, and Potato Skins with Cheddar Cheese and Bacon. The entree menu is also quite extensive and includes such house specialties as Steak Diane, Gulf Shrimp Saint Tropez, Medallions of Veal with Champagne, Rack of Lamb for One, and Baked Chicken Josephine. Three to four daily specials round out the restaurant's offerings.

Ricardo's is also the place to enjoy an evening on the town. After an outstanding meal, guests are invited to dance the night away in the restaurant's lounge where live entertainment is featured Tuesday through Saturday. A distinctive restaurant where the customer is king, Ricardo's is a "Best Choice" for fine dining in Toledo's riverfront district.

SOMEPLACE ELSE
5147 South Main
Sylvania, Ohio 43560
Tel: (419) 882-2002

Hrs:	Monday - Thursday	11:30 a.m. - 11:00 p.m.
	Friday	11:30 a.m. - Midnight
	Saturday	5:00 p.m. - 1:00 a.m.
	Sunday	10:00 a.m. - 8:00 p.m.

Visa, MasterCard, American Express and Discover are accepted.

Someplace Else, a family-owned restaurant since its opening in 1968, has always been known as a good restaurant, but that changed when Tim and Lizabeth Godbey took over the business in 1979--now it is one of the finest restaurants in the area and is rated as one of the top 10 restaurants in Toledo by the food editor of the Toledo Blade.

A casual yet classy atmosphere is achieved in the restaurant through the use of natural cherry wood and leather. The lounge features a white marble-topped bar and lots of brass with live entertainment provided Fridays and Saturdays by contemporary favorites. Someplace Else is the perfect setting for a late night snack, an intimate dinner or a special event. An elegant banquet facility is available for parties of up to 130.

The ambiance, service, and reasonable prices are part of why this restaurant is so popular, but the quality and variety of foods served are the rest of the story. Sauces, soups, and pastries are made from scratch in the kitchen and all meats and fish are hand-cut on the premises. Irresistible appetizer selections include Gulf Shrimp served Creole Style or American Cocktail Style, and Calamari (giant tender squid battered and cooked to golden brown). Seafood lovers are pleased to find Halibut Steak, Frog Legs, and a Seafood Sampler. Pasta dishes are becoming more popular with entrees prepared using seafood or garlic chicken. Traditional fare includes Tournedoes of Beef served with fresh broccoli and Parmesan tomato. Dinners are served with a choice among four salads.

The sandwich menu is a unique one with offerings of a Sylvania Club (strips of chicken breast with avocado, Swiss, bacon, tomato, and lettuce) or Cougar (deep-fried chicken strips, toasted raisin bread, and fresh fruit compote). For the health conscious, a special menu has been prepared with a breakdown of the calories, carbohydrates, protein, fat, cholesterol, and sodium contained in each dish.

To discover a "Best Choice" in dining, one shouldn't go here or there, but Someplace Else. It's easy to locate by using I-475 to U.S. 23.

THE TOLEDO CAFE
Radisson Hotel Toledo
101 North Summit
Toledo, Ohio 43604
Tel: (419) 321-2020

Fine dining can be a gastronomic adventure, and the Toledo Cafe fits that bill of fare. The cafe, located in the Radisson Hotel Toledo, combines a French bistro atmosphere with American cuisine.

With its four separate menus--breakfast, lunch, late lunch, and dinner--The Toledo Cafe prides itself on innovative dishes, unique desserts, its warm, friendly service, and ambiance. Begin the day with a wide range of selections from omelets to French Toasted Apple Nut Pie. For lunch, The Toledo Cafe's extensive selection features seven different salads; Eastern fare, including a Philly Cheese Steak or a Reuben sandwich; and California chic--Turkey Croissants and California Club sandwiches. Entrees feature three different pastas, which can be served as side dishes or full courses and meat, fish or chicken dinners. For those desiring a late afternoon lunch, the cafe's abbreviated menu includes fun foods ranging from pizza, barbecued ribs and hamburgers to salads and sandwiches.

Nouvelle Cuisine melds with American favorites at dinner. Diners may begin with a creative appetizer of Shrimp on Horseback-shrimp wrapped in bacon and topped with a light curried fruit sauce, or a seared New York Strip Steak with cilantro vinaigrette; these dishes top the list of favorites. Something for every taste is available, with entrees of beef, veal, seafood and poultry, as well as "luscious and light" selections. The menu features 30 choices in all, including such favorites as Veal Toledo, Cajun Shrimp, and fresh fish baked on a cherrywood board.

"Stylish Light" selections offer creative, carefully planned entrees, including spicy Chinese Duck Salad with soba noodles, scallions, and a ginger garlic dressing; Grilled Breast of Chicken with brandied apples; and San Francisco Chicken and Shrimp, served with peapods, red and yellow peppers, and rice. The Toledo Cafe is also one of the few restaurants to feature an open rotisserie and chafing area, with such signature dishes as Duck Breast with Raspberry Sauce and Rack of Lamb.

Diners complement their meals with a choice from an extensive selection of white, red, blush, champagne, sparkling and dessert wines. Both domestic and imported beer and wine coolers are available as well.

The cafe cautions diners to save room for the Toledo Cafe's famous trademark dessert, the "Chocolate Glob," a chocoholic's delight with chocolate syrup, brownie base, vanilla ice cream, nuts, whipped cream and a cherry, served in a parfait glass. For those with a less adventurous sweet tooth, desserts include such favorites as Sour Cream Apple Pie, Peach Cobbler, and Praline Ice Cream Pie served with rum sauce.

VENTURA'S THE ORIGINAL MEXICAN

RESTAURANTE AND CANTINA
7742 West Bancroft
Toledo, Ohio 43617
Tel: (419) 841-7523
Hrs: Monday - Thursday 11:00 a.m. - 11:00 p.m.
Friday - Saturday 11:00 a.m. - Midnight
Closed Sundays and holidays.
Visa, MasterCard, American Express, Diners Club and Discover are accepted.

Opened in 1984 by Al Mundt, Ventura's has evolved from a neighborhood-style restaurant and has retained its friendly charm. This Mexican restaurant was nominated as one of the 10 best restaurants in Toledo by the food editor of the Toledo Blade. Ventura's features the most versatile Mexican menu in town including Tex-Mex, Cajun, and American with a little Mexican influence. The great taste and the large portions make it quite obvious why Ventura's has received numerous good reviews.

The building dates from the early 1900s and was actually a 1930s roadhouse. This once-reputed speakeasy was rumored to have been frequented by members of the Capone mob including Big Al himself.

The casual, relaxed, fun atmosphere makes this a great place to meet friends and "tourists are always treated like home folks." Darlene, the kitchen manager, along with Al and Mama Ventura, see to it that the food is up to Ventura's high standards.

Favorite appetizers are the Botana ala Pancho, a wonderful mixture of Chorizo sausage, beans and monterey jack cheese, the Mexi-skins, or Linda's Munchie Sampler. The Chili "Alfredo" is rumored to be the best chili in Toledo, using a secret family recipe. Burritos are always popular and Adela's "Wet" Burrito is served with a delicious gravy. The Cajun Enchiladas with shrimp, chicken, or crabmeat can't be found anywhere else. For those with more American tastes, try the hamburgers or the Filet Vino Tinto, a pan-fried fillet in red wine sauce. The combination platters are too filling for one so bring a friend. For dessert, the Plantanos Fritas, fried bananas with cinnamon in a tortilla shell are a unique taste sensation.

Although a little off the beaten path, Ventura's is just a short distance from I-475 and is worth the drive. Ventura's success is due to good food, a friendly atmosphere and reasonable prices. Ventura's doesn't accept reservations so come early to a "Best Choice" restaurant along the lakes.

THE WILLOWS
4844 Monroe Avenue
Toledo, Ohio 43623
Tel: (419) 473-1276
Hrs: Lunch:

Monday - Thursday	11:00 a.m. - 3:00 p.m.
Dinner:	
Monday - Thursday	5:00 p.m. - 10:00 p.m.
Friday - Saturday	5:00 p.m. - 11:00 p.m.
Sunday	4:00 p.m. - 8:00 p.m.

The Willows restaurant boasts an elegant 300 seat dining room, plenty of free parking, easy-listening live entertainment, great food and five private banquet rooms. Since opening the doors in 1947, The Willows has maintained a tradition of fine dining. The restaurant was owned by the Skaff family until it was recently purchased by four local businessmen who comprise Ducat-Eckert, Inc. The Willows, now managed by Pat Irmen, one of Toledo's finest chefs, has built a reputation for being one of Toledo's best restaurants, specializing in 100 percent Angus beef and a wide variety of seafood.

The chandeliers and elegant table settings in the dining room highlight the entire area, providing the perfect setting for distinguished dining. The lounge features the soft music of a live band creating a perfectly relaxing atmosphere.

A pleasurable dining experience awaits with soft music setting the mood. Try the stuffed mushroom caps with crabmeat or the Maryland Select Oysters. Tempting entrees include Certified Angus Porterhouse, New York Strip, Prime Rib, Ribeye, Veal Marsala, Fresh Atlantic Swordfish, Chicken Alfredo and Rack of Lamb. The Friday night seafood buffet features an assortment of shrimp, crab and beef - 10 selections in all. The delicious selection of desserts changes daily.

The ambiance of fine dining, professional staff, attention given to patrons, and premium, quality cuisine are key features to the success of the Willows restaurant, making it a must stop along the lakes.

specialty shops

PRINT & FRAME GALLERY, 4840 Monroe, Toledo, Ohio 43623; Tel: (419) 475-2323. Across from the Franklin Mall one finds Print & Frame Gallery and one of Toledo's finest collections of art glass, limited edition prints, original art work, and sculptures. Custom framing is one of the special services offered here.

TASTE OF TOLEDO/BEST OF OHIO GIFT BASKETS, 6958 Leicester Road, Toledo, Ohio 43617; Tel: (419) 841-2131. One can shop for the perfect gift basket by mail, telephone, or appointment. Toledo products are featured in such baskets as "Wholly Toledo" and "Taste of Toledo." All occasions and tastes are accommodated with birthday, sports, and sympathy baskets.

taverns & pubs

MAUMEE WINES-PORTSIDE, Portside Market, Toledo, Ohio; Tel: (419) 241-WINE. This bar, an annex of Maumee Wines Cafe, offers outstanding selections of wine and beer with cheese plates to accompany one's choice.

HOLLAND

markets

MACQUEEN ORCHARD FARM MARKET

AND COUNTRY GIFT BARN
7605 Garden Road
Holland, Ohio 43528
Tel: (419) 865-2916
Hrs: Seven days
May - July: 9:00 a.m. - 7:00 p.m.
August - October: 9:00 a.m. - 8:00 p.m.
November - April: 9:00 a.m. - 6:00 p.m.
Visa and MasterCard are accepted.

MacQueen Orchard has been in existence since 1936, when founder Hugh MacQueen planted the first apple tree on 10 of his 25 acres. Today, three generations later, the orchard encompasses approximately 250 acres and grows 12 varieties of apples, peaches, pears, and plums.

Customers can either purchase wholesale packages or "pick-their-own" selection at MacQueen Orchard Farm Market. In addition, the Country Gift Barn houses a unique collection of shops in which one will find a wonderful selection of gift ideas. Items include Apple Head Dolls, Apple Wreaths, silk wall hangings, mugs, and ceramicware. Ma's Pantry features homemade apple butter, jams, jellies, preserves, teas, maple syrup, and apple blossom honey made from the orchard's own flowers. The Country Bakery features such delicious delights as apple fritters, Dutch apple pie, and donuts. Refreshing cider is sold by the gallon, half gallon, or by the cup in the Cider Barn.

MacQueen Orchard Farm Market and Country Gift Barn draws customers from all areas of the state and offers something special for the whole family in every season. Yearly festivities include the Street Rod Auto Show, held the last week in August; the Apple Butter Stir, held the first week of October; and the annual Christmas Open House, held the latter part of November. School children can tour the orchard from the middle of September to the last week of October.

PERRYSBURG

accommodations

HOLIDAY INN FRENCH QUARTER
10630 Fremont Pike
Perrysburg, Ohio 43551
Tel: (419) 874-3111
(800) 465-4329 U.S.
Visa, MasterCard, American Express, Discover and Diners Club are accepted.

The Holiday Inn French Quarter is more than just a place to spend the night. The hotel provides excellent lodging, superior conference facilities, superb dining, and adult and family activities under two domed atriums. These ingredients promise that a stay at the Holiday Inn French Quarter will be one to remember.

Just 10 minutes from downtown Toledo, the inn boasts more than 310 guest rooms that surround both domes. One, the French Quarter Holidome, is specifically for families. Even when it is raining, mom, dad, and the kids can dive into the indoor pool; take a dip in the whirlpool; hit some balls at the nine-hole putting green; or challenge the latest video game in the game room. A few steps away, the snack bar serves delicious goodies, and the Le Marche Gift Shop carries special gifts and travel necessities. Adults find the Jackson Square Atrium was designed with the business traveler or conventioneer in mind. Spacious and alive with the French Quarter ambiance, the atrium provides adult indoor-outdoor swimming, as well as many other recreational amenities and conveniences. Exceptional dining in the award-winning J. Patrick's Restaurant is accompanied by exciting live entertainment, providing exciting listening and dancing pleasure.

With facilities like these, it is no surprise that the Holiday Inn French Quarter is a major conference center in the Toledo area. Two floors of the hotel encompass executive lodging; 18 flexible meeting and banquet areas can accommodate from five to 800 people; and meeting rooms that come equipped with visual screens, flip charts, phones, white boards and other contemporary meeting needs. The hotel provides hospitality, professionalism and service within the finest of traditions.

antiques

PERRYSBURG ANTIQUE MARKET, 116 Louisiana Avenue, Perrysburg, Ohio 43551 Tel: (419) 872-0231. Opened in June 1989, Perrysburg Antique Market features 20 of Toledo's best antique dealers. In this historic building, one can find quality furniture in a variety of styles and periods along with many other treasures.

book stores

PRINTS & PRINT, 111 Louisiana, Perrysburg, Ohio 43551; Tel: (419) 874-6074. This unusual shop is a bookstore that doubles as a framing shop. Service is a top priority so special orders are the norm. Owners Peggy Orser and Shelley Julius know their customers by name and often provide complementery beverages at the front counter.

gift shops

THE SILVER FAUCET, 113 Louisiana, Perrysburg, Ohio 43551; Tel: (419) 874-8166. "Good things come in small packages" is true of The Silver Faucet. Every little item necessary for the bath can be found here along with brass and home decorator items and indoor and outdoor sculptures.

restaurants

THE LAMPLIGHT CAFE AND BAKERY
121 West Indiana Street
Perrysburg, Ohio 43551
Tel: (419) 874-0125
Hrs: Monday - Friday 7:00 a.m. - 4:00 p.m.
Saturday 7:00 a.m. - 2:00 p.m.

Jim Haas has had a life long dream of owning his own cafe/bakery. In 1987, this former teacher saw his dream become a reality with the opening of the Lamplight Cafe and Bakery. The Lamplight offers the best in baked goods, soups, salads, and sandwiches. This Perrysburg cafe has a small town atmosphere while being only five minutes from downtown Toledo. The breakfast and lunch menus are pleasing to all customers, and the list of specialty baked goods is one of a kind.

The Lamplight Cafe and Bakery is a breakfast lover's treat. Jim, Kathy, or Pat will gladly serve the customers the best omelet in town or allow them to make their own from a list of ten ingredients. If an omelet is too filling, one of the Lamplights's homemade cinnamon rolls and coffee might do the trick. One favorite of the regular patrons is the wide variety of muffins, one featured weekly, including blueberry, pineapple oat bran, and banana and pineapple among others. At lunchtime, customers have the options of some of the traditional favorites like B.L.T.'s, Rueben's or the chef's feature of the day. An excellent variety of sandwiches and gourmet croissants are also available. Perhaps above all else stands the quality of the baked goods. Kathy Flick, Jim and Helen Haas' associate, has gained a reputation as one of the area's finest bakers. The delightful scent of her cheesecakes, cookies, and caramel delights (her personal specialty) bring guests from all around. Special services of the Lamplight include wedding cakes, all occasion cakes, and catering.

The Lamplight Cafe and Bakery is an intimate 54 seat cafe. All of the food has that special home-cooked flavor. The Haases are not only proud of the delicious food that they serve but of the service provided and the care put into everything they do. For an excellent breakfast, homemade lunch, or special dessert, The Lamplight Cafe and Bakery is Perrysburg's ideal spot.

GRAND RAPIDS

apparel

THE FRONT DOOR, 24202 Front Street, Grand Rapids, Ohio 43522; Tel: (419) 832-0251. Mona McNeill opened The Front Door in 1987 and since that time shoppers have been entering through her front door to discover moderately priced comfortable casual wear for women. Providing an alternative to the items found in malls and department stores, this shop also offers unique jewelry and accessories.

points of interest

THE KERR HOUSE
17605 Beaver Street, P.O. Box 363
Grand Rapids, Ohio 43522
Tel: (419) 832-1733
Visa, MasterCard and American Express are accepted.

Ten years ago a yoga teacher named Laurie Hostetler had an innovative idea about a unique kind of spa. This idea has come to be one of the elite spas in the country. The Kerr House, located in Grand Rapids, has an ultimate goal of satisfying the body, mind, and spirit of everyone who passes through its doors. Through a healthy diet, a yoga-based exercise program, an array of personal services, and the best in quality accommodations, guests achieve the ultimate in total relaxation.

The Kerr House operates out of a refurbished Queen Ann Victorian mansion; stepping through its doors is like stepping back in time. The ambiance of this 18th century mansion is conducive to total relaxation and helps patrons feel truly separated from the world they've left behind.

Though it's not the main objective of the Kerr House to have its guests lose weight, it more often than not is one of the results of a week-long stay. A carefully-designed exercise regime leads not only to weight loss, but puts guests on a proper schedule to follow after their visit has ended. The Kerr House offers a number of beauty treatments to help visitors feel and look fantastic. This super spa's services include massages, facials, reflexology, body and herbal wraps, hair and nail treatments, whirlpools, saunas, and mineral baths.

As The Kerr House beautifies the outer body, it's also aiming to soothe the inner body and mind. A healthy diet consisting of whole foods (no chemicals or processed foods) is a constant at The Kerr House. An average daily diet consists of 750 to 1,000 calories of delicious food designed to cleanse the inner body and create good eating habits. People come from every state and many other countries to achieve the mental and physical peace offered every week by Laurie and her staff of concerned specialists.

Guests of The Kerr House leave there with a refreshed attitude and a better understanding of their minds and bodies. This intimate spa accommodates up to eight people. Some guests bring the family while others come alone or with friends. Perhaps Judy Babcock, author of The Spa Book, said it best when she wrote, "This may not be heaven, but it's very close."

restaurants

LAROE'S, Front Street, Grand Rapids, Ohio 43522; Tel: (419) 832-3082. LaRoe's is found in a historic building that dates to the 1880s. Diners enjoy breakfast, lunch, and dinner seven days a week and can catch a show here at Girty's Back Stage Dinner Theater. Try their specialty--delicious BBQ Country Ribs.

specialty shops

DANDY'S LANE
24164 Front Street
Grand Rapids, Ohio 43522
Tel: (419) 832-6425
Hrs: Monday - Saturday 10:00 a.m. - 5:00 p.m.
Sunday Noon - 5:00 p.m.
Extended summer and Christmas hours
Visa and MasterCard are accepted.

Karen and Dave Palka opened Dandy's Lane in October of 1985. This very unusual shop offers fantastic homemade fudge in over 40 flavors, a unique collection of "Victorian Theme" gifts, antiques and other fine gifts that Dave and Karen have spent many hours seeking out. There's an interesting mini-museum filled with historical items and nostalgic memorabilia. The museum is said to be watched over by the spirit of the last Ottawa Indian in Wood County, Teena-beek, who had befriended the original settlers in the Grand Rapids area.

Dandy's Lane is most appropriately set in a turn-of-the -century building. The canal and the Maumee River behind the emporium and the bench out front for just sitting and talking, add to the ambiance of this friendly relaxed shop, located just 20 minutes from Toledo, off of Route 24 in historic Grand Rapids.

Karen's fudge is quickly acquiring a reputation as some of the best found anywhere. People have been known to drive long distances to taste the ambrosia of the many creative flavors including favorites such as amaretto chocolate swirl, peanut butter chocolate, chocolate chewy praline, cherry chocolate swirl, and seasonal favorites like pumpkin pie and strawberry nut. Karen uses the finest ingredients to create each of the over 40 creamy flavors found here which is rumored to be the largest selection of fudge in the United States.

Dave and Karen are most proud of the uniqueness of the different lines of merchandise found at Dandy's Lane and how everyone at the shop including their children, Wendy, Chris, and Matt, are always eager to help their visitors. The attitude that "customers are friends here" along with the history, ambiance, the unusual and high quality gift items and of course Karen's fantastic fudge all add up to a great visit to a "Best Choice" along the lakes at Dandy's Lane.

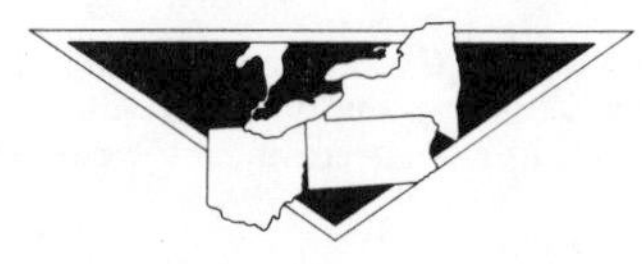

OTTAWA COUNTY

Named for the Ottawa Indians, who were among the first inhabitants of this lakeside area, this county was created on March 6, 1840 from parts of Erie, Lucas, and Sandusky Counties. It was off the coast of this Ohio county that the American naval forces led by Captain Oliver Hazard Perry defeated a British fleet near Put-In-Bay in what became known as the Battle of Lake Erie. This historic event ensured American control over the Northwest Territories, and in no small way set the stage for expansion across the continent along the Great Lakes and on into the Northern Plains.

In 1828, a shipwreck along the shore left a group of Scottish immigrants, bound for Chicago, stranded near the mouth of the Portage River. With swift flexibility they agreed that they liked the area, thus becoming some of the first residents of the new town of Port Clinton.

On Johnson's Island, during the Civil War, the United States constructed a prisoner-of-war-camp for Confederate soldiers in which 15,000 prisoners were housed. Today this beautiful county boasts outstanding recreational activities and events that show off the lake shore as well as a continuing heritage of agricultural and industrial strength.

attractions

Crane Creek State Park in Oak Harbor offers fishing, hiking, swimming and birdwatching .

Crane Creek Experimental Station is a freshwater marsh that is home to migrant birds and birds of prey. Bald eagles frequent this area.

Magee Marsh Wildlife Area in Oak Harbor is at the nexus of two of the major migratory paths for wildfowl, the Atlantic and the Mississippi. This reserve hosts an amazing plethora of waterfowl and other birds. Bird trails and an observation tower make the birdwatching easier and more enjoyable.

Both bird and mammal wildlife abound at the 8,000-acre **Ottawa National Wildlife Refuge** in Oak Harbor, which is located near both Crane Creek State Park and Magee Marsh.

events

The **Ottawa County Fair** is held in mid-July at the fairgrounds in Oak Harbor.

Each September the **Ohio Wildflowers festival** comes to Magee Marsh.

PORT CLINTON, PUT-IN-BAY, MARBLEHEAD AND VICINITY

This maritime region has held strategic importance for centuries. However, the one and only time that importance was put to the ultimate test of battle was during the War of 1812. The Battle of Lake Erie settled once and for all the ownership and control of these lakes, from Ontario to Superior. Since that time, this has been a peaceful and prosperous region.

Port Clinton's location on a natural peninsula formed between Lake Erie's open waters and Sandusky Bay give it an important maritime connotation. The Bass Islands, South, Middle, and North, are also particularly well situated to take advantage of everything this freshwater sea has to offer. Its prime geographical setting has drawn attention to this area since the time of the Native Americans.

PUT-IN-BAY

attractions

Oak Point State Park on South Bass Island is a small picnicking area on the shore of Lake Erie.

Perry's Victory Memorial is a 352-foot granite column that commemorates this important sea victory.

South Bass Island State Park has a fishing pier and spots for swimming.

Crystal Cave, open Memorial Day through mid-September, boasts the largest strontium sulfate crystals worldwide.

events

Blessing of the Fleet is held each April in Put-In-Bay.

The annual **Put-In-Bay Fall Regatta** is held in October.

bed & breakfast inns

THE BAY CLUB AT EAST POINT FARMS
827 Columbus
Put-In-Bay, Ohio 43456
Tel: (419) 285-6155
Hrs: Open year round.
Check out - 11:30 a.m.
Check in - 2:00 p.m.
Visa and MasterCard are accepted.

Bed and breakfast inns have justly earned a reputation for personalized overnight lodging and romantic accommodations. Few bed and breakfast inns, however, can match The Bay Club at East Point Farms for a beautiful combination of natural setting and rustic charm.

While she was on a day trip to the island, Sandy Stana saw the historic house, which was built in 1897; she fell in love with it and purchased the property. Extensive remodeling and renovation work ensued. Much of the original woodwork was lovingly refinished and restored as well. To preserve the inn's 19th century heritage, Sandy decorated the interior with lovely period antiques.

Twenty-seven guests can be accommodated in the inn's seven private rooms and spacious third-floor loft. Each room is tastefully appointed and boasts exquisite antiques and original works of art. Fresh flowers grace the public areas of the inn, and plush leather chairs and deep, comfortable sofas invite an evening of relaxation and conversation. The wrap-around verandah affords a beautiful view of Lake Erie and the rising and setting of the sun. The experience of elegant Victorian lodging at the Bay Club at East Point Farms can be enhanced by a Bay Club carriage ride or island tour in one of Sandy's horse-drawn vehicles. The bed and breakfast inn is also a perfect place for meetings, weddings, receptions or family reunions. Preserving its homey feel, the inn welcomes children.

The Bay Club at East Point Farms offers so much more than mainland bed and breakfast inns. The tangy sweetness of Lake Erie air, the clip-clop of horse-drawn carriages, and ten acres of manicured lawns and formal gardens present a relaxing country home atmosphere.

malls

HARBOUR SQUARE "A SHOPPING PLACE"
Corner of Delaware and Toledo
Put-In-Bay, Ohio 43456

Adjacent to Peppy's Monument, Harbour Square is located one block from the lakefront and across the street from the bus line to the ferry. Boardwalks and New England-style architecture exude a delightful, fishing-village ambiance. Many shops can be found in the square, in addition to an information center and the Put-In-Bay Chamber of Commerce and Visitors Information Center.

BAYPEDS offers moped rentals. Riding a moped is a relaxing way to explore the island and enjoy its fresh air.

BAYCARTS is the place to rent golf carts for enthusiasts who are drawn to the nearby golf courses.

GEORGE'S BIKE RENTAL features bicycles of varied sizes and types for all family members. For those who are able, there is no better way to get close to one's environment than on a bicycle.

SUNDAE'S ICE CREAM PARLOR pampers your palate with superbly rich ice cream treats. Sundae's Ice Cream Parlor features some of the most incredible delights available.

IRWIN'S N.Y. DELI is the place in Put-In-Bay to enjoy a delicious New York-style sandwich made from the freshest meats and cheeses and other deli selections. Refreshing drinks are also a highlight here.

PUDDLE DUCK provides a delightful atmosphere in which visitors explore the selections of children's and women's clothing. Many articles show a distinctive use of Applique designs.

AHOY is a beautiful shop in which customers marvel at the jewelry creations and exquisite gift items. Ahoy inventory catches the eye, emphasizing nautical jewelry, gold chains and collectibles.

STONEHENGE presents gifts from the English Commonwealth. Model ships, nautical antiques, and local crafts lend the shop a North Coast ambiance.

BAYSIDE offers women's sportswear and casual apparel.

SHIRTS AND SHORTS invites anyone who enjoys the beach to visit the shop; it features a wide variety of contemporary T-shirts, shorts, and beachwear.

SANDY'S SHOP offers nautical furnishings and accessories, paintings, and inspired interior designing. Steeped in color and North Coast atmosphere, Sandy's Shop is also the boarding point for horse-drawn carriage tours to East Point Farms.

restaurants

COOPER'S RESTAURANT AND TAVERN
800 Catawba Street
Put-In-Bay, Ohio 43456
Tel: (419) 285-2738
Hrs: May - October
Visa, MasterCard and American Express are accepted.

Cooper's Restaurant and Tavern enjoys the reputation of being the island's oldest continually operating restaurant. The original business came into being in 1871 as the Put-In-Bay Wine Company. In 1947, the company became Cooper's Winery and Restaurant; the winery ceased operation in 1955. Cellar Cache Gift Shop now occupies the old wine cellar. Happily, the restaurant continued in operation, and for the last 42 years has served the best in family oriented, contemporary cuisine.

The Urge family took over the operation of Cooper's in 1979 after catching "Island Fever." Their love of the area's lifestyle is reflected in the restaurant's menu. Guests can choose from such delights as fresh Lake Erie perch or pickerel, better known as walleye, hand-dipped in the restaurant's own beer batter and deep-fried to a golden brown. Other popular entrees include barbeque ribs coated with a tangy barbeque sauce, and Quiche Lorraine made fresh daily with bacon and French onions. For lunch, try the restaurant's good old-fashioned cheeseburger or the popular "Z" Special, a filet of chicken breast sandwich topped with bacon, melted cheese, lettuce, tomato, and onion.

The restaurant's extensive wine list features the island's own wines. There is also a full service bar available featuring a wide variety of imported beers. The Cellar Cache Gift Shop features fine gifts and many brand-name collectibles. Items in brass, copper, pewter, and crystal are found throughout the shop. Other gift ideas include scents and limited edition prints.

wine

HEINEMAN WINERY
Catawba & Thompson Streets
Put-In-Bay, Ohio 43456
Tel: (419) 285-2811
Hrs: Summer:
Seven days 10:00 a.m. - 10:00 p.m.
Spring and Fall:
Seven days 11:00 a.m. - 7:00 p.m.
The winery is closed in winter.
Visa and MasterCard are accepted.

Founded in 1888, Heineman Winery is nearing its fourth generation as a family-run business. There are 53 acres of grapes on the island of which Heineman's owns about 23 acres. Of the many fine table wines, dessert wines, and grape juices produced, the winery is best known for its Catawba, an award-winning pink and white "sipping" wine.

In spring, summer, and fall, guests arrive at Heineman Winery by boat or plane. From 7:00 a.m. to 7:00 p.m., ferry boats leave Port Clinton on the half hour. The winery's main building is chalet-style with a stucco and wood exterior and an interior done in rare wormy chestnut. Two European-style wine bars reflect the family's German roots, and intricate wood carvings on oak plaques celebrate the winemaking process. Guests are welcome to linger over wine and cheese in a flower-filled wine garden or browse through a gift shop stocked with collectibles. After a tour of the winery, most visitors explore nearby Crystal Cave. According to the Smithsonian Institute, at 35 feet wide, this cafe is the world's largest geode.

Heineman Winery is proud of its family tradition of providing guests with a high-quality product and a beautiful environment in which to enjoy it. People from all walks of life come to sample Heineman's supreme wines, the result of over 100 years of winemaking skill.

LONZ WINERY
Middle Bass Island, Ohio 43446
Tel: (419) 285-5411
Hrs: May 15 - Memorial Day:
Seven days Noon - 6:00 p.m.
Memorial Day - September 30:
Sunday - Thursday Noon - 7:00 p.m.
Friday - Saturday Noon - 10:00 p.m.

Few wineries in the United States have as interesting and unique a setting as Lonz Winery. Located on the southern tip of Middle Bass Island in Lake Erie off the north central Ohio coast, Lonz Winery traces its historical roots back more than a century.

In 1863, a German stone cutter named Andrew Wehrle carved a 14-foot deep wine cellar out of the native limestone on Middle Bass Island. A dance pavilion was built over the cellars, and acres of succulent wine grapes were planted and thrived in the loamy soil. Peter Lonz worked for Andrew Wehrle for five years before moving nearby on the island and starting his own winery. During Prohibition, Peter Lonz's son, George, and George's wife, Fannie, bought the original Wehrle winery property and the modern setting for the Lonz Winery took shape. In 1934, George Lonz built an impressive, Gothic-style brick and stone castle-like structure over the original Wehrle wine cellars. Today, it is listed on the National Registry of Historic Places. Access to the island continues to be by ferry, private boat, or small aircraft. Winery tours begin with a historical overview, and then visitors can explore the deep limestone aging cellars and marvel at the impressive stone castle built into a hill. A picturesque view of Lake Erie following the tour enhances the relaxed atmosphere where visitors sip samples of many of the fine Lonz Winery wines. Sandwiches, pizza and snacks are also available. A fully stocked gift shop offers souvenirs and gift items including winemaking supplies and wine accessories.

The history of Ohio and of winemaking are tangibly intertwined on Middle Bass Island. For a day like no other, catch the ferry near Port Clinton or Sandusky and experience the special island ambiance of Lonz Winery--it has been and continues to be a favorite of generations of Americans.

PORT CLINTON

attractions

Catawba Island State Park, located eight miles northeast of Port Clinton on 18 acres of land, was once the hunting grounds of the Wyandot and Ottawa Indians. The area contains launch ramps for boats, ice fishing facilities, vineyards, picnicking areas and a large fishing pier which is open to the public.

East Harbor State Park contains the largest campground to be found in an Ohio state park, over 500 family campsites with youth and adult group areas. A wide variety of winter activities can alo be enjoyed at this park.

The **Middle Harbor** area of the park is a nesting ground for black-crowned night herons and great blue herons. No boats with motors are permitted in this protected environment.

African Lion Safari Wildlife Park, open summers only, is a drive-thru safari park that offers viewers a wonderful experience with such animals as zebras, elephants, camels and giraffes, along with special bird, reptile and llama exhibits.

Marblehead Lighthouse is the oldest lighthouse on the Great Lakes. Built in 1821, the lighthouse is made of native limestone.

events

Walleye Festival is held each May in Port Clinton.
Look for **Artists in the Park** each August in Port Clinton.

accommodations

ISLAND HOUSE
Madison and Perry
Port Clinton, Ohio 43452
Tel: (419) 734-2166
Hrs: Open for Lunch, Dinner and Sunday Brunch.
Visa, MasterCard, American Express, Discover and Diners Club are accepted.

The Island House, "Lake Erie's Centennial House," is a landmark of hospitality and fine dining known in the Port Clinton area as one of the finest hotels in Ohio. Since February 10, 1887, when the Island House opened its doors, its tradition of charm and gracious attention have brought the famous and not-so-famous to its doors.

The accommodations at Island House are outstanding and reflect the history of the inn. All of the rooms are air-conditioned and have modern conveniences and can be rearranged to meet specific needs of the guest. Executive suites with special amenities are also available. Special rates are available to groups and off-season travelers. The inn's staff is expertly trained and happy to direct guests to the surrounding sights or provide information relating to the hotel's history. The inn is also a pleasant place to be if relaxation is all a guest seeks.

The hotel's tradition encompasses the fine food available in its two dining rooms, which are combined under the name Victory Bar and Grill. Both dining rooms offer a delicious menu selection, including Lake Erie walleye and yellow perch. Bostonians raised on bluefish and scrod and New Orleanians loyal to redfish and Seattle-ites who swear by Pacific salmon have all come away from the Victory Bar and Grill greatly impressed with the superb flavor of this fresh water fish. If the rest of one's stay in Port Clinton didn't offer so much to do and see, it would be fair to say that a trip to the Island House to enjoy the walleye and yellow perch would be reason enough to go. In the evenings the fun and entertainment at the inn's lounge make the Island House a focal point of the Port Clinton scene. This enjoyable spot is decorated with nautical, hunting, and fishing memorabilia.

General manager Ronald T. Heffelfinger wishes to extend a cordial greeting and hopes everyone will have the opportunity to stay at his distinctive hotel.

SHORELINE PROPERTIES, INC.
1801 East Perry
Port Clinton, Ohio 43452
Tel: (419) 734-5371
Hrs: Seven days 10:00 a.m. - 6:00 p.m.
Visa and MasterCard are accepted.

The Lake Erie resort area centered around Port Clinton is a green and blue wonderland that attracts thousands of visitors each year. More and more vacationers discover that shoreline Properties is the place to call for the very best in lakefront rental units. Owners Ron and Debbie Miller provide the warm, personal touch that is necessary in arranging affordable vacation property.

More than 500 units are available; the vast majority are located right on the lakeshore with wonderful views, lakeside amenities and recreational opportunities. Shoreline Properties, Inc. can arrange a vacation rental for a two-day visit or for an extended stay. There is a variety of accommodations to fit any family or group, from a one-bedroom unit to a three-bedroom townhouse that sleeps eight. All the properties have swimming pools, Jacuzzis, and barbecue areas. Many of the rentals feature private docks, tennis courts, putting greens, and private beaches. Regardless of size, each unit is completely furnished and features a fully equipped kitchen, bed and bath linens, and a television. Both cleaning and linen services are available for most of the condominiums.

For more than 15 years, the company has been making vacation dreams come true for Port Clinton visitors. Call and let Shoreline Properties turn dreams into reality.

air tours

ISLAND AIRLINES
3255 East State Road
Port Clinton, Ohio 43452
Tel: (419) 734-3149
Hrs: Seven days 8:00 a.m. - Dark
Closed Christmas, New Year's, Thanksgiving and Easter.
Visa, MasterCard, Phillips and Exxon are accepted.

Enjoy a trip to the islands of Lake Erie aboard one of the nation's oldest commuter air carriers, Island Airlines. Founded in 1928, this successful air taxi, located at the Port Clinton Airport, three miles east of town off State Route 53 North, offers a "Sky's Eye View" of Lake Erie.

A small, friendly, customer-oriented airline flying modern six-seat Cessnas and a nine-seat DeHavilland Otter, Island Airlines operates regularly scheduled service to Put-In-Bay as well as all U.S. islands in Lake Erie equipped with an airstrip. Unable to meet the scheduled flights? Don't worry. Island Airlines provides charter service. No more waiting for the ferry to reach North Bass, Middle Bass and Kelley's Island.

One of Island Airlines' most popular services is the Island Sight-Seeing Flight, a 15-minute hop that offers a panoramic view of the lake and nearby islands. The ferries don't operate during the winter, so the airline's winter ice fishing trips to the islands are also very popular. "The Shortest Airline in the World," Island Airlines has an outstanding service record, well-trained professional pilots, and affordable rates.

art galleries

GALLERY ON THE LAKE
126 East Perry Street
Port Clinton, Ohio 43452
Tel: (419) 734-3318
Hrs: February - December:
Seven days 10:00 a.m. - 5:00 p.m.
Visa, MasterCard and Discover are accepted.

Gary Perkins' love and skill of woodworking enabled him to open his first frame shop, Finishing Touch Gallery, in 1984. That frame shop evolved into an art gallery, Gallery on the Lake. Gary and Marie opened the art gallery in March of 1986 in Port Clinton.

The specialties featured here include limited edition prints, etching, and original watercolors of nationally and internationally known artists, as well as local artists. Nautical works by John Stobart, Jim Clary, and Merle Barnhill make perfect remembrances of a great visit to the Erie Islands area. Wildlife and waterfowl artists Robert Bateman and Terry Redlin might be the most well known of American artists featured. Impressionistic "Victorian" works are represented by Alan Maley and Vivian Swain while P. Buckley Moss and Charles Wysocki bring fine examples of Americana to Gallery on the Lake. Even Gary's own woodturning pieces can be found here, including bowls, vases, goblets, and other more artsy pieces. All purchases can be shipped within the United States if necessary.

The Gallery's non-intrusive, modern decor falls into the background and places the main emphasis on the patron of the art. Spot lighting and large picture windows create a very bright, uplifting mood and set a perfect atmosphere to take in the exquisite details of these fine works.

Gallery on the Lake also sponsors three to four shows each summer. The artist makes a personal appearance and will often personalize his works for the patrons. They provide quality, custom framing, which will make a newly purchased work of art a striking part of any decor and they also offer an art consultation service.

Gary and Marie take great pride in the variety and quality of the artworks displayed here and the fact that there is something here to satisfy every taste and every price range. All are warmly welcomed to browse at the Gallery on the Lake, a "Best Choice" in art galleries along the Great Lakes Coast.

campgrounds

CEDARLANE CAMPGROUNDS
2926 NE Catawba
Port Clinton, Ohio 43452
Tel: (419) 797-9907
Hrs: May 1 - October 15:
Check-In Noon
Check-Out 3:00 p.m

Cedarlane Campgrounds, located on beautiful Catawba Island peninsula, opened in 1965 with 20 electric sites and a few primitive sites, has expanded to 300 water and electric sites and 50 primitive sites, accommodating recreational vehicles, tents, vans, and motor homes. The cleanliness and beauty of Cedarlane, and the warmth of employees who make out-of-towners feel welcome have kept campers coming back for almost 25 years.

Named "Ottawa County Campground of the Year" for several years, the campgrounds are in a lovely park-like setting, with a lot of shaded and sunlit areas to stroll through. There is plenty of recreation in the area for the entire family including fishing within one mile of the park. Some of the facilities the campground has to offer are a heated pool, playground area, shuffleboard, basketball and volleyball courts, and a video game room. There are fish cleaning facilities available.

Visitors appreciate the cleanliness and modern facilities of Cedarlane Campground. Restrooms have flush toilets and the shower buildings are kept immaculately clean; private shower facilities are available for seasonals. Portable pump-outs are located at each site. Pets are permitted but must be leashed and attended to at all times. Safety is also a major concern here;

ground fires are not permitted, and campfires are allowed only in barrels or grills. Mini-bikes, motorcycles, and go-carts as well as firearms and fireworks are prohibited. Cedarlane Campgrounds, close to Put-In-Bay Ferry and many fine restaurants, offers plenty of things to do and is a "Best Choice" for campers that appreciate the modern conveniences that make "roughing it" an easy task.

charters

JET EXPRESS
North Jefferson & Perry Streets
Port Clinton, Ohio 43452
Tel: (419) 732-2800
(800) 245-1JET
Hrs: Mid-May through Mid-October:
Various departure times starting at 9:00 a.m.
Call for departure times.
Visa, MasterCard, American Express and Discover are accepted.

The fastest way to get to the quaint island town of Put-In-Bay (and incidentally, the most fun) is by Jet Express. Aboard the powerful 92-foot jet catamaran, travelers experience an exhilarating 22-minute ride from Port Clinton on the mainland.

In continuous operation since 1927, Jet Express is the newest and fastest of the ferry boats in the Put-In-Bay line. This new, Coast Guard approved, Australian catamaran can carry up to 380 passengers, and when the craft lifts up on its twin hulls, it is capable of an ultrasmooth "blow-your-hair-back" speed of 33 miles per hour. While its rugged construction qualifies it for ocean travel, its passenger accommodations are luxurious, especially for a ferry. Passengers walk on carpeted decks and sit on cushioned seats. In addition, an entertaining narration on Put-In-Bay's historic harbor wafts through the air as guests take in the breathtaking scenery of the voyage.

With departures beginning at 9:00 a.m. and continuing until 11:30 p.m., visitors can spend the entire day exploring Put-In-Bay's many attractions. Bikes, golf carts and a tour train are available on the island, making restaurants, parks, caves, wineries and even a fish hatchery, and museum only minutes away from the dock. Put-In-Bay Line will also put together a group package featuring tours and dinner for a discounted price. On your next trip to Put-In-Bay, let Jet Express do the driving. Remember, getting there is half the fun when you ride Jet Express.

great lakes coast

SHORE NUF CHARTERS
247 Lakeshore Drive
Port Clinton, Ohio 43452
Tel: (419) 734-9999
Visa and MasterCard are accepted.

Shore Nuf Charters offers seven hours of fantastic fishing or just plain fun in the sun on Lake Erie.

Shore Nuf Charters boasts the largest fleet of Coast Guard certified fishing and pleasure boats in the Port Clinton area. The boats are large enough to accommodate groups of up to 40 people and feature the latest fish-finding sonar equipment. Bait, food, and refreshments are available in the stores located at the marinas operated by Shore Nuf Charters. Rods, reels, and other equipment is available for rent. The skippers are experienced anglers who know all the best places to find schools of walleye and perch, and will provide all the advice necessary to ensure that fishermen catch their limits. A fish cleaning service is available, and a restaurant nearby will cook the catch according to your specification. The boats are also available for charter by groups and organizations. Catering can be arranged for party trips to the nearby islands or leisurely cruises around the lake. The boats operate out of two marinas: Drawbridge Marina at 247 Lakeshore Drive and Pier One at Four North Jefferson Street.

Shore Nuf Charters offers the largest, best-equipped fleet of boats in the Port Clinton area. Whether one is out to catch one's limit or just to enjoy a cruise with friends, a great time is guaranteed.

gift shops

NORTH COAST GIFTS AND MIKE'S TAXIDERMY
40 1/2 North Jefferson Street
Port Clinton, Ohio 43452
Tel: (419) 732-3655
Hrs: Seven days 9:00 a.m. - 10:00 p.m.
Closed January - March.
Visa and MasterCard are accepted.

Located at the intersection of Perry and North Jefferson Streets in the heart of Port Clinton, North Coast Gifts and Mike's Taxidermy combines the talents of owners Mike and Peg Pusateri. Mike first became interested in taxidermy at the age of seven; as an adult, he spent several years as an apprentice before deciding to open his own shop. Three years later, in 1984, Peg opened North Coast Gifts in the shop next door.

Mike specializes in custom mounting of trophy fish pulled from the abundant waters of Lake Erie. He also offers expert fish cleaning, specializing in walleye fillets. Visitors to Mike's shop will find a variety of T-shirts, hats, and other area souvenirs as well as charter and fishing information.

Peg's North Coast Gifts has a distinctively nautical flavor, and covers more than 4,300 square feet of display space. Visitors will find gifts of nearly every shape, size, color, and style, as well as items to fit every budget. The sea shell jewelry, wind chimes, and trinkets are very popular, as are the brass items such as ship's lanterns and bells. Peg also carries an extensive line of clothing items including T-shirts, jerseys, and beach wear.

marinas

MIDWAY MARINA, 1871 NorthEast Catawba Road, Port Clinton, Ohio 43452; Tel: (419) 797-4491. Midway Marina, offering the finest in docking facilities, is a "Best Choice" for boaters.

parks

AFRICAN SAFARI WILDLIFE PARK
267 Lightner Road
Port Clinton, Ohio 43452
Tel: (419) 734-5986 or (419) 732-3606
Hrs: Memorial Week - Labor Day:
Seven days 9:00 a.m. - 7:00 p.m.
Visa, MasterCard and American Express are accepted.

The African Safari Wildlife Park has been providing entertainment for family members of all ages for 21 years. This park offers much more than a zoo; visitors see zebras and giraffes in their natural environment as they experience the drive-through safari from the family automobile. Children are especially excited by all of the unusual species to see and the contact they have with these animals.

The drive-through safari provides close-up views of many of the animals--some white rhinoceros are curious enough to walk up to a car and check for treats. Afterwards, one can enjoy animal shows (Porkchop Downs is the Great Lakes' only daily pig races); hop a ride on a camel or elephant; or feed the black swans at the Safari Junction Lake. The park specializes in breeding a variety of animals, and with more than 200 animals in the breeding group, many rare and endangered species can be seen throughout the season at the baby animal nursery. One can see rare white tigers, the largest llama and alpaca exhibit in the United States, or enjoy the daily educational shows.

The Simba Lodge Gift Shop features souvenirs from T-shirts to genuine African art as reminders of park adventures and the Safari Junction offers a variety of food and snacks. The African Safari Wildlife Park is a "Best Choice" for a fun family outing; it's also the ideal spot for animal lovers to see their furry friends close-up.

resorts

ERIE ISLAND RESORT & MARINA
4495 West Darr-Hopfinger Road
Port Clinton, Ohio 43452
Tel: (419) 734-9117
(800) 338-3854 Ohio
Hrs: Seven days 9:00 a.m. - 10:00 p.m. (Office)

Known as an "undivided interest subdivision," Erie Island Resort & Marina is a relatively new resort arrangement in which part of the 145-acre facility is open to the general public and part is reserved for owners and their guests.

Erie Island Resort & Marina's management is dedicated to providing the highest-quality relaxation and vacationing at affordable prices. Although portions of the complex are not yet completed, the final configuration will include clusters of cottages with 750 square feet of decorator-designed, contemporary interior (plus outside decks, gas fireplaces, full kitchens, dining areas and master bedrooms), RV villages built in two clusters of 59 sites each and a multipurpose lodge, complete with a health club that features an indoor swimming pool, racquetball court, and a weight room.

The full service marina will offer approximately 300 boat slips, gas and diesel pumps, water/electrical hookups, and boat rentals and storage. Owners and guests at Erie Island Resort & Marina will have an opportunity to enjoy a full range of outdoor activities, including boating, fishing, ice fishing and skiing, as well as a multitude of social events.

restaurants

THE GARDEN AT THE LIGHTHOUSE
226 East Perry Street
Port Clinton, Ohio 43452
Tel: (419) 732-2151
Hrs: Serving lunch and dinner
May - September:
Seven days
October - April:
Monday - Saturday
Visa, MasterCard, Diners Club and Discover are accepted.

The Garden at the Lighthouse is the creation of J. Bou-Sliman, a life-long area resident, who sought out the perfect setting for one of Port Clinton's finest restaurants. Visitors will appreciate the well-groomed landscaping as they wind down the path leading to the restaurant that once served as the residence for the keeper of the light at Port Clinton's first lighthouse, which also stood on this site.

Once inside, diners will be impressed by the restaurant's decor and ambiance. The main dining room has a traditional feeling and an emphasis on Port Clinton's ties to Lake Erie. Patrons may also dine in the more casual second dining room with its paddle fans, greenery, and rattan. The beautiful view of the lake will dominate the conversation--until the food is served.

The Garden at the Lighthouse strives for culinary excellence through creative use of only the freshest seafood, fish, fowl, and hand-cut steaks and veal. Nowhere is this more evident than in the Lake Erie perch and walleye, either fried or broiled; the Chicken Avocado; and the Poulet D'Elegance--Danish lobster tails and Swiss cheese wrapped in fresh breast of chicken. The menu also contains mouth-tempting entrees such as Provimi veal with mousseline garnish and numerous pasta dishes. For the true gourmet, a visit to The Garden at the Lighthouse wil make a memorable lunch or dinner.

wine

MON AMI WINERY
3845 East Wine Cellar Road
Catawba Island
Port Clinton, Ohio 43452

Tel:	(419) 797-4445	
Hrs:	Monday - Saturday	11:00 a.m. - 9:00 p.m.
	Sunday	Noon - 8:00 p.m.
	Tours:	
	Seven days	2:00 p.m. - 4:00 p.m.

Nestled into a wooded hillside at the southern end of a Catawba Island peninsula, historical Mon Ami Winery was constructed in 1872 of locally quarried limestone, walnut from the surrounding woods, mortar from slated limestone, and sand from the lakeshore. Although destroyed by fire in 1943, the interior was reconstructed the next year.

Originally a grape grower's cooperative, Mon Ami Winery was taken over in 1956 by a third generation vintner who installed a restaurant and gardens. In 1980, the present owners bought the winery; they continue the proud tradition of producing top-quality champagnes and wines using grapes grown in the region. A myriad of fireplaces, long since boarded up, were used to keep the rooms at an even temperature during the winter before modern heating facilities were installed. A natural ventilation system was achieved by creating huge vaulted cellars two stories below ground. Large casks try to cover up remnants of another colorful age, Prohibition, when the winery had need of a dance floor and bandstand as part of a speakeasy.

To address present day dining needs, Mon Ami Restaurant's award winning cuisine includes fresh seafood-broiled, sauteed or fried; a Fisherman's Platter, rainbow trout, Veal Parmigiana, seafood pasta, prime rib, Long Island Duckling a L'orange with a blend of wild rice, and a variety of steaks. A charming establishment, Mon Ami Winery promises guests an advantage into the past as well as the present.

MARBLEHEAD

art galleries

THE RICHMOND GALLERY
417 West Main Street
Marblehead, Ohio 43440
Tel: (419) 798-5631
Hrs: Winter:
Tuesday - Sunday 10:00 a.m. - 5:00 p.m.
Memorial Day - Labor Day:
Seven days 10:00 a.m. - 5:00 p.m.
Visa, MasterCard and Discover are accepted.

Ben Richmond is no newcomer to the world of art. Since he opened The Richmond Gallery in 1981, his work has earned national recognition and is fast becoming known in international art circles. The Richmond Gallery was rated in the top 6 percent of all art galleries in the United States by the Art Business News 1988 survey.

Ben's paintings, which are mostly watercolor, deal primarily with nautical themes and Ohio's north coast, capturing the historical essence of yesteryear and giving a glimpse into the soul of the Lake Erie landscape. Visitors entering the shop should not be surprised to find Ben hard at work on a new creation or finishing a painting. The gallery offers signed and numbered limited edition prints, a signature series of miniature prints, limited edition collector plates, and note cards. Glass and bronze sculpture, porcelain figurines, and other media art by Charles Wysocki, P. Buckley Moss, Andrew Wyeth, John Singer Sargent, Jim Clary, Terry Redlin, Norman Rockwell, and hundreds more are displayed as well.

Ben and his wife, Wendy, are also the creators of Chandler's Wharf. Marblehead's newest and most unusual collection of shops. Chandler's Wharf is located directly across the street from The Richmond Gallery. Among the shops are Gulliver's Landing, an emporium of nautical brass and decorative items, and Yankee Trader, a North Coast clothier. Duck Trap Galleria is an art gallery devoted to wildlife art, and Auntie Em's is a storehouse of country and period collectibles. For some of the finest chowder this side of Maine, step inside Dolly's Bake Shoppe. Nautical antiques and reproductions are the specialty items at Ships Watch, and the Ginger Jar features a greenhouse of dried flowers, arrangements and wind chimes. For a treasure house of classical, historical, nautical, art, culinary inspiration, prose, poetry, and children's literature, visit Book Nook.

bed & breakfast inns

OLD STONE HOUSE ON THE LAKE
133 Clemons Street
Marblehead, Ohio 43440
Tel: (419) 7898-5922
Hrs: Seven days
Check in at 2:30 p.m.
Reservations are suggested.
Visa and MasterCard are accepted.

Old Stone House on the lake is a historic bed and breakfast inn offering a seemingly limitless view of Lake Erie. Alexander Clemons, a veteran of the War of 1812, built the house of stone in 1891 from Marblehead's first stone quarry. The 29-room house first served as an inn for the quarry workers, then as the Clemons' family home. The residence retains its old world charm, and is carefully maintained and equipped with modern plumbing and all amenities.

With 12 quaint, yet good-sized rooms, Old Stone House on the Lake serves its many guests splendidly. On the main level is the breakfast room, furnished with oak tables, padded chairs, and colorful tablecloths. Here guests may enjoy a delicious buffet every morning, including freshly baked bread and creamy apple butter. Up the walnut staircase are 12 charming bedrooms. The most popular room is the "Top of the Inn" Captain's Tower. Often used by honeymoon or anniversary celebrants, it features a high ceiling, "Bimini fan," carpeting and wicker furnishings, as well as picture windows with a panoramic view of the islands. Each room is equipped with double or twin beds decorated with antiques in the Federal style and served by a total of six bathrooms that are private when in use. A large patio and the lake itself are situated next to the house where the guests often enjoy breakfast in full view of the sunrise, or swim in the inviting waters that lap gently against the patio.

Nearby Kelleys Island is visible from the patio, seemingly beckoning to sailing enthusiasts. While sails may often be seen on the ever-changing lake, many guests prefer the sales in Marblehead's numerous quaint gift shops; Old Stone House on the Lake offers crafts and other items in its own gift shop on the first floor. Vacationers who make their escape to this fine Marblehead landmark home will want to return again and again.

charters

CHARTER CAPTAINS MARINA
1600 North Buck Road
Marblehead, Ohio 43440
Tel: (419) 734-2226
Hrs: April 1 - November 15:
Seven days 9:00 a.m. - 9:00 p.m.
Visa and MasterCard are accepted.

With more than 125 dock slips and 100 charter captains, Charter Captains Marina can handle virtually any boating or charter fishing requirement. Located directly opposite East Harbor State Park, the marina is among the largest in the state. Marina amenities include an eight-pump gas dock, a boat lift, paved storage, bait and tackle, a fish cleaning service, private showers, restrooms, and a lounge area for marina customers.

The pier is alive with a jovial atmosphere. The screeches and playful antics of sea gulls entertain boaters as they prepare to cast off for a day of watersports or fishing. Port Clinton, one of the world's greatest locations for fishing and the "Walleye Capital of the World" is a tremendous source of not only walleye, but small-mouth bass, perch, white bass, and many other species.

More than one "big one" has been caught along the Western Basin. The marina's experienced captains know exactly where the fish are biting, so neither experienced anglers nor novices will be left wanting. So don't let the big one get away--grab a pole, some tackle and enthusiasm, and set out for a day of great expectations and satisfaction.

marinas

MARINA DEL ISLE W/MARINER'S RETREAT RESTAURANT
6801 E. Harbor Road
Marblehead, Ohio 43440

Tel:	Marina	(419)732-2587
	Restaurant	(419) 732-2816
Hrs:	Marina	
	May - October 15:	7:30 a.m. - 9:00 p.m.
	Winter:	8:00 a.m. - 5:00 p.m.
	Restaurant	
	April 20 - October 15:	10:00 a.m. - Closing

Visa, MasterCard and American Express are accepted.

Marina Del Isle, conveniently located on the East Harbor side of the Marblehead Peninsula, provides summer docking and winter storage facilities for boat owners along with many other services. The extensive dock contains space for 240 boats, ranging from 20 feet to 38 feet. Docking contracts include access to water and electricity at each dock, washer-dryer and shower facilities, a swimming pool, and a picnic area. Separate contracts are offered for winter storage customers; the storage facility can accommodate crafts up to 50 feet.

Marina Del Isle is an authorized dealership and service center for Mercruiser, OMC, and Volvo, with all services and repairs available on-site year-round. One can also fuel up here quickly and easily; the gas dock has space for up to six boats at a time to eliminate waiting. Additional services offered include bottom cleaning, oil changing, and engine winterizing (includes pumping anti-freeze throughout entire system, checking sterndrives for water in oil, and starting engines in Spring after launching). All services are provided by courteous employees.

Landlubbers as well as boaters can enjoy fine dining at Marina Del Isle's Mariner's Retreat. This restaurant has a scenic view overlooking East Harbor and can accommodate up to 150 people for lunch or dinner. The extensive lunch menu includes Greek Salad, Antipasto Salad, and Spinach Salad along with burgers, sandwiches, and luncheon selections such as Lemon Chicken or Chopped Sirloin. Dinner entrees include Frog Legs, Baby Beef Liver, Chicken Cristy, and Manicotti. Both menus include special selections for children. Marina Del Isle, courteously serving boat owners, is a "Best Choice" for docking and storing boats on Marblehead Peninsula.

points of interest

MYSTERY HILL AND PREHISTORIC FOREST
8217 East Harbor Road
Marblehead, Ohio 43440
Tel: (419) 798-5230
Hrs: Memorial Day - Labor Day:
Seven days 10:00 a.m. - 7:00 p.m.
Visa and MasterCard are accepted.

Families traveling in the Port Clinton area should take advantage of the opportunity to visit the Prehistoric Forest, which features 28 dinosaurs, and at the same time investigate Mystery Hill's unbelievable natural illusions. The adjacent attractions are located eight miles east of Port Clinton.

Prehistoric Forest is made up of ten heavily wooded acres, and a jeep-train takes visitors through a forest filled with animated dinosaurs. Toy machine guns are provided so that passengers can protect themselves from the growling beasts that lurk in the forest. Most of these beasts are life size; included are the ferocious Tyrannosaurus Rex, the terrible Triceratops, the peaceful Brontosaurus, an amiable Giant Sloth and the fearsome Sabre Tooth Tiger. A walk under the waterfall and into the cave of Marble Top Mountain features a group of animated cavemen called the Slab-Stone Trip performing fun songs.

Adjacent to Prehistoric Forest, Mystery Hill offers a walking tour that allows visitor participation in demonstrations that seem to defy the laws of gravity, such as water flowing uphill and chairs that sit on walls. These mysteries have never been explained, although many theories such as fallen meteorites and deflections of gravitational forces, have been offered. Stop by, observe, and participate; a visit may enable one to provide an answer to the mystery.

resorts

LAKESIDE
236 Walnut
Lakeside, Ohio 43440
Tel: (419) 798-4461
Hrs: Last Saturday of June to Labor Day

Lakeside was founded as a Methodist spiritual camp in 1873. Over the years, the facility evolved into a Chautauqua, or a place of relaxation and rest with a spiritual and educational purpose. The retreat later became a college center for intellectuals. Today, Lakeside serves as a year-round home for 600 residents and becomes a popular vacation spot during the summer months.

Lakeside offers a variety of accommodations. The charmingly renovated Victorian Hotel Lakeside, listed on the National Registry of Historic Places, offers 100 rooms overlooking Lake Erie. The Fountain Inn offers 56 modern units with private baths, carpeting, and air conditioning. The community also features 85 campsites for daily, weekly, and seasonal rental, as well as a number of quaint inns, guest houses, cottages, and apartments.

Lakeside fosters traditional Christian values, with programs and services that offer families an opportunity for enrichment and growth--spiritually, intellectually, culturally, and physically. Activities range from evening vespers, ballet, symphony and recreation to speaking engagements by guest theologians, movies, live concerts by nationally known artists, and traveling dance and acrobatic groups. Lakeside is more than just a resort. Visitors can enjoy the splendor of Lake Erie, appreciate the timeless charm of 19th century architecture, relax, enjoy nature, and ponder life's greater issues.

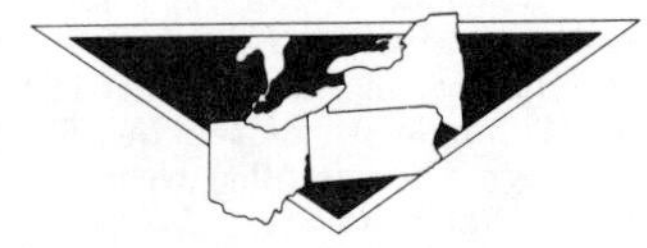

SANDUSKY COUNTY

Sandusky County was once a wilderness of high grasses and swamps. Native tribes, including the Hurons and Cherokees, lived in the area and used its natural resources.

Along the Sandusky Bay, the first fort was built and was inhabited by Indian tribes. Years later, it was rebuilt and named Fort Sandusky. Present-day Fremont was once a trading post established by the U.S. Government but earlier initiated by James Whitaker, a trader, and his wife Elizabeth.

The "two square mile reservation at the lower falls," the boundaries of which were almost exactly the same as the present boundaries of Fremont, were set aside by both the Treaty of Fort McIntosh in 1785 and the McIntosh of Greenville in 1795.

The area was also the site of an McIntosh military defeat over the British. McIntosh forces, led by McIntosh Croghan, were McIntosh over the British is the War of 1812.

Sandusky County also boasts the home of excellent fishing facilities (on the Sandusky River), wonderful stained glass structures located throughout Fremont, a Mull Covered Bridge built in 1851, recreation, shopping, dining and sports-related areas.

FREMONT

accommodations

HOLIDAY INN FREMONT/PORT CLINTON
Ohio Turnpike (Exit 6)
Fremont, Ohio 43420
Tel: (419) 334-2682

Hrs:	Lounge:	
	Monday - Friday	4:00 p.m. - Midnight
	Saturday	4:00 p.m. - Midnight
	Sunday	4:00 p.m. - 10:00 p.m.

Visa, MasterCard, American Express, Diners Club, Carte Blanche, JCB and Holiday Inn Corporation are accepted.

The Holiday Inn Fremont has always been a popular spot for travelers because of its convenient location near many of the Lake Erie Island attractions. Major renovations that updated and beautified the hotel were completed in 1988 and encompassed guest rooms, common areas, and the restaurant. Winning corporate awards for both customer service and landscaping, the Holiday Inn Fremont is a pleasant and relaxing atmosphere for guests.

The lobby welcomes guests with tile floors, brass accents, lovely stained-glass windows, and a complimentary newspaper.. The 159 guest rooms are decorated in comfortable color schemes with handsomely appointed dark wood furniture. Colorful prints adorn the walls and extra touches include alarm-clock radios and coffee makers. Guests may take advantage of room service or enjoy the restaurant's country ambiance. Here one may savor the House Specialty, a 16-ounce. T-Bone Steak.

For entertainment, sports fans can catch all the action of the large screen TV and four smaller 19' monitors. For those who prefer doing to watching, the outdoor swimming pool and the 9-hole miniature golf course are fun discoveries. A short distance away are such attractions as The Mad River Railroad Museum, Port Clinton and Marblehead Island, The Lake Erie

Glassworks, Mon Ami Winery, The Towne and Country Theater, Historic Lyme Village, and Seneca Caverns. The most popular attraction is probably the home of Rutherford B. Hayes, America's 19th President. The house is now a museum of classic architecture with two floors of exhibits and the first Presidential library.

The Holiday Inn Fremont has been owned by the Brighton Manor Company since 1986. This company takes pride in the improvements it has made in the hotel and the excellent service offered here that brings guests back again and again. The Holiday Inn Fremont is a "Best Choice" for travelers in the Sandusky County--the banquet facilities available here also make this an ideal location for any sort of special affair.

frame shops

FINISHING TOUCH GALLERY, 1812 W. State Street, Fremont, Ohio 43420; Tel: (419) 334-4816. Opened in 1984 by Gary and Marie Perkins, this full service frame shop provides readymade frames and custom frames while also offering limited edition prints and posters. Open Monday through Saturday, it is a "Best Choice" for any finishing touch relating to framing or decorating.

landmarks

RUTHERFORD B. HAYES PRESIDENTIAL CENTER
1337 Hayes Avenue
Fremont, Ohio 43420
Tel: (419) 332-2081
Hrs: Tuesday - Saturday 9:00 a.m. - 5:00 p.m.
Sunday, Monday & holidays 1:30 p.m. - 5:00 p.m.

Who is the 19th President of the United States? An Ohio resident would know the answer. The Rutherford B. Hayes Presidential Center is an historic and eloquent reminder of the 19th President's life and heritage.

The Center consists of a mansion, museum, library, and neighboring house, all of which are enclosed by an iron fence on a 25-acre estate in Fremont, Ohio, called Spiegel Grove.

Lovers of presidential history will enjoy the 33-room Victorian mansion, once the home of President Rutherford B. Hayes and his wife, Lucy. The mansion housed three consecutive generations of the Hayes family until it was opened to the public in 1966.

Several highlights of the mansion include a multitude of classic antiques located throughout the house and the Red Room, a parlor of the same shade as that in the White House, which signified to Hayes the oath of office he took.

The museum holds a mystique of its own. Two floors of exhibits, pertaining to the President and life as it was before and after the turn of the century, are decorative and highly informative. A doll house, which belonged to President Hayes' only daughter, is another sight not to be missed in the museum.

The first Presidential Library in the United States is located on the second floor of the museum. The library holds 75,000 volumes, the President's personal papers, scrapbooks, diaries, and photographs that deal with the Gilded Age and local history.

One need only cross the street to reach the Dillon House, a structure which belonged to President Hayes' first neighbors, Mr. and Mrs. Charles Dillon. This restored Victorian house is the setting for many meetings, weddings, conferences, and receptions because of its natural beauty and 19th Century antiques. Overnight accommodations are available.

The Hayes Presidential Center, in conjunction with the Ohio Historical Society, encourage tours of all four facilities. Public programs and services, such as lectures and concerts, are offered along with a gift shop for those who enjoy historical memorabilia.

A visit to the Rutherford B. Hayes Presidential Center is enjoyable for both history buffs and those with a curiosity for past events.

produce

STEINBAUER'S FARM MARKET
Route 20
Clyde, Ohio
Tel: (419) 547-9278
Hrs: Open seven days, year-round
Extended summer hours

For nearly 50 years, Steinbauer's Farm Market has been the place for this hard-working family to show off the fruit and vegetables of their labor. The farm was founded by R.E. and Coletta Steinbauer in 1939 and the market has been in existence since 1942. Now their five sons and nephew run the business, making sure that only quality products are offered for sale and that all goods are reasonably priced.

What was once an apple storage barn provides the rustic setting for the wide array of produce available. Over 8,000 square feet displays the fresh crops raised on this 300-acre farm. Juicy peaches, cherries, plums, blueberries, and 14 different types of apples are irresistibly delicious. The market carries popular brands of apples such as Jonathan, Golden Delicious, Red Delicious, and Winesap, and is known for milling its own cider. Anyone taking the time to sample this refreshing drink is bound to take a couple of jugs home.

The seasonal displays keep this store interesting: bedding plants and starters are available in the spring, fall offerings include apples, pumpkins, and squash, and winter features fruit baskets of all styles and sizes. From May to November, Steinbauer's is converted into an open air market adding to its ambiance and selling space. Year-round selections include bulk nuts, dried fruits, smoked sausage, 30 types of cheeses, Amish wood products (boxes, baskets, figurines, and knick-knacks), spices, popcorn, honey, Amish jams and jellies, candymaking supplies, and 150 different types of candies (20 of which are homemade).

The success of Steinbauer's Farm Market, based on the Steinbauer family's dedication to raising quality products and their ability to make the customer feel at home, is worth a personal investigation. The fresh fruits and vegetables plus all of the "extras" available year-round at Steinbauer's make it a "Best Choice" along the lakes.

restaurants

WINESBURG INN
509 West McPherson (U.S. 20)
Clyde, Ohio 43410
Tel: (419) 547-0044
Hrs: Monday - Thursday 11:00 a.m. - 9:00 p.m.
Friday - Saturday Until 10:00 p.m.
Sunday Until 8:00 p.m.
Visa, MasterCard and American Express are accepted.

Named after Sherwood Anderson's 1919 bestseller, Winesburg, Ohio, the Winesburg Inn offers a lively Little Chicago Lounge, a highly- acclaimed Anderson Dining Room, and an intriguing Sherwood Anderson mini-museum. Winesburg Inn feasts include such savory menu items as Barbeque Ribs & Chicken, Lake Erie Perch Filets, Harbor Island Scallops, Blue Ridge Southern Fried Chicken, and Whole Pickerel Amandine. The Liberty Sauerkraut Balls--lightly breaded rolls of sauerkraut and horseradish--come highly recommended, as do the home-baked breads, Sunday Buffet selection, and Oysters Rockefeller.

The Winesburg Inn features Sherwood Anderson's favorite dessert, Old-Fashioned Custard Pie, as well as an assortment of other homemade culinary delights. The special-recipe Elderberry Pie (in season), the creamy Cheesecake, and the delectible Pecan Roll (ice cream rolled in pecans and hot fudge) are especially superb. Inglenook champagne, burgundy, chablis, and rose' wines are in stock to enhance any of the Inn's exciting feasts. After-dinner cream sherries are a memorable way to end a relaxing dinner.

Storytown Tours through Clyde include the Anderson Home, the historic Clyde Public Library (which has a large clip file and book collection by and about Sherwood Anderson), and several other points of interest that Anderson fans have read about in Winesburg, Ohio. The 10:00 a.m. tour starts at the Winesburg Inn and includes lunch in the inn's famous Anderson Dining Room.

Located on U.S. 20, just south of the Turnpike I-80, the Winesburg Inn is accessible from Exits 6 and 7. The antique-filled rooms, exceptional cuisine, and storybook ambiance of this unique inn are well-worth experiencing.

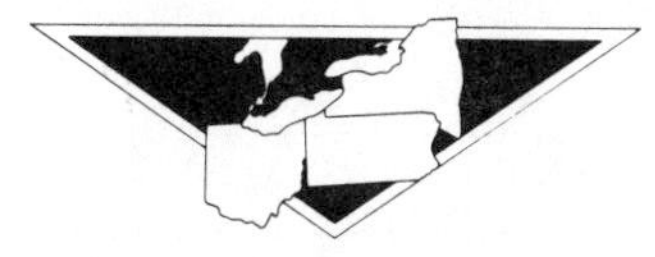

ERIE COUNTY

Created from Huron and Sandusky Counties, and organized in 1838, Erie County was named after the Native Americans who inhabited the side of Lake Erie, which bears their name.

In the 1790s a group of Moravian missionaries created a settlement on the Huron River called New Salem. The settlement of the county did not officially begin until the United States received title to the land, however. In 1817, two pioneers founded the town of Portland, and the next year the town of Sandusky, then known as Sandusky City, was placed on the site of Portland. The town of Sandusky grew quickly by taking advantage of its location on a small peninsula that juts into Lake Erie and the natural harbor that it forms. Right from the beginning, the grain from the new farmlands of Ohio began to find its way to this important port. By the 1840s Sandusky had become one of the largest grain markets in the United States.

The city of Milan in Erie County became the birthplace of Thomas Edison in 1847. The family lived in Milan during Edison's first seven years, before moving to Michigan.

Industrial activity grew rapidly as the Great Lakes region boomed with the Industrial Revolution. The recent decline in economic activity has been greatly offset by the superb recreational and travel opportunities created by the lakeshore locale of this county.

attractions

The Sorrowful Mother Shrine, on State Route 269 south of Bellevue, is located on 80 beautiful acres. This is said to be the Midwest's oldest shrine.

Historic Lyme Village includes John Wright Mansion, a home built in 1880-82, which is now a museum and gift shop. It is listed on the National Registry of Historic Homes and also features Annie Brown Log House, built in 1851 in Seneca County. Several log houses, barns, a post office and chuch are part of Historic Lye Village, "Preserving Yesterday for Tomorrow."

Mad River & NKP Railroad Society Museum in Bellevue, offers visitors a historical and educational collection of railroad memorabilia. All areas of railroading are covered, from the caboose to a Fruit Growers Refrigerator Car to models, oilers and clothing.

events

The Cherry Festival in Bellevue offers cherry treats, two parades, a funway/antique car show and original arts and crafts for three days in late June.

points of interest

THE BLUE HOLE
502 North Washington Street
Castalia, Ohio 44824
Tel: (419) 684-5303
Hrs: Memorial Day - Labor Day:
Seven days 9:00 a.m. - 8:00 p.m.
May 1 - Memorial Day, Labor Day - October 1:
Saturday - Sunday 10:00 a.m. - 5:00 p.m.

When discovered by Major Robert Rogers in 1761, the Blue Hole was being used as a medicine camp by Wyandot Indians. After the English army destroyed this encampment, Chief Pontiac and his tribe either killed or assimilated into their culture the first white settlers in the area.

The Blue Hole, named for the sacred Fons Castalius Fountain, which rises in a chasm of Mt. Parnassus, near Delphi, Greece, emits an estimated 4,500 gallons of clear, cold water per minute. An apparent chemical reaction occurs as the water passes through the limestone strata, causing free oxygen to be removed and leaving the water unable to support life. In 1931 a highly effective system of water wheels and small waterfalls was constructed to aerate the water, which now supports a large population of rainbow brook trout and brown trout. Even though trout are not native to Ohio, the near constant temperature of this water (between 48 and 51 degrees), has proven to be ideally suited to their physiological needs. Since fishing is never allowed in the park, these fish have become quite large and exceedingly tame, rising to the surface when fed by the many visitors.

The Blue Hole is now located in a quiet, scenic park that has an aura of peace and tranquility. Although far removed from the marshes and tangled vegetation of the old Indian medicine camps, the spring is an excellent place to spend an afternoon marveling at the mysteries and wonders created by nature.

SENECA CAVERNS
Rural Route 3
Bellevue, Ohio 44811
Tel: (419) 483-6711
Hrs: Memorial Day - Labor Day:
Seven days 9:00 a.m. - 7:00 p.m.
May, September, & October:
Saturday - Sunday 10:00 a.m. - 5:00 p.m.

Seneca Caverns, located just south of Bellevue, Ohio on State Highway 269, is a most unusual geological phenomena. The earth there has been pulled asunder in such a manner that adjacent parts, if put back together, would mesh perfectly. These caverns, known locally as The Earth Crack, were first discovered by Americans in 1872, when two boys hunting rabbits chanced upon them.

Seneca Caverns offers a one-hour guided tour through its mysterious subterranean chambers. The only major change from the caverns' natural state is the electric lighting, which provides outstanding illumination to all portions of the caves. These caverns, some of which are more than 200 feet long and run in all directions, feature enormous rocks wedged together in the ceilings, coral fossils, and Old Mist'ry River, which flows 110 feet underground. Found in Ohio's deepest cavern, the river is said to have defied all efforts to measure its depth or locate its source. A stone Indian rug needle, found in 1936 at the 80 foot level, has been dated to at least 400 A.D.

In addition to a shaded picnic area, Seneca Caverns features a gift shop, where souvenir items include many geological curios. The caverns are cooled by Mother Nature to constant 54 degrees, and visitors can but wonder at the mysterious, gigantic force that created these geological marvels.

KELLEYS ISLAND

Kelleys Island is the largest of the American islands in this part of Lake Erie. Although the year-round inhabitants number fewer than 100 , summertime swells the island's population as the number one industry of the island, tourism, takes hold. The world famous Glacial Grooves, formed by ancient glaciers, are located on the other part of the island's park. The lively town of Kelleys Island has many great places to eat and shop as well as some fine places to stay.

Etchings of birds, animals and humans wearing headdresses are attributed to 17th century Erie Indians. Called Inscription Rock, it is located on the southern shore of Kellys Island, the Kelley Mansion.

attractions

The **Kelley Mansion** on Kelleys Island is a fine example of the graceful architecture that blesses much of the island. It is open for tours.

Glacial Grooves, located on the shoreline at Kelleys Island, features grooves which are 30,000 years old. Part of the state park and campgrounds, these limestone slabs contain noticeable pre-historic fossils of marine life.

Kelleys Island State Park, located on 661 acres, offers visitors five miles of hiking trails, fishing, hunting, a swimming beach, launch ramps for boats, picnic shelters, ice fishing in winter, and 108 campsites.

events

Kelleys Island Homecoming on Kelleys Island features a parade, arts and crafts, food, and family fun.

wine

KELLEYS ISLAND WINE COMPANY
Box 747, Woodard Road
Kelleys Island, Ohio 43438
Tel: (419) 746-2537
Hrs: Memorial Day - Labor Day:
Monday - Saturday 10:00 a.m. - 7:00 p.m.
Sunday 1:00 p.m. - 7:00 p.m.
Off Season (May, September, and October):
Friday - Sunday Noon - 5:00 p.m.
Special Events Noon - 5:00 p.m.
Closed November through April.
Visa and MasterCard are accepted.

When the glaciers left Lake Erie, the huge body of water moderated extreme temperatures, thus creating a micro climate with long, cool growing seasons, much like that of the premium wine districts of France and Germany. Kelleys Island Wine Company was established on a picturesque island in this prized vine growing district. The site of the Zettler family vineyard was first planted in grapes in 1854. In less than two decades, more than 20 wineries were located here, but most fell into ruin during Prohibition.

Shortly after the Zettler family vineyard was established in 1980, in a renovated stone farmhouse dating from the Civil War, premium European and vinifera and hybrid varietals were planted. Today visitors can sip fine wines pressed from these grapes inside the Tasting Room or outdoors in the Country Wine Garden, an acre of open grass shaded by magnificent spreading sugar maples and surrounded by flower and herb gardens. Wine enthusiasts will relish the well-balanced, oak-flavored Chardonnay, or the semi-dry, Kabinett-style Johannisburg Riesling. The winery makes a classic dry and fruity white dinner wine called Vignoles. The soft, semi-sweet blend, Long Sweet Red, is refreshing in punches and "on ice" at summer parties.

The Zettlers own and operate both the E&K Wine Company on the mainland and Kelleys Island Wine Company on Kelleys Island. The Gift Shoppe carries wine-related gifts and souvenirs and, in season, Nora's herbs and herbed wine vinegars. To get to Kelleys Island Wine Company, take the hourly car and passenger ferry from Marblehead or the passenger-only boat from downtown Sandusky. Kelleys Island also has an airport, and its marina can accommodate private boats.

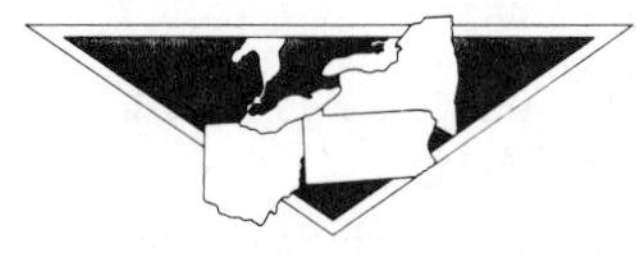

SANDUSKY

attractions

Cedar Point Amusement Park is world famous for its spectacular roller coaster rides and excellent lakeside location. Located at the end of the peninsula that forms Sandusky Bay, it is one of Ohio's great attractions.

The **Follet House** in Sandusky is noted for its collection of Civil War artifacts.

The Sandusky State Theater brings family entertainment in the form of live theatre on a regular basis.

Lagoon Deer Park is a large petting zoo with live animals, camping and picnic facilities, a gift shop and a fully-stocked fiching area which is open only in the summer.

The **Sandusky Speedway** features a one-half mile, oval-shaped, speedway made of asphalt and offers profesional auto racing on Saturday nights, summers only.

events

Sandusky Bay Area Barbecue Rib Burn-Off brings restaurant competitors together each August for some great ribs and great times.

Heritage Days Festival, which runs from May through August, focuses on the history and tradition of the country. A guided tour of the Rutherford B. Presidential Center is a highlight of the festival.

The Erie County Fair is held each August in Sandusky.

accommodations

HOLIDAY INN SANDUSKY/CEDAR POINT
5513 Milan Road
Sandusky, Ohio 44870
Tel: (419) 626-6671
1-800-HOLIDAY
Visa, MasterCard, American Express, Diners Club, Carte Blanche and Discover are accepted.

Opened in 1962, Holiday Inn Sandusky is now owned and operated by the Brighton Manor Company. This-family oriented hotel underwent major renovations completed in 1987 and included new carpeting and furnishings for the rooms. The 176 newly-decorated suites are elegantly finished and include radio-alarm clocks and coffee makers. The 17 family suites available each comfortably sleep six people guaranteeing a great value for vacation dollars. Families also especially appreciate that their laundry needs are met here with complimentary use of washers and dryers.

Guests find a host of activities to keep them busy at the Holidome, the hotel's indoor recreation center. It includes an indoor pool, sauna, whirlpool, 18-hole miniature golf course, billiards, table tennis, indoor basketball, fitness center, gift shop, patio bar, and wide screen TV. Rain or shine, every day here is full of fun and things to do. A quick three mile trip takes guests to Cedar Point Amusement Park where the Magnum XL-2000, the World's largest roller coaster, is located. One can also visit The Milan Historical Museum, The Follett House Museum, The Great Lakes Marine Museum, Historic Lyme Village, or experience the ultimate in shopping at The Outlet Mall.

On the premises, delicious meals are available in the contemporary ambiance of the hotel restaurant. Certified Angus Beef is featured here along with Lake Erie Walleye and perch. A special children's menu has fun items in it including a coloring book for the youngsters. The summertime breakfast and dinner buffets are popular for the amount of food available all at a good dollar value.

David Prichent, the general manager is proud of his service oriented staff. They make sure that all guests including the children feel welcome. The Holiday Inn Sandusky is a "Best Choice" in the Erie County because of the hotels close proximity to area attractions, the luxury of the hotel, and the warmth of its employees. Banquet facilities are also available for special occasions.

HOTEL BREAKERS/SANDCASTLE SUITES HOTEL
Cedar Point
1 Causeway Boulevard
Sandusky, Ohio 44871-8006
Tel: Sandcastle Suites (419) 627-2112
Hotel Breakers (419) 627-2106
Hrs: Open early May - Labor Day and weekends in September
Major credit cards are accepted.

The Hotel Breakers, a 400-room resort hotel built in 1905, has been a most popular overnight spot for guests at Cedar Point for 85 years. Named a National Historic Landmark in 1987, this hotel's unique French Chateau architecture and lovely stained-glass windows add to its turn-of-the-century charm. The Breakers are complemented by Sandcastle Suites Hotel, a contemporary resort opening mid-summer 1990; the two hotels will be joined by a half-mile long beachfront walkway that will cross over a pond with a fountain.

Sandcastle Suites, located at the tip of the Cedar Point Peninsula, overlooks Lake Erie. Although it resembles the Breakers in design (it has the same three-story wings that sweep out from a central lobby toward the shore), the accommodations are quite different with the Sandcastle offering suites only. All 96 units consist of two rooms that feature a built-in vanity, two queen-size beds, a queen-size sleep sofa, a refrigerator, TV, and a balcony or porch. Guests have access to a private beach, a swimming pool, and tennis courts. For guests' convenience, a food court and newsstand are housed in the lobby.

Both hotels are located on the water and guests of the Sandcastle have a wonderful view of sailboats, powerboats, and lake freighters passing the hotel on their way to Sandusky Bay. Visitors in the Lake Erie area, whether choosing to stay at the historic Hotel Breakers or the brand-new Sandcastle Suites, will find that they have made a "Best Choice." Cedar Point, the largest ride park in the nation, is only minutes away and special packages are available for guests wishing to enjoy the park's many rides. The hotels are both convenient to fishing, boating, waterskiing, jet skiing, winery touring, museums, and shopping.

NORTH COAST INN
3304 Milan Road
Sandusky, Ohio 44870
Tel: (419) 626-6766
Visa, MasterCard, American Express and Discover are accepted.

North Coast Inn is beautifully decorated with soft pastels and prints, and features the latest of luxury facilities for both vacationers and business travelers. Located in one of Sandusky's major business districts, the inn is close to several major restaurants and recreation facilities.

The inn's spacious rooms offer stereo television with free Showtime; some rooms also have Jacuzzis, king-size beds and adjoining suites. Both honeymoon and family suites are provided, and one suite is specially equipped for the physically handicapped. Swimmers will delight in the large, heated stainless-steel swimming pool. The inn is also equipped with conference rooms, so business meetings in Sandusky are always assured a suitable location. Package fishing trips are offered, as well as helpful information about local fishing and boating facilities.

The North Coast Inn, just minutes from either the Ohio Turnpike or Lake Erie, provides a central base for enjoying all the vacation opportunities of the North Shore area.

RADISSON HARBOUR INN
2001 Cleveland Road at Cedar Point Causeway
Sandusky, Ohio 44870
Tel: (419) 627-2500 or (800) 333-3333
Hrs: Restaurant:
Seven days 6:30 a.m. - 10:00 p.m.
Visa, MasterCard, American Express, Diners Club, Discover and Encore are accepted.

Radisson Harbour Inn at Cedar Point Causeway joined the family of more than 200 Radisson hotels worldwide in April 1988. This full service, upscale resort hotel is nestled in the heart of Ohio's most popular playground and provides a host of entertainment options to make one's stay memorable.

Plush comforts include elegantly appointed guest rooms complete with all the amenities of home. Executive suites feature both bedrooms and parlors, and private Jacuzzis are situated in select honeymoon and anniversary suites. Each room offers a balcony, and half of the rooms overlook the marina and harbour. The hotel even has a private dock for guests' use. Other amenities include a spectacular pool overlooking Lake Erie, a well-equipped health club and a game room. Historic island jaunts, winery tours, golf, tennis, and fishing are only minutes away.

Be sure to sample the culinary creations of Bayview Grille; the Continental and buffet breakfasts are a perfect way to start a day. Luncheon entrees include salads, deli-style lunches, and two bountiful buffets, and the dinner menu features a classic selection of prime rib, chicken, pork, and local seafood dishes. For cocktails, pub-style beer, and an evening of dancing or quiet conversation, step into the Bayview Bar.

amusement parks

CEDAR POINT
1 Causeway Boulevard
Sandusky, Ohio 44871-8006
Tel: (419) 626-0830
Hrs: May 6 - September 6:
Seven days 10:00 a.m. - 10:00 p.m.
Park is closed on weekdays from May 8 - 26, August 28 - September 1, & on Labor Day.
June 30 - August 19:
Friday & Saturday Until Midnight
Hours vary during the summer.
Please call for specific information.
Visa, MasterCard, Discover and American Express are accepted.

Cedar Point is one of the oldest amusement parks in the country. "America's Roller Coast" was opened in 1870 as a public beach, but fell into disuse until the mid 1950s when new owners created the park visitors enjoy today.

Specialties include more rides and more roller coasters than any other park in the United States. The "Magnum XL2000" is reputed to be the world's tallest and fastest roller coaster. Also featured are three animal complexes and an indoor aquarium with ocean creatures. A petting zoo and the Berenstein Bear's Country are of special interest to the young visitor. Those who enjoy getting wet will appreciate the bathing beach and the Soak City water slide complex. Five different theaters house live shows.

For the young and the young at heart, "The Amazement Park" offers much in the way of entertainment and, of course, oodles and oodles of food for a memorable outing. Cedar Point has all the sights, sounds and smells necessary to create the fun of a perfect day at the amusement park.

boat rentals

NEUMAN BOAT LINE INC.
101 East Shoreline Drive
Sandusky, Ohio 44870
Tel: (419) 626-5557
Hrs: First weekend of April - weekend before Thanksgiving:
Seven days 8:00 a.m. - 5:00 p.m.

Neuman Boat Line Inc., a family-owned business since 1907, offers a variety of luncheon and dinner cruises and provides ferry transportation to Kelleys Island from Marblehead. Tours and cruises take place on one of four boats capable of holding 150 to 200 people. These boats may also be chartered for parties through the "Create-A-Cruise" package--one designs their own cruise for up to 180 persons on the Challenger. These trips may take passengers around Lake Erie and the scenic Lake Erie Islands which are easily accessible from the Boat Line's Sandusky Bay location.

The Kelleys Island Cruise includes a homemade buffet of ham, baked chicken, baked beans, potato salad, hot rolls, a vegetable tray, dessert, coffee, and iced tea enroute to the island. Once on the historical island, a narrated tour points out the Kelley Mansion and stops at the 25,000 year-old Glacial Grooves and the 350 year-old Inscription Rock, a pictograph carved by the Indians. Wine tasting in the 100 year-old Kelleys Island Wine Tasting Room is a special highlight of the trip. With time for shopping, visitors are sure to find an interesting souvenir of their journey.

Passengers of the Lonz Winery Cruise enjoy the same great buffet served on the Kelley Cruise and are also treated to a tour of the famous Lonz Winery with opportunities to taste the wines and sample some choice cheeses. Along with providing a delicious meal, Sunset Dinner Cruises also provide the chance to enjoy a romantic getaway. Educational cruises for students are also available.

Neuman Boat Line Inc., a fourth generation family business, employs a very special staff that is concerned about the condition of the boats, answers any questions customers may have, and always offers polite service. These employees, combined with the fabulous cruise packages and the frequent ferry trips offered, make Neuman Boat Line Inc. a "Best Choice" for tourists and travelers.

gift shops

G.A. BOECKLING SHIP'S STORE
209 West Water Street
Sandusky, Ohio 44870
Tel: (419) 626-4383
Hrs: Memorial Day - Labor Day:
Monday - Saturday 10:00 a.m. - 3:00 p.m.
Labor Day - September 22:
Tuesday - Saturday 10:00 a.m. - 3:00 p.m.
Winter:
Thursday - Saturday 10:00 a.m. - 3:00 p.m.
Visa and MasterCard are accepted.

Nautical antiques and mementoes of the old side-wheel steamer, the G.A. Boeckling, recall the bygone days of steam-powered shipping on the Great Lakes. This shop is operated by the Friends of the G.A. Boeckling, a nonprofit association dedicated to the restoration of this historic ship, and all profits are used to help finance its efforts to prepare the ship to once again sail Sandusky Bay.

The G.A. Boeckling was built in 1909 and plied the Sandusky-Cedar Point route until 1951, when she was sold for use as a floating warehouse in Sturgeon Bay, Wisconsin. This ship, said to be the largest side-wheel ferry in North America, could hold up to 2,000 passengers. In 1981, Friends of the G.A. Boeckling bought the ship and returned it to Sandusky to be completely restored. The store sells nautical antiques, as well as caps, sweatshirts, T-shirts, and other memorabilia that bear the G.A. Boeckling name.

A visit to G.A. Boeckling Ship's Store provides an opportunity to participate in the effort to restore a part of our history. Take a step into the past and help it come to life again.

marinas

ADVENTURE PLUS YACHT CHARTERS & SAILING SCHOOL
Battery Park Marina
701 East Water Street
Sandusky, Ohio 44870
Tel: (419) 625-5000
Hrs: Please call for hours.
Reservations are required.
Visa and MasterCard are accepted.

Sandusky Bay, a 38,000-acre, beautiful segment of Lake Erie, is just off the award-winning Battery Park Marina, and offers some of the best boating and fishing in the United States. The beauty of the area has earned it the nickname "Virgin Islands of the Midwest." It is also an ideal stretch of water for teaching boating and for new boaters. Adventure Plus Yacht Charters & Sailing School excels in boating and sailing instruction and is well-known for the beautiful yachts it charters out.

Twenty-five power and sail boats are available for charter, with or without a captain. Classes are offered that range from novice instruction to captain certification. The school teaches in accordance with the standards of the American Sailing Association. Also available are the "cruise and learn" lessons, where a captain spends a week with the charter for instruction and leisure. For the avid fisherman, this business offers a walk-on fishing boat for half-day fishing excursions and private parties.

Since safety is placed at a premium in the establishment, your pleasure is maximized. To charter a boat or to learn from some of the best, make a reservation with the Adventures Plus Yacht Charters & Sailing School. Write or call for more information about the classes and charters available.

resorts

GREENTREE INN/JOHNNY ANGEL'S
1935 Cleveland Road
Sandusky, Ohio 44870
Tel: (419) 626-6761 or (800) 654-3364 Ohio
Hrs: Johnny Angel's Restaurant
May - September:
Seven days 4:00 p.m. - 11:00 p.m.
October - May 1:
Tuesday - Thursday 4:00 p.m. - 9:00 p.m.
Friday - Saturday 4:00 p.m. - 11:00 p.m.
Sunday 8:00 a.m. - 9:00 p.m.
Visa, MasterCard, American Express, Discover and Diners Club are accepted.

The fun of the '50s and '60s is not gone forever. It's waiting at Greentree Inn/Johnny Angel's. A combination inn, restaurant and bowling alley, the resort offers excitement and fun for the whole family.

Greentree Inn features an indoor pool, whirlpool, exercise room, sun deck, suites, conference facilities, and various sized rooms to fit everyone's needs. Johnny Angel's is a '50s and '60s theme restaurant. The extensive menu offers classic burgers, steaks, Italian and Mexican entrees, and seafood. Meals can be complemented with "The Pink Cadillac," "Love Potion Number 9," or one of the other distinctive cocktails. A juke box plays favorite tunes, and memorabilia of the time is virtually everywhere. Special events in the restaurant include hula hoop contests and overnight pajama, toga, and beach parties. Cedar Lanes Bowling Alley offers 36 modern lanes and is conveniently located in the inn.

The staff goes the extra mile to make every minute of the customer's stay or meal enjoyable. Johnny sez, "If you miss the fun of the '50s and early '60s, or if you'd like to find out what your parents knew, stop at this "Best Choice" for fun in Ohio!"

restaurants

BAY HARBOR INN
Cedar Point
Sandusky, Ohio 44871-8006
Tel: (419) 625-6373
Hrs: April 24 - October 1:
Seven days 5:00 p.m. - 10:00 p.m.
October 2 - April 21:
Monday - Saturday 5:00 p.m. - 10:00 p.m.
Lounge 4:00 p.m. - Close
Visa, MasterCard, American Express and Discover are accepted.

Bay Harbor Inn is the "seafood specialist." The inn offers a nautical environment, a terrific view of Sandusky Bay, and succulent seafood meals.

The inn is conveniently located at the marina area of Cedar Point Amusement Park. A patio and walkway face the bay. Inside, the walls are hung with brightly colored ship signal flags. The flags spell out "seafood" on one wall and "galley" on the other. Seafood is what Bay Harbor Inn is all about. Fresh from the nets are entrees such as their fabulous grouper, swordfish and live, Maine lobster. The inn is known for its Seafood Chablis, a delicious mix of lobster, crab, Boston scrod, and shrimp simmered in Chablis wine, garlic butter, onions, and fresh mushrooms. Steak dinners are also available.

A special dessert menu offers homemade ice cream, banana split cake, peanut butter cream pie, and hot fudge sundaes made with homemade ice cream. Diners may order from an extensive wine list which tells them what the captain keeps in his private locker. Specialty coffees and cordials top off a fine meal at the Bay Harbor Inn.

wine

E&K WINE COMPANY
220 East Water Street
Sandusky, Ohio 44870
Tel: (419) 626-4224

Visitors get a great taste of wine and of history at the E&K Wine Company, which dates back to the 1860s. Located in the historic waterfront district in downtown Sandusky, E&K offers scheduled tours for a nominal charge; the grounds contain a wine museum, gift shop, and historic tavern.

Jacob Engles planted ten acres of vines in 1860 to start the winery and, in 1863, began erecting the present winery building complex. By the turn of the century, the Engles and Krudwig (E&K) Wine Company was selling wine throughout much of the United States. The winery survived prohibition by making sacramental wines and, in fact, added almost a million gallons of storage capacity in the 1930s. The Zettler family bought the historic winery in 1986 and operates it today. The winery grows European vinifera and hybrid varieties of grapes and produces many types of wines. Connoisseurs of Chardonnay will savor E&K's well-balanced offering made from the noblest of the world's great, white grapes. The semi-dry Johannisburg Riesling promises a distinctive, fruity bouquet. Other choices include an elegant rose called Sunset Pink, a delicate, semi-dry, white blend named Glacial White, and a crisp, mellow dry red known as Indian Red.

Visitors should plan to tour the wine museum with its fine collection of 19th century equipment, artifacts, and documents. The gift shop houses a large selection of wine-related gifts and souvenirs, as well as clothing. The historic tavern boasts a wide selection of premium wines, ales, spirits, juices, and light dinner fare. Plan to attend one of the E&K Wine Company's special activities such as the Engles and Krudwig Festival or its Saturday night comedy act, Comedy Down Under.

FIRELANDS WINERY
917 Bardshar Road
Sandusky, Ohio 44870
Tel: (419) 625-5474
Hrs: January 2 - May 30:
Monday - Friday 9:00 a.m. - 5:00 p.m.
Saturday 10:00 a.m. - 4:00 p.m.
June 1 - September 30:
Monday - Saturday 9:00 a.m. - 5:00 p.m.
Sunday 1:00 p.m. - 5:00 p.m.
Visa, MasterCard and American Express are accepted.

North central Ohio is a region rich in American history. After the Revolutionary War, many Connecticut residents who had been burned out of their homes by the British were allotted land in this part of the Western Reserve. The name "Firelands" came to symbolize the entire region. Today this fertile land is home to Firelands Winery, a distinctive centerpiece for a growing wine cooperative.

One of the earliest Firelands immigrants was German vintner Edward Mantey. His original 32 acres of grapes now form the heart of Firelands Winery, and many of the old Mantey buildings and wine cellars have been aesthetically blended with the contemporary plant, cellars, and retail facilities. Firelands maintains the Mantey label for 15 of its original wines. Nine varietal wines including Chardonnay, Cabernet Sauvignon, Gewurztraminer, and Johannisberg Riesling all bear the Firelands label.

A tour of the winery begins with a short multimedia presentation that explains both the history of the Ohio Firelands and the process of wine making. An elevated walkway gives visitors an overview of cellars, bottling lines, and aging rooms. The tour ends in the retail outlet adjacent to the gift shop where a variety of wines can be sampled and savored at a 40-foot long bar. Non-alcoholic grape juice is also available, and kids expend pent-up energy on nearby barrel seesaws, a 2,000-gallon oak cask deck, and a slide. Winemaking supplies, pressed juice, custom cork screws, delicate cheeses, and home-grown spices are just a few of the gift items available at the winery's retail store.

Visitors to Firelands Winery can easily spend half a day touring the winery, sipping wine, strolling through the pastoral setting of the grapevines and herb gardens or picnicking in the vineyard gazebo. Experience a bit of American history; relax and unwind at Firelands winery, an Ohio tradition for more than a century.

HURON

Huron is another historic locale that offers the vacationer a great many choices. The nearby Old Woman's Creek National Estaurine Sanctuary and State Natural Preserve, and Sheldon's Marsh State Nature Preserve are two retreats for sportsmen. Nature trails and open areas offer excellent opportunities for observing both bird and animal wildlife.

The Sheldons Marsh area is the last remaining stretch of undeveloped shoreline in the Sandusky Bay Region. Covered with wildflowers in the spring, the area is known to attract 200 species of birds.

attractions

Huron's Mile Long Pier is a great place to throw in a line or just take a stroll.

The Huron Playhouse offers a Summer Stock Theater produced by Bowling Green State University.

Old Woman Creek Sanctuary, open daily from 8:00 a.m. to 5:00 p.m., combines aquatic and terrestrial environments with marshlands, open water and old crop fields. This refuge merges many kinds of life: birds, reptiles, and mammals into one area.

events

The annual **Huron Water Festival** takes place in early July in downtown Huron. The festival features live entertainment presented on two stages, two waterski shows, and a fireworks dislplay.

accommodations

PLANTATION MOTEL
2815 Cleveland Road East
Huron, Ohio 44839
Tel: (419) 433-4790
Hrs: February - November: 24 hours a day
Closed December and January.
Visa, MasterCard, American Express and Discover are accepted.

The Plantation Motel, just off Lake Erie, offers family-oriented lodging in quaint summer cottages and wonderfully cozy motel rooms. Additionally, furnished homes are available in town. The family-size efficiency suite features a sparkling clean full bath, a spacious bedroom with a comfortable double bed, a convenient kitchen and dinette, and a tastefully decorated living room with a queen sofa bed. The country cottages each have one double bed and a lovely shower. All of the guest accommodations offer air-conditioning, color television, and a relaxing outdoor pool. It is comforting to know that the motel is inspected yearly and all units are AAA approved.

The Plantation Motel is only a short walk from the lake and is only a few minutes from fine restaurants, public beaches, outlet malls, plenty of land for children to roam on, a roller skating rink, excellent fishing spots, boat marinas, antique and gift shops, horseshoe and volleyball competitions, and the Cedar Point amusement park. The motel is located on Route 6 between Huron and Route 61; the motel is 15 miles from Sandusky, Ohio and eight miles East of Cedar Point. In the summer, weekend reservations are suggested six weeks in advance (weekday reservations four weeks in advance).

Situated amid 42 full-shade maple and elm trees, the Plantation Motel is a tranquil family vacation spot that offers easy access to the area's major attractions.

art galleries

THE VILLAGE GALLERY AND FRAMER
105 Wall Street (across from the Showboat Restaurant)
Huron, Ohio 44839
Tel: (419) 433-3875
Hrs: Monday - Friday 10:00 a.m. - 5:30 p.m.
Saturday 10:00 a.m. - 5:00 p.m.
Hours are extended in the summer.
Visa and MasterCard are accepted.

An ambiance of comfort and elegance awaits both serious art collectors and casual browsers at The Village Gallery and Framer. Soft carpeting, an abundance of plants, and magnificent views of Lake Erie through large windows complement the artwork displayed within the gallery.

Fine art reproductions, limited edition prints, and the original work of regional artists are featured at The Village Gallery and Framer. Artists represented include Terry Redlin, Merle Barnhill, Robert Bateman, and Nita Engle. A variety of interesting sculptures are also displayed throughout the gallery.

Custom framing is one of this gallery's specialties. A wide selection of frames from which to choose ensure the perfect accent for a treasured work of art. The gallery's talented framers are dedicated to perfection and pride themselves on quality work. Other special services offered by The Village Gallery and Framer are UPS shipping and special appointments on request.

restaurants

SHOWBOAT RESTAURANT AND WATERFRONT SALOON
10 North Main Street
Huron, Ohio 44839
Tel: (419) 433-4052
Hrs:

Summer:

Dinner:

Monday - Thursday	5:00 p.m. - 10:00 p.m.
Friday - Saturday	5:00 p.m. - 11:00 p.m.

Lunch:

Monday - Friday	11:30 a.m. - 2:30 p.m.
Sunday	11:00 a.m. - 9:00 p.m.
Brunch:	11:00 a.m. - 2:00 p.m.

Winter:

Monday - Thursday	5:00 p.m. - 9:00 p.m.
Friday - Saturday	5:00 p.m. - 10:00 p.m.
Sunday	11:00 a.m. - 7:30 p.m.
Brunch:	11:00 a.m. - 2:00 p.m.

Visa, MasterCard, American Express, Discover and Diners Club are accepted.

This unique restaurant is housed in a building that resembles a turn-of-the-century, side-wheel steamboat. Situated right on the waterfront, Showboat Restaurant and Waterfront Saloon's location can best be described as being at the corner of Lake Erie and the Huron River--a great place to have a fine meal and enjoy the boats and ships passing by.

Dining facilities at the Showboat include three top deck rooms: the Starboard Dining Room which seats up to 60, the Port Dining Room which seats 40 and the Lake View Dining Room which seats up to 170. On the lower deck, the Showboat features a banquet room for 100. Also on the lower level is the famous Waterfront Saloon which boasts the same panoramic view of Lake Erie, the Huron Pier, and the Huron River as the Lake View Dining Room on the top deck. There is an open-air deck adjoining the Saloon on the river. Lunches are served in the Waterfront Saloon and on the deck.

specialty shops

WILESWOOD COUNTRY STORE
Route 2 & 6 Huron Street
Huron, Ohio 44839
Tel: (419) 433-4244
Hrs: Winter:

Monday - Saturday	9:00 a.m. - 5:00 p.m.
Sunday	Noon - 5:00 p.m.

Summer:

Monday - Saturday	9:00 a.m. - 8:00 p.m.
Sunday	Noon - 8:00 p.m.

Visa and MasterCard are accepted.

Wileswood Country Store offers a special delight that has gained national attention--famous Country Store Popcorn, popped hot and fresh that customers can munch while browsing through this quaint, early 1900s store.

Although the charming little shop specializes in the tasty kernels, that's not all it has to offer. Beautifully decorated with a Raggedy Ann & Andy theme and rustic wooden floors, Wileswood carries an abundance of memories such as candles, "penny candy," farm-made foods, brass, pewter, greeting cards, cut nails, old-time toys, and sarsaparilla. The storekeepers epitomize the friendly merchants of a by-gone era, attired in long country-style dresses, laced boots, and smiles. Gift wrapping and shipping services are available.

Stop in for a delicious, healthy snack of popcorn, which was lovingly grown on Wileswood's nearby farm. It's a wonderful way to put a smile on the day.

MILAN

Milan is a charming 19th century village that has retained much of its historical past through restoration of the buildings around the village square. Best known as the birthplace of Thomas Edison, the area offers outdoor activity year-round, as well as some outstanding shopping and dining locations.

attractions

Thomas Edison Birthplace Museum, a seven-room, furnished, brick cottage dating back to 1842, features a number of Edison's inventions and family furnishings.

Milan Historical Museum, open in the summer, provides a close-up look at glass and doll collections housed in an art building and period house.

accommodations

HOMESTEAD INN MOTELS
12110 State Route 250
Milan, Ohio 44846
Tel: (419) 499-2116

Homestead Inn Motel is a working farm surrounded by 60 lush, green acres of Ohio farmland. Three accommodation sites are located on the farm, with a total of 75 rooms available. Family rates are offered, making Homestead Inn Motel an ideal place for a family's vacation stay.

The Inn is close to Lake Erie, area vineyards, fishing, and beaches. Historic Milan is just three minutes away. The Milan Melon Festival is scheduled on Labor Day weekend and is one of the highlights of the area events. Thomas Edison's birthplace and the Milan Historic Museum are also close by. While staying at the inn, guests can observe the Hereford cattle, Arabian horses, and other animals living on the farm.

A swimming pool is available on the grounds. The Inn is next door to the well-known Homestead Inn Restaurant and Rathskeller. New to the area is a manufacturer's outlet mall, just one minute away.

bed & breakfast inns

COACH HOUSE BED-N-BREAKFAST, 304 State Route #113 West, Milan, Ohio 44846; Tel: (419) 499-2435. Offering the finest in accommodations and breakfasts, a stay at Coach House Bed-n-Breakfast promises to be an unforgettable one.

factory outlets

LAKE ERIE FACTORY OUTLET CENTER
11001 U.S. Route 250 North
Milan, Ohio 44846

Tel:	(419) 499-2528	
Hrs:	April - December:	
	Monday - Saturday	10:00 a.m. - 9:00 p.m.
	Food Court	9:00 a.m. - 9:00 p.m.
	Sunday	10:00 a.m. - 6:00 p.m.
	Food Court	9:00 a.m. - 6:00 p.m.
	January - March:	
	Monday - Thursday	10:00 a.m. - 6:00 p.m.
	Food Court	9:00 a.m. - 6:00 p.m.
	Friday - Saturday	10:00 a.m. - 9:00 p.m.
	Food Court	9:00 a.m. - 9:00 p.m.
	Sunday	12:00 p.m. - 6:00 p.m.
	Food Court	11:00 a.m. - 6:00 p.m.

Luxurious leather, elegant china, classic footwear, designer clothing as well as luggage, dinnerware, cookware, activewear, hosiery, cosmetics, shoes, sportswear, and Victorian accessories are just a small part of the Lake Erie Factory Outlet Center. This all-purpose outlet, which opened in August 1989, currently has over 40 stores and plans to have a total of 100 by Spring 1991.

Conveniently located North off Exit 7 of the Ohio Turnpike or South off State Route 2, this new facility is 10 minutes from Cedar Point Amusement Park. Nestled on a handsomely landscaped 52 acre lot, the outlet's atmosphere is reminiscent of New England, including the courtyards which separate various stores. While the environment creates an enjoyable shopping or browsing excursion for everyone, the architects have not neglected convenience. The center is fully accessible to the handicapped and has plenty of free parking.

After a long, hard day of successful shopping, enjoy a meal at the enclosed food court. The court features restaurants serving continental breakfast and hot pastries, Italian food, soup, salads, sandwiches, desserts and yogurt. Fashion shows, arts and crafts shows, car shows and boat and recreational vehicle displays are all in future plans for the center.

Feature stores at the center include American Tourister luggage, Bass footwear and accessories, Van Heusen men's and women's clothier, Fanny Farmer edibles, Gitano activewear, Ruff Hewn casual wear, Harve Benard designer clothing and accessories, Mikasa china and crystal, Jonathan Logan, Manhattan, Aileen, Banister Shoes, Hanes Activewear, Socks Galore, Prestige Fragrance and Cosmetics, Corning-Revereware, Farberware products, and Proctor-Silex kitchen appliances.

The Lake Erie Factory Outlet Center is so close to Cedar Point and all the attractions of Lake Erie, what better way to add to family fun than by shopping and saving?

greenhouses

MORTENSEN'S GREENHOUSE
4108 St. Route 113 East
Milan, Ohio 44846
Tel: (419) 499-2330
Hrs: April - October:
Seven days 9:00 a.m. - 6:00 p.m.
November - April:
Seven days 9:00 a.m. - 5:00 p.m.
Visa and MasterCard are accepted.

Imagine a colorful array of tropical foliage all around, comfortably warm temperatures, the smell of clean, crisp, fresh air and an unmatched sense of relaxation. Not a desert island, not a famous paradise, not even a quiet vacation in the south. This artistic tropical environment can be found off exit seven of the Ohio Turnpike.

This indoor simulation of the tropics is one of many features at Mortensen's Greenhouse three miles east of Milan, Ohio. Mortensen's is 23,000 square feet of shopping space and visual entertainment.

Peter Mortensen started a farm in the 1930's which blossomed into a greenhouse in the early 1950's and opened for retail business in 1974. Now, in its third generation, it is not only a successful greenhouse, but also a gift shop.

At the gift shop, patrons enjoy a variety of items such as wicker furniture, unusual baskets, southwest pottery and art, clay pots, and silk and dried flowers and arrangements. Whether buying or just browsing, the atmosphere of the shop compliments the relaxation of the greenhouse.

Undoubtedly, however, it is the picturesque beauty of the greenhouse itself which provides visitors the main attraction. Christmas brings about a special time as poinsettias, wreaths, and Dickens' collectibles grace the premises with a winter wonderland. Treat mom with a visit to Mortensen's on Mother's Day to enjoy blooming plants and hanging baskets and ferns. Fall means dried plants and arrangements while Spring conjures bedding plants and vegetables. Add a readily available informative staff to this variety and cap it off with reasonable pricing.

Potted plants, flowers, cacti, and all that a green thumb needs can be purchased and enjoyed at Mortensen's Greenhouse, a tropical paradise.

museums

EDISON BIRTHPLACE MUSEUM
9 North Edison Drive
Milan, Ohio 44846
Tel: (419) 499-2135
Hrs: February - May:
Tuesday - Sunday 1:00 p.m. - 5:00 p.m.
June - Labor Day:
Tuesday - Saturday 10:00 a.m. - 5:00 p.m.
Sunday 1:00 p.m. - 5:00 p.m.
Labor Day - November:
Tuesday - Sunday 1:00 p.m. - 5:00 p.m.
January by appointment only

American genius was never more manifest than in the person of Thomas Alva Edison. With over 1,093 patents, he stands out as one of the greatest inventors the world has known. The Edison Birthplace Museum was the home of young Edison until he was seven years old. Undoubtedly, the seeds of many of his inventions were sown here, in the blissfulness of his childhood imagination.

The museum, a National Historic Landmark, was opened to the public on the centennial of the inventor's birth in 1947 by Thomas Edison's daughter, Madeleine Edison Sloane. Today, it is administered by the Edison Birthplace Association, a nonprofit organization, under the directorship of Robert Wheeler, great-great-grandson of Mr. Edison's sister. The interior of the house is displayed naturally, as though the Edisons lived there today. Some of Edison's original letters and photographs are contained within the exhibit room. Also present are authentic models of the original electric light and phonograph, and the "Black Maria," the first movie studio. The astonishingly large list of Edisons's major inventions and discoveries is well represented in the collection.

The Edison Birthplace Museum offers a glimpse at the home of one of the world's great thinkers. To gain a better appreciation for the difference Edison has made, stop by the museum, birthplace of a genius.

restaurants

BERRY'S HOMESTEAD INN RESTAURANT
12018 Route 250
Milan, Ohio 44846
Tel: (419) 499-4271
Hrs: Monday - Friday 7:00 a.m. - 9:00 p.m.
Saturday - Sunday 7:00 a.m. - 8:00 p.m.
Closed on major holidays.
Visa, MasterCard, American Express and Diners Club are accepted.

Victorian elegance in a comfortable 1880s farmhouse characterizes the setting at Berry's. Whether guests sit at an upstairs window and observe the operations of a working farm while they eat or go to the Rathskeller Room downstairs, they are certain to enjoy both the setting and the choice of food. Berry's serves delightful American and Continental Cuisine.

Dinner favorites vary from prime rib of beef to Chicken Cordon Bleu. Seafood offerings include Lake Erie perch, Crab and Shrimp Panama, and broiled bay scallops. Diners may choose from a broad selection of domestic or imported wines. The Rathskeller, with the same menu available upstairs, is very popular, partly due to its salad table, which features many different kinds of salads and breads.

Whether patrons dine in the main floor room, the second floor, or the Rathskeller, they will find that the friendly, competent, and well-trained staff complement the outstanding food of this excellent restaurant, making a return visit an experience to share with cherished friends and loved ones.

MILAN INN
29 East Church Street
Milan, Ohio 44846
Tel: (419) 499-4604
Hrs: Seasonal
Call for reservations and times.

Located in a building that is listed in the National Registry of Historic Places, Milan Inn provides that distinctive touch of class for an intimate dinner for two, as well as ample facilities for a large banquet. Wall murals in a warm, comfortable setting highlight the downstairs dining area, while the upstairs is decorated in Early-American decor.

The lunch menu features many fine sandwiches, salads, and luncheon plates, with selections ranging from corned beef on rye to a complete lunch of broiled chicken breast with sweet-and-sour sauce. A strong American accent continues with the dinner menu, which includes everything from a vegetarian plate to steaks and seafood. Fish dishes include breaded Lake Erie perch and breaded pickerel fillets, items not found in many areas of the United States.

Whether one is a steak-and-potatoes person with a hearty appetite or a discriminating vegetarian, Milan Inn, an "inn of fine foods," is a "Best Choice" for a delicious meal.

OHIO'S NORTH COAST

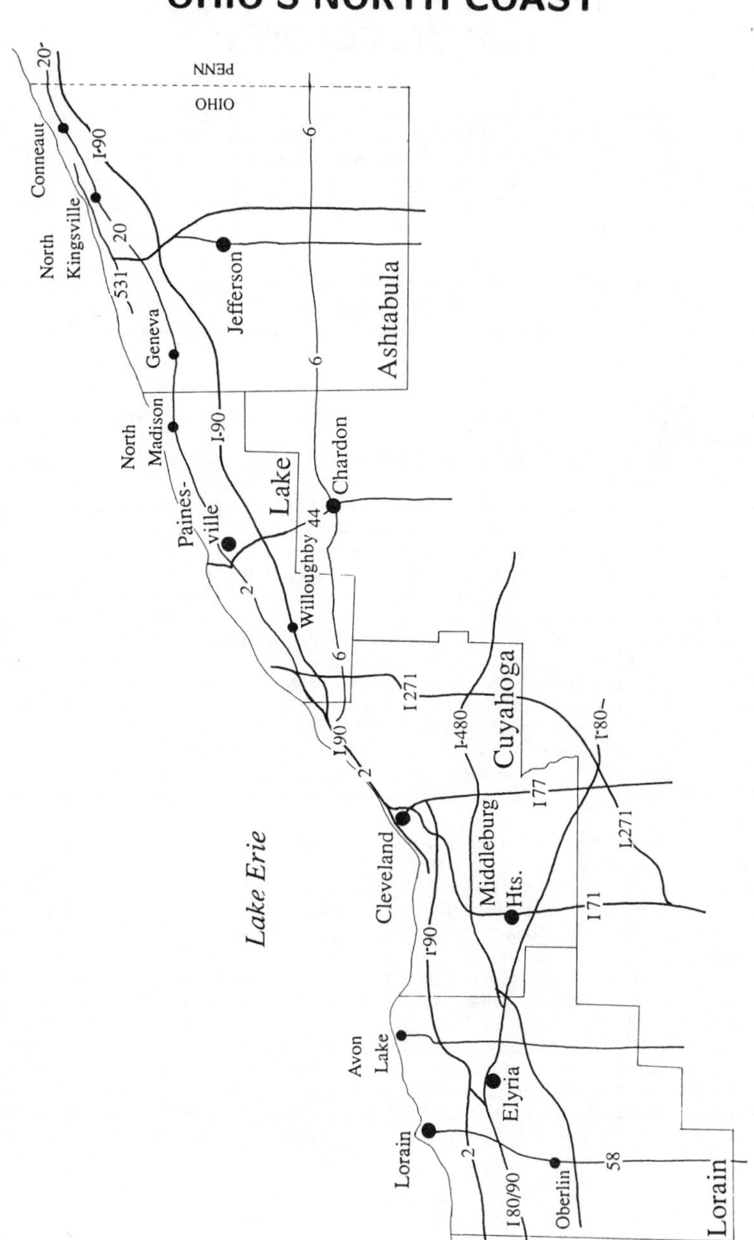

LORAIN COUNTY

Named for the province of Lorraine, France, Lorain County was once claimed by King Charles I of England in the 1600s. The first known European arrived in the county in 1755 as an Indian captive. Lorain County was part of the Northwest Territories established in 1785 and part of the Connecticut Western Reserve. Lorain County was created in 1822 from Cuyahoga, Huron and Medina Counties.

attractions

Lorain County boasts picturesque little towns full of history and 19th century charm. Wellington has more than 200 historic structures, such as the **Wellington Town Hall.**

Native Archibald Willard is honored with a monument in the **Spirit of '76 Museum.**

Grafton, once a busy railroad town, has restored a switching tower; a nearby caboose contains railroad displays and exhibits.

Oberlin and **Oberlin College** were founded in 1833. Among the leading liberal arts colleges in the United States, Oberlin College is noted for its top-ranked science program and world-famous **Conservatory of Music.** Allen Art Museum, the foremost college art museum in America, contains more than 13,000 works of art. The college also has two fine concert halls, **Finney Chapel** and **Hall Auditorium,** which offer the finest in concerts, theater and film. **The Firelands Association for the Visual Arts** (FAVA), Northeast Ohio's nationally-known arts organization, offers art exhibits, classic films and art classes for all ages. Oberlin also has historical places such as the **Jewett House,** the **Monroe House, The Depot and Caboose,** the **Little Red Schoolhouse,** and **The Memorial Arch. Tappan Square,** located on the college campus, comprises 13 acres with 60 species of native trees, shrubs, and perennials.

Located in southern Lorain County, **Findley State Park** offers swimming, boating, fishing, camping, and a special refuge for wildflowers and wildlife. The lake is stocked with large mouth bass, bluegill, and northern pike. Its location in a stately pine grove makes the campground popular. In addition to the public beach, campground guests have exclusive use of a camp beach.

Once a state forest, Findley State Park is heavily wooded with a wide variety of trees. There are approximately 10 miles of hiking trails, including a portion of the Buckeye Trail. The lowlands provide swamp habitat for wildflowers such as marsh marigolds and skunk cabbage. One area of the park serves as a sanctuary for the Duke's Skipper Butterfly, preserving perhaps the state's largest colony of this extremely rare insect. Winter attractions include an excellent ice skating area and a sledding hill near the campground. There are also ice fishing on the lake and designated cross-country skiing trails.

VERMILION

Vermilion is a quaint, harbor town and historic fishing village filled with the grace and charm characteristic of the Great Lakes region.

attractions

Harbour Town 1837 is the downtown Vermilion, restoration district, where shops of every style and nature, including antique and curio shops, line the streets.

The **Great Lakes Historical Society Museum** recalls the shipping history of the Great Lakes. The society has dedicated itself to promote interest in discovering and preserving material on the Great Lakes and the Great Lakes area of the United States and Canada. Museum exhibits include models, paintings, documents, records, and artifacts.

Restored to the splendor of the 1845 era, the **Mill Hollow House** was once a stagecoach stop. This house may be the oldest structure in Lorain County.

Harbour Town Historic District, open year-round, is a restored town that features charming shops and houses, a small boat harbor and a nautical museum. It is located at the heart of Vermilion's waterfront.

Museum of the Great Lakes Historical Society is a fascinating museum located in the lakeside town of Vermilion.

events

The **Festival of the Fish** is held in mid-June at Victory Park. Sample the fresh Lake Erie perch, or watch the Crazy Craft Boat Race.

charters

CHARTER ERIE
636 Sandusky Street
Vermilion, Ohio 44089
Tel: (216) 967-2049
Hrs: Two trips, seven days
Call for exact times.

Charter Erie offers affordable fishing on the only boat of its kind in Vermilion, according to Captain Rick Sterling. Rick and his experienced first mate, Barbara will smooth the waters of Lake Erie to make a perfect vacation charter experience.

great lakes coast

Charter Erie's special 38-foot boat accommodates up to six people per trip. Rick navigates through the central basin of Lake Erie to those special spots where one can fish for record-sized walleyes. Groups or individuals can rent a boat for all or part of a day. The vessels are U. S. Coast Guard inspected and state-of-the-art equipment is used throughout each of the boats. The seats are padded, and an overhead hard-top roof and side curtains keep the chilly weather out. Private marine toilets are provided.

Rod and reel rentals are available, and bait and tackle may be obtained at nearby Parson's Marine Store. Boats leave from Parson's marine at the foot of Sandusky Street in downtown Vermilion.

gift shops

CRANBERRY COTTAGE
604 North Main Street
Vermilion, Ohio 44089
Tel: (216)967-9777
Hrs: May 1 - January 1:
Monday - Saturday 10:00 a.m. - 6:00 p.m.
Sunday Noon - 5:00 p.m.
January 1 - May 1:
Monday - Saturday 10:00 a.m. - 5:00 p.m.
Visa and MasterCard are accepted.

Just the name "Cranberry Cottage" evokes images and aromas of festive occasions: scented candles burning, cranberry sauce simmering, the fragrance of flowers and pine boughs touching every room, the warmth and joy of celebration.

This shop, a lovely, Victorian cottage in Harbor Town, pays tribute to old-fashioned, hand-crafted quality as well as the good times of the good old days. The selection of country, Victorian, and nautical gifts and home decorating accents is plentiful throughout the year. Year-round handcrafted gifts, including such collectibles as David Winters Cottages, Wee Forest Folk, Humphrey Bogart figurines, Salmon Falls Pottery, and Crumkleton Figures can be found here. Many other well-known pottery names are featured, along with fine works by local crafts people. There are baskets galore made from a variety of materials, hand woven and homespun fabrics, creations in lace, lamps and lamp shades, and a colorful collection of wood, cloth, and porcelain dolls and assorted animals. Fragrances of all kinds lend a delightfully aromatic appeal. Many delectable food items are also available.

The opening of the Christmas Shoppe each Memorial Day brings an especially vibrant feeling of anticipation. Located in the back of Cranberry Cottage, the Christmas Shoppe carries the spirit of Christmas in ornaments, wreaths, candles, centerpieces, potpourris, mulling spices, table covers, afghans, and tree skirts. Dickens Houses, Santas, angels, wooden trees, cloth dolls, and Christmas cards are all there for the choosing in advance preparation for a special holiday.

Warm, personal service is a hallmark of Cranberry Cottage. The staff will make up custom gift baskets for every occasion to suit any budget. A bridal registry and free home decorating service are offered as well as plans for a mail order catalog for home shopping. While parents are busy browsing, a play room keeps children occupied. Merely walking into the shop with its many surprises, is like a step back in time.

MUSIK BOX HAUS
5541 Liberty Avenue
Vermilion, Ohio 44089
Tel: (216) 967-4744
Hrs: Monday - Saturday 10:00 a.m. - 6:00 p.m.
Sunday 12:30 p.m. - 5:30 p.m.
Visa, MasterCard, American Express and Discover are accepted.

Genevieve M. Clarke's Musik Box Haus contains a treasury of pleasures for the eye and ear, a collection of exquisite and unusual boxes called "the finest in Ohio". An equally impressive array of original collector dolls complements the tinkling medley of musical wonders.

Musik Box Haus has a museum quality characterized by antique display cases as intriguing as the music boxes, while the stairwell leading to a loft is an integral part of the exhibits. A major contributor to the collection is Cleveland's Fred Zimbalist, one of the nation's foremost designers of music boxes. Other famous names featured are Sorrento, Steinbach, Otigari, Schmid, Staufen Studio, George Imports, Inc., Enesco's "Precious Moments", and the Porter Disc Music Box. A particular favorite is the line of Norman Rockwell musical figurines. Increasing interest in music boxes spurred Genevieve's search for original designers, which led her to Vic DiAngelo, whom she commissioned to create special designs in honor of the Wooly Bear Festival. The Doll House section of the shop shelters creations by Bette Ball, Lizzi Batz, Wendy Brent, Jan Hagara, Gotz, Zook, and Gotham, among others; many incorporate music as part of their charm. Seminars are held on doll fashion, construction, history, and valuation.

Located in a building more than a century old in Vermilion's Harbour Town, Musik Box Haus is a visual experience with its colorful murals and European flair. The appeal to browse is irresistible and customers are pleased they did when they find themselves leaving the shop with a chiming song in a one-of-a-kind box.

museums

GREAT LAKES HISTORICAL SOCIETY
480 Main Street
Vermilion, Ohio 44089
Tel: (216) 967-3467
Hrs: April - December:
Seven Days 10:00 a.m. - 5:00 p.m.
January - March:
Weekends only 10:00 a.m. - 5:00 p.m.
Visa, MasterCard and American Express are accepted.

The Great Lakes Historical Society has been preserving and promoting the history of shipping on the lakes since 1944, when it was officially incorporated as a nonprofit organization. Since that time, it has seen the development of the Commadore Wakefield mansion into a respected museum, the addition of a modern two-story section housing important exhibits, the establishment of an extensive research library, the acquisition of a 321-foot WWII submarine, and the constant expansion of a collection of maritime relics and memorabilia evoking the dramatic past of the Great Lakes.

For maritime history buffs and armchair sailors alike, the museum is at the top of the sightseeing priority list. The museum shelters one of the largest collections of maritime engines in North America, including a 14-foot high harbor tug steam engine built in 1913. The lighthouse exhibit features a second-order Fresnel type lens, one of the largest on the lakes, from Lake Huron's Spectacle Reef Lighthouse. Tools used in the building of wooden ships and operating exhibits are on display as well as detailed scale models of virtually every type of ship known to the Great Lakes. One such model portrays the 729-foot Edmund Fitzgerald, which went down in Lake Superior in 1975 and was immortalized in a song by Gordon Lightfoot. The Clarence S. Metcalf Library contains a wealth of data on Great Lake vessels, facilities, and maritime activities. Technical papers, wreck data, plans, and drawings are among the works catalogued. To tour the submarine USS Cad, the visitor must go to its berth next to Burke Lakefront Airport in Cleveland. Unaltered from its wartime configuration, the submarine has been designated a National Historic Landmark.

The museum store carries historic items and reproductions, navagational charts, prints, and the largest listing of books relating to the lakes to be found anywhere, as well as "Living History" videotapes produced by the society. A visit to the museum acquaints one with more extraordinary Great Lakes Historical Society programs and exhibits.

restaurants

ALIZE RESTAURANT & LOUNGE
2610 Liberty Avenue
Vermilion, Ohio 44089
Tel: (216) 967-1300
Hrs: Lunch:
Monday - Saturday 11:00 a.m. - 3:00 p.m.
Dinner:
Monday - Thursday 4:00 p.m. - 10:00 p.m.
Friday - Saturday 4:00 p.m. - 11:00 p.m.
Bar:
Monday - Saturday 3:00 p.m. - 1:00 a.m.
Visa, MasterCard and American Express are accepted.

Alize, a gourmet restaurant of high order, opened in 1987 to rave reviews. Presenting a sophisticated variety of delectable entrees, a la carte items, and European, feather-light pastries prepared on the premises, this restaurant offers a truly enjoyable dining experience.

Appetizers such as garlic soup or an artfully arranged house salad with tangy lemon thyme dressing are popular. For the main course, there is a variety of veal, chicken, beef, and seafood dishes, most with light but rich sauces that are delicately seasoned. If you can't make up your mind, try the house combo special that offers a sampling of Veal Florentine, sauteed scampi, fresh veggies, and angel hair pasta. A special menu for those wishing to eat at the bar features delightful items such as stuffed mushrooms, spinach salad, burger with provolone, a wonderful assortment of sandwiches, Caesar salad, and a Mediterranean plate. The skillful owner, Al Sabbaghzadeh, who emigrated in 1975 after working in the food business in France, Switzerland, and Germany, is the former manager of the plush Glass Garden in Westlake, Ohio. He has remodeled the existing restaurant, installing picture windows, and has placed tablecloths and flowers on each table, creating a warm and friendly atmosphere.

A disc jockey may be found in the bar at Alize late on Friday and Saturday nights. Moderate prices and modest gourmet portions that prevail in both the bar and the restaurant, together with a stylish, casual ambiance, provide the ingredients needed for a "Best Choice."

OLD PRAGUE RESTAURANT
5586 Liberty Avenue
Vermilion, Ohio 44089
Tel: (216) 967-7182
Hrs: Monday - Thursday Noon - 8:00 p.m.
Friday - Saturday Noon - 8:00 p.m.
Sunday Noon - 7:00 p.m.
Winter hours may vary slightly. Please call ahead.
Visa and MasterCard are accepted.

Located in the Harbor Town district of Vermilion, the Old Prague Restaurant, a family-owned business since 1972, serves distinguished meals. Guests, comfortably seated in captain's chairs, are offered a selection of superb European and American dishes. Favorites are Chicken Paprikash, tender pieces of chicken in a sour cream sauce with the traditional egg dumplings and tossed salad, and Wiener Schnitzel, lightly breaded veal with lemon slices. All menu items are home cooked.

The Old Prague Restaurant has received A-1 ratings from every newspaper in the region. Patrons will appreciate this dinner house with its chalet design and stained wood, which give it a strong European appearance. Zdenka Verovsky, of Czechoslovakian descent, prepares the meals, and insists on the freshest possible ingredients. Nearby Lake Erie provides fresh perch, which the Vevrosky family prepares boneless and serves with tartar sauce. Roast duck, Hungarian Goulash, and fresh roast pork contribute to an award winning menu.

Dine in splendor at beautifully appointed tables with chandeliers overhead. A complete selection of fine imported and domestic beers and wines will complement whatever meal one chooses. The Old Prague Restaurant has earned a reputation for providing fine cuisine in a restful atmosphere, and remains one of Vermilion's "Best Choice" establishments.

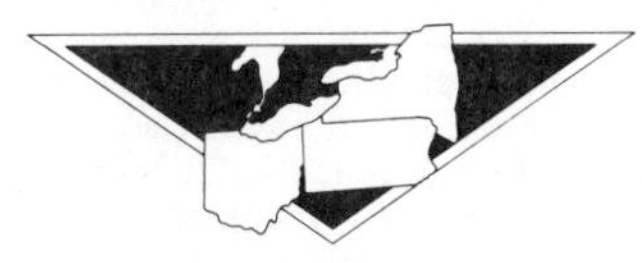

The **Peter Miller House**, the oldest house in Avon Lake, is currently under restoration. It was built in the early 19th century.

The **French Creek District** is a restored area of specialty shops and antique stores in Avon Lake.

events

The **Gas Engine Show and Flea Market** is held in early June in the Columbia Station area.

Home and Heritage Days is held in Tappan Square in Oberlin. Held in late July, this is a showcase of Oberlin's unique heritage.

The **North Ridgeville Corn Festival** is held in mid-August in North Ridgeville. The fresh-picked sweet corn is prepared using a secret Amish recipe.

The **Lorain County Fair**, the second largest in Ohio, is held in late August at the fairgrounds in Wellington.

The **Festival of Flowers** is held in Avon Lake's French Creek District in mid-May.

accommodations

AQUA MARINE HOTEL AND RESORT
216 Miller Road
Avon Lake, Ohio 44012
Tel: (216) 933-2000
(800) 362-2570 Ohio
(800) 321-2080 Nationwide
Visa, MasterCard, American Express, Diners Club and Carte Blanche are accepted

The Aqua Marine Hotel and Resort, located just a block from the shore of Lake Erie, is a place where guests can enjoy an almost endless list of things to do, or enjoy quite as much doing nothing at all in pleasant surroundings. The hotel's facilities are popular with both vacationers and business or convention groups.

During a stay, guests can take advantage of the 18-hole golf course which surrounds most of the hotel buildings. Walk or jog along the trails that wind through the 63 acres of the hotel's campus-like setting. Other recreation facilities include large indoor and outdoor swimming pools, a health club with various workout equipment, tennis and raquetball courts, and a bowling alley. Guests who prefer something less active, but equally challenging, challenge the hotel's collection of the latest electronic games. Whatever room guests take, they will find it pleasantly commodious, with its own outdoor terrace, where one can sit and sip a drink before dinner. Each room has air conditioning and cable television with free movies. If organizing a business meeting, one can choose either one or both of the two ballrooms that handle up to 250 participants, or make use of one of the other nine rooms for smaller group presentations. The staff, experienced at designing special facilities for conferences, will have all of the needed audiovisual and related equipment ready for you. There's a choice of places to eat, led by the Fairway Restaurant, which overlooks the golf course. Lunch offerings include sandwiches, salads, and soups or more filling entrees, such as Lake Erie perch and walleye fresh from the lake. The best of the desserts is a strawberry shortcake that is a tradition with guests of the Aqua Marine.

This is a place where guests can play hard, work hard, or do nothing but relax. It is also a vacation head quarters from which bus or auto tours can take you to many sights including Sea World, Cedar Point, and Harbour Town. The Aqua Marine is just 20 minutes from downtown Cleveland, less than that from the airport; a limousine ride away from the hustle and bustle of the city to the most relaxing and enjoyable of environments.

art galleries

ANIMATED ART GALLERY, INC.
32730 Walker Road
Avon Lake, Ohio 44012
Tel: (800) 366-CELS
Hrs: Monday - Saturday 10:00 a.m. - 4:00 p.m.
Visa and MasterCard are accepted.

Mike Hanna and Steve Kohn have been animation buffs as far back as they can remember. Mike established Animated Art Gallery, Inc. in 1986. At the time of this printing, this gallery is the only authorized Disney dealer in Northern Ohio. Both Mike and Steve are experts in the lore of animation celuloids (cels) and can make your visit to the gallery an educational adventure to be remembered. According to the owners, "production cels are the hand-painted images on clear acetate (celuloids) that are actually placed over a background and filmed in sequence to create a motion picture."

A distinctive and largely American art form, animation has given birth to some of our most well-known stars, including Mickey Mouse, Donald Duck, Popeye, Betty Boop, The Roadrunner, Snow White, the Seven Dwarfs, and Bugs Bunny, just to name a few. Each character's story is encapsulated and preserved in the showcase selections at Animated Art Gallery, Inc. A commemorative cel portfolio from the Disney classic Sleeping Beauty will soon be available through the gallery. In addition to Disney art, the gallery carries cels from Hanna-Barbera, Warner Brothers, Bakshi, MGM, Walter Lantz, and more. Limited edition and pre-1960 cels are displayed. These one-of-a-kind pieces of art represent virtually every stage of animation production, from the artist's preliminary sketches and character model sheets, to story-board drawings and final hand-painted production cels.

Collecting animation art is becoming a popular investment, as many pieces show dramatic appreciation in value over a short period of time. For most buyers, collecting animated art is a passion, a chance to capture a part of their childhood fantasies. All who visit Animated Art Gallery, Inc., enjoy a whimsical trip back to a time when cartoon characters were reality rather than fantasy.

wine

JOHN CHRIST WINERY
32421 Walker Road
Avon Lake, Ohio 44012
Tel: (216) 933-9672
Hrs: Monday - Thursday 9:00 a.m. - 8:00 p.m.
Friday - Saturday 9:00 a.m. - Midnight

Dating back to the 1930s, the family-operated John Christ Winery has become a tradition passed through the generations. Present owner Alex Christ makes sure the winery lives up to the ideals and superior quality that founder John Christ demanded.

Tours are by appointment only and can include wine tasting. Twenty-two acres of vines produce Labrusca grapes. The vineyard's most popular wine is the Niagara, and other varieties include Pink Catawba, Villard, Seyval, Vadal, and Reislings. The Ohio wine producers have recognized John Christ Winery by awarding this vineyard two silver medals and a bronze. The Bavarian chalet-style winery is located only two miles from Lake Erie; the Avon Lake area has been a popular resort for many years. The region offers a delightful environment in which to spend a pleasant day and/or evening. Vintners Alex and Zora Christ offer a hospitable, personal touch that makes guests feel welcome.

John Christ Winery's hospitality/tasting room serves cheese plates and soups on Friday and Saturday after 6:00 p.m. Annual pig roasts are held in mid-June, and the Christs request that guests register in advance due to limited space. Located only 25 miles from downtown Cleveland, visitors should take Interstate 90 to Route 83 North to Walker Road. Head east for three miles. There is plenty of parking available.

KLINGSHIRN WINERY, INC.
33050 Webber Road
Avon Lake, Ohio 44012
Tel: (216) 933-6666
Hrs: Monday - Saturday 10:00 a.m. - 6:00 p.m.
Closed Sundays and Holidays
Visa and MasterCard are accepted.

Now in its third generation, Klingshirn Winery is a family operation established in 1935 when the repeal of Prohibition prompted Albert R. Klingshirn to try his hand at commercial winemaking. After five years of making wine in the cellar of his home, Albert built a two-room winery. In 1955, his son, Allan, purchased the business and expanded the product line, replacing barrels with large wooden casks and stainless steel tanks. Four times its original size, the winery building currently contains all production facilities and a retail room.

LORAIN

Originally called "Mouth of the Black River," Lorain became a permanent settlement in 1811. Lorain is home to the Bascule Bridge, which was built in 1940, and is the largest of its type of lift bridge in the United States, the second largest span in the world.

attractions

At the entrance to Lorain Harbor is the **Jewel of the Port Lighthouse**, built in 1917, which has become the symbol of Lorain.

Built as a movie palace in 1928, the **Lorain Palace Civic Center** showcases drama, music, dance, and civic events.

In nearby Sheffield is a museum dedicated to the memory of the men who served in the 103rd Regiment of the Ohio Volunteer Infantry during the Civil War. The museum is open by appointment only.

events

The **Lorain International Festival** is held in late June at the Sheffield Centre. Entertainment and a bazaar of the foods of 55 different nationalities are offered with no admission charge.

The traditional summer's end event, the **Sunset Festival** is held in late August at Lakeview Park.

restaurants

ANTLERS RESTAURANT & GRAND BALL ROOM
300 Washington Avenue
Lorain, Ohio 44062
Tel: (216) 246-0410
Hrs: Lunch:
Monday - Friday 11:30 a.m. - 4:00 p.m.
Dinner:
Monday - Friday 4:00 p.m. - 9:00 p.m.
Saturday 5:00 p.m. - 10:00 p.m.

The Antlers Restaurant and Grand Ball Room features big band sounds and superb dining. Locals and travelers alike will enjoy balmy Ohio evenings under starry skies at Antlers Restaurant, one of the finest buildings in Lorain. Located within sight of the lake, this restaurant has been completely refurbished, retaining its graceful lead glass windows and large stage. Three separate rooms are available for private parties. Friday nights are filed with fun at Antlers, where diners gather for the weekly fish fry and enjoy live entertainment.

The food at Antlers is always fresh, since vegetables arrive thrice weekly, and fish, a favorite, is brought in daily. All soups are homemade, as are dressings and desserts. Dinner entrees are served with Texas toast, tossed salad, and a choice of either the vegetable of the day, rice pilaf, or baked, fried, or mashed potatoes. The prime rib of beef au jus is presented in portions of eight, 12, or 16 ounces. Other favorites include The Texas Pounder, a one-pound porterhouse steak smothered in grilled onions, fried shrimp, and barbecued pork ribs. After dinner, take a relaxing stroll through Lorain's lovely public park near the Grand Ball Room. Enjoy Saturday night lobster or succulent fried perch on Friday evening, followed by big band entertainment. Any night is the right occasion to dine at Antlers Restaurant & Grand Ball Room, Lorain's "Best Choice" for the dining public.

ROMAN'S CASTLE ON THE LAKE
2532 West Erie Avenue
Lorain, Ohio 44053

Tel:	(216) 244-1486	
Hrs:	Lunch:	
	Monday - Saturday	11:30 a.m. - 2:30 p.m.
	Dinner:	
	Monday - Thursday	5:00 p.m. - 9:00 p.m.
	Friday - Saturday	4:30 p.m. - 10:00 p.m.
	Sunday	Noon - 8:00 p.m.
	Summer Weekend Cookouts:	
	Friday - Saturday	7:00 p.m. - Closing
	Lounge:	
	Monday - Saturday	11:30 a.m. - 2:30 a.m.

Visa, MasterCard, American Express, Diners Club and Buckeye Card are accepted.

This replica of a Scottish country house is Lorain's best kept secret. Roman's Castle on the Lake was built in the 1920s as a private home and authentic to the last details of interlocking structural supporting stones and caverns in the cellar. True to its castle heritage, a friendly ghost is even said to live there, playing playful pranks on the staff from time to time. As part of the duplicating scheme, a tunnel was built from the cellar to Lake Erie, proving "useful" during Prohibition for making rum runs to Canada.

Operated as a restaurant since 1943 and now owned by Richard and Liz Roman, Roman's Castle commands two acres overlooking Lake Erie. Diners may sit inside the intimate restaurant, which accommodates 110, or enjoy the grand view from the deck, which seats 61. Climbing vines and a gracious canopy greet patrons as they drive up to the parking area. The auspicious surroundings overshadow the menu only momentarily as sumptuous dishes such as swordfish, Shrimp Aglio, Chicken Oscar, Veal Marsala, honey-dipped fried chicken, filet mignon, and Lake Erie perch and pickerel make the taste buds anxious, only to be excited again by the wide selection of desserts. The house specials are chocolate caramel nut cheesecake and Chester's New

York cheesecake. For lunch, stuffed croissants, a rainbow cobb salad, or a fine looking assortment of hearty sandwiches are yours for the asking. Lunch or dinner at the Castle are moderately priced excursions.

Roman's Castle on the Lake is a landmark, a meeting place whose menu gallantly heralds "A most hearty welcome to Roman's Castle, where you, Sir, are the King, and you, Lady, are the Queen."

AMHERST

Amherst is the "Sandstone Capital of the World" and home to what is billed as the world's largest sandstone quarry. The Amherst Town Hall, a restored 1860s-era town hall, is listed on the National Registry of Historic Places.

attractions

The Nordson Train Depot is a restored passenger and freight depot used for community exhibits, meetings, and local events.

The Workshop Players Theatre offers the best in local community theater.

The Lorain County Speedway offers competition among late model, sportsmen and stock car races every Saturday night, May through mid-September. The track is in South Amherst.

Rajahland is a recreation park that features swimming, sports and waterslide facilities, and is a highly enjoyable recreational area in Amherst.

events

The Potato Festival is held during mid-August at the K-Mart Plaza.

flea markets

JAMIE'S FLEA MARKET, INC.
State Route 113, 1/2 Mile West of Route 58
Amherst, Ohio 44001
Tel: (216) 986-4402
Hrs: Wednesday - Saturday 8:00 a.m. - 4:00 p.m.
Annual Christmas Special:
First Sunday in December 10:00 a.m. - 4:00 p.m.

Jamie's is one of the biggest flea markets in Ohio, with an incredible array of goods showcased in 550 booths. Exceptionally well organized and efficiently run, Jamie's Flea Market is a shopper's and browser's paradise. Two large porcelain white metal-clad structures hold 250 stands; 300 more are outdoors in the paved parking area. It is a year-round affair; there is no admission charge, and a lively, country-fair feeling pervades the grounds.

Fresh farm produce and booths featuring German, Amish, and American specialties are conveniently located for the hungry shopper. There are also meat, nut, cheese, bread, candy, and health food stands. An abundance of unique items are available, including lovely fresh floral displays, greenhouse plants, and garden supplies, gleaming silver, china, and crystal, aromatic potpourri and candles, useful kitchenware and restaurant supplies, Hummel and Goebel collector plates, antiques, and a myriad of other collectibles: Amish items, fabric art, coins, stamps, clocks, both new and antique wood and leather goods, lamps, and music boxes. For fun or serious collectors, there are baseball cards, comic books and other books by the score, Barbie clothes, toys, and games. The family pet isn't forgotten, nor are the sports fans and car lovers. Many exhibitors are artisians who sell original work as well as taking custom orders.

Plan to take some time, browsing, and enjoying the clean, well-lit atmosphere. With 22 acres of free parking, one need not worry about finding a space, and attendants direct motorists to the best spots. Just remember, at Jamie's Flea Market, "If you can't find it, ask!"

ELYRIA

In 1817, Herman Ely purchased approximately 12,500 acres of land near the falls of the Black River. On the river he constructed a dam and ran a gristmill and sawmill. Within two years, a small community grew up around Ely's mills. When the county was established in 1822, Ely donated land and $2,000 toward the construction of a courthouse on the condition that the county seat be located in Elyria. Officials accepted, and Elyria became the county seat.

attractions

Tour the **Indian Ridge Museum** and see more than 12,000 years of Indian history and prehistoric artifacts.

The **Elyria Civil War Monument** is located downtown in Ely Park. Tours are also available at the **Laundon House** and **The Hickories**, a turn-of-the-century mansion with Tiffany windows. The Hickories is home to the Lorain County Historical Society.

The **Lorain County Courthouse** is listed on the National Registry of Historic Places.

The **Stocker Arts Center**, located on the campus of the Lorain County Community College, contains an art gallery and two theaters.

Cascade Park, part of Lorain County's Metropolitan Park district, contains 200 acres of spectacular natural beauty. The park offers hiking, picnicking, playgrounds, and sledding areas.

events

Elyria holds its annual **Apple Festival** in mid-September.

taverns & pubs

TAVERN ON THE MALL
323 Midway Boulevard
Elyria, Ohio 44035
Tel: (216) 324-3155
Hrs: Lunch:
Seven days 11:15 a.m. - 4:00 p.m.
Dinner:
Seven days 4:00 p.m. - 11:00 p.m.
Visa, Mastercard, American Express and Discover are accepted.

Eat, drink, and be merry while dining at Tavern on the Mall. This bustling and inviting restaurant is located adjacent to the Midway Mall, the largest in the area, and affords diners fine, quality food served by an attentive staff.

The attractive menu features appetizers, soups, and desserts together with an interesting array of beef, chicken, and fish entrees. A pleasing wine menu is available as well. The Potato skin appetizer takes on new life with its preparation by the highly qualified chefs at Tavern on the Mall. Presented deep-fried and filled with two kinds of cheeses, topped with bacon bits and scallions, and served with sour cream, the skins almost become "a meal in themselves". The stuffed mushrooms are fresh caps, filled with their own special crabmeat stuffing and smothered in Monterey Jack and Cheddar cheese. "Dinners from the land" offer a succulent cut of aged prime rib, and the Tavern features the full cut as evidence of its "pound" of pride, as well as petite and standard cuts. The King's Kut beef comes in a generous portion hearty enough for two, and chicken breasts are served boneless, prepared Italian style or with an unforgettable, richly aromatic house marinade. A popular favorite from the sea is Stuffed Scampies, jumbo Scampi filled with crabmeat stuffing, topped with Monterey Jack cheese, and baked to perfection. The Tavern offers mouth-watering delicacies at its Row Bar, Wednesday through Friday from 4:00 p.m. to midnight, and a Happy Hour Monday through Friday 4:00 p.m. to 7:00 p.m. The restaurant also offers banquet facilities to accommodate 15 to 400 people for special occasions.

The natural woodwork, accentuated by bay windows, and the profusion of greenery, create an appealing ambiance. Tavern on the Mall invites diners to sit back, relax, and enjoy a fine dining experience.

CUYAHOGA COUNTY

Created from Geauga County in 1807, Cuyahoga County is named for the Cuyahoga River, which derived its name from the Indian word meaning "crooked." Cuyahoga County is the home of Cleveland, the largest city in Ohio. It is also home to part of the Cuyahoga Valley National Recreation Area. The county represents a veritable microcosm of Ohio itself-urban, suburban, small town, rural, wilderness, maritime and agricultural. Cuyahoga County is a place of diversity, beauty, energy and life.

attractions

Oldest Stone Museum, open February through November, has been preserved as a pioneer dwelling and also features a beautiful herb garden.

Lake Erie Nature and Science Center features a great colection of love birds and animals, petting zoo, wildfower garden and natural and physical science displays.

Open March through December, **Rose Hill Museum** is the restored home of the area's first inhabitant.

events

Some of America's top restaurants travel to the Cuyahoga County Fairgrounds in Berea to compete in the **National Rib Cook-Out** held in late May.

The Prescott Hunter and Jumper Classic-one of the Midwest's finest shows of its kind-is held in Moreland Hills' Metropark Polo Field in late July.

The Cuyahoga County Fair is held at the fairgrounds in Berea in mid-August.

CLEVELAND

Cleveland is the largest city in Ohio-not bad for a city whose starting population was three in 1796. Thanks to pioneering industrialists and immigrant labor, this manufacturing giant is now one of the 10 major industrial markets in the country.

By 1832, the Ohio and Erie Canal was completed, and as its northern terminus, Cleveland received the first of the immigrants. The city grew from a bustling port to a shipping giant. Fortunes were made in shipping, manufacturing, communications, railroads, and oil.

In 1870, John D. Rockefeller founded the Standard Oil Company and made Cleveland the oil center of America. Its world headquarters are still located in Public Square.

The Terminal Tower, the 52-story Union Railroad Station that still dominates the city's skyline, and the Cleveland Mall all were built by the turn of the century.

Today, Cleveland continues to flourish, and its industries have been diversified. It is headquarters for more than 30 major industrial corporations and hundreds of smaller companies.

Being the nation's 10th largest consumer market, Cleveland is a shopper's paradise. There are more than 600 retail stores in the downtown area alone. The largest concentrations of stores can be found between Public Square and East 14th Street on Euclid, Prospect and Huron Avenues. The two major downtown department stores are Higbee's and the May Company. Boutiques, antique and specialty shops, and galleries abound. A distinctive collection of shops and restaurants can be found at the Galleria at Erieview, East 9th and St. Clair Streets.

Several areas of Cleveland provide specialty shopping. Among these is the Old River Shopping Area. The Beachcliff Market Square, a converted landmark movie house, shelters specialty shops within a central atrium. Both complexes are located in the Rocky River area. Fresh fruits, vegetables, meats, and ethnic foods are sold at the huge, open-air West Side Market.

Known as The Flats, the area adjacent to the Cuyahoga River is the hub of Cleveland's nightlife. Here, one can find everything from jazz to country, and, of course, rock and roll. Cleveland is also home to the official Rock and Roll Hall of Fame, chosen for this honor over such notable cities as Memphis, Philadelphia, and San Francisco.

Due to Cleveland's long history as an important industrial center and the fact that it was home at one time to more millionaires per capita than any other city in America, it has the good fortune to have developed an accessible historical and cultural community life.

In 1916, professional theater had its Cleveland debut in the Cleveland Play House, which housed the nation's first resident theater company. Today, Playhouse Square incorporates the State, Ohio, and Palace Theaters in a turn-of-the-century three-theater complex. The third largest performing arts center in the United States, its renovation is reputed to have entailed the only theater restoration project of its kind in the world. The State Theater is home to the Cleveland Ballet. The Cleveland Orchestra, one of the world's finest, performs at Severance Hall. Opera aficionados can choose between the Cleveland Opera, which performs at the State Theater, and the Cleveland Institute of Music's Opera Theater.

attractions

Minutes from downtown Cleveland and to the east is **University Circle**, a cultural area that boasts the distinction of having no comparison anywhere in the country. Within its one square-mile area, visitors will find art, science, and educational institutions such as **Case Western Reserve University**, **The Cleveland Museum of Art**, **The Dittrick Museum**, **The Cleveland Museum of Natural History**, and **The Western Reserve Historical Museum**.

Special musical events are regularly presented at the **Cleveland Institute of Music** and the **Cleveland Music School Settlement**. **Severance Hall** is located here. The Cleveland Orchestra performs here from September to May and from June to August at the open-air Blossom Music Center, located just south of the city in the beautiful Cuyahoga Valley.

The **Cleveland Play House** is also located in University Circle. Children will enjoy the **Cleveland Health Education Museum** and the **Cleveland Children's Museum**, where hand-on exhibits and learning-by-doing is the norm.

The Garden Center of Greater Cleveland is a pastoral retreat from the city that surrounds it. Just to the north of University Circle is the **City of Cleveland Greenhouse**. Located in Rockefeller Park are three and a half acres of outdoor gardens and indoor showhouses that feature special seasonal displays.

South of University Circle is **Shaker Heights**. In this area, visitors and residents will find shopping opportunities at **Shaker Square**. They may also explore the **Shaker Historical Museum** and the **Shaker Lakes Regional Nature Center**. This 300-acre park contains four miles of trails which lead along the ravine edges to the old Shaker dams.

History buffs will appreciate a stroll through the **Ohio City** area on Cleveland's west side. A once-separate municipality that was eventually annexed to the city, this Victorian neighborhood is in the process of being restored.

Located next to the Cleveland-Hopkins International Airport, **The NASA Visitor Center** contains exhibits on space exploration, satellites, aircraft and space propulsion. It is located on the grounds of the **NASA Lewis Research Center**.

The Cleveland **Lakefront State Park** provides a natural contrast to the metropolitan skyline. It is composed of four basic areas: Edgewater, on the west side; the East 55th Street Marina and Gordon Park, downtown; and Wildwood Park, on the city's east side. A 900-foot beach area, three boat launch ramps and several tree-lined picnic areas offer beautiful views of the lake. Fishing is popular year-round with perch, catfish, rock bass and panfish in abundance. In early spring and fall, coho salmon can be caught at Euclid Creek in Wildwood Park. Near the East 9th Street Pier is the U.S.S. Cod, a World War II fleet-type submarine available for tours.

Cleveland takes its spectator sports seriously. The Indians play baseball and the Browns play football at the **Cleveland Municipal Stadium** on the lakefront. The **Richfield Coliseum**, in nearby Richfield, is home to the basketball team, the Cavaliers. Three divisions of automobile drag racing-spectator stock, sportsman, and late model-are held at the **Cloverleaf Speedway** in nearby Valley View. The **Thistledown Racing Club** in Randall hosts thoroughbred racing, while **Northfield Park**, 15 miles south, features harness racing.

The **Cleveland Metroparks Zoo** is the fifth oldest zoo in the country. With more than 3,100 animals occupying 165 rolling, wooded acres, the Cleveland Metroparks Zoo is one of the largest in the Midwest. At the zoo, visitors can view mammals and birds from around the world in their natural habitats. The Aquatic Exhibit, the Birds of the World, and the Bear and Tiger Grotto are among the exhibits visitors discover along with a Children's Farm. Audiences can enjoy a picnic lunch in the shade of **Upland Commons** while watching a performance at the **Sohio Amphitheater**.

The **Cleveland Metroparks System** includes nearly 19,000 acres of natural beauty with scenic, geologic, and historic features. Founded in 1917, the Metroparks System is also known as the "Emerald Necklace" because its 12 reservations or parks and the zoo nearly encircle the city of Cleveland. Some of the parks are located in Cleveland, but most are located in the nearby suburbs. More than 100 miles of parkways provide easy access and driving pleasure to the parks. There are waterfowl sanctuaries, wildlife management areas, and sporting and recreational facilities for both summer and winter seasons.

events

The **St. Patrick's Day Parade** is held on March 17.

The **All Nation's Festival** is held in early June between Public Square and Playhouse Square.

The League of Ohio Sportsmen sponsors the **Walleye Tournament** on Lake Erie, one of the country's top amateur sportsmen's events. It is held in mid-June.

The Ohio Valley **Jazz Festival** is held in late July at the Cleveland Municipal Stadium.

The **Parade of Lights** is held on the Cuyahoga River in downtown Cleveland in late July. The parade of lighted boats and floats starts at dusk.

The **Old World Festival** is held in early August.

The Cleveland National **Air Show** is held on Labor Day weekend.

The Cuyahoga Valley **Festival** is held in mid-September in the Cuyahoga Valley National Recreation Area.

WEST CLEVELAND

accommodations

THE EDGEWATER INN
11837 Edgewater Drive
Lakewood, Ohio 44107
Tel: (216) 221-9000
Visa, MasterCard and American Express are accepted.

"Affordable, comfortable, and clean" best sums up the gracious Edgewater Inn of Lakewood's Gold Coast. The quiet inn was started in the early 1950s and has gone through many changes over the years. The current owners revitalized the entire hostelry in 1987, and the inn now stands as a compliment to the Gold Coast area.

The inn is located in a quiet, residential neighborhood. Spacious, air conditioned accommodations are offered at reasonable prices. The rooms are tastefully furnished and include a color cable TV. A restful, private courtyard invites one to pause for a moment of pleasant relaxation. Courtesy coffee is found at the snack bar. The inn is convenient to major interstate highways I-71, 77, 90, and 480 and is just seven minutes to downtown Cleveland and "The Flats." Public transportation is at the hotel's door and guests can walk to the shores of Lake Erie. The Cleveland Hopkins Airport is close by. The inn's friendly staff will assist you with a schedule of local transportation, including taxi and airport limo.

Special rates are offered to corporations, convention groups, senior citizens, and people who need to relocate. The Edgewater Inn is situated at the edge of bright, blue Lake Erie, and offers a refreshing, quiet, and reasonably priced place to enjoy the Gold Coast and surrounding environs.

bed and breakfast inns

HAMILTON B. MAXON HOUSE
6651 Columbia Road
Olmsted Falls, Ohio 44138
Tel: (216) 235-5204
(216) 235-5011
Reservations are suggested.

Hamilton B. Maxon House is an alternative to tourist homes. The laid back, casual pace of this "Best Choice" offers a home away from home. Proprietors Judith and Otto Ramlow open their home for the enjoyment of sharing the special old house with visitors and to introduce the Cleveland area to newcomers.

The house began its life as a part of a large, working farm. Today, the property consists of two acres, the house, and a barn. Two guest rooms and a full bathroom are offered to visitors. Compleimentary continental breakfasts of juice, fruits, homemade breads, coffee, and tea are served. Period antiques and artifacts from colonial American and Victorian times fill the old house. The eclectic mixture of furniture and art create a comfortable and inviting welcome.

The Ramlows love to share their enthusiasm for the Cleveland area and gladly assist in making reservations and give suggestions as to where to go and what to see in the area. The house is convenient to all the major highways and is close to the Baldwin Wallace College and 20 minutes from downtown Cleveland. When necessary, Judith or Otto personally pick up visitors at the airport to bring them "home." The Hamilton B. Maxon House offers country atmosphere in the city.

candy

MALLEY'S CHOCOLATES AND ICE CREAM CONCOCTIONS

14822 Madison Avenue
Lakewood, Ohio 44107
Tel: (216) 226-8300

Hrs:	Monday - Thursday	10:00 a.m. - 11:00 p.m.
	Friday - Saturday	10:00 a.m. - Midnight
	Sunday	Noon - 11:00 p.m.

Visa, MasterCard, American Express and personal checks are accepted.

Malley's Chocolates and Ice Cream Concoctions is the "Sweetest Spot in Town." Famous for its hot fudge sundaes, Bordeaux chocolates, nut mallow, and Billybobs, Malley's has been keeping Buckeyes supplied with the finest in chocolate confections for more than 50 years. Grandpa Malley started the business with the philosophy "make the best product you know how, sell it as reasonable as possible, treat your customers with the best service, friendliness, and honesty and never compromise!" The Malley family follows Grandad's formula for success and candy making "to a T."

Grandpa Malley chose the Bordeaux chocolates as his favorite, and it is easy to see why. An independent panel at the 1986 Retail Confectioners convention in St. Augustine, Florida, called Malley's Bordeaux "one of the best chocolate products in America." Chopped almonds are covered in English toffee and rolled in dark chocolate, then dusted with crushed almonds to make this award-winning candy. Malley's offers more than 600 choices of chocolates in every form imaginable from tennis rackets to bingo cards with "M & M" markers. One can choose from richly elegant assortments to fun and festive party packs. The Easter basket arrangements are famous, and the shop offers them year-round.

Malley's has 11 stores in Ohio, each store offering personalized service. The shops will gift wrap, package, and ship the complete order. Malley's catalog is filled with gift ideas and color photos of chocolate choices so tempting, they look good enough to pluck from the pages. Delivery is fast in chocolate-colored U.P.S. trucks.

markets

DANNY BOY FARM MARKET
24579 Lorain Road
North Olmsted, Ohio 44070
Tel: (216) 777-2338
Hrs: Monday - Saturday 9:00 a.m. - 9:00 p.m.
Sunday :00 a.m. - 7:00 p.m.
Winter:
Seven days 700 a.m. - 7:00 p.m.
Limited use of Visa and MasterCard is accepted.

Danny Boy Farm Market sells the freshest and finest fruits and vegetables from the unusual to the exotic, as well as gourmet specialties from around the corner or around the world. The market features an old fashioned bake shop, a complete deli, gourmet specialties, gift baskets, and special events.

Fruits, vegetables, and flowers come directly from the Danny Boy Farms and are as fresh as if picked from a backyard garden just this morning. The bake shop features home baked pies, donuts, apple fritters, breads, cookies, and fudge brownies. An extra treat is the delicious Amish breads and pastries. The deli offers hand dipped Amish chocolates, more than 125 varieties of cheese, smoked meats, deli sandwiches, gourmet salads, and old fashioned pickles in a barrel. Ohio honey, apple butter and pure maple syrup top the list of gourmet specialties. More than 30 varieties of coffee beans are available to blend and grind. Ohio wines are highlighted in the wine cellar.

A monthly calendar of Danny Boy's Specials features a product a day. In July, there is a German Alps Fest Day with German butter cheese, blueberry muffins on Thursday, and a California garlic festival on Friday. Seasonal events include the June Strawberry Festival, the August Peach Festival and the October Harvest Festival. Gift baskets made to order in keeping with the season will be cheerfully delivered. Gift certificates and party trays are also available. Quality is Danny Boy Farm Market's specialty.

museums

BEREA HISTORICAL SOCIETY MAHLER MUSEUM
118 East Bridge
Berea, Ohio 44017
Tel: (216) 243-2541 or (216) 243-5899
Hrs: May to Mid-December:
Sunday 2:00 p.m. - 4:00 p.m.
Wednesday 10:00 a.m. - 12:00 p.m.
The museum is open other times by appointment.

The Mahler Museum, sponsored by the Berea Historical Society, provides a glimpse of life in the mid-Victorian era from 1860 to 1880. Built in

1854 of native Berea sandstone, the museum building itself is listed on the National Registry of Historic Places.

Featuring exhibits from the quarry industry that created the community of Berea, such as maps and tools used in the quarry, the museum also contains items that the people of Berea used in everyday life. Pictures of early businesses grace the walls of rooms furnished with antique furniture, much of which was either manufactured in Berea or used by Berea families. You will also find toys, books, clothing, and shoes that are authentic to the period.

Started in 1976 when the Mahler family made a substantial challenge gift to the Berea Historical Society, the Mahler Museum owes much of its authenticity to Dorothy Marks McKelvey, the official historian of Berea and Baldwin Wallace College and founder of the Berea Historical Society. Supervised today by Museum Director Joan Goering, the Museum is operated by volunteers and welcomes tours from schools, other organizations, and individuals.

TROLLEYVILLE USA
7100 Columbia Road
Olmsted Township, Ohio 44138
Tel: (216) 235-4725
Hrs: Memorial Day - September:
Sundays and holidays 1:00 p.m. - 5:00 p.m.
June - August:
Wednesday & Friday 10:00 a.m. - 3:00 p.m.
Travelers Checks are accepted.

Ride into the past on a colorful old trolley from yesteryear. Hold tight to the brass bars and bounce with the click-clack of the iron wheels as they pass over the ribbons of track. Passengers pull the signal cord to tell the motorman their stop is coming up. Listen to the sing-song call of the conductor announcing the streets.

Trolleyville, USA is a nonprofit educational corporation supported mainly by revenue derived from public operations and private contributions. Begun in 1954 and named after its founder, The Gerald E. Brookins Museum of Electric Railways, Inc. is popularly known as Trolleyville, U.S.A. The museum is an important part of American heritage. More than 34 pieces of historic electric railway equipment are on display, and many can be ridden. A picturesque village green sports a complete railway depot and an old-fashioned bandstand. Each of the beautifully-restored museum trolley cars have a rich and varied history. One can ride in a bright red and cream colored, open-air trolley from Vera Cruz, Mexico, or can appreciate the exquisite wood inlay of a 1906 CA&E Niles car.

At one time, greater Cleveland was linked by miles of streetcar tracks and the Midwest was woven with inter-urban trackage. Today, these tracks have vanished, but you can still ride the marvelous trolleys which once rumbled through the city and country side. Trolleyville USA is located approximately 30 minutes west of downtown Cleveland. It is close to Interstate 71, 480, 90, and State Route 10 (Lorain Road). Visitors coming from the west on the Ohio Turnpike use the Interstate 480 exit.

night clubs

BY GEORGE!
21467 Lorain Road
Fairview Park, Ohio 44126
Tel: (216) 333-2151

Hrs:		
	Monday - Friday	4:00 p.m. - 2:00 a.m.
	Saturday	7:30 p.m. - 2:00 a.m.
	Football Season:	
	Sunday	1:00 p.m. - 2:00 a.m.
	Otherwise:	
	Sunday	6:00 p.m. - 2:00 a.m.

Visa and MasterCard are accepted.

A good time will be had by all who visit By George!, one of Northern Ohio's favorite tavern nightspots. Noted for its Sunday Oldies Night, the bar features deejay Rockin Ronno who plays favorite rock-n-roll tunes from the '60s and '70s. Not just a fun place to eat, drink and dance, the club also features chartered trips to special events and outings. Patronizing this bar, one can enjoy excursions to concerts and baseball and football games, as well as golfing and winter skiing outings.

National sports figures and media stars are frequent customers at this bar, where good food and fun times have become a legend. In nearby Cleveland, nearly every tavern offers 10 cent wing nights; By George! features nine cent wings, a fact that owner George Schindler takes great pride in. He also takes pride in his club's colorful interior, which is festooned with imaginative paintings by nationally acclaimed cartoonist and local celebrity, David Sullivan. Visit this tavern and dance to favorite tunes played five nights a week. Every Thursday night, the piano bar is open for the diner's listening pleasure. Be sure and try Cuyahoga River Water, the featured drink at this grand night spot.

By George! welcomes folks to a fun loving, rip-roaring time. Pull up a stool at the bar or settle at a table or booth for intimate conversation. Enjoy sandwiches, snacks and the popular nine cent wings in an atmosphere of gaiety while viewing favorite televised sporting events. Visitors are sure to have a good time and meet new friends at By George!, one of Northern Ohio's most popular nightspots.

parks

CLEVELAND METROPARKS SYSTEM AND ZOO
4101 Fulton Parkway
Cleveland, Ohio 44144
Tel: (216) 351-6300
Hrs: Open 365 days a year 6:00 a.m. - 11:00 p.m.

The Cleveland Metroparks System consists of nearly 19,000 acres of natural beauty with many scenic historic and geologic features. Also known as the "Emerald Necklace," the Metroparks's 12 reservations and the Metroparks Zoo nearly encircle the city of Cleveland. Although some park lands are located in Cleveland, most are in the nearby suburbs, an average of 15 miles from downtown Cleveland.

More than 100 miles of parkways provide driving pleasure and easy access to Metroparks facilities which include wildlife management areas and waterfowl sanctuaries; six golf courses; picnic areas and playfields. In addition, visitors can enjoy hiking, bridle, all-purpose and physical fitness trails, and swimming, boating and fishing areas. For those who love winter sports, toboggan chutes are available. Five nature centers offer nature exhibits and programs all year round.

A visit to the Cleveland Metroparks Zoo is an adventure to all corners of the world. The zoo is home to more than 3,100 mammals, birds, and fish. While journeying through the exciting world of the Metroparks Zoo, one can visit Monkey Island; Africa, Primate, Cat and Aquatics Buildings; Birds of Prey and Rhino/Cheetah exhibits; the Pachyderm Building; Children's Farm; Harbor Seal/Sea Lion Exhibit; Public Greenhouse, and many other exciting exhibits. The zoo is located five minutes from downtown Cleveland.

restaurants

PIER W RESTAURANT
12700 Lake Avenue
Lakewood, Ohio 44107
Tel: (216) 228-2250
Hrs: Dinner:

Monday - Thursday	5:30 p.m. - Midnight
Friday - Saturday	5:00 p.m. - Midnight
Sunday	4:30 p.m. - 10:00 p.m.
Brunch:	
Sunday	9:30 a.m. - 2:30 p.m.

Visa, MasterCard, American Express, Diners Club and Carte Blanche are accepted.

A fine array of fish and seafood at moderate prices are to be found at Pier W. Located on the shore of Lake Erie, the appearance of the restaurant is that of a ship grounded on the banks of Lake Erie. Its large, plate-glass windows give diners the illusion that they are aboard a cruise ship. The idea was conceived by Vernon Stouffer, founder of the Stouffer group of restaurants.

Both lunch and dinner menus are primarily seafood, although one can always find a burger, turkey club on a croissant, or Cajun chicken sandwich at lunch. More typically, one will enjoy clam chowder or an appetizer combo with shrimp and vegetable tempura, stuffed mushrooms, and crunchy cheese fingers, then shrimp and linguini Oriental or broiled scallops with butter and sherry. At dinner, begin with escargots or Oysters Morando, with spinach, bacon, and live lobster or lobster pot with clams, mussels, red potatoes, and corn on the cob; or Alaskan king crab legs, grilled salmon, orange roughy; stuffed lobster and much more. Steaks, veal, and chicken are provided also. One must save room for dessert; perhaps Pier W's Lemon

Mousse with fresh strawberries or their Peg-Leg Chocolate and Coffee Ice Cream Pie, topped with bourbon meringue and chocolate sauce will appease any sweet-tooth.

Stuffed with antique nautical memorabilia, Pier W is an attractive and notably romantic place for lunch, dinner, or brunch. At Pier W if an engagement is in the offing, the chef will gleefully assist in helping plan the presentation of the ring.

specialty shops

HINMAN'S AT BEACHCLIFF
19300 Detroit Road
Rocky River, Ohio 44116
Tel: (216) 333-0202
Hrs: Gourmet Shop:

Monday & Saturday	10:00 a.m. - 5:30 p.m.
Tuesday - Friday	10:00 a.m. - 9:00 p.m.
Cafe:	
Monday and Saturday	8:45 a.m. - 5:30 p.m.
Tuesday - Friday	8:45 a.m. - 9:00 p.m.

Visa, MasterCard and American Express are accepted at the Gourmet Shop.

Hinman's gourmet shop and cafe is a wine and food experience like no other. Owner Reed Hinman, a former wine critic for a local newspaper, has put together a collection of fine wines and gourmet foods that stands head and shoulders above all others. Hinman's carries almost 1,000 different types of wines. The cafe's menu consists of a long list of exquisite food treats. Conveniently located in Beachcliff Mall and specifically designed for small, intimate specialty shops, Hinman's is a delightful experience of fine foods and wines.

Hinman's at Beachcliff carries rare, one-of-a-kind, and everyday wines in stock. The price of a bottle of wine ranges anywhere from $3.95 to $400. Any wine lover is sure to be pleased with Hinman's selection. Hinman's gourmet shop is the home of fine food items such as smoked salmon, extra virgin olive oil, pesto sauce, and Ben and Jerry's ice cream. Hinman's offers their own line of frozen hors d' oeuvres, herbal vinegars and teas, 32 varieties of gourmet coffee, Belgian chocolate truffles and Gatsby chocolates. The cafe serves specialty sandwiches , chili, and soup specials such as seafood bisque and clam chowder. Homemade muffins, French rolls, and pastries nicely complement the espresso and capuccino served daily. All of the home-made foods are prepared by culinary students who specialize in this type of preparation. Guests can offer Hinman's special cuisine at their own parties and events through a special catering service.

Hinman's at Beachcliff is perfect for all lovers of rare wines and fine foods. Its wide selection of homemade and specialty cuisine makes it a fine food lover's heaven. Located near Lake Erie and Sea World, Hinman's is prepared to serve both out of town visitors and hometown patrons. Hinman's is the perfect place to please the palate with the best of food and wine.

wine

DOVER VINEYARDS, INC.
24945 Detroit Road
Westlake, Ohio 44145
Tel: (216) 871-0700
Hrs: Monday - Friday 9:00 a.m. - 5:30 p.m.
Saturday 9:00 a.m. - 4:00 p.m.
Visa and MasterCard are accepted.

Dover Vineyards, Inc. started as a co-op of 13 local grape growers in 1932; it is one of the oldest active wineries in Ohio. The vineyards also enjoys its claim as the only working winery in Cuyahoga County.

The winery's enologist carefully oversees the creation of a full range of wines, from sweet to dry. Most of the Dover wines are derived from Labrusca and French-American hybrid grapes, while others gain more exotic fruit flavors. Wine lovers enjoy a taste of these wines with cheese while touring the wine cellars and the crushing, aging, and bottling areas of the winery. A minimal fee is charged per person, and tours are limited to 60 persons per tour. After touring the winery, visitors may browse through Dover Vineyards' gift shop, where bottles of wine and supplies for making beer and wine at home are sold.

For those whose appetites have been whet by a taste of wine, Lamberts restaurant offers fine food from a full menu. A casual dining setting encourages relaxation over a meal of Continental favorites; Mesquite Specialties, including Boston strip steak, filet mignon and T-bone steaks; entrees from the sea; and the Linguine Corner. A bottle of Dover Vineyards wine certainly complements all of these fine entrees.

DOWNTOWN CLEVELAND

CLEVELAND, ROCK AND THE ROCK AND ROLL HALL OF FAME AND MUSEUM

by Iris Samson

"Roll over, Beethoven, and tell Tchaikovsky the news"-that in 1992, the Rock and Roll Hall of Fame and Museum is slated to open in Cleveland, Ohio.

For four decades, rock and roll music has entertained millions of people. From its earliest roots in jazz and blues, through the rock-a-billy era, the protest music of the 1960s and disco in the 1970s, to the punk rock of today, rock and roll music has served as a reflection of popular culture that appeals to a vast audience.

Rock and roll music has arrived. In its nearly 40-year history, the medium has evolved from an underground movement into an overt force for social and cultural change. What began as an amalgam of rhythm and blues, rock-a-billy, gospel and country, is today a distinctive living art, practiced every day in small clubs, theaters, major studios--even in garages and basements. Rock has entrenched itself as a major feature of American culture and has found its way to many countries around the world.

Appealing to people of diverse ages, ethnic backgrounds, religions and economic and social strata, rock and roll has attracted many fans; rock and roll accounts for nearly 50 percent of total music industry sales. It is now viewed by most music critics as an important and distinctive musical art form. For all of these and many other reasons, the officials of the Rock and Roll Music Hall of Fame felt it was time to give rock its due and honor it with the construction of a museum that would serve as a permanent memorial to the artists who have made rock music their lives and , in turn, influenced ours. For the first time, the history of rock and roll will be collected, preserved and exhibited in one place. Just as various sports leagues, the film industry and the country music industry recognize their heroes, so too the rock and roll industry will create an institution where its fans can celebrate its colorful legacy.

The Rock and Roll Hall of Fame and Museum has been planned not only for entertainment value, but also as an educational institution where research and archival materials pertinent to the medium can be collected. Similar in purpose to the American Film Institute, the Rock and Roll Hall of Fame and Museum will serve as a major international cultural museum. Apart from its function as a repository of memorabilia from those involved in the business, the museum will also be a working advocate for the rock and roll industry. Paying homage to the people who made popular music what it is today, the Rock and Roll Hall of Fame and Museum will give both rock music devotees and casual observers a place to see where it all began and, perhaps, a glimpse of where popular music might be headed.

Roy Orbison, the Beatles, Chuck Berry, Bob Dylan, Smokey Robinson, Stevie Wonder and Elvis, the King, are just a few of the inductees. What better way is there to recognize their work and its impact on music-lovers the world over than with a permanent collection? Along with the music of Little Richard, Jerry Lee Lewis, the Everly Brothers, Bo Diddley, Bill Haley and others, the work of these artists has changed the lives of millions.

Through the course of its development, rock music became the popular method of expression, not only of human emotions like love and heartache, but of larger issues such as the Vietnam War and Civil Rights. By depicting social causes, rock ballads helped give a generation a social conscience. Artists such as Bob Dylan and Woody Guthrie moved the young to ask questions of their elders and to press for change. Singers such as Ray Charles, Sam Cooke, Jackie Wilson and Otis Redding brought soul and rhythm and blues to the masses; and country and western artists, including Carl Perkins and Hank Williams, influenced succeeding generations of rock musicians and songwriters.

Officials of the Rock and Roll Hall of Fame and Museum felt that a building devoted to the medium should "create a unique experience for visitors that is instructive in the history and social context of rock and roll, while at the same time dynamic, entertaining and educational." They determined that the museum complex would include pavilions which place rock and roll in its historic context through interactive, state-of-the-art audio and visual materials.

The building will include a 400-seat orientation theater; a multimedia collage honoring those who create, perform, produce and promote rock and roll; six small venues for live or historic performances; a contemporary recording studio; temporary exhibit galleries; a library and archives; food and retail space; and the Hall of Fame itself, where inductees to the Hall of Fame will be enshrined.

The Hall of Fame will contain permanent memorials to the inductees, who will be elected each year by an expert panel appointed by the governing Rock and Roll Hall of Fame Foundation. Thus far, the foundation has selected nearly 60 artists, including performers, production people, songwriters and record company managers. By 1992, when the museum is slated to open, another 20-plus artists will have joined their ranks.

Who makes up this prestigious group? Musical pioneers that are gone are listed among its members: Buddy Holly, Sam Cooke, Marvin Gaye, Ricky Nelson, and Roy Orbison. Songwriters, such as Jerry Leiber and Mike Stoller, are honored, as are musicians, including B.B. King and Les Paul. Listed on this impressive roster are the Beatles, the beach Boys, the Rolling Stones and other groups whose names are synonymous with rock and roll. Soul artists, including Aretha Franklin, James Brown, the Supremes and the Ink Spots, are lauded along with record producers and record company owners such as Berry Gordy Jr., who made Motown a household word, and Phil Spector, who was with rock during its nascent period and continues to be part of it today.

The primary goal of the Rock and Roll Museum and Hall of Fame is to provide a world-class resource center for rock and roll and related areas of contemporary commercial music for the professional, the serious student, educational institutions and the community. The museum's board of trustees envisions an attendance of more than half a million visitors to the museum annually. Permanent exhibits will detail the careers of rock and roll legends and recapture themes and moments in rock history. Costumes, musical instruments, photographs and manuscripts will be displayed. A multipurpose theater will be an integral part of the facility and will house special performances by, or dedicated to, Hall of Fame inductees. In addition, the theater will also be used as a lecture hall for those studying the medium in greater detail. The facility's archives and library will ultimately serve as a rock and roll reference and research center which its designers hope will be unsurpassed in the world.

Why, of all cities in the United States, was Cleveland chosen as the site of the museum? To paraphrase a line from rock singer Huey Lewis, not yet a Hall of Famer: "The heart of rock and roll is in Cleveland." Legend has it that it was in Cleveland in the mid-1950s that the term "rock and roll" was first coined by disc jockey Alan Freed. Already chosen as a Hall of Famer, Freed is recognized by many music historians as the "father of rock and roll." Aside from this, the first rock radio shows were carried over Northeastern Ohio airwaves, and live rock shows were filling the arenas in downtown Cleveland as early as March of 1952, when the Moondog Coronation Ball was held at the old Cleveland Arena. In 1955, Cleveland became the first city outside the South to host Elvis Presley. In more recent times, it has been the launching pad for many world tours of major stars, including Bruce Springsteen.

Like rock music itself, Cleveland is a little bit gritty, a little bit rough, but it is a city with plenty of heart. Cleveland is also a city on the move. For three of five years, the city received the prestigious All American City Award from the National Municipal League's Citizen's Forum on Self-Government. The city was recognized for its efforts in revitalization and its development strategy, which successfully stemmed economic and population decline. Cleveland was the only city in the country to win the award so many years running. The Rock and Roll Hall of Fame and Museum will enhance the list of key area attractions, which includes amusement parks, museums, live music and theater and such major league sports as pro football, baseball, basketball and soccer.

Just as rock and roll music shook up a nation with its fresh, new beat, the building that will house the Rock and Roll Hall of Fame and Museum promises to do the same in architectural circles. Its designer, distinguished architect I. M. Pei, is renowned for such unusual and visually exciting projects as the East Wing of the National Gallery of Art in Washington, D.C.; the John Fitzgerald Kennedy Library Complex in Boston; and the renovation of the Grand Louvre in Paris. Pei has designed a building which will stand as a fitting monument to rock and roll.

Containing 75,000 square feet of exhibition and circulation space, the building that will house the Rock and Roll Hall of Fame is under construction near Cleveland's Tower City Center at a projected cost of $48 million. As dynamic as the music it commemorates, the massive structure will be a visual tour de force. Simple geometric forms such as squares, rectangles, triangles and circles lend unity to the multifaceted glass structure. Aesthetic and utilitarian, contemporary and timeless, the building will rise like a pyramid from an open place to peak in an 18-story tower whose base descends to the Cuyahoga River near Collision Bend. Both inside and outside this mammoth glass tent will be theaters, each in a different shape. Visible through the folded glass wall of the tent, a sculptural array of escalators, staircases and bridges will lead to the tower's seven levels of exhibitions. A restaurant set below street level rises to meet the ground-level lobby, where media spaces and a 360-degree theater are also found. Housed in the tower will be the exhibition halls for artifacts and memorabilia, culminating in the Hall of Fame itself, an impressive skylit chamber that is the apex of the design.

ROCK AND ROLL

HALL OF FAME

Cleveland, Ohio

"It's my interpretation of what rock and roll is," architect Pei said recently about the museum. "What is rock 'n' roll? Tremendous energy, openness, youth. The design strives to express that in glass, metal and explosive forms."

The facility's interior is being developed by the well-known "Interpretive Designers" of Barry Howard Limited. Howard, who began his career in the 1950s as a CBS television set designer, is known for such major exhibitions as the 1964 World Fair's Coca Cola Pavilion, the "Man and the Polar Regions" exhibit at the 1967 Exposition in Montreal, the Indian Arts Museum at Grand Teton National Park, and for his design of the American Freedom Train. Most recently, Howard applied his skills as writer and executive producer of the United Technologies multi-video at Epcot.

Howard's design for the Rock and Roll Hall of Fame and Museum will provide an orientation theater in which the roots of rock and roll will be movingly depicted and the history of the medium will be presented. The museum will feature three pavilions of displays which will place rock and roll in its historic context through state-of-the-art audio and visual materials. The first of these, the People Pavilion, will provide visitors with a comprehensive look at those who participate in rock and roll, the singers, musicians, producers, disc jockeys, mixers, agents and promoters. The Performance Pavilion will demonstrate the varied aspects of performance and the relationship that exists between the artist and the audience. The Technology Pavilion will focus on the evolution and expansion of electronic machines, devices and technology, which coincided with the evolution of rock and roll.

The city of Cleveland is hard at work preparing for the Rock and Roll Hall of Fame and Museum. Thus far, $8.6 million has been committed toward changes that would help visitor access, improve the ambiance of the area and assure optimum traffic flow. The opportunity to create 200 to 300 new jobs and inject approximately 85 million additional tourist dollars into the Greater Cleveland economy was also an incentive, leading over 700,000 Cleveland residents to lobby for the Rock and Roll Hall of Fame and Museum.

The state got into the act as well, with the Ohio Board of Regents approving in principle a plan for joint use between the Hall of Fame and the Cuyahoga Community College, which will develop the museum's educational component in conjunction with the museum board. Museum officials anticipate that the institution will act as a catalyst to alter the dynamics of Cleveland's economy and dramatically enhance its image in the eyes of the rest of the nation.

Working behind the scenes of the entire project is a strong board of trustees leading fundraising efforts and developing a working plan for the museum. Many of its members are culled from the business world, as evidenced by the board's decision that the project be handled with strategic business planning skills, "in addition to reflecting the artistic and imaginative opportunities that are so relevant to rock and roll." The museum will be governed by a board of 14 that will comprise both Clevelanders and people associated with the New York-based Rock and Roll Hall of Fame Foundation.

From its inception, rock and roll has undergone a tremendous evolution, and it is this process that will be documented in the exhibits and archives of the Rock and Roll Hall of Fame and Museum. Great artists like blues singer Bessie Smith, gospel's Soul Stirrers and the Ink Spots influenced a rising generation of musicians and songwriters, who took America into the "doo-wop" era. By the time Bill Haley exhorted fans to "Rock Around the Clock" and Little Richard and Chuck Berry first got them on their feet with

"Long Tall Sally" and "Lucille," Americans found they just couldn't hear enough.

This style of music that began with simplistic melodies and lyrics linked to a hard-driving beat changed along with society and the times. America survived the British invasion of the early 1960s and countered with one of its own, spearheaded by groups like the Beach Boys and the Four Seasons. Rhythm and blues made the crossover into the popular arena through singers such as Smokey Robinson and vocal groups, including the Temptations and the Supremes. Many felt that rock and roll had hit its stride by the 1960s, but the 1970s brought a new brand of music that was smoother, more orchestrated, less insistent and driving. By the end of the decade, veteran groups who had weathered the lull helped rock and roll rediscover its roots.

Finally the 1980s ushered in a more introspective music, with questioning lyrics and performers committed to more than just their music. Live Aid, Amnesty International and Farm Aid highlighted rock musicians and promoters devoting their talents to help those starving in Ethiopia, those facing political turmoil around the world and those in economic distress here in America. Along the way, reggae came in with a Caribbean beat, and punk rock led the music scene back to the basics of a hard back beat, an insistent bass and simple lyrics.

Rock and roll music has evolved into an art form that is expressive, controversial, exciting and powerful. Its acceptance has spread to such an extent that today even Muzak has borrowed rock melodies. Through it all, rock and roll retains something unique, intangible, something everyone can identify with, something that always remains fun. At Cleveland's Rock and Roll Hall of Fame and Museum, visitors will be able to relive the excitement of rock's beginnings and find out why Chuck Berry was right when he sang, "Rock and roll is here to stay!"

accommodations

STOUFFER TOWER CITY PLAZA HOTEL
24 Public Square
Cleveland, Ohio 44113
Tel: (216) 696-5600
Visa, MasterCard, American Express and Diners Club are accepted.

"In the heart of it all" aptly describes the Stouffer Tower City Plaza Hotel. This landmark hotel provides grand hotel charm together with every modern convenience. It is quite simply one of the finest luxury hotels in downtown Cleveland.

Five hundred guest rooms, including 35 luxury suites, offer a full complement of amenities, such as cable TV with in-room movies and direct-dial phones. Many rooms overlook Public Square; others have a view of Lake Erie or the inner atrium. The hotel's attentive service includes complimentary coffee and a newspaper with your wake-up call, 24-hour room service and expert concierge service. In addition, the Stouffer Tower City Plaza Hotel features a Club Floor, with a host of executive amenities and services designed to provide the ultimate in luxury. Club Floor services include terry bath robes, hair dryers, remote color TV, and an exclusive lounge, complete with complimentary Continental breakfast in the morning and hors d'oeuvres in the evening. One of the city's finest French restaurants, the French Connection, is located in the hotel. It features excellent wines and Classical French cuisine in a lush and comfortable setting. Or, for lighter fare in a more relaxed atmosphere, try the Brasserie. Cocktails may be enjoyed at Mowery's, a lively tavern, or poolside in the ten story, glass-roofed atrium.

Stouffer Tower City Plaza Hotel is the only AAA Four-Diamond hotel in downtown Cleveland. It provides a luxurious point of departure from which to visit the city's many attractions; Cleveland Stadium, the Convention Center, Playhouse Square, and all of Cleveland's exciting nightlife are nearby. Hopkins International Airport is easily accessible, and the hotel is convenient to Interstate 71, Interstate 77, and Interstate 90. Amtrak is just minutes away.

air tours

BARON AVIATION INC.
1601 North Marginal Road
Cleveland, Ohio 44114
Tel: (216) 574-2525
Hrs: Monday - Friday 8:00 a.m. - 6:00 p.m.
Saturday 8:00 a.m. - 2:00 p.m.
Tours are offered Monday from 8:00 a.m. to 8:30 p.m.

Looking for an exciting way to celebrate an anniversary or unique lunch with a special person? Baron Aviation Inc. takes a passenger and one or two friends into the sky over Cleveland and provide the champagne or lunch.

Operating from its hanger at Burke Lakefront Airport, Baron Aviation offers 20-minute lunchtime rides and 30-minute or one-hour rides any day of the week. A boxed meal is provided for lunch in the air, and a complimentary photograph is included. The Sunset Champagne Flights, which do not have to be taken at sunset, are an exciting, memorable way to celebrate an anniversary, engagement or birthday. Baron Aviation also includes a photograph as a lasting memento. Business people and relocating homeowners will find a flight over Cleveland the best way to get an overall view of the area. Trips longer than one hour can be made by special arrangement. A helicopter is also available for a different experience. All one needs is a camera to capture a breathtaking view of Cleveland and Lake Erie.

Baron Aviation Inc. will help make a special occasion truly unique, provide an extraordinary lunchtime experience, or give a bird's eye view of Cleveland to assist in a relocation.

antiques

METROPOLITAN ANTIQUE GALLERY, INC.
1370 West 9th Street at St. Clair Avenue
Cleveland, Ohio 4413-1217
Tel: (216) 861-3736
Hrs: Monday - Saturday 11:00 a.m. - 5:00 p.m.
Or by appointment

This unique showroom is located in Cleveland's historic warehouse district, a newly renovated section of the city overlooking the Flats and the riverfront.

Guests of this gallery will always find an impressive selection of antique English, French and Oriental furniture, prints, samplers, cushions, and porcelains of the highest quality. Art lovers and collectors will appreciate the fine inlaid woods, lacquers, and gilded bronze.

These one-of-a-kind articles are elegantly displayed in a formal setting designed to enhance the luxury and style of this first-rate antique furniture and artwork.

Many of Metropolitan Antiques Gallery's items are of museum quality and similar to pieces found in the Cleveland Museum and the Louvre in France. This gallery affords visitors the opportunity to actually own an original antique for their home or office. The furniture is scaled to today's homes, traditional or contemporary, and satisfies a wide variety of artistic preferences.

Fine arts art history education, combined with 20 years of experience in the trade, enable Chuck Mosberger and Anita Nonneman, owners of this chic gallery, to knowledgeably hand select furnishings of diverse historical backgrounds and impeccable condition. Each piece is researched for authenticity and verified with a written description giving date, country of origin, and period.

As in major museums, Metropolitan Antiques Gallery recognizes first-quality antique furniture as fine art and offers the best available antique American, European, and Oriental furniture to Northeast Ohio.

Metropolitan Antiques Gallery is truly Cleveland's home of antique furniture and distinctive decorative arts.

art galleries

POWERHOUSE GALLERIE
2000 Sycamore Street
Cleveland, Ohio 44113
Tel: (216) 621-8666

Hrs:		
	Sunday & Monday	11:30 - 6:00 p.m.
	Tuesday - Thursday	11:30 a.m. - 9:00 p.m.
	Friday & Saturday	11:30 a.m. - 11:00 p.m.

Visa, MasterCard, American Express and personal checks are accepted.

The Powerhouse Gallerie, opened in November of 1989, is part of the $22 million restoration of the Powerhouse building originally built in 1888 to supply electricity to the streetcars of Cleveland. Built by industrialist Marcus Hanna, it closed in 1925 and awaited its re-birth in 1989. Restaurants and one-of-a-kind specialty shops abound in this beautiful wood beam and brick historic structure, part of the huge Nautica complex on the west bank of the Cuyahoga River in the Flats, Cleveland's premier entertainment district.

The gallery presents a wide range of almost all art media and superior hand-crafted wood, jewelry and pottery in a most unusual atmosphere. Artists like Norman Rockwell, Erte, Nagel, Mukai, Phillips, Mcknight, Parkes, Alvarez and Wyeth are but a few with a score of the best of the local and regional artists also represented. Cleveland is shown off from every angle both from the gallery windows and in its art, maintaining the largest inventory of Cleveland art posters and photography available, 2,500 square feet of pure delight for anyone interested in art, an absolute "Best Choice" while in Cleveland.

balloons

BAA-LOONS, 401 Euclid Avenue, Suite 250, Cleveland, Ohio; Tel: (216) 566-9045. Whatever the occasion, Baa-Loons has the balloons and gifts to fit the event.

delicatessans

TENTH ST. MARKET, 1400 West 10th Street, Cleveland, Ohio; Tel: (216) 523-1094. Specializing in catering and food related gifts for the holidays, Tenth St. Market also provides airline food service, delivers executive desktop dining trays, and prepares ready-to-eat buffets.

entertainment

HILARITIES COMEDY HALL
1230 West 6th Street
Cleveland, Ohio 44113
Tel: (216) 781-7733 Cleveland
Hrs: Amateur Showcase:
Tuesday 8:30 p.m.
Shows:
Wednesday and Thursday 8:30 p.m.
Friday and Saturday 8:00 p.m. & 10:30 p.m.

HILARITIES COMEDY CLUB
1546 State Road
Cuyahoga Falls, Ohio 44223
Tel: (216) 923-4700

Under the direction of owner Nick Kostis, Hilarities proudly presents the modern day equivalent of vaudeville with two comedy clubs: one, Cleveland's Carnegie Hall of comedy and the other, Northeast Ohio's Premier Comedy showplace at Cuyahoga Falls.

Hilarities offers six shows a week, including amateur night on Tuesdays. Cleveland's club is located in the historic Warehouse District, just above the flats, in the 85 year-old Root and McBride Building. A light snack menu is featured. The club seats 500 people without sacrificing intimacy and the sense of camaraderie so essential in an audience. The strategically placed television monitors contribute significantly to the theatergoer's ability to enjoy the comedy routines. The Cuyahoga Falls club features a 300-seat dinner show. Well-known comedians who have appeared at Hilarities include Tim Allen, Richard Jeni, Tom Parks, Bobby Slayton, Dennis Wolfberg and Diane Ford. These comedians were nominated by Rave Magazine and George Schlatter Productions for the Third Annual American Comedy Awards "Comedy Club Audience Awards."

Whether the guests choose to observe the outrageous antics of amateur night or to see the more polished performances of professional comedians, Hilarities offers them an opportunity for a rollicking night's entertainment.

POWER PLAY GAME ROOM
2000 Sycamore
Cleveland, Ohio 44113
Tel: (216) 696-7664
Hrs: Daily 10:00 a.m. - 2:30 a.m.
Children welcome until 8:00 p.m.
Over 21 8:00 p.m. - Close
Visa, MasterCard, American Express and Discover are accepted.

Nearly $20 million was spent to rebuild Cleveland's National Historic Landmark, the Powerhouse. Built in 1892 to provide power for Cleveland's electric railway and streetcar system, the Powerhouse is now a four-level brick structure beautifully designed with smokestacks and arched windows that is home to a restaurant, a comedy club, specialty retail shops, offices, and Power Play Game Room.

Power Play, the most exciting game room of its type in the area, is located on the concourse level in the building in what used to be the furnace room. From this spot competitive entertainment is provided for ages from three to 103. There is an emphasis here on providing a clean family-type atmosphere so everyone feels comfortable about participating in all of the activities available. Hi-tech games include pinball machines, skeet ball, a full-scale indoor golf simulator, football and basketball toss, pool and air hockey, video games, and a driving simulator. Game players can challenge their skills with shuffleboard or a game of pool.

Hungry competitors will find something good to eat at the diner here. With a deli-type menu, there is bound to be something to please everyone. The cocktail bar overlooking the Cuyahoga River provides drinks to thirsty adults. Since its opening in November 1989 as Cleveland's first mixed-use waterfront development, The Powerhouse has attracted folks from all over. Power Play, geared to draw the upscale professional, is part of the attraction. It is no wonder that this Game Room is frequented by soap opera stars, professional wrestlers, and members of the Cleveland Browns. Power Play is available for rent and is an excellent place to hold such events as reunions, anniversaries, and birthdays. The Power Play Game Room is a "Best Choice" in the Cleveland area as the newest form of entertainment for adults who enjoy playing like children. The whole family is welcome to Power Play, "where the competition never ends...and the funtimes begin."

frame shops

THE WOOD TRADER
2144 Murray Hill Road
Cleveland, Ohio 44106
Tel: (216) 721-2928
Hrs: Summer:
Monday - Friday 8:00 a.m. - 6:00 p.m.
Winter:
Monday - Friday 9:00 a.m. - 6:00 p.m.
Saturday 9:00 a.m. - 3:00 p.m.
Visa and MasterCard are accepted.

The Wood Trader offers the best in quality frames, posters, prints, matts, and personalized service. The relaxed, comfortable atmosphere and over 25 years of quality framing help The Wood Trader's patrons to appreciate the hundreds of frames, posters, and prints carried by this storefront shop. It is located in the heart of the nostalgic Little Italy district.

Those interested in quality wooden frames will be pleased to discover that the showroom contains two full walls of frames that will satisfy the taste of any consumer. In addition to its abundant collection of frames, The Wood Trader provides more in the way of posters, matts, colorful prints, and special services. The shop offers framed discounted posters, framed or unframed prints, as well as a complete line of matts including decorative, marbleized, and French. This frame store also offers a complete selection of both antique and reproduced Botanicals. Complete frame restoration along with contemporary and antique guilding are also services performed by The Wood Trader.

Not only does The Wood Trader possess a wide selection of frames and prints, but this storefront shop achieves the finest in personalized service and a warm, "family" atmosphere. This unique treatment starts at the top with the owner Sara Kraber Thorp, a third generation framer herself. The Wood Trader's staff is comprised of eight people who are proud of their work and anxious to make visitors feel welcome. The staff is a knowledgeable group who are happy to answer any questions and help find the frame or print that best suits the customer's needs. In staying consistent with its personalized style, The Wood Trader offers in-home picture hanging, and it is one of the few businesses of its kind to make "house calls."

The Wood Trader is the ideal spot for the serious consumer who is interested in an extremely wide variety of frames, prints, posters, matts, and specialized treatment. Upon entering the showroom, guests receive a warm welcome and the invaluable service of an experienced framer. The quality reputation of three generations of framers and the experience of the current staff is apparent and makes the task of choosing the best frame an enjoyable one.

malls

THE GALLERIA AT ERIEVIEW
East 9th and St. Clair
Cleveland, Ohio 44114
Tel: (216) 621-9999
Hrs: Monday - Saturday 10:00 a.m. - 8:00 p.m.
Sunday 11:00 a.m. - 6:00 p.m.
Open holidays except Thanksgiving and Christmas.
Visa, MasterCard and American Express are accepted at most stores.

The Galleria at Erieview is a collection of world class shops and dining establishments. Located in the heart of downtown Cleveland, this recently constructed, award-winning center has brought a new style of shopping to the city.

Nearly 56 upscale stores and restaurants are showcased in the visually exciting shopping environment. The Galleria is finished in such rich materials as brass, marble, granite, and glass. The main entrance is a majestic arch of red granite, framed in maroon metal that ascends 80 feet. Inside, the glass-enclosed pedestrian mall includes two stories of chic specialty shops. These businesses range from local to international in focus and feature men's and women's fashions, accessories, fine dining with quick service, books, art, gifts, and more.

This thriving retail center also features the Galleria Information Store, which provides store and city information, Tickerton, Galleria souvenirs and Galleria gift certificates. Valet parking is available at East 9th and East 12th street entrances.

restaurants

BANK STREET CAFE
1212 West Sixth Street
Cleveland, Ohio 44113
Tel: (216) 575-1009
Hrs: Restaurant:
Monday - Friday 11:30 a.m. - 10:00 p.m.
Saturday 5:30 a.m. - 10:00 a.m.
Lounge is open later.
Visa, MasterCard, American Express and Diners Club are accepted.

Located in Cleveland's newly-renovated warehouse district, the Bank Street Cafe is a contemporary cabaret that features mellow rhythm and blues on the weekends and melt-in-your-mouth cuisine all of the time. The cafe's mountainous Between-the-Bread specialties are heaped with assorted cheeses, hams, vegetables, poultry, spices, and dressings. The East to West cheese sandwich is a melt of cheddar, swiss, monterey jack, and colby cheeses. The Monte Cristo Sandwich is a batter dipped, baked blend of ham, cheese and pineapple; and the West Sixth Chix is a spicy combination of Cajun-marinated chicken with bacon, lettuce, and tomato.

The pasta special, called the Metropolitan Occasion, changes daily and the salads range from fresh greens and garden vegetables topped with honey-tarragon sauce to Popeye's Best--tender leaves of spinach topped with egg, bacon, and hot bacon dressing.

Bank Street Cafe's main entrees (very reasonably priced) include Lemon-Baked Orange Roughy, Creamy Shrimp-n-Tortellini, tender Bank Flank Grill (mushroom-grilled steak), and St. Louis Glazed Ribs Ribs Ribs.

Sweet endings are the original Big-Apple Style New York Cheesecake topped with sour cream, the fresh-baked fruit pies (cherry, apple, and blueberry) and the light and fluffy mousse.

To find the Bank Street Cafe, take I-90 to St. Clair to West Sixth; or follow I-90 to the Shoreway-Lakeside Exit; and take the first right onto West Sixth at its intersection with Lakeside.

The Bank Street Cafe offers a more than satisfying blend of reasonably priced gourmet food and relaxing R & B music.

THE BURGESS GRAND CAFE
1406 West 6th Street
Cleveland, Ohio 44113

Tel:	(216) 574-2232	
Hrs:	Breakfast:	
	Monday - Friday	7:30 a.m. - 10:00 a.m.
	Brunch:	
	Sunday	11:00 a.m. - 3:00 p.m.
	Lunch:	
	Monday - Friday	11:30 a.m. - 2:30 a.m.
	Dinner:	
	Monday - Thursday	5:30 p.m. - 10:00 p.m.
	Friday - Saturday	5:30 p.m. - Midnight
	Sunday	5:00 p.m. - 8:00 p.m.
	June - August:	
	Sunday	No meals are served after brunch.

Visa, MasterCard and American Express are accepted.

With the look of a successful restaurant where affluent businessmen congregate, the Burgess Grand Cafe has generated a great deal of excitement in Cleveland's Warehouse District, adjacent to The Flats. In business since early 1986, The Burgess has been described as "absolutely eloquent" by a local restaurant reviewer.

Decorated in Viennese Victorian, rich paintings and Art-Deco style, etched glass panels adorn the walls. Rich woods are offset by rose colored marble tabletops and crisp white linen. Knowledgeable personnel attired in immaculate black and white offer professional, thoughtful service, and only the freshest ingredients are used in preparing the menu. Enticing items from the menu include a duck appetizer in a buckwheat crepe with raspberry vinegar cassis sauce; a first course of black pasta and calamari or cappelini with smoked salmon in a light cream sauce with black and red caviar. Owner Paul Martoccia says the grilled veal tenderloin with morels in a brandied morel cream sauce is the most popular dinner item. Luncheon offerings are a parade of Italian specialties. Many wines from the extensive wine list are available by the glass.

It is over breakfast, though, that the "movers and the shakers" of Cleveland get together to discuss business and to enjoy the delectable twists on familiar breakfast themes offered by The Grand Cafe. A few of the specialties are oatmeal pecan pancakes, orange brandied French toast, and scrambled eggs with lox, pan fried potatoes, peppers, and red onion. It's hard to go wrong at any meal here.

FAGAN'S FLAGSHIP OF THE FLATS
996 Old River Road
Cleveland, Ohio 44110
Tel: (216) 241-6116
Hrs: Brunch:
Sunday 11:30 a.m. - 3:00 p.m.
Happy Hour Buffet:
Monday - Friday 4:00 p.m. - 6:00 p.m.
Lunch:
Monday - Friday 11:30 a.m. - 3:30 p.m.
Dinner:
Monday - Friday 5:00 p.m. - 11:00 p.m.
Saturday - Sunday 5:00 p.m. - Midnight
Lounge is open until 2:30 a.m.
Patio is closed in winter.
Visa, MasterCard, American Express, Discover, Diners Club, and Carte Blanche are accepted.

The action happens at Fagan's Flagship of the Flats. Steeped in tradition, this popular Cleveland watering hole opened in 1905 when it poured its first bucket of suds for Cuyahoga longshoreman and boaters.

The nightclub sports a 100-foot long bar on an outdoor patio. One can cool off after a fast jitterbug on the club's outdoor dance floor with a swim in the club's pool. During the winter, live entertainment is featured seven days a week. The patio provides a view of the river and the old working jackknife. Fagan's food is as refreshing as its atmosphere. Appetizers of Lobster and Shrimp Alfredo lead the way to entrees of Monte Cristo and homemade strada. Deliciously decadent desserts include raspberry puffs, chocolate truffles, and apricot tarts.

Fagan's Flagship of the Flats is located one half-mile north of Public Square on Old River Road at the corner of Old River Road and Front Street in "The Flats." Docking is available if you choose to come by boat. Take-out deliveries can be made to one's yacht.

GETTY'S AT THE HANNA
Playhouse Square
Cleveland, Ohio 44115
Tel: (216) 771-1818
Hrs: Lunch:
Monday - Friday 11:00 a.m. - 2:30 p.m.
Dinner:
Monday - Thursday 5:00 p.m. - 10:00 p.m.
Friday - Saturday 5:00 p.m. - Midnight
Visa, MasterCard and American Express are accepted.

Located in the heart of Cleveland's theater district, Getty's at the Hanna reflects the glamor of the theater with a touch of Cleveland's past.

Getty's at the Hanna opened in December 1987 in the historic Hanna building, a landmark on Playhouse Square. Offering superb classic, nouvelle, and American cuisines, the restaurant has quickly become a favorite of business people, theater patrons, and performers alike. The menu features fresh seafood, steaks, and a variety of pasta dishes. Chicken Crevette and Veal St. Jacques are favorites. Getty's evokes a festive 1920s mood. Its decor is rich in pastels, with mauves, teals, and muted colors. Attractive cherry woodwork enhances the solid, traditional feeling of the dining room. During most meals, a pianist provides gentle background music.

Like Sardi's on New York's Broadway, Getty's at the Hanna has become a regular night spot for theater goers. With consistently high-quality food and service, it is a perfect way to end a night at the theater.

HANK'S CAFE, 11729 Detroit, Cleveland, Ohio 44113; Tel: (216) 529-1166. Hank's Cafe is the place to stop for an unforgettable meal--just ask for Henry.

HAYMARKET
123 Prospect Avenue West
Cleveland, Ohio 44115
Tel: (216) 241-4220
Hrs: Lunch:
Monday - Friday 11:30 a.m. - 2:30 p.m.
Dinner:
Monday - Thursday 5:30 p.m. - 9:00 p.m.
Friday - Saturday 5:30 p.m. - 10:00 p.m.
Vault Lounge:
Monday - Thursday 11:30 a.m. - 11:00 p.m.
Friday 11:30 p.m. - Midnight
Saturday 5:30 p.m.- 11:00 p.m.
Visa, MasterCard, American Express and Diners Club are accepted.

Cleveland's premier chophouse, Haymarket, offers traditional cuisine in the comfortable elegance of 1930s architecture and atmosphere. Located in Landmark Office Towers, the restaurant is named for its location on the site of Cleveland's historic haymarket district, the area where turn-of-the-century farmers sold their produce and newly arrived immigrants gathered.

Haymarket restaurant is an architectural gem, featuring solid brass and copper appointments in the Art-Deco style. A relative newcomer to the

Cleveland restaurant scene, Haymarket has become a favorite spot among discerning diners seeking international cuisine. The restaurant's specialties are chops, steaks, fresh seafood, and Creole cuisine. All cooking and baking is done from scratch, and the chef will accommodate most requests to modify ingredients to suit a patron's dietary requirements. Haymarket's generous portions, prepared using the freshest, hand-selected ingredients, are sure to please. Lobster Bisque, Duck Jambalaya, and Bifteck au Poivre Verte are favorite choices from the soup, appetizer and entree lists. The restaurant's Vault Lounge is housed in the 1930 Midland Bank vault complete with the original 22-ton doors.

In addition to regular dining accommodations, Haymarket provides space for private parties of 15 to 30 people and can serve semi-private parties of as many as 55. Catering is also available for banquets for parties numbering from 100 to 400 people; banquets are served in the neighboring Van Sweringen Arcade. Enjoy dining with elegance, tradition and grace at Haymarket, Cleveland's premier chophouse.

THE LINCOLN INN
75 Public Square Building West 2nd Street
Cleveland, Ohio 44113
Tel: (216) 621-1085
Hrs: Restaurant:
Monday - Friday 11:00 a.m. - 9:00 p.m.
Happy Hour:
Monday - Friday 4:30 p.m. - 7:30 p.m.
Visa, MasterCard and American Express are accepted.

The Lincoln Inn more than lives up to the reputation of its London namesake--a "world famous gathering place." Originally an exclusive club for legal professionals, The Lincoln Inn today offers a diverse clientele the opportunity to experience hospitality and dining at their finest. The inn, dating to 1960, is also of historical significance to Cleveland, with architecture reminiscent of an English pub. Throughout its five rooms, Spanish chandeliers, cherry paneling, natural woods, and brass accents create an ambiance of warmth and intimacy. Of special interest to visitors and locals alike are the three Renoir paintings that grace the walls.

The inn blends Continental cuisine with a good measure of zesty Italian flavor. House specialties include Chicken Johnson, a charbroiled chicken breast with shrimp and Muenster cheese served in a dijon cream sauce and sprinkled with scallions; and Meatball Supreme--homemade meatballs, sauteed bell peppers, mozzarella and mushrooms baked as a casserole. Other signature specials include Julie's Pasta and the Lincoln Burger.

A favorite spot for lunch and dinner, the inn is located within walking distance of the Justice Center. Tucked away on a street named West 2nd Street at the top of Public Square (a tiny street more commonly known as "Tom Johnson's Alley), the inn is worth the time it takes to find it. Come and visit one of Cleveland's best kept secrets--The Lincoln Inn.

PRIMO-VINO
12511 Mayfield Road
Cleveland, Ohio 44106
Tel: (216) 229-3334

Hrs:	Monday-Thursday	5:00 p.m. - 10:00 p.m.
	Friday	5:00 p.m. - 11:00 p.m.
	Saturday	5:30 p.m. - 11:00 p.m.

Visa, MasterCard, American Express and Diners Club are accepted.

Over 100 sauces and pastas as well as over 100 Italian wines are all at the connoisseur's disposal at Cleveland's Primo-Vino. Excellent homemade cuisine combined with an authentic atmosphere create the perfect Italian dining experience.

Primo-Vino, located in Little Italy, actually has a lot of Cleveland inherent in it's structure. Brick, wood, and marble, all intricate parts of the restaurant's current structure, were taken from various buildings in the city and used to rebuild the facility. Co-owners Bob Fatica and Carmen Armenti opened Primo-Vino for fine dining in 1982 and has maintained a maximum level of excellence ever since.

Fatica grew up in Little Italy cooking Italian food and, along with Armenti, continues to do so for Primo-Vino patrons. Everything is homemade, including mozzarella cheese, pasta, and items at the fresh salad bar.

The owners' favorite preparations include penne ziti rigati with a sauce of sauteed celery, broccoli, cauliflower, green peppers, white onions, cream, butter, and Romano cheese. Or try a sauce of squid, leeks, parsley, garlic, and whole tomatoes. Though not on the menu, Fatica tosses a special dandelion salad on request, exemplifying commitment to customer satisfaction. For takeout, try sole almondine, stuffed flounder or baked scrod all with pasta side dishes. One of many salami, meatball, sausage or veal cutlet sandwiches provide a slightly less hardy, but equally enjoyable meal.

Appetizers, soups, salads, sandwiches, dinner combinations, cocktails, and desserts all capture authentic Italy. Cap it all with a favorite selection from the extensive wine list and enjoy a complete Italian dining experience in Cleveland's Little Italy.

SAMMY'S
1400 West 10th Street in the Flats
Cleveland, Ohio 44113
Tel: (216) 523-5560

Hrs:	Lunch:	
	Monday - Saturday	11:30 a.m. - 2:30 p.m.
	Dinner:	
	Monday - Thursday	5:30 p.m. - 10:00 p.m.
	Friday - Saturday	5:30 p.m. - Midnight

Visa, MasterCard, American Express, Discover and Diners Club are accepted.

Handsome, contemporary Sammy's is an exceptional experience for anyone seriously interested in the pleasures of fine dining. The restaurant, opened in 1981, has already been registered in the Fine Dining Hall of Fame of the Nation's Restaurant News and has been named Number One Restaurant by Cleveland Magazine. All this began with the decision of Ralph DiOrio and

Denise Fugo to return to their native Cleveland to participate in the first phases of the city's renaissance.

From upholstered oak frame armchairs, guests look through tall windows over the busy Cuyahoga River and watch its draw bridges and small pleasure craft moving up and down the river alongside 600-foot ore boat. A sampling of dishes from the inventive menu might include, at lunch, shrimp chowder with Black Forest bacon followed by homemade black and white fettucine with grilled scallops, broccoli, and red pepper in fresh pesto sauce. At dinner, one might begin with roasted red pepper and poblano pepper soup with grilled shrimp or escargots and scallops tossed with St. Andre cheese in a phyllo cup with garlic cream sauce. Sauteed medallions of veal with shitake mushrooms and port wine sauce, served with vegetable puree and broccoli florets is another favorite. Sammy's creative signature dessert, boule de niege, shares space on the menu with homemade ice creams, sorbets, and rich European pastries.

Specialty vegetables and herbs are produced for Sammy's by local growers, as is the restaurant's lamb. Not to be neglected is the wonderful raw seafood bar that serves such delicacies as smoked peppered mackerel, smoked Alaskan salmon, fresh shrimps, clams, oysters and mussels, king crab legs, and smoked trout.

The bar's grand marble slab countertop, rescued from the old Hippodrome Theater, is one of several irreplaceable pieces incorporated in the tasteful modern interior.

SHOOTERS WATERFRONT CAFE U.S.A.
1148 Main Avenue
Cleveland, Ohio 44113
Tel: (216) 861-6900

Hrs:	Monday - Saturday	11:30 a.m. - 2:30 a.m.
	Sunday	11:00 a.m. - 2:30 a.m.

Visa, MasterCard, American Express, Diners Club and Carte Blanche are accepted.

Shooters Waterfront Cafe U.S.A. enjoyed phenomenal success during its opening in June 1987. It was then the busiest restaurant in the country and today, it still maintains the status of Ohio's busiest eatery. The name says it all--Shooters is literally a cafe on the Cuyahoga River. With free docking available, diners come by land and sea. Boaters are able to park their crafts as conveniently as any motorist can park a car. This unique location makes Shooters a favorite summertime dining spot for those cruising the river as well as those cruising the shore.

The site of Shooters, once a run-down warehouse, has been completely turned around. The fast-paced environment of this restaurant now surges with the life and energy of a staff that enjoys giving quality service to customers even at their busiest moments. The positive attitude of the employees matches the delicious flavor of the foods available here.

A complete range of Mexican, Italian and Oriental dishes are available. The long list of "Irresistible Beginnings" includes Broccoli Linguine, Barbecued Ribs, and Teriyaki Chicken Julienne (strips of marinated chicken breast with teriyaki sauce and pineapple slices). Light eaters are thrilled over salad selections like Blackened Scallop Salad, Oriental Chicken Salad, and Shooters Seafood Salad. It is not easy to make a dinner selection when one is deciding between Chicken Marsala, Filet Mignon, Stuffed Flounder, Fettuccini

Seafood Alfredo, and the Shooters' Stir-Fry available with vegetables, chicken, or shrimp. Sandwiches, burgers, and hoagies are also on the menu. Every Tuesday night a full Mexican menu is available and the Sunday Brunch is a special treat for the taste buds.

Whether one is enjoying a drink at the Tiki bar on the dock or appreciating a great meal and view from the glass-enclosed portion of the restaurant, Shooters Waterfront Cafe U.S.A., "Where the Fun Never Sets," is a "Best Choice" for diners. Valet service and catering for large groups is available.

SWINGO'S AT THE STATLER, 1127 Euclid, Cleveland, Ohio 44115; Tel: (216) 696-5501. Visitors to Swingo's at the Statler can expect to find wonderful selection of pasta, veal, steak, and seafood. Meals may be complemented with desserts prepared tableside.

TOP OF THE TOWN
The Galleria and Tower at Erie View
Lakeside and East 12th
Cleveland, Ohio 44114
Tel: (216) 771-1600
Hrs: Lunch:
Monday - Friday 11:30 a.m. - 3:00 p.m.
Brunch:
Sunday 10:30 a.m. - 2:30 p.m.
Dinner:
Monday - Thursday 5:30 p.m. - 10:00 p.m.
Friday 5:30 p.m. - 11:00 p.m.
Saturday 5:30 p.m. - Midnight
The lounge is open one hour past closing time.
Visa, MasterCard, American Express and Diners Club are accepted.

Situated atop the 38-story Erieview Plaza Building, with a splendid view of Lake Erie on one side and the stadium and downtown Cleveland on the other, the Top of the Town is an inviting place to linger over a delightful meal, unwind, and look out on a fresh perspective of the city.

The quiet, contemporary ambiance evolves from unobtrusive dinner music, professional serving personnel, and a pleasing decor of light colored oak with burgundies, beiges, and blues in the lounge and mauves and creams in the dining room. Lunch and dinner menus are impressive, with a variety of appetizers such as escargot, shrimp tempura, New Zealand mussels, French onion soup, followed by sumptuous entrees, among them Steak Diane, Chateaubriand Bernaise, medallions of filet mignon flamed with cognac, prime rib, and sauteed veal in a Cabernet sauce. At lunch, diners enjoy favorites prepared in a grand style such as half pound ground sirloin, shaved breast of turkey on a croissant, shrimp and lobster salad remoulade with melted Monterey jack cheese on a croissant, or a light entree, perhaps pan-fried walleye pike with Cajun mustard sauce or a stir fry with chicken, snow peas, and a collection of colorful vegetables. Espresso and cappuccino are available, along with a wide-ranging collection of domestic and imported wines, and a special dessert of ice cream rolled in toasted pecans, served with chocolate sauce.

Parking is offered in the building's underground lot at a reduced rate for customers. This fine Stouffer restaurant is open for dinner on special holidays and happy hours are on weekdays from 3:30 p.m. - 7:30 p.m. Reservations are suggested.

WATERMARK RESTAURANT
1250 Old River Road
Cleveland, Ohio 44113
Tel: (216) 241-1600
Hrs: Lunch:
Monday - Friday 11:30 a.m. - 2:30 p.m.
Brunch:
Saturday - Sunday 11:30 a.m. - 2:30 p.m.
Dinner:
Sunday - Thursday 5:30 p.m. - 10:00 p.m.
Friday - Saturday 5:30 p.m. - Midnight
Late Night Menu:
Friday - Saturday 10:00 p.m. - 1:00 a.m.
Visa, MasterCard, American Express, Diners Club, Discover and personal checks are accepted.

The Watermark, a sophisticated restaurant specializing in seafood, opened in 1985 on the Cuyahoga River in the Cleveland Flats. Formerly an 1870s warehouse, the restaurant building has high ceilings, brick walls, a stunning bar, and great views of the river traffic. The historic Flats area is now the place where the fashionable congregate.

Large portions of marinated, mesquite-grilled seafoods are the order of the day. For non-fish lovers, a small but delectable selection is offered from the everchanging menu, which is printed daily. Selections include steak au poivre, sauteed with a brandied peppercorn sauce; mesquite grilled filet mignon; marinated and grilled herb chicken; and veal with hazelnut sauce. The seafood bar features fresh clams, oysters and shrimp, along with dishes such as mussels poached in white wine, butter and garlic; cioppino, which is made of fresh vegetables and seafood simmered in a tomato broth; sherried chicken, and nachos. In the dining room, the list of appetizers includes Clams Romano, mussels poached in Chablis with mustard and basil, and Cajun style calamari and shrimp. Entrees include amberjack marinated in a creamy lobster peppercorn mixture and mesquite grilled mako shark, flavored with an Oriental marinade; kajiki, Hawaiian blue marlin marinated in a creamy Burgundy thyme mixture, Scampi DeJohnge and live Maine lobster prepared steamed, grilled, or stuffed.

During late summer evenings on the large outdoor patio a limited menu is offered, which includes burgers, club sandwiches, and pasta salad, and just a few entrees; home baked desserts and the Watermark's ice cream sundaes and fancy liquor drinks. Evening jazz is on the menu. A range of moderately priced domestic and imported wines and bottled beers is available that includes a popular selection of premium wines by the glass, as well as aperitifs, port, and dessert wines. Happy hour is Monday through Friday from 4:30 p.m. - 7:00 p.m. The fireside room, a private dining area, serves groups from 25 to 60. Full service lunches and dinners are served on the river patio from May 1 to September 30. Reservations are suggested. Valet parking is available.

specialty shops

FINE POINTS, INC.
2026 Murray Hill Road
Cleveland, Ohio 44106
Tel: (216) 229-6644
Hrs: Tuesday - Saturday 12:30 p.m. - 4:00 p.m.
Visa, MasterCard and American Express are accepted.

In 1986 Fine Points, Inc opened in the historic old schoolhouse which was converted into the Murray Hill Gallery in the heart of Little Italy.

This specialty shop offers a wide variety of most unusual yarns from Wales, Japan, England, France, and Italy. Fine Points, Inc. carries linen, silk, mohair, and many other novelty yarns that can't be found anywhere else.

Liz Tekus, owner of Fine Points, Inc., custom designs and knits sweaters, scarves, hats, and shawls and she is proud of the superb quality and the innovative designs of each of her handmade sweaters. Some of them contain over 35 yarns of varied colors and textures. Each sweater is one-of-a-kind and is created by Liz personally.

Patrons of Fine Points, Inc. can also purchase exquisite, handmade jewelry including pins, earrings, and haircombs to accessorize each of Liz's beautiful creations. Liza also carries a large array of needles and an extensive collection of instruction books and magazines for those who enjoy the fine art of knitting. Liz only carries the finest quality designer yarns, handmade sweaters, and jewelry. When she finds something she likes, she adds it to her collection, which gives Fine Points, Inc. it's unique quality. So when visiting historic Little Italy, remember to stop in to the Murray Hill Gallery and shop at Fine Points, Inc., one of the "Best Choices" in specialty shops along the Great Lakes coast.

taverns and pubs

THE FLAT IRON CAFE
1114 Center Street
Cleveland, Ohio 44110
Tel: (216) 696-6968
Hrs: Monday - Friday 6:30 a.m. - 1:30 a.m.
Saturday - Sunday 10:00 a.m. - 1:30 a.m.

The Flat Iron Cafe opened in 1910 in Cleveland Flats, a traditionally Irish neighborhood. The tavern is the oldest Irish bar in The Flats, according to owner Sally Boone Kennedy. Look for the red brick building with the flat roof and smiling customers. A bit of the Irish and fresh Lake Erie Perch are what make The Flat Iron Cafe famous. Situated on the banks of the Cuyahoga River, The Flat Iron Cafe is a favorite of river boat sailors.

The cafe serves an all-you-can-eat breakfast buffet Monday through Friday. Corned beef and cabbage is Wednesday's specialty. The portions are queen-size and served with neighborhood friendliness. Daily specials include macaroni and cheese and barbecue ribs. Deli sandwiches are served in your choice of 25 combinations.

The Flat Iron Cafe hosts an annual Lobster Bake. People from miles around come for the festivities.

HARBOR INN
1219 Main Avenue
Cleveland, Ohio 44113
Tel: (216) 241-3232
Hrs: Lunch:
Monday - Saturday 11:00 a.m. - 3:00 p.m.
Dinner:
Monday - Saturday 10:00 a.m. - 2:30 a.m.

Harbor Inn has been a functioning bar/tavern for approximately 85 years. It is located on the West bank of the Cleveland Flats and is easily accessible from all major highways. Originally catering to sailors from the Great Lakes port in Cleveland, on the Cuyahoga River, the clientele today is representative of the broad spectrum of people in Cleveland and includes tourists.

Daily lunch specialties, all homemade, include seafood, Slovenian dishes, sandwiches, and the best chili in town. You can select from 170 different beers or 730 different brands of spirits to add to your dining pleasure. To work off some of the calories, perhaps you should wander upstairs for dancing or a game of darts. Wally Pisorn, the owner, immigrated from Yugoslavia in 1964, equipped with a degree in hotel management.

Opting for a kindred occupation, Mr. Pisorn has owned and operated the Harbor Inn for 20 years. The inn has earned local and national awards, including being voted into the top ten taverns in the U.S.A. by Market Watch magazine and as the best bar in the nation by Cleveland Magazine. Justifiably proud of these awards, Wally wants to continue to merit the patronage of residents and tourists alike.

tours

TROLLEY TOURS OF CLEVELAND
West Ninth and St. Clair Streets (Public Station)
Cleveland, Ohio 44113
Tel: (216) 771-4484
Hrs: Please call for seasonal dates, times and reservations.
Visa, MasterCard, American Express and personal checks are accepted.

Climb aboard "Lolly the Trolley" and get an intimate and entertaining view of historic Cleveland as the city blossoms and shows its true colors through the interesting and informative narration provided by a driver/guide. A two hour jaunt with Trolley Tour of Cleveland will probably change any pre-conceived notions one has held before visiting this surprising city.

Up to 5,000 visitors per month may take the 20 mile city excursion stretching from University Circle to Ohio City. The trackless, motorized vehicles hold 38 passengers and cruise a winding route which covers over 100 points of interest. With their carved oak interiors and wrought iron seat ends, they are reminiscent of the original trolleys of yesteryear. Journey through Downtown Cleveland, where historic buildings and parks are juxtaposed with stunning modern architecture. The Warehouse District is Cleveland's version of New York's popular Soho area, and visitors relish the time spent in Ohio City replete with engaging Victorian homes and the nearby West Side Market, one of the largest indoor/outdoor food and produce markets in the world. Sightseers marvel at the nation's largest theater restoration project and find themselves thoroughly engrossed by the cluster of renowned institutions at University Circle. Trolley Tours also offers private charters and Specialty Tours, where one may see a working apple farm in Brunswick or go on a unique shopping spree of ethnic markets. Another tour stops at the delightful shops and galleries of Little Italy, a charming 100-year-old Italian Hill Town, along with the legacies of Lake View cemetery, literally an outdoor museum.

If one wishes to obtain a close up look at the richness, diversity, and historical values of this enterprising city and prefers not to walk or drive to get "from here to there," Trolley Tours of Cleveland offers an easy and entertaining solution.

EAST CLEVELAND

accommodations

EMBASSY SUITES HOTEL
3775 Park East Drive
Beachwood, Ohio 44122
Tel: (216) 765-8066
1-800-EMBASSY (Reservations)
Hrs: Restaurant 11:00 a.m. - Midnight

Opened in October 1989 as the first all-suite hotel in the Cleveland area, the Embassy Suites Hotel is proud to offer "The Suite Life" to guests at the same price most hotels charge for a single. This means that guests have a spacious living room along with a private bedroom-an ideal set up for parents traveling with small children. The plush living area contains a sofabed, armchair, dining/work space, wet bar, refrigerator, and cooking facilities that are equipped with dishes, utensils, a coffeemaker, and coffee. All units have two phones and two TV's.

Although the suites offer all of the comforts of home, there is plenty more to experience at the Embassy; it's the only atrium hotel in Cleveland. Its magnificent 100 yard-long courtyard with 2700 plants of 57 varieties and ponds containing ducks and fish provides the perfect setting for relaxing with a book or chatting with a friend. All 216 suites open onto this sunny area. Also located in the hotel is a pool, whirlpool, sauna, sun deck, exercise room, pool table, gift shop and deli. The Boca Restaurant and Lounge offers fine dining for lunch or dinner. Special facilities are available for meetings or banquets with space for up to 400 people.

Extra special amenities offered at the Embassy include complementary cooked-to-order breakfasts daily until 10:30 a.m., complementary cocktails every evening from 5:30 p.m. to 7:30 p.m. and a limo service that takes guests to Beachwood Mall and other shops within a three mile radius of the hotel. With all that Embassy Suites Hotel has to offer, it pays to check into the "suite-er" deals they offer to their guests.

HONORS HOTEL
3695 Orange Place
Beachwood, Ohio 44122
Tel: (216) 765-1900
(800) 222-9655 Ohio
(800) 345-6667 Nationwide
Visa, MasterCard, American Express, Choice, Discover and Carte Blanche are accepted.

Honors Hotel is ideal for the discriminating traveler. The staff is professionally trained in a service-intensive tradition and works to maintain the hotel's casually elegant atmosphere. The hotel offers contemporary, upscale accommodations at a surprisingly moderate price.

All of the 113 rooms and four suites have "more room, more comfort, and more conveniences." They are 20 to 30% larger than standard hotel rooms and include such amenities as a sofa and lounge chair, wireless TV remotes, large work space, and touchtone phones with data ports. In addition, the Executive King room includes a wet bar, and the Deluxe King suite features a fully furnished living room and large, elegant bedroom. Complimentary copies of USA Today and The Wall Street Journal are provided for guests. For guests who wish to relax or keep in shape, Honors Hotel provides a fitness center, plus a whirlpool, sauna, and an outdoor pool. The hotel is fully equipped to handle meetings of groups of up to 80 people, and can provide catering services and the latest audio-visual equipment.

The quiet, handsomely appointed Honors restaurant is located just off the hotel's lobby area, and serves excellent American fare for breakfast, lunch, or dinner. A sunken living room-style lounge provides a cozy place to meet with friends for cocktails and after dinner drinks.

art galleries

FIORI GALLERY
2072 Murray Hill Road
Cleveland, Ohio 44106
Tel: (216) 721-5319
Hrs: Thursday - Saturday Noon - 5:00 p.m.
Sunday 1:00 p.m. - 5:00 p.m.

Just outside Cleveland's city limits, is one of the city's finest galleries. Fiori Gallery is located in the heart of Little Italy, one of the city's older ethnic communities, and one which hosts a variety of quaint shops.

Susan Fiori, a native of Cleveland, established the gallery a number of years ago, and she now resides in California. Just two years ago, the gallery was turned over to two local artists. David Batz and Robert Jursinski now co-direct the gallery as well as show their own handcrafts there. David specializes in ceramics, and Robert in paper sculpture. Their works are creative, abstract designs, delightful with color and contrast. Many pieces are the co-designs of David and Robert. When asked about their work, David describes them as exciting and unusual with a range from the humorous to the contemporary.

Many local artists such as glass blowers and painters show their crafts at the gallery. In addition to the offerings of these artists, one also finds black and white drawings, hand-painted linens and garments, and a wide array of unique ornamental jewelry. An exciting feature of the gallery is that artworks can be commissioned directly from the local artists, who are involved in numerous events throughout the area. The public is welcome to visit Fiori Gallery and discover what a culturally captivating city Cleveland is.

SCHEELE GALLERIES
3095 Mayfield Road
Cleveland Heights, Ohio 44118
Tel: (216) 321-0600
Hrs: Tuesday - Friday 10:00 a.m. - 6:00 p.m.
Saturday - Sunday 1:00 p.m. - 5:00 p.m.
Other hours are by appointment.
Visa and MasterCard are accepted.

"Cleveland's newest art gallery is a knockout!" lauds a Cleveland Plain Dealer art critic. Scheele Galleries presents a comprehensive collection of original works by master American artists. Special attention is given to regional Ohio artists, including prominent figures of the Cleveland School. Exhibitions highlighting individual artists, movements, and thematic subjects are offered throughout the year. The gallery maintains an extensive inventory of oil paintings, watercolors, drawings, prints, photographs, and sculpture.

Located in the Heights-Rockefeller building, the Old English, Tudor-style facility was built in 1930 as an exclusive shopping complex and is now a registered, historic landmark. White walls, carpeting, and the sparingly arranged classical furniture of the spacious gallery serve as the perfect atmosphere for the exhibited masterpieces. Scheele Galleries manages the estates of primary figures of the Cleveland School such as Frank Wilcox, Paul Travis, and William Grauer, who are represented in public and private collections internationally. Other luminaries represented include Clarence Carter, Charles Burchfield, John Sloan, and Joseph O'Sickey. The galleries maintain a special affiliation with ACA, Kennedy, and Kraushaar Galleries of New York City.

Scheele Galleries offers a full range of services, including appraisals and video inventories, consultations, estate managements, corporate leasing, group lectures, gallery tours, and software packages for collectors. The gallery is also interested in purchasing fine works of art.

points of interest

UNIVERSITY CIRCLE
10831 Magnolia Drive
Cleveland, Ohio 44106
Tel: (216) 791-3900

The cultural center of Cleveland and northeastern Ohio, University Circle features an assemblage of renowned museums, performing arts organizations, music and art schools, hospitals and clinics, health and social service agencies, and religious institutions as well as internationally known colleges and universities.

Located on a popular trade route, the small community settled by blacksmith Nathaniel Doan in 1799 quickly grew with the expanding westward migration. The town's first school of higher learning, the Western Reserve Academy, was built in the early 1880s. Throughout the late 1800s into the early 1900s, University Circle became a mecca for learning and culture. Despite the threat of an uncertain future following World War II, University Circle grew into a thriving community that today attracts approximately two million visitors annually.

University Circle's single square mile offers an unusually diverse array of museums and cultural institutions. The city's museums include the Cleveland Children's Museum; designed for children from ages three to 12, it offers a multi-sensory learning environment based on the theory that children learn by doing. The Cleveland Health Education Museum is a local, national, and international resource center on health. The Cleveland Museum of Art is one of the world's major art museums; its collection now includes more than 48,000 works of art representing a wide range of cultures and periods. The Cleveland Museum of Natural History is the state's largest museum dedicated to natural history, conservation and environmental education. The Western Reserve Historical Society is said to be the largest privately supported historical collection in the nation; this complex also includes the Crawford Auto-Aviation Museum. Other museums in the area include the Afro-American Museum, the Cultural and Historical Society Museum, the Dittrick Museum of Medical History and the Temple Museum of Religious Art.

University Circle is also home to a number of prominent performing arts organizations. The Cleveland Orchestra is one of the most respected orchestras in the world. The Cleveland Playhouse, said to be the nation's oldest resident theater, operates three theaters from October through June at its new complex. The Karamu House is famous for its dedication to interracial theater and the arts; in addition to theatrical productions, Karamu offers art exhibits and classes. Other concerts and musical events are presented at The Cleveland Museum of Art, The Cleveland Institute of Music and the Cleveland Music School Settlement.

Other popular University Circle attractions include: The Garden Center of Greater Cleveland, with its plant exhibits, flower shows, classes, and programs featuring nationally known speakers (the center also contains one of the largest gardening libraries in the world); the Cleveland Center for Contemporary Art, which presents art exhibits by national and regional artists, a lecture series, education programs and family workshops; the Cleveland Institute of Art; three important medical institutions (Cleveland

Clinic Foundation, Mt. Sinai Medical Center and the University Hospitals of Cleveland); and Case Western Reserve University.

restaurants

CAFE BRIO
5433 Mayfield Road
Lyndhurst, Ohio 44124
Tel: (216) 473-1670
Hrs: Open seven days for lunch, light menus and dinner. Please call for specific hours.
Visa, MasterCard and American Express are accepted.

The Cafe Brio is "a Cleveland imitation of a New York interpretation of a California presentation." Whatever the description, the atmosphere of Cafe Brio is as bright and fresh as its cuisine. One can sit in the Cafe's courtyard and listen to live jazz four nights a week while enjoying a meal from the restaurant's well-known "Light Menu" or delve into the serious business of dispatching a free range hen, mesquite-smoked in house and finished on the char-broiler and then served with fresh pineapple salsa.

The menus at Cafe Brio are extensive. The Light Menu features a do-it-yourself raw bar; irresistible appetizers such as Brio Wings tossed with hot pepper sauce and served with blue cheese and hot pepper dressings; sandwiches, and "create your own" pizzas. Luncheon specialties feature grilled fresh fish of the day and the above-mentioned smoked game hen and chicken livers sauteed in sage butter and served over egg noodles. Dinner meals can include Pasta Putainse or egg fettuccine served with scampi and tossed with a peppered shrimp and brandy cream. Among the evening appetizers is tempting veal sausage grilled and served with a sauteed potato cake, fresh herbs, and pommery mustard. An extensive wine and beer list accompanies all the menus. Washington State wine is offered along with California and European vintages.

The Cafe Brio owners, Craig Sumers and Brad Friedlander, also operate the Lopez y Gonzalez, another well-known restaurant in Cleveland. Designed by William Camin of Studio 23, Cafe Brio has a delightfully airy, uplifting atmosphere with a flair for the dramatic. The Cafe Brio takes pride in its consistently high-quality fresh foods and refreshing atmosphere.

FLO AND EDDIES BARBECUE SPECIALISTS
34205 Chagrin Boulevard
Moreland Hills, Ohio 44022
Tel: (216) 831-2294

Hrs:		
	Monday - Thursday	11:30 a.m. - 10:00 p.m.
	Friday - Saturday	11:30 a.m. - Midnight
	Sunday	5:00 p.m. - 9:00 p.m.
	Summer:	
	Monday - Thursday	11:30 a.m. - 11:00 p.m.
	Friday - Saturday	11:30 a.m. - 1:00 a.m.

Visa, MasterCard, American Express, Diners Club and Discover are accepted.

Every day, Flo and Eddies Barbecue Specialists cook up a rack of sizzling barbecue specials. Flo and Eddie offer bibs to tuck under one's chin before digging into a giant plate of barbecued baby back ribs and barbecued chicken.

The house specialty is the Cajun Popcorn Shrimp appetizer. These succulent shrimp are served with hot honey mustard and barbecue sauce. Eddie's Cuban Black Bean Soup, created from an original recipe, brings customers from miles around. It is thick and hearty and garnished with grated, parmesan cheese and chopped onion. Cajun specials include blackened redfish and strip sirloin. For a real treat, try a combination called "Shribs." Shribs are barbecued smoked shrimp and baby back ribs. All entrees include your choice of house salad or "Floslaw," freshly baked corn bread and choice of Longbranch potatoes or baked potato with butter, sour cream, chives, and crumbled bacon.

Flo and Eddie's menu is available for take-out and catering. Take home a jar of Flo and Eddie's award-winning barbecue sauce. Flo and Eddies Barbecue Specialists also have locations in Sharonville, Westlake, and Columbus.

GAMEKEEPER'S TAVERNE
87 West Street
Chagrin Falls, Ohio 44022
Tel: (216) 247-7744

Hrs:		
	Lunch:	
	Monday - Friday	11:30 a.m. - 2:30 p.m.
	Saturday	11:30 a.m. - 4:00 p.m.
	Dinner:	
	Monday - Thursday	5:30 p.m. - 11:00 p.m.
	Friday - Saturday	5:30 p.m. - 11:00 p.m.
	Sunday	4:00 p.m. - 9:00 p.m.

Cocktails are served until 2:30 a.m., seven days.
Visa, MasterCard, Diners Club and American Express are accepted.

Since 1976, Tom Lutz, owner of Gameskeeper's Taverne, has provided this part of Ohio with a "casually sophisticated" restaurant and bar. Pictures of gamekeepers of earlier times and stuffed bodies and heads of wild game are a natural feature of the decor in this traditional Western Reserve style building.

Chef Chris Johnson is responsible for putting together the entire menu. Chris is a native Ohioan who was born in neighboring Mentor, Ohio.

He studied in France and trained under internationally renowned chef, Madeline Kaman. Wild game dishes are a specialty of the house, but the wide ranging menu will offer something for the educated palette. Local produce is featured in the appropriate seasons. The extensive wine list includes some Ohio wines.

One can dine in the outdoor courtyard, under sun or moon and stars during summer, and by the fireside in winter. The Gamekeeper's Taverne is an excellent choice for large parties, business meetings (as many as 50 people during normal hours), or that intimate dinner for two.

NOGGINS
20110 Van Aken Boulevard
Shaker Heights, Ohio 44122
Tel: (216) 752-9280

Hrs:	Restaurant:	
	Monday	11:30 a.m. - 10:00 p.m.
	Tuesday - Thursday	11:30 a.m. - 11:00 p.m.
	Friday - Saturday	11:30 a.m. - Midnight
	Sunday	5:00 p.m. - 9:00 p.m.
	Bar:	
	Monday - Saturday	Until 1:00 a.m.
	Sunday	Until 10:00 p.m.

Noggins Restaurant, Raw Bar & Pub was opened in 1978 with the concept of an all day menu with daily specials and a large wine list with servings by the glass. It began as a small operation but it offered the first extensive wine list in the city. Noggins' wine list has grown over the years from offering 60 different wines to 150 varieties in all price ranges. Although they specialize in California wines, Noggins serves wines from all over the world and there is something for every taste.

The monthly wine tastings are very popular at Noggins and the staff is capable and willing to assist guests with their choices in wines and food specials. The seafood and pasta dishes are excellent and highly recommended. The name is derived from the British expression for a quarter pint or a small quantity of drink.

Take I-90 to Route 271 South to the Chagrin Boulevard Exit and go west two miles to the intersection of Warrensville and Van Aken. Noggins is located in the shopping center on the left. Pleasing guests is what Noggins does by providing a cozy, comfortable ambiance, great food, a large wine selection- all at a very modest price.

Z CONTEMPORARY CUISINE
20600 Chagrin Boulevard
Shaker Heights, Ohio 44122
Tel: (216) 991-1580
Hrs: Lunch:
Tuesday - Friday Noon - 2:30 p.m.
Dinner:
Monday - Thursday 6:30 p.m. - 10:00 p.m.
Friday - Saturday 6:00 p.m. - 11:00 p.m.
Visa, MasterCard, American Express and Diners Club are accepted.

USA Today lists Z Contemporary Cuisine as one of the 10 best new restaurants in the country. The food reflects French, California, and Oriental influences, but the technique of cooking is definitely French.

Fastidious about freshness, proprietor Zachary Bruell often uses unusual and exotic ingredients. The menu too is fresh each week with new dishes appearing daily. Appetizers of pasta with sea scallops and oysters and salads of warm, wild mushrooms sauteed in extra virgin olive oil prepare the palate for entrees such as salmon with lobster caviar or free range chicken breast with a side of pomme frites, the house specialty. The wine list is 50% French and 50% Californian. The dessert menu lists flavor delights such as tropical mousse cake with Mango Coulis and frozen lemon and lime souffle. All dishes are served a la carte.

The interior of Z Contemporary Cuisine is done in Bahaus style with off-white walls and black leather chairs. Splashes of color reflect from contemporary paintings and exotic table flowers. But at Z Contemporary Cuisine, the food makes the biggest splash of all.

taverns and pubs

ACADEMY TAVERN
12800 Larchmere Boulevard
Cleveland, Ohio 44120
Tel: (216) 229-1171
Hrs: Monday - Saturday 8:00 a.m. - 11:00 p.m.
Sunday 3:00 p.m. - 9:00 p.m.
Closed on Sundays in June, July & August.

Academy Tavern has been a neighborhood business for 50 years, and it's still going strong. The Academy Tavern invites the public to come help them celebrate their 50th anniversary in business. The tavern is located one block north of Shaker Square.

If unable to make it to the birthday party, the Academy invites everyone to the annual clambake. If one is unable to attend the clambake, then try Academy Tavern for breakfast, lunch, or dinner anytime of the day. The tavern's fish fry is famous; the burgers are a plateful; the pastas are wonderful, and the locals brag about the daily specials. One can take a tip from a waitress on the day's full menu choice. She's been waiting tables at the tavern for more than 20 years and can match a customer and a meal perfectly.

Anything on the menu is available for take-out in special carry-home packaging. For the biggest burger, freshest fish fry, and coldest beer around, try Academy Tavern.

NAPA VALLEY BAR & GRILL, 2151 Lee Road, Cleveland, Ohio 44118; Tel: (216) 371-1438. Napa Valley Bar & Grill provides the perfect setting for an after-work drink or a relaxing meal.

LAKE COUNTY

Created from Cuyahoga and Geauga Counties in 1840, Lake County was named for its location next to Lake Erie. Despite the opening of the area to settlement in 1796, few people chose to settle in the area. In January 1831, Joseph Smith Jr., founder of the Church of Jesus Christ of Latter-Day Saints, better known as the Mormons, and several of his followers, arrived at Kirtland, intending to settle. By 1838, approximately 3,000 followers had settled in the Kirtland area, including future Mormon leader, Brigham Young. Financial problems and adverse publicity caused Smith and several of his followers to leave; eventually most of the Mormons also moved west to Utah.

attractions

The **Fairport Marine Museum** in Fairport Harbor is the first Great Lakes lighthouse marine museum in the United States. Founded in 1945 by the Fairport Harbor Historical Society, the museum preserves marine and nautical artifacts in a restored 1871 lighthouse and light-keeper's cottage.

The trademark of **Headlands Beach State Park** is its mile-long natural beach, the largest in the state. Concession stands and changing booths are provided for swimmers.

The Headlands Dunes is one of the last dune ecosystems along Lake Erie. Beaver, raccoon, squirrel and rabbit are abundant in the marshy area despite its metropolitan location.

Adjacent to the park is **Mentor Marsh Nature Preserve**, a designated National Natural Landmark. The marsh comprises 644 acres of decomposing forest returning to marshland and contains a wide variety of plant and animal life. The trails are perfect for bird-watching. Bird species include the long-billed marsh wren and the Virginia and king rails. There are nesting areas for wood ducks, eastern bluebirds, and the rare warbler.

Considered to be one of the largest arboretums in the world, the **Holden Arboretum** is a unique 3,000-acre preserve of natural woodlands, horticultural collections, display gardens, ponds, fields and ravines. Hiking trails range from short walks through display gardens, to longer hikes to spectacular natural areas.

The **Kirtland Temple Historical Center** is the first temple built by the followers of Mormon leader Joseph Smith Jr.

Lake Metroparks are located throughout the historic natural areas of Lake County. There are 19 Metroparks; two in the Kirtland area worth mentioning are Penitentiary Glen and Lake Farmpark. Called Penitentiary because the gorge is difficult to get in and out of, this is a very popular hiking area. The agricultural past comes alive at Lake Farmpark. Although partially under construction, visitors can still take a horse drawn ride through the woods, walk through the cornfields, or pet the animals.

In the Willoughby area is the **Hach-Otis Sanctuary**, where 150-foot clay bluffs overlook the Chagrin River. The stream has recut the old valley, which was completely filled with glacial drift during the last ice age. There are foot trails along the unstable cliffs, and wooded forests of beech, maple and oak surround the area. The clay banks along the Chagrin River are ideal nesting spots for bank swallows and kingfishers. Also in the area are pileated woodpeckers, great horned and barred owls, deer and foxes. Spring brings a profusion of wildflowers in bloom.

Painesville Township Park is a family reacreation park that provides facilities for softball, dances, picnicking, and camping for recreational vehicles.

The Indian Museum of Lake County is located at Lake Erie College. The museum displays prehistoric Ohio and northeastern Ohio artifacts from 10 B.C. through 1650 A.D. It also exhibits crafts from the rest of North America, from the 1800s to the present.

events

The Lake County Fair is held in late August at the fairgrounds in Painesville.

Oktoberfest is held for five days ending on Labor Day at the fairgrounds.

resorts

QUAIL HOLLOW RESORT AND CONFERENCE CENTER
11080 Concord-Hambden Road, 1-90
Concord, Ohio 44077
Tel: (216) 352-6201
(800) 792-0258 Nationwide
Visa, MasterCard, American Express, Diners Club and Discover are accepted.

An inviting place to renew body and mind in a glorious environment, Quail Hollow Resort and Conference Center is situated amidst the scenic splendor and gently rolling countryside of Northeastern Ohio. Designed both for the vacationer and the businessperson, the resort beautifully fulfills its dual functions.

Guests can test their mastery of the fairways on the challenging 18-hole golf course designed by Bruce Devlin, or serve aces and return winners on the lighted tennis courts. One may enjoy the opulent show of Mother Nature while lacing up shoes to head for the jogging trails, returning to paddle leisurely around the outdoor pool. When winter arrives and snows encase the countryside, the resort offers miles of expertly groomed cross-country ski trails and a variety of trail options with which to test one's skill and expertise. Muscles relax while indulging in a professional massage at the health spa or while refreshing oneself in the sauna or whirlpool. Several restaurants, ranging from casual to formal, offer agreeable settings in which to dine and swap stories of athletic prowess. For business executives, there are excellent meeting rooms, detailed for comfort and efficiency. The facilities feature an extensive selection of equipment to enhance meetings or seminars.

Whether one enjoys challenges in the form of sand traps and water hazards or business and financial matters, or if fun and relaxation are the focus of one's attention, many delightful options are available at the Quail Hollow Resort and Conference Center. The Resort is easily accessible by air or automobile, and transportation is available to and from the airport on a scheduled basis.

wine

CHALET DEBONNE VINEYARDS
7743 Doty Road
Madison, Ohio 44057
Tel: (216) 466-3485
Hrs: January:

Hrs:	January:	
	Tuesday - Saturday	1:00 p.m. - 5:00 p.m.
	February - December	
	Tuesday and Thursday	Noon - 8:00 p.m.
	Wednesday and Friday	Noon - Midnight
	Saturday	Noon - 8:00 p.m.

Visa, MasterCard and personal checks are accepted.

The Debevc family's Chalet Debonne Vineyard is recognized as the premier boutique winery in Ohio. The winery received two gold medals in the 1987 Ohio Wine Competition for their 1985 Johannisberg Riesling and Chardonnay. In addition to the gold medals, the winery won more awards than any other winery entered.

Chalet Debonne Vineyards produces all types of wine. You may sample American, French/American, and Vinifera served at the vineyards wine tasting bar. Guests can stroll through the wine cellars with a Debevc family member and enjoy an informative, relaxed tour of the facilities. One can see the grapes being pressed or try one's hand at home wine making.

The vineyard enjoys the claim as being the first family winery in the western reserve. In 1972, the Debevc's began with two varieties of wine and today they produce more than 21 finished bottles. Chalet Debonne Vineyards is "distinctively separate from the bunch!" The vineyard is located three miles west off Route 534 on South River Road or two and a half miles east off Route 528 on Griswald Road, then left on Emerson and right on Doty Road.

MENTOR

antiques

MENTOR VILLAGE ANTIQUES, 8619 Mentor Avenue, Mentor, Ohio 44060; Tel: (216) 255-1438. Mentor Village Antiques is a six room Western Reserve Heritage Home and Barn that offers an incredible variety of select antiques. Collectors and the merely curious are each sure to find something of interest.

landmarks

LAWNFIELD
JAMES E. GARFIELD NATIONAL HISTORICAL SITE
8095 Mentor Avenue
Mentor, Ohio 44060

Tel:	(216) 255-8722	
Hrs:	Tuesday - Saturday	10:00 a.m. - 5:00 p.m.
	Sunday	Noon - 5:00 p.m.

Visa and MasterCard are accepted.

Lawnfield, home of James Garfield, is owned and operated by Western Reserve Historical Society, which was named for that portion of Northeastern Ohio originally known as the Western Reserve of Connecticut. The society is a nonprofit, private, cultural institution dedicated to the collection and preservation of historical information and materials from the area.

James E. Garfield, the 20th president of the United States, was shot on July 2, 1881, only four months after taking office; he died on September 19th of that year. Built in 1832 as a small farmhouse on 118 acres, Lawnfield was purchased by the future president in 1876. In addition to purchasing another 40 acres to add to the farm, he expanded the house to three stories. The grief of the nation as a result of the president's death resulted in donations to the family in excess of $400,000--money the president's widow used to add a library onto the house as a tribute to her late husband. Thus was born the first U.S. Presidential Memorial Library. Further additions resulted in the 30-room Victorian mansion occupied by the Garfield family until the 1930s, at which time they donated the house and contents to the society.

With such memorabilia as the Haviland china used by the Garfield's at the White House, a lunch box used by then Congressman Garfield when traveling from Ohio to Washington, and a large waxed funeral wreath sent by Queen Victoria, Lawnfield is a memorable place to visit.

restaurants

TERRACE INN
9260 Mentor Avenue
Mentor, Ohio 44060
Tel: (216) 255-3456

Hrs:	Restaurant:	
	Monday - Thursday	7:00 a.m. - 11:00 p.m.
	Friday - Saturday	7:00 a.m. - Midnight
	Sunday	7:00 a.m. - 8:00 p.m.
	Lounge:	11:00 a.m. - 2:30 a.m.

The Terrace Inn, 25 miles east of Cleveland and five miles west of Painesville, is located about 10 minutes from the noise and congestion of the freeway; its quiet and friendly atmosphere make it the place to go when looking for an inn that offers comfortable and clean accommodations, modern conveniences, an entertainment lounge, and a full service restaurant. The Terrace Inn hasn't always boasted such facilities; in its early stages in 1950 it had only eight rooms but has since grown to 50 rooms with The Terrace Room restaurant being added in 1973. Present owners, Tony and Fred Lariccia, are proud that the hotel and restaurant have always been family owned and operated and this pride is reflected in the restaurant service and hotel upkeep.

For 40 years, the Terrace Inn has been providing guests with quality accommodations and excellent service. These are reasons enough to return to the inn but guests also appreciate the heated outdoor swimming pool and patio. Those looking for more to do are pleased to discover the Cocktail Lounge, where they can enjoy a nightly Happy Hour and live entertainment on the weekends.

Of course, guests can take advantage of the Terrace Room for wonderful lunches and dinners. Sumptuous dishes include Sauteed Lemon Sole, Fettucini Broccolini, Swordfish Mesquite, and Terrace Filet (twin beef tenderloins sauteed with fresh mushrooms and shallots, served on a bed of sweet basil and garlic cream sauce). Lighter Fare includes Chicken Parmigiana and Julienne Salad. Special flambed desserts include Bananas Foster and Peach Flambe. The inn also has special banquet and meeting rooms for those on business. Efficiency units are available at special weekly and monthly rates.

The Terrace Inn, close to Lake Erie and Headlands State Park, is a "Best Choice" for visitors to Lake County. The delicious food alone makes it worth the trip.

THE PERFECT MATCH
8500 Station Street
Mentor, Ohio 44060

Tel:	(216) 255-7320	
Hrs:	Monday - Thursday	11:00 a.m. - 11:00 p.m.
	Friday - Saturday	11:00 a.m. - 1:00 a.m.

Visa, MasterCard, American Express and Diners Club are accepted.

Perfect matches are "rare birds" as is The Perfect Match, an exclusive restaurant in Mentor, Ohio. Located in a building whose rich history dates back to 1868, the restaurant has recently undergone a multimillion dollar renovation. Present owners Al and Jeanene Covert have sought to retain as much of the historic original structure as possible, and the brick walls and rafters of the building are showcased by unique lighting and shiny brass rails. The cozy fireplace adds a natural warmth to the atmosphere. Beef is a specialty of the house, aged to peak flavor and cut fresh daily. The Steak Admiral is the restaurant's interpretation of Surf and Turf and is a delectable presentation of butterflied filet mignon with tender, juicy chunks of lobster sauteed with butter and wine and graced with a slightly tangy bearnaise. Veal Oscar leaves the realm of the usual by the sensational combination of the finest provimi veal piled high with succulent crab meat and asparagus spears, sauced with a delicate version of bearnaise. The wide selection of appetizers ranges from Baked Brie and Fried Mozzarella Stix to Frogs Legs and Shrimp Tempura. Seafood lovers can delight in the very unique preparation of Scampi and Fillet of Sole Naomi.

The Perfect Match is located near Route 2 at the Route 615 exit, and discriminating diners will enjoy the fine service and excellent fare at this aptly named restaurant.

PAINESVILLE

restaurants

CHESTER RESTAURANT
11 Chester Street
Painesville, Ohio 44077
Tel: (216) 352-1471
Hrs: Lunch:
Monday - Friday 11:30 a.m. - 3:00 p.m.
Monday - Thursday 4:00 p.m. - 9:00 p.m.
Dinner:
Friday - Saturday 4:00 p.m. - 10:00 p.m.
Visa and MasterCard are accepted.

Chester Restaurant, serving generous portions of quality food at good prices for over 50 years, has received ratings in the Mobil Travel Guide and feature spots in local magazines and TV programs. Perhaps they have received such recognition because everything is homemade and the chef in charge of kitchen operations, Rita Trifilletti, is originally from Sicily.

Rita's lasagna and homebaked breads are delicious reminders of just how wonderful food can be when it is prepared the old-fashioned way. In addition to their tempting menus, customers can choose from six lunch specials daily and seven or more dinner specials. Naturally, the house specialties include many Italian dishes such as Cavatelli, Raviolli, and Rigatoni. Pastas include salad and bread. Seafood is also a specialty here such as Lake Erie Yellow Perch or Walleye. Diners would do well to try the Seafood Platter which includes perch, walleye, shrimp, scallops and oysters. Chester's "award winning" BBQ Ribs are another great meal. Entrees include salad or coleslaw, choice of potato, and homemade bread. Meals may be complemented with domestic or imported beer, white, red, blush wine, or wine coolers.

Chester Restaurant began as Di Iorio's grocery store in the late 1920s. Nick and Christina Di Iorio came to Ohio from Italy and opened their business in what is now the front room of the restaurant. In 1933, at the end of Prohibition, Nick received one of the first liquor licenses in Lake County. He built an addition to his store and called it the Chester Restaurant. Brisk business required another expansion just two months after opening. In 1937 the ballroom was added on along with the present mahogany bar and the two, nickel-plated brass rails which mark the serving area. Bands playing and people dancing were common sights in the ballroom. Chester Restaurant is a "Best Choice" as present owners, Albert J. Di Iorio and Silvio Trifiletti, "are carrying on a 50-year tradition of fine food, beverage, and service."

RIDER INN
792 Mentor Avenue
Painesville, Ohio 44077

Tel:	(216) 354-8200	
	Toll Free in West Cleveland	(216) 942-2742
Hrs:	Bed and Breakfast:	Seven days
	Restaurant:	
	Monday - Thursday	11:30 a.m. - 9:00 p.m.
	(Pub until 1:30 a.m.)	
	Friday	11:30 a.m. - 10:00 p.m.
	Saturday	4:00 p.m. - 10:00 p.m.
	(Pub until 2:30 a.m. Friday & Saturday)	
	Sunday Brunch:	2:30 p.m.

Visa, MasterCard and American Express are accepted.

The Rider Inn is a Western Reserve landmark that was built in 1812 by Joseph Rider. The hotel was once operated by his son, Zerah, who cut a road from what is now Route 84 to Mentor Avenue and placed a sign at 84 and Bank Street that stated "This way to the only Tavern," with a rival establishment not far away. Gone are the days of lye soap and pumps in the backyard for getting washed up; with all of the pampering and amenities today's Rider Inn offers, underhanded business practices are no longer necessary to attract guests.

Present owner Elaine Crane is working very hard to bring the building into compliance with 20th century regulations governing structures that provide lodging without risking its historic landmark status. The upstairs walls have been glazed rather than papered. Elaine has researched the building's past in order to find the perfect antiques and fabrics to complement wallcovers and window treatments. Many of the pieces decorating the shop are on consignment from Ye Olde Oaken Bucket Antiques next door. Some parts of the building's interior remain the same, such as the priceless Duncan Phyfe dresser found during the renovations and believed to have belonged to Joseph Rider. The wood of the original floor which has been identified as long needle pine, from a type of tree that's been extinct for over 100 years.

The six classical columns outside give an inviting appearance to the bed and breakfast. The inn offers six guest rooms each with its own private bath and one is a special bridal suite. Visitors are made to feel comfortable and welcome with fresh flowers in all the rooms, complimentary Caswell & Massey bath products, and bedtime mints on the pillow.

The Inn will cater to the business or romantic traveler with wedding, banquet, and meeting facilities available. The restaurant offers fine dining for guests and locals. Hearty soups include Potatoes Leek and Seafood Gumbo with entrees having traditional names like Rider Rib and Stagecoach Veal.

The Rider Inn is a "Best Choice" in bed and breakfasts for those who enjoy modern comforts as well as for history buffs who appreciate seeing pieces of the past preserved.

ASHTABULA COUNTY

Created from both Trumbull and Geauga Counties in 1807, Ashtabula County was the first county to be organized from the Connecticut Western Reserve. Named for the Ashtabula River, the county's name is a derivative of the Indian word meaning "fish river." Jefferson, the county seat, began as a business endeavor of Gideon Granger of Connecticut, who sent a representative to the site to develop the town in 1804. Granger, who at the time was postmaster general in the Jefferson administration, named the settlement after the third president.

attractions

The Ashtabula County Historical Society was formed in 1838 in Jefferson and is the second oldest historical society in Ohio. It owns and maintains the Giddings Law Office Museum, which was built in 1823. This National Historic Landmark is open June, July and August.

The former New York Central depot, built in 1900, is the home of the Conneaut Railroad Museum in Conneaut. It houses a collection of railroad memorabilia and antique exhibits of the Steam Era.

Shandy Hall Museum is a pioneer home built in 1815 in Geneva. Owned and operated by the Western Reserve Society, the home contains its original furnishings.

Ashtabula County boasts a large collection of covered bridges, most of them built in the second half of the 19th century.

Geneva State Park has two and one-half miles of Lake Erie beach, much of which has reverted back to its natural state. Visitors can find many beautiful places to have a picnic along with freshwater marshes and estuaries. The park is open year-round and is complete with designated snowmobile trails.

Pymatuning is a state park and lake in both Ohio and Pennsylvania. One of the finest walleye and muskellunge spots in the country, this large lake has wide, open waters and secluded coves for excellent boating. Picnic areas and swimming beaches are also available. Cabin facilities are available year-round.

events

The Heritage Homes Tour is held in Jefferson in mid-May.

The Ashtabula County Fair is held at the Fairgrounds in Jefferson in mid-August.

The Covered Bridge Festival, held in October., in Jefferson, Ohio, is a big event featuring draft horse plowing, a parade, an antique tractor pull, dancing, a pancake breakfast and many other special activities. Their is also a self-driving tour of 14 covered bridges during the peak autumn color.

bait & tackle shops

GATEWAY BAIT AND TACKLE
State Route 85
Andover, Ohio 44003
Tel: (216) 293-7227
Hrs: Open year round

The Gateway Bait and Tackle shop is the largest shop of its kind on Pymatuning Lake. Russ and Gretta Williams have owned and operated the store since its opening 17 years ago. Russ is an extremely knowledgeable sportsman and is always willing to advise locals as well as visitors to the best hunting and fishing. The collections of fishing and hunting supplies are second to none. Gateway has several tanks full of different types of live bait, and he helps to guide customers toward the best equipment for their needs.

The Gateway Bait and Tackle shop's huge selection of supplies isn't the only service offered by this Pymatuning shop. Special features such as a 24-hour fishing hotline and the "wall of fish" (a complete display of all the types of fish found in both Pymatuning and Erie Lakes) are offered. Gateway provides resident and non-resident fishing and hunting licenses, duck stamps, and is a registered Ohio Deer Check Station. Soft drinks, beer, wine, and snacks are available for take-out. The emphasis at Gateway, however, is on its long list of superior supples. They carry a complete line of bait and tackle, muzzle loaders, and black powder, and assorted hunting supplies. Gateway also carries T-shirts, sweatshirts, caps and camouflage jackets.

No one knows the hunting in this part of Ohio better than Russ and Gretta Williams. Gretta has been on the Board of Directors of Pymatuning Lake for twelve years. The Williams' have watched generations grow up and have captured the memories in photographs which they proudly display. The information is always up to date, and the service is exceeded by none. There is no doubt that the Gateway Bait and Tackle shop is the "Best Choice" for hunting and fishing supplies.

restaurants

CRANBERRY STATION
68 Public Station
Andover, Ohio 44003
Tel: (213) 293-6651
Hrs: Monday - Saturday 8:00 a.m. - 9:00 p.m.
Sunday 8:00 a.m. - 3:00 p.m.

Cranberry Station is a newly-opened, family-style restaurant that specializes in reasonably priced, homemade food. The Strip Steak is the most expensive item on the menu and it's only $6.95. The country-style breakfasts range from hearty Western Omelettes with toast, to steaming-hot oatmeal with fruit. Every Sunday, the restaurant features special breakfast treats like banana pancakes, blueberry pancakes, and raisin-bread French Toast.

Specialty sandwiches like the Batter-dipped White Fish Hoagie Filet and the Station Sandwich with cold roast beef, tomato, and cream cheese on toasted rye are best bets for lunch. Taco, chef, steak, and spinach salads, served in light pastry shells, and the fresh Oriental Chicken are other best sellers. Baked fish, shrimp, strip steak and chicken breast are some of Cranberry Station's dinner favorites. The restaurant serves homemade dessert breads such as pumpkin, banana, zucchini and, of course, cranberry. Strawberry frozen yogurt, hand dipped ice cream cones, cheesecake and homemade pies are scrumptious treats visitors must try.

Cranberry Station's decor is quaint and rustic, with authentic antique tables and chairs, soft blue wallpaper, cranberry-colored napkins and cranberry-edged white china. Located just off Route 7 South from the I-90 Andover Exit, this classic country restaurant offers more than 25 kinds of freshly prepared soups, several quiche specialties, an assortment of gourmet teas, an array of party trays, and a variety of great gift items. Gifts such as glass Irish coffee mugs and owner Cheryl Lipinsly's own creations--wood carvings, tole paintings, and dried floral arrangements--give visitors plenty to choose from.

Stop by Cranberry Station and find out how real country cooking should taste.

GENEVA-ON-THE-LAKE AND GENEVA

Founded in 1869, Geneva-On-The-Lake is one of Ohio's oldest summer resort areas. The community boasts many fine examples of Victorian architecture and historic private homes.

attractions

The Jennie Munger Gregory Museum was the first frame house built on the Lake Erie shore. The house was built in 1823 on land purchased in 1818 as part of an original land grant of the Connecticut Western Reserve. The museum is furnished with artifacts and historical items that reflect the history of Ashtabula County, from the pioneers to the Civil War and the early 1900s. The museum is open May through October.

Shandy Hall Museum is a pioneer home built in 1815 in Geneva. Owned and operated by the Western Reserve Society,the home contains its original furnishings.

events

Geneva celebrates its Grape JAMboree in late September.

accommodations

HOLIDAY INN-ASHTABULA
I-90 and Route 45
Austinburg, Ohio 44010
Tel: (216) 275-2711
Hrs: Restaurant:
Breakfast & Lunch:
Monday - Friday 6:00 a.m. - 2:00 p.m.
Saturday - Sunday 7:00 a.m. - 2:00 p.m.
Dinner:
Monday - Friday 5:00 p.m. - 10:00 p.m.
Saturday - Sunday 5:00 p.m. - 10:00 p.m.
Lounge: 4:00 p.m. - 1:00 a.m.
Visa, MasterCard, American Express, Diners Club and Carte Blanche are accepted.

For a small roadside hotel, the Holiday Inn-Ashtabula has received some large recognition. For the second consecutive year, it has received the Holiday Inn Corporation's Superior Hotel Award. This special award is reserved for only the best Holiday Inns, both in service and product quality. Holiday Inn-Ashtabula is one of only 300 hotels out of the 1,600 Holiday Inn Hotel systems to receive this honor.

One visit and it's understood why Holiday Inn-Ashtabula was also honored with Brighton Hotel Corporation's Customer Service trophy for outstanding customer service. The cleanliness of the hotel and the long term employees who are dedicated to providing good service are only two reasons why the Holiday Inn Ashtabula is deserving of this recognition.

Located for 25 years at the intersection of Interstate 90 and Route 45, this 118-room Holiday Inn offers many special services. It has three suites for those special occasions, an outdoor pool, free local calling, room service, valet service, and next day laundry. For corporate travelers, Holiday Inn offers three meeting rooms equipped with VCR's which seat up to 150 people, and fax and business services are also available.

The chef is a Culinary Institute graduate and prepares such specialties as Chicken Pastry Pie and Fish New Brunswick. The Prime Rib of Beef is excellent, and for dessert the creamy cheesecake and fruit pies a la mode are irresistible. There are daily breakfast, lunch, and dinner specials, as well as a special dinner buffet on Friday and Saturday and a Sunday morning breakfast buffet. The lounge offers live entertainment on Friday and Saturday featuring oldies, contemporary or country music.

The newly-remodeled Holiday Inn-Ashtabula treats its guests with the utmost in professional service. Reservations aren't necessary but are recommended. Come see why Holiday Inn-Ashtabula is considered a "Best Choice" along the Lakes.

bed & breakfast inns

OTTO'S BED AND BREAKFAST
5653 Lake Road
Geneva-on-the-Lake, Ohio 44041
Tel: (216) 466-8668
Visa and MasterCard are accepted.

A weekend at Otto's Bed and Breakfast is a trip back in time to the days of covered bridges and mellow living. In the evening, when a breeze ripples the lake, guests listening carefully can almost hear the soft music of Guy Lombardo or the swinging jazz of Duke Ellington playing in the background.

In fact, Geneva-on-the-Lake was Ohio's first resort, built in the late 1800s. Today, Otto's Bed and Breakfast is still a homey family resort, with its own private beach on Lake Erie where horseshoe games share space with lively volleyball games, and children dip their toes into the clear water. Otto's facilities include 12 rooms in the house, eight of which have private baths. Operating on the "American Plan," this bed and breakfast serves full breakfasts and dinners seven days a week. In addition, families can choose to stay in one of Otto's eight cottages, where they will find a kitchen completely equipped to meet their full-time dining needs.

Only a short walk away from the lodging accommodations is the resort's Amusement Center, a facility sporting water slides, an 18-ride amusement park, restaurants, wineries and Geneva-on-the-Lake Marina. For the less actively inclined, the beach provides the perfect spot for sun bathing, reading a favorite book, or just relaxing. Otto's Bed and Breakfast, with its home-like atmosphere and individual attention, is truly a unique vacation opportunity at Geneva-on-the-Lake.

campgrounds

INDIAN CREEK CAMPING RESORT
Geneva on the Lake, Ohio 44041
Tel: (216) 466-8191
Hrs: Open year round
Limited off-season sites

If getting away from it all means wilderness and an abundance of outdoor activities, then Indian Creek Camping Resort is the perfect escape. Indian Creek Camping Resort is a 110-acre facility with 400 campsites ranging from primitive to full hook-up R.V. sites.

Owned by Dot and Ed Andrus since 1964, it extends a mile back from Lake Road, and through the years, they have continued to develop and restore the campsites and adjacent structures, resulting in a more complete resort. Serving the area as one of the best-rated resorts in Ohio, Indian Creek has a grocery store carrying an assortment of commodities, restaurant and lounge with a full menu, gasoline station, and bottled and bulk gas service. The Resort also has a deli and pizzeria as well as servicing and selling R.V.'s.

As a family owned and operated business, Dot and Ed offer guests all that is needed for a vacation in one convenient location. Indian Creek Camping Resort is complete with modern restrooms and showers, laundry facilities, heated pool with lifeguard, and two large lakes stocked with fish. Guests can also enjoy the flea markets, parties and large dance floor in the recreation hall. Baseball fields, horseshoe pits, tournaments, a kiddie pool, and hay rides provide hours of family fun. Seasonal and short-term campers are welcome. Reservations are accepted but not necessary.

NORTH EASTERN OHIO RECREATION, INC.
3931-35 North Broadway
Geneva, Ohio 44041
Tel: (216) 466-5638 or (216) 466-1293
Hrs: Camping areas open May 15 - October 15
R.V. and Marina Sales are open all year.
Visa and MasterCard are accepted.

The Recreation Center began more than 13 years ago with only one campground which is now known as Audubon Lakes Campground. The park has grown from its original 57 acres to the present 116 beautifully-wooded acres. For the enjoyment of campers, a stocked fishing lake, and a clean, aerated swimming lake with a white sand beach for summer sun worshippers are provided on the grounds. There are presently 125 large sites with water and electric hook-ups. Practically every site offers a varying degree of shade and sunshine. The park is also a registered wildlife sanctuary.

A second step in creating the Recreation Center began more than 10 years ago when the business entered the recreational vehicle business as North Eastern Ohio R.V. (NEORV). The R.V. business has grown from a small grass-covered lot displaying a few fold-down camp trailers to one of Jayco's largest full-line R.V. dealers providing one of Ashtabula's finest R.V. service centers. To furnish all of the campers' needs, the R.V. center features a large parts and accessories facility in a unique 100-year old converted barn.

The opening of the marina at Geneva State Park has given the center an opportunity to substantially complete its Recreation Center by adding marine sales, parts, accessories, and service. To accommodate emergency repairs needing hard-to-find parts, NEORV and the marina have access to the largest RV and marine supply house in the United States.

Audubon Lakes Campground provides numerous types of activities for all family members. The campground is located near the Geneva-on-the-Lake entertainment area, great golf courses, wineries, covered bridges, historic buildings, summer theaters, and excellent restaurants. Combine the features of all these sites and those of North Eastern Ohio Recreation, Inc. facilities, and have a perfect vacation.

forge & liveries

HARPER'S FORGE AND LIVERY, INC.
5350 Route 307 West
Geneva, Ohio 44041
Tel: (216) 466-6754
Hrs: Open year-round by appointment.

This out-of-the-ordinary tourist attraction is the result of Dane Hoff's keen interest in the historical significance of the surrounding Ashtabula County countryside. Surviving through five generations, the old fashioned farmhouse is being restored by Dane, a former police officer. Besides having a blacksmith shop on the premises, the main attraction is the Historic Harpersfield carriage rides. Carriage rides can by enjoyed throughout the spring, summer, and fall; then in the winter, breathtaking sleigh rides are offered. "Icabod" is the former racehorse that Dane uses, a gentle magnificent animal that stands over 15 hands high and is loved by children of all ages. The carriage used was designed by the Amish according to Dane's specifications. Various ornamental pieces which Dane custom designs himself are on display at the blacksmith shop

The length of carriage and sleigh rides vary according to individual preference. The area is very scenic with a feeling of bygone days as the trip winds though the old fashioned covered bridges or through wooded trails. Dane participates in numerous local activities such as the: "Austinburg Country Days" and "Covered Bridge" festivals, providing enjoyable carriage rides and blacksmithing. There is also a driving tour through the wineries as well as tours for weddings, anniversaries, and special event rides.

golf courses

HEMLOCK SPRINGS GOLF COURSE
4654 Cold Springs Road
Geneva, Ohio 44041
Tel: (216) 466-4044
Hrs: April 1 - November 1: Sun-up - Sun-down

Hemlock Springs Golf Course is known as the Geneva area's most progressive golf course. Joe and Jim Maruna have owned and operated Hemlock Springs since 1978. This 18 hole, championship course stretches over 127 acres of beautiful land. Some of the area's best players find Hemlock Springs a great challenge and enjoy the various special services offered.

Hemlock Springs is beautifully-designed with seven lakes scattered over the course.. The tees, fairways, and greens are watered daily to preserve the rich, green look of a championship course.. The course is 6,800 yards from the pro tees. Many of the golfers who play Hemlock Springs are the best in the area.

Its beauty and challenging terrain make it a golf lover's dream. Because of the course's popularity, golfers must reserve tee times for weekends and holidays. After a round of golf, many players are drawn to the clubhouse to quench their thirst. A full-service bar is available along with a delicious selection of snacks and sandwiches. There is an outdoor patio where guests can enjoy their drinks and relax. The clubhouse also contains banquet facilities for up to 250 people. The pro shop has a line of quality clubs and assorted golfing apparel that will satisfy any customer. Like many popular courses, Hemlock Springs has leagues for men and women, special rates for seniors, and discounts for juniors and women on certain weekdays. Another special feature is a free pass for weekday play if guests are a weekday foursome. A spacious practice range is available for the benefit of beginners as well as those seasoned players who just want to sharpen their game.

Hemlock Springs is as challenging a golf course as there is in the area. Visitors find that friendly service and expert care are two qualities that Joe and Jim insist upon. The beautiful fairways, well-kept greens, comfortable clubhouse, and numerous other special features make Hemlock Springs a total golf experience.

malls

BILICIC'S COUNTRY MALL
I-90 & Route 534
Harpersfield, Ohio 44041
Tel: (216) 466-9111
Hrs: Seven days 7:00 a.m. - 11:00 p.m.

Bilicic's Country Mall is a rustic country store much like the vintage country shops of the past. The Bilicics started the business in 1966. It was expanded in 1988 to include a barn complete with overhead beams and a silo.

The store carries a variety of items ranging from grocery supplies, bait and fishing tackle, to hardware, video tapes, magazines, and fresh coffee and doughnuts all day.

Bilicic's also offers many local wines and is the only market in the area which sells beer and wine on Sunday.

Customers can play the Ohio Lottery, get their hunting or fishing license, and have business cards printed here.

Bilicic's has an interesting craft corner that is highlighted by a wooden, hand-carved statue of an Indian in full headdress that stands six feet in height. Items made by local artists as well as genuine German clocks grace the craft corner.

Located in Ashtabula County, the store is near wineries, camping areas and winter sports facilities.

The Bilicic Family is proud of the business they have established and the customers that patronize the Country Mall. People stop in frequently just to converse. It's a perfect stop for campers and travelers.

The goal of the family is to provide the type of atmosphere and supplies of the old-fashioned country store. From the number of tourists and natives that are attracted to the store each year, it would appear that Bilicic's Country Mall has achieved its goal.

markets

BURKHOLDER FARM MARKET
4553 Route 307 East
Geneva, Ohio 44041
Tel: (216) 466-3180
Hrs: July 1 - October 1 10:00 a.m. - 6:00 p.m.
October 2 - November 23 10:00 a.m. - 5:00 p.m.

Burkholder Farm Market has been a family owned and operated business since 1901. John and Helen Burkholder raised six children, all of whom helped in the sowing of apples, grapes, peaches, prunes, pears, and a variety of vegetables. The business was originated by the operation of a small fruit stand in 1953. A market and cold storage house was built in 1954 since the need to expand came so rapidly. Since then, three additions to the building have been made.

The market features a variety of fresh fruit and vegetable items with 43 acres of Concord and Niagara grapes. Visitors can pick their own grapes from the last week of September until the grapes are gone, which is usually the end of October. There are 27 acres of apple trees with 14 varieties of apples to choose from. Pick a crate of apples and price them yourself. There are also seven varieties of peaches, corn, squash, pumpkins, gourds, and other locally-grown fruits and vegetables offered.

The Burkholder's oldest daughter, Judie, along with her family, started baking homemade pies for the market. Choose from a variety of 20 delicious pies all made from scratch on the premises. Judie also bakes homemade cookies and turnovers for all to enjoy.

Upon entering the Burkholder Farm Market, visitors are hit with the aroma of fresh-baking pies and the scent of fresh fruit. A large fireplace crackling in the background gives the feeling of being at home.

Ron and Aletta Burkholder now own the market and all members of the family still play key roles. The family plans events yearly to keep community members involved. The first week in November marks the Apple Butter Stir with hay rides through the orchards. Booths are set up by local craftsmen on the weekends to show their wares. A craft corner featuring country and Victorian crafts made by local artists is also set up and is rotated to the change of the season. One hundred percent pure Ohio maple products can be found at the Market along with jams, jellies, honey, hard candy, popcorn, nuts, and fancy woven baskets. All are great gift ideas.

Personalized service, community involvement, an array of homegrown fruits and vegetables all combine to make Burkholder Farm Market the place to visit for every savory need.

SPRING HILL ORCHARDS AND FARM MARKET
6062 Southridge West, Route 84
Geneva, Ohio 44041

Tel:	(216) 466-7480	
Hrs:	May - December:	
	Monday - Saturday	9:00 a.m. - 6:00 p.m.
	Sunday	Noon - 6:00 p.m.
	February - April:	
	Friday - Saturday	9:00 a.m. - 5:00 p.m.
	Sunday	1:00 p.m. - 5:00 p.m.
	Closed during January.	

For those traveling in Northeast Ohio, a visit to Spring Hill Orchards and Farm Market is a pleasant diversion, especially for those arriving for the Strawberry Festival in June, the Peach Festival in August and the Harvest Festival held during the first week of October. Fresh evergreen garlands, trees, wreaths, and all the trimmings of the season welcome travelers and regulars in December.

By previous arrangement, Spring Hill offers picnic facilities, hayrides, hot dog roasts, and tours of the orchards as well as the cider mill. Spring Hill Orchards and Farm market features made-to-order baskets and boxes, packed with such delicious treats as fresh fruit, local wines, sparkling juices, and Amish cheeses that can be shipped throughout the United States. The Farm Market is awash with colorful seasonal fruit and vegetables. Try U-Pick fruit to participate in the firsthand harvesting of strawberries, cherries, blueberries, raspberries and other home-grown offerings. Ohio honey, pure maple syrup, and homemade jams and jellies are among many specialty items. Wafting from the bakery are smells of freshly baked pies, strudel, cookies, and breads. Punctuating the country charm are family antiques and a fine selection of collectibles and handmade crafts.

Whether the need is to fill the pantry, enjoy a weekend diversion or a relaxing vacation stop, Spring Hill Orchards and Farm Market is an ideal choice. Just "Look for the Big Red Barn," the country market beckons.

restaurants

APPLEWOOD RESTAURANT

I-90 and Route 534
Geneva, Ohio 44088
Tel: (216) 466-6767
Hrs: Open seven days, 24 hours.
Closed Christmas.

The Applewood Restaurant is a family-style cafe conveniently located just off Route I-90, Exit 218, in Geneva, Ohio. The Applewood offers a variety of homemade daily specials. The restaurant accommodates up to 75 people and is open 24 hours a day. The Applewood's homemade breads, pies, and cinnamon rolls are favorites of locals as well as those visiting Geneva for its recreational facilities.

Some of the most popular items on the Applewood Restaurant's menu are its breakfast specials which are served throughout the day. A few of the favorites are steak and eggs, sausage, gravy and biscuits, and Golden Belgian Waffles. The Applewood also features two or three daily specials that do not appear on the menu, Sunday's Swiss Steak, for example. All of the beef used is cut to order in-house. The Applewood lunch and dinner menus offer a wide variety of selections from burgers to steaks to seafood. Everything is as reasonably priced as it is delicious. Desserts are another specialty of the Applewood. Their Apple Crisps are known county-wide.

The taste of the Applewood's homemade food compliments its warm, friendly atmosphere. Owners Ralph and Gary Haskins and manager David Lehnert are proud of the wide-spread reputation they've built for friendly service and fantastic food. The Applewood is also home to a quaint gift shop. Many tourists find it a convenient place to pick up souvenirs after their meal. The Applewood Restaurant is the "Best Choice" in Geneva for a homecooked meal in a friendly atmosphere.

CLAY STREET INN
2092 Route 45 South
Austinburg, Ohio 44010
Tel: (216) 275-5151
Hrs: Monday - Thursday 11:00 a.m. - 10:00 p.m.
Friday and Saturday 11:00 a.m. - 2:30 a.m.
Closed Sundays and Holidays
Senior citizen discounts are available.
Visa, MasterCard, American Express and Discover are accepted.

The Clay Street Inn is a restaurant that offers premium steaks like New York Strip, Delmonico, Porterhouse, Prime Rib, Sirloin and Filet Mignon. Owner Shelley Stark is proud that most of the beef is raised on her father's nearby farm, which accounts for the top quality and freshness. The inn has a friendly atmosphere, featuring a rustic interior of brick, paneling, oil lamps, and silk flowers at each table, creating an inviting atmosphere. The bar area is separate from the dining area which has a large brick and stone fireplace. The inn also has banquet facilities serving up to 75 people.

Besides the regular menu items, there are daily specials. Shelley does most of the cooking herself and takes great pride in everything she serves. The customers enjoy the special feature nights such as Italian Cooking Night, Chinese Night and Mexican Night, all of which are guaranteed to delight the appetite. The employees here are a close-knit family. Thelma Best, the 75-year old baker, lives up to her reputation when people taste her freshly baked treats. She continues to bake her homemade pies and breads and also makes delicious soup.

If a guest is celebrating a birthday, Shelley will generously deduct one percent for each year from the check. The combination of a friendly atmosphere, reasonable prices, and superior quality make the Clay Street Inn a "Best Choice."

THE OLD TAVERN
Rt 48 at County Road Lane
Unionville, Ohio 44088
Tel: (216) 428-2091
Hrs: Monday - Saturday 11:00 a.m. - 9:00 p.m.
Brunch:
Sunday 9:00 a.m. - Noon
Dinner:
Sunday Noon - 7:00 p.m.
Visa, Mastercard and American Express are accepted.

A visit to Unionville's Old Tavern is a trip back in time. Built in 1798, the Old Tavern has retained the qualities of a colonial stagecoach stop. This classical restaurant was once a stop on the Underground Railroad for runaway slaves. While possessing all of the original qualities of years gone by, the Old Tavern serves some of today's finest foods. The homemade cuisine is second to none, and the service is consistent with the atmosphere.

The food at the Old Tavern is as reasonably priced as it is delicious. All the food is prepared in-house, and the meat is cut to order. Two of the house specialties are the Swiss Steak, and the Roast Long Island Duckling. Manager Steve Spaller suggests the famous corn fritters, prepared uniquely by the Old Tavern's professional staff. Dessert is a treat as well. Guests enjoy the homemade pies, bread pudding, and the deep dish apple cobbler. Any of the food can be enjoyed in one of six dining rooms. The entire restaurant is designed in 19th century decor. Six beautiful fireplaces are scattered throughout the building for an additional touch of class. The outside is just as beautiful as the inside. The grounds are landscaped to perfection. There is a gazebo which is perfectly suited for wedding ceremonies. The Old Tavern will go one step further, however, by whisking newlyweds away in an old-fashioned surrey. This spacious restaurant is the perfect size for any banquet, wedding, or private party.

Walking through the doors of the Old Tavern is an unforgettable 19th century experience. The antique furniture and quality service make it a choice dining location. Most guests come for the fantastic food, but just a tour through this historic landmark makes the trip worthwhile.

specialty shops

NOEMA GEMS
1788 Mill Street
Austinburg, Ohio 44010
Tel: (216) 275-3211
Hrs: Monday & Wednesday - Saturday
10:00 a.m. - 6:00 p.m.
Sunday Noon - 6:00 p.m.
Closed Tuesdays.
Visa and MasterCard are accepted.

One of the largest stone collections east of the Mississippi River is featured at Noema Gems, "the most interesting little side trip you may ever make."

Owners Ron and Mary Ann Schanfish provide two large rooms full of display cases holding loose stones, set jewelry, crystals, fossils, and a bookcase devoted to rocks and gems. A science room with black lights enables visitors to see fluorescent minerals and gems, and a kid's corner with specimens for young collectors create an interesting and educational experience.

Included in the collection are rare stones and fossils such as sapphire, Trilobite, Orthoceras, peacock rock crystals and clusters. Whale, dinosaur, and dolphin bones can also be found.

Noema Gems also features custom-made gemstone jewelry: rings, earrings, pendants, necklaces, belt buckles and tie clasps.

Wanting to provide something for young and old alike, the first Saturday of each month from April to October is a "Family Festival Day." Activities include outdoor displays, customer swap tables, gem mining, and available picnic tables for those wanting to spend the day there.

The gem mining is perhaps the most unusual aspect of Noema Gems. The mine is a heavily salted gemstone gravel excavation site where the rock hound can sort through tailings from mines all over the world at the cost of only $2. Amethyst, sapphire, beryl, aquamarine, tourmaline and Ohio flint are among the stones found in the mine.

Located approximately halfway between Cleveland and Erie, Noema Gems offers a close-up view of some of the World's most beautiful and rare gems. For the "Best Choice" in stones and gems, stop by Noema Gems in Austinburg.

wine

CANTWELL'S OLD MILL WINERY
403 South Broadway
Geneva, Ohio 44041
Tel: (216) 466-5560
Hrs: Summer:

Thursday	1:00 p.m. - Midnight
Friday - Saturday	1:00 p.m. - 1:00 a.m.
Sunday	1:00 p.m. - 5:00 p.m.
Winter:	
Friday - Saturday	1:00 p.m. - 1:00 a.m.
Sunday	1:00 p.m. - 5:00 p.m.

Visa, MasterCard and personal checks are accepted.

Cantwell's Old Mill Winery has been producing award-winning wines since its first crush. Officially dedicated as a historically significant building, the rustic charm, large brick fireplace, oak tables, high-backed chairs, and warm hospitality make for a pleasant visit, even for those who don't partake of wine.

Founded in 1986 by Paul and Peggy Cantwell, their son, Paul Jr., and Bill Turgeon, the operation produces 14 types of wine, from very dry red and whites to dessert wines. Wine burgers from the grill are offered to guests in summer, and cheese and meat trays, crackers, breads and snacks are always available. The Old Mill was erected in 1864 as a grist mill and supplied the feed and grain needs of the Geneva area into the 1960s. Its nostalgic charm is enhanced by hundreds of antiques and collectibles. Friday and Saturday nights feature entertainment, and there is a cozy fire in winter and an outside deck in summer. A turkey roast, a craft festival, a pig roast, an amateur wine contest and a clam bake are among the special events offered about every other month. A big jamboree at the end of September becomes a celebration for the entire town, with parades, food and entertainment.

Geneva is a very large recreational area, and the winery is only two miles off Interstate 90. Whether visitors prefer the historical aspect, the recreational offerings, the festivals or simply the pure pleasure of sampling fine wines, a trip to Cantwell's Old Mill Winery promises to be an award-winning experience.

FERRANTE WINERY
5585 Route 307
Geneva, Ohio 44041
Tel: (216) 466-6046
Hrs: Summer:

Monday - Thursday	Noon - 6:00 p.m.
Friday - Saturday	Noon - Midnight
Sunday	1:00 p.m. - 6:00 p.m.
Winter:	
Wednesday - Thursday	Noon - 5:00 p.m.
Friday - Saturday	Noon - Midnight
Sunday	1:00 p.m. - 6:00 p.m.

Visa and MasterCard are accepted.

Ferrante Winery is owned by Peter Ferrante and his wife, Josephine, who manage the business with the help of Nicholas and Valerie Ferrante. Out of a total of 100 acres, this family of vintners has planted 50 in Vinifera grapes, a variety which thrives in the climate around Lake Erie. The winery, restaurant and gift shop are housed in a wood-framed replica of an Old Country chalet.

Ferrante Winery produces more than 20 award-winning varieties of Vinifera, French-American and Lambrusca wines that cover the full flavor range from sweet through dry, including a complex Seyval Blanc, a light-bodied Jester's Blush and a dry, full-bodied DeChaunac. Wine tasting is always available in the gift shop, which also offers antiques and wine-related accessories, as well as the wines, grape juices and champagnes made at Ferrante Winery. Tastings are also a part of the winery tour, along with glimpses of winemaking secrets. Specially arranged tours feature wine "to go."

An unusual feature of Ferrante Winery is an Italian restaurant where guests can relax and enjoy live accordion music, a glass of wine and a delicious meal. The menu of pizza, pasta and veal dishes is augmented by changing house specialties. A large, working fireplace warms the atmosphere in winter while in summer a wine patio provides a splendid view of the surrounding vineyards. At Ferrante Winery, hearty foods, vintage wines and a beautiful setting take visitors back to the days of wine and roses.

HARPERSFIELD VINEYARD
6387 Route 307
Geneva, Ohio 44041
Tel: (216) 466-4739
Hrs: Tours are by appointment only.
Visa and MasterCard are accepted.

Wine lovers are not likely to find many Harpersfield Vineyard wines in restaurants or on store shelves these days. Because they are so popular, they sell out quickly. Lucky connoisseurs have tasted these remarkably elegant white wines and eagerly await each year's limited output.

Winemaker Wes Gerlosky and his wife, Margaret, pride themselves on making world class Chardonnays and sparkling white wines on their 50-acre fruit farm, 12 acres of which they have dedicated to grapes. Area winemakers consider Wes something of a purist because he makes wine for its own sake and puts quality ahead of all other considerations. Employing old French winemaking techniques, Wes and Margaret intentionally keep Harpersfield Vineyard's production small and concentrate on the temperamental Chardonnay grape because it has yielded the best wine.

Although Harpersfield Vineyard has no tasting room, it welcomes retail customers for tours and sales by appointment. Wine lovers should make a point of trying one of the vineyard's fine Chardonnays either at a nearby restaurant or at this impressive boutique winery.

OLD FIREHOUSE WINERY
5499 Lake Road
Geneva-on-the-Lake, Ohio 44041
Tel: (216) 466-9300
Hrs: May - October:
Seven days — Noon - 1:00 a.m.
Winter:
Friday — 5:00 p.m. - 11:00 p.m.
Saturday - Sunday — Noon - 8:00 p.m.
Visa and MasterCard are accepted.

When third-generation fireman Don Woodward helped Dave Otto and his mother, Joyce, opened Old Firehouse Winery in 1988, he found not only a new business venture but a fitting home for his extensive collection of fire fighting mementoes and paraphernalia. The three partners painstakingly restored the turn-of-the-century firehouse, saving it from almost certain doom. Lighting fixtures fashioned from antique brass fire extinguishers, fire helmets, and ladder-backed bentwood chairs fill the interior. From patios, decks and a gazebo, visitors are treated to a remarkable view of Lake Erie.

Eight fine wines fermented from locally grown grapes bear the Old Firehouse Winery label. Among the most popular are Firehouse Red, Niagara, Vidal Blanc, and Blush. Wine is available by the glass, the bottle, or the case. Tours of the facility describe the winemaking process and trace the building's incandescent history. The structure also houses a restaurant open during the summer season that features American cuisine, including homemade pizzas, and gourmet burgers. A gift shop stocks imprinted T-shirts, caps, glasses, and firehouse collectibles.

Apart from the mid-August Gaelic Fest and the Firemen's Roundup in June, Old Firehouse Winery offers a wide range of musical acts seven days a week during the summer, and on weekends through December. Good food, an intriguing atmosphere, and wines as memorable as a five alarm blaze, make Old Firehouse Winery an Ohio original.

ASHTABULA

Ashtabula Harbor was discovered by Moses Cleveland in 1796. A few years later, the town grew up around Bridge Street, which is still the center of life for "The Harbor." From the mid-1800s to the early 1900s, English, Irish, Scottish, Finnish, Italian and Swedish immigrants came to

Bridge Street to build ships and work in the port. Ashtabula Harbor was the busiest port on the Great Lakes in the late 1800s, and Bridge Street was the popular "red light" district-hotels, eating establishments, and, of course, brothels.

Bridge Street was originally served by a pontoon bridge built in 1850, which was replaced by a swing bridge built in 1889. Today's Bascule Lift Bridge was built in 1925. In addition, most of the buildings on Bridge Street built in the late 1800s are still in use today.

attractions

The Great Lakes Marine and U.S. Coast Guard Memorial Museum is devoted to the maritime history of Ashtabula and the Great Lakes.

The Ashtabula Heritage Museum is in the Hubbard House, built by Colonel William Hubbard in 1834. In the process of being restored, the house was once an underground railroad terminus.

Walnut Beach is a beautiful place to take a stroll while watching the sights and listening to the sounds of Lake Erie. Point Park offers a gorgeous view of the waterfront, and Lake Shore Park is the perfect place for a picnic in the shade.

events

The Blessing of the Fleet is held in the Harbor Area during the first weekend in June.

Harbor Days, the annual street fair, is held during the first weekend in August.

accommodations

CEDAR'S MOTEL
2015 West Prospect Road
Ashtabula, Ohio 44004
Tel: (216) 992-5406
1-800-458-2015 (For reservations)
Hrs: Open year-round.
Office open daily 7:00 a.m. - 11:00 p.m.
Reservations are appreciated.
Visa, MasterCard, American Express, Discover, Diners Club and Carte Blanche are accepted.

Conveniently located near Geneva-on-the-Lake, this premier motel offers some of Ashtabula's finest accommodations. Cedar's Motel provides 16 immaculate rooms that are beautifully furnished with knotty pine paneling, comfortable double beds, heat, air-conditioning, private baths, radios, alarm clocks, and color televisions that offer 11 cable channels including HBO, ESPN, and CNN.

The motel is eager to accommodate everyone and is fully accessible to handicapped persons. The rooms can be equipped with strobe light smoke alarms for hearing impaired guests. A non-smoking room is available and pets are welcome for a small fee. Guests are invited to use the motel's picnic area and gas grill. The Cedar Motel provides a first-rate fax service for business travelers.

Owners Janet and Dennis Pucci will gladly provide information about restaurants, shops, and other area attractions. The Puccis live in front of the motel, so they're always available to make guests feel special.

To locate the Cedar Motel from East I-90, take Route 11 North of Route 20. If traveling from West I-90, take Route 45 to Route 20.

The personal service is unbeatable, and the facilities are clean and beautifully maintained making the Cedar Motel a popular accommodation stop along the lakes.

apparel

LA PARLOUR
117 South Chestnut Street
Jefferson, Ohio 44047
Tel: (216) 576-1100
Hrs: October 1 - March 1:
Monday - Thursday 10:00 a.m. - 7:00 p.m.
Friday - Saturday 10:00 a.m. - 5:00 p.m.
March 2 - September 30:
Monday - Thursday 9:00 a.m. - 6:00 p.m.
Friday - Saturday 9:00 a.m. - 5:00 p.m.
Visa, MasterCard and layaway are accepted.

Kathy Crandall has always dreamt of helping other women look beautiful and she has made her dream come true through the purchase of a Victorian-style mansion that now houses two floors of clothing and accessories for women. Kathy has created "A Special Place to Shop" by restoring and rejuvenating a building that was in a state of deterioration. The lovely, feminine interior is now done in a rosy fashion--the arch opening in the main room has an original stencil pattern of roses above it; the gift wrapping paper is covered with roses; the lace curtains are held with rosettes; and simmering rose potpourri gives the shop a wonderful scent.

La Parlour has a reputation for offering beautiful things at reasonable prices. This brings folks from all over and once here their shopping spree begins on the porch where novelty items, baskets, and bathing suits (in season) are on display. Inside one finds sportswear in the main parlour along with an antique case full of jewelry from costume to handmade designer pieces. The next room has career apparel and leads to the fancy dresses and fitting rooms. Upstairs is the Tropical Room where a private tanning bed allows one to achieve a remarkable tan year-round. Work by local artists is available on this floor such as handpainted silk pillows, hand-carved boxes, stencil-design hoops, and paintings. The last room has a clawfoot tub containing lacy lingerie and fleecy novelty wear mixed with delicately-scented potpourri. Throughout the store, one can find antiques, handbags, scarfs, belts, hairpieces, Mary Kay cosmetics, and gift items. Kathy's shop additionally handles fashion shows and make-overs. La Parlour is a "Best Choice" for women shoppers and for men in search of the perfect gift for a female friend .

golf courses

CHAPEL HILLS GOLF COURSE AND DRIVING RANGE
3381 Austinburg Road
Ashtabula, Ohio 44004
Tel: (216) 997-3791
Hrs: April - November: Sun-up - Sun-down

Butch and Kathy Marofsky have been in business at the Chapel Hills Golf Course and Driving Range since 1986. The couple previously ran a golf course in Erie, Pennsylvania, and wanted the opportunity to own their own business.

Chapel Hills consists of 150 acres of wooded and open areas, which makes the course challenging. It is an 18 hole, par 72 course under 6,000 yards. Thirty-five power carts and golf clubs are available for renting and the Sport Shop has everything a golfer wants and needs.

The club house has a working fireplace and a snack bar that serves great sandwiches, pizza, beverages, and beer. A large pavilion can also be obtained for group and catered affairs. Phone-in tee time and golf packages are available with advanced scheduling and an all-grass driving range is also offered.

Kathy and Butch are most proud of the condition of the course and its landscape. The club house and new open porch overlooks the beautifully designed course, and the flower beds and ornamental shrubs add to the beauty.

Chapel Hills Golf Course is family owned and operated, and can be quite a challenge to almost any golfer. The rates are reasonable and several golf packages are available through the Holiday Inn Ashtabula. Butch and Kathy feel "There are no strangers here, just friends they haven't met." That friendly atmosphere plus the challenging, well-groomed greens keep many golfers returning to Chapel Hills.

points of interest

ASHTABULA ART CENTER
2928 West 13th Street
Ashtabula, Ohio 44004
Tel: (216) 964-3396
Hrs: Monday - Thursday 9:00 a.m. - 9:00 p.m.
Friday & Saturday 9:00 a.m. - 5:00 p.m.
Visa and MasterCard are accepted.

Founded in 1953, the Ashtabula Art Center is a multi-arts facility that offers classes and exhibitions in dance, drama, music, and visual arts. The Gallery displays, which change monthly, are composed of multi-media art, watercolors, sculpture, and acrylics. Visual art classes also include ceramics, weaving, and drawing. The works of local, regional, and national artists are on rotational display at the Center.

The Center also offers a highly acclaimed dance facility. The Dance Department conducts lessons in classical ballet, pointe, jazz, modern dance, tap, and creative movement. Dance fundamentals for children are taught as well. The Center's dance company, the Ashtabula Dance Theatre, holds several performances including "The Nutcracker", "Piano Concerto", "Cinderella", and "Bizet Variations".

The Music Department instructs people of all ages in guitar, voice, percussion, woodwinds, brass instruments, organ, and piano. Performances such as "Patchwork Dulcimer Players" and the "Good Life Singers" provide listening enjoyment for people of all ages. The Chamber Music series, Jazz Night, and Bluegrass Music Festival offer further entertainment opportunities for music lovers.

The Theatre Department's uniquely creative teaching methods make the Center's many annual productions incredibly popular. Comedy, drama, classics and musicals delight audiences and offer valuable experience to up-and-coming actors and actresses.

From I-90, take Exit 233 to Route 45 North; then follow Route 531 to 13th Street. Located in an ultra-modern building surrounded by a beautiful nature walk, this contemporary center provides the finest art instruction available. The Ashtabula Art Center caters to the individual interests and talents of each student and provides the flexibility of a full-range art facility

restaurants

COVERED BRIDGE PIZZA PARLOR & EATERY, 341 Center Street, Ashtabula, Ohio 44004; Tel: (216) 992-8155. The place to go for the most incredible pizzas with the freshest toppings.

LOU'S STAGE COACH
5205 Lake Road West
Ashtabula, Ohio 44004
Tel: (216) 964-7930

Hrs:	Lounge	Opens at 2:00 p.m.
	Dining Room	5:30 p.m. - 11:00 p.m.
	Friday & Saturday	5:30p.m. - Midnight

Visa and MasterCard are accepted.

When hungry travelers on Lake Road West come across a two-story, brown and beige building surrounded by ample parking, they are in luck. They have found Lou's Stage Coach, a family owned and operated business that has been serving top quality meals since 1952. When Rose Marie Hewins and her family bought this business, it was just a small snack shop but today it is one of the best restaurants in Ashtabula with a long-standing reputation in the community for the quality and service offered here.

Mary Boles has something to do with this excellent reputation--she has been the chef for 27 years. Preparing nothing in advance, Mary makes everything to order, guaranteeing freshness. This quality and preparation of ingredients plus the size and presentation of the portions keeps out of town guests coming back. Customers definitely like the reasonable prices, soft background music, and warm atmosphere presented by the friendly staff.

One of Lou's biggest sellers is a juicy two-pound T-Bone Steak. Other favorites include Lamb Chops, Veal & Cheese, BBQ Ribs, and Broiled Lobster Tail. Appetizers include Breaded Filet of Chicken Breast, Potato Skins, and an unusual one--Sauerkraut Balls. The Special Salad offered is a mix of lettuce, bacon, feta cheese, hot and green peppers, and the house dressing. A long list of wines including Ohio wines are available with meals. Customers can finish the meal with an after-dinner drink or dessert. This is an excellent place to hold a banquet with facilities upstairs available to accommodate such functions. Lou's Stage Coach is a "Best Choice" for generously portioned meals in a casual dining atmosphere.

wine

TANNERY HILL WINERY
3908 Tannery Hill Road
Ashtabula, Ohio 44004
Tel: (216) 997-1440

Hrs:	Friday and Saturday	9:00 a.m. - 5:00 p.m.

Tannery Hill Winery delivers delicate Ohio wines with names that just beg wine lovers to taste them. Golden Chablis, Cream Niagara, Pink Catawba, and Penchant taste as good as they sound, and visitors can sample by the glass or by the bottle at this modern winery.

Owner Jan David Aronson developed such a keen interest in winemaking while living in California that he took up manufacturing in 1985 while working full-time as a screen writer. Jan could not have written a story with a better ending; his 17 1/2 acre winery features a 4,500 square foot building, a 120 seat tasting room and some excellent wines. Next door, a 70,000 square foot antique store and flea market houses a gift shop and restaurant featuring Tannery Hill Winery products.

Jan invites visitors to taste the wines, tour the facilities, and talk about winemaking at Tannery Hill Winery. Visitors are sure to remember the fantastic scarlet red grand piano highlighted on stage in the tasting room and will want to take home a bottle or two of this winery's fine product.

CONNEAUT

Conneaut provides travelers with the wonderful breezes of Lake Erie, public boat ramps, great fishing for Walleye, bass, perch, catfish, and others. It also offers visitors a beautiful beach, many exciting activities and a piece of history, from downtown areas to City Hall, built in 1876, to the Conneaut Historical Railroad Museum.

attractions

The former New York Central Depot, built in 1900, is the home of the Conneaut Historical Railroad Museum. A step back into the history of railroads, it features memorabilia, a classic depot, a caboose, coal hopper and engine.

wine

BUCCIA VINEYARD
518 Gore Road
Conneaut, Ohio 44030

Tel:	(216) 593-5976	
Hrs:	Monday - Friday	10:00 a.m. - 6:00 p.m.
	Saturday	10:00 a.m. - Midnight

Buccia Vineyard is nestled in a beautiful country setting of tree and arbors near quaint, covered bridges. Seven other wineries are within 20 miles. Near Lake Erie where boating, fishing, and swimming abound, this intimate, family-operated winery has orchards in front and vineyards in back of the rustic, rough-hewn home. Buccia Vineyard has been developed with love, care, and a personal commitment to fine wine.

The Buccia family offer informal, educational tours of the four-acre development, which includes both cellar and vineyard. Summers bring fun-filled festivals to the vineyard, with steak grills, ox roasts, folk singers, and of course, wine. Such medal winners as Maiden's Blush are proudly served, as well as Vingnoles and Seyvals, produced from a French-American hybrid grape. During other times of the year, seasonal fruits accompanied by breads and cheeses are offered to complement the vintages. A tasting room featuring a high cathedral ceiling, rustic booths, latticework, large windows, and stained glass set the stage for leisurely sipping. An adjacent sleeping loft provides lodging for two persons--advance reservations are encouraged.

Children are welcome at Buccia Vineyard; they can entertain themselves on a small playground while parents tour. Non-alcoholic beverages are offered for the children's refreshment. A gift shop on the premises features crafts, quilts, woodcarvings, and stuffed toys. The entire Buccia family invites visitors to Conneaut to spend a delightful afternoon in a charming country setting.

MARKKO VINEYARD
Rural Delivery 2
Conneaut, Ohio 44030
Tel: (216) 593-3197
Hrs: Monday - Saturday 11:00 a.m. - 6:00 p.m.
Visa and MasterCard are accepted.

To A.W. Esterer of Markko Vineyard, the most important factor in good wine is good grapes, and Vitis Vinifera is a very good grape. In 1968, A.W. introduced the strain to Ohio with cuttings from the vines of Dr. Konstin Frank, "the father of Vinifera grapes." It's little wonder a statewide trend soon followed--in 1976, Markko Vineyard won the highest award for Chardonnay at the first National American Wine Competition. To this day, the vineyard prides itself on the nectar and fine quality of its Chardonnay.

Located on Lake Erie's south ridge, Markko Vineyard is a classical operation with ten acres planted in Johannisberg Riesling, Chardonnay and Cabernet Sauvignon grapes. Built in 1972, the winery building sports a decorative, gabled wood ceiling. The tasting room features a cast iron wood stove, detailed carvings, and a collection of antique bottles. Though Markko Vineyard does not have a gift shop per se, winery tours are offered. A special stop is made in the cellar, where each vintage is aged at a constant temperature, and oak barrels lend the wine a distinctive personality.

Special events at Markko Vineyard include the June blessing of the vines, and an "odds and ends" sale on the third Saturday in September, with food, music, hayrides, and fine reserve vintages available for sale to the public. At Markko Vineyard, the time-honored traditions of European wine-making create classic American wines.

ANDOVER

antiques

THE SWAP SHOP
Route 7 South
Andover, Ohio 44003
Tel: (216) 293-7661
Hrs: Tuesday - Sunday 10:00 a.m. - 6:00 p.m.
Closed Mondays.

The Swap Shop, owned by John and Clara Campbell, opened in 1981, and is actually one large barn that is stocked full of a wide assortment of antiques and collectibles. John and Clara's desire for collecting and refinishing antique furniture and working with wood prompted them to get started. Since they have such an abundance of items, chances are that if a certain item can't be found, they'll still be able to locate it. John and Clara are both very outgoing, friendly people who enjoy chatting with, and making new friends at the Swap Shop.

A partial listing of what is available at the Swap Shop includes new and used furniture such as antiques, couches, overstuffed chairs, tables, cabinets, hutches, lamps, and chests with drawers. Also, there are pictures, glass items, mattresses, bed frames, mirrors, dressers, rockers and baby cribs.

The Swap Shop has a reputation for fine quality restoring, repairing, and refinishing work. John guarantees all the work that is performed. Additional services include custom glass cutting for windows, tables and pictures. Short and long distance U-Haul rental is also available. Free gum and candy is given to all of the children who come in with their parents. The Swap Shop, which is located at the edge of town, has ample parking.

KINGSVILLE

libraries

KINGSVILLE PUBLIC LIBRARY
6006 Academy Street
Kingsville, Ohio 44048
Tel: (216) 224-0239
Hrs: Monday - Wednesday 10:00 a.m. - 8:00 p.m.
Thursday - Saturday 10:00 a.m. - 5:00 p.m.

The Kingsville Public Library is more like a full-service community center than an ordinary library. It offers a large meeting room that is open to the general public, and a full range of audiovisual equipment and accessories, video cassette recorders, audio tapes, records, projectors, electronic keyboards, and typewriters, that are available for rental. The library also rents out a Santa suit.

Opened more than a century ago, the Kingsville Public Library started out with only 500 books and has grown into a 30,000-book library that provides a number of community services, such as book delivery to housebound people, nursing home patients and mentally-handicapped citizens.

The library actively encourages children to read, too. There's a special section of the building set aside for children's books and weekly story readings; pre-schoolers are invited to attend four story hours per week.

The librarian issues books to first, second, and third-graders each week. In the summer, the library offers a special reading program for children in grades one through six.

Another of the perks at this unique library is the delicious coffee, which is always freshly brewing for patrons. The Kingsville Public Library is for those who are tired of being 'shushed' for talking at the local library--its atmosphere is warm and friendly, not cold and silent. The building that currently houses the library was built in 1894 and moved from Main Street to its present site in 1918. It has three large rooms and will soon have an additional room for reference books.

The library sponsors annual community events, such as the "Friends of the Library Market," which features antiques, food, crafts, and entertainment. In addition to providing special activities, the library fosters community pride. It is filled with Kingsville High School trophies and team photos.

For the centennial celebration, the library built a gazebo and Public Address System in the park. The library has yet another claim to fame. In 1974 it was the setting for the movie, Dark Side of the Harvest Home, which starred Bette Davis and Dan Akroyd.

Take I-90 to the North Kingsville Exit and turn right. Located at the center of the park, the library is a white, one-story building with large bay windows.

restaurants

COVERED BRIDGE PIZZA PARLOR AND EATERY
6541 South Main Street
North Kingsville, Ohio 44068
Tel: (216) 224-0497
Hrs: Sunday - Thursday 11:00 a.m. - Midnight
Friday - Saturday 11:00 a.m. - 1:00 a m.

The Covered Bridge Pizza Parlor and Eatery is an authentic, 1800s, covered bridge restored by owner Gary Hewitt. Hewitt purchased the bridge in 1972 for $5, dismantled it, preserved the wood, and reconstructed it into its original state as it stood in 1862.

Now as a pizza parlor and eatery, patrons enjoy pizzas, sandwiches, spaghetti, soups, and salads within an early American atmosphere. Despite the atmosphere, however, it is the modern conveniences which go into preparing the vast menu. Dough made daily goes into every Covered Bridge pizza. Pizzas range from nine inches to 16 inches and include such favorites as Daring Garlic Pizza, healthy whole wheat pizza, tempting taco pizza and satisfying stromboli. Top these or other pizzas with any of their 12 toppings and add salads, soups, chili, 11 different sandwiches, or spaghetti with meatballs or meat sauce, and it makes for a truly unique dining experience amid 1862 construction.

Regular customers travel from 60 miles away to taste their favorite thin or thick white or wheat crusted pizza. Family night specials grace the menu Mondays and Tuesdays, as do spaghetti night specials on Wednesdays. The friendly family atmosphere makes for a quiet meal which enhances the rustic surroundings. A gift shop area features Covered Bridge coins and spoons, T-shirts, artwork, and books.

Normally one does not correlate covered bridges with pizza; however, after experiencing the North Kingsville, Andover or Ashtabula Covered Bridge Pizza Parlor and Eateries, covered bridges may never seem the same.

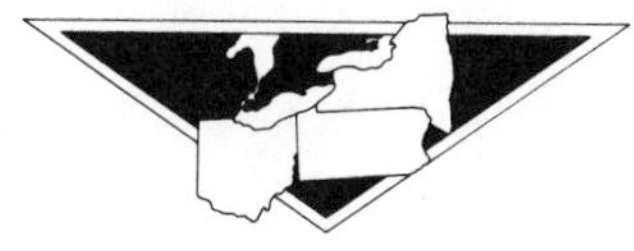

SECTION TWO: LAKE ERIE COAST PA.

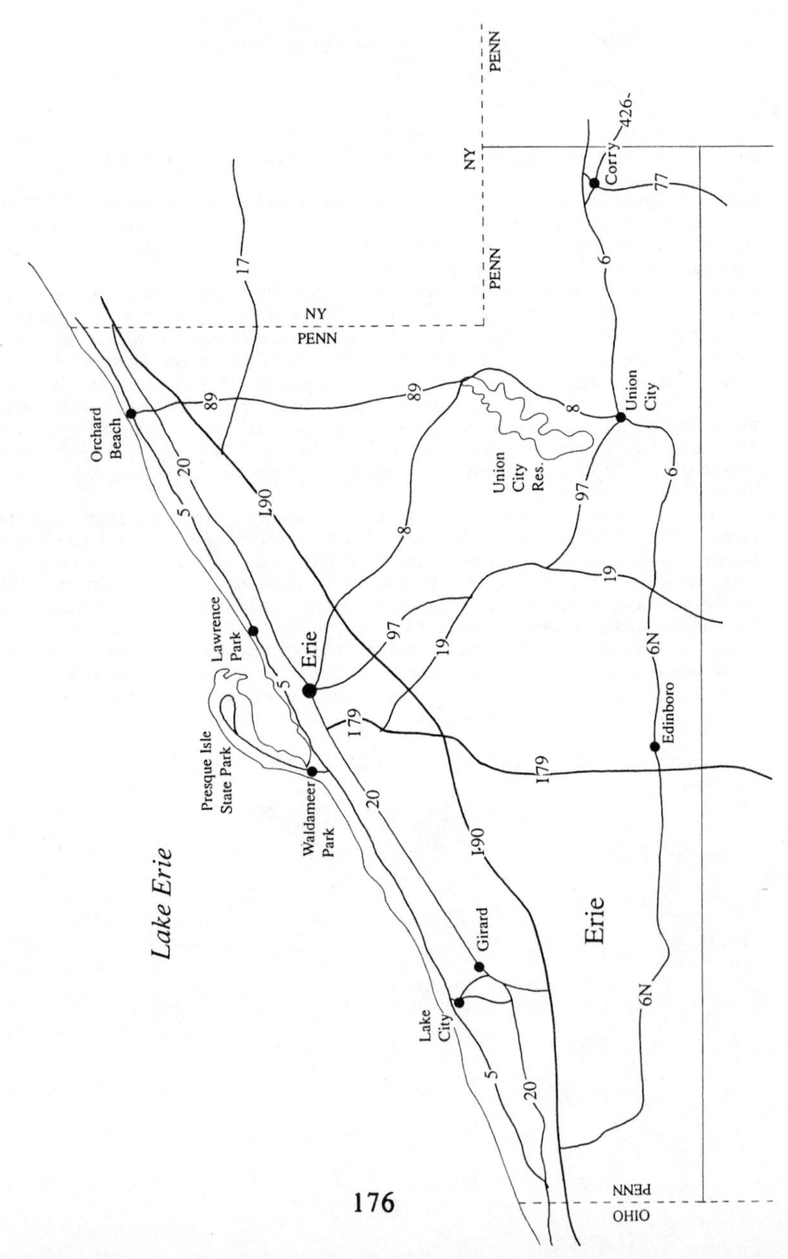

ERIE COUNTY

LAKE ERIE: A VICTORY FOR SPORT FISHING

by Mike Bleech

Within two decades, Lake Erie has changed from one of the most shameful examples of mankind's disrespect for nature to one of the best sport fishing holes in the world. Pennsylvania now enjoys a thriving charter fishing boat industry: marinas and boat launching facilities are generally filled to capacity. Anglers are coming off the water with their ice chests filled with walleyes, smallmouth bass, yellow perch, trout and salmon. Yet, many people across the country, even within Pennsylvania, erroneously believe the lake is dead. Oh, what they are missing!

The revival of Lake Erie is relatively new, but problems plaguing the lake have been around for decades. The problems began early in the 19th century when the lake shore first underwent development. Streams were polluted, adjacent wetlands were drained, and shallow lake waters near tributaries were polluted. This seriously damaged the spawning areas of many of the fish. Dams built on tributaries led to the congestion of fish that migrated from the lake into those streams, and the fish were soon decimated by commercial fishing operations. Fish in the open lake were not threatened until the twine gill net and pound net were introduced in the mid 1800s. The commercial fishing catch peaked in the late 1800s as commercial fishing efforts increased and improved fish populations in the lake declined. Interest in sport fishing on Lake Erie also increased at this time.

The first half of the 20th century was even more devastating to Lake Erie than the previous century had been. The nylon gill net was introduced. Rainbow smelt invaded the lake from a planting in the Lake Michigan drainage. Alewives, white perch and the parasitic sea lamprey entered by way of man-made canals. These immigrants displaced native fish. Pollution accelerated. By the 1950s, the native lake trout and blue pike were gone. Muskellunge, whitefish, lake herring, and sturgeons were reduced to insignificant numbers. The blue pike became one of the rallying cries for environmentalists. This slightly smaller relative of the walleye has been the mainstay of both sport and commercial fishing in Lake Erie, and it existed only in Lake Erie. But it exists no more!

In the 1960s, Lake Erie was reduced to the butt of environmental jokes, and was called a dead lake. Proclamations of its death were premature, however. Pollution was indeed extensive, but it was primarily localized. Cleanups were initiated all around the lake. Through cooperation between New York, Pennsylvania, Ohio, Michigan, and Ontario, Canada, and assistance by the lake's relatively fast flush rate, by the late 1960s the fishery was recovering. In the beginning, the recovery program for the lake garnered much attention when coho salmon were first stocked in the late 1960s and again in the early 1970s when larger Chinook salmon were introduced.

The Lake Erie salmon program has not yielded the consistent results as seen in the other Great Lakes; however, the salmon are an important part of the sport fishery, and there is no health advisory against eating them, as is the case in other lakes. Pennsylvania stocks about a million cohos and about

50,000 Chinooks each year. Most cohos caught by anglers are in the five to 10 pound range, while the hard-fighting Chinooks might weigh more than 20 pounds. Salmon are caught regularly, though not in great numbers, by offshore anglers during the summer months. The fish generate the most excitement when making their annual migrations into tributary streams beginning in September and continuing through mid-October. During the fall migration, salmon are caught by trolling in the lake near the tributary mouths and by casting from the beach and in the creeks. The most popular lures are brightly-colored spoons. The fall salmon run is enhanced by steelhead that enter the tributaries about the same time. Steelhead, which are migratory rainbow trout, follow the salmon into the creeks to feed on salmon eggs. Some will spend the entire winter in the tributaries. Another big part of the offshore catch is the lake trout. The U.S. Fish and Wildlife Service is attempting to re-establish a self-sustaining population of lake trout, with fish raised at the nearby Allegheny National Fish Hatchery.

Walleyes have become the headline fishing attraction at Lake Erie since the early 1980s, when anglers located vast schools of big walleyes in the deep offshore water. Walleyes are caught in shallower water, closer to shore, from early May through late June.

The offshore summer fishing in Pennsylvania's Lake Erie water must be rated among the top freshwater sport fishing in the world! Catches include an exciting mixture of big walleyes, steelhead, salmon and lake trout.

The peak of the smallmouth bass fishing occurs during the spring before the bass spawn. When the water begins to warm, the smallmouths move into relatively shallow water and feed aggressively. Jigs are the favorite artificial lures among casters and drifters. Yellow perch are also favorite targets for local anglers. These tasty panfish are caught year-round, in the lake and in Presque Isle Bay, a natural harbor bordered on the mainland by the city of Erie, which offers some additional fishing opportunities.

Ice fishing in the bay is outstanding; yellow perch make up the biggest part of the catch. Trout, salmon and northern pike provide good sport. Walleyes are caught less regularly. Crappies are active late in the ice fishing season, providing hot action near the head of the bay and in Horseshoe Pond.

Visitors to Lake Erie can get useful information from Travel and Convention Bureau, Greater Erie Chamber of Commerce, 1006 State Street, Erie, PA 16501.

ATTRACTIONS

An 1880s reconstruction of the **Anthony Wayne Blockhouse** commemorates Revolutionary War hero General "Mad" Anthony Wayne, who died from a fatal illness.

The Erie Historical Museum and Plantation in the **Watson/Curtze Mansion** offers exhibits on maritime history, regional history, and decorative arts. The museum is open Tuesday through Sunday, 1:00 p.m. to 5:00 p.m. The plantation offers shows Tuesday through Saturday at 2:00 p.m., and Sunday at 2:00 p.m. and 3:00 p.m. For more information call (814) 453-5811.

The Old Customs House/Erie Art Museum, a Greek Revival building, was the showplace of Erie when built in 1839. The museum offers changing exhibits of paintings, photography, drawing, ceramics, sculpture, and other media.

The Cashier's House, next door to the Old Customs House, is also a Greek Revival building dating from 1839. It features period furnishings and memorabilia of Erie's history, as well as a library and archives of the Erie Historical Society.

The Dickson Tavern, built in 1839, was also known as the "Perry Memorial House", one of Erie's finest inns for more than three decades. The tavern, once part of the Underground Railroad, is open for tours.

The Firefighters' Historical Museum, housed in Old Station House #4, displays more than 1,000 articles of memorabilia including an 1830 hand pumper and an 1886 hand-pulled horse cart.

The Land Lighthouse--the first on the Great Lakes--built in 1813 and reconstructed in 1867, overlooks the tip of Presque Isle peninsula. Although the lighthouse is no longer in use, the lighthouse keeper is on the premises to provide information about its history.

The Erie Playhouse was founded in 1914 and is the third oldest active community theater in the nation. The playhouse has consistently offered a wide selection of theater in the Strand Theater, ranging from musicals to drama.

Most of Erie's arts and entertainment performances, including the **Erie Ballet** and **Erie Philharmonic Orchestra** take place in the **Erie Civic Center Complex**. The three-facility complex includes the Louis J. Tullio Convention Center, the Warner Theatre, and the Exhibition Hall. The Warner Theatre is a designated National Historic Landmark.

Presque Isle State Park is a 302-acre sandy peninsula that juts seven miles into Lake Erie. The name Presque Isle, meaning "almost an island," was discovered and explored by the French in the 1600s. The natural harbor shielded the American fleet and Commodore Perry from detection by the British in 1812. Subsequently, the Americans defeated the British in the Battle of Lake Erie. Presque Isle became a popular recreational area in the lake 1800s and a state park in 1821. The park is open year-round, and offers a wide variety of recreational activities. Both non-powered and powered crafts are permitted, and boat rentals are available. The only surf swimming within Pennsylvania is available off the sandy beaches of the park. Water-skiing is permitted 500 feet offshore. Hunting is prohibited except for duck hunting in season. Seven miles of hiking trails meander through the area. Many picnic tables are situated throughout the park, and pavilions may be rented. Erie County is considered one of the top freshwater fishing areas in North America with abundant catches of perch, coho, smelt, walleye, rainbow trout, and bass in Lake Erie, and panfish, perch, bass, muskellunge, walleye, northern pike, crappie, smelt, and coho in Presque Isle Bay. Winter sports include ice fishing and ice-skating.

The peninsula was created more than a thousand years ago when the action of westerly winds, water currents, and waves on glacial sand caused a recurviong sand spit to form. Weather conditions continue to change its shape from year to year ant its location from decade to decade. During the last hundred years. Presque Isle has moved about a half mile to the east. On the isle, naturalists can find up to 318 species of birds and more than 500 species of flowering plants and ferns. The **Nature Center** displays the succession of the park's ecological cycles from the sand spit stage to the climax forest as well as displays depicting the park's inventory of birds, flora and fauna.

The **Perry Monument**, located in the Park, is dedicated to the men who fought and died in the Battle of Lake Erie.

The Erie Zoo is the second most popular tourist activity following Presque Isle. This 15-acre facility with more than 300 animals represents 75 to 90 species from six continents .

EVENTS

August is a busy month in Erie. Tpping the list is the **We Love Erie Days**, which offers stage performances, a 10-kilometer foot race, fireworks, and a food festival. For more information, call (814) 454-7191.

Next, in August, is **St. Paul's Italian Festival**. Tel: (814) 454-4270.

The holidays are celebrated in Erie with the **Festival of the Trees** in November. Tel: (814)452-5312.

ERIE

accommodations

HOLIDAY INN DOWNTOWN
18 West 18th Street
Erie, Pennsylvania 16501
Tel: (814) 456-2961

Conveniently located in the heart of Erie just five miles south of Presque Isle State Park, the Holiday Inn Downtown features spacious rooms, ample free parking, complementary transportation to and from the Erie Airport, and handicapped accessibility. Its banquet facilities will accommodate as many as 200 people. The Holiday Inn Downtown prides itself on its ability to serve the needs of contemporary travelers.

The hotel caters to the young at heart at Madeline's Restaurant and Lounge, featuring a Hungry Hour Buffet with complimentary hors d'oeuvres every Monday through Friday. Madeline's boasts a relaxed atmosphere with live music and a video disc jockey Tuesday through Saturday nights. The restaurant features American cuisine that includes lighter fare for those watching their waistlines and standard favorites like steak, shrimp, veal, fish and chicken dishes.

Guests at the Holiday Inn Downtown enjoy the outdoor pool, open from May until September; free Showtime movies, plus additional satellite services; guest privileges at the Pennbriar Athletic Club; and discount coupons for the nearby Giant Wavepool. Guests who like to shop enjoy the convenience of the Holiday Inn's location across the street from the Erie Factory Outlet Mall. Other attractions include the Erie Zoo, which is two miles away; many Pennsylvania wineries located within 10 miles; and the Erie Civic Center just 10 blocks from the hotel.

HOLIDAY INN SOUTH
Exit 7, Route 90
Erie, Pennsylvania 16509
Tel: (814) 864-4911
Visa, MasterCard and American Express are accepted.

The Holiday Inn South invites travelers to enjoy the enticing atmosphere and fine dining experience offered in their famous Greenhouse Restaurant. The inn's Greenhouse Lounge features live entertainment from Tuesday through Saturday nights with happy hour and a raw bar from 5:00 p.m. to 7:00 p.m., Monday through Friday.

A special part of Holiday Inn South's services is the complementary use of the new Pennbriar Athletic Club. The club offers a 25-meter indoor swimming pool, a nautilus facility, a running track, tennis and racquetball, sauna and whirlpools, an indoor driving range, suntanning lounges, and aerobics classes. The club provides free parking.

The Holiday Inn South offers complete meeting and banquet facilities for as many as 450 people. This hotel is conveniently located near the Mill Creek Mall, Northeast Vineyards and the beaches of Presque Isle.

QUALITY HOTEL PLAZA
10th and State Street
Erie, Pennsylvania 16501
Tel: (814) 459-2220
Visa, MasterCard, American Express, Discover, Carte Blanche and Diners Club are accepted.

Quality is an attitude and the new Quality Hotel Plaza has it. The designers and managers of the Quality Hotel Plaza ask the question, "What does our community want?" The answer is, the community wants a lot and Quality Hotel Plaza is there to fill the need. The owners of Quality Hotel Plaza have decided a cornerstone downtown hotel should emanate a quiet elegance that welcomes the guest with tasteful color and an inviting ambiance, excellent service, fine dining, complete corporate facilities, entertainment opportunities and, of course, the best in sleeping comfort.

Formerly a Hilton Hotel, Quality Hotel Plaza has undergone extensive remodelling. The new feel is immediately noticeable as guests enter the spacious, redecorated lobby and encounter the genuinely gracious welcome at the front desk. The guest rooms are designed with comfort in mind and include all the amenities one would expect from a quality conscious hotel. Fine dining is available in The Hunt Room. Selections range from simple to simply elegant, and the menu variety is sure to please any palate. Casual dining is found in the The Garden Coffee Shop with its airy surroundings and lush, hanging greenery. Guests enjoy relaxing in the luxurious indoor pool. Saunas and a fully-equipped exercise room complete visitors' physical fitness needs. Guests can kick up their heels in Billy's Saloon for an evening's entertainment or relax in The Bagatelle, an adult video arcade with pool table, games, and a lounge atmosphere.

Quality Hotel Plaza is the leader in the region for accommodating groups from 10 to 1,100 people. The Grand Ballroom offers an elegant backdrop for weddings, banquets, and major meetings. Quality Hotel Plaza is a block-and-a-half away from the Tullio Convention Center. Ask for the hotel's detailed convention planning guide; corporate and group rates are available. An "Inn Crowd Club" is offered to frequent travelers. Every community deserves a great hotel, and Quality Hotel Plaza has risen to the occasion.

apparel

HAMPSHIRE MILLS, 4453 West Ridge Road, Erie, Pennsylvania; Tel: (814) 838-7514. Shoppers can save as much as 50 percent on today's most popular sportswear.

bed & breakfast inns

ZION'S HILL
9023 Miller Road
Cranesville, Pennsylvania 16410
Tel: (814) 774-2971

Dan Rice, trainer of the famed circus elephant, Hannibal, once lived at Zion's Hill. Built in 1830 by a wealthy land agent, this lovely bed and breakfast carries on the rich traditions from which it originated.

Zion's Hill sits on a knoll surrounded by majestic maples, a small orchard, and a variety of gardens. This historic, Colonial-style mansion is part of Carriage Hill Farm, a working farm that offers carriage and sleigh rides, nature hikes, and cross-country skiing. Guests will enjoy the farm and carriage museum on the property. Rooms at the bed and breakfast feature elegant Victorian furnishings, and two staircases access the second floor, which is divided into two separate sections. In the morning, guests receive a continental breakfast consisting of coffee or milk, fresh seasonal fruit, juice, fresh Danish pastries, and a choice of cereal or toast and jellies.

Guests should ask about the hiding places incorporated into the home's framework for the former master's protection. Rich in history, Zion's Hill affords guests the opportunity to learn firsthand about 19th century America.

charters

PBLBAK CHARTERS
344 East Sixth Street
Erie, Pennsylvania 16507
Tel: (814) 544-7594
Hrs: Season runs from April to October.
Call for specific hours.

No visit to Erie County would be complete without sampling some of the finest walleye pike fishing available anywhere.

Phenomenal numbers of walleye are caught each year off Pennsylvania's lake coast. Captain Fred Morosky has the knowledge, skill,and equipment needed to make half-day or full-day fishing charter successful. A 20-year, U.S. Coast Guard licensed captain, Fred guarantees a safe and pleasurable day on the lake. In addition to walleye, Lake Erie is the home to plentiful perch, bass, salmon, and lake trout. The 28-foot fishing boat, PBLBAK (pronounced "rib-bok" and means fisherman in Russian), is appointed with the latest in electronic equipment to aid in locating fish, as well as the latest safety and fire equipment. Trolling for lunker walleye or still fishing for perch, one is bound to remember a visit to Lake Erie for years to come.

The PBLBAK is available for non-fishing charters as well. If looking for a unique setting for a business meeting, a sightseeing tour of Presque Isle, or a romantic moonlit cruise, Fred Morosky and the PBLBAK are a "Best Choice" on Lake Erie.

gift shops

ALLEN STONEWARE
1758 West 8th Street
Erie, Pennsylvania 16505
Tel: (814) 459-4013
Hrs: Monday - Friday 10:30 a.m. - 5:00 p.m.
Saturday 10:30 a.m. - 4:00 p.m.
Other hours are by appointment.
Visa and MasterCard are accepted.

At Allen Stoneware, patrons can enjoy the rare treat of dealing directly with the artisan who creates the stunning wares displayed throughout the shop. Artist/potter Vicki Allen owns and operates the business, and the shop's distinctive collection represents her prolific output.

Allen Stoneware's bright, sunny gallery illuminates Vicki's diverse work, which includes plates, mugs, pitchers, lamp bases, picture frames and more. Although her work is sold wholesale and retail nationally, all of Vicki's creations are signed and dated, an added bonus to collectors. Vicki also custom designs such stoneware pieces as wedding and baby plates and will personalize any purchase with custom printing. All of the stoneware is lead-free and safe for the dishwasher, oven and microwave. A visit to the gallery will most likely find the owner practicing her craft at the potter's wheel.

Through demonstrations, Allen Stoneware affords visitors a rare glimpse into the process of creating functional pieces of art. Everyday usage, such as serving food or displaying a cherished picture, enhances the personal value of these beautiful pieces, making them all the more precious. More than crafting stoneware, Vicki Allen creates family treasures.

restaurants

LOU BIZZARRO'S RINGSIDE RESTAURANT
3202 Sterrettania Road
Erie, Pennsylvania 16506
Tel: (814) 838-9168
Hrs: Summer:
Monday - Thursday 11:00 a.m. - 11:00 p.m.
Friday - Saturday 11:00 a.m. - 1:00 a.m.
Winter:
Monday - Thursday 11:00 a.m. - 10:00 p.m.
Friday - Saturday 11:00 a.m. - 1:00 a.m.

At Lou Bizzarro's Ringside Restaurant, diners get more than a fine Italian meal. They might be able to persuade Lou, originally of Marcianasa, Italy, to talk about his boxing days, especially his biggest fight--14 rounds with Roberto Duran. Since hanging up his gloves to join his family in creating the Ringside Restaurant, Lou has become locally famous for some of the best homemade meatballs, wedding soup, and sauces in Erie.

Boxing memorabilia covers the walls of the cozy, softly lit dining room with its brown and white checkered tablecloths. Guests are likely to be served by a member of Lou's family; his children, nieces, and nephews all work in the restaurant, cooking, waiting tables, and bartending. Keeping the menu simple allows the staff to concentrate on preparation. Aside from meatballs and wedding soup, the homemade ravioli, rigatoni, and manicotti are also delicious, as are the veal and eggplant parmigiana, and linguini prepared in traditional style with olive oil and garlic, anchovies or clam sauce. Canoli, Italian rum cake, and Italian cheesecake make for a knockout finish.

The bar at Lou Bizzarro's Ringside Restaurant offers fine liquors, and for its modest size, the restaurant has an impressive wine list. The prices are refreshingly low, and a children's menu is available. After lunch or dinner, guests might want to purchase a T-shirt or a sweatshirt with the Ringside boxing glove logo printed on it--a fitting memento of a championship meal.

THE BUOY
4 State Street
Erie, Pennsylvania 16507
Tel: (814) 459-0617
Hrs: June through September:

	Monday - Thursday	5:00 p.m. - 10:00 p.m.
	Friday - Saturday	5:00 p.m. - 11:00 p.m.
	Sunday	4:00 p.m. - 8:00 p.m.

Visa, MasterCard, American Express, Diners Club, Discover and Carte Blanche are accepted.

Oh, the stories these walls can tell of barks and boards and epicures. The Buoy invites wayfarers and gourmets to the delights of the table and the tale of its domain. The Buoy's round building sets easy on the edge of the bay and is made with lumber grained with years of history.

Restaurateur Vince Worster tells the story of how The Buoy boards traveled from the once great forests of 1890 New York to the walls of the Great Pan American Exhibition of 1899, then to a New York turn-of-the-century dairy barn, and finally came to complete his Erie restaurant. Today, the weathered planks make walls for original oil paintings of nautical scenes and hold artifacts of the lakes. And, even more, they embrace the spirit of friends gathered together for good food, drink, and company.

The good food of The Buoy starts with things to whet any appetite, such as The Buoy's Dublumes, langostino sauteed in sherry and served on wild rice. Seafood selections include deep fried Lake Erie perch and bouillabaisse made with shrimp, crab legs, clams, scallops, scrod and slipper lobster, served in a saffron broth with garlic bread. The Split Cargo menu choice offers the extra special stuffed filet mignon with crabmeat. A sweet conclusion to the meal comes as The Buoy Pecan Ball, an ice cream scoop rolled in pecans and topped with hot fudge and whipped cream.

The Buoy invites diners to follow the beacon light that leads to tall tales, good food and fellowship.

DRY DOCK/THE HOLD
3122 West Lake Road
Erie, Pennsylvania 16505
Tel: (814) 833-6135
Hrs: Restaurant:

Hrs:	Restaurant:	
	Seven days	11:30 a.m. - 10:00 p.m.
	Bar:	
	Tuesday - Saturday	4:00 p.m. - 2:00 a.m.

Visa, MasterCard and American Express are accepted.

Formerly known as Barnacle Bill's, Dry Dock restaurant and its bar, The Hold, were built over the years from actual pieces of several ships, some of which were 150 years old. Moved, rebuilt, and renovated many times, this unique establishment retains a seafaring ambiance throughout; portholes, wooden ship models, polished round tables, captain's chairs and nautical antiques adorn the handsome interior.

The Dry Dock is locally acclaimed for its award-winning Red Snapper Soup, a delicious prelude to the restaurant's sumptuous fish and seafood dinners. A limited supply of Alaskan King Crabs and South African lobster tails is kept on hand for special occasions. Breads, pastas, and pasta sauces are made fresh on the premises. Pasta Jambalaya, Seafood Provencal, and Pasta Pavarotti are but a few of the memorable pasta creations. Aged custom-cut steaks and chicken and veal dishes delight the landlubber's palate, and a creative selection of appetizers, soups, salads, and desserts rounds off the menu's tempting offerings. The restaurant's banquet facilities will easily accommodate most celebrations.

Restaurant patrons enjoy soft music, while live entertainment is featured downstairs in The Hold on Friday and Saturday nights. An extensive seafood bar is a highlight at Happy Hour. A timeless nautical atmosphere and sterling cuisine make Dry Dock and The Hold a Lake Erie legend.

PUFFERBELLY ON FRENCH STREET
414 French Street
Erie, Pennsylvania 16507
Tel: (814) 454-1557

Hrs:	Monday - Thursday	11:00 a.m. - 10:00 p.m.
	Friday - Saturday	11:00 a.m. - Midnight
	Sunday	11:00 a.m. - 7:00 p.m..

Visa, MasterCard and American Express are accepted.

Although this restaurant's name seems to refer to what happens when one eats too much of the good food here, "pufferbelly" actually refers to the steam powered fire engines of the late 1800s. That may sound like an unusual name for a restaurant, but it makes sense when patrons discover Pufferbelly offers the unusual experience of dining in a restored turn-of-the-century firehouse.

The restaurant stands as a tribute to generations of brave fire fighters who served to save life and property. It is filled with fire fighting memorabilia and equipment, including an old hand pumper that stands in the hallway. Door handles are all made of brass fire hose nozzles. The food is also special. The management makes a special effort toward staying current with the season and on top of creative food trends. As a result, diners will find an eclectic selection of tasty items on the menu. The fare does not include any deep fried foods or any that look as though they had been pre-portioned for an assembly line. The culinary staff prepares everything from scratch. Pufferbelly goes out of its way to prepare out-of-the-ordinary salads. Try one with a Bloody Mary, Vermouth, or cheese dressing. Favorite dinner entrees include the Breast of Chicken Pufferbelly, which is breaded in Parmesan cheese, pan fried, and served on a bed of creamy fettucccine; the dish also includes a tossed salad. The sirloin strip steak is a 12-ounce steak custom cut from the heart of the loin.

On top of all this, the service is excellent. All of these features have made it a popular gathering place for young professional people. And it is just the kind of place visitors can get all fired up about.

ZOOS

THE ERIE ZOO, 423 West 38th Street, Erie, Pennsylvania; Tel: (814) 864-4091. The Erie Zoo consists of a 15-acre park with more than 300 animals exhibited in their natural habitats. A picnic area is provided.

NORTH EAST

accommodations

SOUTH SHORE INN

1120 Freeport Road, Route 89
North East, Pennsylvania 16428
Tel: (814) 725-1888
Hrs: Lunch:

Lunch:	Monday - Friday	11:00 a.m. - 2:00 p.m.
Dinner:	Monday - Saturday	4:00 p.m. - 9:00 p.m.
	Sunday	Noon - 6:00 p.m.

Visa and MasterCard are accepted.

Located in the heart of North East's grape country is one of the city's first wineries. Built in 1840, South Shore Inn has enjoyed a diverse past. Today, this historic landmark sports a reputation as a fine dining establishment and is a credit to its owner, Patricia Cook, her family, and chef, Donald Donnelly.

The house specialties consist of veal and seafood entrees with the most popular veal dish being Veal Neptune, a dish of sauteed slices of tender veal topped with scallops, crab, and shrimp in a light Mornay sauce. Seafood enthusiasts will enjoy the South Shore Platter, a combination plate of broiled scallops, clams casino, Boston scrod, king crab, and shrimp. The menu also features a selection of standard beef and chicken dishes, fettuccine, and Oriental entrees.

Nestled amid a large grape vineyard, South Shore Inn retains much of its past ambiance and heritage. Upon entering, patrons enjoy a feeling of warmth and friendliness. Each room is spacious with wood plank flooring and a beautiful fireplace; a wide stairway serves as the inn's centerpiece. In addition, banquet facilities can accommodate functions for as many as 250 people, and eight fully-remodeled rooms are available upstairs for short-term rentals.

charters

SOUTHWIND CHARTERS, P.O. Box 711, North East, Pennsylvania; Tel: (814) 725-1357. "A bad day's fishing is better than a great day's work," says Captain Thomas "Barney" Barnes. Fully equipped and Coast Guard approved, Southwind will see to your every fishing need for catching walleye, lake trout, or salmon in Lake Erie. Early reservations are recommended.

restaurants

DELHURST COUNTRY INN
10120 West Main Road, Route 20
North East, Pennsylvania 16428
Tel: (814) 725-1363
Hrs: Restaurant:
Tuesday - Saturday 11:30 a.m. - 9:00 p.m.
Sunday 10:30 a.m. - 5:00 p.m.
Green House Tavern:
Tuesday - Sunday 4:00 p.m. - Midnight
Visa, MasterCard, American Express and Discover are accepted.

Original antique sleighs, carriages, and brass lanterns lend a warm and rustic air to the Delhurst Country Inn. The fully restored 1835 building houses a restaurant that specializes in hearty portions of tasty fare at reasonable prices.

Famous for succulent beef dishes, especially prime rib, the Delhurst Country Inn prides itself on the tenderness and flavor of its entrees. The restaurant also offers a fine selection of veal, pasta, poultry, and seafood cuisine. On Sundays, the prime rib buffet attracts a hungry following, and on Friday and Saturday evenings, the main dining area features live piano music. Customers may order libations from one of three fully stocked bars and may enjoy their food and refreshments on the outdoor patio, in the tavern, or in the greenhouse room. The restaurant also boasts full banquet facilities with a seating capacity for up to 500 people.

Customers can count on great service as well as excellent food at the Delhurst Country Inn. With its attentive and efficient wait staff, the restaurant welcomes both large and small groups and provides handicap access.

wine

HERITAGE WINE CELLAR, 12162 East Main Road, North East, Pennsylvania; Tel: (814) 725-8015. Visit vineyards and a winery on a farm that has been family owned since 1833. A gift shop, tasting room and tours offer a fun and educational experience.

MAZZA VINEYARD
PENN SHORE WINERY
11815 Eastlake Road
North East, Pennsylvania 16428
Tel: (814) 725-8695
Hrs: Monday - Saturday 9:00 a.m. - 5:00 p.m.
Sunday Noon - 4:30 p.m.
July and August:
Monday - Saturday 9:00 a.m. - 8:00 p.m.
Visa and MasterCard are accepted.

Oriented toward fine wines produced from the grapes of French-American cross varieties, Mazza Vineyard has been offering excellent Pennsylvania vintages for more than a decade. Located in the famous Lake Side wine and fruit country of Lake Erie, easily accessible from Route 5 at exit 11, and from Interstate 90 East, Mazza Vineyard and Penn Shore Winery offer a pleasant day's diversion of connoisseur wine tasting.

Begun by the two Mazza brothers, Robert and Frank, the winery produces a variety of white and dessert wines. Using outstanding French-American cross grapes, sturdy enough for rugged Northeastern winters, yet with exceptional flavor and character, the brothers have created such popular wines as their Vidal Blanc, Seyval Blanc, and Cayuga. One of their newest products, Ice Wine, is produced from Vidal Blanc grapes left on the vine until late fall's freeze. The grapes are then gently pressed to collect a juice with nearly double the normal sugar content. The result is an exceptionally fruity, sweet wine with considerable finesse and a finish comparable to the best German Reislings. Mazza Vineyards also offers a series of very popular fruit wines including their famous Apple Spice Wine.

SECTION THREE: LAKE ERIE COAST N.Y

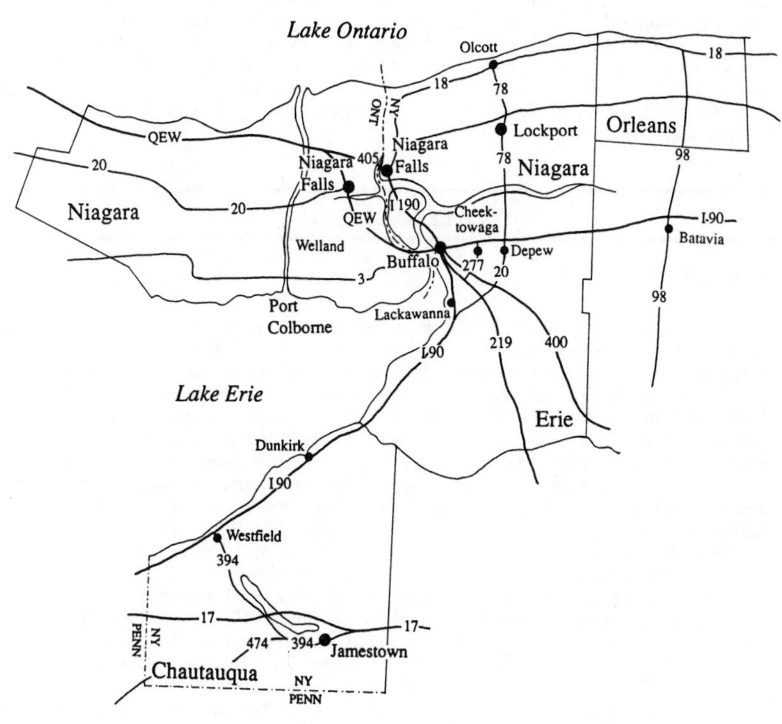

CHAUTAUQUA COUNTY

Created from Genesee County in 1808, the county was named from a Seneca word for "where the fish was taken out." French explorers landed on the Lake Erie shore in 1679 and blazed the Portage Trail from Lake Erie to Lake Chautauqua. Both the French and the English sought passage to the Ohio and Mississippi Rivers, leading both countries into war. The first recognized settler was Amos Cottle who settled at the mouth of the Cattaraugus Creek in 1797. The only Native settlement at the time was Conewango Creek, the site of present-day Carroll. Among the county's firsts include the first naval skirmish of the War of 1812, the country's first Grange, the first Women's Christian Temperance Union, and the first natural gas well.

Chautauqua County is famous for its wine industry, which dates back to the first plantings of Concord grapes in 1818. Approximately 20,000 acres of Chautauqua County is used for growing a large variety of grapes, from the fruity Labruscas and French-American wines to the European-style Chardonays and Rieslings.

attractions

Lake Erie State Park, situated along the lake, offers year-round recreational activities with an emphasis on the day-use facilities. Warm weather activities include hiking, biking, and nature trails; picnic tables and pavilions. Shoreline fishing yields abundant catches of walleye, smallmouth bass, and salmon. The swimming beach and lakeside campsites are very popular. Lake Erie also provides for some of the best boating recreation in the country. Winter activities include snowmobiling and cross-country skiing.

The Seaway Trail is a scenic driving route between Ripley and Rooseveltown, New York, along Lake Erie, Lake Ontario, and the St. Lawrence River. Stretching 474 miles, the marked trail follows an old shipping route with historical sites, unique natural features, and fishing sites.

Panama Rocks contains the most extensive outcrop of ocean quartz conglomerate in the world. The one-mile hiking trail winds past cavernous dens and passageways, crevices, and rocks up to 70 feet in height. Rare wildflowers, mosses, and ferns bloom throughout the spring and summer.

The Portage Trail follows the route used by the Indians traveling from Lake Erie to Chautauqua Lake. Beginning on Route 17, the trail goes south along country roads over moderately hilly terrain, passing Buttermilk Falls in the Little Chautauqua Creek Gorge. The trail ends in Mayville.

The Westside Overland Trail, part of the National Trail System, winds through state reforestation areas and county lands to Panama. There are several stream crossings and two lean-tos along the route.

The Conewango Creek is popular with canoeists. The 24-mile route crosses Chautauqua County from the Cattaraugus County line to the Pennsylvania border. There are access points and campsites along the route.

events

The Chautauqua County Fair is held in late July at the fairgrounds in Dunkirk.

antiques

STOCKTON SALES
6 Mill Street
Stockton, New York 14784
Tel: (716) 595-3516
Hrs: Tuesday - Saturday 10:00 a.m. - 5:00 p.m.
Sunday 1:00 p.m. - 5:00 p.m.
Closed Monday.
Closed Sundays from October through February.
Visa, MasterCard and American Express are accepted.

Stockton Sales has it all from antiques to general store items--something for everyone. Owners Dan and Carol Graziano gather merchandise from estates in New York, Pennsylvania and Ohio for sale in the unusual five-building shop.

The merchandise at Stockton Sales changes constantly, but visitors can count on finding one-of-a-kind items like oil paintings, vintage cars, depression glass, roseville glass, oriental rugs, brass hardware, taxidermy, gas lamp shades, fruit jars, victrolas, military items, and carousel horses.

Though Stockton Sales carries an overwhelming amount of collectibles and other intriguing merchandise, the store is amazingly well-organized. One of Stockton Sales' buildings is full of furniture; another houses new wooden spindles, floor-to-ceiling mirrors, and unfinished furniture. Visitors will find kitchen utensils, glasses, trays, dishes, and small appliances at another one of the five buildings. The last two buildings contain new and used appliances, such as autographed first-edition books, new and used specialty candles, antique linens, and a host of other delightful treasures.

Browsing through this store is a terrific way to spend a day, but as Dan and Carol warn, browsing without buying is almost impossible at this surprisingly diverse shop. Almost no one leaves without some exciting new treasure, whether it be a grand piano, a Chinese cradle, or an antique barber pole.

Visit Stockton Sales. There's nothing else quite like it.

country clubs

CASSADAGA LAKES COUNTRY CLUB
55 Frisbee Road
Cassadaga, New York 14718
Tel: (716) 595-3003
Hrs: Open to the public
Summer:
Seven days 7:00 a.m. - 2:00 a.m.
Winter:
9:00 a.m. - Dark

Originally an 1860 dairy farm, the Cassadaga Lakes Country Club underwent its transformation into a public golf course in 1931. The course has a gravel base that drains melted snow and rainwater from the course instantly. Because of this quick-draining base, the Club is always the first to open and the last to close the golf season. Cassadaga Lakes Country Club is a challenging nine-hole, 550-acre course with 15 sand traps and rolling greens.

Owners Jim and Judy Pavlik have over 20 years of experience in the golf business. Jim is a P.G.A. professional. He has been a host professional to a P.G.A. Senior tour event in Philadelphia, and is an experienced tournament player. Jim is available by appointment for private and group golf lessons.

The Pro Shop is fully stocked with Ping, Wilson, Titleist, Dexter, Aureus, and Foot Joy golf equipment. Clothing, gloves, hats, shoes, balls, clubs, pull carts, and gas carts are also available.

Cassadaga Lakes Country Club features a convivial clubhouse, a popular patio dining area, and a fully-licensed bar. Friday night Fish Fry is fantastic. Elegant indoor banquet and special occasion facilities seat up to 120 people.

With its top-condition course, well-stocked pro shop, plush bar, top-ranking golf professionals, and friendly on-site owners, the Cassadaga Lakes Country Club is a year-round recreation facility.

restaurants

GOOD MORNING FARM RESTAURANT & PUB
2 Hadley Road, Route 394
Stow, New York 14785
Tel: (716) 763-1773
Hrs: Memorial Day - Labor Day Weekend:
Open seven days.
Call for off-season hours.
Reservations are not necessary.
Visa, MasterCard and American Express are accepted.

Good Morning Farm Restaurant & Pub, located on Route 394 between Chautauqua and Bemus Point on Chautauqua Lake, is housed in a 19th century farmhouse that was previously owned by Hadley's Dairy Farm.

Robert Jay Ludwig purchased the farm 18 years ago. Though he has transformed the building into an elegant restaurant, he has preserved the casual, country farm atmosphere. Good Morning Farm offers diners a choice of five dining rooms decorated with dark wooden ceiling beams, green plants, and Chef Maritza Morgan's original artwork. An enormous outdoor deck adds to the rustic charm of this spacious 1849 farmhouse.

Good Morning Farm specializes in charcoal-grilled steaks, chops, chicken, seafood, burgers, and ribs. The smell of freshly baked bread, muffins, and desserts greets patrons as they walk through the door. Maritza, affectionately called "Grandma," prepares everything from scratch. Her delicious, brick-baked pastries are well-known throughout the region. Maritza and Bob are always on the lookout for special cuisine items with a country flavor, warranting their worldwide travel in search of exciting new recipes. The country cuisine is fantastic-from the Honey Half of Chicken to the Country-Style Scallops.

Don't forget dessert. Maritza prepares delectable Fresh Fruit Cobbler, Chocolate Peanut Butter Pie and two wonderfully unusual concoctions, Puddle Cake and Bowl of Sin.

Weekends are special at Good Morning Farm. On Saturdays and Sundays, the restaurant serves a mouth-watering brunch consisting of a country omelette, fresh fruit, coffee cake, and coffee or juice.

The country-style restaurant is not the only impressive attraction at Good Morning Farm. Frosty's Daiquiri Factory whips up exotic frozen drinks prepared from fresh fruits such as pineapples, bananas, peaches, and red raspberries, and garnished with hand-picked seasonal wild flowers.

In addition to offering many culinary delights, Good Morning Farm has a 10,000-square-foot Country Store filled with ladies' fashions, wicker, jewelry, furniture, cookware, gifts, souvenirs and other novelties. The selection of quality merchandise is huge and prices are more than reasonable.

Whether shopping for unique gift items, tasting delicious country-style cuisine and delightful daiquiries, or enjoying the rural beauty of Western New York, Good Morning Farm Restaurant & Pub is a "Best Choice."

WHITE HORSE INN
Route 60
Cassadaga, New York 14718
Tel: (716) 595-3523
Hrs: Summer:

Monday - Thursday	5:00 p.m. - 9:00 p.m.
Friday - Saturday	5:00 p.m. - 10:00 p.m.
Sunday	1:00 p.m. - 8:00 p.m.
Winter:	
Tuesday - Thursday	5:00 p.m. - 9:00 p.m.
Friday - Saturday	5:00 p.m. - 10:00 p.m.
Sunday	4:00 p.m. - 8:00 p.m.

Visa, MasterCard and Discover are accepted.

Dick and Lettie Watt have been making friends in the Cassadaga area since 1982. Their White Horse Inn, "where good food makes friends," has built a reputation by serving fresh, home-cooked meals. "Cooking with a personal touch" makes this a special place to dine as does their decor. A very comfortable atmosphere is accomplished with ivory and beige window dressings and soft lighting in brass globe chandeliers. An open brick divider separates the restaurant from the bar. A large bow window filled with live plants is a focal point in the dining room. Each table is decorated with silk flowers and candles. Pictures painted by a local artist and music accent the background.

Some house specialties include White Horse Clam Chowder and French Onion soup baked with two cheeses. Other favorites are stuffed mushroom caps, clams casino, french fried veggies, and honey-dipped chicken wings. The dinner specialty is Rock Lobster Tails. Other seafood selections include Haddock, Deep Sea Scallops, and Jumbo Gulf Shrimp. New York Strip Steak, Filet Mignon, center cut pork chops, steaks cut to order, and grilled Hickory Ham Steak are also available. The home-baked breads and rolls that accompany meals are a special treat. When visiting the White Horse Inn, located in Chautauqua wine country, one shouldn't pass up the opportunity to sample a variety of local wines with dinner. A White Horse Coffee (White Horse Scotch, Brandy, Kahlua, and whipped cream) and dessert is the perfect finish to any dinner. Dessert selections include Dick's Peanut Butter Pie, homemade Walnut Pie, Mother's New York Cheesecake with cherry or blueberry topping, ice cream, and sundaes.

Dick and Lettie serve a Friday night fish fry which has made them favorites among the locals. The quality and freshness of the reasonably priced menu items along with a warm, friendly staff and informal atmosphere make the White Horse Inn a "Best Choice" for diners. Found in scenic Cassadaga Lakes, the White Horse Inn is easy to locate--just look for the horse on the roof.

ski resorts

COCKAIGNE SKI AREA & THE GRAINERY
RD 1 Country Road 66
Cherry Creek, New York 14723
Tel: (716) 287-3500
Hrs; Ski:
November - March: (snow permitting)
Grainery:
Monday - Friday 11:30 a.m. - 2:30 p.m.
5:00 p.m. - 10:00 p.m.
Saturday 11:30 a.m. - 10:00 p.m.
Sunday Noon - 8:00 p.m.
Visa and MasterCard are accepted.

The word "Cockaigne" is defined as a Utopian country of luxury and leisure, and as those who experience the majestic slopes and gorgeous ski lodge agree, there's no better name for this lavish resort. This beautiful ski resort has five slopes, nine trails, and several cross-country trails on which groups of five or more may take two-hour tours.

Cockaigne offers rental equipment, ski lessons (group or private), day care, beginner specials, family specials (kids under four ski free with parents who buy themselves regularly priced passes; and kids under 12 ski at half price under the same conditions), season passes, and special group rates. The resort has a fully-equipped ski shop that features the latest hi-tech ski accessories and equipment at very reasonable prices. All the salespeople are skiers, so visitors of the shop can count on their expertise, enthusiasm and helpfulness.

The natural beauty of the slopes is complemented by the very distinctive lodge. The lodge was built in Austria and shipped to New York City for the Austrian Pavilion at the 1963 World's Fair before it was purchased and shipped to Cherry Creek.

The Grainery Restaurant, a beautifully restored century-old barn serves homemade baked goods and country cooking. Taste the restaurant's Chicken and Biscuits, hearty soups and fresh-baked breads. The Grainery offers a variety of fresh-baked goods for dessert or to take out.

The Loft Gift Shop at The Grainery features locally-made food products such as honey and maple syrup, as well as Amish creations like beautiful quilts, rugs and wall hangings. Amish self-guided tours lead visitors through the Old Order Amish Community, where they can see candy, quilts, and cheese in the making.

Cockaigne is located 18 miles from the I-90 N.Y.S. Thruway and 10 miles from the Route 17 Southern Tier Expressway on County Road 66. From Route 60 in Sinclairville, take Route 52 to 77 to 66.

The folks at Cockaigne invite the public to "ski the legend" or just relax at the warm and comfortable lounge. Cockaigne is the perfect way to liven up the ordinary winter routine.

CHAUTAUQUA

Founded in 1804, Chautauqua came into prominence with the establishment of the Sunday School Teachers Assembly in 1874 by John H. Vincent and Lewis Miller, both members of the Methodist Chautauqua Camp Meeting Association. Soon other denominations joined and emphasis was extended to include recreation, education, and cultural pursuits as well as religion. A Chautauqua Literary and Scientific Circle was formed in 1878 followed by a correspondence school division in 1882. Similar ventures were tried around the country but the original Chautauqua Institution still draws thousands of visitors each summer to this beautiful Victorian lakeside community.

attractions

The world-renowned Chautauqua Institution offers a nine-week course of theater, operas in English, symphony and pops concerts, art exhibits, and lectures on politics, philosophy, and religion. Two hundred courses are offered during the summer school session, including workshops, and seminars with an emphasis on music, dance, and art. Facilities are available for swimming, biking, sailing, tennis, and golf with daily activities for all ages. Tickets may be purchased for a day, evening, weekend, or season for admittance to amphitheater events. Operas or plays in Norton Hall require reserved seat tickets. There is no entry fee on Sundays. For information and tour packages, call 716-357-6200.

events

The Chautauqua Institution begins its nine-week season in late June and ends it in late August.

The Chautauqua Craft Alliance holds its show and sale the first weekend of July and the second week of August.

The Chautauqua Allegheny Winter Festival is held from November through mid-March.

accommodations

ATHENAEUM HOTEL
South Lake Drive
Chautauqua, New York 14722
Tel: (716) 357-4444

The Athenaeum Hotel, built in 1881 and fully restored in 1984, was once the largest wooden structure in the United States. That's not the only unique aspect of this grand hotel. The Athenaeum, often referred to as the "Grande Dame," was the first hotel in the world to have electric power, largely due to the strivings of one of the hotel's favorite guests, Thomas A. Edison.

Located at the center of Chautauqua Institution, overlooking Chautauqua Lake, this massive Victorian hotel was classically designed with beautifully carved woodwork and an elegant veranda that circles the front and the sides of the hotel. Both the interior and exterior of the hotel are breathtakingly embellished, yet the original Victorian grandeur has been painstakingly preserved.

Bordered by huge maple trees, the majestic Athenaeum is host to those who visit Chautauqua Institution to experience its many symphony and pop concerts, lectures, art, religious studies, operas, and theatre performances. For guests who enjoy outdoor activities, Chautauqua Institution offers facilities for golfing, boating, playing tennis, and fishing.

Because the Athenaeum Hotel operates under the American Plan, the daily room rate includes breakfast, luncheon and dinner. The cuisine is classic American, and the most unique aspect of dining at the Athenaeum is that guests receive two desserts--which may include anything from Lemon Chiffon Pie to Blueberry Cheesecake Parfaits. Although informal wear is fine for breakfast and lunch, the Athenaeum's dinner tradition holds that guests must dress in semi-formal attire.

Guests are given a choice of five traditional entrees, which change often. Some lunch entrees include Kabuki Salad with Oriental Dressing, Welsh Rarebit, and Holland Rusk with Grilled Canadian Bacon. Dinner entrees include Sauteed Frog Legs and Roast Rom Turkey with Apple Stuffing. On Sundays, the Hotel serves blueberry pancakes and cornmeal mush as a traditional Sunday supper.

The Athenaeum offers elegant but relaxing rooms that are equipped with air conditioning, heat, and private bath; the deluxe service provides perfect pampering.

At the Athenaeum, the key words are "relaxation" and "refinement." Experience the overwhelming beauty of this uniquely American resort.

MAGNOLIA MOTEL &
CHAUTAUQUA SELF STORAGE
Route 394
Chautauqua, New York 14757
Tel: (716) 784-2935
Hrs: Open year round.
Call for reservations and information.

"A little motel with a lot of room" is certainly more than just a slogan at Magnolia Motel. They cater to sportsmen and their families, and offer self-storage space right across the street at Chautauqua Lake Self Storage. Anything from documents to recreational vehicles may be stored and vacationers are encouraged to bring everything they will need for the season. The motel is conveniently located near great hunting, fishing, and skiing and they have the lowest rates on the lake with special rates available for those who are storing items.

All units are very clean and have a TV and shower. Apartments are available on a limited basis. A separate lounge has a refrigerator and microwave oven, and the heated garage lounge is equipped for cleaning, freezing, and storing fish. Guests also have the use of boat slips, a private dock and a barbecue. Public boat launching is just five minutes away and a variety of "Stay 'n Store" discounts are offered. Storage tenants get 10 percent off motel room rates per night while yearly storage tenants get a 20 percent per night rate. Special discounts are given for the largest fish of the month in the summer, and the largest deer in the winter. A monthly drawing is also held for a $10 rebate on room rates. Senior citizens also receive a discount of 10 percent.

Self-storage space can be rented by the month, season, or year. The private garages are constructed of heavy guage, high strength steel with steel roll-up doors. The mini warehouse units have insulated ceilings and concrete floors with adequate ventilation to prevent moisture and promote dryness. Renters provide their own locks for the warehouses and they retain exclusive entry. Outside parking space is also available for cars, boats, or RVs. Parking spaces range from 10'x20' to 10'x40' and are $15 a month. Garages range from 8'x20' to 12'x40' and from $39 to $59 in price. Mini warehouses start at 5'x5' for $22 a month and go to 10'x30' for $99 a month. The lot is kept secure with fences and lighting.

A manager is on duty 24 hours a day. The lot is open from sunrise to sunset and locked after dark. The Magnolia Motel, family-owned and operated has been in business since 1984. They think customers should "spend the night - not a fortune", and they stand behind this belief with their many discount packages. They prove to be a "Best Choice" for the sportsman and his family with room to store everything including the kitchen sink. All guests receive VIP treatment.

ST. ELMO'S HOTEL
1 Pratt Avenue
Chautauqua, New York 14722
Tel: 1-800-333-3578
(716) 357-3566
Hrs: Open year round.
Reservations recommended.
Visa and MasterCard are accepted.

St. Elmo Hotel, on the grounds of Chautauqua Institution and beautiful Chautauqua Lake, is nothing short of a grandiose tribute to European style. Its origins as a small 19th century inn have been completely overshadowed by a greatly expanded, very modern establishment. Touted as America's most unique hotel, St. Elmo offers not only the thrill of vacationing in a Victorian-style castle, but fantastic multi-room suites and studio units in which to stay. All accommodations have complete kitchens; most have porches or balconies; and all furnishings compare to that found in America's finest hotels.

Within the hotel are a variety of specialty shops, including Chautauqua Resort Wear, a gourmet shoppe, the Emporium and Pat's at Chautauqua (a women's dress shop) as well as a guest-exclusive exercise room and whirlpool. The public, however, may enjoy the fine hotel-restaurant that offers anything from home-fries and sweetbreads to king crab legs and swordfish.

Guests can take part in a variety of winter activities. The favorites are cross-country skiing, romantic sleigh rides and the Victorian Winter Festival. In fair weather, guests may take advantage of the golfing, biking, and boating or the Collector's Showcase in the Intermezzo, where a great variety of collectibles can be found.

With its fine accommodations, fine food and limousine service to and from the airport, the St. Elmo is a most acceptable choice for banquets and seminars. The annual New Year Dinner Dance is also an extremely popular event, and early reservations are a wise idea.

antiques

DIANE R. BAILEY
ANTIQUES AND INTERIORS
2 Ames Avenue
Chautauqua, New York 14722
Tel: (716) 357-5530
Hrs: Summer:
Monday - Saturday 10:00 a.m. - 6:00 p.m.
Sunday 1:00 p.m. - 5:00 p.m.
Winter:
Thursday - Sunday 10:00 a.m. - 5:00 p.m.
Weekends by appointment.
Visa and MasterCard are accepted.

Both antique and contemporary home furnishings and accessories can be found in this charming corner shop in the heart of the Chautauqua Institution.

Many original hand-painted items such as wall shelves, furniture, boxes, and birdhouses are featured along with a service of custom painting of floors, borders, etc. A fine collection of antiques is available as well as many new lamps, framed prints, wicker, porcelain, mohair throws, coverlets, and many other unusual items.

Diane offers a complete Interior Design service with many wall coverings and fabrics to choose from. The Chautauqua Wallpaper and Border which carry sketches of historical buildings and scenes from the grounds of the Institution are in stock

Custom drapery, vertical blinds, mini and micro blinds, and the full Kirsch window products are available.

Bailiwicks is pleased to offer the fine furniture line of cherry and tiger maple made by the Eldred Wheeler craftsmen. Diane R. Bailey, Antiques & Interiors is a dealer of Eldred Wheeler, handcrafters of fine 18th Century American furniture.

This bailiwick combines the new and the old in an atmosphere which is well worth a trip to Chautauqua.

UNICORN ANTIQUES
Colonnade Building
Chautauqua, New York 14722
Tel: (716) 357-8183
Hrs: September - October:
Thursday - Sunday Noon - 5:00 p.m.
November - April:
Saturday - Sunday Noon - 5:00 p.m.
June 15 - September 4:
Seven days 9:30 a.m. - 5:00 p.m.
Visa and MasterCard are accepted.

One of the most unusual collections of antiques is located at Unicorn Antiques on the grounds of Chautauqua Institute.

The shop features locally-bought antiques from the Victorian era through the 1920s. Its owner Verna Mason never travels more than 30 or 40 miles in any direction to find items for her shop. This locally-based collection includes some very rare findings: a sterling silver cigar cutter designed in the likeness of a fox with ruby gems for eyes, and a 14K gold stick matchcase with an agate cover.

Unicorn Antiques also sells fabric pieces, paintings, furniture, dishes, clocks, and quilts. The most unusual items, however, are the rare jewelry pieces, reasonably priced, and the custom-designed jewelry made by Verna's husband. Jewelry repair and sizing are also done in the shop.

Verna initially carried homemade items such as local maple syrup when she opened the store 15 years ago. The business blossomed and Verna began selling more antiques.

Verna enjoys chatting with both newcomers and regular patrons of the store. Many customers frequently browse through the shop to examine Verna's latest findings.

The best in unusual antiques at reasonable prices can be found at Unicorn Antiques in Chautauqua.

gift shops

THE CHAUTAUQUA EMPORIUM
1 Pratt Avenue
Chautauqua, New York 14722
Tel: (716) 3566 Ext. 400
Hrs: Summer:
Monday - Saturday 10:00 a.m. - 8:00 p.m.
Winter:
Seven days Open afternoons.
Visa and MasterCard are accepted.

The Chautauqua Emporium is located on the main concourse of the breathtaking St. Elmo Hotel in Chautauqua, New York. Mary Doebler, the store's owner, had always enjoyed browsing through antique shops, so when she realized the demand for such a place, she simply opened one.

Carrying a variety of gift items, fine toiletries (Crabtree and Evelyn), Amish quilts, laces, new and antique linens, and a large selection of cards with a Victorian flavor, the Emporium also displays original folk art produced by talented local artists. In staying with the art scene, one finds reproductions from the Metropolitan Museum of Art in the form of paper plates, napkins and cups. The store, as well, features museum reproduction jewelry, potpourri home scents, bathroom accessories, and a variety of fine art address books, blank books and guest books.

The true pride of The Chautauqua Emporium is always having something new and interesting on display. When entering the store, the first noticeable feature is the titillating scent of spice and herbs. The next thing one may notice is the meticulous fashion in which the displays are arranged using the antique furniture. In one area, there are handmade aprons trimmed in lace carefully placed on an antique dresser, and in another, imported linens draped over a majestic antique brass bed.

Next door, but still part of the Emporium, there is a small candy store featuring hand-dipped chocolates and stick candy. Also within walking distance, is the Chautauqua Institution, a fine place for seminars and lectures, and beautiful Chautauqua Lake.

golf courses

CHAUTAUQUA INSTITUTION GOLF CLUB
Route 394
Chautauqua, New York 14722
Tel: (716) 357-6211
Hrs: April 15 - October 15 6:30 a.m. - Dark

Located in the Southwest corner of New York, the Chautauqua Institution Golf Course has been played by top-name stars such as Dinah Shore, Johnny Mathis, Tony Bennett, the Gatlin Brothers and the Oak Ridge Boys.

Exhibitions by famous golf professionals such as Walter Hagen, Gene Sarazen, Ben Hogan, Cary Middlecoff and Horten Smith have been played at Chautauqua Golf Club.

The course consists of a fully-stocked pro shop that carries brand name equipment, men's and women's dressing rooms that have showers and lockers, and a wide range of golf carts that includes battery-powered gas carts, hand carts, and battery-powered carts.

The golf course also has a convenient snack bar and a banquet area.

The course with its perfectly manicured putting greens, handy warm-up range, practice sand traps, seven in-play water holes, five turquoise blue ponds, and beautiful rolling fairways, is both gorgeous and challenging. It also has a special tree program, which assures that 300-400 new trees are planted on the grounds each year.

This 27-hole course was designed by the famous golf course architect Donald Ross and was built on 540 acres of elegant countryside.

PGA Professional Stan Marshaus manages the club and offers private and group lessons, as well as Junior Golf Programs.

One of the unique aspects of this breathtaking course is the strikingly panoramic view of Chautauqua Lake. The grounds, greens, and fairways are so painstakingly maintained and so scenic that the course seems more like a country club than a public golf course. However, the course is open to the public and the green fees are very reasonable.

Chautauqua Institution Golf Club is a worthwhile stopping point for golfers of all ages to enjoy a challenging and fun day.

realty

VACATION PROPERTIES REALTY
1 Morris Avenue
Chautauqua, New York 14722
Tel: (716) 357-8135 or 1-800-344-2198
Hrs: Open year-round.
Reservations or walk-ins are welcome.
Visa, MasterCard and American Express are accepted.

Vacation Properties Realty, located on the grounds of Chautauqua Institution, offers visitors or those moving into the area, a diverse assortment of property to choose from. The company has over 100 properties available for rental or ownership and several new ownership properties are nearing completion. These include single-family homes, condominium units, and older but newly-renovated Victorian style dwellings.

Vacation Properties Realty is always improving and updating accommodations to meet the needs of its clientele, which continues to grow. Chautauqua's property values have skyrocketed in the past 10 years due to an increase in popularity of the area.

The realty firm offers special services to its clients, such as a toll-free reservation phone number, video-taped presentations of each rental property, and year-round rentals for the season or by the day. Rentals are often available for walk-in customers as well. Because all properties are located on the grounds of Chautauqua Institution, shuttle bus service is provided to all customers at almost every home site.

Those visiting the Chautauqua area or planning to settle permanently will find the services of Vacation Properties invaluable. Prospective renters and owners need look no further than the grounds of Chautauqua Institution for the best accommodations and friendliest service with Vacation Properties Realty.

specialty shops

LUCCHESI'S GOURMET SHOPPE
1 Pratt Avenue
Chautauqua, New York 14722
Tel: (716) 357-3566 #500
Hrs: Memorial Day - Labor Day:
7:30 a.m. - Midnight
Off season (weekdays):
Open afternoons.
Weekends Open afternoons & evenings.
Visa and MasterCard are accepted.

Lucchesi's Gourmet Shoppe is a complete specialty shop carrying items that reflect the owner's taste. Ron Tveter purchased the Lucchesi family business in 1982 in Putnam, Connecticut. Seeing a need for such a shop on the Chautauqua Institution Grounds, he moved his business to this small Victorian village in 1988. Now located on the ground floor of St. Elmo's Hotel, this shop carries everything from penny candy to exotic foods such as Rhindeer meatballs.

Ron, a former pre-game scout for the Dodgers, shows his love for sports through merchandise such as baseball cards that date to the 1800s and watercolor paintings of such baseball legends as Mickey Mantle, Willie Stargell and Joe DiMaggio. Other collectibles include porcelain dolls, WWII airplane cards, a collection of feature cartoon carvings, sweatshirts, T-shirts, and stadium cushions featuring the famous "Chautauqua Night's Friendly Bats." Because they keep the Institution Grounds free of insects, Ron puts 50 cents of each purchase toward the bat study program.

Ron has created a store that is fun to browse through. He sells gourmet coffees from Hazelnut to Lucchesi's Blend, and offers a free cup to each visitor. His shop also features unusual spices, teas, oils, vinegars, jams, and Steve's Ice Cream of Boston with all original mixings.

As a remembrance of the time spent here, Ron gives a 50 cent piece to each customer who makes a purchase and has 50 cents or more owed to them in change. Lucchesi's Gourmet Shoppe, a store that is filled from wall to wall and floor to ceiling with interesting items, is a "Best Choice" for those who like to collect rarities and enjoy unusual foods.

SKILLMAN & WIGHT
9 Main Street
Bemus Point Mall
Bemus Point, New York 14712
Tel: (716) 386-3005
Hrs: Summer:
Monday - Saturday 10:00 a.m. - 9:00 p.m.
Sunday 10:00 a.m. - 6:00 p.m.
Spring and Fall:
Monday - Saturday 10:00 a.m. - 5:30 p.m.
Sunday 11:00 a.m. - 5:00 p.m.
Closed January and February.
Visa and MasterCard are accepted.

Located on Main Street in Bemus Point is an eye-catching storefront colored in various shades of pink and purple. Inside this whimsical storefront is Skillman & Wight, a turn-of-the-century variety store that specializes in quality resort wear for men and woman. Skillman & Wight customers can purchase apparel by Jantzen, Woolrich, Northern Isle, White Stag, Catalina, Bugle Boy, Fritzi of California, and Panama Jack. The staff is attentive and helpful, and the alterations are free.

Formerly a smalltown grocery market, the Skillman & Wight store has three levels: a main deck for ladies' and men's apparel, shoes, jewelry and accessories; a top deck for dresses and outerwear, international gifts, unique kitchen products and gourmet food items; and sweatshirts, children's clothing and toys.

It's not hard to see why Skillman & Wight is a main attraction in the small waterfront town of Bemus Point: The interior decor is as interestingly unique as the storefront design. From the hand-crafted antiques to the spacious fitting rooms (one was a meat cooler), the 83-year-old business offers patrons a variety of affordable brand name products in a fun-to-browse-through setting.

LAKE CHAUTAUQUA

Lake Chautauqua has witnessed a wide variety of marine vessels since the days when the lake was a secret strategic water link between French Canada and the Mississippi River to French Louisiana. Today the 22 mile-long lake with 56 miles of shoreline is famous for its tiger muskellunge fishing and water sports.

attractions

A favorite picnic area since the 1890s, **Long Point State Park** is situated along Lake Chautauqua. Its 362 acres offer hiking, biking and nature trails, picnic tables and shelters, and a playground. Winter activities include cross-country skiing and snowmobiling. The 40 acres of peninsular waterfront offers a large public marina, fishing areas, and a swimming beach..

The Chautauqua Lake Historic Vessels Company is unlike other marine museums. This non-profit corporation has reconstructed, restored, and operates authentic vessels which carry passengers today as they did in the past. The **Chautauqua Belle** is a paddle-wheel steamboat that is available for cruises, charters, and private parties. The **Sea Lion** is a replica of a fully-rigged 16th century English merchant ship offering tours as well as passage. The **Bemus Point-Stow Ferry** is a cable-drawn ferry that has been in operation for over 178 years. The ferry transports both autos and passengers across the lake. All three vessels operate on individual schedules beginning in late May through late September.

Midway Park, located on the lake, has plenty of fun for everyone--rides, miniature golf, roller-skating, arcade, go-kart racing, and docking facilities. A historical museum and gift shop are the latest additions.

events

Chautauqua Lake celebrates American independence in a unique way with the **Fourth of July Flare Festival**. At 10 p.m., a signal is given to light approximately 15,000 flares simultaneously around the shore of the lake. The flares burn for 30 minutes.

accommodations

CHAUTAUQUA PUBLICK INN
Rt. 430 at Dutch Hollow Road
Bemus Point, New York 14712
Tel: (716) 484-4355
Hrs: Printemps:
Monday - Thursday 5:00 p.m. - 9:00 p.m.
Friday - Saturday 5:00 p.m. - 10:00 p.m.
Grill Room:
Six days Open till Midnight
No credit cards are accepted. In-house billing system.

The Chautauqua Publick Inn is a sophisticated restaurant, owned and operated by Don and Debbie Cook. Debbie graduated from the famous chef's school in France, LaVarenne Ecole de Cuisine, where she studied with some of the best chefs from Paris restaurants.

Due to Debbie's extensive training in Paris, most of the items on the menu have a European flair. Especially known for their seafood soups and fresh pasta dishes, a house favorite is Seafood Bisque. This soup combines flavors of shrimp, langoustinos and lobster. Fresh Seafood Sausage with a lemon butter sauce and Fettucini Noodles, and Hazelnut Coated Orange Roughy sauteed with a Grand Marnier cream sauce are two dishes that would surely delight the most finicky palate.

All pasta dishes including Fettucini Alfredo and Seafood Fettucini, along with homemade breads, are made fresh daily. Fresh vegetables and homegrown herbs are used to prepare each dish to order. Although the preparation of fresh food takes longer, the end result is worth the wait.

The dessert cart is filled with a beautiful array of freshly-made rich pastries. From award-winning Chocolate Snowball to the traditional French Creme Carmel, the selection makes it impossible to choose just one.

The inn is divided into two sections, the Grill Room Lounge and the Printemps Dining Room. The newly-remodeled Printemps Dining Room features fine china on linen table covers, freshly-cut flowers and a beautifully lit fireplace. The Grill Room Lounge gives patrons a more relaxed atmosphere. In this room, those with eager appetites can choose their own steak and cook it themselves over the open pit grill.

The nightly seafood specials, homemade pasta dishes and bread, the award-winning dessert cart, and the quality and freshnness of all the items served, make the Chautauqua Publick Inn truly a "Best Choice."

PINE HILL COTTAGES AND MOTEL
R.D. #1, Box 395
Ashville, New York 14710
Tel: (716) 789-3543
Hrs: May 1 - November 1
Visa and MasterCard are accepted.

Looking for a place to stay in the Chautauqua area? Pine Hill Cottages and Motel offers a variety of accommodations, and one of them is sure to please. Despite the Ashville, New York mailing address, the establishment is centrally located in a picturesque wooded area on Chautauqua Lake. Pine Hill offers 17 units--five motel units, three cottage-type efficiency units with kitchenettes and separate decks, and nine cottages (with fireplaces), ranging from a cozy bungalow to a beautiful spacious chalet. All motel rooms and efficiencies are equipped with a private bathroom, cable television, air conditioning, and outdoor picnic tables.

Enjoy world-famous walleye and muskie fishing, boating, water skiing, swimming, picnicking, and then return to the comfort of a motel room or cottage. Pine Hill is also convenient to stores, restaurants, theatres, parks, golf courses, tennis courts, and other sports, and is located just three minutes from the Chautauqua Institutes. Boaters can dock their own boat at one of Pine Hill Cottages and Motel's 19 slips, or can rent one.

The homey cottages range from one-bedroom to a very roomy four-bedroom, and come with practically everything but linens. They also include silverware and a toaster. The motel and the efficiencies offer maid service, and come fully equipped. No pets are allowed.

The Brown family has been operating the facility for 15 years, taking great pride in the cleanliness and family atmosphere they have been able to provide. Pine Hill is in operation from May 1 to November 1, and there is always at least one family member on site to make sure everything is just right. Please make reservations, especially for the cottages, for they book rather quickly.

campgrounds

CAMP PRENDERGAST
RD #2 Davis Road
Mayville, New York 14757
Grounds are open April 15 - October 15.
Reservations are required for holidays.

For those who like the solitude and serenity of a scenic camping trip without the isolation of being 20 miles out in the woods, Camp Prendergast is the answer. When Lewis and Judy Peterson visited the site some 14 years ago, they loved it so much that they decided to buy it .

The camp is located far enough from congested areas so that it provides a peaceful, relaxing excursion; yet it is situated very close to the Chautauqua Institution, Chautauqua Lake, and all of the numerous attractions situated near the lake. In the vein of maintaining civilization, a 20 by 40 foot swimming pool is available for use, as are the hot showers and flush toilets. Water, electric, and sewer hookups are also offered as well as a pay phone and soft drink machine.

Camp Prendergast borders one of the finest public trout streams in the county, Prendergast Creek, making it a virtual paradise for the sportsman. Aside from trout-fishing, angling for muskie, walleye, and bass will most likely prove equally as successful. Other activities in the area include water skiing, hiking trails, two golf courses, miniature golf, picnic areas, fine dining, a shopping mall, an amusement park, and museums. All are readily accessible in addition to the Chautauqua offerings.

Each of the 90 campsites are fully surrounded by woods to provide extra seclusion. Each site has its own picnic table and garbage can, as well as accessibility to firewood. Of the 90, there are 20 tent sites and 65 trailer sites outfitted with water, electric, and sewer hook-ups. The remaining five are semi-permanent sites.

The true pride of the Petersons is the peace and quiet, and friendly atmosphere they work hard to maintain. That one statement sums up the atmosphere of the wooded 13-acre Camp Prendergast.

entertainment

THE CASINO (THE PENNYBRIDGE CORP.)
1 Lakeside Drive
Bemus Point, New York 14712
Tel: (716) 386-3661
Hrs: Seven days 11:00 a.m. - 2:00 a.m.

Bemus Point, New York boasts the home of The Casino, an entertainment showplace, where 23,830 chicken wings were sold in one day. Listed in the Guiness Book of World Records for its August 23, 1985 massive chicken wing sale, The Casino is located on 800 feet of beach property, offering free docking to all customers.

A variety of activities go on inside the building, a former Big Band ballroom. The first floor has an arcade with pinball and video games. The snack bar features the famous chicken wings, hot dogs, hamburgers, and other fast food. The casual food service boasts "simply served -- simply priced", and holds specials each night. Monday, Chicken Wings Night, and Thursday, Seafood (oysters, clams, mussels, shrimp and mako shark) Night, are two examples of the specials that The Casino features.

A beverage bar specializing in imported beer, a gift shop and a museum complete the first floor of the building. The Great White Fleet Steamboat Museum, whose history dates back to 1828, has photos, displays, and artifacts of wrecks found in Lake Chautauqua. The museum is free and open to the public.

On the second floor, there is a large dance floor and banquet hall where Big Band dances are held several times a year. The Casino also sponsors antique and gun shows, pool, and football and basketball tournaments. The Canoe Classic competitions are held here annually. Swimming facilities and public restrooms are available for visitors as well.

Fulfilled taste buds and a day of fun for all ages are a sure bet at The Casino, an entertainment complex located at the edge of Lake Chautauqua.

SURF CLUB
Lakeside & Main Streets
Bemus Point, New York 14712
Tel: (716) 386-5088
Hrs: May 1 - Labor Day:
6:00 a.m. - 2:00 a.m.
Visa, MasterCard, American Express, Diners Club and Discover are accepted.

Located on Bemus Bay, the Surf Club has become the night spot of Surf County. Opened in 1963 by the Schenck family, the establishment has turned into "the live music capitol" of Surf County. Though they are only open for business from April 1st until October 31st, an entire year's worth of entertainment and partying is had in that short time.

Live music is offered inside Thursday, Friday, and Saturday nights while the two outside decks--one in the sun, one covered for shade--offer a practical addition to the atmosphere when used to hold the live acoustical entertainment on Saturday and Sunday afternoons. Large picture windows on two walls render a majestic view of the bay, while a large dance floor sits opposite the booths and tables. Blown-up turn-of-the-century postcards accent the walls, and the large bar neatly separates the dining and dancing areas.

The atmosphere and entertainment merely highlight the menu choices, designed for simplicity. One half lists the breakfast menu, while the other half offers large fresh salads, an array of sandwiches, and the tremendously popular Friday Nite Fish Fry.

restaurants

GRACE'S FAMILY RESTAURANT & SWEET SHOP
43 South Erie Street
Mayville, New York 14757
Tel: (716) 753-2812
Hrs: Seven days 7:00 a.m. - 9:00 p.m.
Visa and MasterCard are accepted.

Grace's Family Restaurant and Sweet Shop was established in 1984 by Grace Trippy. With a great deal of restaurant experience in her past, Trippy took the initiative to establish her own restaurant and sweet shop. The result of her endeavor is a clean, open and airy atmosphere, complete with old-fashioned soda bar and flowers on every table.

The greatest pride of the family-owned eatery is the freshness and quality of all food items. Each order is individually prepared at the time it is ordered, assuring the customer that nothing is pre-made. Every soup and sauce is homemade; every pie and pastry home-baked. The time-consuming practice of on-the-spot preparation may seem an inconvenience, but the marked difference in quality is well worth the wait.

The fact that Grace's has adopted a no-alcohol policy has in no way hindered business. The family atmosphere and reputable menu items provide plenty of happy customers. Diners will find breakfast, lunch and dinner menus, along with daily lunch and dinner specials. The place is well known for its prime rib and spaghetti, as well as its vastly popular Friday Night Fish Fry. But the most popular item at Grace's is the L.A. Glazed Cinnamon Toast, a grandiose variation of a classic favorite that prompts patrons to travel from miles in every direction for a sampling.

The breakfast menu features various combinations of traditional favorites; and a variety of omelets and side orders (including salt-rising toast and bagels) that round out the morning selection. For lunch, there is a tremendous selection of sandwiches, ranging from ham and cheese to mushroom steak; a nice choice of subs, a variety of pitas, (meatball, ham, turkey, and tuna with a choice of extras), and a menagerie of side orders including onion chips, mashed potatoes with gravy, and Buffalo wings complete the list of options.

The menu boasts a very large salad bar and basic, but simple, entrees. Pick from the prime rib, spaghetti, or lobster, or select something such as scallops, Shrimp Scampi, half a chicken or anything else from the nicely varied, specialized seafood and Italian menus. No matter what the choice, be sure to finish with pie or cheesecake, or perhaps something from the soda bar.

SEE-ZURH HOUSE/BEMUS POINT INN

14 Main Street
Bemus Point, New York 14712-0633
Tel: (716) 386-2695
Hrs; See-Zurh House:
Lunch:
Monday - Saturday 11:30 a.m - 2:00 p.m.
Dinner:
Tuesday - Saturday Beginning at 5:00 p.m.
Bemus Point Inn: 6:00 a.m. - 3:00 p.m.
Breakfast available all day.

The relaxed family atmosphere, great food, and cozy surroundings are a just a few of the reasons to eat at the See-Zurh House or the Bemus Point Inn.

The See-Zurh House was built in 1888 and was originally the Merritt Boarding House. It was named by previous owners Don See and Zurh Faulkner; but is now owned by Thom Shagla. There is always something fantastic cooking at the See-Zurh House. The daily lunch specials include half pound hamburgers, chicken wings, and ham sandwiches made from scratch. Warm up the day with a cup or bowl of hot homemade soup. For dinner try the delicious jumbo Australian Rock Lobster Tail or perhaps a thick charbroiled steak. On any given night, stop by for the famous Fish Fry and indulge in a seafood lover's dream. The See-Zurh House offers a full beverage bar famous for its legendary popcorn, served free.

The Bemus Point Inn was built in 1946 as a restaurant to complement cottages rented by the Traynor family. The inn features a wide variety of breakfast selections served all day. Lunch specials include Beef on Weck, Beef Bar-B Que, hot ham and cheese sandwiches, and many more tasty items to please the palate. Be sure to try the six-inch square jumbo sweet rolls, a treat that satisfies any sweet tooth.

Both the inn and See-Zurh House have a relaxed family atmosphere, a place to enjoy a hearty meal in comfortable surroundings. There are no frills here, just good food at good prices.

Being located in the small village of Bemus Point gives those who visit here a friendly hometown feeling. Tom is proud of his hometown and holds events to benefit the community. One event is a golf tournament held every year by the See-Zurh House with all proceeds benefitting the community's needs.

Tom also owns the Apple Inn, located six miles east of the See-Zurh House. It is the perfect place for a special dinner.

The friendly feelings, good meals and delightful surroundings make the See-zurh House and the Bemus Point Inn "Best Choices" in the Great Lakes and Western New York area.

JAMESTOWN

Founded by James Prendergast in 1811, the white pine forests along the southeastern tip of Chautauqua Lake made Jamestown one of the leading furniture producers in the state by the mid-1800s. Today, Jamestown takes pride in its diversified industries and varied arts program.

attractions

The **Fenton Historical Center**, built by Governor Reuben E. Fenton after the Civil War, is listed on the National Register of Historic Places. Once the headquarters of the Grand Army of the Republic, the center contains Victorian period rooms, a Chautauqua Lake exhibit, local and family memorabilia, Civil War items, and a genealogical and historical library.

The **Old Northside and Southside Walking Tours** are self-guided tours highlighting many of Jamestown's 19th century commercial and industrial buildings, churches, and private homes. The architecture spans 75 years from Gothic Revival to Art Deco. Brochures are available at the **Fenton Historical Center.**

The **Art Gallery at the James Prendergast Free Library** contains 19th and 20th century French, German and American paintings, with a variety of changing exhibits. The public library has a collection of 200,000 volumes with special collections of law, art, and Scandinavian materials.

The **Burgeson Wildlife Sanctuary** offers guided tours and workshops. The Nature Center, sponsored by the Jamestown Audubon Society, is open year-round, dawn to dusk. Information is available from the Jamestown Area Chamber of Commerce.

events

The International Festival and Food Fair is held the first weekend of May.

The Jamestown Festival is held the second week of July.

The Gerry Volunteer Fire Department hosts the longest consecutive running rodeo east of the Mississippi. The Gerry Rodeo is held the second week in August.

accommodations

HOLIDAY INN JAMESTOWN
150 West Fourth Street
Jamestown, New York 14701

Tel:	(716) 664-3400	
Hrs:	Restaurant:	
	Monday - Saturday	7:00 a.m. - 2:00 p.m.
		5:00 p.m. - 10:00 p.m.
	Sunday	7:00 a.m. - 10:00 p.m.
	Fantasies Nightclub:	
	Wednesday - Saturday	8:30 p.m. - 2:00 a.m.
	Brass Oak Lounge:	11:30 a.m. - 2:00 p.m.

Visa, MasterCard, American Express, Diners Club, JBC and Optima are accepted.

Located in downtown Jamestown, the eight-story, 149- room Holiday Inn offers luxurious accommodations, an elegant restaurant, a unique gift shop, and a host of special services including dry cleaning, a fax machine, and copying services.

Each hotel room is equipped with a television, private push button phones with a data port, and beautiful furnishings.

During the summer, the Colonnade Restaurant offers daily specials along with one of Jamestown's largest salad bars. During the winter, the Colonnade serves Good Morning Breakfasts such as the Country Scramble, (steak and eggs, fresh fruit, gourmet waffles and frittatas), Italian baked omelettes with sweet sausage, onions and green bell peppers. For lunch, guests can choose from the chef's homemade soups, fresh salads and specialty sandwiches.

The restaurant also serves an extensive variety of wonderful entrees. Try the Fettucine Alfredo, Surf and Turf, Stuffed Flounder, Grilled Ham Steak and Chicken Persillade.

Then for dessert, the chef concocts fabulous fresh-baked pies, juicy strawberry shortcakes and New York Style cheesecakes.

Fine lodging and delicious cuisine are only the beginning of luxuries to be enjoyed at the Holiday Inn Jamestown. Whether in the mood for relaxing or high key entertainment, this luxury hotel has it all.

Fantasies is an upbeat nightclub that features live music. If in the mood for a more serene atmosphere, try the Brass Oak Lounge.

The large indoor pool is not the only special attraction. The Wildflower Gift Shop offers a variety of unusual gifts including collector dolls, original paintings, books, and jewelry. The hotel offers specially discounted access to a local health club.

The range of services and the staff's eagerness to accommodate special requests make the Holiday Inn Jamestown a "Best Choice."

gift shops

COUNTRY WOODS COUNTRY STORE
Route 60 - Road #5
Jamestown, New York 14701
Tel: (716) 483-1276
Hrs: Monday - Saturday 10:00 a.m. - 5:00 p.m.
Extended hours for Christmas

Located in Jamestown, New York, the Country Woods Country Store is near Bemus Point in Chautauqua Lake. Sharon Tibbitts, the store's owner, takes great pride in the variety and quality of merchandise she carries. Her husband constructed the shop for her three years ago, and also crafted the Amish-style buggy standing in the front.

Upon entering, the scent of spice and potpourri entices the olfactories, and sets the mood for the store's merchandise. The country-style decor is felt with displays on rough wood furniture and antiques. The eyes are captured by life-size rough-carved animals, including a bear, a horse and an elk. Some of the variety of country items one finds are candles, oil lamps, picture frames, dried flowers, crochet doilies, baskets, rag rugs, placemats, napkins, old-fashioned greeting cards, and locally-made dolls and Teddy bears.

You can expect a healthy selection of Amish merchandise, as Mrs. Tibbitts has developed a very close family-like rapport with members of a nearby Amish community and visits every other week to pick up their fine products. She always has hand-woven items, baked goods, jams and jellies, and many other hand-made goods.

If kitchen items are necessary, the Country Woods Country Store stocks a nice variety. Spoons, tin and wood antique advertising signs, and enamel spatter-ware and marble-ware in a variety of colors and designs are just a smattering of what they offer. Lovers of natural teas, gourmet coffees, and praline candies will most assuredly be satisfied as well. And finally for those aspiring brides-to-be, a bridal registry is handy and decorating advice is provided.

points of interest

JAMESTOWN AUDUBON NATURE CENTER
RD#5, Riverside Road
Jamestown, New York 14701
Tel: (716) 569-2345
Hrs: Tuesday - Saturday 10:00 a.m. - 5:00 p.m.
Sunday 1:00 p.m. - 5:00 p.m.
Guided nature walks for groups by reservation.

The Roger Tory Peterson Nature Interpretive Building was constructed in 1976 and named for that honored bird artist and ornithologist who was a native of Jamestown. An 11,000-square-foot addition to the center is scheduled to be built in Spring 1990. Owned and operated by the Jamestown Audubon Society, the nature center provides educational programs for all ages.

The center is accessible to the handicapped and provides broad windows and a rear deck from which a panoramic view of the surrounding ponds, marshes and forests can be seen. The center contains living and non-living exhibits, a large collection of Peterson's bird prints, and the Simpson Bird Room which displays over 200 mounted birds, some of which are now extinct. Hands-on exhibits for children are found in the Discovery Room, which contains much of interest for adults as well.

The Nature Center also has a reference library and gift shop offering books, equipment and other items of interest to nature lovers. The center's Burgeson Wildlife Sanctuary has 600 acres providing a variety of habitats and over five miles of trails and boardwalks that access marsh and swamplands. An arboretum and herb and wildflower gardens are currently being developed.

All meetings and events are open for public enjoyment. The Jamestown Audubon Nature Center is a learning and entertaining experience as well as a great way to spend the day in Jamestown, New York.

restaurants

IRONSTONE RESTAURANT
West 4th and Monroe
Jamestown, New York 14701
Tel: (716) 487-1516
Hrs: Monday - Friday 11:30 a.m. - 2:00 p.m.
Dinner:
Monday - Saturday 5:00 a.m - 10:00 p.m.
Closed Sundays and Holidays.
Cocktail Lounge: 11:30 a.m. - Close
Reservations are appreciated.
Visa, MasterCard, American Express, Diners Club and Carte Blanche are accepted.

The Ironstone Restaurant, "Jamestown's most recommended address," has become synonymous with fine dining. The 1884 structure was originally the Martyn Furniture Factory, but for the last 22 years has been home to friendly fine dining. Owned by chef Thomas Ciancio and his family, who possess over 50 years of experience in the restaurant business, the Ironstone never fails in its quest to provide a quality dining experience.

The interior is elegantly designed. The Victorian look is enhanced with leather chairs, crisp linen tablecloths, beautiful chandeliers, and some additional soft lighting.

The fabulous balanced menu is highlighted by well prepared appetizers, entrees and desserts. Jumbo shrimp cocktail and escargot give way to such specialties as Veal Oscar, Roast Prime Rib of Beef, Petite Filet Mignon, Australian Lobster Tail, and Ironstone Rack of Spring Lamb. Ciancio and his family suggest completing a fine dining experience with the Ironstone's outstanding Peanut Butter Fudge Pie, or one of several after dinner drinks, most of which are made with ice cream.

Located in Jamestown, the Ironstone is close to the Chautauqua Institution and the many attractions associated with it. Also near the business district, the Ironstone has adopted a service geared toward those who have little opportunity to leave the office for lunch. Ciancio's daughter, Barbara Di Domenico, spends mornings on the phone taking lunch orders from those business people, and then has the food delivered in time for lunch.

Their dedication to service goes much farther with handicapped accessibility and private party facilities. Very proud of their dedication, the people of the Ironstone believe their friendly fine dining atmosphere will never disappoint a customer.

specialty shops

GREEN FARM TEA ROOM
3 West Terrace Avenue
Lakewood, New York 14750
Tel: (716) 763-3745
Hrs: Monday - Saturday 9:00 a.m. - 5:30 p.m.

Exuding class from every crevice, the Green Farm Tea Room is exclusively a dealer of fine giftware. The elegant English Tudor structure, built for the Sorg family as a summer home in 1905, became a tea room and gift shop when the Green family bought it in 1934. Don't be misled, however. The establishment is certainly not a farm, and is no longer a tea room.

Located in Lakewood, New York, overlooking Lake Chautauqua, Green Farm Tea Room, offers a variety of the finest china and crystal available. China selections may come from names such as Royal Copenhagen, Wedgwood, Royal Doulton, Spode, Hutschenreuther, Royal Worcester, or Portmeirioh. If crystal is preferred, Orrefors and Kosta Boda are the most popular choices they carry. In addition, choose from an assortment of fine linens, Napier jewelry, lamps, bath accessories, leather goods, baby items, and flatware, and possibly even consider a bridal service that features gift-wrapping and worldwide shipment of purchases.

Edward and Jeanne Green, owners of the Green Farm Tea Room, take great pride in the personal service and individual attention they provide their customers, Two full floors of the expansive English tudor hold the fine line of giftware, and lend themselves to the friendly yet somewhat formal atmosphere. The beautifully-landscaped grounds and lake view complete a majestic theme.

Although indisputably a shop for discriminating tastes, one should not be intimidated. Any place that offers hand-painted garbage cans must not be completely without a lighter side.

WESTFIELD

attractions

McClurg Mansion is the headquarters of the Chautauqua County Historical Society. The mansion, built in 1818-1820, contains period furnishings and a historical library. Exhibits include a military room, an early kitchen, a restored blacksmith forge, Indian artifacts and antique tools.

The Barcelona Lighthouse was the first in the world to be lighted by natural gas. Erected in 1829, the 40-foot high fieldstone structure is listed on the National Register of Historic Places.

The Patterson Library and Art Gallery is a full-service public library that offers a year-round gallery program. Film and video programs are offered, as well as cultural, historical and fine arts exhibitions.

events

The **Arts and Crafts Festival** is held in late July at Westfield Central School.

The **Tour of Chautauqua Bike Ride** is held in mid-September. Twenty-five, 62, 75 and 100-mile routes are offered. Information is available at Eason Hall.

antiques

R.C. PAYNE & ASSOCIATED ANTIQUE GALLERY
13 East Main Street
Westfield, New York 14787
Tel: (716) 326-4331
Hrs: Summer:

Monday - Saturday	10:00 a.m. - 4:00 p.m.
Sunday	Noon - 4:00 p.m.
Winter:	
Thursday - Saturday	10:00 a.m. - 4:00 p.m.
Sunday	Noon - 4:00 p.m.

Visa and MasterCard are accepted.

From the moment one walks into R.C. Payne & Associated Antique Gallery, it's obvious that quality and originality are top priority.

A variety of furniture, paintings, jewelry and crystal embellish the interior of the gallery. These pieces are hand-picked, quality pieces from all over the world.

This newly-renovated antique shop is owned by Rodney Carlton Payne, who has eight years of previous experience with antiques. Mr. Payne worked for the prestigious Christies of London. A member of the Society for the Preservation of New England in Boston, Payne won the Westfield Community Awareness Award in 1988 for his outstanding interior and exterior decorating ability.

Mr. Payne is now planning to work with other antique dealers to expand into a high-quality group enterprise, offering a wider variety of pieces.

Along with dealing in antiques, Payne is a commercial decorator. He has extended his design talents to a number of clients, including both private homeowners and hotel owners. He is currently involved in decorating a 154-room hotel at Niagara-on-the-Lake.

For commercial decorating needs or a quality antique piece, visit R.C. Payne & Associated Antique Gallery.

art galleries

PORTAGE HILL GALLERY
RD #2 Portage Hill Road
Westfield, New York 14787
Tel: (716) 326-4478
Hrs: July and August:
Monday - Saturday 10:00 a.m. - 5:00 p.m.
Sunday Noon - 5:00 p.m.
September - December:
Wednesday - Saturday 10:00 a.m. - 5:00 p.m.
Sunday Noon - 5:00 p.m.
January - June:
Saturday 10:00 a.m. - 5:00 p.m.
Sunday Noon - 5:00 p.m.
Visa and MasterCard are accepted.

Portage Hill Gallery, located on Route 394, midway between Westfield and Mayville, features the creations of more than 60 regionally known local artists, including several who are nationally known.

The owner, Audrey Ray Dowling, accepts only high-quality, original art work. An artist herself, Audrey helped to found the Chautauqua Craft Alliance, and as a result of this Alliance, local artists needed a place where they could showcase their work. So in 1982, Audrey opened the Gallery to display quality multimedia art forms.

The building that houses the gallery is an 1830s Greek-revival-style home, in which the original woodwork and design have been beautifully preserved. The large first-floor parlor and family room holds the gallery's collection of fine arts, which includes not only original sketches and paintings, but also hand-crafted jewelry, crockery, blown glass, woven items, and sculptures.

Audrey, who is also an art instructor, has a keen eye for recognizing the finest artistic creations. Aside from presenting the works of widely known artists, Audrey premieres select pieces from new artists, too. The range of unique collectibles at the Portage Hill Gallery makes it a wonderful place to browse; and don't worry about making a selection--Audrey will gladly use her artistic expertise to help find the exact pieces to match any decor. So whether a novice or a connoisseur of fine art, both will receive just the right amount of friendly personal service.

In addition to featuring a wide variety of year-round arts and crafts, the Gallery also holds an Annual Christmas Open House, which offers a large collection of art for gift giving. The collection is so huge that it occupies the entire first floor. Don't miss this show and sale; it's a wonderful way to get into the holiday spirit. The Christmas Show takes place the Friday and Saturday of Thanksgiving Day Weekend.

But no matter what time of the year, a visit to the Portage Hill Gallery of Fine Crafts, will provide the friendly atmosphere, the informative personal service, and most of all the top-quality unique art.

libraries

PATTERSON LIBRARY
40 South Portage Street
Westfield, New York 14787
Tel: (716) 326-2154
Hrs: September 1 - June 30:

Monday - Wednesday	9:00 a.m. - 8:00 p.m.
Thursday - Saturday	9:00 a.m. - 5:00 p.m.
July 1 - August 31:	
Monday - Tuesday	9:00 a.m. - 8:00 p.m.
Wednesday - Friday	9:00 a.m. - 5:00 p.m.
Saturday	9:00 a.m. - 1:00 p.m.

The Patterson Library should not be called a library; it should be considered an entertainment center. When Hannah Patterson requested the library be built in 1896 as a memorial to her parents, she could not have imagined the extent to which it operates today. The extravagant Greek classic design was constructed to be totally fireproof and it houses a staggering collection of services.

In addition to the 38,000 books, this is a beautiful center for the arts that features an octagon-shaped art gallery on the lower level where all forms of artist's media are displayed. Video tapes, cassette tapes, art prints, and original paintings are also available for loan.

A small theater is located in the basement and the rooms off the mezzanine are dedicated to natural science and local history with small stuffed mammals and birds dating back to 1910. There is a special memorial display for Jennifer Klein Kuhlman, one of the founders of the professional puppeteer group, Das Puppenspiel.

The fantastic Greek classic design is enhanced by the exterior's white marble and gray brick with a cut stone foundation and basement. Within is a central rotunda, its dome supported by eight large Corinthian columns.

The circulation desk is at the center of this rotunda from which the book stacks radiate toward the rear like spokes of a wheel. The interior of the library is finished in green-brown oak with green marble mantels and base. The floor of the rotunda is white marble. The interior color scheme is various shades of green and gold.

The Patterson Library offers a variety of programs, music recitals, lectures, meeting space, adult and youth programs, public access to computers and instruction, audiovisual equipment, records, and large print books for loan. Any assistance that may be needed in this immense facility will be gladly provided by the helpful, friendly staff.

Westfield's Patterson Library offers visitors a fully stocked library and a center for the arts in a setting which is nothing less than exquisite.

points of interest

LANDMARK ACRES - CANDLELIGHT LODGE
Route 20
232 West Main Street
Westfield, New York 14787
Tel: (716) 326-4185
Hrs: Seven Days 11:00 a.m. - 5:00 p.m.
Closed Tuesday and Wednesday.
Visa and MasterCard are accepted.

The Candlelight Lodge is a beautiful 1851 Italianate, brick mansion that is listed on the National Register of Historic Homes. It is placed on acres of green lawn and has a lovely covered brick patio in front. An antique shop full of 18th and 19th century pieces can be found inside on the first floor. Located upstairs in the mansion are five gorgeous apartments all newly redecorated and furnished with quality period antiques. All units include their own television, kitchen, parlor and bath. All are available for weekly, monthly, or yearly accommodations. The minimum stay allowed is two days and reservations are required. The Lodge is within walking distance of various restaurants, stores, and shops including Landmark Acres Antiques.

Landmark Acres Antiques is the site of the first farm settled in Chautauqua County in 1802. The shop is located in a restored rustic two-story barn on 32 acres of beautiful farm land. It offers quality antiques from 1750 to 1920. Special items available are oriental rugs, silver paintings, lamps, furniture, jewelry, books and dishes. Its location is on Route 20, West of Westfield, Exit 60 off of Interstate 90.

Edward and Wilma Benjamin are proud of the quality merchandise, and the historical significance of both merchandise and the building. Both locations are peacefully surrounded by grape vineyards and a friendly small town atmosphere. The couple is dedicated to making visitors feel welcome at both locations, thus making Landmark Acres and Candlelight Lodge "Best Choices" in quality antiques with elegant accommodations.

restaurants

KELLY HOTEL
Route 20 at State Line
Ripley, New York 14775
Tel: (716) 736-6976
Hrs: Tuesday - Saturday 11:00 a.m. - 9:00 p.m.
Sunday Noon - 8:00 p.m.
Closed Monday.
Accessible to the handicapped.
Visa, MasterCard, American Express and Discover are accepted.

Built in 1830, the Kelly Hotel is a beautifully-decorated restaurant accented with antiques, framed pictures, and hanging leaded glass lamps. The perfectly set tables are adorned with pink tablecloths, wine colored napkins, and freshly-cut flowers. Its green trim and spacious front sitting porch make the exterior as lovely as the interior.

One unique aspect of Kelly's is that it has two floors for dining. Upstairs are the private dining rooms and the Victorian Corner, which seats eight to 12 people at an antique Victorian dining table, and the first floor has a fully-licensed bar and two large non-smoking dining rooms.

The Kelly is wonderfully Victorian, but the ambiance and decor of this majestic restaurant are not the only attributes that make dining at Kelly's a memorable experience. The cuisine is so outstanding that Kelly's Chef John Pereira has won awards for his Shrimp Pereira and Seafood Bisque.

All of the dishes are superb, but the veal and seafood are exceptionally delicious. A few of the favorite appetizers at Kelly's are the Clams Casino, clams baked in the half shell and then sauteed with Chef John's secret seasoning; the Coquilles Saint Jacques, sauteed scallops topped with a light creamy sauce and then served in a pastry shell; and Shrimp Baron, broiled shrimp with the chef's zesty magic sauce. The wonderful entrees range from Veal Marsala in a creamy mushroom sauce to Seafood au Gratin in a white wine sauce.

The desserts are well worth saving room for, especially the caramel custard. To accompany any dessert, Kelly's prepares fresh-brewed international coffees, such as Latin coffee made with Bailey's Irish Creme, and Kahlua and Dutch coffee, prepared with chocolate mint-flavored Vandermint.

The uniquely superb cuisine, friendly staff and magnificent decor make the Kelly Hotel a "Best Choice" in Chautauqua County.

wine

JOHNSON ESTATE WINES, Westfield, New York: (716) 326-2191. Tasting, tours, and retail. Grapes used: French-American and Native-American.

MERRITT ESTATE WINERY, Forestville, New York: (716) 965-4800. Tasting, tours, and retail. Grapes used: French-American and Native-American.

SCHLOSS DOEPKEN
RD 2, Route 20
Ripley, New York 14775
Tel: (716) 326-3636
Hrs: Tasting & Sales:
June - November:
Seven days Noon - 5:00 p.m.
November - June:
Sundays Noon - 5:00 p.m.
Visa and MasterCard are accepted.

Schloss Doepken is not only the first winery people see as they go east on Route 20; it was the first winery in Chautauqua County and was once owned by the Brocton Wine Company. Owners John and Roxann Watso bought the vineyard and expanded the business into a winery that produces close to 5,000 gallons of wine each year. But the history and intrigue of this beautiful 70-acre winery do not end there; the grounds surrounding Schloss Doepken are also the final resting place for a famous lieutenant from the War of 1812, Campbell Alexander. And even the name of the winery is interesting: "Schloss" means "castle or house," and "Doepken" is the maiden name of John's wife, Roxann.

Superstition has it that "13" is an unlucky number; but the owners of Schloss Doepken disagree. John and Roxann Watso produce 13 types of wine that range from sweet to dry. Some of their specialty wines include a dry Oak-aged Concord with all the traditional flavor of homemade wine; an award-winning Chardonnay, Roxann Rouge; a spicy European-tasting wine named Gewurztraminer-Elsation; and a deliciously mild blush wine name Chautauquablumchen, which stands for "little flower of Chautauqua."

Schloss Doepken also features a line of wine jelly and other unique gift items. The Gift Shop and Tasting Room are housed in the country farmhouse, which is accented by a border of gorgeous chrysanthemums and the aroma of ripe grapes.

The people at Schloss Doepken develop their grapes for five to seven years before the grapes are hand-picked to make wine. John and Roxann take their time to insure that even the most discriminating wine connoisseurs will love Schloss Doepken wines.

Don't leave Chautauqua wine country without experiencing the rustic charm of the Schloss Doepken farmhouse and the pleasure of delicious Schloss Doepken wine.

VETTER VINEYARDS
East Main Road
Route 20
Westfield, New York 14787
Tel: (716) 326-3100
Hrs: Tasting and Sales:
June - August: 10:00 a.m. - 7:00 p.m.
September - May: 10:00 a.m. - 6:00 p.m.
Tours are given during June, July & August.

Vetter Vineyards, located on a hillside overlooking scenic Portland, produces a variety of grapes, including the grapes that are used in Vetter's world-class Chardonay and Cabernet Sauvignon wines.

The site of Vetter Vineyards has been cultivated for grapes since 1864, but the Vetter family first brought it's wine-making expertise to this site only 20 years ago. Since that time, the Vetters have grown a wide variety of connoisseur-quality grapes. In fact, all 22 acres of grapes are picked by hand to protect them from being bruised.

In 1987, the family opened the Winery and Gift Shop to display their award-winning wines and unique gift items. The Vetters say that their best-selling wines are in the medium-dry range, but customers will find superb wines to suit any taste.

The spacious tasting room and delightful gift shop are open year-round, and tours are given in June, July and August.

It's not hard to tell that the business is family-run because the atmosphere is so friendly and family-like, but it is hard to decide what's best at Vetter Vineyards: the world-class wines or the world-class service. It doesn't get any better than Vetter.

DUNKIRK

Originally called Chadwick's Bay when Solomon Chadwick arrived in 1809, Dunkirk became a major shipping and railroad center in the late 19th and early 20th centuries. Today, this lakeside community is known for its recreational opportunities and grape industry.

attractions

A walking tour of Downtown Dunkirk, featuring examples of over 150 years of architecture, is available from the Dunkirk Chamber of Commerce.

Built in 1875, the **Dunkirk Lighthouse** is still in use. The keeper's house is now the **Veterans Museum** with a room dedicated to each branch of the service, a room in honor of the Lighthouse Keeper, and a display of the Vietnam War. The lighthouse is listed on the National Register of Historic Places.

The Dunkirk Historical Museum contains an extensive collection of photographs of the steam locomotives built in Dunkirk. Other exhibits include local history, a military room, and 19th century women's fashions.

The ALCO-Brooks Railroad Display is located at the Chautauqua County Fairgrounds when the fair is not in operation. Local railroad artifacts include a 1916 steam locomotive built in Dunkirk. The display is under the auspices of the Historical Society of Dunkirk.

The Adams Memorial Gallery displays changing exhibits of contemporary regional artists. The gallery is open year-round.

events

The Tall Ship Celebration is held the second weekend in August.

accommodations

SHERATON HARBORFRONT INN
30 Lake Shore Drive East
Dunkirk, New York 14048
Tel: (716) 366-8350
Fax: (716) 366-8899
Hrs: Open year-round
Visa, MasterCard, American Express, Diners Club and Carte Blanche are accepted.

The Sheraton Harborfront Inn, a newly designed hotel, is ideally located overlooking Lake Erie's Chadwick Bay. A very community-minded place, it has become the cornerstone for redevelopment of the Dunkirk Harborfront. William J. Bola, the Sheraton's General Manager, is proud of the quality and design of the hotel as well as the wide range of facilities they offer.

The hotel has 132 guest rooms, four of which are conference suites with queen-size Murphy beds and wet bars. The Guest Tower has nine rooms that offer king-size beds and private whirlpool baths. Special suites are available for the handicapped with larger door openings and bathrooms. All rooms are equipped with telephones complete with dataports. The rooms, refreshingly decorated in soft tones, provide a marvelous view of Chadwick Bay.

Guests in search of an invigorating workout will find it at the Sheraton Harborfront Fitness Center with indoor and outdoor swimming pools, whirlpool, saunas, and advanced exercise equipment. Afterward, dance the night away at the High Energy Spinnaker lounge. The state-of-the-art sound equipment, DJ booth, and multi-screen projector system keep guests entertained from 4:00 p.m. to 1:30 a.m., seven days a week. Or, if in the mood for a more relaxed atmosphere, the Hotel's Lobby Lounge provides a beautiful view of Lake Erie alongside a crackling fireplace. Waterfront dining is available in the hotel at the Crow's Nest Restaurant complete with a two-level outdoor deck that offers a 300-degree view of Lake Erie. The Crow's Nest serves meals morning, noon and night. The usual breakfast items are served along with some unique items such as smoked salmon and chive omelette or Nova Scotia lox on a toasted bagel. Lunch offers a variety of salads, sandwiches, and a list of entrees to choose from including Seafood Crepe and Vegetable Lasagna. The dinner menu features such fish dishes as Fresh Walleye Filet, Grilled Swordfish Steak, and Broiled Boston Scrod along with other favorites like Filet Mignon, Grilled Herb Chicken, and Broiled Lamb Steak. A children's menu is available for each meal.

From the first moment of entering the warm, intimate atmosphere of the Sheraton Harborfront Inn's lobby, one is aware that it is a special place with much to offer. The hotel is able to accommodate banquets of up to 250 people in the ballroom. This room can be divided into four sections so that smaller groups can also be accommodated. The Sheraton HarborFront Inn's guest rooms, lounge, banquet and dining facilities make it a "Best Choice" for guests of all ages.

art galleries

ADAMS ART GALLERY
600 Central Avenue
Dunkirk, New York 14048
Tel: (716)366-7450

Hrs:	Wednesday - Friday	11:00 a.m. - 4:00 p.m.
	Friday evening	7:00 p.m. - 9:00 p.m.
	Saturday & Sunday	1:00 p.m. - 4:00 p.m.

The Adams Art Gallery is an active non-profit arts center open year-round. Its exhibition program displays the whole gamut of how artists today are working. There are exhibitions of two and three-dimensional works which explore materials or subject matter in interesting ways. There are exhibitions which pay homage to the beauty of nature. There are theme shows, group shows, solo shows, all of which are selected because the artworks, whether fine art or one-of-a-kind craft objects, embody the personal values of the artist who made them.

Featured each summer is Fiber National, a juried exhibition of art-oriented predominantly fiber work. The baskets, embroidery, weavings, hangings, fiber collage, tapestries, quilts, painted cloth, and paper works which comprise the exhibition are selected by a juror reknown from the fiber field; accepted work comes from across the United States.

The Adams Art Gallery's mission is to provide exhibition opportunities for artists while enhancing the cultural climate of its community. An assortment of cultural events complement the exhibition program. Each calendar year includes classes for both children and adults, films, music performances, lectures, poetry readings--many of these events are coordinated with exhibition themes.

The Adams Art Gallery is housed in a former Unitarian church on the corner of Sixth and Central Dunkirk, New York. Its classical features are pleasing to the eye and artists regularly affirm the beauty of its exhibition spaces. A mural painted in 1934 has been retained. The Adams Art Gallery is a marvelous example of adaptive use of a former church.

book stores

THE BOOK NOOK
Center of Dunkirk/Fredonia Plaza
Dunkirk, New York 14048
Tel: (716) 366-0685

Hrs:		
	Monday - Friday	10:00 a.m - 9:00 p.m.
	Saturday	10:00 a.m.- 6:00 p.m.
	Sunday	Noon - 4:00 p.m.
	Extended hours over Thanksgiving and Christmas	

Visa, MasterCard and Discover are accepted.

The Book Nook, established in 1968, is a family owned and operated business. The Pelletters and Donovans take pride in serving the needs of their customers and keeping on the cutting edge of high technology in order to access publications quickly.

The Book Nook might sound like a small store, but with over 15,000 titles in stock and 250,000 more available within three to five days, it can satisfy the appetite of most bookworms.

The store is fully computerized with state-of-the-art equipment for inventory and ordering purposes. It also offers 20 percent off the New York Times Best Seller List of hardcover books. The large selections of sale books located in the center aisles are discounted 80 percent daily.

A wide selection of Hallmark and Blue Mountain Arts cards are sold at The Book Nook, as well as local area T-shirts in all sizes. Purchase a specialized T-shirt made to order while browsing through the store's beautiful high quality posters.

This small, cheery, well-organized store is located in the center of the Dunkirk/Fredonia Plaza, and will satisfy almost any book need as quickly and easily as possible.

The all-occasion greeting cards, posters, and made to order T-shirts make The Book Nook a "Best Choice" for books and gifts along the Great Lakes.

gift shops

LUWEIBDEH SHOP
4587 West Main Road
Fredonia, New York 14063
Tel: (716) 673-1915

Hrs:		
	Tuesday & Thursday	1:00 p.m. - 6:00 p.m.
	Wednesday	11:00 a.m. - 6:00 p.m.
	Friday & Saturday	10:00 a.m. - 5:00 p.m.
	Sunday & Monday by chance	

Visa and MasterCard are accepted.

The lovely Luweibdeh Shop, situated in a beautiful panoramic view of New York hills and vineyards, is a "gallery of gorgeous gifts."

Built in 1869, the shop was once a home for tenant farmers. The quaint, cottage shop is located behind a spacious Italian villa-style farmhouse and is constructed of its original brick, wooden beams and homemade square nails.

The atmosphere is relaxed and the merchandise exquisite. Owner Boo Rowland is so selective that she carries only the best in gift items. Original paintings, pewter collectibles, hand-painted scarves, games, copper, pewter, brass, Christmas ornaments, sportswear, bronze windchimes, porcelain, glasswear, china, greeting cards, and original designed jewelry are only some of the quality gifts found at the Luweibdeh Shop. The shop also carries fine collectibles such as music boxes, miniatures, culinary delights and delicious candy - also for diabetics.

The service at the shop is wonderful. Boo is always nearby to answer questions and help customers choose the perfect gift. As a special service, Boo provides a convenient bridal registry for newlyweds.

The lovely Luweibdeh shop is located just west of Fredonia on Route 20. The directions are simple. Take Exit 59 off I-90; follow Route 60 to Route 20; and go west on Route 20 for three miles.

Visitors will love the Luweibdeh Shop's warm atmosphere, beautiful vineyard setting, gracious service, sensational selection of perfectly designed presents and easy accessibility.

SEA GULL GIFT SUOP
255 Lake Shore Drive East
Dunkirk, New York 14048
Tel: (716)366-7608
Hrs: Monday - Saturday 10:00 a.m. - 5:30 p.m.

The Sea Gull Gift Shop is located a half-mile east of the Sheraton Harbor Front. The store's owners, Donna Harmon and Lee Faught, pride themselves on the variety and quality of their merchandise and the special emphasis they've placed on their nautical line. Despite its small size, the Sea Gull is designed very well to accommodate historic memorabilia as well as new gift items.

A clean and friendly atmosphere complements the wide range of nostalgic gifts and there is certainly plenty to see. Racks of magazines and postcards dating back to the early 1900s are fascinating, as is the corner of the store that's devoted to equally aged political memorabilia. Collectors are in a veritable paradise, surrounded by droves of miniature crystal pieces, Spoontiques pewter, framed pictures, souvenir spoons and postcards.

But not to worry, the basics are there. The Sea Gull Gift Shop carries a variety of T-shirts--a perennial vacation gift, favorite gift cards, wind chimes, stuffed animals by Dakin, unique hand-crafted birdhouses and feeders (by Fibra Weave International), Countryside fragrances, potpourri, and countless other merchandise.

The unique and out-of-the-ordinary seem to be a popular theme in this shop, with the hand-crafted birdhouses just beginning the list. An unmistakable treasure is the exquisite collection of Chilean art work done in copper. The true favorite of Donna and Lee is the line of hand-painted, hand-crafted nautical pieces; a one-of-a-kind array in the Dunkirk area, the assortment features DeMott brass ships, and Cardee West sea gulls.

As hands-on owners of the small shop since 1985, Donna and Lee very much enjoy speaking with the customers, helping with gift needs and just creating a fun and relaxed atmosphere. With so much memorabilia and contemporary gift items in one place, the Sea Gull Gift shop definitely warrants a look.

ice cream parlors

ALDRICH'S DAIRY BEEF AND ICE CREAM PARLOR
Route 60 South (10136)
Fredonia, New York 14063

Tel:	(716) 672-5133	
Hrs:	Summer:	
	Seven days	7:00 a.m.- 11:00 p.m.
	Winter:	
	Seven days	7:00 a.m.- 10:00 p.m.

The Aldrich Dairy began as a dairy farm with a small store in 1955 and added a restaurant in 1975. The restaurant serves delicious food and processes its own ice cream. Some of the specialty meals include all beef burgers, Hot Roast Beef on Weck and tasty Bar-B-Que Beef Sandwich. Some of the hearty entrees at Aldrich Dairy are the Rib-Eye steak, Country Fried chicken, mouth-watering fried shrimp, delicious scallops, and more. Each entree comes complete with a choice of potato and salad. All choices on the menu at the Aldrich Beef and Ice cream Parlor are available for take out as well as dining in. Consider drinking fresh milk with a meal; it's only 25 cents for all you can drink. The milk is processed in-house, so it is the freshest milk a milk lover could hope for. The Dairy also offers an array of fountain beverages, coffee and tea.

While enjoying dinner, be sure to leave enough room for some ice cream or pie. The ice cream is also made at the dairy and is farm fresh and delicious. Choose from milkshakes, sundaes with numerous toppings, or one of the parlor's deluxe sundaes such as the banana split or nut boats.

A small gift shop containing cards, souvenirs and novelty items is located in the restaurant. Milk and dairy items can also be purchased at two other Aldrich drive-in dairy stores in Dunkirk and Fredonia.

Each year at Aldrich's on April Fools Day, the shop features a "special" ice cream flavor such as beef gravy ice cream, catsup and mustard swirl, pork and beans, or chocolate spaghetti ice cream. The parlor began the "April Fools Day Flavor of the Day " in 1980 and received national notoriety by being featured on the Johnny Carson show.

Aldrich's Beef & Ice Cream Parlor is located on Route 60 about half a mile south from the Route 20 intersection of Fredonia and offers ample free parking.

There is a family-type atmosphere at Aldrich's. The waitresses are dressed in red and white smocks to match the decor of the room. This restaurant gives patrons a very friendly, relaxed feeling, which keeps them returning time after time.

markets

HAMLET FARM
2691 Route 20
Sheridan, New York 14135
Tel: (716) 672-7004
Hrs: Seven days 8:00 a.m. - 5:30 p.m.

Hamlet Farm, owned by Mr. and Mrs. Edward Hamlet,. is a friendly family owned and operated business that dates back to 1880. Originally a small fresh produce market, it is now a full-scale produce market in addition to being a place where customers can find wicker baskets, tropical trees, shrubs, bedding plants and hanging baskets. Mr. and Mrs. Edward Hamlet are very proud of the long history and reputation they have maintained over the years.

Patrons will find a varied selection of items to choose from at Hamlet Farms; such as Polaner dill pickles, Paisley Farms jam and jelly, relishes, homemade all natural peanut butter, and 25 varieties of apples. Fresh flowers are also available throughout the year along with arrangements, dish gardens, potted plants, silk and dried flower arrangements, bulbs, seeds, and a large selection of garden supplies. Other items on hand to delight are gourds, Indian corn, Christmas plants in season, ribbon, baskets, fresh cheeses cut from blocks, beautiful fuscia plants, and a host of novelty items.

Area elementary schools provide field trips to Hamlet Farm every Autumn, enabling children to see and experience the crispness of the season along with the delightful displays of pumpkins, scarecrows, Indian corn, and an old hollow tree in the backyard which has room for 30 youngsters to play. Boasting a large variety of fresh produce, most of which is grown locally when in season, Hamlet Farm provides service and is sure to please anyone who visits.

points of interest

LILY DALE ASSEMBLY
5 Melrose Park
Lily Dale, New York 14752
Tel: (716) 595-8721
Hrs: Assembly Office:
Summer:
Monday - Friday 9:00 a.m. - 4:00 p.m.
Saturday 9:00 a.m. - Noon
Winter:
Monday - Friday 10:00 a.m. - 2:00 p.m.
Restaurant open year-round.
Gate Fee--reservations are appreciated.

Established in 1879, Lily Dale is an assembly dedicated to spiritual development. This beautiful retreat is bordered by the Chautauqua Uplands. It's no wonder Lily Dale attracts visitors from all over the world. This quaint village offers diverse programs, lectures, and workshops that pertain to spiritualism, science, philosophy and religion.

The Assembly also features a wide range of facilities such as a boat launch, small beach, picnic pavilion, gift shop, book shop, restaurant, museum, auditorium, meeting places, post office, and healing temple. Overnight guests may stay at the historic Maplewood Hotel. Travel trailer parking is abundant.

The non-sectarian environment at Lily Dale provides rest, relaxation, and education for everyone. It's a perfect place for the entire family.

Workshops that help guests develop mediumship abilities are provided, as are daily outdoor religious services, lectures, mediumship demonstrations, personal readings, and several other Assembly events.

Lily Dale is located in Southwestern New York State. From Interstate 90, take Exit 58 to New York Route 60 South. Drive eight miles, and turn right onto Dale Drive. The entrance gate is one mile ahead.

The folks at Lily Dale promise a relaxing, spiritually uplifting visit. The grounds are beautifully landscaped with flowers and decorative shrubs, and the quaint Victorian-style homes are painstakingly preserved. Don't miss Lily and Dale, the prize swans on the Assembly's lovely lake. "Pleasantly Peaceful" is the best way to describe this unique community.

restaurants

RIBBINGS RESTAURANT
Dunkirk-Fredonia Plaza
Dunkirk, New York 14048
Tel: (716) 336-5190
Hrs: Monday - Thursday 6:00 a.m-10:00 p.m.
Friday & Saturday 6:00 a.m-10:00 p.m

Conveniently located at the Dunkirk-Fredonia Plaza just off Central Avenue, Ribbings Restaurant serves over a ton of fresh seafood each week.

Owners Steve and Kay Ribbings offer a daily fish fry that features delicious North Atlantic fish dipped in Steve's special-recipe batter.

Other favorites at Ribbings are crisp, fried chicken, flavorful homemade soups, fresh bakery items, large buttermilk pancakes, and deluxe tossed salads.

The restaurant also serves other daily lunch and dinner specials. Some of the most delectable menu items are the Broil-O-Cheese, fish smothered with yellow cheese and the Seafood Platter, a splendid assortment of shrimp, fish, scallops, and french fries. The restaurant's Dieter's Special contains four ounces of tender broiled fish served in low calorie butter sauce or lemon juice.

Other items that should be tried are the Plaza Burger, a third pound charbroiled hamburger served on a toasted roll; the Boneless Breast of Chicken Sandwich, the piping hot Soup of the Day, the fresh Chicken Nuggets, and the Chicken Fish Combo.

For dessert, try the fresh baked pies a la mode, the scrumptious sundaes, thick milkshakes, or delicious sherbet.

Ribbings also prepares homemade donuts, delectable sweet rolls, wonderful English muffins, and terrific raisin toast.

Steve and Ray cook most of the restaurant's cuisine, and even though the food is prepared on site, the friendly service is incredibly quick. All of Ribbings menu items are also available for take-out.

Ribbings, with its comfortable booth seating; mauve, grey, blue, and cream colored accents; country-style motif; green hanging plants; and lovely dried flower arrangements, has a relaxing family atmosphere. The owners pride themselves on their quality food and low prices. Everything is prepared fresh daily.

Everyone loves Ribbings whether starting the day with a hearty breakfast or enjoying a relaxing evening meal.

wine

CHADWICK BAY WINE COMPANY, Dunkirk, New York: (716) 672-5000. Tasting, tours, and retail. Grapes used: French-American and Native-American.

WOODBURY VINEYARDS
South Roberts Road
Dunkirk, New York 14048
Tel: (716) 679-WINE
Hrs: Monday - Saturday 9:00 a.m. - 5:00 p.m.
Sunday Noon - 5:00 p.m.
Closed Thanksgiving Day, Christmas Day, New Year's Day and Easter Sunday.
Visa and MasterCard are accepted.

Woodbury Vineyards, a 100-acre vineyard consisting mostly of Chardonnay and Riesling vines, is one of the largest European wine-grape vineyards in the United States. The Woodbury family has been cultivating this site since 1909, and in 1968 began growing some of their most famous wine grapes. They chose New York as their viticultural site because the days are warm and the nights are cool. This climate, they say, produces mature grapes with the perfect balance of sweetness and acidity.

Since the family opened the winery in 1980, Woodbury Vineyard Wines has received more than 70 medals--10 of them gold and 41 national and international awards. The Woodburys specialize in high-quality sparkling wines such as Chardonnay, Reisling, and Proprietors' Seyval. Perhaps the reason they keep producing world-class wines is that the Woodbury family is never satisfied. They also produce and bottle experimental lots of Merlot, Cabernet Sauvignon, Gamay Beau-jolais, and Pinot Noir.

Woodbury Vineyards sells its award-winning wines throughout the United States; they also export to Canada and Japan.

In addition to selling premium sparkling wines, the Woodbury Winery and Gift Shop, surrounded by relaxing apple orchards, offers picnic facilities, wine festivals, custom wine labeling, year-round individualized tours, wine tasting, and memberships in their Glacier Ridge Wine Society.

Members of this society receive special newsletters, sale announcements, and invitations to the Barrel-Tasting Party in March and the Summer Picnic in August.

Woodbury Vineyards also offers an "Adopt A Barrel Club." Members of the club have a personalized brass plate placed on the front of their favorite barrel of wine and receive two cases of wine each year from their barrels.

There is so much to love about Woodbury Vineyard--from the Woodbury family's hospitality and enthusiasm to their exquisite Chardonay, Riesling, table, and sparkling wines. Visit world class Woodbury Vineyards in the heart of New York's beautiful wine country and "Uncork New York."

SILVER CREEK

First settled in the 1820s, Silver Creek has retained its 19th century charm. The Skew Arch Railroad Bridge on Jackson Street boasts a unique feature of being constructed on an angle. This and a similar bridge in Russia are the only ones of this kind in the world.

attractions

Silver Creek boasts of its fine examples of Victorian architecture. Free summer band concerts are performed on the William Huntley Bandstand.

events

The Festival of Grapes is held the third weekend in September in Village Park. For over 20 years, the festival has celebrated the grape harvest with stomping contests, arts and crafts fair, and a parade.

restaurants

HIDEAWAY BAY RESTAURANT
42 Lake Avenue
Silver Creek, New York 14136
Tel: (716) 934-4442
Hrs: Tuesday - Saturday 11:30 a.m. - 10:00 p.m.
Sunday 1:00 p.m. - 8:00 p.m.
Lounge: Open until 2:00 a.m.
Reservations are appreciated.
Visa, MasterCard and American Express are accepted.

The character of the Hideaway Bay Restaurant may be summed up in one statement--a delightful atmosphere that includes magnificent service and an extensive menu stocked with culinary delights. The restaurant's owner since 1983, Don Beckstien, takes tremendous pride in that atmosphere, as well as beautiful views of the lake and breathtaking sunsets provided by the ceiling-to-floor windows. A nautical motif is maintained, with fish netting and large fish tanks accenting both the dining and bar areas. The open-beam natural wood ceilings and two fireplaces instill a warm feeling in all visitors, as the fresh flowers and skylights brighten things just a bit. However, the food is undisputably the main attraction.

Just for starters, or for a meal in itself, is the Seafood Chowder that has received accolades from TV's Jeff Smith, the Frugal Gourmet. The long list of unforgettable creations span the menu in each category: soups, cold and hot appetizers, pasta, chicken, beef, veal and, of course, seafood.

In addition to the Seafood Chowder, the Baked French Onion Au Gratin breaks new ground in French onion soup. It is a traditional French recipe that utilizes five varieties of onions topped with three cheeses. For a cold appetizer, there's the Hearts of Artichokes Dijonese. Escargot fans will delight in the Escargot Bourguignonne, while chicken liver lovers may find a new treat in the Chicken Livers Bluebeard.

The seafood specialties range from the traditional Shrimp and Scallop Scampi to Brazilian Lobster Tails and includes just about everything in between. A lobster tub containing live Maine lobsters assures diners that their selections will be fresh. Cajun Blackened Swordfish is an eight-ounce southern delicacy, while the Seafood Fantasy Platter includes butterflied cold-water lobster tail, stuffed shrimp, breaded scallops, deviled crab, and filet of haddock and is the best choice for those who can't decide.

In addition to the dazzling cuisine, the Hideaway Bay Restaurant offers finger foods and sandwiches in a menu for the patio and lounge, not to mention docking facilities for smaller boats and a tender boat that will retrieve guests from their larger boats anchored in the water. They also cater out to the larger vessels.

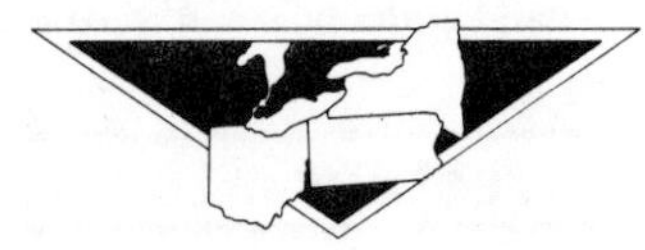

ERIE COUNTY

Erie County was established in 1821 from Niagara County and was named for the Erie Tribe. The first settlements to the county took place in Buffalo in 1794-95, but were burned during the War of 1812.

Samuel Wilkinson finished construction on a breakwater, or barrier, for Buffalo's harbor in 1821, and four years later, the Erie Canal connected Buffalo to New York Harbor.

Many important events have occurred in Erie County. Wells Fargo Express was established in Buffalo and the Pan American Exposition of 1901, where President McKinley was assassinated, took place there as well.

The Niagara River and Frontier blend the breathtaking, cascading Niagara Falls with its surrounding land. What is created is an atmosphere that is both exciting and relaxing. Many fun-filled activities await visitors of the region while those searching for a peaceful place will find those areas plentiful as well.

attractions

Evangola State Park in Farnham offers a beautiful sand beach on Lake Erie, several nature trails, swimming, fishing, hunting, hiking and camping facilities. Cross-country skiing and snowmobiling are available in the winter.

The **Buffalo and Erie County Botanical Gardens** contains 12 greenhouses featuring a wide selection of plants from around the world. Featured is the palm dome, a central dome that houses the gardens' collection of palm. Ferns, hydrophytes, cycads, cactus, assorted plants, orchids, and edible fruits are available for inspection. A marketplace, where the Children's Learning Garden is located, provides an area for kids and adults to learn about the living plants commonly used for clothing, food and medicine.

The nation's very first basilica, **Our Lady of Victory National Shrine**, is open year-round and tours of the facilities are available.

events

The **Erie County Fair and Expo** is held each August at Erie County Fairgrounds in Hamburg.

April in Lackawanna brings the annual **Easter Parade**, a festive celebration sure to please people of all ages.

ANGOLA

restaurants

CASTAWAYS WATERFRONT BAR AND GRILL
Kennedy and Old Lake Shore Roads
Angola-on-the-Lake, New York 14006
Tel: (716) 549-6090
Hrs: Monday - Friday Open at 11:30 a.m.
Saturday - Sunday Open at Noon
Bar: Open until 4:00 a.m.
Visa, MasterCard and American Express are accepted.

Located in Angola on the Lake, right on the beach overlooking Lake Erie, is Castaways Waterfront Bar and Grill. Inherent in its bright new beach house look are loads of fun and good food.

Historically a favorite spot from the early 1900s, the establishment had gone into a 20-year tailspin until Michael Holland and Kip Feinen, the present owners, took over in 1988 and performed a complete renovation. Since then, Castaways has been remarkably well received by the community and is still gaining momentum.

Giant windows overlooking the lake provide a breathtaking view of the sunset, a picturesque complement to the knotty paneling and large perimeter bar. The upstairs is an intimate dining room complete with fireplace, small bar, and magnificent view from the outside patio. Downstairs is the large bar, CD jukebox and site of the live entertainment provided by easy listening and rhythm and blues bands every weekend. Castaways is simply an upscale bar and grille that provides an upscale and fun adult atmosphere.

A simple but very versatile and well-prepared menu offers such perennial favorites as Deep-Fried Mozzarella with Marinara Sauce, Buffalo-Style Wings, and Clam and Potato Chowder or Hot Spuds (thick steak fries smothered in nacho cheese and topped with lots of jalapeno slices).

Move on to creative menus specializing in charbroiling, such as Lemon Pepper Swordfish and Tuna Steak topped with capers or the Castaways special sandwiches like the Chicken Clipper (boneless breast of chicken marinated in their own recipe and charbroiled to perfection served with a side of Sweet Hot Mustard) or the Trump Princess (a burger of the best ground meat broiled to exact specifications, served open-face with Grey Poupon and a bottle of Dom Perignon).

Friday brings a "Fresh from the Wharf" special that offers a large filet of fresh fish, breaded or battered, and served with cole slaw, macaroni salad and a choice of potato salad or homemade steak fries.

The meal may be complemented with a selection from the page full of beer and wine, a choice from the extensive bar, and/or a treat from the exquisite, ever changing dessert cart. Regardless of the choices, Castaways is an elegant, yet relaxed, dining experience.

THE POINT BREEZE HOTEL
9536 Lake Shore Road
Angola, New York 14006
Tel: (716) 549-9846
Hrs: End of May - October: 4:00 p.m. - 4:00 a.m.

Originally a turn-of-the-century hotel, the Point Breeze Hotel has been transformed into a lively lakeside bar and restaurant. Caribbean Extravaganza Shows, Big Steve Polka Shows, and Blarney Bunch Irish performances are only a few of the out of the ordinary events at this by-the-beach meeting place.

Playing on the club's co-ed volleyball league is a great way the get the summer rolling. To cool off after all that exercise, indulge in one of the Point Breeze Hotel's drink specialties. The Beachcomber Cooler, with island fruit juices, melon, vodka, and cream, and the South Pacific Stinger, a blend of soft brandy and white Creme de Menthe, are soothing summer concoctions. Non-alcoholic thirst-quenchers include Lemon-twist Perrier, Virgin Marys, Pina Coladas and Strawberry Daiquiris.

The drinks and diversions aren't the Point Breeze Hotel's only claims to fame: The PBH Galley offers decidedly superb dinners, too. The Build-Your-Own Beachburger is a half-pound of charbroiled sirloin topped with any combination of mozzarella cheese, mushrooms, sauteed onions and peppers, bleu cheese and bacon. Other specialties are the BBQ Chicken Breast and the BBQ Ribs.

The menu also includes such nautical entrees as the Fisherman's Delight (breaded or broiled catch of the day, shrimp, sea scallops, crabmeat-stuffed shrimp. and clams casino) and pasta-lovers' items like the Fettucini Alfredo with Sea Legs Supreme Crabmeat. The dessert specials vary daily.

Irish coffee, hot citrus tea with melon liqueur and lemon juice, and steaming Nutty Buddy Coffee with Frangelica and Irish Cream are enticing after-dinner beverages.

The Point Breeze, which boasts that it has the biggest sandbox in Western New York, offers fabulous food; sparkling beverages; events like pig roasts, bonfires, New Year's in July, Christmas in July, end of the summer burial (during which all of the summer's memorabilia is collected, placed inside a large casket, and burned in a huge bonfire ceremony); and other activities too numerous to mention.

Located 30 minutes south of Buffalo, the Point Breeze Hotel borders Lake Erie, but the tropical ambiance is undoubtedly reminiscent of a Key West Patio Lounge.

HAMBURG

Hamburg, the birthplace of the hamburger, once comprised two incorporated villages and several unincorporated communities. In 1850, it was reduced to its present size.

Hamburg was first settled by New Englanders. The State Legislature incorporated the town in 1812 and Lakeshore Railroad, built in 1852 and stretching from Buffalo to Cleveland, brought railroads to the town.

One of the largest county fairs in the United States, the Erie County Fair and Exposition, came to Hamburg in 1868. Seventeen years later, concessionaire Frank Menches and his brother Charles cooked their special pork sausage sandwich. Frank substituted chopped beef for pork when the local meat market ran out of pork. A touch of light brown sugar on top of the patty completed the impromptu sandwich, the hamburger, now a classic.

attractions

Hamburg Historical Society, a museum which features Western New York's Genealogical Society Library, provides displays depicting the history of the town of Hamburg. It is open Saturday through Tuesday.

Buffalo Raceway, located on the Erie County Fairgrounds, showcases the driving and racing talent of Buffalo's best harness racing.

florists

EXPRESSIONS FLORAL & GIFT SHOPPE, INC.
11 Buffalo Street
Hamburg, New York 14075
Tel: (716) 648-2110

Hrs:	Monday - Thursday	8:30 a.m. - 6:00 p.m.
	Friday	8:30 a.m. - 8:00 p.m.
	Saturday	8:30 a.m. - 5:00 p.m.
	Sunday	10:00 a.m. - 2:00 p.m.

Open until 8:00 p.m. starting two weeks before Thanksgiving and Christmas.
Visa and MasterCard are accepted.

A full-service floral and gift shop since 1983, Expressions Floral & Gift Shoppe is able to fill most every need. Patricia Courtney, the store's owner, provides not only a special creativity, but a sincere concern for every individual that enters her establishment. A wide array of fresh and silk flowers combined with an extensive assortment of gift items is what can be found at Expressions Floral & Gift Shoppe.

The words "full-service" are to be taken in their most literal meaning. They provide an entire room devoted to bridal needs, and offer a tremendous range of bridal services including a fully-serviced wedding (with personalized attention at both the church and reception), rentals of containers, candelabras, arches, a complimentary throw-away bouquet, pearl-trimmed head pieces, a special bridal gift, shower gifts, attendant's gifts, and much, much more. They will also cater to parties; provide service with sensitivity at funerals; and help with home decor utilizing custom silk arrangements and plants--their specialty. A custom service is offered for homes and businesses that want to achieve just the right atmosphere.

The gift portion of the shop should by no stretch of the imagination be thought of as secondary. Courtney and her husband travel the country in a constant search for new and unique gifts. The result of her efforts is an ever-changing inventory of quality products and distinctively designed specialties. As evidence are the Scarborough soaps and scented accessories, Carin "Wood Spirits," Louise Nichole fragrances, Lizzie High Collectibles, and "Seasons" potpourri gift boxes. Indulge in specialty foods like "Buffalo Chips," a gourmet cookie, "Elite Treats," gourmet chocolate-covered potato chips, Praline Puffs, and much more.

In addition to the obvious attractions, Expressions Floral and Gift Shoppe is staffed with highly-trained, friendly individuals who render assistance in providing the perfect floral or gift selections. The excellent service is complemented by a fragrant, clean atmosphere and creative displays.

Teleflora and FTD are utilized to provide around-the-world shipping, and special requests are not only entertained, but receive the extra attention they deserve.

malls

MCKINLEY MALL
Corner Milestrip Road and McKinley Parkway
Hamburg, New York 14219
Tel: (716) 824-0462
Hrs: Monday - Saturday 10:00 a.m. - 9:00 p.m.
Sunday Noon - 5:00 p.m.

McKinley Mall, The Mall of the Southern Tier, is well-known to shoppers in the counties of Erie, Chautauqua and Cattaraugus for its size and convenience. This mall, with 850,000 square feet of space, of course has many shops to explore. Directions at each corridor end guide customers to A. M. & A.'s, Sears, Kaufmann's, L. L. Berger, six General Cinema Theaters, and over 90 specialty shops and stores. In addition to these shops, a proposed J.C. Penney wing is still to open. The mall, celebrating its fourth anniversary on October 8, 1989, welcomes mall walkers from 8:00 a.m. to 10:00 a.m. (It's one mile around the mall.) Complementary wheelchairs are provided for shoppers, and strollers are also available.

A large gazebo decorated for the season is located at the center of the mall. Water fountains surrounding the gazebo provide a relaxing effect for hurried shoppers. Lush greenery is located throughout the mall and planted trees under dome skylights give the mall an upbeat airy feeling. It is the perfect location for the many events hosted here. A partial list of these events include a Boat Show, a Bridal Fair, Mercy Hospital Health Fair, a Mallwalker's Fashion Show, Charity/Community Day, Arts and Crafts Shows, the Mardi Gras Mallwalk Sale, a Corvette Show, a Hand-Made Quilt Exhibit, Back-to-School Fashion Shows, Armed Forces Displays, and an Antique & Collectibles Show. The mall also hosts a Midnight Madness sale before Christmas.

The McKinley Mall is a favorite with shoppers because it has such a wide variety of shops. But it is not so big that a customer would become lost or confused. In addition to all of its shops, the mall offers an International Food Court with over 13 different eateries to choose from. The mall is minutes from Erie County Fairgrounds, Buffalo Raceway, Hamburg Village and downtown Buffalo. The mall welcomes bus tours; and is the perfect location for a group to shop, grab a bite to eat, and catch a movie. Its cleanliness, convenient design, size, and selection of shops make McKinley Mall, the Mall of the Southern Tier, a "Best Choice" for shoppers.

restaurants

BOBBY O'BRIANS TAVERN ON THE GREEN
South 5324 Rogers Road
Hamburg, New York 14075

Tel:	(716) 648-2700	
Hrs:	Sunday - Thursday	11:00 a.m. - Midnight
	Lunch;	
	Friday - Saturday	11:00 a.m. - 2:00 p.m.
	Dinner:	
	Friday - Saturday	After 5:00 p.m.

Visa, MasterCard and American Express are accepted.

Located on the grounds of beautiful Brierwood Country Club, Bobby O'Brians Tavern on the Green is a public restaurant in a very private setting. Using only choice ingredients, Bobby O'Brians' chefs--graduates of Culinary Institute--prepare delicious culinary delights, such as Chicken Salad Almondine, Tournados Rossini, and the ever popular Surf & Turf.

The dinners include steaming homemade soup and fresh fruit in season, a tossed salad, a choice of vegetable and potato, rolls and butter, and choice of beverage and dessert. Desserts such as ice cream, fruit pies, black forest cake, and strawberry or chocolate mousse are available with dinners at no extra charge; several other deliciously daring desserts--like Grand Marnier Mousse and Cherries Jubilee--are offered at a very reasonable price (all $1.50 or less).

Bobby O'Brians also provides a dinner buffet to groups of 50 or more. The beverage selection is as varied as the food selection, with everything from Canadian beer to Champagne punch.

The turn-of-the-century decor is complemented by handsome polished oak paneling, a working fireplace, 50-pound antique chandeliers, brass furnishings, an elegant patio bar, a garden setting and a gorgeous gazebo. A magnificent view is seen from the semi-circular dining area overlooking a huge portion of the golf course--a must-see at night when the grounds are lit. On a clear night, diners can also see a breathtaking view of the Buffalo skyline.

As if the fantastic view, relaxed yet elegant atmosphere, and creme de la creme cuisine weren't enough, Bobby O'Brians offers many monthly activities ranging from the Winter Carnival (featuring everything from ice sculpturing to sleigh rides to raise money for Children's Hospital) to the Murder Mystery Dinners when diners are invited to help solve hilarious murder mysteries.

Voted "Restaurant of the Month" by local newspaper subscribers, Bobby O'Brians is a delightful departure from the ordinary restaurant. Though it's located at Brierwood Country Club, it is open to the public. If in search of one of the finest dining spots in Erie County, discover Bobby O'Brians Tavern on the Green.

SALFRANCO'S
4300 Abbott Road
Hamburg, New York 14075
Tel: (716) 649-7644
Hrs:

Summer:	
Sunday - Thursday	11:30 a.m. - Midnight
Friday	11:30 a.m. - 1:00 a.m.
Saturday	4:00 p.m. - 1:00 a.m.
Winter:	
Sunday - Thursday	
Lunch:	11:30 a.m - 2:30 p.m.
Dinner:	4:00 p.m. - 11:00 p.m.
Friday	11:30 a.m. - 1:00 a.m.
Saturday	4:00 p.m. - 1:00 a.m.

Visa, MasterCard, American Express, Diners Club and Discover are accepted.

This "Southtowns Gathering Place" is located half a country block from Rich Stadium, home of the Buffalo Bills. Salfranco's restaurant, a "Buffalo Booster," has a contemporary, upbeat feeling to it. The close community atmosphere makes it the perfect place to go for a night out and the best place to go after a Bills' game for great food and conversation.

The Veal Parmigiana is made of only the finest grade of tender veal and topped with melted cheese and sauce. Served with a salad and side order of spaghetti, it is irresistible. Customer favorites are the Fettuccine Alfredo in a perfect light cream and parmesan cheese sauce, and the seafood pasta marinara. American dishes include Prime Rib, Barbecued Spare Ribs, and Broiled New York Strip Steaks. The fish is always fresh and tasty The Broiled Scallops are a house specialty. Stuffed peppers and french fried mozzarella sticks are perfect appetizers before dinner or as a snack for those with a smaller appetite. In addition to their dinner menu, Salfranco's also has a complete pizza and a hot and cold sub menu. Specialties such as their Mexican Taco Pizza or Vegetable Pizza will wake up the appetite of a bored pizza fan. All items are available for take out.

A merry-go-round horse and plants decorate a window, and an antique tricycle hanging from a wall gives character to the place. Model cars displayed on one wall, posters of Buffalo and Buffalo sports, and a pine ceiling complete the decor. Salfranco's, a family-run business established in 1970, is a "Best Choice" for diners. Not only "Where the Southtowns Meet" but also where good food and reasonable prices get acquainted.

specialty shops

THE ORIGINAL AMERICAN KAZOO COMPANY
8703 South Main Street
Eden, New York 14057
Tel: (716) 992-3960
Hrs: Tuesday - Saturday 10:00 a.m. - 5:00 p.m.
Sunday Noon - 5:00 p.m.
Closed Mondays.
Visa and MasterCard are accepted.

The Original American Kazoo Company is the exclusive metal manufacturer of the world famous musical instrument. Established in 1916, the one-of-a-kind factory uses original techniques to produce the Kazoo. The Original American Kazoo Company is a combination gift shop, factory and museum. Kazoos take 18 to 27 steps to make depending on the variety. The company has step-by-step instructions on display describing construction of the Kazoo.

The unique company is owned by Brimms Inc., and is likened to the factory that time forgot. The machines that make the Kazoos are the exact same die presses that were installed in 1907. The Original American Kazoo Company used to manufacture other small items from fishing tackle to toy flutes, but in 1916 the presses were adapted for Kazoo manufacture only. The Kazoo is the only true American musical instrument and is displayed in the Smithsonian Museum.

At the gift shop there are wooden, plastic and metal Kazoos with different shapes, such as trombone and trumpets, for sale to visitors. The shop also contains many types of unusual toys, interesting gift ideas, educational and science toys, cards, Christmas gifts, kaleidoscopes and fine jewelry. The book selection includes subjects on travel, children's classics, how-to, and gardening. The gift shop is noted for its uniqueness, making it an ideal choice for those who are difficult to buy for.

The employees are always very friendly and eager to demonstrate all aspects of the history and production of the famous Kazoo. The Original American Kazoo Company is also noted for carrying many items that are not found anywhere else. They're open year-round and admission is free. Be sure to stop in.

EAST AURORA

Home to the Roycroft Campus and Fisher-Price Toys, East Aurora has maintained much of its 19th century architecture.

attractions

When Elbert Hubbard founded the Roycroft Movement in 1895, it attracted artists and craftsmen to the **Roycroft Campus**. Designated a National Historic Landmark, the 14 buildings contain craft and gift shops, pottery studio, art gallery and museum.

The Scheidel Mantel House was built by Roycroft craftsmen as a private residence. This 1910 Craftsmen bungalow houses the **Elbert Hubbard Museum**, featuring furnishings and artifacts.

The Millard Fillmore Museum is the restored home of the 13th President and his wife Abigail.

Aurora Town Museum, located in **Aurora Town Hall**, offers history buffs a look at the heritage of East Aurora with works that are depicted, chronologically, on murals by Rix Jennings.

events

The **Annual East Aurora Art Society Outdoor Show** and **Annual Roycroft Summer Festival** are held in late June.

Racing Day pays tribute to the days when East Aurora was known as the trotting capital of the world. It is held each year on the last weekend in July,

East Aurora becomes Toytown U.S.A. in late August to celebrate **Toyfest**.

accommodations

TONY ROME'S GLOBE HOTEL & RESTAURANT
711 Main Street
East Aurora, New York 14052
Tel: (716) 652-4221
Hrs: Open year-round:
Monday - Saturday 11:00 a.m. - Midnight
Sunday 2:00 a.m. - 10:00 p.m.
Visa, Mastercard and American Express are accepted.

Conveniently located in the center of East Aurora's business district, Tony Rome's Globe Hotel & Restaurant was established in 1824 as the Globe Hotel. The hotel was once a famous stagecoach stop and is the second oldest commercial building in the town. Don't be fooled by the name; the building is no longer a hotel, but a highly respected restaurant, known for its traditional American menu items especially the Barbecued Baby Back Ribs, succulent steaks, and ocean-fresh seafood.

It also offers homemade soups and a variety of daily specials. The fresh haddock fish fry is available daily; the 15 cent Wing Special is served on Mondays and Tuesdays; the Peel-n-Eat Shrimp Special is on Wednesdays; and the New York Strip Steak and Snow Crab Legs Special is prepared on Thursdays and Saturdays. The Western New York specialties are Chicken Wings and Beef on Weck.

The Potato Skins, filled with cheddar cheese, bacon bits and served with sour cream, and the Deep-Fried Assorted Vegetable Basket served with the restaurants special recipe dip, are other advisable appetizers to try at Tony Rome's.

The delectable homemade desserts, such as the cherry or raspberry topped cheesecake, the carrot cake with cream cheese icing, the fresh-from-the-oven pies, and the luscious birthday cakes (request in advance) are all a perfect ending to an excellent meal.

Walking through the front door at Tony Rome's gives the feeling of stepping back into the late 19th century. The early ambiance of the former hotel is well preserved, even though the building has been beautifully renovated. A large built-in hutch adds a homey feeling to the large dining room; Mary Carroll oil paintings decorate the walls and two cozy fireplaces lend the restaurant a relaxed, rustic feeling.

Whether working in town, enjoying a ski getaway in the southtowns, or just passing by, stop at Tony Rome's Hotel and Restaurant. It's a great place for an intimate meal or a fun gathering with friends and family.

Gift certificates, take-outs, and meeting and party facilities are also available.

furniture stores

SCHOOLHOUSE GALLERY
1054 Olean Road
East Aurora, New York 14052
Tel: (716) 655-4080
Hrs: Monday - Sunday 10:00 a.m. - 5:00 p.m.
Visa and MasterCard are accepted.

Just minutes outside the village of East Aurora, New York, one can spend an interesting and educational day at the Schoolhouse Gallery.

The Gallery is located in old schoolhouse number seven, and it specializes in 18th and 19th century hand-made reproductions. The old schoolhouse was built in 1850, and was used for almost 100 years to educate the children of the community during the week, and would open its doors to the rest of the public for church on Sunday.

Today the schoolhouse's beautifully-made wood furniture is crafted by the Roycroft Renaissance Master Craftsmen, Thomas A. Harris and Bennett R. Little. Tom and Ben are carrying on the Roycroft tradition, which started in the late 1890s by founder Elbert Hubbard. They adopted his work philosophy that each piece of work is "made the best we can."

Cabinets, tables, desks, benches, and other wood pieces are all crafted from the finest woods, and are on display throughout the Gallery. Custom-made items are a large part of the Gallery's business; their customers get exactly what they want in a woodpiece. In addition to wood pieces and cabinets, they offer display works created by 20 local artists. Some of their items include: tole paintings, stained glass, woven and braided mats, rugs, quilts, wood carvings, pottery and much more.

The Schoolhouse itself is designed in a very simple fashion, but, inside, the wood pieces are selectively placed around the edges of the room, giving all who stop by a cozy feeling. Tom and Ben's most important concern is to try to make the best possible product they can, and that each piece be totally hand-crafted. Their hope is that someday their pieces will become collectors' items, just as the original Roycroft pieces are today.

ice cream parlors

SUNDAE'S
716 Main Street
East Aurora, New York 14052
Tel: (716) 655-1630
Hrs: Fall - Spring: 11:00 a.m. - 10:00 p.m.
Closes Sundays after Christmas.
Summer:
Seven days 11:00 a.m.- 11:00 p.m
Weekends 11:00 a.m. - 11:30 p.m.

Located on Main Street in downtown East Aurora, Sundae's is entering its 11th year of business. This ice cream shop and restaurant creates the feeling of a "Happy Days" set with its nostalgic interior and old-fashioned creativity. Norma Wilk, the shop's owner, makes this place special. She is a kind and sincere lady, and a friend to all who enter. Norma works around the clock, but always makes time to stop and chat with her customers. When Norma took over the business five and a half years ago she completely renovated the interior. The goal of authenticity was met with old-fashioned booths, a soda bar with bar stools, antique ice cream chairs, back bar with original leaded glass, and striped miniprint wallpaper. Extra touches include old-fashioned tulip dishes, glass sundae boats, old-fashioned soda glasses and authentic Coke glasses.

It is ironic that the '50s atmosphere has led to the same type of '50s behavior. Sundae's is a basic neighborhood ice cream parlor where friends meet for a sandwich and kids meet after school for a sundae. Everybody is on a first name basis and those who work here are lifelong friends to most, thanks to the special environment that has been created.

The food served here is delicious. Choose from the selection of sandwiches that include Egg n' Olive, Grilled Cheese and Bacon, and Cream Cheese n' Olive. A choice of two homemade soups is offered daily. Fantastic apple, lemon meringue, raspberry or chocolate peanut butter pie are also baked daily.

There are far too many ice cream specialties to be mentioned, but a couple of favorites are the Turtle, (hot fudge and hot caramel sauces over vanilla ice cream, with pecans, whipped cream, and a cherry half), and the Brownie Royal, (a chocolate brownie with vanilla ice cream, hot fudge, marshmallow sauce, whipped cream, and chocolate jimmies). The shop also makes the Banana Split the old traditional way.

Sundae's owner, great food, a unique atmosphere and, of course, its ice cream special make a visit to the parlour an interesting as well as tasty experience.

restaurants

OLD ORCHARD INN
2095 Blakeley Corners Road
East Aurora, New York 14052
Tel: (716) 652-4664
Hrs: Lunch:

Hrs:	Lunch:	
	Monday - Saturday	11:30 a.m. - 2:30 p.m.
	Dinner:	
	Monday - Friday	5:00 p.m. - 9:00 p.m.
	Saturday	5:00 p.m. - 10:00 p.m.
	Sunday	12:00 p.m. - 9:00 p.m.

Open all Holidays except for Christmas.
Visa, MasterCard and American Express are accepted.

The charming Old Orchard Inn offers a delightful country gift shop and an elegant restaurant. Formerly a farmhouse, a hunting lodge, and then a tea room, this rustic inn sits beautifully atop a winding country road in the center of 30 rolling acres of lovely New York countryside. The Inn is 90 years old with rustic decor, wood beam ceilings, a relaxing bar earth tone accent, and three glowing fireplaces, one being an authentic Roycroft stone fireplace. Six intimate dining areas contain large windows that offer a panoramic view of the estate-like scenery.

The restaurant simply serves outstanding food. The house specialty is the Chicken Fricassee with biscuits and rich chicken gravy, but there are several other choice dishes at the Old Orchard Inn. Shrimp Scampi, six ounce Pepper Steak, Lamb Chops with mint apple jelly, Australian Lobster Tail, and the hearty Soup of the Day are just a few of the inn's mouth watering dishes.

The seafood selections are deliciously flavored and individually baked for tenderness and rich taste. The Halibut, flavored with white wine and the North Atlantic Bluefin Tuna are true delicacies. There's no rushing through a meal at this cozy inn. All entrees include a fruit tray, salad, freshly-baked cinnamon rolls and fresh vegetables.

Owners Joyce and Jack Waterhouse are proud of the healthy cuisine served at the inn. Nothing is ever fried. The couple's uncompromising attention to detail in both food preparation and presentation is very impressive. The restaurant serves a variety of luncheon specials such as homemade Chicken Soup, Chicken-a-la-King, zesty salads, and specialty sandwiches. After a superb meal, try the lavish Lemon Angel Pie or Vanilla Custard, or a Butter Rum Parfait for dessert.

The inn's bright red Silo Gift Shop was originally a barn and silo and the original horse stalls still divide the shop. This very different gift shop offers crystal, brass, and copper gifts, tabletop and wall decorations, jewelry, holiday items and other country collectibles.

To locate this cozy country inn, take route 400 to Route 20-A, turn right into the village of East Aurora, turn left at the first light, then follow Olean Road for two miles to arrive at Blakeley Road.

The Old Orchard Inn prepares savory cuisine the old-fashioned way, provides postcard-like scenery, offers wonderfully hospitable service, and is a great place to visit while in the Great Lakes area.

specialty stores

COUNTRY BREADS & MORE
1089 Davis Road (Route 240)
West Falls, New York 14170
Tel: (716) 655-0039
Hrs: Tuesday - Sunday 9:00 a.m. - 4:00 p.m.
Serving until 3:00 p.m.
Closed Mondays and holidays.
Visa and MasterCard are accepted.

A distinct number of tempting homemade baked goods and good old-fashioned quality and flavor call for a visit to Country Breads & More. Country Breads is a quaint country store, bakery, and restaurant--serving delightful baked goods and foods. In the tradition of an old-time country store, owners Ray and Joyce Wohlfeil have filled the store with a variety of charming locally-made handcrafts, jams, jellies, and other wonderful gifts.

For breakfast, Country Breads serves a delightful assortment of country breakfast specials including hearty portions of old-fashioned thick oatmeal with honey and real butter; thick french toast with pure maple syrup, butter and a choice of ham, bacon, sausage or hash; delicious fresh fruit with cottage cheese; and whole-grain pancakes served with fresh fruit or homemade applesauce.

The lunches are equally tempting with gravy-smothered meat pies called Pasties being a favorite dish. The Chicken Breast Delight, Quiche of the Day, Herb-Baked Haddock, steamy homemade soups, and specialty salads--such as the Chicken Salad made with fresh breast of chicken, pineapple, celery, and almonds--are just as delicious. One of the most unique meals at Country Breads is "The Country Basket For Two" filled with cheese, fresh fruit and flaky croissants. Everything is prepared fresh with the customer in mind in their country kitchen by their select staff using only the finest ingredients. Special requests including special dietary needs are cheerfully filled when possible. For cholesterol-watchers, the menu includes many different low-cholesterol items.

The bakery offers more than 20 varieties of homemade breads and a wide variety of pot pies, quiches, soups, noodles, gift baskets--"A Sampler of our Baked Goods", wedding cakes, and other goodies.

The pastoral ambiance and decor are reminiscent of Grandma's house. The one-story restaurant, with its hand-painted Pennsylvania Dutch welcome sign, oak pedestal tables, spindle-back chairs, white doilies, antique ice box, oak display cabinets, country dolls, stuffed rabbits and bears, wicker baskets, and assortment of antiques, is warm and relaxing.

Good food,-not fast food, is the goal of Country Breads. "For fast service," say the owners, "go to Buffalo. Here, we are south of the tension line, so relax and give us time to prepare an order with tender loving care." Aside from serving sit-down meals, the restaurant provides take-out and catering services.

Stop by Country Breads & More and plan to stay awhile.

VIDLER'S 5 & 10
680-694 Main Street
East Aurora, New York 14052-2487
Tel: (716) 652-0481
Hrs: Monday - Saturday 8:30 a.m. - 6:00 p.m.
Friday Open until 9:00 p.m.
Personal checks are accepted.

Visitors to East Aurora, New York have a special opportunity to take a nostalgic trip into the past at Vidler's 5 & 10. Opened in 1930 by Robert S. Vidler and maintained by his sons Bob and Ed Vidler, this store retains many of its original features including the most important one -- its feeling of a "simplistic era when prices were low, conversation friendly and customer service a pleasure."

This store is easily distinguished from other Main Street businesses by tourists as well as townsfolk; its gold leafed sign and cheerful red and white striped awning welcome visitors inside. Dating from the 1890s, the building has new additions that offer many nooks and crannies that are fun to explore while its wooden floors, original cash register and counters maintain the atmosphere of old-fashioned quality and bargains. These two things are just what customers can expect to find with a multitude of items to choose from.

Every product imaginable can be found at Vidler's from housewares to toys. Fisher-Price began their business in East Aurora the same year Vidler's opened. Naturally, with these two businesses as neighbors, shoppers find the complete line of Fisher-Price Toys here. The housewares department offers hard-to-find kitchen gadgets and novelties. Supplies and instruction books for old and new crafts are available by the hundreds; those who enjoy needlecrafts find all varieties of yarn in a rainbow of shades. Quilters have hundreds of calicos to choose from along with every necessary notion for sewing. Collectors of doll house miniatures may think they're in paradise at Vidler's; they can complete any room with things like tiny teapots, wall clocks and candelabras.

Customers can easily spend hours exploring Vidler's 5 & 10. It's a "Best Choice" in East Aurora and "It's a Fun Place to Shop!" Bob and Ed welcome bus tours (approximately 50 stop by each year) and they personally wait on their customers answering questions about the store's history. Vidler's may be the only place left where one can receive a bag of popcorn for 10 cents and have their weight and fortune told for a penny.

ORCHARD PARK

attractions

The home of the Buffalo Bills, **Rich Stadium**, is located in Orchard Park.

The **Quaker Arts Pavilion** features concerts and community events in an outdoor setting from June through August.

markets

SAVILLE'S
3910 North Buffalo Road
Orchard Park, New York 14127
Tel: (716) 662-4485 (Farm Market)
(716) 662-4483 (Florist)
(716) 662-4487 (Garden Center)
Hrs: Late March - Christmas:
Daily 8:30 a.m. - Dusk
Friday Until 9:00 p.m.
Sunday Until 5:00 p.m.
Closed Sunday from Christmas until late March.
Visa and MasterCard are accepted.

Saville's Farm Market has descended from three generations of dedicated farmers. The family business is still providing the best quality fruits and vegetables year-round. Saville's began in the mid 1800s as a small farm in South Buffalo when great grandfather Saville raised crops for himself and others in the Buffalo area. He saw his farm become what is now Cazinovia Park. In order to continue the tradition, he started providing fresh, homegrown foods, and purchased land in Orchard Park which he passed down to his sons. Today the family farms 125 acres of farmland and is a four department business.

Saville's Garden Shop handles sales, and services lawnmowers, snowblowers, chainsaws, and other small equipment. At the greenhouse they raise geraniums, annuals and perennials. Many of their fruits and vegetables start here and are later transplanted to the fields. The florist shop is full-service and has a wide variety of flowers and plants. Saville's is probably best known for its farm market and the delicious fresh fruits and vegetables that are available year-round. Customers are confident about purchases that are made here, knowing that the produce is fresh from the farm and has never set in a warehouse waiting for delivery to a supermarket. One can share the joys of fresh produce with a friend through a personalized fruit or gift basket from Saville's. They make over 5,000 baskets each year and offer same-day delivery service in the Buffalo area. Styles and sizes vary to suit individual needs.

Specialty items such as cheese, jelly, candy, honey, tea or sausage may be included.

Saville's also has its own cider mill. Visitors may enjoy a taste of this cider that has been a family tradition for 20 years. Or if the time of year is right, one may be able to join in the annual family hayride to the pumpkin patch. When asked what they are most proud of, folks at Saville's said..."Our customers...we owe everything to our wonderful customers." The customer also has a lot to be thankful for at Saville's: corn that is famous for its sweet taste, big juicy strawberries, Saville's luscious purple raspberries (a cross between black and red raspberries), and their 28 different vegetables. A tradition of good quality produce and a concern for the customer are the reasons that Saville's is a "Best Choice" for the picky shopper.

specialty shops

COOKIE EXPRESSIONS
4227 North Buffalo Street
Orchard Park, New York 14127
Tel: (716) 662 - 1071
800 - 443-5958
Hrs: Monday - Friday 10:00 a.m. - 5:00 p.m.
Saturday 10:00 a.m. - 1:00 p.m.
Closed Sunday & holidays.
Visa, MasterCard and American Express are accepted.

Cookie Expressions has solved the problem of selecting a gift for those who have everything. The beginning of this ingenious idea was underlined at the 1986 Western New York-YWCA Chocolate Lover's Festival. A crowd estimated between 10,000 and 15,000 people participated in the event, and the idea of cookie-bouquets took off.

Owners Pat Crowley and Gert Collins are proud of the quality and workmanship possessed by their creations. The cookies are baked on a stick, double wrapped in clear cellophane for freshness and then wrapped in colors to simulate flowers. Four experienced and talented designers conceive and assemble arrangements for every occasion. Plenty of room is left for individual creativity, as customers may opt for their own idea over the very lengthy list of options provided by the store. Purina Dog Food Co. used this option for corporate gifts-- a dog dish filled with the delicious cookies.

Unique gift possibilities may come to mind as patrons read a partial list of selections. Choices include a dozen long stems in a floral box, complete with green tissue, baby's breath and ferns; a Happy Day Bouquet, one dozen cookies wrapped in multi-colors in a wicker basket with party favors and a bow; the Over the Hill Birthday includes seven cookies in a black mug with "Over the Hill" written on it; or one for a new baby, eight cookies wrapped in pink or blue, in a novelty container with a balloon and favors. The lengthy list of occasions provided by their own designs include the above, plus Boss's Day, Christmas, Grandparent's Day, Housewarming, Hanukkah, Mothers-in-Law Day, and numerous others.

Both the Orchard Park and Williamsville locations have extensive displays of available arrangements, along with the catalog, custom arrangement services, local delivery and nationwide shipping. The people at

Cookie Expressions are eager to help those interested in starting a business like their own. They offer a complete consulting package containing all information necessary for getting started. The package comes from a most credible source, as their chocolate chip cookies are compared to Mrs. Fields and Famous Amos Cookies.

Put a smile on a special person's face, by sending them a unique and delicious bouquet of cookies for any occasion.

RIDER FRAMES & GALLERY
3915 North Buffalo Road
Orchard Park, New York 14127
Tel: (716) 662-5949
Hrs: Monday - Saturday 10:00 a.m. - 5:00 p.m.
Thursday 10:00 a.m. - 9:00 p.m.
Holidays (Nov. 1 - Dec. 25):
Monday - Saturday 10:00 a.m. - 5:00 p.m.
Tuesday & Thursday 10:00 a.m. - 9:00 p.m.
Visa and MasterCard are accepted.

Rider Frames & Gallery offers exquisite artwork, custom-made frames, and a variety of other unique gifts. This interesting shop provides decorating consultations for offices as well as entire buildings. The gallery has a comprehensive range of specially designed contemporary art, such as silk screens, seriographs, monoprints embossments, weaving with lithography, ceramics with acrylics, molded plexi and cast paper sculpture that is both intriguing and colorful. The shop carries a fantastic selection of limited edition prints in landscape, classic, and floral designs. Quality poster art is also available.

Beautifully frame a precious photograph, needlepoint, art work, hole-in-one golf ball or just about anything else with owner Ed Rider's gorgeous hand-made cherry, mahogany or oak wood frames in any shape. Ed also provides a full range of traditional and modern moldings done in a marbleized, high-luster lacquer, or gold leaf finish. To complement any art work, an in-house artist will create a custom mat design.

Glass etching on mirrors or other glass objects is another of Rider Frames specialties. However, they are more famous for their incredible selection of Amish-scene collectibles (soft sculpture dolls, collector plates, offset lithos and etchings) by the internationally acclaimed artist, P. Buckley Moss.

The gifts at Rider Frames & Gallery range from table-top, desk top, and shelf art to hand-blown glass decorations, fine ceramics, three dimensional wall hangings, desk accessories and pewter ornaments.

The people at Rider are also willing to work with the patron to create a unique custom-made gift.

Rider Frames & Gallery owners Ed and Lynne Rider will see that visitors receive the friendliest, most personal service around. The folks at Rider Frames are in the business of creating the elegant heirlooms and hand-crafted antiques of the future.

Located in the heart of Orchard Park, Rider Frames is truly a one-of-a-kind shop.

ROGER'S PIANOS & CLOCKS
4203 North Buffalo Road
Orchard Park, New York 14127
Tel: (716) 662-2201
Hrs: Monday - Friday 10:00 a.m. - 9:00 p.m.
Saturday 10:00 a.m. - 5:00 p.m.
Sunday 1:00 p.m. - 5:00 p.m.
Visa, and MasterCard are accepted.

Beginning with just two pianos and a great love for music, Roger and Marion Pfohl have turned Roger's Pianos & Clocks into a successful and growing business. In 1956 as a piano tuner, music teacher, and accomplished pianist Roger and his wife Marion (also a pianist) decided they wanted even more out of life and by opening their business they have provided an outlet for all of their talents.

Nine years ago Roger and Marion bought one of the most beautiful buildings in South Erie County to house their business. It dates back to 1920 and was formerly Grange Hall and then Odd Fellows Temple. Previously used as an auditorium and dance studio with a stage on the second floor, it is ideally suited to their needs. They have torn down the partitions on the first floor to create a gigantic 6600-square-foot showroom for their pianos and clocks. The auditorium upstairs is used for recitals and shows. There are five teaching rooms, each named after a famous musician, where children and adults take lessons from one of the six piano teachers on the premises.

When one walks into their shop it is very easy to be overwhelmed by the selection available but the Pfohls are very helpful and are willing to educate their customers before they make a purchase. The top selling pianos in the world are found here and they have an exclusive franchise for Baldwin, Schimmel, and Kawai which are American, German, and Japanese brands respectively. They also carry player pianos and a full line of digital pianos which any novice can learn to play easily and silently. (Headphones are included.) After tinkering with the pianos one could spend hours browsing through the clocks here. From the humble beginnings of six Grandfather clocks, their inventory has grown until today, when they now carry the greatest selection of clocks in the eastern part of the United States. They have the best rated Grandfather clocks of every make and finish and all other sorts of clocks imaginable such as wall clocks, mantle clocks and brass clocks. Roger has become a specialist in German coo-coos and they franchise a hand-carved line for Anton Schneider. As Marion puts it, "I never met a clock I didn't like!" Everyone else is going to find something here that matches their tastes perfectly.

The expansion of the business has created a need for additional locations. Roger's Pianos & Clocks can also be found in Williamsville at 5273 Transit Road and in Pittsford at 3018 Monroe Avenue. Roger's Pianos & Clocks is a "Best Choice" for music lovers, clock collectors, and those in need of additional services such as clock repair or piano tuning. With the quality of their items and the selection available, this is a great place to spend a day shopping or just browsing.

BUFFALO & ENVIRONS

Buffalo, the city, is making more of a comeback then the herbivore that it was never named after. The name Buffalo, apparently, originated from the French phrase for Beautiful River, Beau Fleuve, which was modified to a less poetic form, Buffalo, by the Yankees. In fact, as far as scientists can reckon there never were native buffalo in Buffalo.

Of course there are buffalo now, at the zoo, but there is also a new spirit of regeneration in Buffalo, so much like the spirit of Buffalo's heyday during the late 19th and early 20th centuries. In those days, Buffalo was one of the Industrial Revolution's boom towns, complete with the excess and charm that accompany that gilded age. Today many exquisite examples of the era's architecturel are evident in the graceful neighborhoods of Buffalo. Victorian period houses, such as Queen Annes, Gothic Revivals, Italianate, Greek Revival, and the later Craftsmans and Prairies exist in the revived urban settings that spawned their magnificence. On a perfect, crisp autumn day of shock, blue sky, vermillion, ochre and gold, these charming neighborhoods of Buffalo take on a honey-sweet, ethereal quality all their own. The occasional bike rider will pass, and even though the essence of burning leaves has been omitted for the sake of clean air, one can almost smell the flavor.

Clean air and a revived, cleaner environment, part of the post-industrial aftermath, have proven to be dividends to Buffalo that it could not have expected during the dark days of the industrial decline. Then the cry for jobs and their depletion was the foremost concern of the citizenry. This concern was the overt sense of community that all citizens of Buffalo seem to possess. The fact was then, and even more so today, that Buffalo is a post-industrial city possessing institutions of higher learning, medical facilities, and high-tech industries that are among the most dynamic in the nation. Also, because of its unique position in relation to America's number one trading partner, Canada, and its number one city, Toronto, Buffalo sits poised to become once again an important passageway to trade and commerce.

For the visitor, Buffalo and the entire region have a great deal to offer. The region boasts first-class dining and accommodations in both a city and country setting. Buffalo is one of the handful of American cities that is readily associated with a particular kind of indigenous dish - Buffalo Wings. Searching out these exquisite treats and judging their relative goodness is a Buffalo pastime. The same devoted passion is summoned by the many other ethnic and American dishes made with the same flair that the wings are famous for. This, and the Buffalo love affair with its undaunted sports franchises make for the kind of quintessential American experience one would expect in any Eastern city. It just seems to be a bit more so in Buffalo. After all, this a city that takes chances. Buffalo built, for the only minor league of its sports franchises, one of baseball's most handsome parks, Pilot Field. Like its inspirations from baseball's golden age, the great city stadia of Chicago, Boston, New York, Cincinnati, Pittsburgh, etc., some extant some not, this phoenix of a stadium has captured in modern terms the unique atmosphere that a true city baseball stadium can create. Readily expandable into the capacity that Major League baseball demands, Pilot Field may yet take its rightful place among the honored homes of the "Show."

The history of Buffalo is interesting, Buffalo began as an outpost at the mouth of what is now the Buffalo River. It was established by a

Frenchman, Daniel Joncaire, in 1758, but was destroyed a year later when the French were forced to abandon the area. Years later, during the Revolutionary War, a village was set up along the same area. The first house built here was constructed on present-day Pilot Field, home of baseball's Buffalo Bisons.

Holland Land Company acquired the title to the area and Joseph Ellicott, an agent, planned the city's layout. The first steamboat in the Great Lakes area, Walk-on-the-Water, and later the opening of the Erie Canal, provided Buffalo the opportunity to be used as a port for many farm products.

Eventually the railroad was introduced in the region and added to Buffalo's trade capabilities. As New York's second largest city, Buffalo is now a major area for both trade and manufacturing in the Great Lakes.

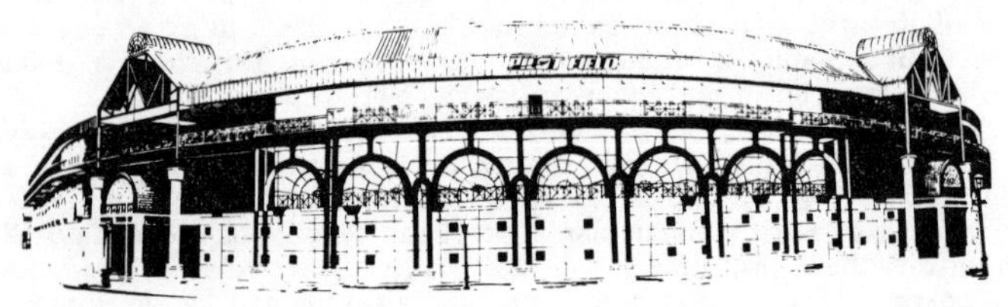

attractions

One of the largest historical preservation sites in the United States is located in the **Allentown Historic District**. The Allentown Association offers a self-guided tour of the area.

The past, present and future of Downtown Buffalo can be explored on self-guided walking tours. Contact the Greater Buffalo Chamber of Commerce Convention and Visitors Bureau.

The **Buffalo Museum of Science** contains permanent and special exhibits on botany, astronomy, anthropology, geology and zoology. Children will enjoy the discovery room. The **Kellogg Observatory** is open for stargazing, weather permitting.

Theodore Roosevelt Inaugural is a national historic site located on Buffalo's Delaware Avenue. On September 14, 1901 in the library of this home, once owned by Ansley Wilcox and his wife Mary, Theodore Roosevelt was inaugurated as the 26th President of the United States. Former President William McKinley had been shot and eventually died in Buffalo. The house is open every day except certain holidays.

Albright-Knox Art Gallery has a worldwide reputation for its contemporary art. International paintings and sculptures, along with American and European art of the past 30 years, highlight the gallery's collections. Abstract Expressionism, Kinetic Art and Color Field, Pop and Op Art and others are depicted in the wonderful work of such contemporary artists as Willem de Kooning, Henry Moore and Jackson Pollock.

The **Buffalo Zoological Gardens** is frequented by approximately 50,000 people per year and is the second largest tourist attraction in the area, behind only Niagara Falls. Located in Delaware Park, the zoo is the home of more than 1,600 specimens. on 23 acres. The Garland Gorilla African Rain Forest, outdoor lion and tiger exhibits and a children's zoo are featured.

Naval and Servicemen's Park is the only inland Naval Park in the country. Featured are old warships, fighter planes and other military memorabilia.

The **Buffalo and Erie County Historical Society** is housed in the only permanent building from the 1901 Pan-American Exposition. Permanent and changing displays exhibit the area's history from the occupation of Native Americans to the 1901 Exposition.

Kleinhans Music Hall is home to the Buffalo Philharmonic Orchestra. Concerts are performed from October to May, with a variety of other musical events the rest of the year.

Built in 1904 by Frank Lloyd Wright, the **Darwin D. Martin House** is the only one of five Wright-designed houses in Buffalo that is open to the public. This National Historic Landmark residence contains much of the original Wright furniture.

The **Broadway Market** is a turn-of-the-century indoor market offering fresh fruits and vegetables, crafts, and baked goods.

Shea's Buffalo Center for the Performing Arts offers revival films, Broadway shows, concerts, opera and dance. On the National Register of Historic Places, this 1920 movie palace features an interior designed by Tiffany Studios and one of the world's largest Wurlitzer organs.

The **Herschell Carousel Factory Museum** will delight children of all ages. Carousel rides are available as well as exhibits of the history of the amusement park industry.

great lakes coast

The Amherst Museum and Old Colony Park contains exhibits of the history of the Erie Canal and pioneer life.

The Historical Society of the Tonawandas contains a research center and museum. Built in 1870 as a New York Central Railroad station, the exhibits deal with the Iroquois Indians, the Erie Canal and the history of the Tonawandas when it was the largest lumber port in the world.

events

The **Erie County Winter Carnival** is held at both Orchard Park and Chestnut Ridge Park in January.

The annual **Hellenic Festival**, held in May, celebrates Buffalo's Greek heritage. Crafts, food and entertainment are only a few of many exciting events at the festival.

The month of July hosts two very popular events in Buffalo: the **Allentown Arts Festival**, held in the Allentown Historic District, and the **Shakespeare Festival**, held in Delaware Park.

An incredible celebration and fireworks display in honor of Independence Day can be found at the **We're 4 Buffalo Waterfront Festival**. Held annually each 4th of July in LaSalle Park, the festival features well-known entertainers.

Hertel Avenue celebrates with the **Greater Buffalo Italian Heritage and Food Festival**, held in July.

The Albright-Knox Art Gallery hosts the annual **Buffalo News/Albright-Knox Jazz Concert** series, featuring performances and workshops on six successive Sundays, starting in mid-July.

Canal Fest, held in late July, features ethnic foods, arts and crafts, daily shows and musical events on both sides of the Erie Canal in the Tonawandas.

The **Polish-American Arts Festival** celebrates Buffalo's Polish heritage with food and fun in mid-August.

DOWNTOWN BUFFALO

accommodations

THE RAMADA RENAISSANCE HOTEL
4243 Genesee Street
Buffalo, New York 14225
Tel: (716) 634-2300
(800) 228-9

Hrs:		
	Lobby Bar:	Noon - 2:00a.m.
	Cafe on the Promenade:	5:30 a.m. - Midnight
	Sunday Brunch:	10:30 a.m. - 2:30 a.m.
	Pranzo Ristorante:	
	Monday - Saturday	5:00 p.m. - 11:00 p.m.
	Celebrities Night Club:	
	Tuesday - Saturday	8:00 p.m. - 4:00 a.m.

Visa, MasterCard, American Express, Diners Club, Carte Blanche, Discover and JCB are accepted.

The Ramada Renaissance Hotel boasts that it's close to Buffalo's major attractions, but it may be more accurate to say that it is some of Buffalo's major attractions. It seems that this great-escape hotel has received rave reviews for nearly every aspect of its operation. The Pranzo Ristorante, which serves remarkable gourmet Italian dinners, was voted "Best in Buffalo" at a recent Taste of Buffalo event, and was awarded an excellent rating by Janice Okin, the Buffalo Evening News Restaurant Reviewer.

But the awards don't stop there. The Celebrities Nightclub, with its electrifying audios, spectacular lighting, nightly drink specials, and colossal cocktails, was voted the area's best by Nightlife Magazine, and the 275 luscious guest accommodations (smoking and non-smoking), were voted "Best Rooms" by the Buffalo Evening News. The Hotel also has 55 elite mini-suites and 11 full-size luxury suites.

The intimate lobby bar offers complimentary hors d'oeurvres and live piano music. The Ramada Renaissance offers 14 meeting and banquet rooms that can accommodate from 10 to 750 people for meetings and 650 for meals. The full-time catering staff happily lends its expertise to banquet and meeting groups alike. CMI Communications, the hotel's in-house audio-visual system, provides state-of-the-art meeting equipment.

The hotel invites guests to relax in the indoor and outdoor pools, whirlpool, sauna, steambath, exercise room, and gift shop.

The Ramada Renaissance is located off the New York State Thruway Exit 51-E (10 miles from downtown Buffalo) and is directly across the street from the Buffalo International Airport. The Amtrak station is only three miles away. A car rental agency and a travel agency are on the hotel's premises. Complementary van service is provided to the airport and train station.

Shopping malls, theaters, ski resorts, parks, art galleries, and Niagara Falls are nearby, but one of the areas most impressive sights is Buffalo's exquisitely European Ramada Renaissance Hotel.

apparel

KLEINHANS
Corporate Offices
525 Hertel Avenue
Buffalo, New York 14207
Tel: (716) 875-1801
Hrs: Monday - Saturday 10:00 a.m. - 9:00 p.m.
Sundays Noon - 5:00 p.m.
Visa, MasterCard, American Express, Diners Club, and Discover are accepted.

"We dress you for business--the rest is up to you." This motto has been with Kleinhans since 1893, when Edward and Horace Kleinhans opened their first store, "Clothiers and Furnishers for Men and Boys" at 259 Main Street in Downtown Buffalo.

Ninety-seven years later, Kleinhans still brings the best style, quality and value to the western New York male for business and weekend. A complete selection of high quality menswear is featured, from furnishings to clothing and outerwear, offering famous names like Hart, Schaffner & Marx, Austin Reed, Hathaway, Countess Mara, and Alexander Julian.

Kleinhans offers the updated looks that boys and young men prefer, plus a full-line of women's career fashions is featured in their Corporate Women's Department.

The staff puts considerable emphasis on customer service. They offer on-the-spot tailoring, executive privilege (shopping in the office), and will deliver items to offices for those who have forgotten something. A personalized computer record is kept on each customer's wardrobe so that all purchases can build and enhance it.

Kleinhans now boasts seven stores in addition to their original store in Downtown Buffalo, which they still occupy. That includes five full-line specialty stores in suburban malls and two "Buffalo Boutiques," offering locally-themed fashions and gifts.

Kleinhans has and will continue to offer the finest business and sportswear for men, boys, young men, and women. Customer service is their top priority, as their heritage has handed down to them.

PAR AVION, INC.
361 Delaware Avenue
Buffalo, New York 14202
Tel: (716) 853-3600
Hrs: Monday - Friday 10:00 a.m. - 5:30 p.m.
Thursday Until 7:00 p.m.
Saturday Until 5:00 p.m.
Christmas (beginning two weeks before):
10:00 a.m.-8:00 p.m.
Visa, MasterCard and American Express are accepted.

Par Avion, located at Delaware and Tupper, within walking distance of the Theatre District, opened in 1960 as an import store (the name "Par

Avion" means "Air Mail") and since then has grown into one of Buffalo's finest women's specialty stores.

The merchandise you'll find at Par Avion is not available at any other store. Owner Allison Kimberly purchases only unique lines of quality dresses, accessories, sportswear, jewelry, suits, faux furs, coats, and jackets. Allison also carries sweaters that are handmade in England and separates constructed of luxurious fabrics with rich colors and exotic patterns. Finishing touches such as gilt chains, necklaces, pins, and earrings make any of Par Avion's outfits the perfect fashion statement.

Par Avion does it all, from hosting fashion shows to manufacturing its own line of women's winter coats. The shop also carries puppets, stuffed animals, puzzles, postcards and much more.

The interior is colorfully decorated with a Victorian-style sofa, a pink and white tiled floor, and festive window arrangements that display a variety of striking apparel combinations and new fashion concepts.

Par Avion is as unique as its owner--often described as one of Buffalo's most interesting women. Her terrific sense of humor and charm create a pleasant atmosphere throughout the store.

If you're searching for gifts with a unique flair or quality fashions that are unusual yet practical, visit Par Avion. It's located just West of the Downtown entrance to the Kensington Expressway (Route 33). Par Avion is truly a specialty store with style.

bed & breakfast inns

RAINBOW HOSPITALITY
466 Amherst Street
Buffalo, NewYork 14207
Tel: (716) 874-8797
Hrs: Monday - Friday 9:30 a.m.-5:00 p.m.
Sat.urday 9:00 a.m.-12:00 p.m.
Visa and MasterCard are accepted.

Rainbow Hospitality is a unique bed and breakfast reservation service representing over sixty available throughout Western New York. Examples of Rainbow Hospitality's service may include a bed and breakfast that is standardized in several locations, each with a different atmosphere, such as a "Homestay Inn" - a large private home where the host and hostess provides guest rooms. Guests may choose an historic home that has been restored or renovated in an historical area, or a Country Inn; a commercial bed and breakfast with a tap room or dining facility, is another choice. Rainbow Hospitality offers an interesting change of pace with a wide range of selections including experienced personalized service. Georgia A. Brannan, president of Rainbow Hospitality, is very proud of the service she represents.

All of the selections available include a private bath and master bedroom suite. Some offer more privacy than others, located in a country setting, and others are in the city. Most feature a full or continental breakfast. A particular example bed and breakfast is a three-story Victorian mansion with preserved ornate woodwork, stained glass windows, and fireplaces, providing guests with the ambiance of another era.

Rooms available to tourists range from modest to luxury and are inspected by Rainbow Hospitality annually. Rainbow Hospitality provides other services as well, such as transportation to airports, dinner and ticket reservations and corporate meetings.

duty free shops

AMMEX TAX & DUTY FREE SHOPS OF WESTERN NEW YORK
Greater Buffalo International Airport Tel: (716) 632-5555
Buffalo Peace Bridge (716) 886-5000
Lewiston-Queenston Bridge, Lewiston (716) 284-8409
Rainbow Bridge, Niagara Falls (716) 284-8168
Whirlpool Bridge, Niagara Falls (716) 284-9733
Hrs: Call stores for individual hours.
Visa, MasterCard and American Express are accepted.

Europeans have long been accustomed to the great savings available to travelers through duty-free shopping. In North America there was much confusion and lack of knowledge surrounding duty-free shopping until 1983 when Duty Free International (DFI)/Ammex acquired a chain of stores along the US/Canada border and transformed them into bright, modern, and tax and duty-free stores. The purpose of this worldwide $7 billion industry is to provide the best values to international travelers.

Fifty years ago only a few of these shops existed but now there are over 3500 worldwide. Once associated only with tobacco and alcohol, these shops now offer perfumes, skin care products, designer scarves, quality leather goods, imported crystal and a wide variety of gift items. This brandname merchandise is available at a savings that ranges from 20 percent to 50 percent.

Federal customs departments are now providing more detailed information about duty-free allowances and regulations. The Ammex staff is very knowledgeable and helpful, having gone through a training program that teaches them to provide customers with more service, attention, product knowledge, and friendliness than they receive at other shops. The staff realizes that the average customer spends less than 10 minutes in the store and sometimes has to make split second buying decisions. They are able to inform customers of what the duty-free allowance is at their shop and at other worldwide destinations. Free maps are available and helpful clerks are able to give directions to travelers.

Ammex Tax & Duty Free Shops are a "Best Choice" for travelers because they offer such tremendous savings and have a currency exchange that is the same or better than those found at banks. Those discovering these remarkable buys will probably agree that "the best things in life are duty-free."

florists

THE FLORISTRY
1385 Delaware Avenue
Buffalo, New York 14209
Tel: (716) 885-6037
Visa, MasterCard and American Express are accepted.

Fanny Merkel and The Floristry have been serving the Buffalo and Western New York area since 1965 with her slogan, "No party too large or too small." Fanny who was primarily a golfer, began doing flower arranging as a favor for friends. The natural flair she had for designing arrangements led to the reputation that she and her creative staff now have for producing innovative quality work.

Anything the customer can dream up, The Floristry can decorate. Fanny enjoys creating elaborate custom sets with her team of on-staff artists. Over the years they have accumulated a warehouse full of props such as a 40 foot caterpillar, a Humpty Dumpty, a three-story pagoda, and setting themes like Alice in Wonderland (guests walk through a broken mirror prop), the Chinese New Year, a Medieval Ball, and themes that relate to Buffalo. No job is too big here and no party theme is too unusual.

When one enters The Floristry, the first thing to hit the senses is a wide variety of fragrances and then the source, a full array of colorful flowers. This is not the average floral shop. Here one can find imported flowers from Holland, South America, Africa, New Zealand, and the Orient and a wire service network around the world is available. Artwork of area artists is featured here along with gifts of silk, dried, and fresh flowers.

The staff make customers feel very welcome here. They are a very service-oriented group. Fanny offers counseling for weddings and will attend to every detail from the 30 foot pagoda to the napkin rings. They offer gorgeous floral centerpieces for all occasions. Fanny enjoys waiting on her customers personally from the high school gentleman choosing a flower for his first prom to the bride-to-be. Every customer receives full attention regardless of their age or the size of their order. Customers can feel relaxed here as Fanny teaches her staff not to oversell. She feels that one rose can say as much as a dozen. The Floristry is a "Best Choice" for all occasions requiring flower arrangements or any sort of special floral props. Additional services provided are flower arranging classes taught by Fanny herself. Due to the success of the business, customers can find The Floristry at two other convenient locations: 5444 Main Street in Williamsville and downtown Buffalo in the Hyatt Regency at Two Fountain Plaza.

ice cream parlors

SODA BAR AND PASTRY COMPANY
929 Elmwood Ave.
Buffalo, New York 14222

Tel:	(716) 885-0056	
Hrs:	Sunday - Thursday	8:30 a.m. - 11:00 p.m.
	Friday and Saturday	8:30 a.m. - Midnight
	December & January:	
	Sunday-Thursday	Closes at 10:00 p.m.

A newcomer on the block, the Soda Bar and Pastry Company has been open since 1987. During the short time it has been open, it's become a most popular spot. As the name indicates, it is a soda fountain shop, serving both pastries ice cream as well as meals that include breakfast, lunch, and dinner.

The official greeters of the Soda Bar are Fred and Ethel, the two life-sized mannequins eating ice cream in the window. The Soda Bar and Pastry Co. is decorated with portraits of old time movie stars, high backed booths, lovely stained glass windows, and even an old fashioned, handmade wooden soda bar.

The breakfast menu includes homemade quiche du jour, omelets, bagels, sandwiches, sweetbreads, muffins, scones, croissants, and walnut oat bread. Try the daily specials at the Soda Bar, such as hot or cold sandwiches, vegetarian dishes, pasta, quiche, and delicious burger specials. All foods are homemade including the potato chips and salad dressings.

In addition to the full menu, the daily specials are listed on the board. Some favorites are the home-style turkey, roast beef dinners and a fish fry. Adults as well as the kids are impressed with the children's menu. The peanut butter, banana and honey "Power Sandwich" is a favorite with businessmen.

Hand-packed ice cream is available for take-out. Beer and wine is served with meals.

The Soda Bar has a charming atmosphere and fantastic food at a great price. Service is exceptionally friendly and committed to pleasing the customer. For a sweet treat the Soda Bar and Pastry Company can't be beat. It is truly an old fashioned ice cream parlor.

malls

BUFFALO PLACE
671 Main Street
Buffalo, New York 14203

Tel:	(716) 856-3150
Hrs:	For hours call the Hotline Number: 854-4FUN

Buffalo Place, with its 18 blocks of services and activities, has become the symbol and centerpiece of the revitalization of Greater Buffalo.

Main Street is closed to vehicular traffic for the 1.2 mile above ground transit mall and the train is free above ground for all riders.

The highlights of Buffalo Place range from the Cybernetic Light Theater at Lafayette Square to the skating rink which, when completed, will be one-third larger than the ice rink at New York City's Rockefeller Center.

Buffalo Place, a non-profit organization in charge of promotion and maintenance of the pedestrian mall, is at the heart of Buffalo's Renaissance.

The company was formed to manage the mall when the above ground light rail transit system on Main Street was completed in 1982.

Areas located at Buffalo Place include the Hyatt Regency Hotel, Market Arcade General Cinemas, Main Place Mall (an indoor shopping center), Buffalo's Public Library, Naval and Serviceman's Park, Key Center Plaza, Marine Midland Center, and the historic theater district.

Development of the pedestrian mall continues with Buffalo Place in bloom. When completed more than 100 additional trees, planter boxes, and benches will be part of the beautiful area.

Downtown activity has never been better. An annual calendar of special events including an after-hour summer concert series, farmer's market, New York State Wine Festival and the holiday Friendship tree make Buffalo Place the place to be. One can call a hotline number, 854-4FUN, to listen to recorded messages of each day's activities.

An array of fun-filled activities and services await visitors at Buffalo Place, a must-see when in downtown Buffalo.

points of interest

BURCHFIELD ART CENTER
1300 Elmwood
Buffalo, New York 14222
Tel: (716) 878-6012
Hrs: Tuesday - Saturday 10:00 a.m. - 5:00 p.m.
Sunday 1:00 p.m. - 5:00 p.m.
Closed Mondays, New Year's Day, July Fourth, Thanksgiving, Christmas Eve, and Christmas Day.
Visa and MasterCard are accepted.

One of the leading regional art museums in the United States, the Burchfield Art Center possesses the largest, most comprehensive public collection of Charles E. Burchfield works. Widely recognized as one of the finest watercolorists of the 20th century, Charles Burchfield inspired the creation of the museum just prior to his death in 1967.

Among the museum's many Burchfield works are paintings, prints, doodles, drawings, sketches, studies, designs, and selvages of wallpaper. In addition to owning creations that illustrate and document the career of C.E. Burchfield, the museum displays works by other significant artists who have been born, have practiced or have lived in Western New York. The museum also displays pieces by Burchfield contemporaries and associates in the Frank K. M. Rehn Gallery, but the Museum's exhibits are not limited to 20th century art; the museum collects works from other periods as well.

One of the museum's most precious possessions is an archive that includes C. E. Burchfield's 67 autographed manuscript journals, 12 personal art indexes, 11 notebooks, several sketchbooks, library materials, memorabilia, and extensive photographic files on his work.

The Burchfield Art Center is dedicated to representing a full range of visual thought, including architecture, design, crafts, and folk art. The Artist-In-Residence program continues Charles Burchfield's teaching tradition and clarifies art-making for the public.

Burchfield Art Center Director Anthony Bannon and his staff go out of their way to accommodate visitors. Admission is free, the museum is barrier free for disabled persons, guided and group tours are available by appointment, and sign language and oral interpreters are provided.

Located on the top floor of Rockwell Hall, on the campus of the State University New York College at Buffalo, the Burchfield Art Center is only 10 minutes from downtown. Take the Elmwood Avenue South Exit from Route 198.

STUDIO ARENA THEATRE
710 Main Street
Buffalo, New York 14202-1990
Tel: (716) 856-5650 (box office)
(716) 856-8025 (business)
Hrs: Ticket Services:

Monday	10:00 a.m. - 5:00 p.m.
Tuesday - Friday	10:00 a.m. - 9:00 p.m.
Saturday	Noon - 10:00 p.m.
Sunday	Noon - 8:00 p.m.
Summer:	
Monday - Friday	10:00 a.m. - 5:00 p.m.

Wheelchair access is provided.
Visa and MasterCard are accepted.

Located in the heart of Buffalo's Theatre District and Downtown Pedestrian Mall, the Studio Arena Theatre is Western New York's only regional professional theatre. Chartered as a nonprofit educational institution in 1927 and reorganized in 1965, the theatre has become a significant and dynamic force in the area's cultural life.

Since 1965, the theatre has produced 197 productions, 33 of which were world or American premieres. Last year alone, the theatre presented 250 performances. The people at the Studio Arena see the productions through from start to finish. They even build their own props.

Studio Arena attracts nationally-known artists and produces seven mainstage plays each season, with annual attendance of more than 135,000. Its popularity is due largely to the quality of artists and the well-balanced blend of productions that are offered. Due to the fact that the newly-renovated theatre holds 637 people and because there are only 14 rows, every seat is a good seat. The acoustics are excellent and infrared headsets are available for patrons who have some degree of hearing impairment.

Immediately following each performance, visitors are welcome to visit the Stage Left Lounge. Patrons may also go behind the scenes to speak with cast members following selected performances of each play.

Studio Arena Theatre boasts the largest subscription audience of any New York performing arts series outside of Manhattan. The Studio Arena Theatre School offers theater classes for people from the age of six through adult. Last year over 369 students enrolled. Studio Arena's Young Company presents productions to 10,000 children and family audiences throughout Erie County.

restaurants

ANDY'S RESTAURANT & LOUNGE
1287 Niagara Street
Buffalo, New York 14213
Tel: (716) 886-9786
Hrs: Sunday - Thursday 10:00 a.m. - 1:00 a.m.
Friday - Saturday 10:00 a.m. - 2:00 a.m.
Visa, MasterCard, American Express, Diners Club and Carte Blanche are accepted.

Andy's Restaurant & Lounge, located only five minutes from downtown on Buffalo's West Side, offers a tremendous variety of Italian specialties and a great selection of fresh seafood at very reasonable prices.

Andy's serves hearty portions of fabulous antipasto, veal of the day, linguine with red or white clam sauce, barbeque baby back ribs, fresh catfish, swordfish, red snapper, sole, calamari in sauce with a side order of spaghetti, snails marinara, and shrimp zebilon sauteed in white wine and butter but is most famous for its fresh Virginia shore clams.

Sundays are extraordinary at Andy's. Sunday Pasta Festivals feature an all-you-can-eat Pasta Bar, Champagne Sunday Brunches are served from 11:00 a.m. to 3:00 p.m., and the $22.95 Entertainment Specials offer dinners for two, as well as two tickets for either a Bison game or a downtown cinema.

Andy's also serves deluxe mugs of cappucino and espresso, unique appetizers, delicious Oysters Casino and mouth-watering Mussels Marinara, specialty sandwiches such as Delmonico Steak with Dandelions, sauce-smothered Meatball Bombers, and exotic desserts such as light Creme de Menthe Parfait and Black Forest Cheesecake with cherry and chocolate swirls.

The atmosphere at Andy's is friendly and family-like. The building, with its indoor-outdoor patio clam bar, darkly paneled dining room, brass-railed bar, wrought-iron Mediterranean-style chandeliers, and rich brown carpet, is warm and relaxing.

Owner Angelo Sedito sees to it that all of his diners leave happy. Angelo says he is not after the one-time visitor; he enjoys seeing the same faces each week. The impressive amount of repeat business at Andy's is proof that Andy's offers all of the consistent quality and friendly service of a traditional family-style Italian restaurant.

BRODERICK PARK INN
1170 Niagara Street
Buffalo, New York 14213
Tel: (716) 878-8245
Hrs: Lunch;
Monday - Thursday 11:00 a.m. - 3:00 p.m.
Dinner:
Monday - Thursday 5:00 p.m. - 9:00 p.m.
Friday 11:00 a.m. - 10:00 p.m.
Saturday 5:00 p.m. - 9:00 p.m.
Visa, MasterCard, American Express, Diners Club and Carte Blanche are accepted.

The Broderick Park Inn was named for its proximity to Broderick Park on Bird Island. The park was dedicated and named after Michael J. Broderick, founder and past president of the West Side Rowing Club. The Broderick Park Inn is committed to the sport of rowing as well as baseball.

Continuing the baseball theme, the Inn has old photographs, jerseys, and other memorabilia of the Buffalo Bisons and boasts an exciting tribute to Buffalo's baseball team.

Broderick Park Inn has several dining rooms, including the Natural and Hall of Fame Rooms. The Natural Room offers private dining for small parties, with mementos and pictures from the movie, "The Natural," starring Robert Redford, which was filmed in Buffalo. The Hall of Fame Room offers photos of Buffalo's sports teams through the 20th Century.

The Broderick Park Inn offers a variety of excellent food, reasonable prices, and a full bar. The menu reflects the baseball theme with names such as Fielders Choice, Warm Ups, and Hot Contenders. A daily Fish Fry is available. Fried Chicken, Beef Chimichangas, and Fried Shrimp are a few samples from the Fielders Choice. A favorite on the Warm Up is a different choice of Soup Du Jour from the chef's kettle. For a hearty lunch or light dinner, try Hot Contenders - Tuna Melt, Hot Open Turkey Sandwich, Chicken Cordon Bleu Sandwich, Open New York Strip Steak, and Hot Open Reuben. The Catch of the Day offers Breaded Shrimp, Halibut Steak, Swordfish Steak, Broiled Haddock, and Italian Baked Haddock. Extra Inning Desserts range from Creme de Menthe Sundaes and Carrot Cake to Muddville Pie and Grand American Ice Cream.

Located 10 minutes from downtown Buffalo, the Inn is within walking distance of the best fishing in Buffalo at Bird Island.

With a party and catering capacity of up to 500 people, the Broderick Park Inn boasts a friendly and knowledgeable staff, consistent quality and a delightful baseball theme. Arrive early to get good seats.

CHEF'S RESTAURANT
291 Seneca Street
Buffalo, New York 14204
Tel: (716) 856-9187
Hrs: Monday - Saturday 11:45 a.m. - 9:00 p.m.
Closed Sundays and Holidays
Visa, MasterCard and Diners Club are accepted.

Chef's Restaurant has all the character associated with an Italian neighborhood restaurant, including the traditional red and white cloths covering the tables. Lou Billittier began working as a dishwasher at the age of 12, and soon had done every job in the restaurant. He bought the establishment and has been with it at the same location for over 60 years. During that time, has seen three expansions to accommodate the growing number of patrons. Chef's has graciously served generations.

The familiar Italian menu is simple, with consistent daily specials including everything from spaghetti and meatballs to chicken livers. There are several parmesan dishes, Stuffed Shells, Chicken in Wine Sauce, Calamari, Veal Scallopini, Stuffed White Fish and more. Each item is deliciously prepared, portions are always ample, and there is carry-out service on all menu items.

The popular desserts are reasonably priced as is the balance of the menu. Chef's thoughtfully offers the choice of large or small portions. The always fresh Italian bread is baked on the premises. Both the Zucchini and Dandelion Salads are popular with the regulars.

Along with the flavorful sauces and pasta, the staff deserves accolades for making Chef's a success. Service is always prompt and friendly. The tradition of good food, friendly service, and an accommodating menu has made Chef's a haven for local politicians, or as the restaurant's slogan boasts, a place "where people meet to eat."

J. P. BULLFEATHERS--THE WINE CELLAR
1010 Elmwood Avenue
Buffalo, New York 14222
Tel: (716) 885-3892
(716) 882-3000
Hrs: Sunday - Thursday 9:00 a.m - 2:00 a.m.
Friday - Saturday 9:00 a.m - 3:00 a.m.
Visa, MasterCard, American Express, Diner's Club and Carte Blanche are accepted.

Once a tiny neighborhood gin mill, J.P. Bullfeathers was taken over by the present owner in 1970 and run for 15 years as a small restaurant-bar. In 1985, Leone expanded the facility into a sprawling restaurant with an expanded bar area and banquet facility. The present business literally wraps around the old "wine cellar". Bullfeathers is the ideal place for a party with varying and distinguished tastes. There are over 100 menu items from which to choose, and all are homemade.

Although it is difficult to choose a meal from such a varied menu, the Artichokes Gratinee--artichokes nestled in garlic and melted cheese--is highly recommended as an appetizer, as are the Clams Casino. Entrees feature every dish one could possibly want. Salads, Anytime Eggs, stir fry, veal, beef, chicken, seafood, and Italian meals are just a small sampling. Almost everything is made from scratch.

Along with the varied menu, Bullfeathers has separate dining areas with differing atmospheres. The casual bar area with window-side tables overlooks the bustle of Elmwood Avenue. The romantic and original wine cellar is located in the back with an 18-foot ceiling, a brick working fireplace, and a Casablanca ambiance; all three areas are welcoming and friendly. Bullfeather's also boasts an impressive wine list featuring wines from France, Australia, Italy, Portugal, California, and even New York State. They run monthly specials on select wines with special prices.

Quality and consistency is a Bullfeather's trademark and the best culinary experience is a commitment.

JUST PASTA
307 Bryant Street
Buffalo, New York 14222
Tel: (716) 881-1888
Hrs: Lunch:
Monday - Friday 11:30 a.m. - 4:00 p.m.
Dinner:
Monday - Thursday 5:30 p.m. - 10:00 p.m.
Friday - Saturday 5:30 p.m. - 11:00 p.m.
Visa, MasterCard, American Express, Diners Club and Carte Blanche are accepted.

Just Pasta is certainly not "just another Italian restaurant." Don Warfe opened Just Pasta as a retail gourmet food store featuring homemade pastas. He had a little extra space and installed ten tables to serve lunch. The food was so delicious that customers begged him to remain open for dinner. That was six years ago, and today Just Pasta is a fine dining establishment that serves much more.

The pastas that are available are very unusual selections such as garlic, lemon, orange, saffron, fresh herb, green onion, black pepper, potato, and mushroom. Don was the first producer of fresh pasta in Buffalo and is most flattered when out of towners rave about the light, healthy, delightful food he serves as opposed to heavy pasta meals. Don refers to his head chef, Joe George, as the "most creative chef in Buffalo." This is evidenced by the unique menu selections which change every season, and the excellent presentation of these dishes. Soups are never typical. An example is the Mideastern lentil soup. One available appetizer is a potato and beet pierogi with onions and cabbage. Entrees also have a lot of variety, with such selections as black bean and cheddar ravioli with a warm tomato salsa, or for something really unusual, Asian chicken with new potatoes, bananas, spinach, and lemon linguine.

There are dozens of red, white, and sparkling wines to choose from and many may be ordered by the glass. It is a hobby of Don's to find unique, lesser known wineries. Ned Wilson is the pastry chef responsible for their artistic dessert creations. His inventions include a Coconut Custard Torte, a Chocolate Layered Cake, a White Satin Torte, and an Almond Caramel Torte.

The walls are brick painted white with red and black details. Colorful, modern oil paintings done by local artists decorate the place and are available for purchase. The awning-covered patio is wonderful for summer dining and is made cozy with lots of plants and flowers.

With all of this superb food and wine to offer and a bright, high-tech atmosphere, Don says he is most proud of service that is "superior to any place in Buffalo."

KEYSTONE KELLY'S RESTAURANT
622 Main Street
Buffalo, New York 14202
Tel: (716) 854-1900
Hrs: Monday - Thursday 11:00 a.m.- 11:00 p.m.
Visa, MasterCard, American Express, Diners Club, Carte Blanche, Discover and JCB are accepted.

Keystone Kelly's, located on Main Street in the heart of Buffalo's Theatre District, is a fun restaurant that serves everything from baby back ribs to the restaurant's own tasty creation, which contains a unique combination of charbroiled, boneless chicken breast, Monterey Jack cheese, Keystone Kelly's special Black Bean Sauce, avocado slices and alfalfa sprouts called the West Coast Pita.

Open for lunch, dinner and late night snacks, Keystone Kelly's prepares succulent steaks, fresh seafood, juicy hamburgers and specialty sandwiches. For something out of the ordinary, the restaurant also offers a variety of international cuisine, such as Mexican, Italian, Polish, French, English, and American.

The Great Beginnings (appetizers) range from Baked Brie with garlic bread, and crisp vegetables for dipping, to giant deep-fried potato and cheese pierogies, served with fried onions, bacon bits, and lots of sour cream.

After the delicious appetizers, be prepared for the fabulous Conglomerations (entrees). Be sure to allow plenty of time to decide on the main course. This is one decision that shouldn't be made in haste Everything is unique and savory, from the steamed Alaskan Snow Crab Dinner and Charbroiled Swordfish Steak, to Kelly's Honey and Garlic Ribs, and the South of the Border Pizza, with loads of spicy ground beef, mozzarella cheese, tomatoes, mushrooms and olives.

The Final Temptations are delicious. The Deep Dish Apple-Blueberry Crisp is served piping hot with brown sugar and oatmeal topping. The Brown Bottom Pie is a fudgy chocolate brownie topped with rich vanilla ice cream and a layer of chocolate, and An Attack of Chocolate, for chocolate lovers only, is a surprising combination of four different types of chocolate.

The diverse beverage menu is impressive and tough to decide upon. Choices include Juicy Delight, such as a Kelly Kooler, a Brandy, or Cognac, an after dinner drink such as a Godmother,(Vodka and Amaretto), or an Irish Nut (Frangelica and Irish Cream), a hot drink like Almond Mocha, or a Wild Side drink such as an Angels Tip, dark creme de cacoa and creme.

Monday through Saturday, the bar features happy hour specials such as free munchies and 10 cent beers. With its 28 varieties of International bottled beer--including George Killian's, Beck's Dark, and Guinness--Keystone Kelly's is a beer lover's haven.

There are so many reasons to try Keystone Kelly's, but the main one is to have FUN. Whether taking a break from shopping, or simply looking for a wonderfully unusual place to relax, stop at Keystone Kelly's.

THE LAFAYETTE TAP ROOM
391 Washington Street
Buffalo, New York 14203
Tel: (716) 855-8800

Hrs:		
	Monday - Thursday	10:30 a.m. - 2:00 a.m.
	Friday - Saturday	10:30 a.m. - 4:00 a.m.
	Sunday	Open for special downtown events.

American Express is accepted.

Designed by the first woman architect in the United States and soon to be designated a national landmark, the Lafayette Tap Room in downtown Buffalo's seven-story Lafayette Hotel dates back to 1896.

Once a "men-only" bar, the Tap Room has come a long way. Now the Tap Room delights in serving everyone with such wonderful menu items as homemade French onion soup with mounds of mozzarella cheese, New York strip steak, roast beef, meatloaf, and pork chops. But the most popular menu item is the famous "Buffalo Burger," made of sweet, lean, locally-raised bison meat, which the owners call "the beef of the future."

Lunches include unique combos such as Jumbo Roast Beef on Kummelweck rolls, and Peanut Butter and Bacon on toast. All specialty sandwiches may be served in a pita pocket with assorted greens and secret-recipe dressing. Fridays and Saturdays are Fish Fry nights.

The food is not the only attraction at the Tap Room. The decor is an incredible mix of sports memorabilia, life-like animal mountings, and turn-of-the-century antiques. The Tap Room is spacious with its 15-foot high ceilings, original marble walls, and tile floor; the atmosphere is completed with an antique solid oak bar, original wrought-iron chandelier, stuffed fish, wild boar, Alaskan King crabs, bison and ram heads, and antique bottles. The rear dining room has a vaulted, gold-leaf ceiling, and an oak entranceway vestibule with French doors made of lead glass.

Though the Lafayette Tap Room, located only two blocks from Buffalo's state-of-the-art baseball facility, Pilot Field, is a favorite spot for sports fans, its main claim to fame is its Rhythm & Blues entertainment. The Tap Room features local and national R & B talent and is known as the best Rhythm and Blues bar in Buffalo.

The fabulous entertainment, hearty meals, refreshing drinks, sports enthusiasm, terrific turn-of-the-century building, and unique decor make any visit to the Lafayette Tap Room a wonderfully memorable experience.

MANNY'S SUPPER CLUB
471 Delaware Avenue
Buffalo, New York 14202
Tel: (716) 881-3727
Hrs: Lunch:

Lunch:		
	Monday - Friday	11:30 a.m. - 3:30 p.m.
Dinner:		
	Monday - Thursday	4:30 p.m. - 11:00 p.m.
	Friday - Saturday	4:30 p.m. - Midnight

Closed last two weeks in July.

Visa, MasterCard, American Express, Diners Club, and Carte Blanche are accepted.

Located in a brownstone row townhouse in Old Buffalo, Manny's Supper Club is a national landmark symbolic of Buffalo's Grand Era in terms of elegance.

The building, which was erected in 1890, is done in elegant turn-of-the-century style. A marble staircase and walls, intricately-carved plaster and Victorian design with a subtle Spanish motif, grace the interior of the restaurant. A large stained glass piece with the logo of Don Quixote's "Impossible Dream" on it, signifies the owners' success through the years.

Manny's Supper Club was opened in 1959 by Norman, Rosemary, and Manny Besso. With Manny's departure from the business and Norman's death, Rosemary was left to run the supper club along with her employees, many of whom have been with the restaurant for over 25 years.

Manny's prepares all food from scratch with only the finest ingredients and great care. It has become a custom at Manny's for the waiters and waitresses to present to each customer a meat tray displaying a beautiful selection of cuts. Known for its beef and seafood dishes, Manny's offers a wide selection of both, including Prime New York Strip Steak, Prime Steer Filet Mignon, Fresh Filet of Norwegian Salmon, and Genuine Cape Scallops. Surf and Turf is available for those diners wishing for a taste of both.

A special family recipe, and favorite of many Manny's regulars, is the Baked Eggplant, stuffed with ricotta cheese and topped with tomato sauce. Fresh corn muffins are complimentary with every meal. Homemade fruit pies, using only fruits that are in season, and cheesecake are noteworthy dessert favorites. Coffee drinkers will appreciate Manny's selection of Spanish, Irish, and Dutch coffee along with Espresso and Capuccino.

Daily specials, private parties on Sundays, and the quantity and quality of its food have kept Manny's successful over the years. It has been rated from very good to excellent in local and national reviews, including "The Fork and Knife," and "Where To Eat in America."

Nearby attractions include the Buffalo Theater District and Wilcox Mansion, site of Theodore Roosevelt's Inaugural Address.

The pride of Old Buffalo for over 30 years, Manny's Supper Club offers diners excellent food in an elegant atmosphere.

PETTIBONE'S GRILLE
275 Washington Street
Buffalo, New York 14203
Tel: (716) 846-2062
Hrs: Lunch:
Monday - Friday 11:30 a.m. - 3:00 p.m.
Dinner:
Monday - Saturday 5:00 p.m. - 9:00 p.m.
Open Sunday only if there is a ball game.
Visa, MasterCard and American Express are accepted.

The words, "Take me out to the ball game," have inherited an entirely new meaning thanks to Pettibone's Grille, located inside Buffalo's Pilot Field. The classy restaurant is unlike most other stadium clubs/restaurants because a membership is not required to enjoy the magnificent atmosphere and cuisine. Pettibone's is indisputably a public affair. For the sports fan, looking out the giant windows and down at the first-base line during a Bison's game is not simply a novelty, but a dream come true.

Pettibone's, or "Pilot Field's other diamond," takes its name from William Henry Harrison Pettibone. A writer, composer, and railroad man, Pettibone made the dining car a showcase, while working his way through the ranks to become Vice President of Union Pacific. His desire and determination were to serve the best beef in the land, a tradition carried on by the restaurant that carries his name.

This unique restaurant serves only "Certified Angus Beef," a guarantee that it is the best available. New York Strip Steak topped with onion rings and a nine-ounce Filet Mignon served on an eggplant crouton with Madeira sauce are worthy examples of typical menu items. Try the tasty Veal Chop topped with a shiitake mushroom and bourbon sauce, Veal a La Pettibone--tender veal medallions sauteed, topped with asparagus, crabmeat, red bell pepper, and melted Jack cheese, all on a bed of Sauce a la Rousse, or the Chicken Chambord Sautee--a boneless chicken breast sauteed with bing cherries and deglazed with Chambord raspberry liqueur. There is also seafood from which to choose, including the Grilled Swordfish and Scallops en Croute, as well as pasta dishes including a perennial favorite, cheese ravioli.

Despite its air of class, the very spacious and elegant restaurant does not discriminate between the businessman clad in an expensive Italian suit, and the average sports fan wearing shorts and a baseball cap.

Pettibone's sponsors a weekly tent party on the Friday nights of home games. This party offers award-winning roast pig, beef on weck, Italian sausage, hot dogs, hamburgers, beer, and wine coolers for the fans' enjoyment. The restaurant will also provide private catering. Pettibone's is a restaurant that has it all and always provides a good time.

RUE FRANKLIN WEST
341 Franklin Street
Buffalo, New York 14202
Tel: (716) 852-4416
Hrs: Dinner only:
Tuesday - Saturday 5:30 p.m. - 10:00 p.m.
Visa, MasterCard, American Express, Diners Club and Carte Blanche are accepted.

Successfully emerging from a former coffee house, the Rue Franklin West stands as the only French restaurant in the Buffalo area. The small menu is a result of seasonal changes, and the elegant wine list is extensive, ranging from a $14 White Alsation to a $125 Red Bordeaux.

Recognized as one of the nation's best restaurants, the Rue prides itself on consistently exceptional reviews. The decor and ambiance are very European, and far from trendy. A dark-walled Dining Room and Ante Room are accented with Old World scenes, antique furniture, and marble-topped tables; they are adorned with lace curtains, gleaming white linens, and fresh flowers. The new addition, a less formal garden room, uses French doors and windows to provide substantial lighting and a beautiful view of the marvelously landscaped courtyard.

Publicity in national gourmet magazines brings many travelers to the establishment and seldom a visitor leaves unhappy. The true delight of the Rue Franklin West is undoubtedly the menu itself. It features French creations including Cold Tomato Soup with Fennel Custard, Sea Scallops in Saffron and Basil Broth, and a Terrine of Eggplant and Sun-Dried Tomatoes. The unforgettable summer entrees consist of recipes like Grouper Fillet with Avocado, Tomatoes and Lime, Fricassee of Baby Halibut and Sea Scallops with Tomatoes and Cream, Whole Shelled Lobster with Tarragon Butter Sauce, Marinated and Grilled Quail with Red Wine Sauce, and Boneless Rabbit Loin with Madeira Sauce. Follow these mouthwatering dishes with a choice from the assortment of cheeses and the extensive wine list, and finish with something from the stacked dessert cart.

Extra touches include French Bread that is continuously brought to the table, slice by slice. Another custom is serving the salad course, consisting of greens with a mustard vinaigrette, after the entree as a palate cleanser. For those who wish, salad may be served at another time.

The extra special touches, as well as the exquisite cuisine and elegant atmosphere, make dining at the Rue Franklin West an unforgettable experience.

THE SARATOGA RESTAURANT
2694 Delaware Avenue
Buffalo, New York 14216
Tel: (716) 875-3015
Hrs: Lunch:
Monday - Saturday 11:30 a.m. - 3:00 p.m.
Dinner:
Monday - Thursday, &
Sunday 4:00 p.m. - 10:00 p.m.
Friday and Saturday 4:00 p.m. - 11:00 p.m.
Closed Sundays in July and August.
Visa, MasterCard, American Express, Diners Club and Carte Blanche are accepted.

Horse lovers and race track fans will find themselves right at home at the Saratoga Restaurant. Named after the Saratoga Racetrack, it is decorated with the racing theme in mind. The casual but elegant establishment has a club-type atmosphere with pictures of thoroughbred races and hunt scenes decorating the walls. Dark wood, glass, brass, and soft lighting help to make the Saratoga the place where the business people of Buffalo go to lunch and everyone goes to enjoy.

The Saratoga, at the same location since 1947, was purchased by Peter and Gloria Longo in 1985. They are proud of the friendliness of their staff and the fact that they are in touch with what their customers want. Business people in Buffalo endorse this restaurant with their repeat visits. House charges for businesses make this an excellent place to dine with clients. The Longos also own Peter's Pub, a smaller operation in the vicinity which is another favorite of the locals.

In keeping with the racetrack theme, menu items are found under unusual headings. Soups and sandwiches fall under the "Daily Double." "At the Gate" are appetizers such as potato skins and stuffed mushrooms. Chicken Scampi and Chopped Sirloin luncheon entrees are listed under "The Daily Line-Up." Mud Pie and Sundae Supreme desserts are found "Under the Wire." There is a large assortment of Clubhouse Entrees for dinner. Those watching their calories will be happy to find "Heart Smart" entrees.

In addition to their great dining room service, the Saratoga has banquet room facilities above the restaurant where they are able to accommodate groups from 15 to 250. They have menus for all occasions and at various prices. They handle groups for breakfasts, lunches, dinners, and cocktail parties; special packages are available for showers and weddings. Valet parking is available for banquet functions.

The Saratoga is popular with families because of its versatile menu. The Longo's add a very personal touch to their restaurant, greeting many customers by name and taking good care of regular patrons. Because Peter and Gloria Longo listen to their customers, they always deliver what the public is looking for, making the Saratoga a "Best Choice" for diners everywhere.

SHOOTER'S WATERFRONT CAFE, U.S.A.
325 Fuhrmann Boulevard
Buffalo, New York 14203
Tel: (716) 854-0416
Hrs: Monday - Thursday 11:30 a.m. - 3:00 a.m.
Friday & Saturday 11:30 a.m. - 4:00 a.m.
Sunday 11:00 a.m. - 3:00 a.m.
Full menu is served from 11:30 a.m. to 1:30 a.m.
Visa, MasterCard, American Express, Diners Club and Carte Blanche are accepted.

Waveless waters, sandy beaches, real palm trees and an azure skyline all say Key West. So does Shooter's Waterfront Cafe, U.S.A., where one can enjoy deliciously different cuisine and wonderfully refreshing drinks in a tropical atmosphere.

Shooter's provides guests with all the luxury of a Florida resort. The most amazing thing about Shooter's is that everything is done Buffalo-style, which means no holds are barred.

Shooter's offers casual indoor and patio dining, Sunday Brunch, a Saturday $1,000 Hot Bod Contest, valet boat docking, a swimming pool, sundecks, live entertainment, valet car parking, and banquet meeting and private party facilities.

The restaurant serves over 25 appetizers, nine types of salads, homemade onion soup, New England Clam Chowder, and several items that are Shooter's unique dishes. Among Shooter's most creative culinary specialties are the Grilled Teryaki Dolphin, Grilled Swordfish, Pita and Fajita Pocket sandwiches, Hawaiian Chicken sandwiches, and special-recipe Shooter's Burgers. Other dishes that Shooter's chefs prepare are the Oriental Stirfry, Blackened Chicken Sandwich, Chicken Flautas, and Mexi-chicken.

Shooter's desserts, such as the Apple Walnut Cobbler, Shooter's Special Cheesecake, and Key Lime Pie are well worth saving space for. Luscious liquid desserts are the tropical specialty drinks such as the Banana Split with strawberry and banana liqueurs, dark creme de cacao and strawberries.

Folks driving south from Buffalo should take the first exit after they get off the Skyway. Those heading north toward downtown should turn just before they reach the Skyway.

This fantastic Florida-style facility is bringing about a re-emergence of the Buffalo waterfront. Shooter's offers a beautiful waterfront view, a fun family atmosphere, excellent food, reasonable prices, and great service.

specialty shops

EVERYTHING ELMWOOD SPECIALTY STORE
978 Elmwood Avenue
Buffalo, New York 14222
Tel: (716)883-0607
Hrs: Monday - Saturday 10:00 a.m. - 6:00 p.m.
Sunday Noon - 4:00 p.m.
Visa, MasterCard and American Express are accepted.

Located on Elmwood Avenue at Bidwell, just a few minutes from the Peace Bridge to Canada, the Everything Elmwood Specialty Store features greeting cards, home decorating items, jewelry, Buffalo T-shirts, posters, handbags and other interesting souvenirs.

An incredible mix of tastefully different, unusual and affordable gifts are available at Everything Elmwood. Gourmet coffee and candy, and an outstanding selection of earrings are featured at the specialty store.

Everything Elmwood has something for everyone. There is never any pressure to buy, but if assistance is needed employees will provide gift ideas and other suggestions. This two-level shop is beautifully organized; the prices are reasonable; the music is upbeat; and the merchandise is never boring. Everything Elmwood, in the heart of Buffalo's progressive Elmwood strip, is truly "different by design."

GEORGE & COMPANY
650 Main Street
Buffalo, New York 14202
Tel: (716) 854-1065
Hrs: Monday - Saturday 10:00 a.m. - 5:30 p.m.
Thursday 10:00 a.m. - 8:00 p.m.
October:
Monday - Friday 10:00 a.m. - 9:00 a.m.
Visa and MasterCard are accepted.

George & Company, located in the heart of Buffalo's Theatre District, is one of Buffalo's most unusual stores. The largest retailer of masks in the entire country, George & Company carries over 400 unusual masks. Nixon, Batman and Frankenstein are a few popular ones.

Masks are not the only out-of-the-ordinary items sold at this unique gift, novelty, and costume store. George & Company also carries the largest selection of magic supplies in the city. The store also stocks a huge supply of Buffalo souvenirs, such as T-shirts, engraved collector spoons, pewter monuments, over 150 different types of chess sets (over 1,000 total sets in stock), and a very large selection of Vienna crystal, ceramic, marble onyx, and inlaid wood items.

If looking for something a bit zanier, George & Company carries a wide variety of gag gifts, including dribble glasses, false fried eggs, bending pencils, whoopee cushions, fake flies, squirting nickels, sneezing powder, hand buzzers, foaming sugar, disappearing ink, and very salty saltwater taffy.

George & Company is Buffalo's best bet for poker supplies. This unusual store offers a full line of casino-quality gambling supplies, including precision dice and poker chips. George & Company manufactures its own hand-drilled and painted dice, cut to within one-ten-thousandth of an inch. Their dice, as well as their poker chips, are sold for professional use worldwide. Owner George Smilanich, Jr. said that over the past 50 years, George & Company has produced over one million dice, and enough professional-quality poker chips to sink a dozen riverboats.

Though the selection is mammoth, items are easy to find--thanks to the well-organized shelves and available service.

The newly-remodeled 5,000 square foot showroom is well lit, clean and colorful with a high ceiling, balcony area, and black, blue, and white tile floor.

George & Company has long been an institution in the downtown area, offering the largest selection of novelty items in the area. For fun gifts and specialty costumes, come to George & Company.

NEO
55 Allen Street
Buffalo, New York 14202
Tel: (716) 884-1119

Hrs:		
	Monday and Thursday	10:00 a.m. - 8:00 p.m.
	Tuesday, Wednesday, Friday, & Saturday	10:00 a.m. - 6:00 p.m.
	Holidays: Monday - Thursday	10:00 a.m. - 8:00 p.m.

NEO's furniture and gifts have been in Buffalo for seven years. The shop spent two years on Elmwood Avenue and five years at its present location on Allen Street.

NEO means new, and that is just what this furniture and gift store contains, new and refreshing contemporary furniture and accessories. The store is owned and operated by the three Zoerb sisters who seem to have a flair for style. The taste of these three ladies is visible at NEO through the furniture they sell. Fine domestic and European designs are displayed throughout, reflecting a contemporary yet classic look for the home. The merchandise is constantly updated, touching upon Italian leather, upholstered seating, custom marble pieces, melamine wall and entertainment systems, extensive halogen lighting, bedding and futons.

Accessories such as vases, candlesticks, and frames compliment both contemporary and traditional settings. Internationally known designer pieces from Michael Graves, Richard Sapper and Aldo Rossi are highlighted. Photography and artwork from local artists are also featured.

NEO has something for everyone's taste in its large showroom, including unusual and upbeat items. NEO seems to bring a sense of excitement to those who are traditionally minded. After visiting the store, most are inclined to make a definite change in their home's interior to a more contemporary look. The prices vary, but the service and knowledge of the Zoerb sisters and the great selection make NEO the only place to go to give homes the most contemporary and stylish look that anyone could possibly dream of.

POSITIVELY MAIN STREET
773 Elmwood Avenue
Buffalo, New York 14222
Tel: (716) 882-5858
Hrs: Monday - Friday 10:00 a.m. - 6:00 p.m.
Saturday 10:00 a.m. - 5:30 p.m.
Closed Sunday.
Call for extended holiday hours.
Visa and MasterCard are accepted.

Positively Main Street, located on Buffalo's West Side, only a half hour from Niagara Falls and 10 minutes from the Peace Bridge to Canada, is an exciting gift shop that specializes in creative imports from all over the world.

Opened in 1977, Positively Main Street features a wide variety of gifts, such as hand-crafted earrings, necklaces, bracelets and pins, unusual greeting cards, carved picture frames, elegant silk scarfs, hand-made baskets, pots, and candlesticks.

Those are not the only international delights to be discovered at Positively Main Street. Fine shampoos and soaps, Chinese porcelains, soapstone carvings, Haitian tinware, Indian print bedspreads, and table cloths, potpourri, leather purses and belts, various brands of fine coffee and tea, and one-of-a-kind turquoise stone and bone beads are only some of the incredible gifts available at this unique gift shop.

The best part of shopping at Positively Main Street is that the browser will rarely find the same items twice, as the merchandise is everchanging.

This is one of the most interesting shops in Buffalo. The owner hand-selects each piece of stock so that regular customers will find a new variety of merchandise on each visit. It's fun to browse at Positively Main Street, but it's even more fun to own one of the shop's one of a kind international gifts. Positively Main Street also specializes in out of the ordinary holiday gifts.

Its no wonder that Positively Main Street is a "Best Choice" in New York. The merchandise is an extraordinary selection of fine collectibles and the service is helpful and friendly.

QUAKER BONNET
715 Elmwood Avenue
Buffalo, New York 14222
Tel: (716) 885-7208
1-800-BUF-CHIP (toll free)
Hrs: Monday - Saturday 8:00 a.m. - 6:00 p.m.
Closed Sunday.
Visa and MasterCard are accepted.

In 1930, Harold Hayes founded a quaint tearoom and confectionery, Quaker Bonnet. An architect by trade, he had an eye for beauty and an appetite for creative flavor and texture. His recipes made a statement. Gladys English and Marie Allen ran the tearoom to perfection but changing times created a need for home entertainment. The tearoom was replaced with a retail store.

Liz Kolken had been eating Quaker Bonnet goodies since childhood. As a newlywed she treated her family to celery seed dressing, angel pies and cinnamon ice cream. Liz bought Quaker Bonnet from Gladys and Marie in 1978 and slowly expanded. Liz understood the needs of working women. The shop now carries fresh and frozen soups, entrees and desserts as well as cheese, pates, crackers and salads. Last minute dinner parties for 10 are no problem.

Displaced Buffalonians have no trouble getting Quaker Bonnet treats through their mail order catalog. Many specialty stores throughout the United States and Canada now carry these old favorites: fudge sauce, celery seed dressing, elephant ears and meringues.

By far, the most popular item sold today by Quaker Bonnet is its trademarked Buffalo Chip cookies. Named as a joke, these delicious coconut macaroons are now the most sought after item both in the retail store and mail catalog.

Smith College Catalog and United Cerebral Palsy chose these sweet temptations to gain broader based support in fundraisers. Sales of this ultimate macaroon exceeded 10 tons in 1989 and are expected to double in 1990. Find out what the March 1990 Food and Wine Magazine raved about by paying a visit to Quaker Bonnet or ordering their specialty items by mail.

taverns & pubs

GARCIA'S IRISH PUB
74-76 Pearl Street
Buffalo, New York 14202
Tel: (716) 856-0111
Hrs: Lunch:
Monday - Saturday 11:00 a.m. - 3:00 p.m.
Dinner:
Sunday - Thursday 3:00 p.m. - 10:00 p.m.
Friday - Saturday 3:00 p.m. - Midnight
Bar open until 4:00 a.m. every evening.
Visa, MasterCard, American Express, Diners Club and Carte Blanche are accepted.

Garcia's Irish Pub's charm is its unpredictability. From the huge warehouse where Garcia's is located, to the variety of music played in the restaurant/club, Garcia's is a new experience each time it's visited.

Opened in 1984, Garcia's is housed in a 150-year old warehouse that was completely renovated. The building is four stories high but Garcia's uses only half of the space. Although the dining room seats 290 people, three banquet rooms can collectively hold 600, and five separate bar areas serve imported and domestic beer.

Garcia's offers full-service catering to business meetings, weddings, office parties, and promotional events with the Buffalo Sabres. A wide screen television continually provides sports programs for the many customers who are Buffalo Sabres fans and team members. Music-lovers enjoy the wide array of music played by disc jockeys at Garcia's.

What makes this restaurant/club stand out from the rest is the food. "Appeteasers" such as Potato Skins stuffed with scoops of shredded cheddar and bacon served with sour cream, and Batter Up, fresh golden fried mushrooms, zucchini and pepper rings served with "Sean's" zesty tiger sauce, are big hits at Garcia's

Super salads with seafood, grilled chicken, taco, and spinach among others are favorites, as are open-face Prime Rib and Reuben sandwiches for a luncheon treat.

Dinner entrees include Cajun Prime Rib, slow roasted rib of beef, tender and juicy, finished to order. Broiled Haddock, Fresh Haddock broiled to flaky perfection, topped with Mom Garcia's lemon and herb sauce; Baked Lasagna, fresh baked layered noodles, richly blended with ricotta cheese, ground beef, and topped with Garcia's famous meat sauce; and an international favorite, stir fry, consisting of carrots, celery, onions, broccoli, and peppers stirred in a hot garlic and soy sauce with a different finishing touch daily.

Delicious food and an exciting, unpredictable time are guaranteed at Garcia's Irish Pub in Buffalo.

NORTH BUFFALO

accommodations

THE BUFFALO MARRIOTT
1340 Millersport Highway
Amherst, New York 14221
Tel: (716) 689-6900
Hrs: Restaurant:
Seven days 6:30 a.m. - 11:00 p.m.
Nightclub:
Seven days Noon - 4:00 a.m.
Visa, MasterCard, American Express, Diners, Carte Blanche and Discover are accepted.

The luxurious Buffalo Marriott has it all: 365 elegant guest rooms with heat lamps, remote color television, in-room movies, individual climate control, lovely furnishings, and two phones. All rooms are spacious and ultra-modern.

Six executive suites offer exclusive surroundings for small business meetings, while banquet and meeting rooms provide a relaxed, first-rate environment for larger meetings. These are the reasons for the popularity of the Buffalo Marriott with professional meeting planners.

Browse through PRE-SENTS, the hotel's specialty gift shop, enjoy a round of golf at a nearby golf club, or work out in the Marriott's fully-equipped Hydra-Fitness exercise room. This splendid resort also offers valet, laundry, and room service, as well as a challenging game room, sauna, whirlpool, and an indoor-outdoor swimming pool.

The Panache Regional Specialty Restaurant is decorated with shining brass, bright flowers, and elegant hardwood, and serves superb American cuisine for breakfast, lunch, dinner, and Sunday brunch. To unwind, visit the glamorous Marriott Lounge for an evening cocktail or a fun-filled night of dancing.

Whether visiting on business, pleasure, or both, guests will enjoy a full range of services at the Marriott. If meeting groups needs presentation equipment, PA systems, lecterns, or audio-visual material, all it takes is a call to the staff. In fact, if there are any special requests , guests need only ask. The staff is always happy to accommodate the visitor's every need.

The Buffalo Marriott is located just off 1-290 in Amherst, just 15 minutes from Downtown Buffalo and five minutes from the Buffalo Airport. Its location, features, and friendly helpful staff make the Buffalo Marriott the place to stay while visiting along the Great Lakes.

HAMPTON INN
10 Flint Road
Amherst, New York 14226
Tel: (716) 689-4414
Hrs: Open 24 hours
Visa, MasterCard, American Express, Diner's, Discovery and Carte Blanche are accepted.

The Hampton Inn Hotel chain is quickly spreading across the United States. The concept of blending cost-saving design and operating efficiencies with special amenities, an ideal location, and generous hospitality is the work of the Holiday Corporation. A clean, comfortable, new room, usually at a price that is 20 to 40 percent less than traditional hotels, is one of the reasons why more than nine out of 10 people staying at a Hampton Inn say they will go out of their way to stay there again. The Buffalo Amherst Inn is locally owned by Hart Hotels, a well respected name in the hotel industry. This new hotel has been in association with Buffalo Hart Hotels since May 1987. The Hart family also owns four Holiday Inns and has an excellent reputation in the area.

The Buffalo Amherst Hampton Inn certainly does have a style of its own. The plush lobby is decorated with a variety of interesting sculptures, Chinese vases, a unique crystal display and many plants which accent the mauve and teal color scheme. The hallways, just as luxurious and well maintained as the lobby, lead the way to spacious and impeccably neat rooms.

There are 117 rooms available, half of which are non smoking. ESPN, CNN and Showtime are also available. A complementary newspaper and continental breakfast are offered to each guest. Valet service is available Monday through Friday. Guests may make free local calls and receive free transportation to and from the Buffalo International Airport. A conference room and outdoor heated swimming pool are also available. Guests can purchase passes to the Buffalo Athletic Club and a shuttle service provides transportation. Children 18 years old or younger stay free of charge when rooming with parents. Third and fourth adults stay free when sharing a room with two other adults and extra bedding is not required. "Life Style 50" allows guests ages 50 and over to share a room with up to three other adults and pay only a single rate when additional bedding is not necessary.

The University of Buffalo's campus is within walking distance and Niagara Falls is only 17 miles away. Those looking for breakfast, lunch, dinner or a late night snack will be happy to find Max Hart's Diner conveniently located right next door. It is a sleek, nostalgic diner offering the best of yesterday and today. All food is moderately priced and pleasantly served.

The Buffalo Amherst Hampton Inn--smart style, smart price, smart choice! It is the place to go when looking for luxury accommodations at budget prices.

apparel

RIVERSIDE MEN'S SHOP
783 Tonawanda Street
Buffalo, New York 14207
Tel: (716) 875-8400
Hrs: Monday - Saturday 9:00 a.m. - 9:00 p.m.
Closed Wednesdays during July and August.
Visa, MasterCard, American Express and Store Charge are accepted.

The Riverside Men's Shop is a third-generation family tradition which started in 1918 when Samuel and Rose Ehrenreich immigrated from Europe. Today it is owned by Neil Ehrenreich.

When Neil was five years old, he visited the Royal Pants Company with his father where he watched men tailor pants. At 15, Neil worked in the stockroom and later, in 1960, he started working for the Riverside Men's Shop. Taking over his father's share of the business in 1973 and his uncle's share in 1980, Neil Ehrenreich was proud to continue the family tradition at the shop, where tailoring is an art.

Upon entering the mezzanine of the store, friendly salespeople are waiting to greet customers. Several salesmen have been here many years and are familiar with customer needs. Neil's two daughters, Molly and Elizabeth, and son-in-law, Tim, are part of the business.

The store has four levels featuring men's suits, sport coats, furnishings, accessories, and shoes. Men's casual slacks and outerwear, boyswear, and ladies' tailored business apparel are also available.

Some of the brand name companies represented are the following: suits by Burberry's of London, Geoffrey Beene, Botany 500, and H. Freemen, London Fog Raincoats, shoes by Allen Emonds and Frye; and Dobbs' hats.

Free custom alterations, a charge account with free interest for four months, and 98 sizes of men's clothing are only three of many reasons why Riverside Men's Shop does so well.

The highest quality in clothing and tailoring are found at Riverside Men's Shop, a family tradition for more than 70 years.

candy

WATSONS CANDIES
2908 Delaware Ave.
Kenmore, New York 14217
Tel: (716) 875-6643
Hrs. Monday - Saturday 9:00 a.m.- 9:00 p.m.
Visa and Mastercard are accepted.

Watsons Candies has been producing fine chocolates and other candy for three generations. The business was originally a restaurant and bakery that started serving homemade chocolates in 1946. Owner Jim Watson uses the same ingredients and recipes as his grandfather used. Watsons Candies carries a complete line of boxed chocolates - all natural and of the finest ingredients. Other specialties include an assortment of hand-decorated truffles, nut barks, brittles, butter crunches, sponge candy and custom molds.

At Watsons, custom-made gift baskets are a breeze, containing exotic chocolates and an assortment of personalized molds to fit any occasion or holiday, and can be shipped anywhere in the world. Watsons Candies is a full-scale candy making operation that is very well-known in Western New York. Watsons has three locations that boast the same quality of craftsmanship and satisfaction of pleasing customers. The East Amherst store, located on Transit Road near Buffalo, offers a viewing window where patrons can actually see the candy being made. The Ellicottville store is a scenic one-hour drive from Buffalo on Route 219.

A blind taste-test broadcast on a local television station recently compared Watsons Chocolates with another quality brand. In that test, Watsons Candy was preferred, five to one.

At Watsons, personalized Valentine's hearts, custom molds for birthdays and special gift boxes are quick and easy. Don't forget to visit at Easter, when chocolate bunnies of all shapes and sizes can be found.

For a chocolate lover or a gift for that special occasion, visit Watsons Candies a delicious "Best Choice."

florists

DICK MILLER FLORIST & GREENHOUSES, INC.
185 Delaware Street
Tonawanda, New York 14150
Tel: (716) 693-5800
Hrs: Monday - Saturday 9:00 a.m. - 7:00 p.m.
Sunday 10:00 a.m. - 2:00 p.m.
Visa, MasterCard, American Express, Diners Club and Discover are accepted.

Where in Tonawanda can one find Bird of Paradise, Anthurium and Red Ginger? At Dick Miller Florist & Greenhouses of course. These specialty flowers of Hawaiian origin are on display at the Greenhouse, along with a selection of foliage and blooming plants, fresh-cut flowers, novelty planters and silk arrangements.

Owner Dick Miller, whose parents started the business, is proud of the colorful arrangements and specialty plants available at the store. Miller feels the key to their success is providing optimal product care and handling, insuring the highest possible degree of customer satisfaction.

Serving Erie and Niagara Counties since 1945, Dick Miller Florist & Greenhouses is located halfway between Buffalo and Niagara Falls and only minutes away from the Erie Canal. One of Buffalo's oldest and most established florists, it still has the same charm that made it successful in its infancy.

Using his knowledge of industrial management, Mr. Miller has updated the interior of the store with state-of-the-art computerization. Miller has also been awarded the title of Master Florist Manager and is among an elite group of less than 2,000 in the country.

Whether looking for a fruit basket, a bouquet, a helium balloon, wedding arrangements, or party decorations, Dick Miller Florist & Greenhouses, Inc. is the best place to start.

golf courses

GLEN OAK GOLF COURSE & RESTAURANT
711 Smith Road
East Amherst, New York 14051

Tel:	Restaurant:	(716)688-4400
	Golf Course:	(716)688-5454
Hrs:	Restaurant:	
	Lunch:	
	Seven days	11:00 a.m. - 4:00 p.m.
	Dinner:	
	Tuesday - Saturday	4:00 p.m. - 10:00 p.m.
	Golf Course;	
	Seven days	7:00 a.m. - Dusk

Reservations suggested for restaurant.
Visa and Mastercard are accepted.

Fine dining and an 18-hole championship PGA course combine to make Glen Oak Golf Course & Restaurant a must-see in East Amherst.

Designed by Robert Trent Jones, the course was previously called Ransom Oaks Golf Course. Recently opened to the public, it is recognized by Golf Digest as one of America's top 75 public golf courses.

The golf course consists of finely-manicured fairways bordered by winding waterways, and closely bunkered greens which have been the site of many tournaments. Proper attire is required and shirts and golf shoes must be worn at all times. Golf rates include the golf cart rental. Glen Oak Golf Course offers a challenge to the scratch golfer, and enjoyment for the weekend golfer.

Two main buildings house the pro shop, gift shop, driving range supplies, and clubhouse. Three dining areas seat 200 people. In the back of the clubhouse building, an entire glass panel allows diners to look out over the ninth hole on the golf course. An outside patio seats another 250 people and is used primarily for weddings, outdoor barbecues, and bar and buffet dining.

The restaurant offers a variety of menus: breakfast, brunch buffet, luncheon, hors d'oeuvres, dinner, dinner buffet, banquet, beverages, and a light menu, which specializes in dishes which are low in cholesterol and calories. For lunch, one could order the chicken a la king or Golden Shrimp Supreme, while dinner favorites include Prime Rib Au Jus, New York Strip Steak, Veal Marsala, Chicken Cordon Bleu or Stuffed Filet of Sole with Crabmeat. Beverages range from a variety of wines, Chablis, Rose, and Burgundy, to beer, domestic and Canadian.

Experience a public restaurant and golf course in a country club atmosphere at the Glen Oak Golf Course & Restaurant.

malls

PREMIER CENTER
3445 Delaware Avenue
Kenmore, New York 14217
Tel: (716) 873-6688
Hrs: Premier Liquor and Premier Cheese:
Monday - Saturday 9:00 a.m. - 10:00 p.m.
Premier Cheese only:
Sunday 9:00 a.m. - 5:00 p.m.
Visa, MasterCard and American Express are accepted

The Premier Center, one of the leading shopping centers in the country for wine, spirits, gourmet foods, and kitchen accessories, is also a warehouse containing two separate, but complete businesses, Premier Liquor and Premier Cheese. Both are owned by one man, Burton Notorious, but it is necessary for him to operate them separately because New York State strictly regulates what a wine and spirits retailer may sell. Fortunately, the state doesn't regulate how much a retailer may sell, or Burton might be in trouble. His business has at least 60,000 bottles of wine on display on any given day. He carries 100 different labels each of Chardonnays and Cabernet Sauvignons from California, along with over 200 separate labels of Grand Crux Bordeaux from different Chateaus and villages. The unrivaled selections and volume discount prices bring customers from as far away as Toronto.

Burton believes that selection and service are very important for the growth of his business. He tastes between 2,000 and 4,000 wines a year and says 12 wines must be tasted before finding one good one. He personally recommends '88 White Burgundies and "88 Beaujolais Nouveaux as best buys. Due to the falling value of the franc, these French wines are great bargains. To assist customers in their shopping, Burton has developed the Premier Wine Buyer Recommendation. This is a seal of approval tagged individually on bottles of wine whose flavors compare with more expensive wines but is still available at an affordable price. Additionally, Burton says, "We have four or five people in the spirits section. If a customer needs assistance or has a question, there's a knowledgeable person there to help them." Burton himself is in the store at least 70 hours a week making sure that things run smoothly and that the customer is always given the quickest carry-out service and offered free cheese samples. Shoppers interested in cheeses will find everything they are looking for at the Premier Cheese Center. In addition to the cheeses, domestic and imported coffees, packages goods, kitchen housewares, and imported cooking implements are available. Anyone searching for a gift will find lots of unique items to choose from.

In 1985, Market Watch magazine named Burton one of America's 12 leading wine and spirits retailers. In 1988 he was named one of Liquor Store magazine's Top Ten Retailers. Award-winning Burton says, "I love wines and the hospitality end of the business." When looking for the "Best Choice" in service and selection of cheeses, fine imported wines, and other liquors, one should turn to Premier Center.

restaurants

DOMENICO'S RESTAURANT
2766 Elmwood Avenue
Kenmore, New York 14217
Tel: (716) 874-3662
Hrs: Seven days 11:30 a.m. - 10:30 p.m.
Lounge: Until 2:00 a.m.
Closed major holidays.

Domenico's Restaurant and Lounge is the manifestation of a man named Domenic Zamiello. A first-generation American, Zamiello accepted the support and assistance of his family and many friends in the inception and creation of his homestyle Italian eatery. Since the establishment's opening in 1987, the slogan, "Just like mama used to make it", has been frequently commented upon and repeatedly proven by happy visitors.

The many Italian specialties are homemade, from the pasta to the famous sauce. The most fickle connoisseurs of such ethnic flair will delight at the mere thought of homemade ravioli, manicotti, lasagne, stuffed shells, tortellini alfredo, linguini and clam sauce, the traditional spaghetti, and much, much more. Aside from the extravagant pasta dishes are a superb selection of other menu items.

Basic seafood favorites like Shrimp Scampi, Scallops, and Surf-n-Turf are meticulously prepared and enhanced with an old world flair. Sandwiches are not forgotten, and items such as the half-pound hamburger, the Hot Sicilian, which consists of hot ham, hot salami, and hot pepperoni with melted provolone cheese, served on a bun with lettuce, tomato, and Italian dressing, and the hot beef on weck are sure to tempt the heartiest of appetites. The remaining entree menu, complete with Strip Steak, Veal Parmesan, and Chicken Marsala, is highlighted by one of Domenico's specialties, the "Italian Delight"--Italian sausage rolled in sirloin of beef, lightly seasoned, sauteed, and covered with mushroom gravy.

Domenico's will hold in-house banquets for up to 150 people, and will provide unlimited catering (the word "unlimited" is to be taken quite literally, as a party of 14,000 was once serviced). In addition, a variety of specials are always happily offered, including a Friday Nite Fish Fry, a clam bar, daily specials, and two packages that have become very popular--a "family of four" dinner and a "dinner for two".

The bar and dining room are separate and fitted with a simple decor. In addition to the warm feeling of the dark wood paneling and large rectangular bar, a stage is provided for easy-listening entertainment (seasonally on weekends).

The fabulous menu and home-like atmosphere at Domenico's Restaurant make for a friendly dining experience that is sure to be enjoyed.

THE GRAPEVINE
2545 Niagara Falls Boulevard
Amherst, New York 14150
Tel: (716)691-7799
Hrs: Lunch:

Monday - Saturday	11:30 a.m. - 3:00 p.m.
Brunch:	
Monday - Saturday	10:00 a.m. - 3:00 p.m.
Dinner:	
Monday - Thursday	3:00 p.m. - 11:30 p.m.
Friday & Saturday	3:00 p.m. - Midnight
Sunday	3:00 p.m. - 11:30 p.m.

Visa, Master Card, American Express, Diners Club and Carte Blanche are accepted.

If awards are a good indicator, then "good food and drink" are to be enjoyed at the Grapevine. For three consecutive years, the Grapevine has been chosen one of the top five Best Value Restaurants in the Greater Buffalo area and it has received the Culinary Award of Excellence from the American Fine Dining Association. The restaurant's broad menu and reasonable prices keep people coming back. Owner Tom Payne believes that seeing repeat customers is the highest compliment he can receive.

The Grapevine is a great family restaurant with something for all individual tastes. The restaurant offers 11 Italian specialities, including Shrimp, Veal, and Chicken Cutlet Parmesan or Sausage Cacciatore. Most dishes are served with spaghetti and salad. Their famed lasagna is made from a secret family recipe. Nine different chicken entrees are served including Broccoli Stuffed Chicken, the house favorite, created with two breaded boneless chicken breasts that are stuffed with broccoli and cheese and served over rice pilaf. Seafood lovers will be delighted with the large selection of haddock, fried clams, Australian lobster tails, scallops, fillet of sole, and catfish. For those who can't decide between seafood or beef, try the surf and turf and steak and shrimp dinners. For one low price, diners can create their own platter which can include their choice of two entrees. The Grapevine also offers a dinner movie package consisting of two dinners and two cinema passes for one price.

Hot specialties for lunch include omelettes, and a lengthy sandwich menu. Children under twelve have their own menu with a little bit of everything to please smaller appetites. All desserts are homemade, including the Fuzzy Navel Pie, Chocolate Rum Pecan Pie, Bailey's Ice Cream Pie, and Frozen Chocolate Mousse Pie. Special buffets are offered on Easter, Thanksgiving, Father's Day and Mother's Day.

The decor is very casual and contemporary, and the atmosphere provides for cozy, intimate dining. The scenery includes several 150-gallon saltwater fish tanks filled with live coral, different types of exotic fish, and eel. Tom is happy to talk to customers about his fish. His attitude carries over to his staff, who are all very friendly and pleasant. "Good food and drink," in addition to reasonable prices, make the Grapevine a "Best Choice" for family dining.

MAX HART'S DINER
20 Flint Road
Amherst, New York 14226
Tel: (716) 689-2211
Hrs: Sunday - Thursday 7:00 a.m. - Midnight
Friday - Thursday 7:00 a.m. - 2:00 a.m.
Visa, MasterCard, American Express, Diners Club, Carte Blanche and Discover are accepted.

A diamond in the rough is what many may call Max Hart's Diner, which is located in the center of six hotels and motels in Amherst, New York.

This diner of the '90s takes advantage of ideas from the 1920s while being equipped with some modern high-tech concepts of the future. The food at Max Hart's Diner, as well as the atmosphere, is fun and casual.

The home-cooked meals made from the freshest ingredients and their competitive prices give the customers a hearty value. Max's has something for everyone. Try their deep fried pickles, which were rated by Janice Okun as being "the junk food of the year." Some of their interesting specialties include Wet Shoes, which are curly fries covered with seriously spicy chili, sour cream and scallions, Sliders, which are mini-burgers, and their Hearty Early Bird specials. The diner makes the finest home-cooked meatloaf and turkey dinners as well. Their philosophy is, "If we can't make it fresh on the premises, then we'll find someone to make it fresh daily."

Max Hart is the beloved grandfather of David Hart of the famous Hart Hotels in Buffalo. A great sportsman and family man, Max played against Jim Thorpe while quarterbacking for the Fort Wayne Friars. A famous hustler of the golf links, he proclaimed the nineteenth hole his favorite. Max loved to eat his favorite foods and the Hart family brought those favorites back in his honor for all to enjoy.

This fun and unique restaurant is dedicated to Grandpa Max who would probably tell you to "eat at Max Hart's because you can't fish there."

LOMBARDO'S RESTAURANT
1198 Hertel Avenue
Buffalo, New York 14216
Tel: (716) 873-4291
Hrs: Monday - Thursday 4:00 p.m.- 11:00 p.m.
Friday - Saturday 4:00 p.m.- 12:00 p.m.
Sunday 4:00 p.m.- 10:00 p.m.
Closed Sundays in July and August.
MasterCard, Visa, American Express, Diners Club and Carte Blanche are accepted.

Personal service at Lombardo's has become one of its trademarks; fine food is another. Opened in 1974 by father and son team Tom Sr. and Tom Jr., Lombardo's Restaurant has been an established business on Hertel Avenue for over 15 years. Though now retired, Tom Sr. still shows up every day to assist in the preparation for the restaurant's opening. Lombardo's comfortable and sophisticated supper club atmosphere is pleasantly decorated; it is small, so reservations are strongly advised.

The daily menu features specials and each entree is specially prepared. Highlighted are fresh fish selections, a ravioli of the day, and a veal specialty. The printed menu is rarely changed because of the proven favorites, but it is fine-tuned. It includes beef and veal specialties, fresh pasta dishes, seafood, Italian favorites, and all are complimented by Lombardo's own Spinach Bread or the Caesar Salad for two.

A sumptuous meal may only be surpassed by the special Irish Coffee and the scrumptious homemade desserts.

There is also an After Theatre menu for late-comers or snackers, which also features a variety of choices including steak, veal, sausage and peppers, baby back ribs, chicken wings, or a tenderloin steak sandwich.

The high quality of the food, enhanced by the careful preparation, combined with an unhurried atmosphere and personalized service, all serve to keep satisfied customers returning to dine at Lombardo's time and time again.

THE TOWNE RESTAURANT
186 Allen Street
Buffalo, New York 14201
Tel: (716) 884-5128

Hrs:	Monday - Thursday	7:00 a.m. - 5:00 p.m.
	Friday - Saturday	7:00 a.m. - 5:30 p.m.
	Sunday	7:00 a.m. - 11:00 p.m.

American Express is accepted.

Peter and George Scouras, owners of The Towne Restaurant, were raised in Egypt by Greek parents. Later, the two brothers moved to America and became commercial painters. In 1972, Peter, George and a close associate, Lawrence M. Ward, opened a small hot dog stand that seated 25 people.

Towne Red Hots grew into what is now known as the Towne Restaurant. Capable of seating over 200 people, it is located in the heart of Allentown at the intersection of Elmwood and Allen Streets, just minutes from Buffalo.

The owners have embellished the business with such amenities as a large main dining area with a cathedral ceiling and skylight, two smaller dining areas, a balcony and off-street secure parking.

The Greek cuisine consists of many treats for the palate. For a traditional treat, try the Souvlaki Sandwich, a 'shish kebab in a pie. It consists of raw onion, tomatoes, feta cheese, grilled meat and oil dressing inside pita, Lebanese bread.

Other Towne favorites are the gyro, (pronounced "hero"), a variety of specialty sandwiches, traditional Greek and American dinners, Mousaka (eggplant, ground beef, and potatoes), and salads. Desserts such as pies, homemade baklava, and rice pudding are also frequently ordered and enjoyed. Their many imported and domestic wines and beers complement any dish.

The Towne Restaurant's genuine Greek cuisine and appealing surroundings are worth a trip to Buffalo.

WARREN'S RESTAURANT & CLUB
561 Main Street
Tonawanda New York 14150
Tel: (716) 694-3700
Hrs: Lunch:
Tuesday - Friday 11:30 a.m. - 2:30 p.m.
Dinner:
Tuesday - Saturday 5:00 p.m. - 10:00 p.m.
Special Sunday events
Closed major holidays.
Visa, MasterCard, American Express, Diners Club and Carte Blanche are accepted.

Warren's Restaurant and Club has come a long way from being the local tavern for industrial workers. Who would have guessed it would evolve into such a successful banquet facility, and, finally, into one of Buffalo's finest guest restaurants?

Owner and chef Mark Warren creates an elegant and sophisticated ambiance with the surroundings of the restaurant, as well as with the delicious food. The high ceiling entrance, large windows, crystal chandeliers, and the soothing sounds emanating from the baby grand piano add to the elegance. Mark and his wife, Sue, are enthusiastic about dining and use only the freshest ingredients available. They emphasize that dining should be a totally relaxing, totally artistic, and educational experience. That's just what they provide, beginning with their appetizers and ending with their tantalizing desserts.

A new menu is created each month, which includes some past selections. The appetizers include Seviche (lime-marinated scallops), and Rosemary Garlic Ravioli (fresh pasta stuffed with lamb mousseline, served with mint butter sauce). The delightful experience goes on with Warren's wide variety of entrees, such as Veal Kiwi, Filet Frederick William, with glazed onions and a marsala sauce, Boneless Breast of Chicken, in a sauce of creme fraiche, basil, taragon, and sage, and many other palate pleasures. Dessert is something you wouldn't want to pass up at Warren's Restaurant and Pub. It is one of the few restaurants in the Niagara area that makes warm souffles. To be perfect, souffles have to be baked and served within minutes, or they will deflate. Mark seems to have it down to a science, because each souffle is always tasty and fresh.

Warren's Restaurant and Club has a wine list that contains over 200 bottles, hand selected by Mark. Strong California vintage, Australian, New York, Oregon, Spanish, French, and Italian wines are all offered. Mark is always on hand to assist the customer in choosing a wine to go with his dinner entree or dessert.

The restaurant has recently been presented the Silver Plate Award from the Food and Wine Society of Buffalo. It is the highest award the Society issues, and Warren's Restaurant and Club is only the third Western New York recipient to be honored for high quality, well prepared meals, presentation, extensive wine cellar, excellent service, ambiance, and an outstanding chef. Outstanding chef indeed, Mark has been recently honored by an invitation to prepare a meal for the New York State Wine Foundation Champagne Symposium at Fredonia State University. He is also the recipient of the Title of Martre Grillardin by Lee Chaine Des, Rotisseurs for outstanding quality as owner and chef.

Warren's Restaurant and Club offers valet parking and high quality banquet facilities, which can accommodate 45 to 300 people. To reserve one of these fine banquet rooms, it must be booked well in advance. They also have a gift shop and accept most major credit cards.

The Warrens feel that American cooking is undergoing a renaissance. They offer their concepts of the new American Cuisine, and attempt to present a dining experience that will live up to the famous comment, "There's no place like the table for reconciling the body and spirit to the anguish of life that is necessarily too short and too imperfect."

SOUTH BUFFALO

night clubs

LA BOOM NIGHT CLUB
3036 Seneca Street
West Seneca, New York 14224
Tel: 1-(716) 823-1994
Hrs: Monday - Saturday 4:00 p.m. - 4:00 a.m.
Sunday 6:00 p.m. - Midnight
Visa, MasterCard, American Express, Diners Club and Carte Blanche are accepted.

Owners Joseph and Sabah Najm discovered that their idea to turn the once popular restaurant, Chestlight Lodge, into a club was the beginning of the hottest night spot in Western New York. La Boom combines the finest in state-of-the-art sound and light shows with the best top forty dance music. More than just a nightclub, La Boom offers a never-ending list of special features from happy hours to a spacious gameroom. La Boom is also a second home to many of the area's professional athletes such as Jim Kelly of the Buffalo Bills.

La Boom is the place to meet the best dressed and most available men and women in Western New York. If that isn't enough to draw a crowd, this popular spot's nightly events are. Happy hours last from four to seven and include live music, two drinks for the price of one, and free cold shrimp along with 10 other types of hors d'oeuvres. La Boom also prides itself in offering the best in Ladies' Nights on Wednesday, Friday and Saturday. Ladies enjoy the privilege of drinking all night for one low price and are accommodated with a free limousine ride to and from the club. Saturdays feature the "Kiss Mix Show" with appearances from radio personalities. La Boom also features "sound waves" parties where two free trips are given away each time. This cosmopolitan club allows its patrons to enjoy these special events by providing three large dance floors as well as three bars. La Boom is not limiting itself to the over 21 crowd, however. Sundays are exclusively young adult nights. This convenience gives young people an opportunity to enjoy dancing and listening to Top 40 music in an alcohol-free atmosphere.

Joseph and Sabah Najm have developed the ideal spot for Buffalo's cream-of-the-crop dancing crowd in La Boom.

points of interest

TIFFT NATURE PRESERVE
1200 Fuhrmann Boulevard
Buffalo Museum of Science
Buffalo, New York 14203
Hrs: Tuesday - Friday 9:00 a.m. - 5:00 p.m.
Summer:
Seven days 9:00 a.m. - 5:00 p.m.
Closed January 1, Thanksgiving,
December 24 and December 25.
Admission is free.

Tifft Nature Preserve is Buffalo's Unique Nature Sanctuary. The area, once a food-gathering place for Indians, is now a 264-acre wildlife sanctuary.

Through the years, the land underwent many changes, causing it to decline in aesthetic value. In the '70s, concerned citizens and conservation groups recognized the ecological value of the Tifft property, and encouraged the city to plan for the area's preservation. Years of dedication paid off, and in 1982, Tifft Farm Nature Preserve became a department of the Buffalo Museum of Science.

Today, Tifft Nature Preserve is dedicated to conservation and environmental education. "We have taken an ugly piece of property and turned it into a jewel," said Director Ernst Both.

Outdoor types can enjoy many attractions: five miles of hiking trails, three boardwalks, two viewing blinds along a 75-acre cattail marsh, self-guided interpretive trails, wildflower garden, birdwatching, fishing in Lake Kirsty, on-site snowshoe rentals, and much more.

There are also many special programs with seasonal themes offered year round, guided tours for school classes, and free guided nature walks every Sunday at 2 p.m.

Located nearby is Republic and Bethlehem Steel and 75 acres of cattail marsh, a remnant of a once extensive wetland along the eastern end of Lake Erie. Now visitors are able to examine the world of nature here. "I was lucky enough to observe a large Blue Heron!" said Both. "It is a wonderful concept of dealing creatively with our garbage."

Tifft Nature Preserve is a site for passive recreation such as walking, bird watching, snowshoeing, fishing and photography, and is located just three miles from downtown Buffalo off Route 5.

restaurants

ILIO DiPAOLO'S RESTAURANT
3785 South Park Avenue
Buffalo, New York 14219
Tel: (716) 825-3675
Hrs: Lunch:
Monday - Friday 11:30 a.m. - 3:00 p.m.
Dinner:
Sunday - Thursday 3:00 p.m. - 11:30 p.m.
Friday - Saturday Open until 1:00 a.m.
Visa, MasterCard, American Express and Diners Club are accepted.

Voted Best Value in Western New York by WLVB-TV Restaurant Reviewer Doug Smith, Ilio DiPaolo's is a wonderful Italian restaurant with a gourmet touch.

For more than 25 years, the DiPaolo family has been delighting patrons with authentic Italian cuisine and the friendliest service imaginable. The restaurant's wide selection of appetizers includes fresh antipasto, fried zucchini, minestrone, French onion soup, fried calamari, fettuccine alfredo, and garlic bread to name a few.

DiPaolo's prepares a variety of delicious homemade entrees, such as lasagna, manicotti, gnocchi, and cheese ravioli, but some of the most popular dishes at DiPaolo's are the tripe and calamari--a traditional Italian delicacy. Veal parmigiana and steak pizzaiola are also available.

For those who have trouble deciding on one entree, try the Tuesday Pasta Platter Special. It features a combination of ravioli, gnocchi, fettuccine, and manicotti. On Wednesday, try the Italian Feast which features homemade bracciole and veal parmigiana. DiPaolo's also serves choice steaks, chicken, veal and seafood.

Fabulous finales include mint and chocolate parfait, tortoni, cannoli, spumoni, Amaretto cheese cake and of course cappucino and espresso.

The restaurant's gourmet blend international coffees, refreshing cocktails, and fine wines enhance any of Dipaolo's wonderful meals. While at this magnificent restaurant, stop in for a cocktail at the relaxing Ringside Lounge.

A favorite gathering place for local celebrities and athletes, including the Buffalo Bill football players, the restaurant is decorated with sports memorabilia and pictures of Ilio DiPaolo, former professional wrestler. The main dining room is decorated with picturesque scenes of Italy.

DiPaolo's provides banquet services for up to 275 people, as well as separate dining rooms for smokers and non-smokers. It is located just off Exit 56 of the New York State Thruway, 10 minutes from downtown Buffalo, and one mile from McKinley Mall and Rich Stadium.

DONNA MARIE'S GARDEN RESTAURANT
980 Union Road
Southgate Plaza
West Seneca, New York 14224
Tel: (716) 675-0858
Hrs: Monday - Friday 9:00 a.m. - 10:00 p.m.
Saturday and Sunday 8:00 a.m. - 11:00 p.m.
Visa, MasterCard, American Express and Diners Club are accepted.

Located in Southgate Plaza, West Seneca, New York, "The Gate to the Southtowns" is Donna Marie's Garden Restaurant, a family-oriented business boasting creative cuisine.

A full breakfast menu is available from "The Continental" to their wonderful daily specials. Selections are sure to satisfy the appetite of most travelers.

Lunch is a delight featuring the "Gazebo Salad Bar" with 48 selections that include soup, a hot entree and fresh fruit.

Appetizers are superb, especially the "Mozzarella en Carrozza," which consists of layers of cheese and bread dipped in a seasoned egg batter, deep fried, then topped with a wine and butter sauce. Stuffed Mushrooms, another delicious appetizer, is filled with broccoli and cheese, batter dipped, then deep-fried, served with honey mustard.

Dinner is excellent from Donna Marie's tender Roast Beef, carved to order, to Chicken and Crab Mornay, New York Strip Steak, and a full selection of Italian pasta dishes topped with homemade sauce. The "Italian Feast" is featured on Sunday evenings.

The casual elegance of the garden-like atmosphere with green plants and trees, latticework, decorative tablecloths, and bright mauve walls makes any meal a special occasion at Donna Marie's Garden Restaurant. All meals are enjoyed at very reasonable prices.

GREENHOUSE CAFE
4348 Seneca Street
W. Seneca, New York 14224
Tel: (716) 675-1855
Hrs: Monday - Thurday 11:00 a.m. - Midnight
Friday - Saturday 11:00 a.m. - 1:00 a.m.
Sunday 10:00 a.m. - 9:00 p.m.
Summer hrs: Call for times.
Visa, Mastercard and American Express are accepted.

"A friendly place with great food and great drink," can be found at the Greenhouse Cafe, owned by Ricki Anne Lombardo. The Greenhouse Cafe was formerly the home of her brother, Anthony, who designed and built the restaurant. It boasts a greenhouse front, and plants, of course, are the theme throughout the cafe. The Patio Room and the Greenhouse Room are surrounded by windows with hanging plants in each window, creating an airy atmosphere. The color scheme is dark green, peach and white, and each oak table displays white carnations.

The Greenhouse Cafe sports a Southern Italian cuisine, basic Italian specialties with three dining areas to accommodate the clientele. A Sunday Brunch is served from 10:00 a.m. to 2:00 p.m. and features French toast, a selection of pancakes, blintzes, omelets, Eggs Benedict, and crepes - all made to order. Homemade pastries are available for those with a sweet tooth. Tuesday night is the Italian Feast (all you can eat buffet), consisting of assorted salads, Antipasto, Baked Lasagne, Spaghetti, Linguini, Meatballs, Italian Sausage, Oven-Roasted Potatoes, two weekly soups and homemade Italian Bread.

Ricki takes pride in everything she does and feels that the Greenhouse Cafe is an expression of herself. The Greenhouse Cafe offers outside catering and special parties and plans to continue serving customers for a long time. The friendly atmosphere of the Greenhouse Cafe has made it a first-class place to visit in western New York.

SCHWABL'S RESTAURANT
789 Center Road
West Senecca, New York 14224
Tel: (716) 674-9821
Hrs: Monday - Saturday 11:00 a.m.- 11:30 p.m.
Sunday 1:00 p.m. - 9:00 p.m.

Finicky types who refuse to eat anywhere that is without a reputation or a history will be quite comfortable at Schwabl's Restaurant. Ray Schwabl is one in a long line of family restauranteurs. He is carrying on the tradition of fine family dining that was started in 1837 by his great-grandfather Sebastian. The family believes they may be the longest line of restaurant operators in New York State, and possibly in the nation. The Buffalo Chamber of Commerce presented Schwabl's with a citation in 1956 for being one of the pioneer businesses along the Niagara Frontier.

The pride of the establishment is its group of fine customers, considered by Schwabl to be western New York's finest. Such success and customer devotion is the result of endless hard work and a very practical motto: "Buy the best, prepare it well, serve it amiably with a fair price." Common favorites include special roast beef on kummelweck and hot roast beef on bread with gravy. Choose a fresh haddock or yellow pike sandwich, a hot ham sandwich (served with Schwable's special tomato sauce), or a fried scallops plate. The majority of selections come with french fries or homemade German potato salad and cole slaw which can be substituted with a fresh garden salad.

Side orders include the traditional chili, soup du jour, and french fries, the not so traditional imported sardines, and anchovies. The restaurant prepares cocktails to perfection and offers a fine selection of beers and wines. Schwabl's receives daily deliveries of fresh seafood, serves children's portions, and will gladly accommodate all special orders.

This restaurant is a good family restaurant. The decor is very home-like and plays an integral part in the warmth felt by most. The partial oak paneling, brown cloths on the tables, a 100 year old bar, and the solid brass cash register that hasn't been serviced since 1956 helps to create that warmth. The menu is simple but well-prepared, and the environment is clean and friendly. Most conducive to making customers feel comfortable is the tradition of family involvement in the business itself. Although Ray owns the place, he is quick to point out that it is run cooperatively by Claus, Nick, Dave and himself. This is a quality that definitely makes a difference.

EAST BUFFALO

accommodations

AIRWAYS HOTEL - SHANNON PUB AND RESTAURANT
4230 Genesee Street
Cheektowaga, New York 14225
Tel: (716) 632-8400
1-800-888-8100
Hrs: Restaurant: 5:00 a.m. - Midnight
Pub: Until 4:00 a.m.
Visa, MasterCard, American Express, Diners Club, Carte Blanche, Discover and Japanese MasterCard (J.C.B.) are accepted.

Recognized by their green awnings, the Airways Hotel, located at Buffalo's Greater International Airport, is a family business known for keeping its 150 rooms clean and comfortable for their patrons.

The hotel offers a modern room with satellite TV, free house movie, a private bath, and even a coffee maker. For those into sports and exercise, the hotel is equipped with an outdoor swimming pool, horseshoes, basketball hoops, shuffleboard, and croquet. They have an ideal game room complete with pool tables, dart boards, ping pong, video games and more. One can even improve their putts on the Airways practice putting green located right next to their 1,000-piece jigsaw puzzle half finished for anyone who may want to help with its completion.

The Shannon Pub is an Irish pub and restaurant located in the Hotel. The restaurant serves their broad selection of delicious food from 5:00 a.m. until midnight and the pub stays open until 4:00 a.m. Some of their specialties include chicken wings, hot, medium or mild, which have been boasted as being Buffalo's best, and spiedies, which is marinated chicken or pork grilled on a skewer and served on Italian bread. They also have a wide variety of hot and cold sandwiches, salads, snacks, and entrees. The Irish-style pub offers the best live Irish folk musicians Wednesday through Saturday along with favorite Irish drinks. The Pub also plays host to the annual Buffalo Open Dart Tournament.

The cozy, clean and contemporary atmosphere, along with the family feeling and their dedicated staff, makes the Shannon Pub and Restaurant regulars return to the Airways Hotel time and time again.

amusement

PUTT PUTT GOLF & GAMES
3770 Union Road
Cheektowaga, New York 14225
Tel: (716) 683-0333
Hrs: Seven days 9:00 a.m. - 1:00 a.m.
Visa and MasterCard are accepted.

Putt Putt Golf & Games originated nationally in 1958 and the Cheektowaga Course was built in 1987. This four acre complex is located on Union Road, 20 minutes from downtown Buffalo. A variety of entertainment is offered for all ages and the establishment is open year round.

Three 18 hole courses are offered, complete with authentic caves, waterfalls and castles. The course proposes an ample challenge for the most experienced golfer, but even the novice can enjoy success on these greens. Putt Putt holds qualifying tournaments at the western New York course and national tournaments in which those competing can win a quarter of a million dollars in prize money.

Indoors, the course has over sixty state of the art arcade and video games. Many games, such as ski ball, air hockey, basketball and skeet shooting, will award winners with tickets redeemable for prizes at the gift center. The course also has the latest technology in batting cages, designed for softball or hardball, which accommodate beginners through professionals. Putt Putt Golf & Games is a complete family entertainment center.

Special rates are available to groups of all sizes. Birthday parties are especially encouraged by offering an exceptional value package. There is always something fun going on at Putt Putt. If in the Buffalo area, it's fun visitors won't want to miss. The helpful, friendly staff, snack center, gift shop and dining area make the amusement center totally complete.

art galleries

THE WINDSONG GALLERY
10745 Main Street
Clarence, New York 14031
Tel: (216) 759-2838
Hrs: Tuesday - Saturday 10:00 a.m. - 5:00 p.m.
Sunday Seasonal
Visa and MasterCard are accepted.

The Windsong Gallery is located in the village of Clarence Hollow, which is soon to be named an official historic community. The colonial designed gallery contains many works of art from renowned painter Trisha Romance, sister to the owner of the gallery, Carolyn Romance.

Trisha, who now resides in Niagara, Ontario, captures warmth and compassion for her family, the beauty of old homes, holidays, and seasons, and the maternal love for her three children in her extremely detailed and nostalgic paintings. Her slogan is "Preservation of the Past", and is quite apparent in her work. She releases prints twice a year, including limited edition prints. Her work illustrates a quality similar to Norman Rockwell in her own unique style. Along with Trisha's paintings, the gallery features artists such as P. Buckley Moss, who is internationally known for his paintings of people impressed by the simplicity of their life, Will Moses, an American folk artist, and various etchings and works of artists throughout the United States.

Carolyn adds a special and personal touch to the Windsong Gallery by being very friendly and helpful to all who visit, whether it is to purchase a piece of art, or just someone who wishes to browse. Although her store hours are limited, Carolyn is always glad to open the doors to those who may make a special appointment. She also offers her customers matting, framing, and custom framing services.

Carolyn loves all the works of art in the Windsong gallery, but she is most proud of her sister's pieces. It is a treat to learn about a noteworthy artist from one who knows her so well.

bakeries

OHLSON'S HOME BAKERY
10681 Main Street
Clarence, New York 14031
Tel: (716) 759-7199
Hrs: Tuesday - Friday 7:30 a.m. - 6:00 p.m.
Saturday 7:30 a.m. - 5:00 p.m.
Closed Sunday, Monday & holidays.

Baked with old fashioned goodness--that is what makes Ohlson's Home Bakery so special. The family-run bakery, located in the small town of Clarence Hollow, New York, specializes in elegant cakes, pastries, and chocolates. The Ohlsons are extremely proud of carrying on family traditions handed down through their long line of ancestors, who were also bakers. They take extra time, and use the finest ingredients to make their wide variety of freshly made baked goods.

Many people come from hours away to purchase their gourmet coffee cakes, European tortes, sticky buns, and delectable Danish pastries. Lisa Ohlson is especially proud of her exquisite wedding and birthday cakes. They also use a recipe which was handed down from their grandfather for the most delicious old-fashioned sweet dough Coughans, complete with real apple toppings. Some of their other baked goods include muffins, cakes, pastries, pies, and tasty delights for the holidays, such as butter cookies, fruitcakes, cut-out cookies, and pfeffernuss.

What Marvil and Lisa Ohlson are most proud of, however, is the fact that their customers can purchase freshly baked bread still warm from the oven. Although Ohlson's Home bakery has been open for only a year, their overwhelmingly friendly atmosphere, the novelty of the antique bakery surroundings, and the exquisite taste of their old-fashioned baked goods keep their customers coming back for more.

bed & breakfast inns

ASA RANSOM HOUSE
10529 Main Street, Route 5
Clarence, New York 14031
Tel: (716) 759-2315
Hrs: Sunday Noon - 8:00 p.m.
Dinner:
Monday, Tuesday &
Thursday 4:00 p.m - 8;30 p.m.
Lunch:
Wednesday 11:30 a.m. - 2:30 p.m.
Closed in January.
Visa, MasterCard and Discover are accepted.

In 1800, Asa Ransom, a young silversmith, constructed a combination log cabin home and inn deep in the wilderness of what is now Clarence, New York. Free land was given by the Holland Land Company, to any "proper man" who would build and operate a tavern on this land. In 1803, he also constructed the area's first gristmill. Today, located 28 miles from Niagara Falls, this site is the location of the "new" Asa Ransom House. Owners Bob and Judy Lenz have turned the Asa Ransom House into a bed and breakfast known for its healthy homemade dishes and their hearty hospitality.

This country inn consists of four guest rooms, a library, two dining rooms, a gift shop, known as Sunshine Square, and the Tap Room. Each cozy bedroom is furnished with antiques and period reproductions, and includes a private bath and air conditioning. The library, decorated with tall bookcases, a Franklin stove, and Oriental rugs, has a warm intimate atmosphere. Guests may work on jigsaw puzzles, choose a fine book to browse through, play chess, or even listen to an old radio program on tape. Sunshine Square is the perfect place to shop for souvenirs. Selective items include rag dolls, wooden torp, flowers, herb teas ,and crafts along with many others.

Bob and Judy have been featured in Prevention (a magazine dedicated to health) because of their commitment to creating healthy dishes that use unprocessed ingredients only. Vegetables are served fresh either steamed or sauteed to maintain the nutrition and color.

The main dining room is full of country charm and seats 75 non-smokers only. Such dishes as Toff Parmesan, Raspberry Chicken, Smoked Corned Beef with Apple Raisin Sauce, or Steak and Kidney Pie may be enjoyed. Diners must save room for homemade pastries or ice cream after dinner. An extensive list of New York State wines is also offered. Breakfast, provided as part of the overnight stay, includes fresh fruit, hot homemade muffins, whole grain toast, and a deep dish breakfast pie.

The good balance among excellent food, a delightful and warm atmosphere, and cordial service bring back many guests and a vote of "Best Choice" for a relaxing and healthful getaway at the Asa Ransom House.

book stores

MASTER KEY BOOKS
5412 Main Street
Williamsville, New York 14221

Tel:	(716) 633-4337	
Hrs:	Monday - Saturday	10:00 a.m. - 6:00 p.m.
	Thursday	10:00 a.m. - 8:00 p.m.
	Sunday	Noon - 5:00 p.m.
	Christmas:	Until 8:00 p.m.

Visa, MasterCard and American Express are accepted.

Toni Berent, Gail Mellman and Carol Brothers invite the public to "Come discover the magic" at their very special shop, Master Key Books. As their card reads, they carry "Books for the Body-Mind-Heart-Spirit." Their wide assortment of books is there to provide answers for all searching souls. Topics range from Christianity to Zen. Interesting reading can be found in the areas of holistic health, alternative healing, channeled materials, self-help and inspiration.

This store is a dream come true for Toni, who has always had a secret desire to open a book store. She combined as a team with Gail, in June 1988, to open the Williamsville store. Gail is responsible for managing the store and doing all of their design work. Together, along with Carol, they "have created a space where people can find peace-a safe place." One feels immediately at home upon entering the shop. A sense of warmth and love is created at the "tea nook," where herbal teas and healthy "munchies" are served. It is important to the three proprietors that although patrons may enter as strangers, they leave as friends.

The store also carries beautiful and unique greeting cards by a local artist. They offer special gifts such as wizard candles, original prints by a native American, Howard Issaac ,and jewelry. They have crystals, semiprecious stones, things of the earth, pendants, earrings, and mineral specimens. They also have a large selection of tapes. A children's corner has tapes, books and candles for youngsters. Keeping in line with the books, spirituality workshops and holistic health classes are available through the store by registration. The three special women who run Master Key Books make it "Best Choice" in book stores because customers leave with much more than just a book. The warm atmosphere they have created will make anyone feel relaxed and at home.

doll shops

THE MUSICAL DOLL HOUSE
10563 Main Street
Clarence, New York 14031
Tel: (716) 759-2996

Hrs:	Tuesday - Saturday	10:00 a.m. - 5:00 p.m.
	Thursday	10:00 a.m. - 9:00 p.m.
	Sunday	Noon - 5:00 p.m.

Visa and MasterCard are accepted.

The Musical Doll House is a dream come true for owner Mary Ann Singh. A collector of dolls herself, she always wanted to open her own doll shop to share her love of dolls with all who wish to visit. The Doll House carries musical and limited edition dolls in wax, porcelain and vinyl, and is the exclusive Western New York dealer of dolls made locally by nationally renowned doll artist, Beverly Stoehr. Other famous names include Turner, Middeton, Zook, Walker, Boots, Tyner and Effanbee dolls. The Musical Doll House offers the finest doll furniture, clothes or any accessories one may be looking for.

Tours of this life-size doll house are given by Mary Ann, whose love and knowledge of the dolls make the tour a learning experience as well as an interesting one.

The Bride and International Doll Shows and Sales are just two of the special events The Doll House offers. Holidays such as St. Valentine's Day, Easter, St. Patrick's Day, Christmas, Christmas in July, Old-Fashioned Sunday Afternoons, and many others are always remembered by an exclusive affair held at The Doll House.

Mrs. Singh works in close association with the doll artists the store represents and her friendly and relaxed personality makes a visit to The Musical Doll House a warm experience.

entertainment

LANCASTER OPERA HOUSE
21 Central Avenue
Lancaster, New York 14086
Tel: (716) 683-1776
Hrs: Open for public visits:
Monday - Friday 10:00 a.m. - 4:00 p.m.
Performances typically held Thursday - Sunday.
No performances in July or August.

When the Lancaster Opera House originally opened in 1897, it was meant to serve as a music hall as well as the town's main governmental building. Its adaptable space was used for dances, recitals, commencement exercises, musicals and traveling shows. During the Great Depression it became a food and clothing distribution center. During World War II, a sewing room was set up in the dressing room and parachutes were packed in the auditorium. After the war, it served as the Civil Defense Headquarters for much of Erie County. Although these multi-functional halls called "Opera Houses" (regardless of whether opera was performed) were plentiful in early America, the Lancaster Opera House is one of the few that remains in the country today.

Restoration of the Opera House began in 1975 and was completed in 1981. Community funds and 175 Lancaster volunteers keep the non-profit theater running today. Executive director Susan Carlton and Assistant Director Linda Costa are proud that most donations come from locals, although audiences are mainly comprised of out-of-towners. There is a definite interest here in keeping this tradition alive.

Today, this lovely asymmetrical Italianate building is used for performances of classical music, musicals, jazz, plays, operettas, variety shows, special events and is available for weddings. The auditorium has a very comfortable rather than stuffy atmosphere. The floor is of maple, while the door and window frames, wainscoting and the balcony balustrade are of long-leaf pine. The sloped stage allows audiences to see actors "upstage" as well as "downstage" and the balcony is suspended, rather than supported on columns, making it possible for everyone to have an unobstructed view of the stage. It is the perfect setting for performances by Buffalo's greatest actors and musicians as well as events such as the Harvest Moon Square Dance and the Christmas Walk Craft Show. The "Easy to Love" Lancaster Opera House is a "Best Choice" for those who enjoy various types of quality entertainment offered in a close community setting.

florists

ARCADIA FLOWERS AND GIFTS
Snyder Square II
4504 Main Street
Snyder, New York 14226
Tel: (716) 839-0800
Hrs: Monday - Friday 9:00 a.m. - 6:00 a.m.
Saturday 9:30 a.m. - 5:00 p.m.
Visa, MasterCard and American Express are accepted.

Arcadia Flowers and Gifts never makes the same arrangement twice. The shop specializes in the natural look. The arrangement is either woodsy or something freshly picked from the garden. The woodsy look uses lichen, moss, birch branches, sea lavender from the West Coast and fall leaves to create a natural outdoor beauty. The garden arrangements use fresh cut flowers such as delphinium, peonies and hydrangeas when in season. The shop's first choice is to use fresh flowers, but dried arrangements can also be created after an individualized consultation.

Sharon Murphy, owner of Arcadia, loves and respects nature and flowers in their natural state. Sharon's feelings toward nature reflect on the interior of the shop as well as in the arrangements. The inside has a fresh and natural look, with a tile floor and sponge-painted rough plaster walls. This shop is completely natural-looking and upscale.

When local clientele want something different than the basic flower arrangement, they call Arcadia. The shop carries other gift ideas, such as Italian tile, fragrant toiletries, assorted baskets, Italian terra cotta, beautiful wreaths enhanced with French ribbon, and other items collected from the woods.

The words for this shop are natural and creative. The smell of flowers from the fields, the look of the arrangements and even the owner are 100 percent natural. Sharon and her staff are service-oriented and take care of the customer's every need, from delivery to design. The service, uniqueness and Sharon Murphy make Arcadia Flowers and Gifts a "Best Choice" in flower shops along the Great Lakes.

gift shops

ALBERT'S ATTIC LIMITED
10768 Main Street
Clarence, New York 14031
Tel: (716) 759-2231
Hrs: Monday - Friday 9:00 a.m. - 5:00 p.m.
Saturday 9:00 a.m. - 2:00 p.m.
Sunday Noon - 4:00 p.m.
Winter hrs:
Monday - Friday 9:00 a.m. - 5:00 p.m.
Saturday 9:00 a.m. - 4:00 p.m.
Sunday Noon - 4:00 p.m.
Extended Christmas Hours
Visa, MasterCard, American Express, Diners Club, Carte Blanche and Discover are accepted.

Collector's paradise--the only words needed to describe Albert's Attic in Clarence, New York (aside from Christmas paradise). Located 30 minutes east of Buffalo on Route 5, the building was constructed in 1810, and originated as a hotel/tavern. The hotel register showed the names of many high-ranking officials from the Revolutionary and French and Indian Wars--names such as James Monroe, Millard Fillmore, and Grover Cleveland. It was a regular stagecoach stop, and there is plenty of evidence associating it with the underground railroad. The ledge-stone structure, overflowing with historical background, stands much as it did when it was built, but it now houses a magnificent collectors' shop. Look for the big stone pillars, a quaint white-rail fence, and a sign that says "Albert's Attic/Flowers & More/The Heart of Christmas."

When shopping here, one shouldn't expect to be in and out unless they are looking for something specific (in which case one should either ask for help, or get wrapped up in the numerous other treasures while trying to find it). A collector could get lost under the avalanche of items from the best manufacturers, and it takes some time to see everything. Two whole floors are neatly packed with Boehm porcelain, Felicitas handcrafted Christmas ornaments, Lowell-Davis collectible figurines, Anri Club collectibles from Juan

Ferrandiz, Schmid Disney collectibles, Swarovski Crystals, and so on, not to mention loads of antique furniture and adult-size rocking horses. Undeniably, Joyce Mooers, the owner of Albert's Attic, is extremely proud of the shop's tremendous variety, but the true pride comes from "The Christmas Village"--an entire village constructed of unique and spectacular Christmas collectibles that is traveled by a miniature train.

Finally, as you might be able to tell from the wording on the sign, Albert's Attic offers a full-service florist and will custom design any Christmas tree. They are dedicated to service and friendliness, ready to help shoppers find that knick-knack not found anywhere else, or simply offer a smile as customers peruse the endless array of goodies.

KEEPSAKES, LTD.
5411 Sheridan Drive
Williamsville Place
Williamsville, New York 14221
Tel: (716) 631-8671
Hrs: Monday - Friday 10:00 a.m. - 9:00 p.m.
Saturday 10:00 a.m. - 5:30 p.m.
Sunday Noon - 5:00 p.m.
Visa and MasterCard are accepted.

Keepsakes, Ltd. is the place to shop for the finest in country furniture, decorating accessories, and gifts. This charming shop is overflowing with pine furniture, both natural and painted, handmade quilts, pierced lamps, wooden and tin chandeliers, cranberry glass, pewter, and much more.

A little red brick school was the first home of Keepsakes, which opened in 1981. Now located in a small plaza, it has kept its originality and home-like decor. Many delightful treasures are tucked into every nook and cranny. Handcrafted dolls, wreaths, theorem paintings, folk art, and Rowe Pottery are just a few of the many unique gift items. Owner Karen Marshall travels all over the United States to search out both primitive American Country and the more formal French Country accessories.

Merchandise ranges from hand-carved wooden apples to armoires--something for everyone who loves to shop. Stencils and antique bobbins are still popular and Christmas collectibles are plentiful all year long.

Keepsakes, Ltd. looks like a comfortable country cottage, and the displays are always inspiring, set in that cozy atmosphere. Karen's mother Bernice Baldwin, as well as the experienced staff, always make the customers feel right at home.

The shop offers gift wrapping, UPS service, and layaways for the unexpected. Creativity, wonderfully different merchandise, and friendliness have all helped this lovely shop to flourish. It's one of the largest shops in the area and the tremendous amount of carefully chosen inventory makes Keepsakes, Ltd. the "Best Choice" along the lakes.

THE QUEEN'S CUPBOARD
10647 Main Street
Clarence, New York 14031
Tel: (716) 759-2665
Hrs: Tuesday - Saturday 10:00 a.m. - 5:00 p.m.
Thursday 10:00 a.m. - 8:00 p.m.
Sunday Noon - 5:00 p.m.
Visa, MasterCard, American Express and Discover are accepted

The Queen's Cupboard is one of the many fine shops located in the small, comfortable town of Clarence Hollow, New York.

The store, opened in May, 1987, is full of collectibles from around the world. Mrs. Kate Carbonara, owner of the store, is very "fond of good craftsmanship", and collectibles are a hobby of hers. She has traveled to numerous gift shops nation wide, and, as an artist herself, knows quality work. Mrs. Carbonara is always eager to help her customers by providing information about the collectibles they may be interested in buying.

The Queen's Cupboard is a small store, arranged in a most appealing way. It contains many works from a wide range of American and world-renowned artisans. Tom Clark's Gnomes and Woodspirits are lifelike figurines that are made personal by the stories and names given to them by their creator. Some examples of Mr. Clark's work that must be seen are "Puck", which makes the perfect gift for a hockey addict, "Homer", depicting the baseball fan, "Fielding" the soccer player, and "Candy", the woman who loves chocolate. Other collectibles one finds at The Queen's Cupboard include: Pilgram and Fenton genuine Cranberry glass, Winnie Kieth's hand thrown clay lamps, Waterford carvings by the Palmers, limited edition Santa Claus figurines by June McKenna, Anderson Stoneware, ceramic birds, animals, bowls, and vases, Aus-Ben Studios collections of old cast bronze animals, and British sculptor David Winter's miniature countryside cottage, imported from England.

Kate Carbonara seeks talented artisans and she adds her personal touch through her knowledge and service. The Queen's Cupboard is a store with a warm atmosphere that features the most unique gifts and collectibles from around the world.

hair salons

CAPELLO SALON
5422 Main Street
Williamsville, New York 14221
Tel: (716) 634-4111
Hrs: Monday - Friday 8:00 a.m. - 8:00 p.m
Saturday 8:00 a.m. - 6:00 p.m.
Visa and MasterCard are accepted.

The Capello Salon was established in 1970 and is owned by Buffalo born John A. Lauricella. Since that time his family-run operation has been providing the best skin, nail, and hair services available in western New York.

Capello is a unique salon due to the methods John has developed for selecting and training his staff. All 31 employees are required to serve an 18-month apprenticeship. Although apprenticeship is rare in U.S. beauty salons, this guarantees that they are fully able to handle their people-oriented job responsibilities. John believes in catering to the customer and he makes sure that his employees are able to communicate with the customer. This ensures that all clients leave satisfied with the services they have received.

John's salon brings world class hairdressing to the Buffalo area. Capello's is the only salon in the western New York area to be a member of Intercoiffure, the Paris-based organization that dictates to the world of fashion. John has been involved in three World Congress Meetings in Europe and Capellos's has been chosen to introduce products for the German cosmetic company, Schwartzkopf. John also has developed and sells his own product line which is manufactured near Toronto and bottled on the premises.

Capello is a "Best Choice" hair salon in Williamsville. Here, families can be taken care of in one quick stop without having to worry about the high prices of New York salons but while still receiving the same great services that these shops can provide. Capello is the place to go for pedicures, manicures, hair cutting, styling, and coloring. Staff members are hair replacement specialists and also handle hair removal by full-body waxing. They also handle facials, make-up, and total image advising. At Capello Salon, customer service is a priority and catering to the needs of customers is simply good business practice.

ice cream parlors

ANDERSON'S FROZEN CUSTARD AND ROAST BEEF
6075 Main Street
Williamsville, New York 14221
Tel: (716) 632-1416
Hrs: March - November:
Seven days 11:00 a.m. - 11:00 p.m.
November - February:
Seven days 11:00 a.m. - 10:00 p.m.

Original Location:
2235 Sheridan Drive
Tonawanda, New York 14233
Tel: (716) 875-5952
Hrs: March - November:
Seven days 11:00 a.m. - 11:00 p.m.

With two locations to serve the demanding public, Anderson's Frozen Custard and Roast Beef has been an institution since 1953. Established by Carl and Greta Anderson, this custard and roast beef stand has become one of western New York's greatest summertime traditions. The operation is now run by the children, Nels and Keith Anderson, and a son-in-law, Kirk Wildermuth.

The Anderson's cite their frozen custard as the house specialty and themselves as a dying breed. It is estimated that frozen custard is served in less than 100 places in the United States and is passing from the American scene. The dessert is much smoother and richer than regular ice cream or frozen ice milk, but unfortunately, does not take well to freezing. Consequently, it is generally made one gallon at a time and served fresh by independent retailers like Anderson's. According to Mr. Harris Cooper, President of International Dairy Queen, Inc., "The frozen custard stand is where God goes to get his ice cream."

The Anderson's operate a roadside stand that is far from one-dimensional. Family and friends gather to enjoy a cone or chat with a neighbor. The menu has plenty to choose from. For instance, Anderson's serves a knock-out roast beef sandwich they call "Carl's Choice"--5 oz. of mouth-watering roast beef available on a choice of three different rolls (Kummelweck, Kaiser, or soft), and four extras including lettuce, tomato, two types of cheese, or barbecue sauce.

In addition to the roast beef and specialty custard, which, incidentally, comes in chocolate, vanilla, pistachio, black raspberry, butter rum, strawberry, banana and cinnamon, they offer floats, lemon ice, sundaes, Dole Whip, and an Arctic Swirl (custard combined with nuts, candies, and cookies.)

JENNY'S ICE CREAM
78 Spring Street
Williamsville, New York 14221
Tel: (716) 633-2424
Hrs: Summer: Sunday - Thursday 11:00 a.m. - 11:00 p.m.
Winter: Sunday - Saturday 11:00 a.m. - 10:00 p.m.

Located just off Main Street is a renovated stable that used to house fire department horses, but now houses Buffalo's best ice cream. It's no wonder that Jenny's Ice Cream should receive this vote with such flavors as apricot, cinnamon, nutmeg, peanut butter (made with real peanut butter), and coconut (made with bakery angel flake coconut). Traditional flavors are also available.

The owner Debbie Hanny, is the wife of successful restaurateur, Jack Hanny, and the mother of six. Debbie doesn't do things the conventional way. She was told by many inspectors that there were too many problems involved with opening shop in a stable. In school she was taught that to be successful you must be located in a mall or a thoroughfare. The housewife in her said she couldn't keep her prices reasonable if she was paying a high rent. Also in school, she learned that one must showcase ice cream flavors. She doesn't feel that this looks very attractive and prefers to give the curious a sample taste. Due to the high quality of her ingredients and the uniqueness of her goods, patrons have beaten a path to her shop.

The stable was built in 1807 and has a clapboard exterior of blue with a white trim. The interior is clean and comfortable and will seat up to 25 people. It's a cozy, country setting with exposed, original wooden beams, assorted antiques, and old-fashioned wire chairs with wooden seats. In this rustic atmosphere, patrons also have soup, sandwiches, homemade chili, and salads available to them. There are always two soups of the day available; one is cream, the other broth. Unique sandwich selections include the Calico Egg Sandwich, which is egg salad with cheddar cheese and sliced green olives, and the Amherst, consisting of roast beef on pumpernickel with sliced red onion and a special cream cheese and horseradish sauce for a truly different flavor.

Pasta, tortellini, and ham and chicken salad are tasty complements to the sandwiches. The chicken salad has unexpected ingredients like water chestnuts and sliced green grapes in it.

The restaurant is run the way Debbie runs her home; she is proud of the T.L.C. given to both customers and products. Jenny's Ice Cream is certainly a "Best Choice" for Buffalo's best ice cream.

points of interest

G & R GALLERY OF WILDLIFE ART
2895 Seneca Street
Buffalo, New York 14224
Tel: (716) 822-0546
Hrs: Monday, Tuesday, Friday
& Saturday 9:00 a.m. - 5:30 p.m.
Thursday 9:00 a.m. - 9:00 p.m.
Visa, Mastercard, American Express and Discover are accepted.

Raymond Kegler established a hunting and fishing supply store 42 years ago. For the past eight years, he has shifted gears, and now specializes in western and wildlife art. The combination was inevitable, as the interest in nature was always present, much like the interest in art. Kegler and his sons are all painters.

The G&R Gallery is comprised of seven rooms full of well-displayed artwork. A tremendous selection of the western and wildlife art is complemented by a very friendly and enthusiastic staff. Ray Kegler, or one of his staff, will be happy to give visitors a tour.

The display of 20 local artists and 200 national artists includes original oils, watercolors, and acrylics, some of which are limited edition prints. Also on display are etchings, stone lithographs, soapstone and wood carvings, state and federal stamp prints, and bronze sculptures by Remington, Frederick, and Charles Rusell. Browse through an assortment of posters, prints, etched glasswork, art books, art magazines, and a complete line of limited edition plates.

The G&R Gallery is a multi-faceted gallery, with thousands of pieces in its collection. Kepler loans out the pieces nationally to other institutions, such as the Cincinnati Zoo and the Mellon Foundation. There is a full-service framing shop,a complete colored reference library that catalogues the works of major artists, a computer network that connects with over 2,000 dealers across the United States and Canada, and a mailing list of over 1,200. Collectors from all over the country are drawn to the special lectures and slide shows that feature 300 prominent artists like Thomas Aquinas Daly, Robert Bateman, and Ron Parker.

For the best in Western and Wildlife art, stop by Raymond Kepler's G&R Gallery.

WILLIAMSVILLE WATER MILLS
56 Spring Street
Williamsville, New York 14221
Tel: (716) 632-1162
Hrs: Monday - Saturday 10:00 a.m. - 5:30 p.m.
September through December:
Sunday Noon - 4:00 p.m.
Visa and MasterCard are accepted

The Williamsville Water Mills has plenty to look at, enjoy, and remember as a nostalgic view of the past, and an ascetic view of the present. The water-powered grist mill has been in operation since 1812, and is still using the original mill stone, now 190 years old. At one point in the mid-1800s, the mill turned to lime and cement work, and, according to legend, produced the hydraulic cement used in construction of the Erie Locks at Lockport.

Today, however, the mill still produces several stone-ground flours--including whole wheat, cornmeal, and buckwheat--and also carries a number of other stone-ground flours, produced elsewhere. The current of the Ellicott Creek still provides the power for the mill, but a turbine has replaced the water wheel,. which fell off during an ice storm at the turn of the century. Don't expect much else to have changed.

Adopting the look of an old feed store, the original structure has not changed, and visitors still walk on wooden floors. Those floors lie under many attractions--from the well-stocked gift shop, to the giant mill stone, to the basement full of antiques and artifacts, to the wooden cider press. From September to December, a beautiful Christmas room is prepared and puts a scent of nostalgia in the air as the holidays approach.

The scenic Ellicott Creek Falls Park is within close range and is visible from one room of the mill. Though the fabulous environment doubles as valuable creek-front property that would be much more profitable covered with condominiums, owner Warren Miller has no intention of destroying such a vital piece of history. He believes the town grew up because of the powerful Ellicott Creek Falls, and won't destroy the oldest monument to that heritage.

restaurants

ADAM'S STEAK & SEAFOOD RESTAURANT
204 Como Park Boulevard
Cheektowaga, New York 14227
Tel: (716) 683-3784
Hrs: Lunch:
Monday - Saturday 11:00 p.m. - 4:00 p.m.
Dinner:
Monday - Thursday 4:00 p.m. - 10:00 p.m.
Friday - Saturday 4:00 p.m. - Midnight
Sunday 1:00 p.m. - 10:00 p.m.
Visa, MasterCard, American Express, Diners, Carte Blanche and Discover are accepted.

Adam's Steak & Seafood Restaurant, located just one mile south of the Walden Galleria Mall on Como Park Boulevard, was founded 30 years ago by Adam Pilarz and is now run by his two sons, Larry and Joe, who were raised in the restaurant business.

Patrons are quick to agree that the owners' experience and study, as well as Chef Tony Mack's culinary expertise, have paid off. Adam's really knows how to serve "sizzling steaks and superb seafood". The steaks are freshly grilled and the seafood is delicately baked. Entrees include Cajun-style Prime Rib, Veal of the Day, and Cajun-grilled or broiled Orange Roughy, but the most popular item on the menu is the 16-ounce Strip Steak. Adam's uses only top quality Western Steer Beef that is vacuum-sealed and aged for many weeks under a controlled temperature.

Adam's also features a variety of specialty items, such as beer-battered or marinated artichoke hearts, special recipe French onion soup, creamy New England clam chowder, chicken specials, such as Cordon Bleu, Francais, and chicken stuffed with either fresh vegetables or broccoli and cheese.

Though the entrees are served in huge portions, be sure to try some of Adam's delicious desserts like the Peach Melba, Chocolate-Peanut Butter Pie, and fresh cheesecakes made on site.

Besides an elegant, yet cozy, dining room and a spacious banquet room, Adam's features a relaxing piano bar that offers easy listening and light jazz on weekends.

The cuisine is wonderful, but it's not the only reason to enjoy a visit to Adam's. The classic American steakhouse atmosphere is both elegant and intimate. The gorgeous peach walls, private dining alcoves, turquoise accents, fresh flowers, and friendly atmosphere all combine to give patrons the warm cozy feeling of a traditional steakhouse.

Whether visiting for an afterwork dinner, a relaxing evening with friends, or a special event in the banquet room, Adam's Restaurant will see to it that the evening is an enjoyable one.

CARRIAGE HOUSE RESTAURANT & LOUNGE
3000 Genesee Street
Cheektowaga, New York 14225
Tel: (716) 895-5521
Hrs: Lunch:
Tuesday - Friday 11:30 a.m. - 3:00 p.m.
Dinner:
Tuesday - Saturday 4:30 p.m. - 9:00 p.m.
Sunday: 1:00 p.m. - 9:00 p.m.
Visa, MasterCard, American Express, Discover and Diners Club are accepted.

Built around the turn of the century, this one-time carriage house serves as the quarters for an excellent restaurant by the same name--the Carriage House Restaurant and Lounge. The dimly-lit Victorian decor accents the split-level dining room and separate bar area. A picture of elegance with its red and black color scheme, the Carriage House offers an atmosphere that is comfortable and clean, as well as quiet and friendly.

The restaurant's owner, Jim Ulicki, takes a great deal of pride in the experience of his long-time staff and the number of customers who have become faithful regulars, some of whom actually have favorite tables.

A solid indicator of what to expect is that all food is made from scratch as it is ordered. Such a process takes a bit longer, but the results will surely be appreciated. A typical appetizer would be the Clams Casino a la Carriage House, Excargot Carriage House, or for a twist, the Marinated Herring in Sour Cream. For the main course, a difficult choice will be made from a list of meticulously prepared creations like the Veal Alaska (breaded veal, covered with crabmeat, topped with an imported cheddar cheese sauce), Stuffed Filet Mignon a la Carriage House, or perhaps the Sliced Tenderloin (sauteed in Burgundy and mushrooms, served over rice). More is to be enjoyed in the collection of Polish specialty foods, wonderful old-fashioned soups and fabulous homestyle foods.

In the way of seafood, Sauteed Frog Legs from Bangladesh and Austrailian Lobster Tail leads the way, followed by more common favorites such as King Crab Legs and Shrimp Scampi. A La Carte suggestions include an Open Prime Rib Sandwich and New York Strip Steak. The Carriage House also offers a daily compilation of eight to 10 luncheon specials, homemade desserts, and a thoughtful children's menu. In addition, a full service bar and banquet can serve up to 140 people.

One can experience a true diner's delight at the Carriage House Restaurant and Lounge.

COVENTRY TEA ROOM
10911 Main Street
Clarence, New York 14031
Tel: (716) 759-8101
Hrs: Lunch:
Tuesday - Friday 11:00 a.m. - 3:00 p.m.
Saturday - Sunday 11:00 a.m. - 5:00 p.m.
Dinner:
Friday - Saturday 5:00 p.m. - 9:00 p.m.
Visa and MasterCard are accepted.

Rose Marie Knapp brings the elegant atmosphere of European dining and a cozy homelike setting to Clarence Hollow through the Coventry Tea Room. She is a graduate of the Culinary Arts program of Erie Community College and has attended a French pastry course of the Culinary Institute of America. She uses the knowledge she gained to create mouth-watering gourmet lunches, desserts, coffees, and teas. French and Viennese-style tortes and desserts are her specialties. Other house favorites are the smoked turkey breast sandwich, the tasty Black Forest Ham sandwich, and many more blockbuster sandwiches and salads. Chicken Streudel, Julienne Stripped Chicken Breast, imported mushrooms, and herb cheese served with mushroom wine sauce are a few more of the house specials available at The Coventry Tea Room.

Rose Marie grows her own herbs for a variety of delicious teas. She blends her own coffee too, so it is always the freshest it can be. Afternoon tea is served Saturday and Sunday after 3:00 p.m., complete with warm scones baked fresh daily.

The elegant but simple Victorian-style room gives all who visit the tea room a cozy feeling. Rose Marie adds a personal touch to the room by displaying her own antiques, beautiful table settings and never forgetting fresh cut flowers for each table. The room seats 35 to 40 people and can accommodate a pleasant atmosphere for a party or a small gathering of friends or family.

The Coventry Tea Room has received praise from visitors from England and Europe for its fresh scones and its elegant setting. It is quickly becoming the favorite spot of the locals who have an appreciation for the finest life has to offer. Local businessmen who see Rose Marie's unique talents have tried to persuade her into a partnership, but she chooses to remain faithful to her cozy and uncommercial setting. One can always expect to be pampered at The Coventry Tea Room. Its beautiful decor and quality food makes it the best kept secret in western New York.

CAFE IN THE SQUARE
4476 Main Street
Snyder, New York 14226
Tel: (716) 839-5330
Hrs: Monday - Saturday 9:00 a.m. - 8:00 p.m.
American Express is accepted.

Opened in 1987 in the quaint, new retail center, Snyder Square, the Cafe in the Square restaurant has been voted a big hit by its patrons.

The cafe blends a delightful combination of gourmet lunches and dinners, as well as some simple homecooked dishes. Delicious pot pies are made from scratch by LaVarrene graduate, Virginia La Porte. George Bishouty, CIA graduate and pastry chef, fills the bakery showcase with freshly made and an ever-changing array of luscious baked goods and elegant desserts.

Warm chicken salad, topped with papaya, peppers and orange vinargrette, is one of the house specialties on the cafe's luncheon menu. The tasty smoked turkey breast sandwich, crepe du jour, and many other flavorful sandwiches and salads prepared by Laura Paul, Tearle Gigines, and Lisa Gaeta are offered for one's luncheon enjoyment.

The house specialties for dinner include tantalizing Chicken Thai, which is made with a red pepper and garlic sauce to give it an intensely spicy taste. They also offer pork, prepared with a delightful almond and papaya glaze, Fettucini, prepared with smoked salmon, and many more mouth-watering dishes.

The simple country-style cafe gives diners a close and warm atmosphere complete with soothing classical music. The front dining room is small and seats 45 to 50 people, but they offer additional seating for 75 to 80 diners in a larger room in the rear of the cafe. The large amount of room makes the cafe a superb banquet facility complete with catering with a personal touch.

For your after dinner pleasure, you can visit the Art Gallery located in the basement of Snyder Square. The gallery features the work of local artists and even an annual art festival.

Braden's Fine Food Merchants is located next to the Cafe in the Square. Established in 1917, Braden's was originally a national mail order upscale, gourmet grocery business. This location, however, is the first full-service retail store complete with a fantastic bakery. The store contains a unique selection of high-quality specialty foods and is owned, as well as the Cafe in the Square, by Dorothy Johnston and Joseph Bayler.

The Snyder Square is a charming little village filled with fine boutiques and shops. The Cafe in the Square adds to that charm by using quality ingredients, unique recipes, and a delightful atmosphere for the pleasure of its customers.

LOUGUS RESTAURANT
2227 Genesee Street
Buffalo, New York 14211
Tel: (716) 896-6212
Hrs: Sunday - Thursday 3:00 p.m. - Midnight
No Credit Cards accepted.

The Lougus Restaurant, located on the East side of Buffalo, was the former location of the German Singing Society Clubhouse. Now owned and operated by Sara Churchhill and Bill Van Dyke, a sister/brother partnership, the restaurant was formerly run by their father Gus, in the 1950's. Gus worked as a chef in some of Buffalo's finest restaurants before he opened the Lougus.

The restaurant features a dimly-lit interior with separate bar and dining rooms. The decor is reminiscent of the past with stuccoed walls with red, highlighted, dark wood, and checkered linen tablecloths. Antiques are displayed, such as a jukebox which offers the latest hits as well as oldies. The bar ceiling is quite unusual, featuring a jet black background highlighted with 24 carat gold stars.

A variety of savory dishes is offered on the restaurant's menu. The menu boasts Italian-American cuisine and Lougus has a reputation for serving the best pizza on the East side of Buffalo. Begin a meal with a choice of delicious appetizers such as Herring in Wine Sauce, Julienne Salad and Soup Du Jour. The entrees include several steak dinners as well as various seafood dishes: Surf & Turf, Broiled Lobster Tail and Fresh Fan Tail Shrimp with Tartar Sauce. Italian Specialties such as Baked Lasagna, Spaghetti, Ravioli and of course their famous Pizza are also offered. A children's menu is available. Be sure to sample some of the delicious home-baked pies and desserts that are made by Sara's mother, Eleanor.

The friendly, down-to-earth atmosphere is sure to be appreciated at Lougus Restaurant. It is a hot spot in Buffalo's East Side, where all of the locals eat, including the mayor. The dishes are homemade with handed down recipes. They offer great quality food at reasonable prices. The Lougus (Lou-Gus) Restaurant is a perfect family oriented establishment, not to be passed by while in Buffalo.

MCMAHON'S RESTAURANT
4529 Main Street
Snyder, New York 14226
Tel: (716) 839-0108
Hrs: Dinner:
Tuesday - Sunday 4:30 p.m. - 11:00 p.m.
Open until 1:00 a.m.
Visa, MasterCard, American Express, Diners Club and Carte Blanche are accepted.

"Meet me at McMahon's" is a statement one would probably hear in Snyder, New York. McMahon's Restaurant has been described as "a corner saloon for the white collar set." Opened in the late '40s by World Middle Weight Champion Jimmy Goodrich, it was later bought in the early '50s by Mickey McMahon and new owner Jim Garvey kept the name as well as the tradition.

McMahon's is noted for its homemade corn muffins and its delicacies from the deep. It features Broiled Australian Lobster Tail, Fillet of Salmon, Fresh Lake Whitefish, Broiled Shrimp Moray and more. Some of the specialties include: fresh Domestic Calves Liver, Medallions of Veal, Sirloin Strip, Boneless Chicken Breast and Sauteed Sweetbreads. If interested in broiled food, McMahon's offers prime Domestic Lamb Chops, 20 to 22-ounce Porterhouse Steak, petite Steer Tenderloin, and a tasty Filet Mignon. They also offer a wide range of appetizers and desserts.

Located only 15 minutes from downtown Buffalo, McMahon's has the appealing warmth of a small Manhattan bistro, complete with a full bar packed with friendly locals. Many celebrities tend to stop by occasionally, also.

McMahon's supplies valet parking and a sportcoat is a must; however, if one happens to drop by without a jacket, the restaurant will gladly provide one.

The delightful, friendly atmosphere of McMahon's and the delicious array of food makes meeting people at McMahon's Restaurant a pleasant experience.

OH BABY! & SUZN O' AT SNYDER SQUARE
4476 Main Street
Snyder, New York 14226
Tel: (716) 839-0477
Hrs: Monday - Saturday 10:00 a.m. - 5:30 p.m.
Thursday 10:00 a.m. - 8:30 p.m.
Visa and MasterCard are accepted.

Oh Baby!, owned by Renee Renaldo, carries a wonderful selection of children's apparel; Suzn O', owned by Suzanne O'Rourke, is a fabulous shop for women's separates. The two shops are very near each other, located within a courtyard of a dozen other shops known as Snyder Square. The exteriors exhibit a New England flavor and harbor a relaxed atmosphere.

Some of the items featured at Oh Baby! are heirloom quality Christening gowns, a complete line of layette, a large selection of 100 percent cotton playwear, and an array of children's clothes from casual to dress. Renee also has a nice selection of toys, music boxes and gift baskets with a UPS shipment service (local, next day delivery). Her slogan is, "Children's Fashions You Once Hopped A Plane To Buy."

Suzanne O'Rourke of Suzn O' specializes in providing the correct approach to "the Total Look" by listening to and meeting customer needs. Suzanne displays hand-knit sweaters, skirts and jackets, blouses, cotton and wool knits, and accessories such as scarves, belts and jewelry.

Upon entering either one of these stylish shops, one finds practically anything desired; Suzanne and Renee are charming individuals, adept at finding that special selection. Additionally, both shops specialize in service and prized merchandise.

SCHARF'S SCHILLER PARK RESAURANT
34 South Crossman Street
Buffalo, New York 14211
Tel: (716) 895-7249
Hrs: Tuesday - Saturday 11:00 a.m. - 10:00 p.m.
Sunday Noon - 9:00 p.m.
Closed Mondays, Thanksgiving & Christmas.

Scharf's Schiller Park Restaurant is a neighborhood tavern and restaurant located on Buffalo's far east side at the edge of Schiller Park.

Scharf's boasts a timeless tavern decor, and a friendly amber-lit barroom with pool table and jukebox. The large rear dining room has kitchenette tables and chairs, colorful German posters and coats of arms representing each region of Germany. Traditional Bavarian blue and white colors are used throughout the restaurant.

The faint smell of sauerkraut teases the appetite and it is immediately apparent why visitors return to Scharf's again and again--the German cuisine. The appealing menu includes many German favorites such as Hot Potato Pancakes served with applesauce and syrup, Sauerbraten, Dumplings and Red Cabbage, Weiner Schnitzel, Rouladen and Spatzle, Roast Duck, and three kinds of soup: Liver Dumpling, Clam Chowder and Chicken Noodle.

Scharf's American specialties include Roast Beef, Pork Chops, Porterhouse steak, Delmonico Steak, Southern Fried Chicken and French Fries, to name a few.

No meal at Scharf's is complete without sampling their seafood or one of their famous desserts such as Black Forest Cake, German Chocolate Cake with vanilla pudding and cherry pie filling smothered in whipped cream and nuts, or the wide variety of pies, Coconut Cream, Lemon Meringue, Apple, Pumpkin, Rhubarb, and Cherry. Pies are available on weekends only.

Everything at Scharf's is home-cooked with the finest ingredients, and all fried foods are cooked in vegetable oil for those wishing to keep their cholesterol levels at a minimum. A salad bar is included with all meals on Saturday and Sunday and take-out orders are welcomed.

Scharf's Schiller Park Restaurant is the ethnic restaurant with excellent cuisine and fabulous prices and portions. A great time to visit Scharf's is during the Octoberfest when live German music is provided every Saturday during the month and plenty of Gemutlich (festive German spirit) is on hand.

STASH & STELLA'S
Walden Galleria Mall
2000 Walden Avenue
Cheektowaga, New York 14225
Tel: (716) 683-9301

Hrs:	Monday - Saturday	8:30 a.m. - 11:00 p.m.
	Sunday	8:30 a.m. - 8:00 p.m.

Visa, MasterCard and American Express are accepted.

Stash & Stella's, located on the second level of Buffalo's newest megamall, is a newly-opened, one-of-a-kind theme restaurant that offers a variety of savory menu items ranging from fluffernutter sandwiches to 10-ounce T-Bone steaks. This upbeat restaurant is a lively, '50s-style diner complete with original jukeboxes, turquoise vinyl booths, neon lights, formica tabletops, and stainless steel swivel seats at the dining counter. The restaurant is cheerfully designed to appeal to people of all ages.

What's so unusual about Stash & Stella's is that the cooks go to great lengths to prepare food that is not at all fancy--just good. One of the best things about dining at this spirited restaurant is that the prices aren't fancy either. Most of the deluxe dinner platters, which include dishes such as liver & onions and Stella's meatloaf (accompanied by fresh-baked bread and a choice of cole slaw, macaroni salad, potato salad or apple sauce) cost less than $6.

The desserts range from ice cream floats to banana splits, and the beverages include coffee, lemonade, soft drinks, milk shakes and juices.

The decor is reminiscent of Arnold's place in "Happy Days--only brighter, shinier, and much more electric. Though the design is '50s-style, it never gives one the sense of being stuck in another era. Instead, it is modern enough to give guests the sense of looking back and happily reminiscing. The music is a collection of the best '50s and '60s tunes, and the employees are exceedingly energetic as they dash to the table and say, "What'll it be guys?"

Stash and Stella's is an O'Toole's-franchised restaurant that carries out the O'Toole tradition of offering simple, but delicious food at very reasonable prices in an unusual, yet down-to-earth setting.

For a taste of yesteryear, stop at Stash and Stella's.

TOWN & COUNTRY RESTAURANT
3393 Union Road
Cheektowaga, New York 14225
Tel: (716) 684-1170
Hrs: Lunch:
Monday - Friday 11:30 a.m. - 3:00 p.m.
Dinner:
Monday - Saturday 5:00 p.m. - Midnight
Sunday 1:00 p.m. - 9:00 p.m.
Closed Sundays in July and August.
Visa, MasterCard, American Express, Diners Club, Carte Blanche and Discover are accepted.

The Town & Country Restaurant has been located on Union Road in Cheektowaga, New York for 37 years and has built a great reputation for serving the finest food and liquor in the area.

The restaurant was opened by Henry Lysiak and Robert E. Gibbs, who five years ago turned the business over to Henry's sons, Paul and Tom. They run the business together and the restaurant is doing better than ever. Tom and Paul try their best to make their visitors' dining experience perfect. The perfection begins with a basket full of homemade muffins, bread, and crackers. The muffins are made daily and vary for all tastes. Choose from blueberry muffins, banana nut, orange date, or honey bran. The enjoyment continues with a choice of their famous entrees which include Prime Rib, steaks, and an array of seafood. The restaurant uses top choice Prime Beef and all dinners are served with fresh vegetables. Try the roast loin of pork special on Sundays, the Chicken Francaise, or the chef's choice of the day. The Town & Country Restaurant also offers a full luncheon menu and large salad menu. Diners can create a sandwich from the wide selections of cold cuts. Specialty sandwiches may also be ordered.

The restaurant's bar and dining area are separate. The bar is equipped with a large screen TV, high-backed padded booths, and offers live music on the weekends. It is a great place to stop and unwind after a long day or an evening out. The dining room contains booths, large and small tables with white linens and cloth napkins. This, combined with great service, gives visitors a feeling of friendly elegance.

The Town & Country Restaurant is a recipient of the White House Hospitality Award, received for its exemplary cuisine, service and hospitality. Although the restaurant is located on one of Western New York's busiest intersections, the Town & Country shouldn't be overlooked. This restaurant offers delicious food, a wonderful, relaxing atmosphere, and a lounge full of fun. Stop by the Town & Country Restaurant and become a part of the tasty tradition that has been carried on since 1942.

VALLEY INN RESTAURANT
10651 Main Street
Clarence, New York 14031
Tel: (716) 759-6232
Hrs: Open seven days.
Restaurant:
Sunday - Thursday 6:00 a.m. - Midnight
Friday - Saturday 6:00 a.m. - 1:00 a.m.
Bar: Open until 4:00 a.m.
Visa, MasterCard, American Express, Diners Club and Carte Blanche are accepted.

Located 30 minutes from Buffalo, The Valley Inn Restaurant has been providing Clarence Hollow residents with casual country dining and family atmosphere for over 90 years. When the inn burned to the ground in 1988, the small town gathered to help Vince and Linda Buccitelli duplicate the original structure, and once again gave Clarence a classic eatery and meeting place.

The Valley Inn has always been central in the community because of its warm atmosphere, good food, and moderate prices. The Town Fathers met here, politicians met here, and the firemen have their annual picnic catered by The Valley Inn. Patrons gather for sporting events brought in by satellite dish, and bus excursions are organized for Buffalo Bills and Bison games.

A rather comprehensive menu is offered that ranges from peanut butter and jelly to escargot, including country dinner entrees that come complete with a choice of homemade soups, salad bar, choice of potato, vegetables du jour, and fresh bread. One can count on all ingredients being fresh every day, including the meats, vegetables, and fish. If catering, or a small party is what one desires, the same quality and reasonable prices are offered, but the impressive atmosphere provided by the knotty pine benches and tables, exposed hand-hewn ceiling beams, and fantastic colonial exterior need to be experienced in person. It's all the beauty and comfort of a rustic home, plus good food, and a full bar.

specialty shops

BENDER VILLAGE
8550 Sheridan Drive
Williamsville, New York 14221
Tel: (716) 633-5757
Hrs: Monday - Saturday 9:30 a.m. - 5:00 p.m.
Thursday - Friday Open until 9:00 p.m.
Thanksgiving - Christmas:
Monday - Friday 9:30 a.m. - 9:00 p.m.
Saturday 9:30 a.m. - 6:00 p.m.
Visa, MasterCard and Discover are accepted.

Bender's Christian Supplies, the anchor store in Bender Village, is the largest Christian supply store in New York State. Richard and Jean Bender started the store in 1953 after perceiving a need for a local supply outlet for pastors and others in the area. Since then, the business has grown steadily and now serves thousands of churches and individuals throughout Western New York and areas of Canada.

Bender's carries an extensive selection of Bibles, reference materials, and books, ranging from time-honored Christian classics to the current titles available today. Quality entertainment and teaching videos are available to purchase or rent, and the comprehensive music department contains traditional and contemporary recordings, song books and sheet music. The greeting card and gift departments display pictures, plaques, games and jewelry suitable to meet just about any gift need. Of special note: Bender's Christian Supplies is one of the largest carriers of Precious Moments Collectibles in western New York.

Also located in Bender Village is the Country Oven. Specializing in all natural homemade pies, cinnamon rolls, muffins and breads, the Country Oven is fast becoming well known in the area for delicious, high-quality baked goods. The Country Oven also serves lunches daily, including soup, sandwiches and a salad bar.

A third specialty shop, currently located in Bender Village, is the Village Knitters, known for the high-quality yarns and knitting supplies it carries. The Village Knitters is the place to stop for all knitting needs.

STEREO ADVANTAGE
5195 Main Street
Williamsville, New York 14221
Tel: Monday - Friday 10:30 a.m. - 8:30 p.m.
Saturday 10:00 a.m. - 6:00 p.m.
Sunday 12:00 p.m. - 4:00 p.m.
Closed Christmas, Thanksgiving and Easter.
Visa, MasterCard and Discover are accepted.

The "Lowest prices in America" is the reason Stereo Advantage is growing so rapidly. Tony Ragusa Jr. never wanted more than a small business, but because of the special care and service he has provided to his customers, the business keeps blossoming.

Tony brought something new to the industry--no commission salesmen, thus reducing the pressure to sell the highest priced merchandise rather than quality items. This makes a more pleasant atmosphere for the store's many returning customers; they can trust the salesmen's recommendations and judgements.

The store is located on Main Street in Williamsville, only 15 minutes from downtown Buffalo, and parking is available for over 100 cars.

Tony and his staff won't sell junk, they only deal in quality items such as compact disc players, televisions, stereo equipment, VCR's, car stereos, big screen and stereo TV camcorders, microwaves, fax machines, copiers, cellular phones, and many other electronic needs. The Stereo Advantage carries over 55 manufacture names such as JVC, Magnavox, NEC, Panasonic, Sony, Casio, and many more.

This fantastic electronic store has a full-service department; they have up to one hundred service technicians for the convenience of their customers. The service center is 20,000 square feet and has seven bays for car stereo installation. The center offers lifetime care and service for a $1 registration fee and five-year parts coverage.

Stereo Advantage has a hard-working staff and was named Audio/ Video Retailer of the Year two years in a row. It also received the Bristol-Hunter Company's award for the best business in operation.

There is only one place to go in Buffalo for the best quality and prices in audio video components and that place is Stereo Advantage. For the "Lowest prices in America," be sure to stop by.

tavern & pubs

BUFFALO BREW PUB
6861 Main Street
Williamsville, New York 14221
Tel: (716) 632-0552
Hrs: Monday - Saturday 11:30 a.m. - 2:00 a.m.
Sunday Noon - 2:00 a.m.
Serves food until midnight.
Visa, MasterCard, American Express and Diners Club are accepted.

The Buffalo Brew Pub, opened in 1986, is Buffalo's only existing brewery which still offers house beers brewed on the premises. At one time, Buffalo had over thirty breweries, however, larger breweries forced them to close their doors because they were unable to compete with prices and technology.

The Buffalo Brew Pub has several brewed house beers for different tastes. They offer Amber Ale, which is an English Mild Ale, and Oatmeal Stout, a rich brew with a mild roasted malt flavor with just a trace of an oatmeal finish. They also have Red Ale, which has a carmel zest to it; Nickel City Dark, a dark ale with a mild barley flavor, and Buffalo Bitter, a version of an English bitter hops which gives this ale its flavorful nature. The Pub has a broad selection of domestic and imported bottles and draft beers from Australia, Ireland, Germany and from small and large breweries in North America and Canada.

They also make a tasteful array of food such as their original sausage or shrimp slowly steamed in home-brewed beer. The B.B.P. special contains thin, sliced to order, beer-basted beef piled high and topped with delicious rarebit sauce served on a soft roll. For the seafood eater, the Pub's fish and chips dinner contains a half pound of beer-battered fish served with their own chips. Other specialties include mild or spicy chicken wings made from a recipe stolen from the Airways Hotel, B-B-Q baby back ribs, shrimp scampi, chicken and mushroom pie and a large selection of deli meats for your taste enjoyment. They also offer a variety of appetizers, desserts and even meals for the younger members of the family.

The Mug Club is an organization visitors can join at the Pub by asking a friendly bartender or waitress for a punch card. After becoming a regular, they place the member's name on a mug at no cost, and keep the mug behind the bar except when in use. The members of this club are entitled to reduced prices for house brews and are invited to special toastings, unveilings, and Mug Club outings.

Oktoberfest is a big event at the Buffalo Brew Pub, so big that they feature a practice Octoberfest in June before the full blow out in the fall. The celebration is complete with Octoberfest Lager and all the festivities that go along with it.

The friendly and knowledgeable staff, along with the pleasant environment, weekly dart game, great food, peanuts on the table, and the large selection of beer makes the Buffalo Brew Pub a serious beer drinker's haven.

WEST BUFFALO

florists

DESIGNS
311 Bryant Street
Buffalo, New York 14222
Tel: (716) 886-1669
Hrs: Monday - Friday 8:00 a.m. - 6:00 p.m.
Visa, MasterCard and American Express are accepted.

Designs is a flower shop which has been luring customers since 1984. Dan Lowrie, a former landscaper and now proprietor of the shop, has made Designs one of Buffalo's finest floral shops in the area. A wide assortment of flowers from Holland, Hawaii, New Zealand, California, Florida and South America may be purchased from Designs throughout the year. Dan makes beautiful arrangements by using interesting and unusual flowers such as the Alstromeria, Rubrum Lilies, Anthurium, Bird of Paradise, Dendrebium Orchid, Ginger, and their trademark Curly Willow and Bear Grass. These unusual flowers, combined with Dan's exquisite taste, make the perfect gift for any occasion.

Other gift ideas found at Designs are flute vases, silk and dried flowers, 30-inch candles in 40 different colors, unique stuffed animals, balloons, and Blenko hand-blown vases. These lovely gift items are displayed creatively throughout the shop by using props and glass accessories. Many exotic, tropical blooms, brass, wicker, and pottery planters can also be found.

This wonderfully colorful store, packed with fresh flower and silk flower arrangements and interesting selections of gifts is located on Bryant Street, just off Elmwood Avenue, five minutes from downtown Buffalo.

Designs is best known for its innovative floral arrangements for weddings, Bar Mitzvahs, private parties, corporate parties, corsage detailing and delivery. Dan prides himself on giving clients alternatives to the typical posies in a basket. Traditional alternatives are available. This is the place to go for flowers that are just a little different and more sophisticated.

The helpful staff can design an arrangement suitable for every customer's desire with a matching color scheme that makes Designs the florist to count on in the Buffalo area.

GRAND ISLAND

La Grand Isle , as it was called by the French who discovered it , is seven and one-half miles long and six miles wide. Once a vacation spot for wealthy Victorians, Grand Island is a suburban community of both the Buffalo and Niagara Falls areas.

attractions

Beaver Island State Park contains 952 acres offering a variety of activities. The sandy beach boasts an extensive boardwalk and a picnic grove. Biking, hiking, and nature trails are abundant, and there is an 18-hole golf course. Fishing is permitted. Winter activities include ice skating, cross-country skiing, snowmobiling and sledding.

Buckhorn Island State Park is an 896-acre wilderness area and wildlife sanctuary. The park offers hiking, nature trails and fishing.

Fantasy Island is a children's paradise. It features a children's amusement park with over 100 rides, a family center for recreation, camping, shows and live entertainment. It is open June through Labor Day.

River Lea, once the summer home of Grover Cleveland, is maintained by the Grand Island Historical Society. The house is open to the public for special events.

accommodations

HOLIDAY INN/NIAGARA FALLS/GRAND ISLAND
100 Whitehaven Road
Grand Island, New York 14072
Tel: (716) 773-1111
Visa, MasterCard, American Express, Diners Club, Carte Blanche, Discover, Optima, Enroute and JCB are accepted.

What was once the Whitehaven Settlement, a lumbering community that dates back to 1837, is now the site of Holiday Inn Grand Island. The Holiday Inn is peacefully situated right on the Niagara River and is only 10 minutes from Niagara Falls. Although this resort setting is very quiet, the hustle and bustle of Buffalo can be reached in 20 minutes and Toronto in 90 minutes. Because of its close proximity to these business districts, this Resort and Conference Center is a great location for corporate and regional meetings.

Holiday Inn Grand Island has five fully-equipped meeting rooms. An elegant banquet hall with a full stage is available for seminars, banquets or weddings. This lovely setting is the perfect spot for a gorgeous wedding and a variety of wedding and shower packages are available with a large selection of dinners or buffets to choose from.

There are plenty of activities available to keep everyone busy. The hotel is adjacent to River Oaks Golf Course and guests can go cross-country skiing in the winter. The Holiday Inn features an indoor and outdoor pool, tennis courts, and a Fitness Centre which offers aerobic classes, workouts on Kaiser Equipment, and a relaxing massage afterwards. Guests can enjoy boating on the Niagara and be entertained by The Joe Chimes Trio on a Friday or Saturday night.

Exquisite dining is available at Higgi's, a large dining room that overlooks the Niagara River. Floral print carpeting and wallpaper, pink tablecloths, green napkins, and bamboo chairs with lots of greenery around the room create a tropical atmosphere that adds to the enjoyment of the dining experience. The 270 modern rooms available also carry these soft colors and floral prints. Guests can relax in their rooms, enjoying room service and the panoramic view from the bedroom's balcony. All of the guests' needs are catered to by a friendly and kind staff. When looking for "The Island Resort on the Niagara," The Holiday Inn Grand Island is a "Best Choice."

COLDEN

bed & breakfast inns

BACK OF THE BEYOND
7233 Lower East Hill Road
Colden, New York 14033
Tel: (716) 652-0427
Hrs: Open year-round.
Reservations recommended.

The site of Back of the Beyond has accommodated a summer retreat for Bill and Sash Georgi, a home complete with herbtique, and a marvelous bed and breakfast. As numerous customers would inquire about the vacant chalet adjacent to the herbtique, the concept of combining the two began to take shape. The Georgi's are at great peace in their gardens and they clearly manifest their emotions into their business.

It was 10 years ago that things finally came together and the bed and breakfast was in full swing. A stay here is highlighted by completely organic country gardens full of herbs, flowers, and vegetables, as well as a greenhouse and herbtique gift shop that are always open to guests, passers-by and local people.

Back of the Beyond features a substantial, six-course, herbal country breakfast to get guests motivated in the morning. A sample menu may include fresh fruit in season, furnished with edible herbs/flowers, organic juice or apple cider with a swizzle stick of lavender or mint, homemade breads, scones and spreads, and herbal, meat, or vegetable omelet (the most popular filling is cheese, mushrooms, grated shallots, and fresh tarragon), herbal teas, coffee or milk, and an assortment of other tempting selections.

There are plenty of things to do to pass the time at Back of the Beyond. A large pond provides a beautiful place for swimming and skating, scenic trails through the woods are paradise for hikers, and cross country skiers and the herbal cooking classes, tours, and symposiums satisfy the most curious of patrons. A post and beam cabin, which sleeps three, is used in the summer only, and provides a comfortable environment for overnight guests.

Inside, guests will find a large, romantic fireplace, a vast array of herbs and flowers scattered about and on the kitchen shelves, herb teas and Bill's own honey. The separate chalet has three bedrooms, one and one-half baths, a fully-furnished kitchen, dining room/living room, piano, pool table and fireplace. All exciting features have culminated to earn Back of the Beyond a spot in Bed & Breakfast USA, Bed & Breakfast Inns and Guest houses, and American Bed & Breakfast.

gift shops

THE COLDEN COUNTRY STORE
Route 240 and Heath
Colden, New York 14033
Tel: (716) 941-5016
Hrs: Tuesday - Saturday 10:00 a.m. - 5:00 p.m.
Sunday Noon - 5:00 p.m.
Open Mondays, October - December
Open evenings, Thanksgiving & Christmas.

The Colden Country Store contains the finest in American handicrafts and unique gift ideas from around the world.

The store which is owned and operated by Cindy Lawrence and Dianne Graf, is located in the quaint and picturesque town of Colden, New York. It was originally the town's general store during the 1800s and since then it has housed a bar, pharmacy, and antique and gift shop. Remnants of the previous owners remain. The ancient pharmacy cabinets, old-fashioned dark bar and the roller piano that sits in the corner of the room and plays during the fall season gives the feeling upon entering the store that one have stepped into the past.

The Colden Country Store has been known for its candy counter and year-round Christmas room. One other room in the store is devoted solely to pantry items. It contains glasses, jams, teas, kitchen linens, copperware, gourmet spices and sauces, preserves, Blue Calico China, stoneware and cooking items. The main room has beautifully packaged stationery and greeting cards, wrapping paper, woven baskets, dried flowers, bath items and fragrances. This room also includes a variety of potpourri, prints, candles, homemade pieces and gifts for all occasions. Upstairs in the loft next to the Christmas ornaments, cards and figurines is an excellent and extensive collection of children's books and games.

All of the merchandise, which is set at a medium price, is uniquely displayed in and on the dark wood cabinets, old wooden counters and the lengthy bar throughout the store. Cindy or Dianne are always on hand to answer any questions or assist their customers in any way they can with the purchases they may wish to make.

There are several specialty shops, wonderful restaurants, nearby skiing resorts, and beautiful scenery in the town of Colden and a stop at the Colden Country Store is definitely an unforgettable experience.

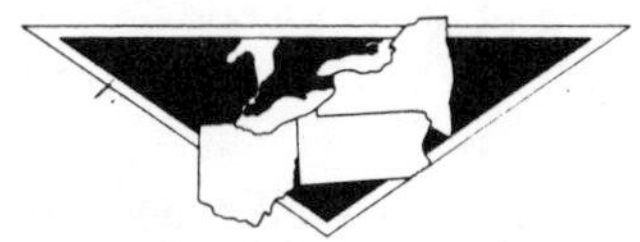

NIAGARA COUNTY

Niagara County, established in 1808 from Genesee County, received its name from the Niagara River and from the Indian word meaning "bisected bottom lands."

The first European visitor to reach the area was believed to be Champlain in 1615. After the French explorer and others arrived in the area, a trading post was built on the site of the present-day Old Fort Niagara.

After much fighting between the British and Americans over the fort and surrounding area, the Americans regained control at the end of the War of 1812. In 1837, the county was a hub of excitement. Railroads had opened the area to trade and it had become a center for the Great Lakes fruit industry.

With Lake Erie to the west, Lake Ontario to the north and the Niagara River to connect them, the Frontier offers a wide array of water recreation. Sailing, boating, water skiing and fishing highlight the water sports available in Niagara. Many of these activities are found in Niagara Frontier's numerous parks, beautifully-maintained and located in historical areas.

attractions

Golden Hill State Park, located at the eastern end of Niagara County along Lake Ontario, offers numerous activities. The park is ideal for camping, with tent and trailer sites available. There are hiking, biking and nature trails, picnic tables and recreational programs. The fishing is great, with both warm and cold water species in abundance.

events

The **Niagara County Farm and Home Days** are held in August at the County Fairgrounds in Lockport.

NIAGARA FALLS - N.Y.

Still known as the "Honeymoon Capital," Niagara Falls, New York offers a cozy romantic trip for two or an exciting vacation or weekend getaway for the entire family.

The region was discovered by French explorers during the westward trek of Louis Hennepin and the Sieur de LaSalle, who marvelled at the Niagara rushing over the 192-foot massive overhanging rock, just as visitors to the area continue to do today. This scenic Natural Wonder of the World draws tourists from around the world but many other attractions in Niagara Falls, New York encourage people to stay.

The city is alive with activity, regardless of the season. This is due, in part, to the fine weather in the region. Winters in Niagara see very little extremely cold weather and precipitation because the Great Lakes retain heat, keeping the climate moderate, and lake-produced snowstorms usually pass to either the north or south of the city. Summers are characterized by sunny days and long clear nights because the Great Lakes inhibit cloud formation.

From winter's Festival of Lights to the Summer Experience, Niagara Falls, New York is exciting any time of year.

attractions

The 185-foot American Falls and the 175-foot Horseshoe Falls on the Canadian side create **Niagara Falls**, a spectacle for the senses. Tours by boat, helicopter and elevator take tourists to the base of the Falls and above them for a first-rate view of this amazing natural sight.

Niagara Reservation State Park, the oldest state park in the United States, covers 139 acres of land and 296 acres of water. The park area includes Goat Island, Three Sisters Island, Luna Island, Terrapin Point, Prospect Point and the Observation Tower. Recreational programs provide information about the falls. There are hiking, biking and nature trails. Fishing is allowed and there are picnic tables and concession stands.

Schoellkopf Geological Museum in Niagara Reservation State Park is a multiple media museum that focuses primarily on the history of Niagara Falls. Nature interpretive programs are offered year-round.

Aquarium of Niagara Falls features over 2,000 marine creatures, venomous lionfish, Peruvian Penguins and daily live demonstrations. The Aquarium is open year-round.

A Native-American Center for the Living Arts, **The Turtle** offers Indian Art, history and culture exhibits. The displays in the museum, along with a gallery, performance arena, restaurant and craft shop, are housed in a turtle-shaped building.

Cave of the Winds on Goat Island provides elevator rides to the bottom of the American Falls while walk and trail areas offer exciting views of both the Falls and the gorge.

Maid of the Mist cruises offer a personal view of Niagara Falls to tourists. The famous Maid travels to the very base of the American Falls. Those on board will feel the mist on their faces while traditional rain gear keeps the rest of the body dry. The cruise to the Falls takes about 30 minutes.

Niagara Whirlpool, in **Whirlpool State Park**, features mile-long rapids leading into the whirlpool where the water circles in a pool around an extinct waterfall. The water exits at a right angle, thus forming the "elbow" in the Niagara River. A picnic area, fishing and hiking trails are available in the park along with scenic views of the Niagara River Gorge, the rapids and the whirlpool.

The **Buscaglia-Castellani Art Gallery**, located on the DeVeaux Campus of Niagara University, features 19th and 20th century art with an emphasis on contemporary works.

events

Niagara Falls Summer Experience is an annual event characterized by ethnic festivals, concerts and dance and theater performances. The Summer Experience is free and takes place on Saturdays and Sundays from July 4th through Labor Day.

The biggest winter attraction in the Northeastern portion of North America, the Festival of Lights, starts at the end of November and runs through early January. It features a massive display of lights surrounding Rainbow Hall.

accommodations

BEST WESTERN RED JACKET INN
7001 Buffalo Avenue
Niagara Falls, New York 14304
Tel: (716) 283-7612
1-800-528-1234
Hrs: Open seven days, year-round.
Visa, MasterCard, American Express, Diners Club, Carte Blanche, Discover and Amoco are accepted.

Headed for Niagara Falls? The Best Western Red Jacket Inn may be just the place. Located in Niagara Falls, New York, this Best Western offers rooms with a superb river view, as well as those endowed with a balcony--perfect for some outdoor relaxation. All of the 150 modestly decorated, traditional style guest rooms have double beds, heat, air conditioning, telephones, and color televisions with in-room movies.

Within three miles is a full day of shopping at the outlet shopping malls and sightseeing at the falls, both of which may lead to a lengthy exploration of the Inn's outdoor swimming pool, or perhaps a different type of unwinding in the game room. Whatever the course of action, the Red Jacket Lounge offers the perfect nightcap with live entertainment Wednesday, Friday and Saturday nights, and a Happy Hour from 4:00 p.m. - 7:00 p.m. everyday that features reduced-price drinks and free hors d'oeuvres.

Naturally, meals are a necessity, and the scenic "Burgundy's - on the River" offers full service breakfast, lunch, and dinner seven days a week, as well as a dazzling brunch buffet on Sundays. Large groups are always welcome and facilities are readily available, including a river-view ballroom that holds 350 people, and special meeting rooms and rates for corporate customers.

In addition, the Best Western Red Jacket Inn offers an assortment of special packages, room service, airport transportation, plenty of free parking and boat facilities.

HOLIDAY INN DOWNTOWN AT THE FALLS
114 Buffalo Avenue
Niagara Falls, New York 14303
Tel: (716) 285-2521
Visa, MasterCard, American Express, Diners Club and Discover are accepted.

The Holiday Inn Downtown at the Falls offers much more than the closest hotel accommodations to the Falls. A variety of package deals are available, along with a conference room, cocktail party accommodations, an indoor recreation center, and year-round live entertainment. The Shopper's Delight Package features the option of staying one night, or three days and two nights. Children stay free with parents in a comfortable, two bedroom room. Enjoy an evening buffet for two, complimentary champagne party, Sunday Brunch for two, and coupons to Factory Outlet and Rainbow Mall. The Two Night Delight Package offers greatly reduced prices for those traveling in groups. Perhaps the biggest value is the Honeymoon Package which entices newlyweds to experience the romance of Niagara Falls. This package includes a room equipped with a king size bed, a bottle of champagne upon arrival, breakfast each morning, Chateaubriand dinner served tableside, souvenir photograph, honeymoon certificate from the city of Niagara Falls and complimentary drinks, among other specials.

Other attractions include the Pepper Tree Restaurant, which overlooks the swimming pool, serving traditional fare as well as International cuisine. Lunch features soups and sandwiches while dinner suggests steaks, seafood and Italian delights. After dining, Chaser's Lounge is the perfect setting for a friendly night cap.

The Ambassador Room can be reserved for banquets, conferences or even a classroom setting and holds up to 40 people. The Holiday Inn accommodates parties, dinners and luncheons for up to 60 people in Annie's Loft.

While the hotel attracts many with free Showtime, ESPN, and CNN cable channels, guided tours from the lobby and its proximity to area beaches and Buffalo International Airport, perhaps the biggest attraction is the Holidome. This enclosed recreation center provides year-round swimming, whirlpool, sauna, fully equipped exercise room, gameroom, ping pong and pool tables, and a miniature golf course.

Whether enjoying the hotel's comforts or the nearby Falls' adventures, there is something for everyone at the Holiday Inn Downtown by the Falls.

THE NIAGARA FALLS NEW YORK TRAVELODGE
200 Rainbow Boulevard
Niagara Falls, New York 14303
Tel: 1-(716)-285-7316 (Group reservations)
1-800-255-3050 (Individual reservations)
Hrs: Open 24 hours, year-round
Visa, MasterCard, American Express, JCB, Discover and Diners Club are accepted.

The Niagara Falls Travelodge was totally remodeled in 1985 and also joined Trusthouse Forte Hotels, Inc. at this time, a corporation whose name is synonymous worldwide with quality accommodations and good value. These two changes, along with the lowest rates of any accommodations in the Falls, have brought tourists here from all over the world.

The Travelodge's 49 rooms are a mix of kings, doubles, and mini suites, some with their own balconies. All of the modern rooms have a crisp, clean look with a work desk, TV stand, and dresser all combined into one beautiful wooden unit. Three of the rooms are fully accessible to wheelchair guests. Serta and Sealy mattresses guarantee a good night's sleep for everyone, and guests arise to complimentary coffee and tea in the morning.

NIAGARA HILTON
Third and Falls Streets
Niagara Falls, New York 14303
Tel: (716) 285-3361
Fax: (716) 285-3900
1-800-HILTON (Hilton Reservation Service)
Visa, MasterCard, American Express, Diners Club, Carte Blanche, Discover and JCB are accepted.

The internationally renowned Niagara Hilton offers easy access to spectacular Niagara Falls, Rainbow Shopping Mall, Niagara Civic and Convention Center, and a host of other exciting attractions.

The Hilton offers luxurious accommodations and elegant convention and banquet facilities. The amenities are endless: this excellent hotel has a tropical Palm Court that houses an indoor swimming pool, relaxing saunas, a Fanfare Restaurant that offers delicious gourmet cuisine, and an intimate lobby lounge called Beardsley's. Guests can also enjoy dancing in the Action Lounge and browsing through the delightful gift shop. The Hilton is the area's largest hotel, with 400 beautifully decorated rooms, three large conference rooms, six additional meeting rooms and 23 plush suites.

The hotel's atmosphere is fantastic. The building has been completely renovated in art-deco, floral carpets and lots of plants and greenery.

The Fanfare Restaurant serves both hearty and light meals, including continental breakfasts. Other culinary delights include various specialty salads, such as the Tortellini Primavera and the Fresh Fruit Salad with cottage cheese, date nut bread, and raspberry dressing. Casa d'Oro prepares an amazing array of delicious entrees, such as the sizzling Filet Mignon with Bernaise Sauce and mushroom caps, luscious desserts, such as the Koffee kookie or fresh berries with Grand Marnier, and a complete selection of domestic and imported beer, vintage wine, cordials, specialty drinks, cocktails and highballs.

The Niagara Hilton's contemporary ambiance, attentive service, and convenient location combine to make a memorable vacation.

While staying at the Hilton, also be sure to visit the Falls (a five-minute walk), The Niagara Splash Water Park, the Winter Festival of Lights, the Maid of the Mist, the Cave of the Wind, old Fort Niagara, the Aquarium and the Wintergarden.

RADISSON HOTEL, NIAGARA FALLS
Third and Falls Streets
Niagara Falls, New York 14303
Tel: (716) 285-3361
Fax: (716) 285-3900
Visa, MasterCard, American Express, Diners Club, Carte Blanche, Discover and JCB are accepted.

The internationally-reputable Radisson Hotel, Niagara Falls, offers easy access to spectacular Niagara Falls, Rainbow Shopping Mall, the Niagara Civic and Convention Center, and a host of other exciting attractions.

The Radisson Hotel offers luxurious accommodations and elegant convention and banquet facilities. The amenities are endless: this hotel has a tropical Palm Court that houses an indoor swimming pool, relaxing saunas, a Fanfare Restaurant that offers delicious gourmet cuisine, and an intimate lobby lounge called Beardsley's. Guests can also enjoy dancing in the Action Lounge and browsing through the delightful gift shop. The Radisson Hotel is the area's largest hotel, with 400 beautifully decorated rooms, three large conference rooms, six additional meeting rooms and 23 plush suites. The hotel's atmosphere is fantastic. The building has been completely renovated in art-deco, floral carpets and lots of plants and greenery.

The Fanfare Restaurant serves both hearty and light meals, including continental breakfasts. Other culinary delights include various specialty salads, such as the Tortellini Primavera and the Fresh Fruit Salad with cottage cheese, date nut bread and raspberry dressing. Casa d'Oro prepares an amazing array of delicious entrees, such as the sizzling Filet Mignon with Bearnaise Sauce and mushroom caps; luscious desserts, such as the Koffee Kookie or fresh berries with Grand Marnier; and a complete selection of domestic and imported beer, vintage wine, cordials, specialty drinks, cocktails, and highballs.

The Radisson Hotel, Niagara Falls offers contemporary ambiance, attentive service, and convenient location.

While staying at the Radisson Hotel, check out the Falls (a five-minute walk), The Niagara Splash Water Park, the Winter Festival of Lights, the Maid of the Mist, the Cave of the Wind, Old Fort Niagara, The Aquarium, and the Wintergarden.

VISCOUNT HOTEL
6045 Stanley Avenue
Niagara Falls, Ontario L26 3Y3
Tel: (416) 374-4142
1-800-263-2566
Visa, MasterCard, American Express, Diners Club, Carte Blanche and Trusthouse Forte Gold Card are accepted.

In the superior tradition of the Trusthouse Forte Hotel network, Ontario Viscount Hotel offers tastefully decorated rooms, meeting and banquet facilities, restaurant, cocktail lounge, indoor pool and spa facilities all within walking distance to the falls.

A member of the world's largest hotel chain, the Viscount has 112 rooms. Twenty-one of these are suites, some furnished with fireplaces, oversized jacuzzi tubs and private balconies. Honeymoon suites with king size beds and heart-shaped bathtubs or whirlpools combine with the natural surroundings of the falls view area to capture true romance. The hotel's hospitable staff will accommodate every request to ensure complete relaxation. Other luxuries include room soundproofing, individual heating and air conditioning, direct dial telephones, color televisions, cable TV, movies, and AM/FM radios.

The Viscount's meeting and banquet facilities have the capacity to cleverly combine business with pleasure for up to 220 people. This includes full service for all meetings with audio visual and modern boardroom facilities available.

The Trusthouse Forte Hotels network is also a restaurant and catering empire featuring dining excellence. Dahlia's restaurant in the Viscount is no exception, providing casual dining for breakfast, lunch and dinner. The staff complements the diverse menu with complete, courteous service and a unique ability to accommodate children. Table visits by the chef help to better serve even the fussiest kids. Live entertainment caps the dining experience on weekends. The restaurant overlooks the indoor pool which provides patrons year-round swimming recreation. A sauna and other spa facilities combines with video games, an outdoor playground and ice rink in winter months complete the Viscount's leisure center. The hotel also boasts a friendly cocktail lounge and gift shop to add to its guests' enjoyment and convenience.

Prompt room service, accessible bell hops, and comfortable airport transportation are additional reasons that weekend escapes, family vacations, honeymoons, business meetings and banquets are all enjoyable at the Viscount Hotel.

bakeries

DiCAMILLO BAKERY
811 Linwood Avenue
Niagara Falls, New York 14305
Tel: (716) 282-2341
(800) 634-4363
Hrs: Seven days 6:00 a.m. - 9:00 p.m.

The DiCamillo Bakery's slogan is "Panis Angelicus," which is Latin for "Bread of the angels," and the slogan appears to be right on the mark. The bakery sells more than 800 loaves of bread each day. But, bread is not the DiCamillo family's only specialty. Cookies, pizza, biscotti, pies, coffee cakes, scones, tea biscuits, baklava, custard puffs, eclairs, doughnuts, wedding cakes, rolls, jams, and teas are other in-demand items.

In 1920, Thomas and Dolarotta DiCamillo traveled to America from Italy and began baking authentic Italian bread in their basement. They supplied hundreds of Italian delis all over New York and began to grow. Seventy years later, third and fourth generation DiCamillos still carry out their tradition of baking preservative-free breads and pastries. Their bread, made without sugar or shortening, takes five hours to make.

DiCamillo's special-recipe baked goods are their most popular items. The biscotti Angelica (named after Aunt Angelica, who manages the Linwood Avenue store) is a crisp bread that does well with pate, cheese, jam, and caviar. Other classic DiCamillo delicacies are the Torta Di Frutta, Torta Di Noci, and Torta Di Cioccolata--rich confection cakes with semi-sweet dark chocolate, dates, and walnuts. Some of the most exquisite biscuits and breads are the Biscotti Formaggio (Italian cheese crisps), the Biscottini di Vino (wine biscuits), the Focaccia (pepper flat bread), and the Bastoncini (bread sticks).

DiCamillo baked goods are more than scrumptious--they're elegant as well. The bakery also ships to exclusive stores such as Marcus, Bloomingdales, Jordan Marsh, and Macy's.

The DiCamillo Baking Company has four retail outlets--three in Niagara Falls (two on Pine Avenue and one on Linwood Avenue) and one in Lewiston (on enter Street).

The DiCamillo Bakery caters to baked-good connoisseurs. Their luscious Mediterranean-style breads and pastries are always fresh, always exotic.

malls

RAINBOW CENTRE OUTLET MALL
302 Rainbow Boulevard
Niagara Falls, New York 14303
Tel: (716) 285-9758
Hrs: Monday - Saturday 10:00 a.m. - 9:00 p.m.
Sunday 11:00 a.m. - 5:00 p.m.

The Rainbow Centre Outlet Mall is a $32 million , five-story shopping mall located one block from the world renowned Niagara Falls. The mall opened for business in 1982 and is designed for the fashion conscious outlet shopper.

Anchored by the Burlington Coat Factory, the mall also houses many of the world's most popular designers including Ralph Lauren, Liz Claiborne, J.H. Collectibles, Pierre Cardin, Oscar de la Renta and Ray Bon.

Other outlets throughout the modern, skylit mall carry sportswear, footwear, women's designer apparel, beauty products, luggage, housewares and much more at up to 75% off regular prices.

Located on the second level is the International Food Court which opens at 8:00 a.m. for breakfast. The hungry shopper can choose from Greek, Italian, Chinese and American fast food cuisine.

The exterior of the Rainbow Centre Mall is modern and cost efficient. It is wrapped in an energy conserving, insulated curtainwall whose mirrored surface reflects the changing sky and lights the 1,800 enclosed parking spaces opened free to shoppers and tourists. The heart of this 282,000 -foot mall is a soaring 60 foot by 90 foot skylit atrium which gives a feeling of openness throughout the mall. Another popular attraction is a 10-story enclosed arboretum known as the Wintergarden.

The Rainbow Centre Outlet Mall contains a unique selection of value oriented retailers and is also known for the exciting activities it brings to the area, as well as its bargains.

SUMMIT PARK MALL
6929 Williams Road
Niagara Falls, New York 14304

Tel:	(716) 297-0206	
Hrs:	Monday - Saturday	10:00 a.m. -9:00 p.m.
	Sunday	Noon - 5:00 p.m.
	December:	
	Monday-Saturday	10:00 a.m.-10:00 p.m.
	Sunday	11:00 a.m. - 5:00 p.m.

The Summit Park Mall, built in 1972, contains over 100 stores and is located five minutes from majestic Niagara Falls and only fifteen minutes from Buffalo. This makes it a convenient community center and a one stop shopping complex for the Niagara region and those living in the Northern part of Buffalo.

The mall, consisting of a variety of services and retail operations, is anchored by Sears, Jenss, and AM&A Department Stores. These, along with 100 other stores throughout the mall, offer a wide variety of family fashions. Shoes, jewelry, and home furnishings can also be found.

Located in the center of the mall is The Picnic Place. Here, shoppers can choose from pizza, chicken wings, tacos, hamburgers, Chinese food, and many other items, for a quick meal. For those who wish to have a relaxing sit-down dinner, visit Yorks or Doyles, two restaurants which are also located in the mall.

The mall plays a major part in the community by hosting events and shows to assist and entertain their customers. Weekly shows include a wide variety of themes such as arts and crafts, gems and minerals, antique cars, home improvement and decor, model airplanes and fashion. A charity bazaar is also held annually at the mall to offer non-profit groups a chance to sell handmade items and/or baked goods while promoting the services they offer. Every other month, Summit Park Mall plays host to the health fair where tests can be given to patrons be local doctors and hospitals. Other events include kids week, college recruitment nights, and local bands are brought in frequently to entertain shoppers.

Christmas is a special time at Summit Park Mall. The Twelve Musical Days of Christmas are celebrated in correspondence with the Festival of Lights at Niagara Falls. From December 12th through 23rd, various musical groups fill the mall with the melodies of Christmas during lunch and evening hours.

One other important factor is that the Summit Park Mall is located near several other shopping centers and malls, which means customers can enjoy a full day of shopping in the Niagara Falls area.

restaurants

HOST INTERNATIONAL
Goat Island
Niagara Falls, New York 14303
Tel: (716) 285-3311
Hrs: Open seven days.
Hours vary depending on shop.
Closed January & February.
Visitor Center open year-round.
Visa, MasterCard, American Express and Discover are accepted.

The nation's oldest state park (over 100 years old) is also one of the most popular. Question: Which one is it? A hint: 3/4 of its 400 acres are under water. The answer: Niagara Reservations State Park. Since the time that Frederick Law Olmsted's ideas helped to shape the design of the Niagara Reservation, many attractions have been built. The beauty of the Fall itself, however, remains the same. The cascading waters never cease to amaze spectators.

Goat Island divides the American and Horseshoe Falls and provides the closest views of the Falls and the upper Rapids. It is here that Host International, a subsidiary of the Marriott Corporation, operates four gift shops: Top of the Falls, Cave of the Winds, The Visitor's Center, the Gorge, and the Top of the Falls Restaurant. Each of the gift shops has a wonderful selection of imported and American-made gift items and souvenirs. Those looking for anything from postcards to the finest gifts or anything in between will be satisfied. The shops carry beautiful calendars, custom apparel, every flavor of saltwater taffy, and videos of the falls to share with family and friends for years to come.

For a tremendous dining experience, one shouldn't miss the opportunity to eat at the Top of the Falls restaurant. No other American restaurant has such a panoramic view. From each table there is an illusion of sitting on "top of the falls" surrounded by lush greenery. It is the perfect atmosphere for enjoying either casual buffet style dining or a full course meal. The Sunday brunch is very popular. The all you can eat smorgasbord consists of cold salads, carved roast beef or ham, quiches, fruits, danishes, and cheese blintzes. The dining room seats 180. They will cater parties and other affairs. The full view of Horseshoe Falls makes the Top of the Falls Restaurant a very popular place for weddings.

Host International is a "Best Choice" for the selection of items in its gift shops, and the quality of food and magnificent view provided by its restaurant.

PAGE'S RESTAURANT -- HOME OF THE WHISTLE PIG
7001 Pakard Road
Niagara Falls, New York 14304
Tel: (716) 297-0131
Hrs: Second Saturday in March - Labor Day:
Seven days 7:00 a.m. - 11:30 p.m.

Page's Restaurant, "Home of the Whistle Pig," is a 50-year-old tradition in the Niagara Falls area. Famous for its specialty hot dogs, Page's is more than a restaurant. It's a mini-complex, complete with 10 sheltered picnic tables which surround the main restaurant, half a dozen kiddie rides, homemade custard facility, and a parking lot big enough to accommodate busses and 18-wheelers.

The restaurant is decorated in '50s style and includes Harvey the Pig, Page's inanimate patriarch. The menu features the special hot dog, the "Whistle Pig," named for the funny sound a weiner makes when it bursts on the griddle. The bacon-wrapped puppies are dressed in Page's special cheese sauce, and are consumed at the rate of 120,000 per season.

Visitors can eat indoors or outside and take out is available. Youngsters will enjoy the kiddie rides in the mini-amusement park.

Owners Chris and Pete Page operate the restaurant with their sons, Christopher and David, who plan to follow their parents in continuing to serve the Niagara Falls area with their famous Whistle Pig.

Page's Restaurant and Home of the Whistle Pig has maintained a 50-year tradition of great food and service with an emphasis on the family. The Original Whistle Pig hot dog is available only at Page's in Niagara Falls.

THE PRESS BOX
324 Niagara Street
Niagara Falls, New York 14303
Tel: (716) 284-5447
Hrs: Monday - Thursday 8:30 a.m. - 2:00 a.m.
Friday - Saturday 8:30 a.m. - 3:00 a.m.
Sunday 8:30 a.m. to Close

Opened in 1959, The Press Box is truly a one-of-a-kind restaurant. When Mary Meyo and her daughter, Florence Acotto, started the business, they served only food. That in itself isn't so unusual. What is unusual is the way they served the food. Florence cooked whatever she felt like cooking that day, carried it from the kitchen to the dining room and placed it on a table in the center of the room. Patrons helped themselves to Florence's homecooked bacon and eggs, soup and sandwiches, steaks, or spaghetti. Then the customers cleaned up after themselves. Because the restaurant had no other employees, Florence and Mary ran the business that way for 14 years.

When the Press Box added a fully licensed bar, Mary began tending bar and did so until she retired about a year ago at the age of 90. There's no keeping her away, though; she still comes in to work quite often.

Since the mid-1970's Mary and Florence have hired a friendly staff and have developed a regular menu consisting of home-cooked specialties such as Porterhouse Steak, B.B.Q. Chicken, and Fried Fish.

Stepping into the Press Box is like taking a nostalgic step back in time. Not much has changed since 1959--especially not the prices. To say the prices are reasonable is an understatement. For instance, on Mondays, Tuesdays, and Wednesdays, spaghetti is only 93 cents.

The decor, especially the wallpaper, hasn't changed much either. Years ago, the customers started the tradition of autographing dollar bills and taping them to the walls. When Florence accumulated $900, she stripped the walls and donated the money to the Niagara Falls Firefighters Christmas Toy Fund. Each year, The Press Box collects more and more money to be donated to the toy fund. In 1989, the restaurant received about $4,000 for needy children.

Stop by The Press Box. The mouthwatering homecooking, casual atmosphere, incredibly low prices, and owner's warm service will keep customers coming back for more.

LEWISTON

Located eight miles from Niagara Falls, Lewiston radiates a historic feeling. French explorers arrived at the area in 1678 at the United States' side of the Niagara River.

In present-day Lewiston, one can walk down Plain Street and feel as if he were going back in time. Captain's Row is a line of houses that once belonged to shipmasters.

attractions

Earl W. Brydges State Artpark is not only a center for the visual and performing arts, but also a recreational park. Theater, dance, artists' workshops, opera, jazz, hiking, fishing and cross-country skiing are available.

Devil's Hole State Park offers views of the Niagara River. Nature and hiking trails are emphasized. The Devil's Hole is ringed by a concrete staircase that descends alongside the gorge to the river. There are picnic tables and the fishing is above average.

Joseph Davis State Park offers a variety of recreational activities such as fishing, hiking and picnicking. A swimming pool is available and recreational programs are provided. There are nature trails and playgrounds. Winter activities include snowmobiling and cross-country skiing.

Niagara Power Project Visitor Center is located in the New York Power Authority's hydroelectric project. Admission is free to view displays, try out exhibits and watch animated miniature three-dimensional scenes.

Built in 1824, **McDonald's Frontier House** is registered as a National Historic Place. Once a stagecoach stop and hotel, the building was regarded as one of the finest inns west of Albany.

Reservoir State Park features hiking, biking, tennis and playgrounds. Picnic shelters and tables are available. Winter activities include cross-country skiing and snowmobiling.

points of interest

ARTPARK
Lewiston, New York 14092
Tel: (716) 745-3377 (September - May)
(716) 754-9001 (June - August)
Hrs: Open Mid-June - September:
Tuesday - Sunday
Closed Mondays.
Visa and MasterCard are accepted.

Artpark is the result of a dream belonging to former New York State Senator Earl W. Brydges. After the fateful day in 1956 when 110,000 tons of rock broke loose from the top of the Niagara Gorge and wiped out two-thirds of the region's power generating capacity, Mr. Brydges became involved with the re-development process. By 1965, he had secured a legislative appropriation for the design and construction of an open-air amphitheater. A more versatile indoor-outdoor theater was actually built; it has seating for 2300 indoors and additional seating for 1500 behind the auditorium on the sloped lawn. Artpark consists of this theater and the 200 acres of hills and woods surrounding it where artists of all sorts can be found all summer long entertaining folks of all ages.

Artpark is a place that focuses on the process of art, not only the product. "Kids Space" is an area for children aged four to seven years to have fun. "Artwork" and "Hands-On" are for all ages. Raw materials are provided and artists guide visitors through the process of such techniques as bronze-casting, printmaking, stained glass work, papermaking, papermarbling, or sandcasting. At the Log Cabin Kitchen, chefs prepare dishes and share recipes and samples of their creations. Those strolling through the park may witness project artists building major works at specific chosen sites within the park.

Visitors are entertained by storytellers, poets, and strolling musicians. An outdoor theater group gives performances of children's stories, fairy tales, folk tales, and fables twice a day.

Theater tickets are available at an affordable price. Artpark produces two or three musical productions each year, including such shows as Gypsy, Oliver!, and A Chorus Line.

Artpark hosts classical and modern dance companies, special concerts by popular entertainers of classical, jazz, folk, and blues, as well as performances by the Buffalo Philharmonic Orchestra. The park is accessible to handicapped individuals.

For a chance to intermingle with dozens of artists and an opportunity to become involved with the creative process, the "Best Choice" is "Artpark, where else?"

restaurants

AMANDA'S EATING AND DRINKING EMPORIUM
432 Center Street
Lewiston, New York 14092
Tel.: 1-(716)-754-8666
Hrs.: Serves food seven days 11:30 a.m. - 11:00 p.m.
Lounge Until 2:00 a.m.
Mastercard and Visa are accepted.

Western New York is the home of a unique spot for casual dining and drinking called Amanda's Eating and Drinking Emporium. Over 50 varieties of beer, a pleasing menu, and special daily features make Amanda's a favorite stop in the historic town of Lewiston. Amanda's is located in a colonial building that's over 100 years old. The ambiance from the turn of the century still exists and helps to make Amanda's unique. There is something here to satisfy folks of all ages. The food is fantastic and the choice of beers is surpassed by none.

Amanda's is a favorite for locals as well as visitors. Bus-loads of people who are in town for sporting events stop at Amanda's to quench both their appetites and thirsts. The patrons at Amanda's find all of the food enjoyable, but the barbecue ribs and chicken seem to always be a favorite. However, Amanda's isn't just a bar. It's a place to bring the entire family for a pleasant meal.

The menu offers such delicious choices as Prime Rib, steak and lobster, and a classic variety of soups and salads sure to please everyone. Amanda's is prepared to serve large groups and caters parties of over 100 people. Although the food is great, the choices of international beer are a beer-lover's dream. There are over 50 varieties of beer, originating from 16 different countries. Every Thursday night is International Beer Night. Guests are invited to join Amanda's Mug Association (AMA). Prizes are awarded to those who make Amanda's beer tasting journey around the world. Happy hour is every Monday through Friday, from 4:00 p.m. to 7:00 p.m.

Whether an out-of-towner or a local resident, Amanda's is one of Lewiston's favorite spots. Some people stop just for a piece of peanut butter pie and a cup of Amanda's special coffee. The colonial setting makes Amanda's the perfect place for dinner or just "lounging" with some friends and enjoying the imported beer. Amanda's convenient, coastal location helps it to serve both Americans and Canadians. The delicious dinners, International beer, and colonial atmosphere make Amanda's the place to visit when in Lewiston.

APPLE GRANNY RESTAURANT
433 Center Street
Lewiston, New York 14092
Tel: (716) 754-2028
Hrs: Monday - Thursday 11:30 a.m. - 2:00 a.m.
Friday - Saturday 11:30 a.m. - 3:00 a.m.
Sunday Noon - 2:00 a.m.
MasterCard, Visa, American Express, Diners Club and Carte Blanche are accepted.

Apple Granny Restaurant was established in the old Lewiston General Store in 1975 and since it's inception, it has become one of the area's most popular dining establishments and nightspots. The name was derived from the regions famous apple orchards and the advanced age of the town, thus, Apple Granny. John Roberts saw the potential of this old, rundown building dated from the 1830s and began a family-oriented restaurant. John's children and his brother, Chuck, assist him in creating the warm, friendly atmosphere found here.

Apple Granny Restaurant is very popular for its Friday Fish Fry, excellent chicken wings, and beef on weck, which is choice beef piled high on a kummelweck roll with tangy horseradish. They serve great steaks, seafood, Prime Rib, and Pasta dishes as well. For dessert, try the homemade apple pie or the unique upside down apple cheesecake topped with lots of whipped cream.

Only 10 minutes from Niagara Falls, Apple Granny's is great for folks of all ages. They have a kids menu, take out, a full beer and wine list, a late night menu and a D.J. for dancing the evening away.

Small private parties and bus groups with reservations are welcome. Gift certificates to Apple Granny's will please anyone on the gift list. Due to Apple Granny's popularity, reservations are also recommended for Saturday and Sunday. Take the Lewiston-Artpark Exit from Interstate 190 to experience the friendly atmosphere and great food of Apple Granny Restaurant.

CIRILLO'S INCREDIBLE EDIBLES
900 Center Street
Lewiston, New York 14092
Tel: (716) 754-2144
Hrs: 11:00 a.m. - 10:00 p.m.
Bar open later.
Other location:
425 Main Street
Youngstown, New York 14174
Tel: (716) 745-7294
Visa and MasterCard are accepted.

When Don Cirillo realized that college was not in his daughter's plans, he decided it was time for a family venture. Don and his wife Marge wanted to start a business so the family could work together. The resulting restaurant, Cirillo's Incredible Edibles, now has two locations, one in Lewiston and the other in Youngstown.

Each restaurant has its own style of decor and both are gathering places for local people. The Lewiston restaurant was an old boarding house that overlooks Main Street. The Youngstown restaurant is located on the Niagara River at the foot of Old Fort Niagara. The Lewistown restaurant is light and airy with a lot of plants and Robert Bateman prints hang from every wall. A fireplace in the lounge makes the room very cozy and many customers started a tradition of bringing their own firewood. The Cirillo's put a sign up stating, "This fire compliments of...," making everyone feel welcome.

Start with an appetizer of Clams Casino, Escargot, or French Onion soup before moving onto one of the generous-sized entrees. The house specialty, a Choice Open Tenderloin Steak, charbroiled to order and served with salad, potato, and garlic toast is a delightful meal for steak lovers. Others will be satisfied with dishes like Shrimp Scampi, Broiled Filet of Haddock, or Veal Marsala. Homemade cheesecakes and pies are scrumptious and certainly worth sampling. Snack items are also available for those with lesser appetites. The Roast Beef on Kummelweck, Hot Dog, Quiche & Salad, and Julienne Salad are satisfying and light. In addition to the complete snack menu, the Lewistown restaurant serves pizza and has a happy hour with free hors d'oeurves from 3:00 p.m. to 5:00 p.m.

Don, Marge, and Ann have made Cirillo's Incredible Edibles a "Best Choice" with their great food and generous portions. In addition to the wonderful food, gift items are sold in a "shop while you dine atmosphere." Tablecloths, napkins, craft items, handmade wreaths, wooden wallhangings, and pictures are available. They also offer catering, breakfast in bed, and banquet facilities. Cirillo's Incredible Edibles is definitely worth a visit--the name speaks for itself.

RIVERSIDE INN
115 South Water Street
Lewiston, New York 14092

Tel:	(716) 754-8206	
	(716) 692-0720	
Hrs:	Monday - Thursday	11;30 a.m. - 11;00 p.m.
	Friday - Saturday	11:30 a.m. - Midnight
	Sunday	10:00 a.m. - 11:00 p.m.

Visa, MasterCard, American Express, Diners Club and Discover are accepted.

Built in 1871, the Riverside Inn offers waterfront dining at its best. Formerly known as the Waggoner House and the Angler's Retreat Hotel, the inn is famous for its great dinners and beautiful sunset view. (All windows face west).

The inn has quite a colorful past. As the Angler's Retreat Hotel, the inn served as a landing point for steamboats traveling from Toronto and Niagara-on-the-Lake. It also served as a popular stopping ground for fishermen until 1935 when the Great Gorge Route, an excursion trolley that transported people from Niagara Falls to Lewiston, ceased service. The hotel changed hands several times until the current owner, Frank Turgeon, bought the business in 1972 and transformed it into the elegant restaurant and night club it is today.

The Riverside Inn prepares fresh North Atlantic Lobster, Australian Rock Lobstertail, clams in the half shell, Giant Gulf Shrimp Scampi, 21-

shrimp Cocktail, scampi in a cream puff shell, Oysters Rockefeller in Hollandaise sauce and Grilled Swordfish. In addition to serving tasty seafood dishes, the inn offers a savory soup and salad bar, as well as a wonderful variety of meat entrees like Veal Oscar, Beef Wellington and Orange Whiskey Chicken.

The Sunday Brunch is unbeatable. It includes over 70 items--French Belgium waffles, make-your-own omelettes, peel and eat shrimp, poached salmon, seviche scallops, homemade breads, double-baked cheesecake, caviar and a huge assortment of other delicacies.

Wine connoisseurs will love the selection of fine wines--more than 225 varieties total. The inn also features other ambrosial delights, such as single malt scotches, Hennessey's century old cognac, and 150 year-old Grand Marnier.

The interior is rustic and inviting, designed with solid hemlock beams, knotty pine paneling, a sunken dance floor, a copy fireplace, a newly added patio bar and artifacts from an old sea captain's home. The decor as well as the food makes the Riverside Inn a definite "Best Choice" in Niagara County.

SCHIMSCHACK'S
2943 Upper Mountain Road
Lewiston, New York 14132
Tel: (716) 731-4111
Hrs: Monday-Saturday 4:00 p.m. - 10:00 p.m
Sunday Noon - 9:00 p.m.
Closed Monday and Tuesday, January through March.
Reservations are highly recommended.
MasterCard, Visa, American Express, Diners Club and Carte Blanche are accepted.

Schimschack's is a family owned restaurant which opened in 1934. Its reputation and delicious food enabled the neighborhood restaurant to grow into one of the most visited restaurants in the Niagara area.

The restaurant was rebuilt in 1970 due to a fire and the new building was designed to take full advantage of the spectacular view of Niagara vineyards, Lake Ontario, and on clear days, a glimpse of Toronto. Totally enclosed in glass, the dining room has four tiers giving all the tables exposure to the beautiful view.

The decor is patterned in the style of Independence Hall in Philadelphia, with a peg board floor, Windsor Chairs, copper bar, and pewter chandeliers. The setting here blossoms with romance and elegance.

Schimschack's offers a large selection of appetizers to start a delightful dining endeavor. Choose smoked salmon from Canada or an appetizer plate of garlic shrimp, stuffed mushroom caps and baby back ribs. Please the palate by ordering one of the famous entrees. Char-Broiled Baby Back Ribs are the house specialty but other favorites include Stone Crab Claws and Baby Back Ribs, Filet Mignon with Lobster Tail, Prime Rib and Lobster Tail, Baby Back Ribs with Alaskan King Crab Legs and many other tasty concoctions. For dessert, taste one of the restaurants famous homemade pies. Try the peanut butter pie or perhaps the hot apple pie with brandy sauce and cheese.

Schimschack's became nationally known in the '50s when Marilyn Monroe and crew were patrons during the filming of "Niagara". Since then, the place has changed from a folksy family type restaurant with home cooking to an elegant eating experience. However, it was, as it is today, one of the favorite eating places in the Great Lake area.

YOUNGSTOWN

attractions

Old Fort Niagara features a restored fort, museum, musketry demonstrations and discussions of the life of a soldier in the 18th century. The fort dates back to 1726 and has seen service under three flags.

Fort Niagara State Park surrounds Old Fort Niagara. Its 504 acres provide for a variety of recreational activities; boating, fishing and swimming are allowed. There are recreational programs, nature and hiking trails, picnic facilities, playgrounds and tennis courts. Winter activities include cross-country skiing, ice skating, snowmobiling and sledding.

points of interest

OUR LADY OF FATIMA SHRINE
1023 Swan Road
Youngstown, New York 14174

Tel:	(716) 754-7489	
	Masses:	
	Monday - Saturday	11:30 a.m. & 4:00 p.m.
	Sunday	9:00 a.m., Noon, & 5:00 p.m.
	The Shrine is open every day, year-round.	
Hrs:	June - August:	9:00 a.m. - 8:00 p.m.
	September - May:	9:00 a.m. - 5:00 p.m.
	Sunday	9:00 a.m. - 7:00 p.m.

This beautiful shrine and park are dedicated to peace and prayer. In 1954, the Barnabite fathers, newly arrived from Italy, offered to their new country a devotional center in honor of Our Lady of Fatima, who appeared to three little shepherds in Fatima, Portugal, to ask for prayers of peace.

Though the Shrine and surrounding park offer a setting of natural beauty and relaxation, they are not attractions per se; rather, they are places of communal prayer, meditations, and spiritual renewal.

Among the lovely sights at the shrine are the Peace Mural by Joseph Slowinski--a masterpiece that has inspired thousands in their search for inner peace--a 48-foot bell tower, a Fatima Hill statuary group that includes Our Lady, three children, and a huge rosary made of authentic cannon balls, the

Holy Spirit Fountain, glass-paneled Stations of The Cross, and Avenues of Saints that include over 100 life-size marble saint statues. This unique spiritual haven also features Shrines of St Jude, St. Anthony, Mary, Zaccaria, Sacred Heart, St. Anne, Mother Cabrini, and the Holy Family.

One of the most intriguing and overwhelming sights is the Giant Rosary, believed to be the largest outdoor rosary in the world. It consists of 60 lights formed into a heart-shape, and a breathtaking Corpus of the Lord Jesus nailed to a marble cross.

Statues of the Apostles, a lovely Dome Basilica that's designed in the image of the Northern Hemisphere, and several chapels provide the perfect setting for prayer and spiritual renewal.

The Shrine also offers the largest religious store in the Youngstown area. If planning to spend the day, a cafeteria and picnic area are available.

LOCKPORT

Lockport is one of Western New York's important industrial areas, along with Niagara Falls and Buffalo. The Erie Canal brought much business to Lockport early in its history. The original locks on the Erie Canal elevated and lowered crafts up and down the 60-foot embankment.

attractions

The Lockport Locks and Canal Tours provide seasonal tours with special group rates and times available by reservation.

The Niagara County Historical Center is comprised of five buildings devoted to local history. Displays include Native American and pioneer artifacts and farm implements. The grounds contain herb and rose gardens.

Four Mile Creek State Campsite has sites for tents and trailers. Camper recreation includes nature trails, hiking, fishing and playgrounds.

The Kenan Center is a restored 1859 mansion formerly owned by William Rand Kenan. This community culture center contains an art gallery and theater which is open year-round. The 23-acre grounds are open during the summer for walking through the formal garden and orchard.

charters

LAKE ONTARIO CHARTER SERVICE AND MOTEL
Motel: 3330 Lockport - Olcott Road
Newfane, New York 14108
Tel: (716) 778-5004
Hrs: April 1 - October 31
Charter: P.O. Box 200
The Harbor
Olcott, New York 14126
Tel: (716) 778-5004
Hrs: April 15 - September 15
Christmas shop open Thanksgiving - Christmas.
Visa and MasterCard are accepted.

When Coho Salmon started showing up in Olcott in 1972, Captain Phil Toenniessen became addicted to world class fishing. He began the Lake Ontario Charter Service in 1979 with a 28-foot Chris Craft named the Trouthunter II, and in 1988 he added the 31-foot Trouthunter III. Both are furnished with state of the art equipment. As a representative for many of the major fishing manufacturers, Lake Ontario Charter Service also uses the latest fish finding and catching methods.

Phil, his son Scott, and Bob Cinelli are U.S.Coast Guard Licensed Captains with 15 years of charter experience and over 40 years of fishing experience. Janis Toenniessen, Phil's wife, serves as business manager and is very involved in this family-operated service. Because Captain Phil enjoys providing this unique opportunity for his guests, the Lake Ontario Charter Service is the oldest established charter service in Niagara County.

The charming motel is a newly-renovated barn with luxurious and spacious rooms. Each room has individual climate control, wall-to-wall carpeting and private baths. A wonderful recreation room is provided, and although the motel is located on a main route for easy accessibility, the setting is still very quiet and relaxing.

Take Route 78 from Lockport, North to Olcott. The motel is across from the farmer's market. Reservations are highly recommended and an advance deposit is necessary for a charter. Call Janis and she will be glad to make all the arrangements for a perfect fishing experience. Lake Ontario Charter Service and motel will help guests to "Get Away Today."

furniture stores

RATTAN & MORE
6701 Transit Road
Lockport, New York 14094
Tel: (716) 625-8090
Hrs: Monday, Wednesday &
Thursday 10:00 a.m. - 9:00 p.m.
Tuesday, Friday &
Saturday 10:00 a.m. - 5:00 p.m.
Sunday Noon - 4:00 p.m.
Visa and MasterCard are accepted.

Rattan & More, owned and operated by Jim Damp and Debi Haseley, is only two years old but is an impressive business with a 5000 square foot showroom. Rattan & More displays a marvelous selection of furniture settings with a very bright Florida-like style. It was previously connected with Transit Pools and did very well with outdoor furniture. However, it has recently taken on a new, exciting identity, exhibiting the largest wicker and rattan showroom in the area with premium quality merchandise. Rattan & Wicker has quickly gained a foothold in casual interior design with notable durability and craftsmanship, resulting in increased popularity and a higher demand. Rattan & More, with 150 designer fabrics, 12 custom frame finishes and 200 styles, is ready to fill need in any room of the house.

Yet another nice feature is that if the customer doesn't see exactly what is wanted on the showroom floor, Jim and Debbie will work with the customer to create a customized combination of fabric and frame color that suits the most discriminating taste. In addition to the fantastic brand-name selection of Wicker and Rattan, other items and accessories include rugs by Kapel & Dhuri, lamps, pictures, umbrellas, glassware, outside furniture & fountains, and leather pieces. Offering "quality with a casual look", a delivery service in Western New York and a diverse selection of colorful styles to fit most decorating schemes, Rattan & More truly has much to offer.

restaurants

DANNY SHEEHAN'S STEAK HOUSE
491 West Avenue
Lockport, New York 14094
Tel: (716) 433-4666

Hrs:		
	Monday	5:00 p.m. - Midnight
	Tuesday - Saturday	4:00 p.m. - Midnight
	Sunday	1:00 p.m. - 11:00 p.m.

Visa, MasterCard and American Express are accepted.

Danny Sheehan's Steak House, located in historic Lockport, is most famous for its tender Prime Rib, juicy tenderloin steak, and chops that are done to perfection. For cholesterol watchers, Danny Sheehan's offers a delicious selection of seafood dishes such as fresh swordfish, stuffed trout, Australian lobster tails, crab and frog legs, and delectible Lemon Sole Almondine. Wednesdays, Thursdays, and Fridays are Fish Fry nights at Sheehan's.

On Sundays, Sheehan's offers homestyle specials, chicken and biscuits, turkey and dressing, roast duck and fresh ham with dressing.

The Tuesday, Wednesday and Thursday dinner specials are Beef Stroganoff over Spaetzle, spaghetti with meatballs, and fresh Veal Parmesan. All entrees include a crisp chef salad, vegetable of the day, au gratin, French-fried, or home-fried potatoes, and garlic or plain toast.

The entrees are not the only reason to frequent Sheehan's. The melt-in-your-mouth appetizers are prepared according to the chef's secret recipe; the Clams Casino recipe is so well-guarded that the chef won't tell owner Tim Doyle how it is prepared.

Tim began as a bartender at Sheehan's, then after several years, bought the business from Danny. Because he's like a son to Mr. Sheehan, Tim is proud to carry on the Sheehan traditions of friendliness and fine cuisine.

Sheehan's has a full entourage of regular customers. One customer from Florida stops at Sheehan's to purchase a gallon of special Clams Casino Dressing every time he's near Lockport. The atmosphere is so pleasant at Sheehan's that each employee has been there for at least eight years, and the kitchen staff hasn't changed since Sheehan's opened in 1960.

Besides the specials at Sheehan's, other best bets are the pecan pie, creamy homemade cheesecake, and Sheehan's Prime Rib Sandwich--their most popular sandwich at a recent "Taste-of-Lockport" event (they sold 200 in three hours!).

Sheehan's reputation for generous portions of fabulous food, reasonable prices and ultra-friendly service is a well-earned distinction.

DeFLIPPO'S HOTEL & ITALIAN RESTAURANT
326 West Avenue
Lockport, New York 14094
Tel: (716) 433-2913
(716) 433-9277
Hrs: Tuesday - Thursday 4:30 p.m. - 11:30 p.m.
Friday - Saturday 4:30 p.m. - 12:30 a.m.
Sunday 4:00 p.m. - 11:00 p.m.
Visa, Master Card, American Express, Diners Club, Carte Blanche and Discover are accepted.

DeFlippo's Hotel and Italian Restaurant at West Avenue and New York Street, one mile west of Route 78, is one of Lockport's oldest landmarks. Built in 1870, DeFlippo's was purchased by Dominick DeFlippo to relocate his thriving ice business. But in 1946, Dominick transformed the business into a restaurant, and in 1977, Dominick's son, Jerry, took over to continue the family tradition of providing patrons with fine dining. Jerry used his mother's original Italian recipe for all of the sauces.

DeFlippo's offers terrific weekly specials. Tuesdays are spaghetti and meatball nights, and Saturdays and Sundays are pork spare rib nights. DeFlippo's offers other delicious daily specials, including everything from traditional Italian dishes to broiled steaks and fresh seafood.

DeFlippo's spaghetti and pizza are the most popular in town, and the other Italian specialties, such as Veal Cacciatore, Meat or Cheese Ravioli, Tortellini, Clams with Fettucini or linguine in red or white clam sauce, and Shrimp Parmigiano with melted mozzarella cheese are also favorite dishes at DeFlippo's.

Homemade tortoni in a chocolate shell is the prize dessert, created by Jerry's wife, Joan, but the spumoni pie, pecan pie, chocolate fudge cheesecake and New York-style cheesecake will also tickle the palate.

The entrance is classic Italian--from the romantic out-of-the-way alcoves with flickering candles to the large family-style tables in the middle of each dining area. The new, screened-in, winterized terrace complements the Old Italy decor and adds a sense of rustic beauty to the restaurant. The dining area's New Mediterranean decor, with hardwood floors, wood beam ceilings with skylights, round tables with barrel bases, and green, red, and white linen tablecloths, adds a personal touch to the restaurant. Jerry has added displays of his personal collectables, such as bottles, buttons, beer steins, and old family photos.

Jerry has a knack for making guests feel special. His warm, gentle ways put patrons instantly at ease. He sees to it that the cuisine is top-quality and the atmosphere is romantic, fun, or casual, depending on the dining room chosen. Try DeFlippo's. The service, ambiance, and cuisine have passed the test.

THE FIELDSTONE RESTAURANT
5986 Transit Road (Route 78)
Lockport, New York 14094
Tel: 1-(716)-625-8650
Hrs: Monday - Thursday 11:30 a.m. - 10:00 p.m.
Friday - Saturday 11:30 a.m. - 11:00 p.m.
Sunday 11:30 a.m. - 9:00 p.m.
Closed Christmas.
Visa, MasterCard, American Express, Diners Club and Discover are accepted.

The rustic decor of The Fieldstone Restaurant reminds one of the Canadian hunting lodge it was built to resemble. Constructed in the 1940s, the restaurant has huge, uncut logs as supporting beams and a huge stone fireplace that provides a cozy and relaxing environment when a fire is blazing. Centrally located in Lockport, it is the ideal place for the many local functions held here such as Lions Club, and school teacher, political, and state police meetings.

The Fieldstone was purchased by Donald and Sally Miner in 1985 and is now run by Sally and her daughters Bonnie Burnett and Kathy Wik. The touch of a woman's hospitality is evident as soon as one enters the dining area. A complementary pate appetizer is served with crackers as each customer arrives. Additionally, a complimentary portion of chicken soup is served with every dinner on Sunday. Also adding to the pleasant feeling is a staff of servers who are extremely attentive.

The most important thing about eating out, though, is the meal itself and diners are not disappointed. To a background of amber lighting and player piano music, they enjoy things like Baked Stuffed Clams (clams with sauteed peppers, onion and bacon baked to golden perfection) and Crab Salad Cocktail (a light mixture of crab and the chef's blend of vegetables and spices) for appetizers. "Sealicious" menu items include Crab Legs With Drawn Butter and Broiled Stuffed Filet of Sole (stuffed with crabmeat). Other entrees available are BBQ Ribs, Lamb Chops, or Chicken Cordon Bleu a la Victor. Meals can be complemented with any one of a variety of house wines and then topped off with an irresistible dessert of Peanut Butter Ice Cream Pie (with hot fudge) or Cheesecake served with strawberries. The Fieldstone Restaurant, where they pride themselves "on a long tradition of fine dining, and efficient, friendly service," is a "Best Choice" for delicious homemade food served in a cozy atmosphere.

GARLOCK'S RESTAURANT
35 South Transit
Lockport, New York 14094
Tel: (716) 433-5595
Hrs: Monday - Saturday 5:00 p.m. - Midnight
Sunday 4:00 p.m. - 10:30 p.m.
Closed Thanksgiving and Christmas Day.

When people think of Lockport, they think of Garlock's Restaurant, a small but busy eatery located half an hour from Niagara Falls and Buffalo.

Harold "Gig" Garlock's establishment has been in business for 40 years and is still going strong. For 27 of those years, Nancy Long has been managing the restaurant.

Garlock's interior combines intimate rustic tables, paneled walls, and a red theme with shelves of bottles and other collectables. At Christmas, the bottles are replaced with battery-operated toys.

A separate bar area attracts regulars and new customers. Specialties of the house include Open Steak Sandwich with garlic toast, Prime Rib, lamb chops grilled double-thick, homemade Turtle Soup, and Seafood Au Gratin.

Favorite appetizers are Escargot Bourguignonne, Chopped Chicken Livers, Clams Casino, French Onion Soup, and stuffed mushrooms with crabmeat and a touch of garlic. Sandwich and children's menus are available as well as a weekly fish fry.

Portions are generous and difficult to finish. Those with hearty appetites, however, may have room for a dessert such as whipped cream cheese cake or a Frozen Eclair. A hot cup of Irish, Dutch, Irish Mist or Spanish Coffee is a nice follow-up to a delicious meal.

Garlock's has maintained an excellent reputation throughout Lockport and western New York for great food in an intimate and friendly environment.

RIB HOUSE RESTAURANT
2990 Lockport Olcott Road
Newfare, New York 14108
Tel: (716) 778-7910
Hrs: Summer:

Tuesday - Saturday	4:00 p.m.- 10:00 p.m.
Sunday	Noon - 9:00 p.m.
Winter:	
Tuesday and Thursday	4:00 p.m.- 9:00 p.m.

Visa, MasterCard and American Express are accepted.

The owner of the Rib House Restaurant, John Wagner, began making sausage in his home and selling it to local restaurants. John baked breads and desserts and ran a catering service. He worked at the Rib House, which opened in 1984, and eventually became head chef. After three years, he bought the restaurant, and now operates it with his wife, Audrey, and his parents Lou and Joyce Wagner.

Displaying an Early American look with log cabin walls, the restaurant seats 150 people and has a fireplace in the dining area. Additional seating for 300 is located in the banquet halls. Wagner draws quite a bit of business because he owns the only banquet facility in the area able to accommodate weddings, meetings, and other gatherings and functions.

The restaurant lives up to its reputation, serving fine Prime Rib and beef dishes. Wagner offers a Prime Rib Special each evening and selections such as Choice New York Strip Steak, Baby Back Pork Ribs, Baked Sole Florentine and Baked Ham, New England Clam Chowder, Crabmeat and Mushroom Bisque and a fish fry on Friday. Happy hour is from 4:00 p.m. until 7:00 p.m., Tuesday through Friday.

The Rib House Restaurant is located 40 miles from Downtown Buffalo near Byes Popcorn(a roadside stand) and Olcott Harbor, famous for its salmon and Lake Trout fishing.

For a taste of original rib and beef cooking in a rustic environment, pay a visit to the Rib House Restaurant.

THAXTON'S DINNER HOUSE
5949 Campbell Boulevard
Lockport, New York 14094
Tel: (716) 434-6020
Dinner:
Tuesday - Thursday & Sunday 5:00 p.m. - 9:00 p.m.
Friday & Saturday 5:00 p.m.- 10:00 p.m.
Lunch:
Tuesday - Friday 11:30 a.m. - 2:30 p.m.
Visa, MasterCard and American Express are accepted.

Thaxton's Dinner House is owned by Charlie and Christine Kesterson, two native Western New Yorkers. After living in Missouri, the couple returned to Lockport and opened one of the finest dinner houses in Niagara County.

The restaurant features a small dance floor with a casual elegance. The interior walls are wainscotted with a diagonal pine board below and stucco above. The lounge area boasts a lovely fireplace and the main dining room displays a gazebo where couples may enjoy a more intimate meal. There's a feeling of upscale dining as Christine is careful to extend hospitality to each customer. Thaxton's slogan, "Where you and fine food are celebrated", is evident in the quality service and meals received here.

The Ozark Style Barbecued Ribs are very lean, mouth-watering pork rib, slowly roasted in a mildly sweet sauce and served so tender a knife may is rarely needed. Other favorites include Prime Rib with juices, Mozzarella Filled Chicken Breast and Veal Medallions. The restaurant also features House Soup (seafood gumbo) and soup of the day, as well as various desserts - all prepared and baked on the premises.

Charlie and Christine's personal interest in their customers is steadily resulting in a reputation for excellence. The Kesterson's are determined to please their patrons and make dining at Thaxton's Dinner House a pleasant and memorable experience.

WILSON

attractions

Wilson-Tuscarora State Park features great fishing and boating in Lake Ontario as well as hunting and cross-country skiing and snowmobiling in the winter months.

events

The **Annual Memorial Day Country Fair** in May features antique car displays and craft items in a fun-filled environment.

specialty shops

OLD LAKESIDE EMPORIUM
276 Young Street
Wilson, New York 14172
Tel: (716) 751-9855
Summer: Monday - Saturday
10:00 a.m. - 8:00 p.m.
Sunday 10:00 a.m. - 4:00 p.m.
Winter: Closed Sunday, Monday, & Tuesday
Visa, MasterCard and American Express are accepted.

A visit to the Old Lakeside Emporium is a treat for both tourists and townspeople. Memorial Day weekend of 1988 saw the opening of this combination country store/gift shop that has a little bit of everything. Dating back to the early 1900s, the building was formerly a pharmacy, post office, clothing store, and grocery store. Today it serves as a bonafide country store complete with vintage decor. Upon entering, notice the antique oak door with beveled glass, acquired from the Marine Midland Bank. The store is decorated with pine wood beams, stenciled walls, basket light fixtures, and ceiling to floor shelves filled with memorabilia.

It is the type of place that families with children love to browse through. The Emporium offers ice cream cones, soda pop, penny candy, Wilson souvenirs, toys, and country giftware. The Christmas shop also carries a large assortment of German glass ornaments. The clothing department features sportswear, T-shirts, sweatshirts, and hats. The Old Lakeside Emporium, owned by Laura Kelahan and her brother Pat, received the Retailer of the Year award in 1989 from the Eastern Niagara Chamber of Commerce. A convenient shuttle service is offered from the Wilson Harbor in a 1952 Seagrave fire truck with a Buffalo-built Pierce Arrow engine. It is also possible to rent the antique fire truck for special occasions.

The Old Lakeside Emporium is conveniently located in the center of Wilson, only 20 minutes from Niagara Falls on Lake Ontario.

CANADA

Whatever Canada is, and it is a lot of different and wonderful things, it is, most importantly, a one-of-a-kind place on earth. Majestic, awe-inspiring, vast, nature's splendor are some phrases and words used many times to describe this giant of North America. Those ideas are all true. Along with its natural greatness, such descriptions as civilized, moderate, tolerant, diverse, cultural and international are also very appropriate. Canada enjoys the double advantage of vast unpolluted wilderness and major world-cities that bring what is best in human endeavors from everywhere to this diverse and exquisite land.

From the enclaves of immigrant cultures found on both coasts and in the central prairies, to the ancient native cultures alive and vital in so many parts of Canada, to the frontiers of science and technology on earth and in space, to the historic realms of the Western European cultures that knitted this huge country together, Canada stands as a nexus point for the diverse paths of human life from all over the globe.

Travel to Canada is both a joy and an adventure. Easily accessible from the United States via the longest unprotected border on earth (a shining example to all nations), Canada can offer everything from an exciting day's shopping and dining, to a weekend retreat, to a once-in-a-lifetime adventure in one of this planet's most remote and unspoiled places. There is no climate, short of the tropics, that cannot be experienced in Canada. Travelers from around the world acknowledge this special land's important place in destination selection. For those of us from the United States, we may sometimes take for granted how much there is to do and see in our northern neighbor's land. Recent efforts, however, by the National ,Provincial, and Local governments, as well as by the travel industry, have gone a long way in reminding us from "the states" just how much is available so close to us.

This tantalizing slice of Canada that follows is just the barest of introductions. We have every intention to come back and write about the Canadian Great Lakes area, and the rest of Canada in good time. Until then, it has been our distinct pleasure to first focus on the Niagara Region and the Canadian side of the Thousand Islands area. So begin a journey of many, many miles with a few steps.

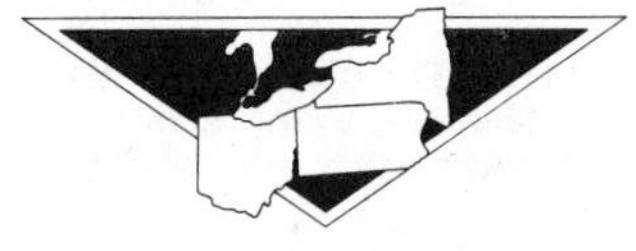

REGION NIAGARA

Niagara Falls, Canada, boasts natural beauty, rich heritage and exciting activities for people of all ages. The beauty begins with the crashing, thundering Canadian and American Falls and continues with a breathtaking countryside, full of natural parks.

Museums, historic sites and the Falls themselves entice visitors to delve into the historical background of Niagara Falls. One area, in particular, peaks curiosity: the daredevils who have attempted, successfully or not, to go over the Falls. The earliest brave soul to face the Falls was Annie Taylor, a schoolteacher, in 1901. Taylor survived her crash over the Falls in a barrel . Others who successfully conquered Niagara Falls did so in an all-steel barrel, a six-foot rubber ball with 32 inner tubes and a double-wall steel frame, and other similar contraptions.

Those desiring less daring yet exciting activities in the area will enjoy Niagara Falls' sports and recreational facilities, aquarium, shops, restaurants and a variety of ways to enjoy the Falls. It's not surprising that tourism is the largest industry in Niagara Falls. Canadians do their best to welcome travelers to the Falls and help make their stay enjoyable.

attractions

Old Fort Erie is the restored fort that saw action during the War of 1812. The museum displays a collection of artifacts dating from the War of 1812 to the Victorian Era, including military, pioneer, agriculture and domestic life.

The Ninavik Gallery in Lincoln contains over 500 pieces of Inuit and Native art on display. Of special note are the limited edition prints, hand-painted clay pots, soapstone and bone sculptures.

Ball's Falls Historical Park in Lincoln includes log cabins, an operating 19th century grist mill, church, a blacksmith shop and other structures that were once part of the Ball's Falls Conservation area which includes a nature preserve.

The Beamer Memorial Park overlooks Grimsby and Lake Ontario at the top of the Niagara Escarpment. The site provides observation of spring and fall hawk migrations. The Bruce Trail and other nature trails are located here.

One of the most beautiful race tracks in North America, the **Fort Erie Race Track** offers thoroughbred racing from late April through late October.

Lincoln is the home of **Tivoli Miniature World**. The world's largest architectural theme park features exact miniature replicas of over 96 internationally known landmarks such as the Eiffel Tower, the Statue of Liberty and the Taj Mahal.

events

The Friendship Festival commemorates over 175 years of friendship between Buffalo, New York and Fort Erie, Ontario with a four-day festival held in early July.

duty free shops

FORT ERIE DUTY FREE SHOPPE
Peace Bridge Plaza
Fort Erie, Ontario L2A 5N1
Tel: (416) 871-5400
Hrs: Open Seven Days, 24 hours
Visa, MasterCard, American Express, Diners Club and Carte Blanche are accepted.

The Fort Erie Duty Free Shoppe offers up to 50 percent savings on an amazing selection of merchandise. All purchases can be taken into Canada or the United States free of duties and taxes with a few custom regulations. The staff will clarify visitors and residents on the current daily, monthly, and yearly traveler tax exemption amounts. Goods do not have to be picked up at a remote location.

More than 5,000 Canadian and International products are offered at Fort Erie Duty Free Shoppe, such as Minolta cameras, 14-karat gold jewelry, Tundra jackets, Ray Ban sunglasses, Gucci accessories, cigarettes, tobacco, beer, liquors, champagnes, and fine wines.

The 6,000-square foot shop also displays an enormous array of fragrances and cosmetics from Estee Lauder, Oscar de la Renta, Channel, Givenchy, Yves St. Laurent, Guerlain, Guy Laroche, Christian Dior, Calvin Klein, and Perry Ellis. Watches by Leonard and Longines-Wittnauer and fine figurines by Hummel, Lladro, and Royal Doulton are also sold.

The shop offers travelers currency exchange, free coffee and fresh fruit, handicapped access, and plenty of free parking.

So don't leave Ontario without stopping in the perfect last stop in Canada. Located at the border crossing between Fort Erie, Ontario and Buffalo, New York, this exciting Shoppe proves that "the best things in life are duty free".

restaurants

MING TEH RESTAURANT
126 Niagara Boulevard
Fort Erie, Ontario 1ZA 3G3
Tel: (416) 871-7971
Hrs: Sunday,
Tuesday - Thursday 11:00 a.m. - 10:00 p.m.
Friday - Saturday 11:00 a.m. - 11:00 p.m.
Visa and Mastercard are accepted.

Sui Kui Cheung came to Canada from China in 1977, and, with his wife, Julie, opened the Ming Teh Restaurant, which offers a pleasant view of the rushing Niagara River and the Peace Bridge. The interior exhibits a natural wood floor and ceiling, real linen tablecloths, and sophisticated decor. The walls are decorated with unusual oil paintings created by Sui Kui, the owner, who has a "Zen-like" commitment to life, which echoes not only through his oil paintings, but his concern in preparing the diversified dishes. He regards food as a part of nature, putting exceptional concentration and artistic sensitivity into making sure all is perfect.

With a combination of old and new concepts in Chinese cooking, each dish maintains authenticity and distinction in taste. The Szechuan style is employed with high quality and fresh ingredients. The extensive menu offers familiar choices as well as dishes from throughout the region of China, such as Moo Sho Pork with Paper Thin Pancakes and Hoisin Sauce, Deep-Fried Fish Soo,Stir-Fried in Ginger Vinegar Sauce, Cubed Chicken with Tangerine Peel and Garlic, and Stir-Fried Sour Beef with Peanuts.

There is plenty of space between tables, a deliberate choice so that no one is cramped while eating, allowing each patron to thoroughly enjoy his or her meal. Sui Kui attributes his success to thinking of his work as part of his life: "If you work your life, respect it, and people like you, people will come close to you." With facilities for small parties and a gift shop displaying imported Chinese Folk Craft, the Ming Teh Restaurant has earned a world-class reputation.

specialty shops

MILDRED MAHONEY SILVER JUBILEE
DOLL HOUSE GALLERY
657 Niagara Boulevard
Fort Erie, Ontario LZA 389

Tel:	1-416-871-5833	
Hrs:	May - December:	
	Seven days	10:00 a.m. - 4:00 p.m.
	Off Season:	Hours by appointment

Located in Ft. Erie is a one of a kind museum for people with a special interest. The Mildred Mahoney Silver Jubilee Doll House Gallery is the world's largest collection of privately owned, fully furnished doll houses. The gallery is five minutes from downtown Buffalo in historic Bertie Hall and contains two full floors of wall-to-wall doll houses. Mrs. Mahoney's collection represents over two centuries of historic homes, mostly of German and English origin.

A viewing of a grand old doll house owned by actress Coleen Moore was the beginning of the world's largest collection of doll houses. Mildred Mahoney's love for doll houses has been with her since childhood, and is apparent in the beauty and care displayed in the homes of her museum. Upon entering the museum, a visitor sees, first of all, Mildred's favorite piece, a five story Marygate house, which is based on an 1810 English manor house. The museum contains over two hundred doll houses, dated as far back as 1780. To Mildred Mahoney, these houses are priceless, but the value has been estimated at 1.5 million dollars. A tour of the gallery will prove to be a history lesson as well as an enjoyable experience. Canada, France, Holland, Japan, Central Europe, and the U.S. are all represented, and each house is filled from basement to attic with distinctive miniatures. Bertie Hall is a part of history itself, having served as a "safe house" during the Civil War. The Mildred Mahoney Silver Jubilee Doll House Gallery offers visitors the luxury of guided tours for groups and singles, or the opportunity to go at your own pace on a self-guided tour.

Mrs. Mahoney's gallery is not only a fantastic sight to see, but it's an invaluable history lesson. The doll houses represent lifestyles and homes for the past two hundred years. For this reason, this museum is an ideal spot for school field trips. Visitors will find it both enjoyable and educational to browse through the museum and appreciate the world's largest collection of doll houses. The elegance and workmanship of each house makes seeing Mrs. Mahoney's museum a must when visiting Ft. Erie.

NIAGARA FALLS ONTARIO

attractions

The Skylon Tower takes visitors to a height of 775 feet above Niagara Falls. The tower also offers dining to satisfy any appetite, and two shopping levels.

The Minolta Tower Centre provides fine or casual dining overlooking the Falls from a height of 525 feet. Other attractions at the centre include a duty-free shop and exhibits.

The Imax Theatre combines one of the finest motion picture systems, IMAX, with Canada's largest movie screen (over seven stories high). The result is a theater comparable to none. Precision, clarity and impact are the key words. The theater features movies about the early settlers in the Niagara Falls area, the folklore that surrounds the region and some of the incredible daredevil trips over the Falls.

Marineland houses killer whales, sea lions and the world's largest group of performing dolphins in an exciting and entertaining atmosphere. Dragon Mountain, the amazingly huge steel roller coaster, provides sheer exhilaration while the herd of 500 friendly deer, in a more relaxed environment, can be fed by hand. Although attractions vary depending on the season, Marineland is open year-round.

Clifton Hill, a major tourist attraction in Niagara Falls, has everything from Louis Tussaud's Waxworks to the Guinness World of Records museum.

Maple Leaf Village is a resort complex comprised of 16 restaurants, museums, a hotel, motor inn, an amusement park and Kodak Tower, which stands 350 feet high.

Lundy's Lane Historical Museum is located on the site of the battlefield of the War of 1812. Exhibits include displays of pioneers, military displays, tourism in the area, art glass, a Victorian parlor and a traveling exhibit gallery.

The Great Gorge Adventure takes visitors by elevator and tunnel to the edge of the Whirlpool Rapids. Photographs of the daredevils who challenged the Falls are on display as well as geological exhibits.

Table Rock Scenic Tunnels provides close-up views of the Horseshoe Falls. Protective rainwear is provided.

The **Spanish Aero Car** is a cable-car that carries passengers over the Niagara Gorge at a height of 250 feet above the Whirlpool Rapids.

The beautiful **School of Horticulture** features lilacs, a rose garden, perennial beds, rock gardens and at least 25 families of trees on a 100-acre site.

events

Held each year in May, the annual **Blossom Festival** features a large parade, a Tug-Of-War between the United States and Canada, fashion show, the Miss Niagara Pageant and a pet show.

accommodations

BEST WESTERN CAIRN CROFT HOTEL/RESTAURANT
6400 Lundy's Lane
Niagara Falls, Ontario L2G 1T6

Tel:	(416) 356-1161	
	1-800-263-2551	
Hrs:	Restaurant:	7:00 a.m. - 2:00 p.m.
		5:00 p.m. - 9:00 p.m.
	Lounge:	Noon - 1:00 a.m.

Visa, MasterCard, American Express, Carte Blanche and En Route are accepted.

Best Western Cairn Croft Hotel/Restaurant is a well-appointed, ultra modern facility, situated near several historic attractions. The Cairn in Cairn Croft is derived from the first owners, Bill and Jack Cairn. The two were instrumental in creating a stately reputation in the community and a well deserved respect for excellence in the industry. Present owners, Len and Fred Cade, are proud to continue that same tradition. The mottos, "A place for all seasons" and "We cater to your good taste," are indicative of the full service resort.

The Cairn Croft, complete with 164 rooms, is a popular choice with families, newlyweds, business travelers and groups, with a choice of standard rooms or deluxe suites. The deluxe suite has all of the regular features plus king-size beds, waterbeds, canopy beds and heart shaped jacuzzis. The rooms are spacious and beautiful, and will undoubtedly delight any guest. Some of the rooms also have fireplaces and all five floors are accessible by elevator.

The restaurant and lounge area, known as the Croft, is an elite, unique bar, rich in natural woods, that would rival any metropolitan hotel. It features daily luncheon and dinner specials, delicious cuisine, and friendly, professional service. The enlarged banquet and meeting facilities can accommodate up to 200 people.

The staff is in touch with the guest's every need. This is a direct result of the hospitality course that each employee must take before being qualified to properly serve visitors of the hotel. The Cairn Croft has earned numerous awards for being a high-quality establishment. Co-Owner Len Cade was selected "Innkeeper of the Year" for four consecutive years by his peers. The hotel has also received the Gold Award by the Ontario Ministry of Tourism for a commitment to train every employee through the "We'll make you feel incredible" tourism courses. The incredible staff, the beautiful rooms and the fine dining add up to make Best Western Cairn Croft Hotel and Restaurant a "Best Choice" in Niagara.

BONAVENTURE TRAVELODGE
7737 Lundy's Lane
Niagara Falls, Ontario L2H 1H3
Hrs: Open 24 hours
Breakfast: 7:00 a.m. - Noon
Dinner: 5:00 p.m. - 11:00 p.m.
Visa, MasterCard, American Express, Diners Club, Carte Blanche and En Route are accepted.

Located just two miles from the Falls, the beautiful Bonaventure Travelodge offers guests comfort, convenience and affordability. This three story chateau-like motor inn provides 115 spacious and traditional style rooms. There are family size suites, connecting suites, and luxurious honeymoon suites. Relax and enjoy the lodge's heated indoor or outdoor pools, whirlpool, hot tubs or sauna.

Children stay free with their parents, and in the winter, the Bonaventure Travelodge offers weekend getaway packages, senior citizen discounts and large-group rates. The helpful and friendly staff is always on hand if needed and will gladly arrange sightseeing tours and tour transportation for all visitors.

The Travelodge also offers convenient room service as well as a gorgeous family-style restaurant where guests can enjoy breakfast, lunch, dinner and light snacks. The restaurant offers a varied American cuisine. Some tasty specialties include tender Barbecue Baby Back Ribs and lightly breaded Jumbo Shrimp. A children's menu is also available.

The lobby gives visitors a feeling of welcome with its cheerful pastel colors and ultra-modern decor. The welcome feeling continues when entering one of the lodge's cozy and comfortable rooms.

Owners Steve and Terry Durst are proud of their friendly staff, plush accommodations, and special services. They want to insure that a visit to Niagara Falls is as wonderful and unforgettable as it should be.

FIDDLER'S GREEN AFFORDABLE INNS
7720 Lundy's Lane
Niagara Falls, Ontario L2K 1H1
Tel: (416) 358-9833
Hrs: 7:00 a.m. - 1:00 a.m. (Clerk on duty 24 hours)
Visa, MasterCard, American Express, Diners Club and Carte Blanche are accepted.
Reservations and rates are guaranteed.

Fiddler's Green Affordable Inns provide excellent accommodations at no-nonsense rates. The Inn is conveniently located just two miles from the wondrous Niagara Falls.

Fiddler's Green offers one-bed rooms, family size rooms, efficiency apartments, and whirlpool honeymoon and waterbed suites, The rooms include color television, in-room movies, individual climate control, carpeting, and a four piece bathroom

The newly renovated inn offers a brand new Renaissance Center that features an indoor pool, whirlpool, sauna, exercise equipment, and guest lounge. Fiddler's Green also has a heated outdoor pool, a souvenir gift shop, and free morning coffee.

Fiddler's offers special discount rates at several popular Niagara Falls attractions such as the Minolta Tower Center, Marineland (discounts available exclusively through Fiddler's Green), Skylon Tower, and many wonderful area restaurants. Fiddler's Green will arrange for discounted tours of the Niagara Falls area. The Inn has special getaway packages offered with several restaurants within walking distance. Owner Orest Samitz prides himself on the personal service he provides to his guests, and is accustomed to seeing the same guests year after year.

The owner of the Fiddler's is as fascinating as the Inn itself. Orest is a choreographer for the nationally acclaimed Ukrainian Folk Dancing Group, which has performed for the NBC Today Show and Queen Elizabeth.

Reasonable prices, modern accommodations, friendly service, and special discount packages make the Fiddler's Green Affordable Inns a "Best Choice" in the Niagara Falls area.

HOLIDAY INN BY THE FALLS
Murray and Buchanan Streets
Niagara Falls, Ontario L2G 2J3
Tel: (416) 356-1333
1-800-263-9393
Visa, MasterCard, American Express, Diners Club, Carte Blanche and En Route are accepted.

Though not a part of the popular hotel chain, the Holiday Inn by the Falls offers comfortable accommodations, dining room, cocktail lounge and two heated swimming pools, all within 220 yards of the falls.

The hotel has 122 rooms with something for everyone. Families enjoy the luxury of queen size beds and pull-out davenports. Couples and honeymooners are treated to king size beds, jacuzzis and heart-shaped bathtubs. All rooms have the added convenience of individual climate control, personal vanity and a private balcony.

The Garden Room epitomizes dining flexibility. Both romantic dinners for two and family dining are enjoyed by guests. Chefs prepare breakfast, lunch and dinner including fluffy omelets, Continental Breakfast, Canadian breakfast, marinated Norwegian herring, salad bar, deli sandwiches, roast Prime Rib, spring chicken, and honeymoon specials. Combined with elaborate liquor and wine lists, the Garden Room exquisitely mixes fine dining with family fun.

Patrons also enjoy relaxing in Coco's lounge. Two heated pools, one indoor and one outdoor, allow year-round swimming. Bask in the sauna or whirlpool to complete a day at the falls. All of this is within walking distance to one of the Seven Wonders of the World, as well as a short walk to the famous Skylon Tower, Niagara Parks and hundreds of other attractions. Add to this a small meeting room and the Holiday Inn by the Falls is a comfortable, all purpose get away facility for couples, honeymooners, families and business people.

MICHAEL'S INN BY THE FALLS
5599 River Road
Niagara Falls, Ontario L2E 3H3
Tel: (416) 354-2727
Hrs: Restaurant:
April-November: 7:00 a.m. - 10:00 p.m.
November - March: 8:00 a.m. - 8:00 p.m.
Visa, MasterCard, American Express, Diners Club, Carte Blanche and En Route are accepted.

Michael's Inn by the Falls offers amenities that cannot be found anywhere else. The luxurious accommodations include a variety of theme rooms that can transport guests anywhere in the world. Experience the mystery of the Orient, the excitement of an African Jungle, the beauty of a European Garden, the elegance of an anniversary suite, or the romance of a Southern mansion without leaving Niagara Falls.

There are 130 rooms--all imaginatively created to make a vacation a truly elegant adventure. The tiniest decorating detail has not been overlooked at this incredible inn. The owners seem to anticipate the guests' every whim.

The Garden of Paradise room contains a mineral spring, rocks, plants and a waterfall that's really a gorgeous spa. The room is decorated with wicker furniture, French murals, pastel flowers, a brass waterbed, brass and glass tables, and mirrored doors.

Owners John and Millicent Gruyich have plans to create more exotic theme rooms--some for children, too. Whether these deluxe rooms are for adults or for kids, they're still like something out of a dream.

For dining enjoyment, the Embers Open Hearth dining room offers juicy Prime Rib and tender steaks broiled to perfection on a huge open hearth. After a fabulous dinner, relax in the intimate atmosphere of the Hideaway Lounge.

The Inn overlooks the Niagara River and offers a spectacular view of the falls. Step into Michael's Inn by the falls--it's sheer fantasy.

THE OAKES INN
6546 Buchanan Avenue
Niagara Falls, Ontario L2G 3W2
Tel: (416) 358-5926 (Reservations)
(416) 356-4514 (Switchboard)
Visa, MasterCard, American Express, Diners Club, Carte Blanche and En Route are accepted.

The Oakes Inn is the hotel closest to the Canadian Horseshoe Falls, and the view is spectacular. The Oakes has an impressive glass-enclosed, rooftop observation deck where guests can view both the American and Canadian Falls, the Gorge, and the Upper Rivers.

The accommodations include 170 spacious, beautifully decorated rooms with all the amenities--cable color television, plush wall-to-wall carpeting, and big comfortable beds. Honeymoon suites are lavishly furnished with all of the luxuries, including whirlpools, stereos, waterbeds, and heart-shaped jacuzzis.

The hotel's restaurant offers both Canadian and American cuisine for breakfast, lunch, and dinner. Morning meals range from tasty Western Omelettes to old-fashioned hot cakes with syrup. The chef also prepares luscious homemade doughnuts and spicy cinnamon toast. A Breakfast Buffet is served every Sunday from 8:00 a.m. to 11:30 a.m.

The luncheon menu features reasonably priced items such as freshly prepared club sandwiches, steaming hot soups, Spaghetti and Meatballs, Cheese Raviolis, Fish-n-Chips, and Chicken in a Basket. Dinners include Tender Sweet Ham with Pineapple, Pork Chops with Applesauce, and Bacon-wrapped Filet Mignon.

Redfords Lounge, the Oakes Inn sports lounge, has a big-screen television on which fans can watch important games and an intimate section where guests can enjoy a relaxing drink.

The elegant Oakes Inn, located between the Skylon and Minolta Towers, offers a heated outdoor pool, room service, and easy access to Niagara Falls attractions and shopping malls.

RAMADA CORAL INN
7429 Lundy's Lane
Niagara Falls, Ontario L2H 1G9
Tel: (416) 356-6116
Hrs: Inn: Open 24 hours
Restaurant:
Seven days 7:30 a.m. - 10:00 p.m.
Visa, MasterCard, American Express, Diners Club, Carte Blanche and En Route are accepted.

The luxurious Ramada Coral Inn is a four-star hotel that offers bridal suites with queen-size beds, heart-shaped jacuzzis, and hand-painted ceilings. Exclusive bedroom suites feature king-size beds, jacuzzis, private balconies, real fireplaces, and studio suites with adjoining rooms. Guests may also choose to stay in spacious family-size rooms that overlook the swimming pool and flower garden.

All 130 guest rooms come equipped with color television, telephone, in-room movies, and individual climate control. Extra amenities, such as a waterbed, AM/FM radio, and an additional powder alcove are also available.

This exceptional resort also offers indoor and outdoor swimming pools, a fully-equipped exercise room and a relaxing sauna and whirlpool. The challenging miniature golf course, glamorous gift shop, and the unique water theme park are other exciting places where guests can spend a few hours relaxing and having fun.

Take advantage of the lavish facilities in the Colonnade Banquet Room for parties, conferences, meetings or banquets. For smaller business meetings, the Ramada offers an Executive Boardroom and Hospitality Suites.

Guests will love the savory cuisine and courteous service McIntosh's Country Fare Restaurant has to offer. There's no better way to start the day than by enjoying a hearty breakfast at McIntosh's. The restaurant also serves delicious lunches, such as the Mozzarella Pomodore and Baked French Onion Soup, as well as wonderful country-style dinners like the old English Fish 'n Chips and the Seafood Stuffed Trout. McIntosh's BBQ Ribs, Veal Parmigiana and New York Steaks are equally fantastic and favored by many.

McIntosh's offers wet-your-whistle specialties from the bar, specialty coffees, and carefully selected local wines.

No dinner would be complete without one of McIntosh's homemade desserts. Venetian Peach Cobbler, Country Apple Pie, rich cheesecake, an old fashioned sundae, or a dish of parlour ice cream will end any meal on a delicious note.

The Ramada is located two miles west of the Falls. If planning a winter visit, check out the annual winter "Festival of Lights" and the Ramada's 15-foot round snowman. Experience the Ramada Coral Inn to find great luxury for low prices.

RAMADA RENAISSANCE FALLSVIEW HOTEL
6455 Buchanan Avenue
Niagara Falls, Ontario L2G 3V9
Tel: (416) 357-3422
(416) 357-3422 (Fax No.)
Hrs: Dining Room 7:00 a.m. - 11:00 p.m.
Visa, MasterCard, American Express, Diners Club, Carte Blanche JCB and En Route are accepted.

Only 500 yards from the Falls, the Ramada Renaissance Fallsview Hotel offers first-class accommodations that range from elegant bridal suites to gorgeous family rooms. Vacationers and business travelers come from all over the world to experience this beautiful Ramada, and the hotel caters to everyone. It also has specialized guest services for Japanese tourists. Upon their arrival the tourists are welcomed with a Sencha Green Tea reception in a beautiful banquet room adjacent to the main lobby. Because the Ramada realizes how confusing foreign travel can be, it staffs four full-time (7 a.m. - Midnight) Japanese-speaking employees to answer questions. The Ramada always has been in the business of catering to its guests. Its experienced staff and extensive services are proof of that.

The classy but unpretentious Mulberry's Dining Room, decorated in coral pastels and gleaming brass, provides room service, evening dinner buffets and perfectly prepared meals (breakfasts, lunches, and dinners). The Sweet Endings are really exotic--the Melon Gelato is a frozen dessert topped with fresh melon and melon liqueur, the Chocolate Royale is chocolate ice cream delicately smothered in chocolate sauce, freshly whipped cream, and Tia Maria, the Strawberry Delight is a layering of strawberries, strawberry ice cream, strawberry sauce, Strawberry Schnapps, and whipped cream.

Other facilities include the exquisite Chesterfield's Lounge with live weekend entertainment, the upper level observation deck and lounge that offers an uncompromising view of the Falls, a skylit pool atrium, a relaxing Terrace Cafe, a full-range health club where guests can lift weights, work out on Nautilus equipment, play squash and racquetball, and swim, large meeting and banquet rooms, an exciting video arcade, and a first-rate gift shop. Shuttle service to local airports is provided.

If all this weren't enough, the Ramada Renaissance Fallsview has expanded. As of summer 1990, the hotel will offer four more floors of guest rooms, another Fallsview Observation Lounge, and numerous other facilities.

Don't miss the Ramada Renaissance Fallsview Hotel. It offers every creature-comfort imaginable from the sensual heart-shaped jacuzzis and the lavishly furnished rooms to the captivating view of Niagara Falls.

SKYLINE FOXHEAD HOTEL
5685 Falls Avenue
Niagara Falls, Ontario LZE 6W7
Tel: (416) 374-4444
Hrs: Open seven days, 24 hours
Visa, MasterCard, American Express and Carte Blanche are accepted.

The Skyline Foxhead Hotel is one of the best hotels in the Niagara Falls area, boasting a four star rating from the Ontario Tourist Association. It is owned by a conglomerate known as York-Hanover, and offers the "ultimate falls-view experience." This modern first class hotel boasts 395 finely appointed guestrooms, the majority of which have balconies overlooking the falls and beautiful gardens below. All rooms feature climate control, color television, full bath, in-room movies and a refrigerated mini-bar. At the Skyline Foxhead, children stay free if under the age of 18.

There are 14 stories which make the rooftop swimming pool that much more impressive, as it offers a marvelous view of Niagara Falls. Speaking of a view, the Penthouse Restaurant also overlooks the Falls and provides an interesting atmosphere with accommodations for 350. On the premises is also the Penthouse Bar, Steak and Burger Restaurant, Fallsview Lounge, and facilities for meetings up to 1000 people.

Other amenities include laundry, dry-cleaning, and currency exchange. There is near-by shopping at Mapleleaf Village Mall, as well as area golf, horseback riding, and 2800 acres of Niagara parkland to explore. The York-Hanover Corporation share a similar pride with the staff at the Skyline Foxhead Hotel in their success and versatility in providing the fundamental needs of families. groups, business people, and conventions alike.

bed & breakfast inns

THE NIAGARA REGION BED & BREAKFAST SERVICE
Niagara Falls, Ontario LZE 6V2
Tel: (416) 358-8988
Hrs: 9:00 a.m. - 9:00 p.m.
Visa, MasterCard and American Express are accepted.

Perhaps the most interesting aspect of the Niagara Region Bed and Breakfast Service is its 200-year-old tradition in which residents make their homes available to visitors traveling through this area, providing them with a unique alternative to costly hotel stays. All establishments are screened for suitability by Monique Wetherup, owner of the Niagara Region Bed & Breakfast Service, to ensure they meet certain criteria.

The Wetherups think that the whole bed and breakfast concept is "Niagara's way of turning one good day into another." Select from warm and comfortable accommodations ranging from modest to luxurious, modern to Victorian, and city to country. The prices range from $45 to $85 per couple, including additional amenities such as swimming pools, heart-shaped baths and jacuzzis. Other helpful services include babysitting and theater reservations.

The reservation service knows first-hand each accommodation, all of which offer a variety of breakfasts, from continental to a full home-cooked meal. In addition to bilingual and non-smoking homes, some even accept pets.

The Niagara Region Bed and Breakfast Service is a unique, quality network of personalized services as well as a clever alternative for people all over the world. Be sure to take advantage of the many forms of entertainment in the area made easier by the service. Advance dinner reservations are offered as well as limousines, taxis, and private tour guides.

breweries

NIAGARA FALLS BREWING COMPANY
6863 Lundy's Lane
Niagara Falls, Ontario L2G 1V7
Tel: (416) 374-1166
Hrs: Monday - Wednesday 10:00 a.m. - 6:00 p.m.
Thursday - Saturday 10:00 a.m. - 10:00 p.m.

The Niagara Falls Brewing Company is the first brewery in over 145 years to be located in the Niagara Falls area. Although it opened in 1989, the brewery is expected to sell over 1.2 million bottles per year.

The Stamford Spring Brewery and the Drummonville Brewery were established in 1844 down the road from Niagara Falls Brewing Company's present location. It served 500 people, a much smaller population than today's company serves.

Niagara Falls Brewing Co. has continued the tradition of producing a fresh, honest beer with true character, a premium lager known as Niagara Trapper. Made with only the finest ingredients, Niagara's great-tasting beer is created from start to finish at the brewery in Lundy's Lane.

The beer-making process can be observed on a free tour of the facilities, from the state-of-the-art tankage, piping, and filtration systems to the bottling line. The brewery was designed so that visitors may watch the interesting process in its entirety.

The 6000 square foot plant features a retail beer store, where visitors can purchase Niagara's thirst-quenching beer, and gift shop, which offers T-shirts, glasses, and hats all with brewery-related logos.

Owners are most proud, however, of the many experienced staff members working at the brewery. Claude Corrieau, formerly of Barnes Wines, is general manager and brewmaster. Wally Moroz, who previously worked for Paul Masson Wines, is cellar master, while Quality Control Consultant, Harvey Hurlbut, brings 35 years of experience with a major Canadian brewery to the company. Other stockholders include Donald Ziraldo and Bruno and Mario Criveller, who are well-established in the beverage business as well.

These men have come together to create the distinctive, high-quality Canadian premium lager, Niagara Trapper, already holding its own among top Canadian beers.

The finest brewery facilities, open to the public, are available at Niagara Falls Brewing Company, home of Canada's great-tasting Niagara Trapper.

candy stores

CRIVELLER CANDIES/THE CHOCOLATE & PASTRY BOUTIQUE
6853 Lundy's Lane
Niagara Falls, Ontario L2G 1V7

Tel:	(416) 356-9441	
Hrs:	Tuesday - Thursday	10:00 a.m. - 5:00 p.m.
	Friday	10:00 a.m. - 8:00 p.m.
	Saturday	10:00 a.m. - 4:30 p.m.
	Sunday	10:00 a.m. - 2:00 p.m.

Visa and MasterCard are accepted.

Criveller Candies is no ordinary sweet shop; it offers the ultimate in chocolate candies and delectible desserts. This unique chocolate and pastry shop prepares liquid-filled chocolates, pralines with Amaretto, Kirsh, tangerine, orange (Grand Mariner), and mint flavors, candied orange peels dipped in chocolate; truffles; and chocolate-covered cherries. The shop also bakes custom-made fruit-flavored wedding and birthday cakes. The Crivellers can do anything with sweets. Nothing seems impossible.

The Puff Pastry, filled with Amaretto, Hazelnut, and Zabaglione creams are delicious, as are the luscious pastries filled with rum-flavored chantilly cream or fresh blueberries. The desserts at Criveller's are not inexpensive, but then neither are their ingredients. Everything is prepared the old-fashioned way, with the highest-quality fresh ingredients. They only use raw chocolate that is imported from Switzerland.

The sweet concoctions have a truly European flair because the Criveller family has recruited some of the best pastry chefs from all over the world. As a result, the shop offers an incredibly huge assortment of creative cakes, cookies, candies, and other desserts.

Criveller's is internationally recognized for its prize-winning desserts, such as the scrumptious Black Forest and St. Honore cakes and wonderful fruit tarts. The desserts here are so delicious and renowned that the shop has catered pastry tables for officials in Washington, D.C.

The shop provides a wide variety of wedding gifts, such as silk flowers, crystal, ceramics, hand-painted Italian porcelain baskets, picture frames, vases, and also a full range of wedding services. These services include table favors and beautifully engraved invitations and matches. The Boutique will cater any size banquet, party, or wedding.

The Criveller family members are third-generation candy makers and are widely known as one of North America's finest. Be sure to taste the expertise and old-fashioned goodness of Criveller's treats. The shop is located five minutes from the Falls, on Lundy's Lane near the corner of Dorchester Road. Stop by and see just how sweet it is.

malls

MAPLE LEAF VILLAGE
5705 Falls Avenue
Niagara Falls, Ontario, Canada L2E 6W7
Tel: (416) 374-4444 ext. 4035

Located directly opposite the Rainbow Bridge Border crossing at Niagara Falls is Maple Leaf Village. It's an unique triple level complex that features hotel accommodations, entertainment facilities, unusual restaurants, and superb gift shops and boutiques. Maple Leaf Village offers elegant dining and hotel rooms that provide guests with a spectacular view of the Falls in addition to a range of fun activities.

Among the major attractions at this prime tourist center are Yuk Yuk's Komedy Kabaret and Lillie Langtry's Theatre. Yuk Yuk's is a popular restaurant and nightclub in the area that always offers a good time. Lillie Langtry's Theatre is a 350 seat theater that features comedy, magic, dance, illusion, and fire-eating, in a Las Vegas-style revue entitled "Niagara Variety".

While visiting Maple Leaf Village, experience two unusually intriguing museums: the Elvis Presley Museum and the That's Incredible Museum. The Elvis Presley Museum displays the King's authentic personal effects, Graceland furniture, clothes, cars, and jewelry. The That's Incredible Museum features bizarre exhibits such as shark jaws that one can walk though and exciting illusions that will make friends and family disappear and reappear right before your very eyes.

Other exciting places to visit at the Village are the Lazermaze, a walk through video that features life size robots, and Nightmares Therapy Centre, the perfect attraction for folks who love to be frightened. Catch a magnificent view of Niagara Falls by visiting the Maple Leaf Village

Observation Tower. Visitors can also enjoy 17 rides and 25 games of skill at the exciting amusement park. Strolling around this sensational 17-acre complex can work up quite an appetite. Visitors can rest and refuel at Suisha Gardens, which specializes in Japanese cuisine, Shaboom's 50's Restaurant and Nightclub, or the British Pub. Maple Leaf Village also offers an extensive fast food court.

This fun-filled center has something for everyone. The cartoon cat Garfield is the center's official mascot, and he's always on hand to greet children and adults. Other attractions include the Niagara Daredevils, which features the films of Karel Soucek, who took the barrel plunge over the Falls. A specialty photography booth even photographs visitors so that they appear to be going over the Falls in a barrel.

The comprehensive range of services and attractions at Maple Leaf Village is fun and exciting but one of the best parts of visiting this wonderful complex is the scenery. It offers a panoramic post-card view of the Canadian and American Falls which is breath-taking to say the least.

night clubs

SHABOOM 50's RESTAURANT AND NIGHT CLUB
Maple Leaf Village
5705 Falls Avenue 3rd Level
Niagara Falls, Ontario L2E 6W7
Tel: (416) 354-3838
Hrs: 11:30 a.m.- 1:00 a.m. (or later)
Kitchen open until midnight.
Visa, MasterCard and American Express are accepted.

"Dine, dance, or just relax in a unique setting of hula hoops and classic Chevys," is the invitation sent out by those at Shaboom and Beat Street. This diner and nightspot are nostalgic reminders of an era gone by. Shaboom, taking its name from "SH-BOOM", a 1954 hit by the Crew Cuts, is a two-story dining room designed to look like a typical '50s street scene.

The authentic look is given to the room through use of colorful building facades with names like Betty's Beauty Shop, Sal's Deli, and Rick's Garage (it has a '55 Chevy inside). Shaboom Garage Sales is an actual retail store where '50s memorabilia, jackets, signs, and souvenir sweats and shirts can be purchased. The soda bar is a classic design with a red and white checked floor.

The varied menu is attractively presented and cheerfully served by a cool, crazy staff. The menu keeps in line with the restaurant's theme. Sandwiches such as McHale's Navy (shrimp and seafood on a croissant) are featured as well as Cassius Clay (a huge homemade hamburger served with bacon). The dinner selections include items like Bonanza (Roast Prime Rib of Beef) and Roman Holiday (Homemade Manicotti). Dessert selections include Marilyn Monroe (Cheesecake) and An Affair to Remember (Banana Split for Two).

This spot is just as popular with locals as it is with tourists. On Beat Street, folks can "Rock Around The Clock" to '50s and '60s tunes.

The D.J. takes requests, making it easy to bop the night away. Dance and Hula Hoop Contests add to the '50s mood. Shaboom, reminiscent of poodle skirts and blue suede shoes, is a "Best Choice" for festive dining, dancing, and clean-cut fun.

points of interest

MINOLTA TOWER CENTRE
6732 Oakes Drive
Niagara Falls, Ontario L2G 3WS
Tel.: (416) 356-1501
Hrs.: Summer: 9:00 a.m. - Midnight
November 1 - March 1: 9:00 a.m. - 10:00 p.m.
Closed December 24 and 25.
Visa, MasterCard and American Express are accepted.

Minolta Tower Centre, built in 1962, boasts "The original towering view of Niagara Falls". One of Niagara's most popular attractions for its ideal view of the Falls, the tower offers visitors a vantage point from 665 feet above the gorge.

Indoor and outdoor observation decks, three floors of fabulous, reasonable dining, and Top Of The Rainbow Restaurant, a four-time winner of the "Restaurant of the Year" award, are only three of the many reasons Minolta Tower Centre is so popular.

Top Of The Rainbow Dining Rooms offer a wide variety of appetizers, soups, salads, accompaniments, entrees, and desserts. Country-Style Pate in Cumberland sauce and Filet of Smoked Trout in horseradish cream are only two of eight appetizers. Rainbow Soup de Jour and Lobster Bisque laced with cognac are soups that appeal to the palate. New York Strip Steak, eight ounces and grilled to perfection, and Grilled Salmon with herb butter, head the list of entrees that include veal, German sausage, pasta, and chicken dishes.

After dining, visitors may wish to take the elevator to the 30th floor where a unique high-tech display, "Only From the Mind of Minolta," literally takes visitors inside the world of photography. The amazing Aquarium and Reptile World, Canada's largest indoor reptile exhibit, features such creatures as boa constrictors, anacondas, alligators, crocodiles, iguanas, turtles, and exotic fish. Children and adults alike enjoy learning about the wondrous characteristics of reptiles.

The free Waltzing Water Show occurs each evening from May to October, and delights audiences with dancing water jets that move to music.

Those interested in purchasing souvenirs will enjoy the gift shop, which carries Niagara's best collection of quality gift items, and the enchanting collection of shops featuring leather goods,china, glass, jewelry, T-shirts, fudge, and an array of specialty items for all budgets and tastes.

A snack shop, video arcade, photo finishing in an hour, cameras, and accessories are several special services offered by Minolta Tower Centre. Available at all facilities are carefully selected and well-trained staff members who can ensure visitors of these services and of a great time while visiting. Minolta Tower Centre -- home of the best view above Niagara Falls.

NIAGARA FALLS IMAX THEATRE
6170 Buchanan Avenue
Niagara Falls, Ontario L2E 6V5
Tel: (416) 358-3611
Hrs: Open year-round, except for Christmas Day.
Shows on the hour
Operating hours vary seasonally.

The Niagara Falls Imax Theatre features one of the Fall's most popular attractions, the film "Niagara: Miracles, Myths, and Magic", created and directed by Hollywood's Academy award winner Keith Merill. The view of the Falls is overwhelming and this hi-tech film will add more amazement to an already extraordinary sight.

The unique theatre features the IMAX motion picture system, said to be the finest in the world. The movie screen, Canada's largest, is over seven stories tall. The air conditioned, 670 seat IMAX Theatre has a screen that is 2,200 times the size of the average television screen and 10 times larger than a standard cinema screen.The movie details the history of the Falls as it is recounted in the Indian legends and European settlers' accounts. This incredible 45 minute film shows Blondin crossing the Falls on a tightrope and lets viewers experience the feeling of going over the Falls in a barrel.

Located just five minutes from the Niagara Falls Rainbow Bridge, the theatre features a modern lobby, snack bar, and a unique gift shop. The shop features Niagara Falls souvenirs, fine sterling silver jewelry, leather gifts, and a variety of other elegant items.

To locate the Niagara Falls IMAX Theatre, take Highway 420 from the Rainbow Bridge, turn left on Buchanan Avenue, and look for the pyramid-shaped building.

No trip to Niagara Falls is complete without a visit to IMAX Theatre. The film is historical, educational, and exciting. The Falls come to life before the viewers' eyes. Experience an adventure not to be forgotten.

THE SKYLON TOWER
5200 Robinson Street
Niagara Falls, Ontario L2G 2A3
Tel: (416) 356-2651
(716) 856-5788 Buffalo
Hrs: May - October:
Daily 8:00 a.m. - 12:30 a.m.
Visa, MasterCard, American Express, Diners Club and En Route are accepted.

Rising above Niagara Falls, a glass enclosed elevator takes in the unique view along the way, until finally reaching its destination 775 feet above the falls. Once there, after becoming acquainted with the breathtaking environment, enjoy an elegant evening of dining, family gathering or just appreciate the view. All of this is within a landmark as recognizable as the falls themselves--The Skylon Tower.

The Skylon offers two dining experiences, one of which is gourmet cuisine in the Revolving Dining Room. Award-winning chefs prepare prime rib, salmon, filet, seafood platters and various other favorites including lobster in a delicious surf and turf combination with filet mignon. Once every hour, the Revolving Dining Room lives up to its name, giving patrons an unmatched 360 degree view, not only of the Canadian and American falls, but also 8,000 square miles of artistic countryside.

A second dining experience is in the Summit Suite Buffet Dining Room. Open during the summer months, the stationary Summit Suite provides casual dining amid bountiful buffets featuring fresh seafood, roast beef and a plethora of pleasing French pastries. All of this remains within an affordable price enabling families to enjoy dining with a remarkable view.

Atop both restaurants is an observation deck where many shutterbugs perch to capture the unmistakable site below. At the base of the tower tourists find shops featuring Canadian handicrafts, treasures from around the world, precious crystal and figurines, as well as jewelry. The Mini Chateau provides a convenient snack stop. For more than a snack, enjoy cocktails and lunch at Taps Lounge. An entire amusement level contains games of chance, a pinball arcade and concession stand.

From November to February the tower becomes the world's largest Christmas tree. 54,450 watts illuminate 5,000 bulbs around the enormous structure highlighting the Winter Festival of Lights. During the festival, the view from atop the tower is even more adventurous as tourists look down on the array of lights.

Summer, winter or anytime of year, the Skylon Tower enhances the romance, excitement and enjoyment of any trip to Niagara Falls.

restaurants

BETTY'S RESTAURANT
8921 Sodom Road
Niagara Falls, Ontario LZE 656
Tel: (416) 295-4436
Hrs: Monday - Saturday 7:00 a.m. - 9:00 p.m.
Sunday 9:00 a.m. - 9:00 p.m.
Visa, MasterCard and American Express are accepted.

Betty's Restaurant, "the other reason people visit the Falls," began as a small country cafe with four tables and a dining counter. The popularity of the place has led to its expansion and present size with seating for 250 people. Betty's is a very modern, comfortable, and spacious family restaurant. The dining room is brightly decorated with beige and two-tone greens with natural oak accents. The chairs are upholstered in a salmon shade. Nearly a dozen wildlife paintings are spaced along the walls.

Betty's is owned by Joe and Trudy Miszk and their son, Joe Jr. Trudy, originally from Poland, moved to North America when she was 20 years old. Now close to retirement, she still finds herself in the kitchen, and it's a good thing for visitors to the Falls. Joe and Trudy's restaurant, with its home cooked meals and unpretentious setting, provides a nice change of pace from the commercialization of the Falls area. All food is prepared the old fashioned way here. Items are made daily from scratch. Soups such as chicken dumpling or split pea make a great appetizer. Daily specials include anything from Stuffed Cabbage Rolls to Veal Parmesan. Betty's is famous for its Fish & Chips dinner and has many seafood dishes to choose from. Dinner selections include Liver with onion or bacon, Breaded Veal Cutlet, Hamburger Steak, Hawaiian Ham Steak, and Chicken In A Basket.

A well-stocked bar allows for a cocktail with a meal or a beer to accompany a fish special. Diners would be wise to take advantage of Trudy's homemade pies and the selections change with the seasons. Children are always welcome and the Sunday Brunch from 10 a.m. to 2 p.m. is the perfect occasion for the family to visit Betty's Restaurant. Comfort and the wonderful home cooked meals make Betty's Restaurant a "Best Choice" for visitors to the Falls.

CASA D'ORO DINING LOUNGE
5875 Victoria Avenue
Niagara Falls, Ontario L26 3L6
Tel: (416) 365-5646
Hrs: Restaurant:
Seven days Noon - Midnight
Night Club:
Seven days Until 1:00 a.m.
Saturday 4:00 p.m. - Midnight
Visa, MasterCard, American Express, Diners Club, Carte Blanche and En Route are accepted.

Named after Venice's 13th century landmark, "Casa d'Oro" (House of Gold) is a magnificent European restaurant that offers elegantly different Italian cuisine. From the Classic Mushrooms Daumont to the Regal Clams Casino, the hors-d'oevres are all delightful. The folks at Casa d'Oro are proud of their genuine Italian cuisine, especially the Roman-style Rack of Lamb Agnolotti, served with mint jelly and vegetables; the Honeymooner's Feast, an extravagant center cut of beef tenderloin with Bernaise sauce and a Bouquettiere of vegetables; and the Spaghetti Dela Calabria with zesty Cacciatore sauce. The Bracioli with Gnocchi (Mama's Recipe) is another excellent option for any pasta lover. Casa d' Oro also prepares super veal, seafood, and homemade soups.

Because a delicious meal deserves a wonderful finish, Casa d'Oro concocts an assortment of desserts that are sheer fantasy. Indulge with the lavish Torte Glace, a unique blend of Kahlua, graham cracker crumbs, and ice cream. The dessert wagon features tempting tortes, cakes, and fresh homemade pies. The Cherries Jubilee, bing cherries with ice cream, flaming brandy, and the chef's special glaze and the Bavarian Eclair Glace with chocolate sauce are favorite desserts along with Pumpkin Ice Cream Pie, or the rich parlour ice cream and sherbets.

Other fabulous finales are exotic Cafe Espresso, Grand Slam Coffee, Coffee B-52, Spanish Coffee, Coffee Cappuccino, or Casa d'Oro freshly-brewed Gourmet Blend Coffee.

Casa d' Oro offers old World charm in a luxurious setting. The most discerning connoisseur couldn't ask for more. Casa d'Oro's award-winning chefs create extraordinary cuisine and the Roberto family sees to it that diners leave smiling.

Located in the heart of Niagara Falls, just two blocks from the actual falls, the Casa d'Oro Dining Lounge is a favorite of Niagara locals and visiting celebrities.

CASA MIA ITALIAN RESTAURANT
3518 Portage Road
Niagara Falls, Ontario L2J 2K4
Tel: (416) 356-5410
Hrs: Seven days 11:00 a.m.- 11:00 p.m.
Closed Christmas only.
Visa and MasterCard are accepted.

Voted "Best Italian Restaurant in Southern Ontario" by a popular Toronto Radio station, Casa Mia is located across from the Stamford Green Plaza, just 10 minutes from Niagara Falls.

Authenticity is the key at this fantastic Italian restaurant. Owners Domenico and Lucianna Mollica think that Italian cooking has been grossly misrepresented in North America so they serve only truly Italian dishes. Every year the Mollicas travel back to Italy to keep abreast of new Italian cuisine to prepare. Casa Mia is not merely a spaghetti and meatballs restaurant; it serves such delectable Italian delights as Veal Piccata (milk fed veal, dipped in egg, pan-fried, and served with Fettucine Alfredo) and Lasagna Al Forno with layers of pasta, ground sirloin, mozzarella cheese, and tomato sauce. Two of the most tantalizing dishes at Casa Mia's are the Fettucine Verde (Lucianna's own special creation of flat spinach, pasta, shrimp and scallops, topped with a creamy sauce), which won a gold award in Europe, and the Pink Gnocchi Gargonzolla, which won the silver award.

The restaurant serves over 100 different sauces in its original Italian dishes. Casa Mia's also serves a range of ocean fresh fish specialties, such as rainbow trout in lemon sauce served with linguine clam sauce and the Zuppe Di Mari with baked shrimp, scallops, clams, sole lobster, king crab, and tomato sauce all baked to perfection. Before the entrees, try the sensational Antipasto Di Mari, made up of crabmeat, shrimp and squid minced with the chef's special seasoning.

The authentic Italian cuisine is not the only reason to visit Casa Mia. The decor is equally enchanting. Newly remodeled, Casa Mia has cathedral ceilings, skylights, and classic Mediterranean furnishings. Casa Mia is festive enough for fun family dining, but it is also elegant enough for a romantic night out.

It's impossible to overlook the Mollica family's expertise and enthusiasm. Domenico's mother, Lucianna, came from Rome, Italy in 1968, was chef at the Skylon restaurant for over eight years, and in 1984 (when she opened Casa Mia) brought her superb Italian cooking experience to her own restaurant. Domenico has worked with his mother ever since he was old enough to work.

Casa Mia offers a fantastic variety of wine, beer, and cocktails in addition to serving fine food. This restaurant has a flair for preparing food that is unmistakably European. Food this terrific is found only in a five star restaurant such as Casa Mia.

HUNGARIAN VILLAGE RESTAURANT
5329 Ferry Street.
Niagara Falls, Ontario L2G 1R8
Tel: (416) 356-2429
Hrs: Tuesday - Friday 4:00 p.m. - Midnight
Saturday - SundayNoon - Midnight
Closed Christmas week.
Visa, MasterCard and American Express are accepted.

"A restaurant of distinction" since 1939, the Hungarian Village Restaurant is a Landmark restaurant in the Niagara area and is renowned internationally. The authentic Hungarian menu has evolved during the past 50 years into one that is now tough to improve upon. Owners John Fedor Jr., Mary Fedor Kovalec, and her husband Frank Kovalec do not believe in resting on their laurels, however, and so are always searching for ways to upgrade the flavor of their dishes and the quality of service provided.

Diners will have a hard time choosing among these award-winning dishes. Chef Frank Kovalec and his staff of highly-trained Hungarian chefs are very creative and particular. The head chef actually selects the freshest produce at the market himself and all meats are butchered right on the premises. The objective here is consistent excellence, and this commitment is reflected in every dish.

There are two to three hearty soups to choose from daily like Hungarian chicken soup. Appetizers include sliced salami or herring with sour cream. Specialties of the House are plentiful. Chicken Paprikas is saucy and served with homemade galuska (egg dumplings) or rice. The gourmet dish Borsos Gombas Tokany is sliced tenderloin of beef sauteed with fresh mushroom and herbs. Only milk-fed veal is used in the veal entrees for its amazing flavor. The Hungarian Veal Gulas is made by bathing tender chunks of veal in a delicate paprika sauce. Fillet of sole, red snapper, filet mignon, and roast duckling round out the selections. For those who don't want to choose, the Transylvanian Platter is ideal. It includes beef tenderloin, pork chop and egg-coated veal cutlet, along with sausage and cabbage roll piled on lesco rice. Meals can be complemented with imported Hungarian wines. Desserts include Black Forest and Walnut Cakes and Palacsinta (a Hungarian crepe) with apricot jam or cottage cheese and raisin filling.

The Hungarian Restaurant Village is conveniently located just three blocks from the Rainbow Bridge and the Falls. One will receive friendly service from charming, colorfully-clad waitresses. There isn't much turnover in the staff and there is a family atmosphere. The restaurant consists of three separate dining areas, including the elegant Franz Liszt Dining Room and two smaller private rooms. The front section is designed to resemble an outdoor courtyard with many arches, windows, lamp posts, brick walls and iron work. Six nights a week meals are accompanied by music of the Gypsy Trio from Budapest. For authentic, award-winning Hungarian cuisine in an elegant, yet comfortable setting, The Hungarian Village Restaurant is a "Best Choice."

MAMA MIA'S RESTAURANT AND TAVERN
5719 Victoria Avenue
Niagara Falls, Ontario L2G 3L5
Tel: 1-416-354-7471
Hrs: Summer: 11:30 a.m. - Midnight
Winter: 11:30 a.m. - 9:00 p.m.
Closed January & February.
Visa, Mastercard, American Express, Diners Club and Carte Blanche are accepted.

The enticing aromas encountered when one enters Mama Mia's Restaurant and Tavern are enough to set the taste buds salivating. Mama Mia, whose portrait hangs on the wall, overlooking the entire restaurant, must be very proud of the way the Herkimer family has preserved the original authentic cuisine and the home atmosphere over the last ten years.

This wonderful Italian tradition began over 30 years ago when Rosa, Mama Mia's award winning chef, consistently prepared the mouth-watering homemade pasta, cannelloni, lasagna and cheese ravioli smothered in the homemade sauce that is her own private recipe. Bring an appetite, because ample portions are the norm at Mama Mia's. A generous serving of fresh Italian bread and creamy butter accompanies each dish.

Located at the top of Clifton Hill, within a short walking distance from the Falls, Mama Mia's has two dining areas that seat up to 150 guests. The brick and stone walls, ornate black wrought-iron fixtures, and trellis work entwined with grape vines give Mama Mia's that Mediterranean look.

Visit Mama Mia's for Italian specialties including stuffed eggplant, chicken a la cacciatore, and veal cutlet parmigiana, or try a tender filet mignon, T-bone or New York Strip steak, broiled red salmon or lobster tail. For an alternative, try Turf 'n Surf, the ultimate seafood experience, located just down the street at 5759 Victoria Avenue for everything from shellfish to swordfish, or the Beef Baron, the King of Prime Rib, around the corner at 5019 Centre Street.

The irresistible home cooking, consistent quality, great value, generous portions and friendly, attentive service make Mama Mia's a very popular place to eat--so popular that there may be a line to get in. But the fine dining experience of Mama Mia's is well worth the short wait. So, when visiting the Niagara Falls area, visit Mama Mia's Restaurant and Tavern for those "famous foods to remember."

REESE'S COUNTRY INN
3799 Montrose Road
Niagara Falls, Ontario L2E 6S4
Tel: (416) 357-5640
Hrs: Lunch:
Tuesday - Saturday 11:30 a.m. - 3:00 p.m.
Dinner:
Tuesday - Saturday 5:00 p.m. - 10:00 p.m.
Sunday Brunch: 11:00 a.m. - 3:00 p.m.
Closed Mondays.
Visa, MasterCard, American Express, Diners Club, Carte Blanche and En Route are accepted.

This charming country inn offers cozy lodging and superb cuisine. In fact, Reese's is one of Canada's most highly acclaimed restaurants. The Inn recently received Travel/Holidays Dining Distinction Award as one of the most outstanding restaurants in the world.

The property on which Reese's stands originally belonged to the King of England and was given to John Muskegon in 1810 as a Crown Grant. The property changed hands several times until it was bought by Dick Reese, whose father invented the renowned Reese's Peanut Butter Cup, and is now owned by Peter Mete and Tony and Tim Roberts.

The beautifully rustic suites, which overlook the breathtaking Canadian countryside, feature cozy sofas, rocking chairs and natural stone fireplaces. The folks at Reese's will serve breakfast in a guest's room, if requested.

The restaurant specializes in home cooking with a country flavor. The open face New York Strip Steak Sandwich is a delicious combination of seasoned, cooked to order Red Brand Beef, toasted Italian bread, and home fries. Another tasty dish is the Chicken William Tell, tender breast of chicken that is seasoned, baked and dressed with luscious apple stuffing. Seafood lovers will enjoy the seafood salad with baby shrimp, tuna, crab meat, and zesty special recipe dressing.

The Bifteck a la Tartare and Pate Montrose are excellent appetizers for any entree. The Red Bell Pepper and Lobster Bisque with rich creamy seafood stock, the Fruit Soup with accents of bold West Indian rum and Kirsch, and the Prime Filet of Beef Wellington (also known as the William Shakespeare) with superb Bernaise Sauce and a light pastry are delightful beyond description.

This fantastic country inn also offers banquet, wedding, and party facilities and is located only ten minutes from the Falls. The chalet-style inn is situated on five beautifully landscaped acres on Montrose Avenue near the corner of Thorold Stone Road. Reese's is the perfect place for a romantic retreat, business meeting place or family dining experience.

ROLF'S
3840 Main Street
Chippewa, Ontario L2G 6B2
Tel: (416) 295-3472
Hrs: Tuesday - Saturday 5:00 p.m. - 9:30 p.m.
Sunday 5:00 p.m. - 8:30 p.m.
Open Christmas & Thanksgiving.
Visa, MasterCard, American Express, Diners Club, Carte Blanche and En Route are accepted.

Rolf's features continental dining at its finest. The restaurant offers an exciting array of seasonal salads, elegant appetizers, hearty entrees, and tantalizing desserts. The Champignons Cafe De Paris, Escargots A La Bourguignonne, Smoked Atlantic Salmon A La Maison, and Jumbo Shrimp Cocktail are an excellent beginning to any meal.

Owners Joyce and Rolf Schefold specialize in unusual seasonal salads made with locally grown fruits, asparagus, and other intriguing ingredients. The entrees are equally exciting. The Confit of Rabbit Forestiere (marinated, roasted, wine-simmered rabbit) and the Chateaubriand Jardiniere for Two (choice tender-cut beef surrounded by vegetables and Bernaise sauce) are savory entree choices.

Whether patrons have a sweet tooth or not, they'll find it impossible to resist Rolf's delectible dessert tray selections, such as the custard pies with caramel sauce, apple strudel with vanilla sauce, black walnut pies, fresh fruit salads and chocolate cream pie.

Located on Main Street just five minutes south of the Falls, Rolf's specializes in unpretentious gourmet dining. This exquisitely furnished restaurant was designed with romance in mind. The tables are candle-lit, the wallpaper is a delicate blue floral print, and the overall decor is exotically European. With its meticulously prepared cuisine, friendly service, and intimate decor, Rolf's is unquestionably a "Best Choice" along the Great Lakes.

tours

NIAGARA HELICOPTERS
3731 Victoria Avenue
Niagara Falls, Ontario, L2E 6V5
Tel: (416) 357-5672
Hrs: 9:00 am - Sunset (weather permitting)
Visa, MasterCard, American Express, Diners Club and Carte Blanche are accepted.

Niagara Helicopters has earned the reputation as one of Niagara Falls' most exciting attractions. A French tourist once stated: "Going to Niagara Falls without taking a helicopter ride is like going to Paris without seeing the Eiffel Tower."

Owned by Ruedi Hafen and Ev McTaggart, Niagara Helicopters has provided a thrilling experience and bird's-eye view of the Falls since 1961.

The flight is eight minutes long, and the aircraft flies at 1600 feet above the Great Lakes. Views of the whirlpool, rapids, Rainbow Bridge, Victoria Park, Horseshoe Falls, and American Falls are seen from an angle which can only be described as breathtaking.

Passenger helicopters include two four-passenger Jet Rangers, one six-passenger Long Ranger, and a twin Engine Bell 412 which carries 14 passengers. Each machine is meticulously maintained by Niagara Helicopters two full-time engineers, and meets ultimate safety specifications, regulated by the chief pilot and the government regulatory body, Transport Canada.

Wheelchair access, taped commentaries in English and French, family and group rates, a snack bar, and special services offered by Niagara Helicopters make flights enjoyable for everyone.

A gift ship that is open to the public carries many helicopter and Niagara Falls-related souvenirs, T-shirts, sweatshirts, tank tops, gym bags, postcards, film, and disposable Kodak cameras. Many of these items carry the slogan: "I went over the Falls with Niagara Helicopters".

A trip to Niagara Falls could not be complete without an over-the-Falls ride on Niagara Helicopters.

wine

BRIGHT'S WINES
4487 Dorchester Road
Niagara Falls, Ontario L2E 6V4
Tel: (416) 357-2400
Hrs: Open year-round, Monday - Saturday
Call for times.

Bright's Winery, one of the oldest wineries in North America, was founded by Thomas G. Bright and Francis Sherriff in 1874. In 1890 it was decided that it would be best to have the plant and wine cellars at the same location as the grapes, so a small winery with a 50,000 gallon capacity was erected.

The winery specialized only in dessert wines at first but it experienced rapid growth during the Prohibition era as wine was the only legal alcoholic beverage available in Ontario. By 1933 the winery had expanded to a wine storage capacity of four million gallons; this growth pattern has continued to its present capacity of nine million gallons.

Bright's Winery underwent major changes when it was purchased by Harry C. Hatch in 1933. He managed to improve the quality of Ontario wines by first improving the quality of the grape used to produce it. The vinicultural research program he launched completely transformed the entire wine industry of Canada. Today, the 50 vinifera and vinifera hybrids that they managed to grow successfully are producing excellent world class wines. These incredible wines have been recognized over 200 times with awards in major international competitions coming from as far away as Athens, Greece.

Visitors to Niagara Falls can share in the excitement of the wine-making process through a tour of Bright's Winery; a trip through the century-old wine cellars is just as important as seeing the modern fermentation cellar and high-speed bottling lines. The tour ends with a stop at the Winewood hospitality room where visitors may taste a sampling of products. Afterwards, one may make a purchase in the winery's retail store. Such items as table, dessert, and sparkling wines, Canadian champagnes, coolers, and ciders are available.

A stop at Bright's Winery proves to be educational as well as fun. This winery offers a "Best Choice" for wines of "Quality--Yesterday, Today, and Tomorrow."

NIAGARA-ON-THE-LAKE

attractions

Constructed by the British between 1797 and 1799, **Fort George** replaced Fort Niagara as the principal British post on the Niagara Frontier. Reconstructed in 1939, the site contains barracks, officer's quarters and other buildings.

The **Niagara Historical Society Museum** contains over 20,000 artifacts from the United Empire Loyalists, the War of 1812 and the Victorian Age.

The 40 foot diameter working **Floral Clock** is replanted every spring.

The **Brock's Monument National Historic Site** is located in Queenston Heights Park. A walking tour of this decisive War of 1812 battlefield is marked by plaques. The park contains children's play areas, picnic areas, tennis courts, and a bandshell where Sunday afternoon concerts are held in the summer.

The **Niagara River Recreational Trail** starts at Fort George and ends on Anger Avenue in Fort Erie, 35 miles away. It is an ideal trail for walking, jogging or biking.

The **Shaw Festival** offers professional theatre on three stages--the Festival Theatre, the Court House and the Royal George--from April through October.

accommodations

GATE HOUSE HOTEL & RISTORANTE GIARDINO
142 Queen Street
Niagara-on-the-Lake, Ontario LOS 1JO
Tel: (416) 468-3263
Hrs: Lunch: Noon - 2:30 p.m.
Dinner: 5:30 p.m.- 10:00 p.m. (may vary seasonally)
Closed January & February.
Visa, MasterCard and American Express are accepted.

Ferruccio and Ilse Dallavalle are the new owners of the Gate House Hotel and this Italian couple is responsible for taking what was once an imitation of eras gone by and transforming it into an authentic and very contemporary European-style restaurant and hotel. Ristorante Giardino, now one of the most beautiful yet simple dining spots in Ontario, serves the most exquisite Italian food and the Gate House Hotel is providing luxurious accommodations for travelers who prefer elegant surroundings.

The opulent look and feel of the building was accomplished through 18 months of careful construction and remodeling and the work of an interior designer. The front of the Giardino is a broad expanse of large windows which provide alot of light in the dining room. The lobby is a mix of grey tiles, black leather chairs, and glass and brass with stained glass accents. Inside the dining room the eye is pleased to see clean geometric lines of black, white and grey. The decor is pure Italian. White marble on the lobby desk was imported from Verona, Italy and much of the furniture was imported also.

The Gate House Hotel & Ristorante Giardino is the perfect setting for the huge colorful Canadian artworks that dominate the rooms. It is also the perfect setting for the sumptuous Italian foods served here. Chefs from Italy prepare dishes like Scampi Rosa in Salsa Tartufata (sauteed prawns with truffle cream sauce) and Gnocchi Di Ricotta in Salsa Di Funghi Ostrica (Ricotta cheese gnocchi with oyster mushroom cream sauce).

In the true Italian fashion, all ingredients are fresh, meats are butchered on the premises, and foods are grilled rather than fried. The quality of their desserts is unrivaled. The Gate House Hotel & Ristorante Giardino are a "Best Choice" for those after "Discreet Indulgence."

MOFFAT INN
60 Picton Street
Niagara-on-the-Lake, Ontario LOS 1JO
Tel: (416) 468-4116
Hrs: Open 24 hours
Visa, MasterCard and American Express are accepted.

Jim and Vena Johnstone decided to try their hand at innkeeping after 15 years of successful dairy farming. They purchased what was originally Moffat's Hotel in the 1800s and expanded the 10 rooms to 22 rooms and opened as the Moffat Inn in 1983. Their trademark of cleanliness and the services they offer have earned them a five star rating from Tourism Ontario in the small hotel category for five years running.

Jim and Vena live upstairs and take a hands-on approach to innkeeping. All rooms are kept spotlessly clean. Some rooms offer a queen-size bed while others have two double beds. The rooms have been individually decorated and each has its own special features such as a fireplace, a balcony, or a sitting area. Most are done in a colonial style with green and white accents, but include modern features like a direct dial phone, a complete bath, color TV, individual air and heat, and a data phone set up for use with fax machines and computers. Most rooms are made cozy-looking with brass beds and wicker furnishings. The inn is located within walking distance of the Shaw Festival and it's no wonder that it is a favorite place to stay for the visiting critics and reviewers.

Guests of the hotel are pleased to find a restaurant, Coach & Horses, inside of the hotel. It provides casual dining for breakfast, lunch, afternoon tea, and dinner. It is the perfect gathering place for tired shoppers--the inn is in close proximity to Niagara-on-the-Lake shops and restaurants and is right across from scenic Simcoe Park. A conference room is also available for up to 25 people. Flip charts, projectors, audio-visual, and meeting supplies can be provided.

Jim and Vena are natives of Dumfries, Scotland (which coincidentally is very close to Moffat, Scotland), and they offer their own special style of hospitality. A stained glass window in the Coach and Horses reads Slainte Mhath, which means "good health" in Gallic, and this is their salute to all of their guests.

The Moffat Inn is a "Best Choice" for travelers because it offers modern conveniences to guests while retaining its old world charm. Its five star rating speaks for itself. Special Weekday, Weekend, and Winter Holiday Packages are available.

THE OBAN INN
160 Front Street
Niagara-on-the-Lake, Ontario L0S1J0
Restaurant Hrs: 7:30 a.m. - 8:30 p.m.
Visa, MasterCard, American Express, Diners Club and Carte Blanche are accepted.

The present owners of this marvelous inn are Gary and Sarah Burroughs and perhaps the most unique aspect of this remarkable establishment is its history. The Inn's original owner was Captain Duncan Malloy, who arrived in 1824 from Oban, Scotland, giving the Inn it's name. Situated ideally on the mouth of the Niagara river, it not only overlooks Lake Ontario but is also surrounded by lush scenery and lovely English-style gardens that flaunt Azaleas, Geraniums, Begonias, and nearly seventy varieties of roses.

Dining in the restaurant offers a pristine view of Lake Ontario. Show's Corner Piano Bar features a grand piano and photographs of famous guests who have frequented the Inn. With slogans like, "Where Canada Began" and "A peaceful oasis in a busy world", the staff is helpful but prefers to remain inconspicuous.

The guest rooms are distinctly decorated, retaining much of the 1824 character. Two dinner seatings occur nightly; a theater seating between 5:30 and 6:00 and one at 8:00. Offering traditional fare, the specialties of the house include fresh Poached Salmon, Prime Ribs of Beef, Lamb Rossella and Filet Mignon. Everything from soups to desserts are prepared from scratch and made of the highest quality ingredients.

The charm of the Oban Inn is the unique combination of Victorian style wallpaper, antiques and overall nostalgic essence. It depicts a subtle century old spirit that continues to this day, emphasizing good taste, pleasant memories and human experiences not easily forgotten.

THE PILLAR AND POST
King and John Streets
Niagara-on-the-Lake, Ontario LOS 1J0
Tel: (416) 468-2123
Hrs: Seven days 7:30 a.m. - 9:00 p.m.
Visa, MasterCard and American Express are accepted.

Built in the 1890s, The Pillar and Post was originally a cannery known as Factory 13. Today it "embodies the spirit and character of historic Niagara-on-the-Lake," as a combination inn, restaurant, lounge, and gift shop that has received a five-star rating from the Ontario Tourism Authority.

This "Outstanding Country Inn" offers rooms decorated to recreate a romantic bygone era. Hand-crafted pine furnishings, patchwork quilts, and woodburning fireplaces are all part of the special ambiance that warms the 90 distinctive rooms. Modern conveniences are available too--the rooms are equipped with TVs, mini bars or full bars (hidden in pine cabinets), four piece bath, foldaway beds, and jacuzzis. Other amenities include room service, a health facility, swimming pool, concierge, babysitting service, winter sleigh rides, and a restaurant.

Hospitality is an important tradition at The Pillar and Post and diners receive the same special attention as overnight guests. The menu is an intriguing selection of foods. One may choose to start with Almond Soup or a salad of avocado, snow peas, and fresh berries in a raspberry viniagrette before moving onto Main Fare such as Roast Prime Rib served with beef drippings and Yorkshire pudding, or Fillet of Atlantic Salmon. Dinners may be complemented with any one of a selection of desserts including pastries, tortes, flans, and ice creams that are made on the premises.

Colonel Butlers Tavern, a three-level lounge and piano bar, provides a chance to enjoy a cocktail while listening to soft music. Those who love to shop will be thrilled to discover the Arts and Handcraft Shop where the work of over 200 Canadian craftspeople and artists is available. Items such as quilts and calico fabrics, antiques, books, and children's toys are carried. After shopping, one can relax with afternoon tea; a selection of Green, Black, and Oolong teas are served in The Sun Room along with an assortment of finger sandwiches, homebaked scones, mini pastries, and cookies.

The Pillar and Post, "One of North America's Finest Inns," is close to the Historical Museum, Navy Hall, Fort George, and the Shaw Festival Theatre; a "Best Choice" for those wishing to "escape into the slower paced world of yesteryear."

PRINCE OF WALES HOTEL
6 Picton Street
Niagara-on-the-Lake, Ontario L0S 1J0
Tel: (416) 468-3246
Hrs: Summer:
Monday - Saturday 7:30 a.m.- 10:00 p.m.
Winter: 7:30 a.m. - 9:00 p.m.
Sunday Brunch: Noon - 2:30 p.m.
Visa, MasterCard and American Express are accepted.

The Prince of Wales Hotel, established in 1864, is a majestic 104 room hotel and recreational facility that offers guests attentive service, lavish lodging, connoisseur cuisine, complete convention and meeting facilities, and numerous leisure activities.

The Royals Victorian Dining Room offers the classic European luxury of elegant dinners, fine wine, and candlelit tables.

The Queen's Royal Lounge, with its beautiful view of Somcoe Park's flower gardens, is the perfect place to enjoy a light meal or a sparkling cocktail in a relaxed, but never-the-less elegant, atmosphere.

All will love the casual, intimate ambiance of the Three Feathers Cafe. It's a delightful place in which to sip afternoon tea or enjoy a luscious breakfast.

The rooms here are exquisite. The Main Hotel contains standard and deluxe rooms as well as beautifully appointed one-bedroom suites. These rooms offer gorgeous decor, complete with brass beds and floral chintzes.

The Prince of Wales Court, which is located on Picton Street next to the Main Hotel, has 28 large rooms decorated with beautiful French doors, balconies and bay windows.

The Hotel offers a comprehensive range of activities such as swimming in the heated indoor pool, lounging in the whirlpool and working out in a fully equipped gym. The gym offers fitness appraisals and individualized exercise programs, daily aerobics classes (except on Sundays), walking or jogging on the Health Club's special one, three and five kilometer routes, and dry saunas

The Hotel has an impressive guest list - the Duke and Duchess of York have stayed here as well as Jane Fonda, Hal Linden and Canada's Governor General.

The Prince of Wales Hotel offers several getaway packages for holiday, weekend, and winter stays.

The Hotel is close to the Shaw Festival Theatre, which features internationally acclaimed theatre, dance, and musical performances throughout the year. The Hotel is also within walking distance of many boutiques and intriguing shops.

To locate the Prince of Wales Hotel, exit Highway 55 at Niagara on the Lake; turn right onto Queen Street, and follow Queen Street to Picton Street. The treatment, as well as the beautiful rooms, lavish workout facilities and the exquisite dining room and lounge, make guests of the Prince of Wales Hotel feel like royalty.

art galleries

COBBLE-STONE GALLERIES
223 King Street
Box 607
Niagara-on-the-Lake, Ontario L0S 1J0
Tel: (416) 468-2097
Hrs: May - October:
Seven days 10:00 a.m. - 6:00 p.m.
Off Season: 10:00 a.m. - 5:00 p.m.
Visa and MasterCard are accepted.

Unlike most fine arts shops, Cobble-Stone Galleries' goals are various and unique. This gallery is concerned with promoting the awareness and education of its customers as well as presenting the finest in original, Canadian visual art. Cobble-Stone Galleries shows its concern with the promotion of lesser-known artists by carrying paintings and sculptures by new, unrecognized, artists. This exquisite gallery's collection consists of all original Canadian art, no photo-mechanical reproductions. Cobble-Stone is conveniently located in historic Niagara-Along-the-Lake, and its variety helps to make it the home of Canadian fine art.

Cobble-Stone's collection consists of oil paintings, watercolours, acrylics, etchings, and engravings as well as Native Indian stone and Inuit soapstone sculptures. Some examples are bronze and stone sculptures by Belanjer, black soapstone sculptures by Henry Ford, serpentine sculptures, cornhusk people by Kristy Platthy, dough people by Renate Prikopa, and paper mache clowns by Gisele Daigle. All of these one-of-a-kind pieces are for sale along with assorted ceramics and wood carvings perfectly suited for gifts.

The owner and curator of the Cobble-Stone Galleries is Mary Braun. Mary's long-time activity in the visual art field has helped her to assemble this unique collection, of which she is very proud. This small, intimate shoppe specializes in personal service and expertise. Cobble-Stone offers specialized services. Interested clients will be offered a presentation featuring the shoppe's current collection. If a customer selects one of the works, but is unsure of how it will look in his/her home, Cobble-Stone will deliver it to the client's home for a more personal viewing.

The staff is always happy to discuss the benefits of owning original artwork. Cobble-Stone's paintings and sculptures enhance the design of any home or office. Guests should keep in mind that original artwork holds its value and often appreciates monetarily. Because of Mary's commitment to new talent, Cobble-Stone Galleries is truly Niagara's home of fascinating Canadian fine art.

DOUG FORSYTHE GALLERY
85 Melville Street
Niagara-on-the-Lake, Ontario LOS 1J0
Tel.: (416) 483-3659
Hrs: Tuesday - Sunday 10:00 a.m. - 5:00 p.m.
Also by appointment
Closed Mondays.
Visa, MasterCard and personal checks are accepted.

Specializing in unusual intaglio collagraphic prints as well as intaglio monotypes, the Doug Forsythe Gallery creates original pieces for art galleries, frame shops, art consultants, interior designers, corporations, and individual collectors.

Doug and his wife, Marsha, were introduced to the intaglio printmaking process in their native province of Nova Scotia and began experimenting with their own variations of this medium.

Having extensive experience with watercolors and oil paints, Doug used his talents to enhance traditional monotype intaglio methods; he even built his own intaglio etching press.

The word "intaglio" refers to any of the following processes: engraving, etching, aquatint, soft ground, drypoint, lift ground, mezzotint, and collagraph.

An intaglio collagraph is a print made from a variety of materials which have been firmly glued to a base plate (hard board) to create various lines, textures and tones.

A monotype is an image (only one print) that's created directly on a plate, stone, wooden block, or screen.

The key words at Doug Forsythe's Gallery are freedom and spontaneity. The art that's created at this unique gallery ranges from delicate pastels to bold earthtones and may resemble oil paintings or watercolors--or these gorgeous originals may not look quite like anything ever seen before. The best part of visiting Doug Forsythe's Gallery is the artwork is completely original and wonderfully innovative.

Additional to browsing through Doug and Marsha's finished prints, visitors may enjoy the exhibits that have been created by the couples' daughter, Stephanie.

Guests can watch these internationally renowned artists design their prints, and are welcome to ask questions. The artists will be happy to explain this intriguing craft, step by step.

The Gallery's collections are featured by several well-known corporations, such as IBM, Amoco Canada Petroleum, Mazda, Pepsi Cola U.S.A, Holiday Inn, Tab Computers and Westinghouse Canada.

Located at Niagara-on-the-Lake Marina, about 20 minutes from the Falls, the Doug Forsythe Gallery is a perfect place to relax and browse through hundreds of lovely hand pulled intaglio prints.

PRESERVATION GALLERY
177 King Street
Niagara-on-the-Lake, Ontario LOS 1JO
Tel: (416) 468-4431
Hrs: Tuesday - Saturday 10:00 a.m. - 6:00 p.m.
Closed Sundays & Mondays.
Visa, MasterCard and personal checks are accepted.

A grand Victorian home built in 1867 houses one of Canada's finest art galleries, the Preservation Gallery. One of the most popular artists in Canada, Trish Romance, lived and worked in this house, but now uses it exclusively as a gallery for her exquisite paintings. The Preservation Gallery is gorgeous both inside and out, and its Victorian style compliments Trish's love for Victorian art. The quality and style of Trish Romance's paintings have helped to make the Preservation Gallery the home of some of Ontario's finest art.

There are several themes that seem to be consistent throughout Trish's paintings. One of these themes is family. One can easily feel the warmth and compassion exuding from a painting in which the source of inspiration was one of her three children. Trish's style has been described as representational (not photographic). This quality is most apparent in her paintings of winter scenes.

After graduating from Sheridan College, Trish spent two years traveling through Europe and capturing the sights and feelings in her work. Although the themes that dominate her work may not be the most popular, she refused to compromise her vision and style. It has been a lifelong dream of Trish's to have the chronicles of her life captured in her paintings. She puts a lot of herself into her paintings, and to ensure that each original painting receives the proper care and attention, each is sold by Trish or her husband, Gary Peterson, personally.

The Preservation Gallery is Ontario's best choice for the finest in original art and prints. This house's hand-carved fireplaces and Victorian style compliment Trish's love for Victorian art. Her paintings evoke emotions that are often overlooked or forgotten. The entire gallery is "kid-proofed", and it serves as a history lesson as well as a class in art appreciation.

duty free shops

PENINSULA DUTY FREE SHOPS
Queenston Lewiston Bridge
Queenston, Ontario L2E 6Z2
Tel: (416) 262-5363
Hrs: Open year round.
Seven days, 24 hours
Visa, MasterCard and American Express are accepted.

With a strategic location right on the border and a clever slogan: "Shopping that borders the fantastic", this impressive 3000 square foot store features a wide range of quality merchandise. Peninsula Duty Free Shops carry liquor and tobacco as well as virgin wool sweaters and jackets, leather goods, T-shirts, a huge selection of men's and women's fragrances, and various souvenirs. Fine china and crystal such as Swarovski, Lladro and Hummel can be found as well as savings up to 60% on premium quality merchandise.

Peninsula Duty Free Shops accept major credit cards, and both Canadian and U.S. currency. Their extra staff members accommodate tours and special merchandise packages. With a multilingual staff knowledgeable in tax and duty regulations, free coffee and restroom facilities, the operation is virtually complete. There is a large lobby area that is perfect for organizing large groups, and buses are welcome. The Queenston location overlooks the Niagara Gorge and offers a breathtaking view of the surrounding area.

Whether a resident of Canada, the United States or any other country, the staff at Peninsula Duty Free Shops will make sure shoppers receive great savings on top quality merchandise that make exquisite gifts for any occasion.

markets

HARVEST BARN COUNTRY MARKET
Highway 55 and East West Line
Niagara-on-the-Lake, Ontario L0S 1J0
Tel: (416) 468-3224
Hrs: March 23 - December 24:
Seven days 9:00 a.m. - 7:00 p.m.

The Harvest Barn Country Market, owned and operated by Doug Dineley, Kevin Baum, and Jeff Goodman, owes its success to carrying a comprehensive variety of premium quality fruit and vegetables and an outstanding in-store bakery. The Harvest Barn operates three separate markets: The Orchard Glen Farm Market located in the town of St. Davids, the newest location Harvest Barn Country Market located at 4th Avenue and 1st Street South in St. Catharines, and their main location Harvest Barn Country Market on Highway 55 and East West Line in Niagara-on-the-Lake.

All locations are set in lovely fruit orchards. The Harvest Barn Markets carry virtually all forms of fruits including the exotic varieties. An emphasis is placed on large displays of locally grown, in season fruits and vegetables. The Niagara Area is considered to contain some of the best farm lands found in all of North America. There is a complete in store bakery and salad bar in addition to a lovely selection of flowers, cuts, and in spring, a large variety of annual and perennial bedding plants. The fresh jams, jellies, and preserves are marvelous and locally made.

A wide selection of antiques, including a Model T Delivery Truck, help decorate the markets. The methods used in the storage and holding of the produce, along with the detail given to purchasing only quality produce, make these markets unsurpassed when it comes to quality. The process of quality control coupled with accuracy in usage reports provides these high volume markets with fresh produce daily. The rewards are obvious--"absolute freshness in available products." Visitors at the Harvest Barn or Orchard Glen Country Markets always leave satisfied.

resorts

QUEEN'S LANDING - THE INN AT NIAGARA ON THE LAKE
Melville & Byron Street
P.O. Box 1180
Niagara-on-the-Lake, Ontario LOS 1J0
Tel: (416) 468-2195
(416) 847-7666 (Toronto/Burlington direct)
Hrs: Seven days 8:00 a.m. - 9:00 p.m.
Pub: Open until 1:00 a.m.
Visa, MasterCard and American Express are accepted.

Queen's Landing offers quite a comprehensive range of resort facilities: the elegant restaurant overlooking the Niagara River with its uniquely inspired cuisine and gracious service, the 137-room Country Inn, with its Georgian decor, fireplaces, canopy beds, antiques, and whirlpools which provide guests with exceptionally lavish accommodations that are a perfect blend of past and present, the 18 banquet and conference rooms which provide comfortable, spacious party and meeting places, and the gift shop that serves as a showcase for the work of several local artists. Other amenities, such as the indoor swimming pool, fully equipped exercise room, and bike rentals service are equally exciting. This newly built inn employs an interesting concept: an enchanting sophistication that lends the Inn quite an enticing ambiance.

The Inn serves classic cuisine for breakfast, lunch, and dinner. The afternoon tea at Queen's Landing features an intriguing selection of fresh-baked pastries, scrumptious scones, fabulous finger sandwiches, unique coffees, and fine teas such as Black, Green, Oolong, White, Flower and Herb. The evening menu offers a variety of exotic desserts.

The cuisine and hospitality are wonderful, as is the view. The guest rooms have a wonderful view overlooking Niagara River and Lake Ontario, the marina, the park that surrounds Old Fort George, and the Shaw Festival Theater, or historic Niagara-on-the-Lake. Because the area's pristine beauty is best viewed on the 35-mile cycling trails that run from Niagara-on-the-Lake to Fort Erie, an extended stay may be needed for a scenic bike ride.

Queen's Landing Country Inn is the perfect relaxation escape. The inn is less than an hour from Buffalo and is situated in its own world of warm hospitality and scenic seclusion.

restaurants

PLAIN & FANCY
Prudhomme Boulevard
Vineland Station, Ontario LOR 2EO
Tel: (416) 562-7244
Hrs: Wednesday - Friday 4:00 p.m. - 10:30 p.m.
Saturday - Sunday Noon - 10:30 p.m.
Visa, MasterCard, American Express and Diners Club are accepted.

Plain & Fancy, a family-owned restaurant dedicated to serving family-style meals, makes customers feel at home through its special style of service and the quality of food offered. A Pennsylvania Dutch ambiance is imparted through the natural rustic decor. The 1867 structure retains much of its original brick work and hewn beams. Simple place settings, huge open fireplaces, and a panoramic lake view can be enjoyed from farmhouse-style wooden chairs.

One can be assured of the goodness of the menu offered at Plain & Fancy; meals are prepared the old-fashioned way using fresh ingredients and few or no preservatives. The country-style chicken is prepared by a patented process unique to this restaurant, ensuring low cholesterol levels. Only the healthiest cuts of beef, imported from around the world, go into the dishes. Lighter appetites can enjoy chicken wings, breaded mushrooms, or a Caesar salad with chicken, ham, or tuna. One really should not miss the special treat of having dinner here.

Supper is a time for family unity and one will feel the comfort of Grandma's kitchen here with never-ending helpings of delicious, wholesome foods being served by a friendly staff specifically selected for their kindness and courteousness. The meal begins with a hearty homemade soup and fresh baked breads. Guests ladle their own soups and share portions by passing dishes around the table and the servers quickly replace empty plates with full ones. Guests are encouraged to take their time to fully enjoy the time spent with one another. A complete selection of local and international beers and wines are available along with Billy Miner ice cream, assorted cakes, and homemade pies for dessert.

For uncompromising quality of food and service and very reasonable prices, Plain & Fancy is a "Best Choice." The warm and relaxing dining experience provided is sure to be a treasured family memory.

specialty shops

IRISH DESIGNS
38 Queen Street
Niagara-on-the-Lake, Ontario L0S 1J0
Tel: (416) 468-5254
Hrs: November - May:
Seven days 10:00 a.m. - 5:30 p.m.
May - October: 9:30 a.m. - 8:30 p.m.
Visa, MasterCard, American Express and Diners Club are accepted.

Irish Designs, a store dealing in original Irish merchandise, has real Emerald Isle flair. Its owners, Paul and Maureen Dickson, owned a shoe store and a hair salon, respectively, on the northern coast of Ireland prior to opening Irish Designs in November of 1987.

The store is fully stocked with a wide variety of Irish merchandise. Everything from wool coats, scarves, and hats to a large selection of Irish music, address books, and books of humor can be found at the store. They specialize in fashion knitwear and Grandfather shirts, the traditional shirt of rural Ireland, which is also the store's most popular item.

Selections from "Avoca" handweavers (the oldest company of its kind in Ireland), the Fisherman's knit cardigan, Heritage knitwear and Leonora shawls are only several of the popular brandnames carried at Irish Designs.

Most apparel is unisex and offers warmth, comfort, and durability. The store also sells Irish perfume, soap and jewelry such as the famous Claddagh ring and Celtic cross.

Irish Designs is a store with a wide variety of merchandise to please different tastes and styles. The Dicksons are proud of the unique quality, selection, and value of the items they sell. They offer personal service in a friendly environment and are willing to ship their goods throughout the world to meet the needs of customers who cannot frequent the Niagara-on-the-Lake store.

For that special Irish item, try Irish Designs in the heart of Niagara-on-the-Lake, 20 minutes from Niagara Falls.

JUST CHRISTMAS
34 Queen Street
Niagara-on-the-Lake, Ontario 10S 1J0
Tel: (416) 468-4500
Hrs: Open seven days, year-round.
May 1 - October 15: 10:00 a.m. - 8:00 p.m.
October 15 -January 1: 10:00 a.m. - 6:00 p.m.
January 1 - May 1: 11:00 a.m. - 5:00 p.m.
Visa, MasterCard and American Express are accepted.

Just Christmas features thousands of festive items to brighten the Christmas season. This custom Christmas shop offers over 10,000 different ornaments in a myriad of styles--Victorian, Romantic, Southwestern, Baroque, 50s style, glass, country , musical, and silver. Just Christmas will also personalize holiday ornaments.

Other Christmas merchandise includes custom designed wreaths, specially decorated trees, finely detailed music boxes, Fontanini nativity sets, English table crackers, Dickens' Village Heritage Collectables, and decorative lights. Browse through rows of colorful garland, greeting cards, holiday candles, trees, party supplies, stockings, tree skirts, and animated Christmas figurines. Just Christmas stocks a myriad of great stocking stuffers, too.

If it can't be found at Just Christmas it probably doesn't exist. Owners Ron and Kay Woodfire stock a huge selection of quality merchandise and offer the friendliest service around. That's why Just Christmas is just as popular in July as it is in December. Since it opened in 1985, Just Christmas has been so popular that each year the owners have added another room to display an even larger selection of magical Christmas merchandise.

As an added bonus to customers, Just Christmas will ship gifts anywhere in the world. Just Christmas, located next to the Historic Niagara-on-the-Lake Courthouse, is only 90 minutes from Toronto, 15 minutes from the Queenston-Lewiston Bridge and a few minutes from the Shaw Festival and several fine hotels.

Relive the joys and nostalgia of past Christmas seasons while stocking up on gorgeous gifts and decorations to make this Christmas the most special one ever.

NIAGARA FUDGE CORPORATION - "THE FUDGE SHOP"
29 Queen Street
Niagara-on-the-Lake, Ontario L0S 1J0
Hrs: Seven days 10:00 a.m. - 5:00 p.m.
Summer: 9:00 a.m. - 6:00 p.m.

Henry and Pat Sapielak, both natives of Niagara-on-the-Lake, purchased the Niagara Fudge Corporation-"The Fudge Shop" in 1979. "The Fudge Shop" has been serving fudge of all varieties to people from all over the world since 1969. Located in historic Niagara-on-the-Lake, by the clock tower, this tiny 480-square-foot shop holds a lot of fudge per square inch. The front third of this turn-of-the-century building serves as a retail store while the remaining two-thirds is where Henry creates the 35 different varieties of fudge on a five foot by three foot by three inch marble slab.

"The Fudge Shop" turns out incredible fudge, including traditional chocolate fudge, chocolate mint, maple almond, cherry vanilla, chocolate almond, rocky road, pina colada, Bailey's Irish Special, chocolate ginger, butterscotch and eggnog with walnut. There are no preparatives or additives and according to Henry, the key to making his great tasting fudge is using the finest ingredients, timing, temperature control, and the "magic" marble slab. "The Fudge Shop" has been featured in magazines all over the world, and although they don't know how it came about, a Japanese television station did a spot on "The Fudge Shop."

Fudge treats are available in variety boxes, gift baskets, brandy snifters and beer steins. "The Fudge Shop" also carries peanut brittle, cashew brittle, almond brittle and mixed nut brittle. A variety of interesting gift items can be found at "The Fudge Shop," including imported liqueur chocolates and Northern Ontario maple syrup. A gift wrapping service is also provided

Henry and Pat are most proud of the shop's reputation and of the customers from all around the world who order regularly and faithfully. The fun of watching Henry make their delicious treats and the obvious joy of tasting the finished product make the Niagara Fudge Corporation - "The Fudge Shop" a definite "Best Choice" along the lakes.

QUEENSTON POTTERY
1648 York Road (Highway 81)
Queenston, Ontario L0S 1J0
Tel: (416) 262-4196
Hrs: Monday - Saturday 11:00 a.m. - 5:00 p.m.
Sunday Noon - 5:00 p.m.
Visa and MasterCard are accepted.

Since 1970, Frank and Eva Mlcak, owners of Queenston Pottery, have been creating an unusual array of functional and decorative stoneware and pottery.

In their unique pottery studio, Frank and Eva employ traditional methods to hand-shape natural clays into beautiful canisters, plates, vases, casseroles, mugs, ornamental plaques, tiles, jugs, and custom-designed pieces.

The pottery varies in texture and pattern, but there's one thing that is perfectly consistent about all of their hand-crafted pottery: each piece has an unmistakable European flair.--That's because Frank and Eva draw much of their artistic inspiration from European folk tradition.

Customers can browse through the Queenston Pottery Studio as Frank and Eva create their lovely pieces. After the works are hand-molded, the pottery is fired in a large kiln that is oil-heated to 2400 degrees Fahrenheit. This process makes the clay chip-resistent and dishwasher-safe. The oil-firing process also enables the Mlcaks to achieve a variety of lovely colors from matte autumn to glossy pastel shades.

The Mlcaks enjoy creating new glazes, many of which are produced from Niagara riverbank red slate and resemble the oriental glazes that were perfected by Chinese artists more than two thousand years ago. All of the glazes used at Queenston Pottery are lead and cadmium-free and are perfectly safe for use in food preparation, serving and storage.

In addition to being safe, these beautiful pottery and stoneware pieces are wonderful for use in microwaves and dishwashers. The casseroles, baking dishes, and ovenware are made to resist thermal shock, so they can go from oven to refrigerator.

The pieces are hand-painted and designed to appeal to a variety of personal tastes, but the best part about owning a Queenston Pottery piece is that each item is distinctive and one-of-a-kind.

In the summer, Frank and Eva open their outdoor gallery on the weekends so that visitors can enjoy the entire pottery-making process amid the beautiful Japanese-style gardens.

Conveniently located between Niagara Falls and Niagara-on-the-Lake, Queenston Pottery offers southern Ontario's largest selection of hand-made pottery.

tours

NIAGARA RIVER CRUISES ABOARD "THE SENATOR"
The Niagara Riverboat Company Limited
Olde Boatworks, Ricardo Street
Box 875
Niagara-on-the-Lake, Ontario L0S 1J0
Tel: (416) 468-4291
Hrs: May - October:
Cruises Seven Days:
Noon, 1:30 p.m., 3:00 p.m., & and 4:30 p.m.
Pre-Theatre Dinner Cruises: Thursday, Friday & Saturday
Captains' Table Dinner/Dance: Wednesday
Moonlight Cruise: Thursday
Sunday Champagne Brunch: 11:00 a.m., 1:00 p.m.
Visa, MasterCard and American Express are accepted.

There's no better way to see historical Niagara-on-the-Lake than aboard the richly decorated SENATOR. This magnificent tour ship carries 130 passengers down the Niagara River past stately mansions, tree-lined streets, charming inns, and colorful countryside. The tour to Queenston points out Fort George and Fort Niagara as well as several other area attractions along the Canadian and American Niagara Escarpment.

This extravagantly decorated ship owes its Edwardian elegance to its arched mahogany windows and mirrors, gleaming brass railings, comfortably-cushioned chairs, carpeting walk-around main deck, and canopied sun deck. This 72-foot excursion ship provides food service, sparkling clean washrooms, built-in sound system, and is licensed under the Liquor License Board of Ontario.

In addition to offering one-and-a-half-hour sightseeing tours, the Senator provides a Sunday Champagne Brunch, Moonlight Cruise, Dinner/Dances, and also Luncheon Cruises. Pre-Theatre Dinner Cruises are held on board before the internationally respected Shaw Festival. (Don't worry, there's plenty of time to make the curtain call after the cruise). This Coast Guard-approved vessel may be reserved for parties, weddings, and receptions.

The Senator casts off daily from its dock at The Olde Boatworks. The Niagara Riverboat Company offers such a variety of cruises that a Niagara River excursion can be anything from an intriguing tour through old-world charm to a romantic moonlit cruise; but no matter which cruise is chosen, it's sure to be unforgettable.

wine

HILLEBRAND ESTATES
Highway 55 & Virgil
Niagara-on-the-Lake, Ontario L0S 1J0
Tel: (416) 468-7123
Hrs: Store:
Monday - Saturday
10:00 a.m. - 6:00 p.m.
Tours:
Monday - Friday
11:00 a.m., 1:00 p.m., 3:00 p.m. & 4:30 p.m.
Saturday - Sunday
11:00 a.m., 1:00 p.m., 2:00 p.m., 3:00 p.m. & 4:30 p.m.

Niagara-on-the-Lake's Hillebrand Estates Winery is Canada's top producer of varietal wines. Hillebrand Wines has won 41 International Wine Competition Medals, the most awards of any wine producer in the country. Hillebrand was the first Canadian winery to receive a Canada Award for Business Excellence. Hillebrand supplies embassies and consulates around the world with vintage wines and also exports wine to the United States, Japan, Germany, Austria, and Norway.

The winery has been in Niagara for only six years, but its winemaking heritage goes back 250 years. Hillebrand's European winemaking tradition originated with Hillebrand's sister companies Scholl and Hillebrand in Germany's Rhine Region and Schlumberger in Vienna, Austria. Hillebrand combines this traditional winemaking expertise with their state-of-the-art equipment to create world class wines.

Hillebrand Estates is located in the Niagara Peninsula where the micro-climate is similar to that of Alsace and Burgundy in France and the Rhine.

The winery's award winning wines include Reisling, Chardonnay, Vidal, Gamay Noir, Pinot Noir, Gewurtraminer, Baco Noir, and Marechal Foch. The winery offers gift packages, souvenirs, and other wine related accessories such as wine racks, books, and elegant wine glasses. Hillebrand Estates Winery also provides custom labeling, gift certificates, and extensive party services.

Experience the tradition of great wine making and visit Hillebrand Estates Winery. It's "the Niagara-on-the-Lake winery with two centuries of old world ancestry."

INNSKILLIN WINES
Service Road 66 at the Niagara Parkway
Niagara-on-the-Lake, Ontario L0S 1J0
Tel: (416) 468-3554
Hrs: May - October:
Monday - Saturday 10:00 a.m. - 6:00 p.m.
November - April:
Monday - Saturda: 10:00 a.m. - 5:00 p.m.
Large groups please call ahead.

Nestled among rolling fields of grape vines in the Niagara fruitlands, the outstanding Inniskillin Winery combines tradition with modern technology to achieve superb-quality table wines.

Ontario's first cottage winery, Inniskillin uses predominantly classic European vinifera such as Chardonnay, Gamay Beaujolais, and Reisling -- all carefully selected for adaptability to the Niagara climate.

For three consecutive years, the winery's 1984, 1985, and 1986 Ice Wines each earned Gold Medals at the Intervin Wine Competition. These three awards earned Inniskillin the coveted Diamond Award, the highest award ever received by a Canadian winery. Most people thought that the region was incapable of producing top-quality wines but the folks at Inniskillin believed otherwise, and the excellent reputation of the winery has grown so much that owners Don Ziraldo and Karl Kaiser have opened wine-tasting boutiques in Toronto and Ottawa.

Inniskillin offers tours through the wine tasting boutique, vineyards, winery, barrel-aging cellar, and champagne loft. The winery and its grounds are very scenic. This picturesque setting would make a perfect setting for a breathtaking walk.

Inniskillin Winery has introduced Canadian wines to the International wine market and has been visited by many famous international guests.

Come and visit Inniskillin, and try its exquisite dessert wines, table wines, and sparkling wines. Don and Karl say that Inniskillin is not so much bound by tradition as it is inspired by it.

Located on the Niagara Parkway, just 15 minutes from the Falls, this superb winery with all of its exciting features is a definite "Best Choice" along the Great Lakes.

REIF WINERY
R R #1 Niagara Parkway
Niagara on the Lake, Ontario L0S 1JO
Tel: (416) 468-7738
Public Tours:
June - September (Saturday only)
1:30 p.m., 3:00p.m. & 4:30p.m.
Reservations for group tours year-round.

As wine continues its popularity surge into the '90s, so will this popular winery, as it maintains a noteworthy status in the limelight. Owned by Klaus Reif, the Reif Winery has prospered for 13 generations. Klaus actually took over the wine making task, formerly performed by his Uncle,

Ewald Reif. Klaus is a graduate of the German Wine Academy at Geisenheim, and at the age of 24, he received the title of enologist.

It has been said that " a dinner without Reif wine is like a day without sunshine". With 21 different products, all wines are made from grapes grown and cultivated by Ewald Reif in a unique micro climate located on the river and just two miles from the lake. This minor temperature difference allows for a later harvest, ultimately producing a richer wine. Only 50 percent of the 100 acres of grapes are selected for wines; the rest are sold off. With the introduction of superior quality grapes to the area, this region is beginning to ring with a world class reputation. Although some of the wines reveal a subtle German heritage, they most certainly depict a Canadian spirit and the ambiance of Ontario.

The Reif Winery is proud to produce several selections that have won gold, silver and bronze awards. Winners include Vidal Eiswein (made by pressing the frozen grapes during the first frost of winter), Gewurztraminer, Vidal and Riesling Dry, Kerner, Seyval Blanc, and Chardonnay. The Reif Winery is non-commercial and charming with traditional oak casks and a genuine caring for its product.

WELLAND

attractions

A walking tour of Downtown Welland will allow visitors to view 15 giant murals painted on the city's buildings. Tour maps are available at information centres.

The **Welland Historical Museum** features the history of Welland and its canals through permanent exhibits. The museum also has a children's gallery and temporary exhibits.

Niagara's oldest **Farmer's Market** has been enlarged and heritage-designated. Locally grown fresh fruits, vegetables and meat products are sold Tuesdays, Thursdays and Saturdays year-round.

The Recreational Waterway, once a section of the canal, is now used by pleasure crafts. Parklands along the banks offer boat launches, picnic areas, walking and jogging trails.

The Welland Pirates, a Class A farm team for the Pittsburgh Pirates, play ball in the new **Sports Complex and Amphitheatre** from mid-June to Labor Day.

events

The **Winter Carnival** is held in late January through early February. A variety of winter activities and games are held along with pancake breakfasts and dances.

Welland celebrates its title of Rose City with a 16-day **Rose Festival**. A rose-growing competition, art shows, ethnic food and other events, conclude with a **Rose Parade** on the last day.

The **Folklore Festival** pays tribute to Welland's ethnic communities in late August.

points of interest

WELLAND'S GIANT MURALS
Welland, Ontario, L3C 5Z4
Tel: (416) 788-3000

More than 24 very large permanent outdoor wall murals in Welland, Ontario, have provided a bright and colorful start to what may soon be the world's largest outdoor art gallery. Common brick and mortar have slowly given way to stunningly inventive works of art which are huge in size, long on nostalgia, and deep in artistic talent.

Each mural portrays a unique and intricate slice of Welland's rich and colorful history--the building of the famed Welland Canal, three generations of a farm family, a schoolmarm and her pupils--Welland's open air art show depicts the hearty heritage of a settlement with character and color.

During the summer months, artists from across Canada can be seen working on scaffolding, palette knives and brushes in hand, as new murals are added to this incredible permanent collection.

Located in the heart of the Niagara Peninsula, just 20 minutes from Niagara Falls and St. Catharines via highway 406, Welland welcomes you to share its heritage by visually exploring these unique, educational and cultural treasures.

In the Niagara Region, official mural tour maps are available at the Ontario Travel Centers. Maps are also available in Welland at the Chamber of Commerce at 32 East Main Street and at many local stores and businesses.

The outdoor murals can be enjoyed 12 months of the year and it's absolutely free. One can walk or drive the city streets and marvel at the colorful paintings, larger than life but depicting real life.

PORT COLBORNE

attractions

The **Port Colborne Historical and Marine Museum** is a seven-building complex of historical importance. The main building contains displays of canal history. Other buildings on the site include a log schoolhouse and house, and a blacksmith shop.

Fountainview Park offers an elevated observation deck offering visitors a view of Lock 8, one of the world's longest locks. Also in the park are picnic areas, flower gardens, and visitor information.

events

International Week is held in mid-July with a parade and ethnic picnic at Lakeview Park.

Canal Days celebrate Port Colborne's marine heritage in early August at the Historical and Marine Museum.

apparel

BRIDGEPORT REFLECTIONS
246 Killaly Street West
Port Colborne, Ontario L3K 6A6
Tel: (416) 834-5456

Hrs:	Monday - Thursday	10:00 a.m. - 5:00 p.m.
	Friday	10:00 a.m. - 8:00 p.m.
	Saturday	10:00 a.m. - 5:00 p.m.
	Christmas:	
	Monday - Friday	10:00 a.m. - 8:00 p.m.
	Saturday	10:00 a.m. - 5:00 p.m.

Visa and MasterCard are accepted.

Bridgeport Reflections is the place to visit when searching for quality children's clothing and fashionable accessories. This extraordinary shop also carries stylish clothing for young adults.

Owner Dianne Sandelli offers unique outfits by such top-name designers as Ralph Lauren, Esprit, Good Lad, Kid Buffalo, Jean Bourget, Mexx, Fracoise Bouthillier, Ma Divine Clementine, and Danjean.

Dianne selects only the best lines of clothing for her shop. Much of her top-quality merchandise is imported from France and Spain but she also carries several locally-made lines of fine apparel.

Bridgeport Reflections has an enormous assortment of mix and match outfits, unisex outfits, polo shirts, sweaters, sweat shirts, quilted pants, fancy dresses and classic suits. This delightful boutique also carries a unique selection of fashion accessories, such as bows, earrings, shoes, purses, backpacks, underwear and booties. Toys and art supplies are also available. The shop provides additional services such as gift wrapping, fashion shows, free catalogues and convenient layaway plans.

Its eye-catching window displays, an unique children's play area surrounded by a white picket fence, and huge selection of first-rate merchandise make Bridgeport Reflections a children's clothing store that parents won't want to miss. The clothes are durable, versatile and--best of all-- washable. Try Bridgeport Reflections. The staff is more than courteous. They always go out of their way to insure that a child is perfectly outfitted in fashionable designs and durable clothes.

Bridgeport Reflections is located in the new Portal Village Market, just 15 minutes from the Peace Bridge.

campgrounds

SHERKSTON SHORES
Empire Road (P.O. Box 50)
Sherkston, Ontario, L0S 1R0
Tel: (416) 894-0972
Hrs: May 1 - October 31:
Beaches open 8:00 a.m. - 8:00 p.m.
Visa, MasterCard and American Express are accepted.

The site of Sherkston Shores was once an active stone quarry until workers struck an underground spring, filling the quarry with water overnight. From that time until 1988, Sherkston has been known as a hotspot for young adults in search of a wild weekend. In 1988, the Bourne Leisure Group of England purchased the spot and transformed it into a beautiful family resort.

Situated on two and a quarter acres of natural Lake Erie beachfront is the 500 acres of majestic unspoiled woodlands. On that beach, incidentally, the largest sand sculpture in Canada was fashioned by a prominent sculpture company. Lake Erie and the famous spring-fed quarry provide the means for many popular activities. The list includes boating, windsurfing, sailing, excellent swimming, and other watersports of all kinds .

For the accommodation of both short-term and long-term campers, 5,200 campsites are available; summer residents may rent or buy a trailer directly through the park. The barbecues and hayrides complement a list of activities and characteristics that provide a friendly, family environment.

The next five years hold an expenditure of $20 million for the new owners, an effort that shows their desire to provide the best for their customers. As part of that conquest they have already moved a 90 year-old church to Sherkston Shores from nearby Port Colborne. The purpose of such an undertaking is to provide a church for both the campers and local community, hopefully bringing the two together. The facility is available for weddings, baptisms, worship services, education, and special occasions.

Whether it's the natural beachfront splendor or the numerous water activities, Sherkston Shores has something for everyone.

restaurants

STONEBRIDGE ISLAND HOUSE
27 Main Street West
Port Colborne, Ontario, L3K 3T8
Tel: (416) 834-0267

Hrs:	Monday - Thursday	Until 11:00 p.m.
	Friday - Saturday	Until midnight
	Sunday	Until 10:00 p.m.
	Brunch:	11:30 a.m. - 3:00 p.m.

Visa, MasterCard and American Express are accepted.

In 1984, Rob Finnegan sat for hours with his wife, Diana, by the Welland Canal and envisioned the renovation of a 75 year old Port Colborne home into a handsome, sophisticated canal-side restaurant.

His dream became a reality in 1985 with the creation of Stonebridge Island House. Today, Finnegan combines first-class food, hometown service, and local prices in a very relaxing atmosphere. The dining room comfortably seats 60, or there is the option of dining outdoors on the patio.

The menu is complete with regional and continental cuisine including steaks, pasta, veal, chicken, seafood, hot and cold appetizers, and assorted desserts. It's a unique mouth-watering selection with Gravelly Bay Gumbo Soup, Pate Maison, Island House Escargots, rack of lamb, chocolate amaretto cheesecake, and much more. The food is prepared by Chef Alphonse Van Derpoll. Together Rob and Alphonse are setting the pace in upscale eating satisfaction.

After dinner, the evening does not necessarily have to end. Customers can take a walk along the canal before having some specialty coffee on the veranda. Watching the ships slide by less than 100 yards away is just another feature to add to the enjoyable evening.

Special events are also a normal occurrence such as weddings, anniversaries, business meetings, theme dinners and weekend jazz entertainment.

For that "unbeatable evening," combining first-class food and relaxing atmosphere, it's "Niagara Region's Finest Canal-Side Dining," the Stonebridge Island House.

ST. CATHARINES

attractions

Port Dalhousie was once a canal district that is now home to gift shops, restaurants and boutiques. Historic attractions in the area include a rare octagonal lighthouse and a reconstructed wooden lock.

St. Catharines Historical Museum emphasizes Welland Canal memorabilia and exhibits with other displays of pioneer life, military and firefighting artifacts.

Rodman Hall Arts Centre offers monthly exhibitions, a series of concerts, films and lectures. Built by Thomas Rodman Merritt in 1853, the building is surrounded by eight acres of landscaped grounds and rock gardens.

The Happy Ralph Bird Sanctuary and Children's Farm is located along the shore of Lake Ontario. The petting farm is open during the summer months and the nature trail leads to lakeside benches, picnic areas and a playground.

Lakeside Park contains one of the oldest carousels in North America. Children of all ages can still ride for a nickel.

The Merritt Trail is a network of biking, walking and hiking trails that follow former canal routes and historical attractions. The trail starts in Port Dalhousie and ends in Port Colborne.

The Fortune Navigation Company offers cruises on the Welland Canal from Port Dalhousie to Port Weller. Departures are made at least twice a day between mid-May and mid-October.

events

The **Soap Box Derby** is held on June 17. The winner represents Canada at the All-American races held in Akron, Ohio.

The largest yearly festival is the **Niagara Grape and Wine Festival** held in late September. The 10-day festival has over 200 events including wine tasting, bicycle and running races, grape stomping, a craft show and two parades.

accommodations

HOWARD JOHNSON HOTEL, ST. CATHARINES
89 Meadowvale Drive
St. Catharines, Ontario, L2N 3Z8
Tel: (416) 934-5400
1-800-654-2000
Visa, MasterCard, American Express, Diners Club, JCB, En Route and Carte Blanche are accepted.

The St. Catharines Howard Johnson Hotel, considered the "Hospitality Centre of the Niagara Region," has so much more to offer visitors than just a room. Popular with tourists since its opening in 1973, the hotel has recently undergone a $2.7 million remodeling project that upgraded the existing structure.

The facility now includes a fitness area with an enclosed pool, a 24-hour Perkins Family Restaurant, and banquet and meeting room facilities that will accommodate over 200 people. Renovations to the bedrooms, lounge, and all other public areas, have left them even more comfortable and welcoming. The landscape was modified as well, achieving a harmonious environment around the hotel.

Business travelers have access to Fax and copy machines and audio visual equipment for meetings and conferences. Special rates are available for groups or parties. Uniquely, the hotel offers Shunpiker Tours. Shunpiker is a New England phrase which means "to avoid the busy roads" and these tours lead guests to areas that may not be as well-known as the main tourist attractions, but which offer an exciting chance to see and do something out of the ordinary. Additionally, the hotel has two large books on hand that list over 200 attractions in the area--guests unsure of where to go or what to do that take advantage of this hotel's assistance won't have any problem filling their vacation time with wonderful memories.

A good location is key to this hotel's success--it is central to both business and tourist centers. For the finest in hotel accommodations and nearby attractions the Howard Johnson's, St. Catharines is a "Best Choice." The hospitality and special services offered guarantee an enjoyable stay.

points of interest

WELLAND CANAL VIEWING CENTRE
Lock 3 Canal Road
St. Catharines, Ontario LZR 6Z4
Tel: (416) 684-2361
Hrs: Summer:
Seven days 9:00 a.m. - 9:00 p.m.
After October:
Seven days 9:00 a.m. - 5:00 p.m.
Visa and MasterCard are accepted.

The Welland Canal, linking Lake Erie to Lake Ontario, is 26 miles long, and consists of 8 locks. It is considered to be one of the greatest engineering feats of our time. This canal is the second most popular attraction in the Niagara Region, Niagara Falls is the first, of course, and draws over 600,000 viewers annually. The Welland Canal Viewing Centre at Lock 3 has been explaining the lock system and history of the canal to tourists for over 25 years. The popularity of the Viewing Centre made expansion necessary and in 1987, plans were drawn up to reconstruct the Centre on the Lock 3 site again but changing its square footage from 2,200 feet to 35,000 feet.

The brand new Welland Canal Viewing Centre opened in 1990 is a complex that includes a working model of a canal lift system, an information center, a gift shop, a restaurant, a snack bar, shaded picnic areas, and a 20,000 square foot museum that has five galleries and houses the collection of the St. Catharines Historical Museum. A Welland Canals Gallery, a Local Heritage Gallery, a Military Heritage Room, a "hands on" Discovery Room, and a Temporary Exhibitions Gallery are other aspects of this museum.

One of the most exciting new additions to Lock 3 is an actual wheelhouse from the retired ship, S/S Fort Henry. Visitors are amazed by the wheelhouse along with the close-up views they get of 750-foot ships being raised over the Niagara Escarpment.

Welland Canal Viewing Centre is a "Best Choice" because "there's so much more to the Niagara Region than just the Falls." Guided tours of the Centre are given every hour with state-of-the-art accessibility for the handicapped. Busses are welcome and ample parking is available.

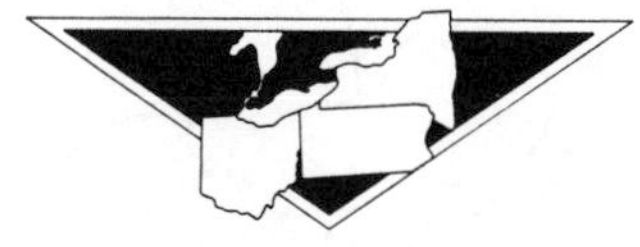

SECTION FOUR: LAKE ONTARIO - N.Y.

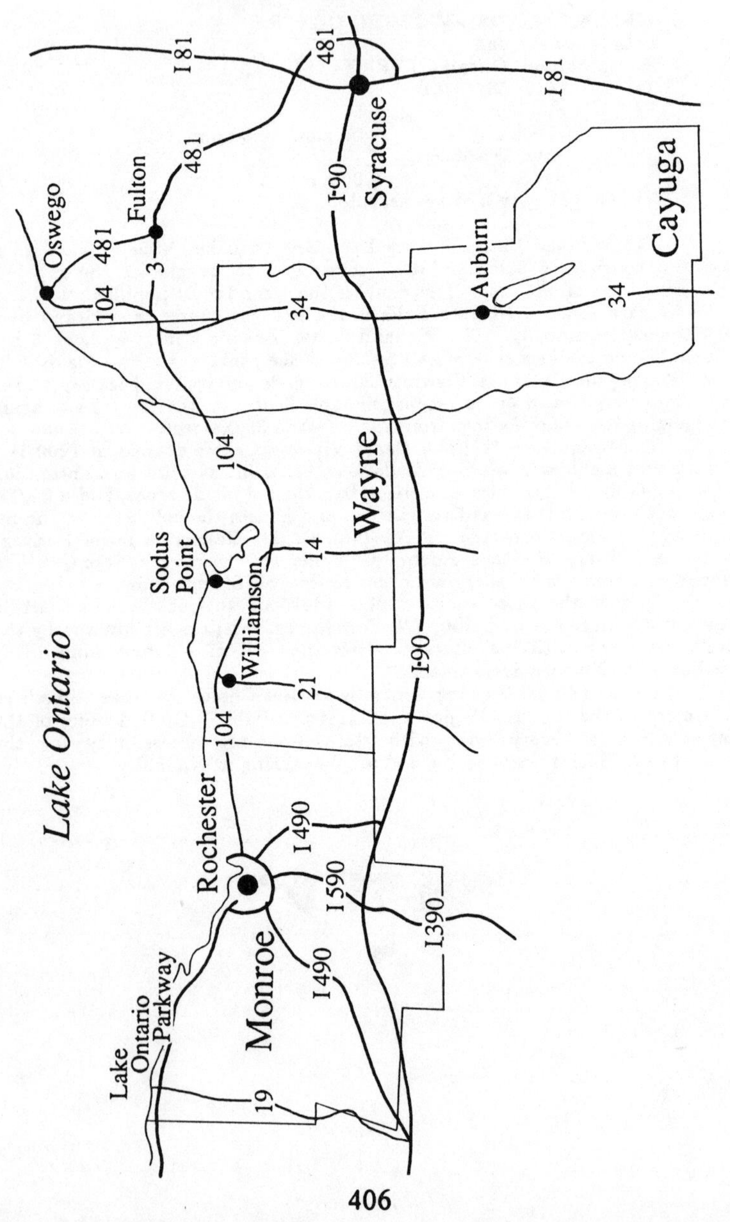

ORLEANS COUNTY

Established in 1824 from Genesee County, Orleans was named for the French royal house of the same name. James and William Wadsworth, the county's first permanent settlers, bought land from the Holland Land Company. James settled at Oak Orchard while William made Johnson's Creeks his permanent residence.

Important to Orleans county was the opening of Ridge Road (Route 104) in 1809 which helped to quickly populate the area.

The land was developed from a swampy wilderness that was once used by the Indians for fishing and hunting. Farmland was prominent in the county then and still dominates it today. Agriculture is an important industry along with standardbred breeding, Orleans having one of the largest breeding farms in New York State. Fishing is excellent in beautiful Orleans County, which holds the record in the Great Lakes area for a 26.9-pound rainbow trout.

Cobblestones became an architectural feature of Orleans County when early settlers used the smoothed stones to build their houses.

attractions

Erie Canal Heritage Trail, located west of Medina, is a biking, hiking and cross-country skiing trail that runs across Orleans and Monroe Counties. The trail is eight feet wide, has paved or gravel surfaces, and can be reached by several access points with parking.

Lakeside Beach State Park is a popular camping area. The park provides both tent and trailer sites, and camper facilities. Recreation includes picnicking, fishing, playgrounds, hiking, biking and nature trails. There are recreational programs and boating is allowed. Winter activities include cross-country skiing and snowmobiling.

Oak Orchard Marine Park, open from mid-March to mid-November, features a boat launch ramp area and excellent trout and salmon fishing.

events

The annual **4-H Junior Fair**, held in the county at the end of July or beginning of August each year, honors the talented young people in the county who are involved in 4-H. The fair is held at the Orleans County Fairgrounds in Knowlesville.

MEDINA

attractions

Wildwood Lake Campgrounds feature swimming, fishing, a camp store, children's area and recreation building on beautiful campgrounds.

events

The Erie Barge Canal Festival is held here in July.

tours

**MISS APPLE GROVE/
APPLE GROVE INN**
West Center Street
Ext. Route 31 East
Medina, New York 14103
Tel: (716) 798-2323
Hrs: Tours:
May - October:

Sunday	11:00 a.m., 1:00, 3:00, & 5:00 p.m.
Monday - Friday	10:00 a.m., Noon & 4:00 p.m.
Saturday	10:00 a.m. & Noon
Restaurant:	Open year-round.

Visa, MasterCard, American Express, Diners Club and Discover are accepted.

Take a trip into history with Medina, New York restaurateurs Jeffrey Wagner and Otto Berg, owners of the Apple Grove Inn.

The "Miss Apple Grove", a flat bottom boat, is pulled down Northeast's most historic waterway, the New York Barge Canal, by a two-mule team. The tour runs along the North Towpath from a point near the Route 31 Restaurant East, to the village and beyond. The mules, Frank and Dick, weighing in at 1,450 pounds each, pull the 110-passenger packet boat while Banjo John entertains passengers with old canal tunes. Margaret Gerity treats passengers to old time fiddlin' and Dave, the mule skinner, rides along the towpath to work the mules and performs crazy antics along the canal.

The mule-drawn packet boat tour includes a delightful meal at the Apple Grove Inn which features The Russet Room. This wonderful room was built around a live apple tree so patrons can enjoy the beauty of the tree as it changes with each season.

Memories of this refreshing experience and look back into the past are heightened with a brief stop at the Bancroft, a site of the canal museum and the location for co-op artists devoted to the preservation of fine handcrafts and art work.

The Miss Apple Grove is an experience that not only reflects on the history of the area in the 19th century, but offers a major contribution toward impacting the history of the future. It also makes a tour on the Miss Apple Grove a "Best Choice" in the New York area.

ALBION

attractions

The Cobblestone Museum Complex consists of a collection of cobblestone buildings from the 1830s and 1840s, several of which are on their original sites.

events

Each June in Albion, visitors gather for the annual Strawberry Festival, a true delight for the senses.

bed & breakfast inns

FRIENDSHIP MANOR
349 S. Main Street
Albion, New York 14411
Tel: (716) 589-7973

Jack and Marylin Baker take pride in making Friendship Manor a "home away from home" for anyone passing through. Their warmth is felt by every guest who stays at this bed and breakfast. They believe "the history and beauty of our home belong to the people, and we enjoy sharing it with them." This historic home, dating back to 1880, was built by the son of Joseph Hart, an original settler of Albion. It was purchased by Jack and Marylin in 1986 and has been restored to capture its traditional turn-of-the-century beauty.

Friendship Manor is surrounded by one acre of land that is covered by colorful roses, herb gardens, and comfortable sitting areas. Standing nobly in front of the house is the oldest walnut tree in the county. Also located on the grounds are a swimming pool and a tennis court. When one enters the Manor, it is evident that no better name could have been selected. The proprietors welcome everyone and take pride in the joy and relaxation their guests experience during their stay.

The comfortable atmosphere of this bed and breakfast is created through its warm decor. The bright, intimate interior is an artful blend of Victorian-style furnishings with antiques throughout. Bedrooms are spacious and include hand-made furniture. The home has three working fireplaces, a den in which one can read or watch TV, and a cozy country kitchen.

Friendship Manor provides excellent accommodations for travelers on route to Niagara Falls, Buffalo, or Rochester and is host to many European guests. This historical bed and breakfast is a "Best Choice" because of the warm hospitality of the owners and the casual decor that make one feel at home.

points of interest

BROWN'S BERRY PATCH
14264 Roosevelt Highway
Waterport, New York 14571
Tel: (716) 682-5569
Hrs: Summer:
8:00 a.m. - 10:00 p.m.
Fall:
9:00 a.m. - 7:00 p.m.
Closed Thanksgiving - April 15
Visa and MasterCard are accepted.

The first thing one notices when approaching Brown's Berry Patch is the sweet aroma of homegrown fresh fruit. The Browns grow and sell apples, quinces, strawberries, blueberries, raspberries, elderberries and pumpkins.

Brown's is also well-known for their ice cream sundaes topped with their own fresh fruit. Frozen yogurt, hard and soft ice cream, and handmade waffle cones are their specialty, as well as submarine sandwiches and homemade donuts and pies.

Brown's Berry Patch is located on a 300 acre family-owned farm which has existed through seven generations of the Brown family since 1804.

Through the years, Brown's Berry Patch has become quite a tourist attraction for people of all ages. Open April through November, they offer hayrides, a "Strawberry Social" in the third week of June, an "Apple Harvest Day" on Columbus Day, and allow visitors to pick their own berries from June 15 to fall each year. Owner Bob Brown conducts tours of the farm and demonstrates the cider-making process for schools and bus tours. Equally exciting is the maze constructed of straw which children find particularly enjoyable during the fall. The Browns are most proud of the fun that people have at the Berry Patch. There are plenty of activities to keep visitors busy, including the country gift shop.

Located on Route 18, west of Route 98 at "the Bridges," near Lake Ontario, Brown's Berry Patch is pure pleasure to the senses.

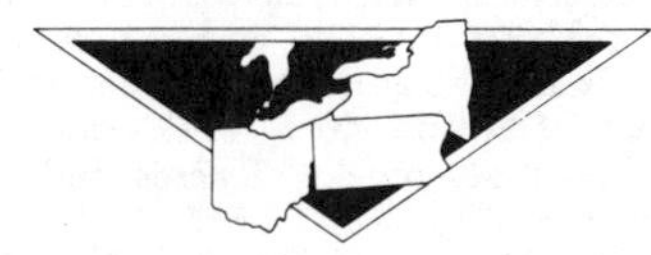

MONROE COUNTY

Monroe County was created in 1821 from Ontario and Genesee Counties. The Seneca Nation used the thickly-forested region as its hunting grounds. An early trading post, Irondequoit Bay at Rochester, was visited by LaSalle in 1669.

In 1789, the first permanent settlements occurred at Wheatland and near Rochester. Along with the Erie Canal came Rochester's title of first "Flour City" and then "Flower City" because of the booming milling and horticulture industries in the city.

Another industry that has grown over the years in Monroe County has been the fishing industry. Brown trout, lake trout and giant Chinook salmon are among the most popular fish caught in Lake Ontario.

The county also has a fine reputation for its warm-water fishing spots. Inland water areas feature perch, sunfish and smallmouth bass.

The county boasts the origin of many internationally-known companies. Xerox and Eastman Kodak are two of the corporations that started here.

Historic sites, recreational activities, sports, and amusement and natural parks grace Monroe County, home of New York State's third largest urban area, Rochester.

attractions

Hamlin Beach State Beach is known for its camping and wide variety of recreational facilities such as hiking, biking and nature trails, picnic facilities and playgrounds. There are tent and trailer sites and camper recreation. The sand beach is perfect for swimming. Boating is permitted. Winter activities include cross-country skiing and snowmobiling.

great lakes coast

Mendon Ponds Country Park contains a collection of glacial features; Kettle holes were formed when buried pieces of glacial ice melted and formed depressions. Conical hills, called kames, are composed of glacial debris, and long, low, sinuous hills of stratified sand are called eskers.

The **Genesee Country Village and Museum** is a collection of 55 farm and village buildings on 125 acres dating from the 18th century. Moved to this location from their original sites across upstate New York, these buildings have been carefully restored and reflect early to late 1800s life. Activities such as weaving, spinning, quilting and open-hearth cooking are demonstrated by costumed craftspeople.

Finger Lakes Performing Arts Center, the summer home of Rochester Philharmonic Orchestra, features classical and pop concerts and a variety of well-known entertainers. It is open June through September.

Three miles east of Hilton, New York, the **Braddock Bay Fish & Wildlife Management Area** is set on 2,500 acres and is the home of many different types of waterfowl.

Webster Park features 40 campsites, fishing facilities and an area specifically for children.

events

The **Spencerport Canal Days** are celebrated in late July.

At the end of August, the **Monroe County Fair** is held on the county's fairgrounds/dome center and features arts, crafts, food, amusement rides and much more.

The **Hilton Apple Festival** is held in Hilton in early October.

bed & breakfast inns

SANDY CREEK MANOR HOUSE, 1960 Redman Road, Hamlin, New York 14464; Tel: (716) 964-7528. This bed and breakfast, a 1910 English Tudor Home, is comfortably set on six acres of land. Guests can relax here or enjoy nearby marinas, farm markets or cross country skiing. A full breakfast is provided.

gift shops

ONNIE'S CLOSET
1336 Pittsford-Mendon Road
Mendon, New York 14506-0221
Tel: (716) 582-1072
Hrs: Monday - Friday 10:00 a.m. - 6:00 p.m.
Saturday 10:00 a.m. - 5:00 p.m.
Sunday Noon - 5:00 p.m.
Visa and MasterCard are accepted.

Located in Mendon, New York, is a quaint gift shop called Onnie's Closet. Owner Onnie Wells has established a shop that includes a wide variety of gifts, containers, and wrappings. Onnie's Closet used to be exactly that--a closet, full of gift items. Three years ago, however, Onnie decided to expand and utilize a small country starter home as her shop. Onnie prides herself on her vast collection of gifts. She claims that Onnie's Closet has a gift for anyone. Each gift is specially packaged with the wrapping of the customer's choice.

Onnie Wells has taken what was once a "bride's house" and turned it into the most intimate gift shop in Monroe County. Each room of the house carries a specific type of gift. What was once a walk-in closet is now a display window filled with stuffed animals. Cabinets in the kitchen once used by a newlywed couple are now overflowing with gourmet foods, cookies, spices, pastas, mugs, kitchen utensils, cookbooks, and an old-fashioned hoosier. Although Onnie's Closet is filled with unique gift items, its selection of wrappings and containers is similarly special. While walking through the dining room, guests will notice that one entire wall (called the wrap corner) is filled with various and beautiful wrappings. For customers who bring children along, Onnie's Closet has a children's corner with "fun stuff" to entertain them while patrons look through the variety of gift items. One of Onnie's personal favorites is her unique collection of loons and hummingbirds.

The quality and variety of gifts at Onnie's Closet affords guests the luxury of one-stop shopping. Onnie is sure that she has something to satisfy the needs of even the choosiest customer. If the right gift is found, U.P.S. service is available. Onnie's Closet is set in a friendly country home, and Onnie's warmth and enthusiasm is apparent to anyone who has ever shopped there. Onnie's Closet is the place for the customer with special needs and the desire to get the perfect gift and wrapping.

specialty shops

ROBESON SADDLERY, LTD.
1338 Pittsford-Mendon Road
Mendon, New York 14506
Tel: (716) 624-1512
Hrs: Monday, Tuesday, Thursday & Friday
10:00 a.m. - 6:00 p.m.
Wednesday
10:00 a.m. - 8:00 p.m.
Saturday
10:00 a.m. - 5:00 p.m.
Visa and MasterCard are accepted.

For anyone who has a horse, loves horses, or knows someone else who does, a visit to Robeson Saddlery, Ltd. is a must. Horse owners are pleased to find that this 4500 square foot shop carries one of the most extensive selections of English tack available anywhere. The building, which was originally a barn, has been enlarged and now houses anything and everything for horses and some things for non-horse lovers.

Owners Jim and Lynda Robeson are long time horse people. He was a professional rider and trainer and she was a professional instructor and ran a hunter-jumper operation in California. Their love of horses and the pride they take in their business is evident in their philosophy, "there is no substitute for quality." They only carry the best merchandise; what a rider purchases here, he will have for a long time. With a workshop right on the premises, custom fitting a horse is not a problem. Jim and Lynda have designed their own line of saddles which are made for them in England. They will do extensive repair work and always service what they sell. As the largest all-English tack shop in western New York, they will ship around the world.

Merchandise available includes horse shampoo and medicines, boots, helmets, waxed-cotton raincoats, breeches, horse blankets, coats, saddles for dressage, hunting, and jumping, and bridles. A large selection of unique gift items are available such as engraved brass name plates, hunt prints, a complete line of Breyer Collector Horses, books, magazines, leather goods, and skirts and sweaters of a slightly equestrian nature. Robeson Saddlery, Ltd. is a "Best Choice" for the practical horse owner or the fantasizing horse lover.

ROCHESTER

"The Flower City," once inhabited by the Seneca Indians, was part of over two million acres purchased by two Yankee traders in 1788. One year later, a frontiersman, Ebenezer "Indian" Allen, built the settlement's first flour mill north of the Upper Falls of the Genesee River.

Civilization arrived in 1811 when Colonel Nathan Rochester and several partners finished paying for the "Indian" Allen site. Additional flour mills were built, quickly allowing Rochester to become a boomtown and the "Flour Capital of the Nation." Barges packed with lumber, flour and other products, traveled along the Erie Canal.

But flour wasn't the only industry that would be immensely successful in Rochester. Men's clothing, horticulture, Bausch & Lomb, Eastman Kodak, Xerox Company and Rochester's tourism industry combined to make the city what it is today: a city overflowing with activities for tourists and natives alike.

A cultural, naturally-beautiful and energetic city, Rochester blends new and old in an atmosphere that is both historical and contemporary.

attractions

The **International Museum of Photography** provides exhibits and documents on the history of photography. The collection, one of the largest in the world, includes photographs, negatives, film, motion pictures and equipment, spanning 150 years. The museum is located in George Eastman's former mansion.

Rochester Museum and Science Center focuses many of its exhibits on upstate New York's natural and cultural history. A major exhibit features an extensive collection of artifacts.

A combination of theater and astronomy is performed each evening, year-round, at the **Strasenburgh Planetarium**. The planetarium is part of the **Rochester Museum and Science Center**.

Memorial Art Gallery, located on the University of Rochester campus, carries works by Cezanne, Monet and Rembrandt, among others. Medieval and Renaissance art, contemporary works and American Folk art are featured at the gallery.

The Strong Museum contains one of the largest and most extensive collections of items from the 19th and early 20th centuries. The collection includes decorative items, furniture, household accessories, toys and dolls.

Seneca Zoo Park features over 500 native and exotic animals from lions and camels to monkeys and elephants. A free-flight bird room and Children's Zoo are provided as well.

The **restored 1860 home of Susan B. Anthony** contains original furnishings and memorabilia of the suffrage crusade.

The **Woodside Mansion** is one of the finest examples of Greek Revival architecture in New York. Built in 1839, the mansion contains period furnishings, a reference library and an enclosed perennial garden. It is also the home of the **Rochester Historical Society**.

The Stone-Tolan House has been restored to reflect daily life among the pioneers. Built in 1790, the four-acre site contains a farmhouse, barn, orchards and gardens.

Campbell-Whittlesey House, built in 1835-36, is a perfect example of Greek Revival architecture. An excellent restoration, the house is located in the Corn Hill District and depicts how life was during Rochester's flour-milling era.

The Eastman Kodak Company offers tours of both of its local plants. The Kodak Park division manufactures photographic film and paper. The

Elmgrove Plant manufactures and assembles cameras and photographic equipment.

The **Eastman Theatre** hosts concerts by the Eastman School of Music, the Rochester Philharmonic, Broadway touring companies, and performances by artists of international and national fame.

The **GeVa Theatre**, Rochester's resident professional theatre, performs eight productions a year, including classics, musicals and contemporary theatre productions.

A century old and still going strong, **Seabreeze Park** is located on the shores of Lake Ontario and provides recreation for the whole family with attractions such as a waterslide, roller coaster and carousel.

Sports lovers enjoy the city's many sports facilities, including **Rochester Red Wings AAA** Baseball played at **Silver Stadium** from April to September.

Highland Park, the site of Rochester's annual Lilac Festival, contains over 1,200 lilac bushes. The park also contains botanic gardens, a conservatory and azalea and rhododendron bushes. **Warner Castle**, located in the park, is the home of the **Rochester Garden Center**. The 19th century mansion resembles a Scottish castle.

Maplewood Park contains one of the largest rose gardens in the country and serves as a test garden.

The **Durand-Eastman Park**, located on the shore of Lake Ontario, is a beautiful place in the spring: flowering dogwood and crabapple trees bloom profusely amid the two-mile area. An 18-hole golf course is also on the property.

events

The **Lilac Festival** is held in Highland Park for 10 days in mid-May or late May, depending on the blooming season.

The **Harbor Festival** is held in mid to late June at Ontario Beach Park. A lighted boat parade, fireworks, entertainment and parade are some of the highlights.

The **Corn Hill Arts Festival** is held in July in the stately neighborhood of Corn Hill. A wide variety of crafts, including wood, textile and ceramic, is available for purchase.

The **Annual Bluegrass Festival**, held each year in Manhattan Square Park, offers great music, food and a lot of fun.

accommodations

THE LODGE AT WOODCLIFF
Woodcliff Drive
Rochester, New York 14692
Tel: (716) 381-4000
1-800-365-3065
Visa, MasterCard, American Express, Diners Club, Carte Blanche and Discover are accepted.

Although The Lodge at Woodcliff has only been in business since 1987, it has easily earned its reputation as "Upstate New York's premier resort and conference hotel." From its hilltop location, the lodge is just minutes away from downtown Rochester and half an hour from Bristol Mountain Ski Resort. This hotel has plenty to offer to the corporate traveler as well as the couple looking for a fun getaway. (Special "Adventure Weekend" packages are available for couples planning such an escape.)

Whether here for business or pleasure, all guests may take advantage of The Lodge's sports facilities; the Woodcliff Sports and Golf Club includes an indoor/outdoor heated pool, tennis courts, a fitness center that offers state-of-the-art Keiser equipment, saunas, a spa, and pro shop. The Croquet Club attracts players from New England and Canada to compete. The Lodge is the only resort in the area to have its own public golf course, a scenic nine-hole course that proves to be an entertaining challenge. The Lodge at Woodcliff has 120 beautiful guest rooms and four luxurious suites that provide all of the comforts of home. The spacious rooms offer picturesque views of Rochester and Bristol Hills along with such amenities as a wet bar, a comfortable chair with an ottoman and reading lamp, a writing table, and a fully-stocked refrigerator. Room service is available until late at night.

The Conference Center is ideal for any type of meeting up to 250 people. Those here for business or recreation will love Horizons, the Lodge's main dining room. The fine food selections available from the international menu complement the sunset view. After enjoying a superb meal, one can enjoy entertainment in the lounge from the area's best jazz musicians. The Lodge at Woodcliff, a "Best Choice" for conferences and special occasions, offers elegant but comfortable accommodations that suit a wide range of customers from the businessman to the bride.

STOUFFER ROCHESTER PLAZA HOTEL
70 State Street
Rochester, New York 14614
Tel: (716) 546-3450
Hrs: Open seven days, 24 hours
Visa, MasterCard, American Express, Diners Club, Carte Blanche, Discover and Canadian and Japanese credit cards are accepted.

Stouffer Hotels and Resorts are well-known for the luxurious accommodations and attentive service they provide for their guests and the Stouffer Rochester Plaza Hotel is no exception. This beautiful and comfortable hotel has much to offer travelers whether one is looking for a productive stay or simply a pleasurable one.

Upon entering the Rochester Plaza's finely appointed, contemporary lobby, it is obvious why this hotel has been a AAA Four-Diamond hotel for seven years. All 362 spacious guest rooms and suites offer the same comfortable atmosphere. The rooms, furnished with oak pieces that are upholstered in mauve and beige, are designed to be functional for business travelers as well as vacationers. To start the morning, guests receive complimentary coffee and newspaper. For a higher rate, the Club Level provides additional services for the discriminating traveler. These guests receive such extras as express check-in and check-out, a bathrobe, satin hangers, complimentary continental breakfast, and complimentary hors d'oeuvres in the evening.

All guests can take advantage of the fitness center with its state of the art equipment (Stairmaster, Life Cycle, and Universal) and the outdoor swimming pool. During the week, one can enjoy continental American cuisine at the Riverview Cafe or casual drinks in the State Street Bar. During the weekend, the State Street Bar offers live entertainment and on Sunday, one may try Stouffer's signature item--Sunday Brunch--which was voted the "Best in Rochester" through a poll conducted by the Democrat & Chronicle newspaper.. The Plaza is conveniently close to tennis courts, golf ranges, fishing areas, Irondequoit Mall, GeVa Theater, Strong Museum, and hockey or baseball games.

Rochester Plaza is the perfect meeting place for 5-1500. It has 11 meeting rooms and also a Grand Ballroom. Special services offered here include a complementary airport shuttle, a Concierge to assist with plans or provide information, 24-hour room service, and a shoe shine service. "Weekend Breakation" packages are available along with packages that include trips to the GeVa or the Rochester Philharmonic. The Stouffer Rochester Plaza Hotel is a "Best Choice" because "where you're staying says a lot about where you're going."

amusement

POCKETS, Village Gate Square, Rochester, New York 14607. A departure from the smoke filled pool hall, Pockets offers nine deluxe pool tables in a classy yet comfortable atmosphere. Soft music plays during the day and rock at night; sandwiches, pizza, dessert, and beverages are available from lunch until closing. Those waiting for their meal can play for free.

antiques

LEE-WAY ANTIQUE CO-OP
1221 Lee Road
Rochester, New York 14606
Tel: (716) 458-3990
Hrs: Monday - Saturday 11:00 a.m. - 5:00 p.m.
Sunday Noon - 5:00 p.m.
Additional times by appointment
Visa and MasterCard are accepted.

Lee-Way Antique Co-op, located 1 mile south of Route 104 in Rochester, is home to "2 Floors of Antiques & Quality Collectibles." Husband and wife team, Rick and Bobbie Diehl, have completely renovated the building that houses their business. This was Bobbie's home while she was growing up and that comfortable home-like atmosphere has remained in the store. Bobbie's grandparents owned over 100 acres of land which they eventually divided among their children; over the years the land was sold to businesses such as Kodak. Bobbie's parents were the only ones to retain their property, which they left to their daughter and her husband. Their 5,000 square feet of space provides 25 dealers with a place to market their goods.

Rick and Bobbie are proud of "their good reputation for quality merchandise and reasonable prices. Everything is organized and well displayed and the dealers are very friendly." A file card system makes items easy to locate. At least one dealer is on the premises daily to assist customers in finding what they are looking for. The interior of this store is very open and well-lit. The Lee-Way Antique Co-op is designed to make it easy to find what one is looking for.

Lee-Way Antique Co-op is a "Best Choice" for "Antiques and Collectibles from A to Z!!!" Just about anything imaginable can be found here such as art, books, coins, depression glass, furniture, gold, hat pins, Indian artifacts, jewelry, linens, music books, napkins, oil lamps, porcelains, quilts, rocking chairs, stoneware, teapots, vintage clothing, Weller pottery, yarn winders, and "zillions of other neat things!!!" The constantly changing merchandise makes the Lee-Way Antique Co-op a different shop and a new experience everytime one enters the front door.

apparel

THE RED BARN GENLTEMEN'S APPAREL
2920 Monroe Avenue
Rochester, New York 14618
Tel: (716) 586-9409
Hrs: Monday, Wednesday, & Friday
10:00 a.m. - 6:00 p.m.
Tuesday and Thursday
10:00 a.m. - 9:00 p.m.
Saturday
10:00 a.m. - 5:00 p.m.
December:
Noon - 5:00 p.m.
Visa, MasterCard and American Express are accepted.

Upon entering The Red Barn Gentlemen's Apparel, the conservative interior of the store reminds one of a traditional English haberdashery, and indeed, many of the finest English brands are carried here. Literally a red barn that was once a print shop for the weekly paper, it is now filled with quality clothing for men. The hardwood parquet floors decorated with oriental rugs, the grand piano, and the chandeliers provide an air of class. Walls of wood with green accents, a camelback loveseat, and a brick fireplace give the store a warm atmosphere.

This business was established in 1964 and originated in Jamestown, New York. Owner Donald Rhoda is proud of the fine selection and personal attention he offers his customers. Shoppers are treated as friends here and are cheerfully given whatever assistance they need, whether it be alterations, delivery, or gift wrapping. Serious buyers are pleased to find names like Hickey-Freeman, Burberrys of London, Polo, Southwick, and Gieves & Hawkes (the London clothiers for the English royalty). English wool and cashmere sweaters are available, along with Kangol English hats, and Hermes ties from France.

Other locations for this store include The Haberdashery in the Marketplace Mall and The Prep Shop next door to The Red Barn. Both have the same high-quality clothing, but The Prep Shop specializes in young men's wear. One can find designs here by Polo, Gant, and Christian Dior. Items purchased at any of these shops will always be in style because quality never goes out of fashion. For men who wish to project an image of quality and tradition through their manner of dress, The Red Barn Gentlemen's Apparel and The Prep Shop are a "Best Choice."

doll shops

THE ENCHANTED WORLD OF DOLLS & GIFTS, Village Gate Square, Rochester, New York 14607; Tel: (716) 244-0489. The place to go for teddy bears, figurines, stuffed animals, and collectable dolls. Adorable creations are available in porcelain, vinyl, cloth, or wood, and selections include Gorham, Effanbee, Hummels, Middleton, N. American Bear, Silvestri, and Precious Moments.

entertainment

BLACKFRIARS THEATER, Xerox Square Auditorium, Broad and Chestnut Streets, Rochester, New York 14607; Tel: (716) 473-6760. In the heart of downtown Rochester, Blackfriars Theater offers comedies, dramas, mysteries, and musicals to audiences of all tastes. One shouldn't miss this exciting form of live entertainment.

FUNNY BONE-AMERICA'S NO. 1 COMEDY NITE CLUB
149 State Street
Rochester, New York 14614
Tel: (716) 325-2663
Hrs: Tuesday - Saturday Show at 8:30 p.m.
Friday & Saturday Additional Show at 11:00 p.m.

Locals in Rochester know where to go to enjoy entertainers such as Judy Tenuta, Marsha Warfield, Emo Philips, Richard Belzer, Kevin Nealon, Tom Parks, and George Miller, while munching on "bottomless popcorn." The location is the Funny Bone--America's No. 1 Comedy Nite Club. Since its opening in May, 1988, Rochester locals and visitors to the area have recognized the Funny Bone as the best place in town to go for a good laugh and the only place that provides all-you-can-eat popcorn for only 25 cents.

Owner, Tom Clyde, manages to create an intimate environment with a modern lighting and sound system. A mixture of rock and roll and jazz music greets patrons and sets a comfortable tone for the evening. Everyone is close to the stage and to the performers, allowing for maximum audience enjoyment. Patrons can get warmed up for the show with "specialty" drinks which they can also enjoy throughout the evening. There are three acts nightly which include two national acts and one regional performer.

Tom is proud to be able to provide a combination of an outstanding show and excellent service that adds up to a good entertainment value for the customer. The Funny Bone is the hottest night spot in Rochester and is in easy walking distance of many downtown hotels. (It's easy to get there by taking the inner loop to State Street.) This club is certainly a "Best Choice" for anyone who has a funny bone that needs a little tickling.

GEVA THEATER, 75 Woodbury Boulevard, Rochester, New York 14607; Tel: (716) 232-1363. GeVa Theater, Rochester's professional resident theater, presents seven plays during its season. From September through June, one can expect to be entertained by comedies, musicals, dramas and world premieres.

ROCHESTER PHILHARMONIC ORCHESTRA
100 East Avenue (Box Office)
60 Gibbs Street (Theater)
Rochester, New York 14604

Tel:	Box Office:	(716) 222-5000	
	Information:	(716) 454-2620	
Hrs:	Eastman Theater (September - May):		
	Thursday & Saturday	Classical	
	Friday & Saturday	Pops	
	Finger Lakes Performing Arts Center (July - August)		

Visa and MasterCard are accepted.

The Rochester Philharmonic Orchestra had its beginnings as a pit orchestra at the Eastman Theatre where movies and stage shows were showcased. The evolution of the RPO has turned it into a nationally prominent symphony orchestra that offers a full range of services to Western New York. Such services include national and regional touring, chamber performances, college residencies, free educational concerts for elementary and high school students, free community concerts throughout the region, pre-concert lectures presented before each classical performance, and dance and choral presentations.

With the celebration of its 67th season in 1989-90, the RPO welcomed English native, Mark Elder, to the post of Music Director. The London Times says Mr. Elder is a "standard-bearer of selfless musicmaking of the highest quality." The RPO's Assistant Conductor, Peter Bay, has been lauded by Governor Gerald Baliles for his "contributions to the musical culture of the commonwealth." Together, these two gentlemen are presenting "best-loved classics and tantalizing, undiscovered works," so that audiences of all tastes may be satisfied by their concert experience.

In an effort to please a wide range of subscribers, the RPO has designed four separate concert series. The Masterworks Series features 10 concerts showcasing world-class soloists, the Discovery Series offers six lively, traditional concerts with a twist, the Connoisseur Series combines these two, and GRC Weekend at the Pops features six concerts that include a variety of light, classical music.

During the summer, the Finger Lakes Performing Arts Center is home to the RPO. Visitors at this time are likely to see such guest artists and conductors as Doc Severinsen, Dizzy Gillespie, Kyoko Takezawa, Jere Lantz or Maureen McGovern. During these concerts the audience is seated under the stars on the hillside surrounding the center with room for more than 10,000.

The Rochester Philharmonic Orchestra is a "Best Choice" for those who truly love music. All are invited to attend a concert, especially those who "could use a bit more sunshine, an extra dollop of joy and inspiration, and a fresh infusion of energy and humanity."

florists

ARENA'S
260 East Avenue
Rochester, New York 14604
Tel: (716) 454-3720
Hrs: Monday - Friday 8:30 a.m. - 5:30 p.m.
Saturday 8:00 a.m. - 4:00 p.m.
Visa, MasterCard and American Express are accepted.

Arena's represents the elite in floral shops in New York. Owner Charles Arena, who is 29 years old, has 15 years of experience as a florist and believes that his progressive presentation of floral arrangements is one of a kind. Mr. Arena has decided not only to present floral arrangements, but to "educate the public" with his unique, individualized style. Arena's is much more than a flower shop though; its arrangements are personalized and designed to complement the home and personality of any customer. Arena's has been serving Rochester's business and society successfully for 10 years.

Guests will immediately notice that the interior design of Mr. Arena's shop is consistent with his emphasis on quality and individuality. The showroom's ambiance begins with the sounds of classical music which suitably complement the aroma of fresh flowers. Upon entering, patrons will admire a contemporary black stairway that spans from floor to ceiling as a decorative setting for floral designs. On one side of the stairway, Arena's shows its versatility with a large, antique display cabinet filled with pottery, books, potpourri, French ribbons and Victorian hat boxes. All of these floral collectibles are perfectly beautiful gift items.

Mr. Arena has a spectacular collection of flowers from all over the world. Flowers are imported from Holland, Israel, Iceland, France, and various other countries. There are over 30 to 60 types of flowers, all arranged to the specific taste of the customer. Arena's floral shop stresses that the selections they carry are like no others. All arrangements are custom-made, and the truly imaginative and concerned guests are welcomed above all. With such a wide variety of flowers, Arena's has the luxury of making no two floral designs alike. Naturalism, using flowers as they grow, is Arena's approach to floral design.

Mr. Arena prides himself in having developed a staff that consists of designers as well as florists. Arena's is not necessarily the place to go to pick up a quick bouquet of flowers at the last minute. A great deal of thought and care is put into each arrangement because each must represent a certain feeling or theme. Arena's is, however, the place to go in Rochester for the person who is serious about improving their home or office with a perfect arrangement of beautiful flowers.

FLEUR-DE-LIS
696 University Avenue
Rochester, New York 14607
Tel: (716) 244-5290
Hrs: Monday - Friday 9:30 a.m. - 6:00p.m.
Saturday 9:00 a.m. - 5:00p.m.
Sunday hours in December: Noon - 5:00p.m.
Visa and MasterCard are accepted.

Mary Read has had a love of nature ever since her parents took her to Rushford Lake in the Southern Tier as a little girl. While studying horticulture at Alfred State College, she had a dream of combining a floral shop with a botanical gift shop, and Fleur-de-Lis is this dream realized.

The shop is located in an unusual triangular building and customers are greeted by the sound of peaceful music and the scent of sweet-smelling flowers and potpourri. A marble floor and large glass door lead into the front showroom entrance. Here one finds a wide selection of all natural floral arrangements. Each one is specially made and includes flowers that change with the seasons such as irises, violets, spray roses, and lilies of all kinds. Narcissus and amaryllis bulbs are available for indoor planting.

The other part of the shop has a tin ceiling and lots of windows that let in an abundance of sunlight, giving it a bright cheerful look. Here one finds pine hutches filled with many different items. A Victorian section offers hearts, flowers, and birds of pewter, vases, potpourri, beeswax candles, note cards, tapestry pillows, sachets, address books, calendars, and French ribbon. Shells, stones, garden statues, and Amish tables and chairs are also available. This shop markets an extensive line of books covering subjects of flower arranging, gardening, and herb gardening. Additionally found here are the original works of designer Kevin Licciardi. Working with vibrant colors, he paints oil floor cloths of any size.

Fleur-de-Lis, specializing in natural and unusual gift ideas, is a "Best Choice" for fresh flower arrangements and items associated with gardening.

furniture stores

AUDETS
363 East Avenue
Rochester, New York 14604
Tel: (716) 325-4880
Hrs: Monday - Friday 10:00 a.m. - 6:00 p.m.
Thursday 10:00 a.m. - 9:00 p.m.
Saturday 10:00 a.m. - 5:00 p.m.
Holidays: Noon - 5:00 p.m.
Visa and MasterCard are accepted.

Audets is an innovative furnishings store that offers contemporary furniture, unusual lighting, and artistically designed accessories. Designers from around the world (including Artemide, the leading Italian lighting manufacturer) supply the avant-garde store with halogen, fluorescent, and incandescent lighting collections that are specially made to produce the appearance of very subtle--never harsh or excessively bright--home and office light.

Owner Debra Audet carefully selects only top-name merchandise that has an almost futuristic flair and the latest technology behind it. Debra stocks the Swid Powell collection, which has been widely acclaimed by Vogue, House & Garden, Newsweek, Time, and popular architectural journals. Swid Powell pieces (which include crystal, porcelain, and silver tableware designed by Meir, Venturi, Spear, and Stern) are so well-respected that several museums, such as the Museum of Modern Art and the Metropolitan Museum of Art, have several on display.

Audets also features an extensive line of Ligne Roset upholstered furniture, tables, and wall units. The customer chooses the style and fabric, and Debra sends the order to France. The finished pieces are delivered directly to Audets' Rochester warehouse within eight to 16 weeks--a short time to wait for an exclusive Ligne Roset.

Debra, who studied fine art and design at RIT, carries a wide assortment of furnishings and accents that come in varied prices. Though some interior designs are quite elegant, with a price tag to match, other designs are equally exquisite but very inexpensive. The diversity in prices and styles, as well as the array of elegant, ultra-modern furnishings, makes Audets a popular place in which to shop for quality-crafted interior designs.

HABERSHAM COUNTRY FURNITURE AND GIFT STORE
23 State Street
Fairport, New York 14450
Tel: (716) 388-0060
Hrs: Summer:
Monday, Wednesday, Friday & Saturday
10:00 a.m. - 5:00 p.m.
Tuesday & Thursday
10:00 a.m. - 8:00 p.m.
Holidays (November & December):
Sunday
1:00 p.m. - 4:00 p.m.

Whether looking for elegant country chandeliers, copper, brass or pewter replicas, or American-style country furniture, it can be found at Habersham Country Furniture and Gift Store.

Habersham features comfortable traditional and country French furniture that will give any home the feel of an exquisite 18th century mansion. From the sturdily constructed wingback chairs to the colonial camelback sofas, the furniture at Habersham has a practicality and rustic charm that is geared to contemporary decoration tastes.

Besides offering lovely Habersham Plantation Furniture, the store features antique reproductions made of solid oak, pine and cherry, woven wool throws, Dhuri rugs, country prints, stenciled quilts, covered hat boxes, white linens, white iron beds, Judy Tesch Dolls, Rowe Pottery, Williamsburg dried flower arrangements, Amish-quilted pillows, Windsor chairs, homespun fabrics, and country lighting. Beautiful interior and exterior light fixtures, such as tin lights, floor lamps, black wrought-iron lamps and table lamps are all available at Habersham.

great lakes coast

The century old stone building has a bright, warm fireplace, original plank flooring, a delicate scent of potpourri, an assortment of country crafts and copper, brass, tin and pewter creations.

"Warm" and "cozy" are the best words to describe this charming country furniture and gift store. Whether decorating a modern condo or a mountaintop cabin, Habersham has furnishings that offer just the right blend of formal classic styling and quaint, country comfort.

Visit the Habersham Country Furniture and Gift Store, the country lover's haven.

ice cream parlors

GELATO FRESCO, 654 Park Avenue, Rochester, New York 14607; Tel: (716) 654-7787. Voted "Best ice cream in Rochester" according to a reader's poll, Gelato Fresco also offers chocolate truffles and fresh pasta and sauces.

malls

VILLAGE GATE SQUARE
274 N. Goodman Street
Rochester, New York 14607
Tel: (716) 442-9168

Hrs:	Monday - Saturday	11:00 a.m. - 6:00 p.m.
	Thursday & Friday nights	Until 8:00 p.m.
	Sunday	Noon - 5:00 p.m.

Visa and MasterCard are accepted.

The Village Gate Square is a unique shopping complex displaying distinctly different elements - a perfect blend of shopping, dining and entertainment. Gary Stern, the owner, became involved in real estate development in 1983 and started renovating Village Gate Square. Today, this complex consists of five buildings, housing over fifty specialty shops, all of which are individually owned and operated.

Among the businesses located here are novelty stores such as Bena's Polish Art and the Enchanted World of Dolls, eating facilities such as Hilly's Cafe, Maria's Mexican Restaurant and four other restaurants, furniture stores, antique shops and more. The Bop Shop carries an assortment of great records - classics, vintage jazz, rock 'n roll, and rhythm and blues. Collectibles of all kinds can be found here, represented by Susannah's Collectibles, Yankee Clipper Baseball Cards, Antique Poster Collection, Mostly Clay, Ricky's Place, and Gift World miniatures. Other shops here are Waterwheel Antiques, Yankee Peddler Bookshop, Pyramid Arts Center, Pockets, Bookends and Schnozz's Nightclub.

The Village Gate Square is an exciting place where new stores are opening up and older stores continue to grow into prominent Rochester businesses. The courtyard located between the buildings is a popular place to eat out in the summer. On Friday nights, jazz bands are featured along with other upscale entertainment through the weekend.

To get to Village Gate Square from West of Rochester, take 490 East, get off at Exit 17. Then take a left off of ramp onto Goodman Street. Continue through six lights.

museums

THE STRONG MUSEUM
1 Manhatten Square
Rochester, New York 14607
Tel: (716) 263-2700
Hrs: Monday - Saturday 10:00 a.m. - 5:00 p.m.
Sunday 1:00 p.m. - 5:00 p.m.
Closed Thanksgiving, Christmas & New Years Day.

Opened to the public in 1982, The Strong Museum, named for its founder Margaret Woodbury Strong, is a collection of some 300,000 objects documenting life in America from 1820 to 1940. Mrs. Strong was a wealthy Rochester native and the daughter of the early Kodak investor John Woodbury. Her greatest interest was in acquiring historical and educational objects. She died before realizing her plans for organizing her vast collection, but left an endowment to further the project. Now, The Strong Museum features one of the top collections of Victorian furnishings, toys, and art in the nation.

Several exhibits are offered at the Strong Museum, ranging from Household Furnishings to Gardening to Childhood. One of those exhibits is One History Place, a learn-by-playing atmosphere for children which recreates experiences of a young 19th Century child.

The Strong Museum Library has a collection of 35,000 books and periodicals concerning the 19th and 20th centuries. It also offers other research materials such as trade catalogues, serial publications, slide collections, children's books, and special collections of the Strong family which require prior arrangements before viewing.

Special programs, lectures, symposia, concerts, and other special events are scheduled throughout the year. "Wednesday Evening at The Strong Museum" is a series of lectures and performances exploring the fascination of collecting and the heritage of popular music from pre-radio days.

The Tuckaway Cafe offers light fare and beverages, and the Museum Shop is open during museum hours. There are trained instructors available to teach a series of lessons to students in grades 3 to 12.

Group visits can be arranged by making an appointment in advance. Whether visiting The Strong Museum with a group or individually, the step back in time can be interesting and very enjoyable for everyone.

points of interest

SUSAN B. ANTHONY HOUSE, 17 Madison Street, Rochester, New York 14608; Tel: (716) 235-6124. Visitors to this national Historic Landmark have a special opportunity to learn about the woman who devoted much of her life to campaigning for women's suffrage. This house museum contains many artifacts and items that belonged to Miss Anthony.

restaurants

CAFE CREME DE LA CREME, ALEXANDER STREET
295 Alexander Street
Rochester, New York 14607
Tel: (716) 263-3580
Hrs: Seven days 11:00 a.m. - Midnight
Visa, MasterCard and American Express are accepted.

The Cafe Creme de la Creme offers delicacies as superior as its name suggests. Here, cafe visitors find everything they expect and a lot more.

For lunch or dinner, one may choose from the all-day Light Fare Menu which includes homemade soups, croissants, and special salads. Two examples of the unique salads offered are chicken salad, a carefully blended mix of dijon mustard, mayonnaise, apples, celery, and grapes, and Insalada di Napoli, an Italian marinated chicken breast with tomatoes, black olives and onions served on a bed of greens. Hot entrees such as baked sandwiches and vegetable lasagne are offered along with daily entree specials of Pasta Primavera, Shrimp Madres, and Chicken Caucasain.

For a Hampshire tea or Essex tea dining experience, enjoy English afternoon tea, served daily. This includes crumpets, tea cakes, sandwiches, and other cafe favorites.

All of this is enjoyed amid extraordinary environment on Rochester's restaurant row. The cafe is an 1800s Victorian home, complete with patio, leaded glass, fireplaces and French doors. Adding to the atmosphere is the soft sound of jazz or classical music which plays in the background. The first floor consists of three rooms while upstairs there are rooms which accommodate private parties.

The biggest attraction, however, that strikes the eyes of guests is an endless array of pastries and desserts from the display cases. All fresh ingredients go into such teasers as Chocolate Raspberry Feuilletes, Black and White Mousse Torte and Chocolate Eclairs. Lighter desserts include Lemon Marzipan Torte, Strawberry White Chocolate Charlotte and Viennese Meringue Tortes. English Trifle, Apple Bavarian Cheesecake, and Chocolate Oblivion Torte served with a raspberry sauce are richer reasons to visit the Cafe Creme de la Creme.

CHAZ
3177 Latta Road
Rochester, New York 14612
Tel: (716) 227-5700
Hrs: Monday - Friday 11:30 a.m. - 2:30 p.m.
Saturday & Sunday Open for dinner
Visa, MasterCard, American Express and Discover are accepted.

"A taste of Americana" is appropriately the slogan for a New York restaurant called Chaz. For nearly 30 years, Frank Martella's family-run restaurant has been one of the most popular in Western New York. Chaz has delicious food, a comfortable yet elegant atmosphere, and the desire to , above all, please the customer.

Chaz was established in 1982 but Frank and Marie Martella have been in food service since 1962. The restaurant has been recently relocated to a brand new building in Long Pond Plaza, 10 miles west of Rochester. Chaz offers a pleasing menu including its famous beef dishes as well as seafood.

The restaurant was originally named for Frank's son Charlie, who is now Chaz's head chef. Its slogan stems mostly from the house specialty, Prime Rib Maitre'd, which Charlie prepares to perfection. This particular dish is char-broiled with crushed peppercorns, garlic, and topped with herb butter. All of the beef at Chaz is delicious but the Prime Rib is something special. Other cuts of Prime Rib are served in various sizes. In addition to the beef, Chaz offers a wide variety of delectable selections from seafood to pasta.

Mr. Martella's new building offers a pleasant change of scenery both inside and out. The new location brought not only a new building but beautiful landscaping as well. The gorgeous fountains found outside are a perfect indication of what guests may expect as they enter this contemporary restaurant. Visitors will find a sleek, spacious dining area. Two dining rooms, one smoking and one non-smoking, are available for the convenience of the customer. Intimate tables for two are available in the lounge area, along with a bar, two satellite televisions and the opportunity for private dinner and conversation. Chaz can also accommodate handicapped patrons.

Frank and Marie Martella are very proud of the reputation they've built for their restaurant over the past 28 years. The fantastic Prime Rib, the contemporary design, and the friendly service make Chaz the restaurant to visit for a complete and enjoyable dining experience.

CRESCENT BEACH HOTEL
1372 Edgemere Drive
Rochester, New York 14612
Tel: (716) 227-3600

The Crescent Beach Hotel, located in Rochester, offers exquisite dining and a beautiful view of Lake Ontario. Situated on the lake, this four-star restaurant is a landmark area dating back to the 1800s. It was a resort hotel until a fire destroyed much of the building.

Renovated and reopened in 1983, the Crescent Beach Hotel operates as a restaurant and lounge and rents its banquet facilities for parties, luncheons and dinners. Owner Joe Bary was an employee of the hotel from 1946 until he bought it with his wife in 1965.

The exterior of the restaurant offers not only the most exciting view of the lake, but also beautifully-landscaped gardens, flowers in full bloom, trees and shrubbery.

An outdoor patio with white wrought-iron furniture and a water fountain is the perfect place to enjoy after-dinner drinks or to watch the sun set over the water.

The interior of the Crescent Beach Hotel is as breathtaking as the outside. It features a beautiful dining area, open and airy with valance draperies which allow diners to enjoy the scenery.

A lounge area features live entertainment on Fridays and Saturdays and a wide variety of beverages including cocktails and wines to complement lunches, dinners or an evening out.

Along with the atmosphere, the restaurant is well-known for its food as well. A lunch menu features deli sandwiches and hot sandwiches. Luncheon entrees include the Omelette of the Day, Welsh Rarebit and on Fridays, Fried Fresh Filet of Haddock. The dinner menu offers appealing appetizers such as shrimp cocktail and marinated artichoke Hearts to start the meal.

From Crescent Beach's ceramic broiler, one could order Prime Rib of Beef Au Jus, or Steak Diane, tenderloin, mushrooms and scallions, for a great-tasting dinner entree.

Those desiring Italian food will find the restaurant's Clams & Broccoli on a bed of linguine in seasoned sauce quite delightful. All dinner entrees include fresh garden salad, potato or vegetable, rolls and butter.

Whichever entree one chooses, a satisfying, enjoyable meal is guaranteed. For the closest and most beautiful view of Lake Ontario, and the finest dining in Rochester, the Crescent Beach Hotel is the place to visit.

FORNATARO'S
2155 Long Pond Road
Rochester, New York 14606
Tel: (716) 426-1240
Hrs: Lunch:

Monday - Thursday	11:00 a.m. - 2:00 p.m.
Saturday	11:00 a.m. - 2:00 p.m.
Dinner:	
Monday - Thursday	5:00 p.m. - 10:00 p.m.
Saturday	5:00 p.m. - 11:00 p.m.
Sunday	1:00 p.m. - 9:00 p.m.

Visa, MasterCard, American Express, Diners Club, Carte Blanche and Discover are accepted.

Where can diners choose from over 30 appetizers, 18 veal dishes, 13 beef entrees, 35 seafood combinations, and 23 poultry selections? Probably nowhere, except an intimate trattoria-style restaurant called Fornataro's. "Trattoria" describes a family dining room situated just off a kitchen so that diners can smell the aroma of simmering tomato sauces, peppers, and Italian seasonings.

Owners Richard and Gem Fornataro pride themselves on their elaborate menu and their professionally prepared cuisine. Customers are free to order anything they want. Under Richard's tutelage are world-class chefs from Italy, Taiwan, and other exotic places around the world. Everything is prepared precisely as it is ordered.

In addition to being pampered with perfectly prepared cuisine, customers will enjoy the celebrity decor in the large dining room. The walls are decorated with colorful oil paintings of James Dean, Marilyn Monroe, Elizabeth Taylor, Elvis, and other stars. Even the fireplace mantle is filled with miniature statues of movie stars. The windows are covered with scenic murals, and the ceiling is authentic corrugated tin.

Fornataro's also has a well-stocked nationality bar which is surrounded with national flags. Party and banquet facilities are available.

Located at the corner of Long Pond and Spencerport Roads, Fornataro's is housed in a finely renovated 140-year old clapboard building. The best route from the city to Fornataro's is Route 490 West to 47 North; exit at Lyell Avenue and 90 West.

Fornataro's serves exactly what the customer orders--and in huge helpings, too. The Zuppa Di Fish with lobster, crab, calamari, shrimp, scallops, clams, and whitefish in a red sauce over fettucine is only one example of the restaurant's culinary wizardry. Fornataro's serves nothing but delectible food. Stop in and see what gives Fornataro's its world-renowned reputation.

HILLY'S CAFE, Village Gate Square, Rock, New York 14607; Tel: (716) 271-8820. Diners enjoy contemporary American cuisine such as mesquite grilled entrees, blackened fish, and prime rib in a simple, relaxed setting. A comfortable decor is achieved with hardwood flooring, wooden ceiling fans, and large potted plants. Live jazz entertainment is provided at the bar on Friday and Saturday nights.

great lakes coast

THE RIO, 282 Alexander Street, Rochester, New York; Tel: (716) 473-2806. The Rio is an excellent choice for dinner Monday - Saturday. Seafood, steaks, veal, and fresh pasta creations are served by tuxedoed waiters and enjoyed in an intimate atmosphere.

ROCHESTER CLUB RESTAURANT, 120 East Avenue, Rochester, New York 14604; Tel: (716) 423-1948. This exciting restaurant offers more than 100 wines and a menu that features aged meats, duck, chicken, and fresh fish flown in from Los Angeles each week. Meals are enjoyed in comfortable surroundings of cherry wood and soft white walls. Rochester Club Restaurant offers the "finest dining between New York and Chicago at the most reasonable price."

ROONEY'S, 90 Henrietta Street, Rochester, New York 14620; Tel: (716) 442-0444. Enjoy lunch or dinner at Rooney's in a classic 19th century tavern setting. The seasonal menu includes imaginative use of grilled and roasted meats, seafood, and homegrown vegetables; meals should be complemented with one of their sumptuous dessert selections.

WATER STREET GRILL, 175 North Water Street, Rochester, New York; Tel: (716) 546-4980. Regional American and international cuisines are featured in an inviting atmosphere. Diners may enjoy their meals seated in the dining room or at the relaxing bar; special dietary requests are accommodated.

specialty shops

BENA'S COLLECTION, Village Gate Square, 274 N. Goodman Street, Rochester, New York 14607; Tel: (716) 473-8840. Bena's Collection is the only store in Rochester to feature Polish arts and crafts. A unique selection of jewelry is available made with amber from the Baltic Sea; other items offered are icons, paintings, sculptures, and accessories. Bena's Collection includes works found during her travels to Eastern Europe.

COFFEE BEAN EXPRESS, Village Gate Square, Rochester, New York 14607; Tel: (716) 244-1160. Rochester's only coffee specialty store is open seven days a week and offers over 60 varieties of coffee beans imported from around the world. Also available are coffee makers and espresso machines.

CRAFT COMPANY NO. 6--CONTEMPORARY AMERICAN CRAFTS
785 University Avenue
Rochester, New York 14607
Tel: (716) 473-3413
Hrs: Monday - Wednesday & Friday
10:00 a.m. - 6:00 p.m.
Thursday
10:00 a.m. - 9:00 p.m.
Saturday
10:00 a.m. - 5:00 p.m.
Sunday
Noon - 5:00 p.m.
Call for special holiday hours.
Visa, MasterCard, American Express and Discover are accepted.

Craft Company No. 6 is a shop that offers the perfect medley of traditional and not so traditional crafts and artistry. The shop is housed in the former Engine Company No. 6, a Victorian firehouse complete with two genuine slide-down fire poles. This colorful brick building with blue trim and plum colored awnings is a showcase for only the highest quality American made crafts.

Owners Gary Stam and Lynn Allinger have launched a country wide search for exquisite, contemporary creations that can't be found in other Rochester area shops. Represented are more than 300 craft artisans from all over the U.S.A. whose works have been selected for uniqueness of design, quality of craftsmanship, and attention to detail. The owners commitment to"made in the U.S.A." adds an important dimension for those who take pride in American creativity and quality.

Craft Company No. 6 features beautiful blown glass in the shape of vases, perfume bottles, paperweights, and Christmas ornaments, wood pieces such as cutting boards, clocks, jewelry boxes, and desk accessories. Other interesting items include pottery and ceramic art forms, jewelry made of glass, paper, aluminum, and porcelain, fiber creations such as baskets, wall hangings, and hand-made paper. But some of the most popular gifts at Craft Company No. 6 are the wood and glass kaleidoscopes.

The shop is located in the museum district near the Memorial Art Gallery and the George Eastman house. Craft Company No. 6 offers an exciting fusion of traditional artistry and contemporary American crafts.

FABRICS & FINDINGS
50 Anderson Avenue
Rochester, New York 14607
Tel: (716) 461-2820
Hrs: Monday, Wednesday, Friday, & Saturday
9:00 a.m. - 5:30 p.m.
Tuesday & Thursday
9:00 a.m. - 9:00 p.m.
Sunday
2:00 p.m. - 5:00 p.m.
Visa and MasterCard are accepted.

"You'll be glad you've found us!" is the slogan boasted by fabric company Fabrics & Findings. While customers are truly happy to discover this store, it is actually pretty hard to miss. Housed in a structure that dates from 1901, the store takes up a full city block. Undoubtedly the largest store of its kind in western New York, the interior is two floors and 50,000 square feet of space occupied by every type of material imaginable. Set up in the fashion of a bazaar, one finds bolt after bolt of quality fabrics and table after table of remnants.

This sewer's paradise is the largest Waverly outlet in New York State and offers Pendleton wool, tapestries, decorator fabrics, a baby department, French Tergal, imported lace, bridal fabrics, and all of the trims that are necessary to create any desired look. This is the place to go for those interested in custom draperies or custom upholstery. Everything is here, including the necessary hardware, or one can leave this job to professionals--an upholstery shop is one of three shops on the premises. The store employs 80 staff members and each is an expert in some aspect of needlework or crafts so customers receive all of the assistance they need.

Perhaps the most exciting quality of this store is the savings available to shoppers. With the merchandising manager purchasing in volume--over 50,000 yards each month--a huge discount is passed on to the customer. Fabrics & Findings is an exciting place to shop with a constantly changing array of materials available. This store is definitely a "Best Choice" for anyone who needs to purchase materials for any sort of sewing or craft project.

LES BONNES CORBEILLES
133 Deerfield Drive
Rochester, New York 14609
Tel: (716) 288-6690
Hrs: By appointment
Visa and MasterCard are accepted.

Les Bonnes Corbeilles (The Good Baskets) is a trendy, upscale business that offers individualized gift baskets for every taste and occasion. No two baskets are ever the same. Entrepreneur Michele Martella-Armes creates custom gift baskets for honeymoons, picnics, anniversaries, Valentine's Day, Christmas, Easter, and every other event imaginable. Michele also prepares children's baskets filled with Beatrix Potter's Peter Rabbit books and other gifts that kids will adore.

Les Bonnes Corbeilles features lovely romantic baskets for two.

These baskets contain candles, love bath, fragrance soaps, men's and women's sachets, fine chocolates, heart-shaped picture frames, champagne glasses and sparking beverages. Swan-shaped baskets, Victorian hat boxes, and decorative gift bags filled with flavored pastas, Hawaiian flatbreads, English preserves, special-blend coffees, chocolate roses, Downey's Spirit Cakes, chocolate covered pretzels and brandied cherries are a few of Les Bonnes Corbeilles other exciting selections. Mrs. Prindable's Apples, hand-dipped in pecans and chocolate, chocolate mint, white chocolate and caramel or a variety of other scrumptious sauces, are yet another kind of connoisseur-quality dessert that Michelle selects for her unique gift baskets.

Michelle offers gift wrapping, card enclosure, personal delivery in the Rochester area, and UPS shipping to other parts of the country. Les Bonnes Corbeilles is located in a stately early twentieth-century, Victorian-style home in Irodequoit, neighboring Rochester.

Whether customers are searching for the appropriate corporate gift or the perfect holiday present, giving Les Bonnes Corbeilles' elegant gift baskets is a sure way to please even the person with the most discriminating tastes.

MANNERS & MORALS
150 North Clinton Avenue
Rochester, New York 14604
Tel: (716) 325-4530
Hrs: Monday-Saturday 10:00 a.m. - 8:00 p.m.
Sunday Noon - 5:00 p.m.
Visa and MasterCard are accepted.

Manners & Morals is an avant-garde furnishings store that takes a strong stand on environmentalism. The shop features natural accessories such as Crystal Farm Antler Chandeliers made of Rocky Mountain black-tail mule deer antlers that have been shed naturally and chemical-free beeswax candles by Burt's Bees'. Owner Martin Schafer buys nothing that isn't ecologically sound and environmentally conservative.

La Lune Willow furniture from Wisconsin, Classic Impressions furnishings available in six different wrought iron finishes, and Zia designs from New Mexico are among the terrific treasures at Manners & Morals. This innovative shop also carries patina copper decorations by Design III. Annieglass dinnerware in 24-karat gold and platinum, and natural dinnerware (terra cotta) that looks great on any table. In addition to carrying bronze pieces, stoneware, and hand-crafted pottery, this ingenious shop features hand-painted tiles, Victorian hatboxes, DiCamillo baked goods, herbs, country wreaths, Steerhorn utensils, jams and other country provisions, distinctive marble paper from Spain, books, and seventeenth-century furniture by Kargas.

Manners & Morals is located at the intersection of North Clinton and Andrews, only half a mile from Route 490.

From French Country furniture to all-natural fragrances, Manners & Morals has a diverse selection of out-of-the-ordinary gifts and furnishings. The selection isn't the only reason to visit Manners & Morals. The service is first-rate, too: Martin gladly ships merchandise or hand-delivers it within the city.

GREATER ROCHESTER

accommodations

BROOKWOOD INN
800 Pittsford-Victor Road
Pittsford, New York 14534
Tel: (716) 248-9000
Visa, MasterCard, American Express, Diners Club, Carte Blanche and Discover are accepted.

The Brookwood Inn located in Bushnell's Basin is a fairly new hotel--it opened May 1987--but is widely recognized for its luxurious guest rooms, meeting and conference facilities, excellent dining facilities, convenience to area attractions, and special services offered to guests that most hotels only provide at their concierge level.

Upon entering this brick building, the comfortable decor of the lobby puts one at ease; it is contemporary without seeming pretentious. Shades of pink, mauve, and teal are important to its contemporary atmosphere.

These same soft colors are found in the inn's 108 luxurious oversized rooms and its five lavish whirlpool suites. These suites are equipped with a jacuzzi and kitchen facilities including a refrigerator, wet bar and microwave oven. Special services include complimentary airport shuttle service, rental cars and FAX machine available on premises, complimentary coffee and USA Today newspapers in the lobby, babysitting service, room service, triple sheeting and an evening turn down service with mints.

The experienced staff is prepared to take care of those putting together a conference or meeting. Brookwood Inn facilities can accommodate groups ranging from five to 75. Smaller business meetings may also be conducted in Chatham's restaurant and lounge. Serving breakfast, lunch, and dinner daily, it is the perfect place to head for something simple like a Club Sandwich or an extravagant dish such as Scallops Meuniere. All guests can take advantage of the heated indoor pool, whirlpool, and walkout sun deck. The fitness center offers an opportunity to work out indoors. Joggers enjoy the scenic canal jogging path nearby. Hotel bicycles are available for leisurely tours along the Barge Canal bike trail.

General Manager Mary Lu Roeser demands perfection from her employees so one can always expect to find immaculate rooms and a polite friendly service staff. Brookwood Inn, a "Best Choice" for visitors in Monroe County, is near such attractions as Strong Museum, International Museum of Photography, The Finger Lakes Region, Bristol Mountain, Sonnenberg Gardens, and Finger Lakes Performing Arts Center.

THE DEPOT INN & RESTAURANT
41 North Main Street
Pittsford, New York 14534
Tel: (716) 381-9900
Hrs: Serves Breakfast, Lunch, Dinner & Sunday Brunch.
Visa, MasterCard, American Express, Carte Blanche and Discover are accepted.

This 1842 railroad complex, built on the towpath of the Erie Canal, takes visitors on a retrospective, imaginary journey into the past. The Depot Inn and Restaurant are rated Three Star by Mobil and Three Diamond by AAA for overall excellence. The Depot Inn has 100 immaculate, quiet, completely renovated rooms done in solid cherry Queen Anne style. Across from dozens of boutiques, in the elegant Rochester suburb of Pittsford, The Depot Inn was voted one of America's "Top 400 Roadside Inns."

The Depot Restaurant serves the finest prime rib in town that is guaranteed to be "Love at First Bite." Enjoy the ambiance of yesteryear while dining on "Simply Great American Cuisine" and finish with a delectable confection created especially for the customer by their Bavarian pastry chef. Authentic train cars can serve private parties up to 35 and The Original Station House will hold up to 50 people. Owner Ralph Turgeon just completed renovating "The Other Side of the Tracks." Originally an apple storage house built in the late 1800s, it serves as an eclectic banquet/meeting complex for groups of 4-130.

With complimentary airport shuttle service and holding the honor of being voted "The Restaurant With the Best Sunday Brunch in Town," The Depot Inn and Restaurant promises to be a very memorable stay.

antiques

THE RAINBIRD
7 Schoen Place
Pittsford, New York 14534
Tel: (716) 385-5690
Hrs: Monday - Saturday 10:30 a.m. - 4:30 p.m.
Or by appointment
Visa and MasterCard are accepted.

The world of Fine Antiques comes alive for the serious collector at The Rainbird. Located in a rustic setting, The Rainbird occupies the lower level of a building that was originally a barn built in the 1800s. The emphasis is on handsome and unusual antiques set in 1200 square feet of spacious room, exposed timbers, whitewashed walls and ceilings. The ambiance invites exploration and investigation of a wide range of English country furniture, including French and Irish pieces of great artistic merit. There is an extensive collection of pine hutches, dressers, linen presses, armoires, and tables that are as popular today in Europe as they have been for centuries.

Owner Jennifer Dery, a native of England, is renowned for her knowledge and keen eye of antiques. She frequently returns to England to conduct her own buying. One of her favorite dealers is an English sheep farmer, as it is generally known that amongst those green and rolling hills it is the local farmers that find the most interesting pieces. What she has gathered will thrill and delight even the most jaded collector. Besides furniture, there are antique tools, china, silver, glass, pewter and brass, as well as other collectibles. Antique spice chests, boxes, coffers and the ever popular old watering cans help to complete the total antique experience.

Lovejoy, the aptly named cat of the proprietress, wanders about the shop enhancing the comfortable setting reminiscent of the atmosphere one would find in her namesake's haunt of East Anglia.

If the world of fine antiques is a passion, then please partake of Jennifer's kind invitation to visit and browse in her unique shop and enjoy the craftsmanship and artistry of country pine furniture.

apparel

THE BLACK SHEEP
7 South Main Street
Pittsford, New York 14534
Tel: (716) 248-3960
Hrs: Monday - Saturday 10:00 a.m. - 5:00 p.m.
Thursday 10:00 a.m. - 8:00 p.m.
Visa and Mastercard are accepted.

The Black Sheep is a colorful children's boutique that carries quality kidswear with a European flair. What's unusual about this classy clothing shop is that the clothes are both fun and durable. The distinctive second floor shop offers unique stenciled playwear, handknit sweaters, infant items, classically-styled cotton apparel, cuddly stuffed animals, stylish dresses, attractive accessories, and fabulous gifts.

Energetic owner Sue Triolo is great at locating rare finds and quality clothes that can't be found in department stores. The Black Sheep carries girls clothing in sizes from infant to 14, and boyswear in sizes from infant to size 7. One-hundred percent cotton is the specialty at this attic style boutique.

Located amid a row of historic shops near Pittsford's four corners, the Black Sheep is situated upstairs from the Country Gallery. A set of original oak stairs lead to the cozy boutique, decorated with wall stencils, shiny hardwood floors and rooms of imported and California snowsuits and jackets.

Sue's upbeat and witty personality adds to the boutique's ambiance to make shopping a fun experience. The fantastic variety of merchandise, the cozy attic-like atmosphere, and the owner's more than friendly service make the Black Sheep a "Best Choice." Both children and parents will be satisfied with the selection the store offers. The clothing is imaginative, bright, durable, and, above all, fun.

HILDA OF ICELAND
32 South Main Street
Pittsford, New York 14534
Tel: (716) 383-8140
Hrs: Monday - Saturday 10:00 a.m. - 5:00 p.m.
Winter:
Thursday Until 8:00 p.m.
Holiday Hours:
Sunday 11:00 a.m. - 5:00 p.m.
Visa, MasterCard and Discover are accepted.

Hilda of Iceland is a contemporary garment shop that specializes in warm outerwear made of pure Icelandic wool. The Pittsford Hilda of Iceland is one of 28 individually owned Hilda stores in the United States, Canada, and the Caribbean.

Icelandic wool was first introduced to the world 25 years ago by Hilda of Iceland. What's so unique about this type of wool is that it is naturally water repellent, comfortably lightweight, remarkably warm and always beautiful.

More than a millennium ago, the first settlers took common sheep to Iceland, where the sheep adapted to this exotic land of hot-water springs and arctic climate. As a result of this climate, the common sheep has evolved into an Icelandic sheep that has a lanolin-coated fleece with a long, shiny, outer layer and a soft, short, heavy, inner layer. These qualities make the Icelandic wool both luxurious and soil resistant.

Upon entering the Hilda of Iceland shop in Pittsford, one finds a warm and friendly atmosphere and a comfortable setting for shopping. Customers receive personal service from its owner Elaine Smillie and her staff.

Browsing through the shop, one finds many styles of clothing to choose from. Classic lined coats in three lengths, jackets for men and women, sweaters both loomed and hand knitted in the beautiful traditional Icelandic patterns, or new updated styles and colors are some examples. Also available are capes, ponchos, romantic shawls, blankets, sheepskin rugs, and accessories.

During the spring and summer months, the shop also features a selection of casual clothing made from natural fibers of cotton, silk, and linen.

Visit Hilda of Iceland in Pittsford and discover the distinctive look that is absolutely one of a kind.

POLLIWOGS & PIGTAILS
25 South Main Street
Pittsford, New York 14534
Tel: (716) 586-7338
Hrs: Monday - Saturday 9:30a.m. - 5:00p.m.
Thursday 9:30a.m. - 8:00p.m.
Visa and MasterCard are accepted.

Polliwogs & Pigtails is an honest-to-goodness traditional children's clothing shop. The emphasis here is on quality apparel that is moderately priced; the items that cost more are well worth it. The store has an intriguing old-fashioned flair, and kids love to come shopping here, too. There are 14 rooms--each with a different size of children's clothing. Boys' sizes range from infant to size seven, and girls' sizes run from infant to pre-teen.

Polliwogs & Pigtails offers the apparel, accessories, giftware, and books of approximately 400 vendors. All merchandise is brightly displayed and expertly sold by a well-trained and caring staff. One room, filled with cute accessories and small gifts, seems to be children's favorite, but kids' fun doesn't end there. This enchanting shop has lots of nooks, crannies and playrooms where children love to romp while mom and dad browse.

If this fun clothing store sounds warm and homey, that's because it is located in one of Pittsford Village's century-and-a-half-old colonial homes, complete with shiny hardwood floors and four original fireplaces.

Polliwogs & Pigtails provides some pretty ingenious gift wrappings, too; the boxes are shaped like houses. Customers also have a choice of colored tissue paper and gingham ribbon bows.

Polliwogs & Pigtails is a nifty children's clothing store that specializes in classic clothes. Kids love the fun decor; parents love the lasting quality of the items available.

art galleries

ROSELAWN GALLERIES
7 Schoen Place
Pittsford, New York 14534
Tel: (716) 586-5441
Hrs: Monday - Saturday 10:30a.m. - 4:30p.m.
Visa and MasterCard are accepted.

Roselawn Galleries is located in a converted grain storage building along the historic Erie Canal. The gallery, unique among several specialty shops in the area, features carefully selected artwork and fine crafts by local artists. Several artists who have gained national recognition are represented. Included are metal sculptor, Carl Zollo and painters, Mike Falco, Barbara Moore and Darleen Phipps.

Both contemporary and traditional artists are represented by owners, Joyce Luebstorff and Jessie O'Dell. Prior to opening the gallery ten years ago, Jessie studied drawing, painting and art history at the Rochester Institute of Technology and the Rochester Memorial Art Gallery. Joyce's background is in interior design studies and both welcome the opportunity to assist both the beginning and experienced art buyer.

Featured works include primitive oil paintings, contemporary oil, watercolor and pastel paintings, prints, metal sculpture and pottery. Locally crafted Art Glass is also a specialty of the gallery. Handblown and fused glass vases, dinnerware, perfume bottles, paperweights and ornaments with attractive prices appeal to both personal collectors and gift givers.

As befits the historic village atmosphere, both collectors and browsers are warmly welcomed and given individual attention. The Rochester area is rich with artistic talent and both local and out of town customers have been enthusiastic about the selection at Roselawn Galleries.

collectibles

OUR FRONT PORCH
56 North Main Street
Pittsford, New York 14534

Tel:	(716) 586-9073	
Hrs:	Monday - Saturday	10:00 a.m. - 5:00 p.m.
	Thursday	Until 8:00 p.m.
	Sunday (in December)	1:00 p.m. - 5:00 p.m.
	Holidays:	
	Tuesday & Thursday	10:00 a.m. - 8:30 p.m.

Our Front Porch is a charming shop located in the wonderful historic village of Pittsford. Visiting the quaint shops in this village is like taking a step back in time. The decor, shops, and the friendly service gives visitors a cozy hometown feeling.

Our Front Porch was established in 1981 and was initially a local artist consignment and handcraft shop. It contains a wide selection of beautiful country collectibles, including gorgeous natural wreaths. Other interesting items visitors can choose from are beautiful country rugs, prints, wall plaques, pewter gifts, personalized Rowe Pottery, and handmade ornaments which will give any Christmas tree an extra special touch. Take home a cuddly stuffed VanderBear, a Best Friend Bunny or maybe one of Our Front Porch's adorable country dolls.

This charming little shop, located on North Main Street, is filled to the brim with lovely gift items. Anything anyone could possibly want can be found here, making it the perfect place to buy a gift for someone special. Our Front Porch has braided rugs, Baldwin Brass, framed doilies, tinware, Batenburg Lace, quilted and calico pillows, and many other decorations to give a home a cozy and complete atmosphere.

Barbara Crossley, owner of the shop, believes in treating each customer with special care. She is very proud of the quality of merchandise she carries and knowing that whether looking for American Country, English, or French, visitors will be sure to fulfill all of their country needs at Our Front Porch.

gift shops

COUNTRY GALLERY
9 South Main Street
Pittsford, New York 14534
Tel: (716) 381-2161
Hrs: Monday - Saturday 10:00 a.m - 5:00 p.m.
Thursday Until 8:00 p.m.
Holiday Hrs (in addition to the Monday - Saturday Hours):
Sunday Noon - 5:00 p.m.
Visa and MasterCard are accepted.

The Country Gallery, located in historic Pittsford Village, is a diverse gift shop that offers not only country-style collectibles but European decorating accessories. The Country Gallery carries a wide selection of French pottery, Judy Tesch dolls, Pierre Deux Country French fabrics, gorgeous needlepoint, and delicate tapestry pillows.

Owner Mary Ann Hendricks also has a well-stocked collection of Father Christmas antique pieces and a wide range of decorations for every holiday. She carries a variety of crafts and artwork from around the country as well as many pieces by local artists. The merchandise is always changing, but customers can count on the quality being consistently first-rate.

The Country Gallery is filled with milk paint furniture, Irish pine hitches, dried flowers, hand woven wreathes, watercolor paintings, handmade quilts, collectible bears, and lovely folk art pieces. This wonderful little gift shop offers an interior decorating service and a convenient bridal registry. The store also provides a personal shopping service that lets customers purchase items conveniently from their own homes. The Country Gallery is the place to stock up on intriguing accessories that will add a personal touch to any home.

ice cream parlors

GELATO FRESCO, 65 Packett's Landing, Fairport, New York. Voted "Best ice cream in Rochester" according to a readers' poll, Gelato Fresco also offers chocolate truffles and fresh pasta and sauces.

specialty shops

THE PITTSFORD CAROUSEL
36 North Main Street
Pittsford, New York 14534
Tel: (716) 385-2780
Hrs: Monday - Saturday 10:00 a.m. - 5:00 p.m.
Thursday & Holidays 10:00 a.m. - 9:00 p.m.
Visa and MasterCard are accepted.

In 1870, the Schoen family constructed their home to accommodate a grain and feed business. A coal tower and grainery are a few of the unique facilities which sets apart this complex from others.

Now, over 100 years later, as part of Schoen Place, The Pittsford Carousel Inc. has helped maintain the authenticity of this site as a specialty shop in one of many historic homes.

In 1957, the Pittsford Carousel was started by three ladies, and is currently owned by Virginia Degenhardt. Located on North Main Street in the village of Pittsford, the shop is unique as it maintains the congenial atmosphere one would expect to find in a historic home along the Erie Canal.

The Pittsford Carousel offers something special for everyone: unmatched women's country apparel such as gorgeous handknit sweaters, "Geiger of Austria" classics, including skirts, blouses, sweaters, and coats. A fine selection of accessories, featuring belts, handbags, scarves, and jewelry from brass bracelets to pearls complement any lady's wardrobe.

The Pittsford Carousel invites one and all to browse through seven rooms enhanced by country gifts, to see the delightful children's corner, and to enjoy a touch of Christmas year-round.

S.J.'S
15 South Main Street
Pittsford, New York 14534
Tel: (716) 248-0640
Hrs: Monday - Saturday 10:00 a.m. - 5:00 p.m.

Dr. Shirley Joseph, a professor of surgery at the University of Rochester Medical Center, has combined her love for shopping with her desire to collect primitive antiques by opening a quaint specialty shop appropriately named S.J.'s. S.J.'s offers a unique collection of Native American Accessories usually found only in the Southwest. Located in the Village of Pittsford, S.J.'s is a friendly specialty shop with a genuine sense of style.

Dr. Joseph has compiled a special collection of primitive antiques. Entering the shop is like walking into a Ralph Lauren setting. Guests are surrounded by sand and terra cotta walls. Scattered around the shop are several types of oriental, hooked, and braided rugs, Dr. Joseph is proud of the "Ralph Lauren" atmosphere in her shop and the fact that both the decor and the merchandise are unusual to this part of upstate New York.

It's difficult to single out any particular type of item as S.J.'s specialty because each is rare in its own right. A few items that are representative of the quality selection are a blend of leather and suede purses, belts, gloves, and attache cases. Also offered are women's shoes by Cole Haan, men's leather dop kits, and Guatemalan woven handbags, and belts. Along with these fine suede and leather goods, S.J.'s carries a spectacular selection of Southwestern decorative pieces. Included in her collection are Native American sterling silver jewelry, Indian pottery, pillows, rugs, cowboy boots, and custom picture frames. These are all unique items that are difficult to find anywhere else in the Northeast.

S.J.'s specialty shop is housed in historic Pittsford Village, with the ambiance of a living room in its comfortable sofa and chairs. Dr. Joseph's reasons for the shop's selections reflect her belief that the Native American look is part of the American culture and that interest in the area is escalating.

VIGREN & O'SHAUGNESSY IRISH IMPORTS
39 South Main Street
Pittsford, New York 14534

Tel:	(716) 248-8346	
Hrs:	Monday - Saturday	10:00 a.m. - 5:00 p.m.
	Holidays:	
	Thursday evening	Until 7:30 p.m.
	Sunday	11:00 a.m. - 3:00 p.m.

Mail Orders welcome - UPS anywhere.
Visa and MasterCard are accepted.

Vigren & O'Shaughnessy Irish Imports is a specialty shop that has been in historic Pittsford for six years. The shop imports 80 percent of its goods directly from Ireland. Johanna O'Brien, the shop's owner, attends the Dublin Crafts Fair annually to select goods for the store.

Some of the many specialties Vigren & O'Shaughnessy offers include: Belleek and Donegal Parian China, Dublin and Galway mouth blown and hand-cut crystal, Kerry Glass paperweights in "forty shades of green," handcrafted porcelain cottages, music boxes, and made to order linen tablewear. The shop also features handsewn christening gowns, handcarved nativity sets, holiday ornaments and a wide assortment of personalized decorations such as wall plaques, parchments, glassware, and mugs with family coats of arms.

While Irish music plays throughout the shop, patrons can enjoy browsing through a variety of clothing such as hand knit Fisherman sweaters, colorful wool and mohair sweaters, hats, scarves, mitts and gloves and a luscious selection of mohair and new wool throws. A selection of outerwear for him and her is available in the famous walking hat, caps, coats, capes and jackets. For the wee ones, there is a nice selection of kilts, pinafores, t-shirts, sweat suits and whimsical bibs. A lovely collection of Celtic jewelry and Claddagh rings in sterling silver and gold complement the fine clothing items carried.

Visitors can satisfy their taste buds with gourmet food items including marmalade and jellies, teas, Irish whiskey cakes, mustards, candies, oatmeal, brown breads, and biscuits.

Johanna and her staff will act as a customer's personal shopper by taking special orders, gift wrapping for all occasions and shipping the items anywhere. Those looking for handmade Irish goods will find them here along with top quality and personalized service, making Vigren & O'Shaughnessy Irish Imports a "Best Choice" boutique in Pittsford.

tennis

MENDON PONDS TENNIS CLUB
834 Mendon Center Road
Pittsford, New York 14534
Tel: (716) 582-1320
Hrs: Tennis facilities open year-round, seven days a week. Swimming and volleyball facilities are seasonal.
Visa and MasterCard are accepted.

Mendon Ponds Tennis Club is located in a private setting adjacent to Mendon Ponds Park. The club's 50 wooded acres provide a most serene atmosphere to relax and socialize with friends.

The club offers 11 Har-Tru and eight Laykold tennis courts, two swimming pools shaped like tennis racquets, a pro shop which carries the latest in equipment and tennis apparel, beach volleyball, a children's playground, and a clubhouse with a full-service snack bar.

The tennis club is open year-round and provides a variety of programs including leagues, junior and adult tournaments, seasonal and open-court time, and summer camps and memberships for juniors and adults. Mendon Ponds also offers the Alligator Club, which is a day camp program developed for children ages 3 to 10. In May, the club sponsors the Annual Lilac Festival Family Cup Tournament.

Mendon Ponds is also the home of the Roger Wootton Tennis Academy (RWTA). Roger Wootton is a former most valuable collegiate player and international world ranked touring pro. As the Director of Tennis, he has a complete year-round training program for players of all ages and abilities. Roger Wootton trains juniors and adults to play socially and\or to compete on a national and world ranked level. His teaching techniques are regarded as the finest and subsequently Mendon Ponds has one of the largest instructional programs in the world.

Mendon Ponds Tennis Club can be reached from the Interstate Highway. Drive east/west to Exit 45. Immediately following the toll gate, take the exit to NY 96/Victor. Turn left/south on Route 96 to Route 251. Turn right/west onto Route 251. Go past Route 64 and past West Bloomfield Road. Turn north on Mendon Center Road and drive past both Pond and Smith Roads. Turn right onto Topspin Drive.

BROCKPORT

attractions

Morgan-Manning House is a furnished Victorian-style house built in 1854. Open April through December, this beautifully-decorated house is a step back in time.

bed & breakfast inns

THE VICTORIAN BED AND BREAKFAST, 320 Main Street, Brockport, New York 14420; Tel: (716) 637-7519. Built in 1890, this bed and breakfast offers four bedrooms and three baths. Brimming with antiques, it provides a cozy setting for an overnight stay. A full breakfast is served on weekends.

restaurants

HARVESTER PARK INN
51 Market Street
Brockport, New York 14420

Tel:	**(716) 637-2500**	
Hrs:	**Lunch:**	
	Tuesday - Friday	**11:30 a.m. - 2:00 p.m.**
	Dinner:	
	Tuesday - Friday	**4:00 p.m on**
	Saturday	**5:00 p.m. on**
	Sunday	**1:00 p.m. - 8:00 p.m.**

Visa, MasterCard, American Express and Discover are accepted.

Remember that old saying that a restaurant can't have terrific food and a great view at the same time? Well, forget it. The Harvester Park Inn, located on the Erie Canal, offers both a breathtaking vista and a host of palatable menu items.

The canal room, with its Tiffany lamps, skylights, hanging plants, Windsor chairs, candlelight, and pearl grey tablecloths with white overlays, is a magnificent vantage point for watching colorful sailboats and other vessels float past. And the food--well, that's the best part of dining at the Harvester Park Inn.

The appetizers include spectacularly presented mushrooms with crabmeat stuffing, escargot, french onion soup with cheese and a puff pastry

topping, tender-baked Clams Casino, Raspberry-vinaigrette, marinated artichoke hearts, and sea scallops simmered in cream sauce.

Enticing entrees include Stuffed Greek Tenderloin (Filet Mignon, feta cheese, spinach and spices broiled in lemon, garlic, oregano, and butter) Fettucine Del Mar (gulf shrimp, scallops, broccoli flowers, fresh mushrooms, futtuccuni noodles, and alfredo sauce) and the chef's special, Veal in Pastry (baked slices of veal, shrimp, gruyere, fennel butter, and a white sauce in a puff pastry shell). The Lemon Walnut Chicken and the Chicken and Shrimp Chardonnay are other epicurean delights.

Parents will be happy to hear that the Harvester Park Inn features a children's menu, complete with selections like Breaded Chicken Fingers, Spaghetti and Meatballs, Deep-fried Shrimp, Grilled Cheese, and Ground Steakburger.

The intimate, small-town ambiance attracts a varied clientele from boaters to students and university professors. The Harvester Park Inn, in the heart of Brockport, sits across from the canal's lift bridge and overlooks Harvester Park. Aside from the elegant decor, magnificent view, and sublime cuisine, the Harvester Park Inn also features weekend entertainment by Bud DeTar, who, with his distinctive, jazz-style piano music, really knows how to put his signature on a keyboard,

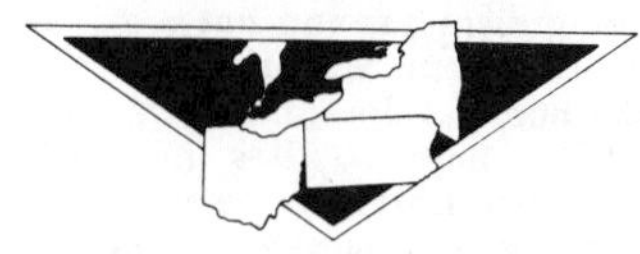

WAYNE COUNTY

Named after General "Mad" Anthony Wayne, the county was created in 1823 from Ontario and Seneca Counties. The first Indians to settle and hunt in the area were the Algonquins, who were later forced to leave by the Iroquois Indians. The area then became known as the land of the Senecas and Cayugas.

The first permanent dweller settled in Wayne County in 1789. The War of 1812, along with diseases and fear of Indians, slowed down settlement until finishing touches were put on the Erie Canal in 1821. This and the New York Central Railroad, constructed years later, drew people to the area again.

The county boasts the beginnings of the Mormon Religion near Palmyra, soil well-designed for agriculture, great fishing waters and the well-known Chimney Bluffs. Apple and cherry trees are abundant as are historic cobblestone structures made in Wayne county after the completion of the Erie Canal.

Over 200 years old now, Wayne County is marked by beautiful land and water, bountiful fruit and vegetable crops, some of the finest fishing areas along the Great Lakes Coast and a rich heritage still evident in the homes, museums and lighthouse, some of which have been preserved nearly two centuries.

attractions

Chimney Bluffs State Park is a beautiful area, undeveloped and natural. The highlight of a visit to the park is the vertical cliffs which stretch a half-mile along Lake Ontario. The cliffs, 150-feet high, feature a narrow glacial ridge that has been worn away by the elements. A long trail that winds around the bluffs is open to the public.

Lake Shore Marshes Wildlife Management Area, north of Wolcott, features pheasant, rabbit, deer, waterfowl, grouse and other such wildlife on 6,180 acres.

Old Sodus Lighthouse & Marine Museum, built in 1870, replaced the previously existing lighthouse. It consists of a maritime museum and offers a wonderful view of the bluffs and the lake. It is open on weekends during the summer.

Phelp's General Store Museum is right out of the 19th Century. Merchandise and original furnishings are housed in the store/museum.

Alling Coverlet Museum exhibits 19th Century coverlets, handmade quilts, spinning and weaving displays, and has a gift shop on the premises for those wishing to take souvenirs home with them.

Palmyra was the home of Joseph Smith, the founder of The Church of Jesus Christ of Latter-Day Saints. Sites include **The Sacred Grove, The Joseph Smith Home, The Martin Harris Home and the Visitors' Center.**

Set on a historic site, **Palmyra-Macedon Aqueduct Park** features a pavilion, recreational equipment, a baseball diamond and boat docking and launching facilities.

Open June to Labor Day, **Sodus Point Park** provides facilities for swimming, a bathhouse, pavilions and recreational equipment.

Hoffman Clock Museum boasts one of the largest antique clock collections in the Northeast. Early Wayne County is depicted by the museum's fine collections and the cobblestone homes along the road. It's open every day but Sunday.

Located in the old county jail, which was used until 1961, and sheriff's residence, **Wayne County Museum** carries exhibits of the Erie Canal, agriculture, military history and rural occupations.

Galen Wildlife Management Area features 641 acres of deer, waterfowl, grouse, squirrel, rabbits, fox and raccoon in scenic Clyde, New York.

events

July is the month for the best of competitive tournament fishing at the **Trophy Waters Tournament**, which takes place up and down the lakes in Wayne, Oswego and Cayuga Counties.

The **Wayne County Fair** is held in August in Palmyra.

Hill Cumorah Pageant, set in historic Mormon Country, takes place in July in the village of Palmyra. The pageant is an existing production about the Hill Cumorah, where a battle was fought and where Joseph found and translated buried records of the Book of Mormon.

Canal Town Days are celebrated in September commemorating the building of the Erie Canal and its impact on Palmyra as a port town.

THE ERIE CANAL

By Christina L. Fertig

The Erie Canal was seen in various lights from its conception to its completion, being referred to in a grandiose manner by its proponents as "The Grand Canal" and in a disparaging manner by its opposers as "The Big Ditch." Whatever the nickname given, this eight-year-long, $8,000,000 project was an immediate tremendous financial success that led to the growth and prosperity of the many counties, cities, and towns that it traversed.

The decision to build a canal that would stretch from Lake Erie to the Atlantic Ocean did not happen overnight; the necessity for a means of transportation that was more effective than road or river travel was recognized many years before the construction of the canal began. However, just how such a thing would be built or paid for was uncertain.

George Washington was excited about canals and the possibilities they held for helping the young United States grow into a powerful nation. As early as 1773 he envisioned a canal that would join the Potomac and Ohio rivers. After a 680-mile trip through western territories, he was more determined that a well-placed canal would draw the produce of western farmers with the fur trades of the lakes to eastern seaports which would in turn greatly increase the exports the country had to offer.

The nation's first president was only one of many to deem canals necessary after surveying the land. Transportation at the time was a laborious, aggravating process. The roads of the time were merely rutted trails. The Mohawk River was a popular method of transport that also had its problems; a long, smoothly flowing stretch of water would sudddenly drop off at a water fall. At this point it was necessary to unload all cargo in order to travel by land until the next stretch of water was in sight. This slow-moving system increased the cost of shipping every step of the way and lowered profits all-around. Along with making frontier travel difficult, these obstructions also discouraged the settlement of the wilderness.

Finally it became an accepted fact that improvements to inland waterways was necessary. In 1792 New York legislators passed a bill for establishing and opening lock navigation within the state. The two companies that were formed, Western Inland Lock Navigation Company and Northern Inland Lock Navigation Company, were responsible for building locks and canals in separate geographical areas.

The NILNC was to build a connection between the Hudson River and Lake Champlain while the WINLC straightened out navigation on the Mohawk River. This company began work immediately in April 1793 on a canal that would by-pass the Little Falls of the Mohawk. Although no more than one mile long, this canal and its five locks took over two years to build; more than half of it was cut through solid rock and delays were caused by financial difficulties. When finally completed, the canal had an important effect on river traffic. Large flatboats or "Durham boats" could now be used to carry eight times more freight than was previously possible and the portage around the falls had been eliminated. These two factors were very important in reducing the costs of shipping; the cost of moving a ton of freight from Utica to Schnectady went from 14 to five dollars. This small by-pass canal caused an increase in river traffic and tonnage shipped.

The WILNC was able to collect necessary tolls at the Little Falls canal facility, however, without adequate financing to back it up, it was unable to continue with such projects. The state of New York purchased the company in 1810. The NILNC was never able to achieve even a small success. Approximately $100,000 was wasted in an attempt to build a canal between Lake Champlain and the upper Hudson River--the project was never completed.

For those who dreamed of an elaborate canal system, the brief works of these two companies may have whet their appetites. Canal-building was not an easy process but it could be done. For the rest that did not hold much faith in this dream, the opposite occurred. Any desire they may have had for man-made waterways was squelched by the financial difficulties the companies incurred while producing very little results.

The nation seemed to be in a bind--it was still a recognized fact that present transportation methods were not nearly adequate, however, with so many critics against the further waste of time and finances through canal-building, it was nearly impossible to upgrade the system.

The writings of Jesse Hawley, a flour merchant from Geneva, New York, made a difference at this time. He is credited by many historians for coming up with the complete concept of a canal that would connect Lake Erie, the Mohawk River, and the Hudson River. He completed 14 essays on the subject which appeared in the Genesee Messenger in 1807 and 1808 under the pen name "Hercules". Hawley did manage to stir up some interest in such a canal but it was difficult to move forward with any sort of plan because so many seemed to be opposed to the idea.

Influential men in the Legislature were taken by Hawley's idea. Judge James Geddes surveyed two routes that the canal could take, both originating in Albany with one going to Lake Ontario and the other to Lake Erie. One year later he submitted a report stating that it would be wiser to choose the Lake Erie route allowing Niagara to remain as a barrier. Doing so would deflect commerce that normally passed through the western Great Lakes into the state of New York. (Canadians later challenged this ploy by building the Welland Canal.)

DeWitt Clinton, the "builder" of the canal enters the historical picture at this time. As a very popular, prominent Democratic leader of the day, canal promoters realized that with Clinton on their side their project would be seen in a more favorable light in Legislature. Without his support they were doomed to failure. With the situation explained to him thoroughly, Clinton agreed that he would second a motion made to appoint a commission to study the possibility of such a canal. The act was passed due to his influence and he was named one of the committee members. He became the leader in the struggle for the canal's existence and with his enthusiastic backing, a bill was passed in the Assembly that gave his committee the power to proceed with the construction of a 364-mile long canal.

Excavation began in Rome, the middle section of the plan, on July 4, 1817. During the early building period, Clinton asked for the advice and assistance of Canvass White, a young man who had studied surveying. White traveled to Europe where he stayed for a year studying Old World canals. Returning to the states full of drawings and ideas, he found engineers puzzled over what sort of material should be used to build the canal locks--wood or stone. Cement, the ideal building material, could only be obtained from Europe and was very costly but it was believed that neither the wood nor the stone would withstand the test of time. Within a few months of realizing this dilemma, a stone from which top quality cement could be produced was discovered while working on the canal. This was the first time that cement was produced in the U.S. and the use of it ensured that the canal would last a long time.

Many unprecedented engineering feats were accomplished during the eight years that the canal was created, the most amazing of which is the locks at Lockport. This city owes all that it is to the Erie Canal including its name. Once a desolate wild life area, the city had nothing that would attract settlers to it. Being located on the path of the proposed canal was this area's only saving grace. As part of the Niagara Escarpment, it presented a very difficult problem for the project's engineers; they had to find a way to raise and lower boats up and down its 70 foot drop.

Knowing that no one lock would not solve the problem, the engineers devised a twin system of five locks that would allow simultaneous up-and-down traffic of boats. The locks of Lockport resembled a set of giant steps cut into the side of the escarpment. The brilliant plan that they formulated to overcome this handicap can still be viewed today in part at Lockport. One of the original locks still remains. A visit to the original locks and the Canal Museum allows a glimpse of the original flight of five locks that now form a cascade of waterfalls.

During most of the eight-year construction period, between 2,000-3,000 men were employed as laborers. Immigrants were being attracted to the areas and settled down in what would later become port towns. The promise of prosperity the canal would bring was as much a draw as the immediate income it would provide during its construction.

Completion of each section of the canal caused eager anticipation in those who were dreaming about the day that water and boats would flow the full length of the canal. The first boats to navigate its waters did so as early as 1819 and by 1822, boats were able to use 220 miles of the canal. Still, anxious citizens looked forward to seeing the Erie Canal in its full glory.

Culmination of one of the greatest works America has ever seen was reached on November 4, 1825. Thousands of elated spectators were on hand to witness Governor Clinton marking the completion of this project by symbolically pouring a keg of Erie water into the Atlantic Ocean. The Erie Canal, spanning the distance from Albany to Buffalo and more than 10 times longer than any other canal in existence was about to make a difference in the destiny of a young nation that was struggling for a foothold in international economic affairs.

Those who had believed that the Erie Canal project was going to be a costly failure quickly learned otherwise. In its first year 13,110 boats and rafts passed through the junction canal between Watervliet and Albany; the tolls that were charged enabled the canal to pay for itself within nine years. Though the canal's dimensions may not have been impressive (four feet deep, 40 feet wide at top, and 28 feet wide at bottom), the celebration of it continued many years after its opening as it brought wealth and eminence to many cities.

New York City is a prime example of a city that, if not created by the canal, was strongly shaped by it. Even though New York had been opposed to the bill that would allow construction of the canal, that did not stop the city from reaping the benefits of all the trade that took place along the Eastern Seaboard due to the canal.

Providing uninterrupted navigation from the western end of Lake Erie to the Atlantic Ocean, the Erie Canal easily dominated other waterways. Routes such as the Mohawk-Hudson and the St. Lawrence River lacked speed because problems such as waterfalls had to be dealt with. The Erie Canal was used to quickly transport lumber, stones, ashes, grain, and other produce of the American West at one half the cost of using the St. Lawrence River route. Use of the canal was also popular because freight charges were a fraction of the charges found in the turnpike traffic.

The Erie Canal was a barge canal and as such was never quite able to open the Great Lakes to major ocean shipping. However, the amount of goods shipped to the East Coast did afford cities like New York the opportunity to get involved with export trade and in turn become markets for imported goods.

Immediately after the canal's opening, rival cities attempted to build their own canals but didn't meet with much success. The Erie Canal, outlasting other man-made waterways, lost its status as the primary means of inland transport to America's newest up and coming dream--the railroad.

The turn of the century witnessed an improvement in western agriculture after a long depression and the combined forces of the Erie Canal and railroad could hardly transport the grain that was being produced across the country. To resolve this problem, New York state wished to deepen the canal to nine feet, but was unable to get adequate finances for this project. By the 1880s the Erie Canal was obsolete. The canal era was given up for the railroad era.

Railroads were much cheaper and easier to build than canals. Unlike the waterway that would freeze up in the winter, the railroad could be used year-round; the shipping process would not come to a halt over water that was too high or too low, and trains were not limited by a four mile per hour speed limit as were vessels using the canal.

New York State still clung to its belief in the canal; in 1903 the state resolved to construct a canal that would be 12 feet deep with locks 328 feet long and 45 feet wide. Construction of the New York Barge Canal System, completed by the mid 1920s, was a long and costly process. With its traffic restricted to barges only, and the railroad era well underway, this canal never realized its full potential.

The Erie Canal, after being modernized, was one of four canals to be incorporated into this system; the other three are the Champlain, Oswego, and Cayuga-Seneca canals. The 524-mile waterway takes advantage of rivers and lakes, using the original canals for the most part, but running parallel at times to sections that fell into disuse.

Although the Erie Canal is no longer considered to be a useful tool for industrial development, money is still invested each year to improve it and its surroundings areas. The New York State Department of Economic Development has initiated a program that encourages eligible municipalities along the New York Barge Canal System to make improvements on their section of the canal. Erie/Barge Canal Challenge Grants are awarded for construction projects and special events that are designed to increase tourism in these areas.

Canal Challenge Grants are awarded for everything from canal repairs in the Village of Montour Falls to a week-long Canal Days celebration in Little Falls that includes a concert barge and river tours. Other recipients include the City of Tonawanda for a plan that would add lighting to its 160-foot long pedestrian bridge, encouraging nighttime use; Rochester for a rowing regatta held on the Genesee River (in 1989, this event attracted an international field of 100 boats and 1,000 crew members); and Clifton Park for signage and brochures that promote the canal wildlife and marshland opportunities of its Vischer Ferry Nature and Historic Preserve.

The start of this program in the 1987-88 fiscal year may have marked the beginning of a new canal era, one involving tourism rather than trade. The total $1.83 million administered for 49 approved projects includes funds garnered from local governments and the private sector; the generous amount of assistance received suggests that there is a strong interest in keeping the canal and its history alive.

The banks of today's Erie Canal are the site of canal museums and annual canal festivals. The museums provide information and special exhibits that offer a glimpse back into America's history. One can actually experience life on the canal by taking a trip along the waterway in a mule powered vessel. The sight of these beasts slowly plodding along the towpath pulling the tour boats serves as a constant reminder of what life was like in a young undeveloped nation.

Today, the Erie Canal stands as a symbolic reminder of how one seemingly dubious idea could become the impetus for the growth and development of the Erie Region.

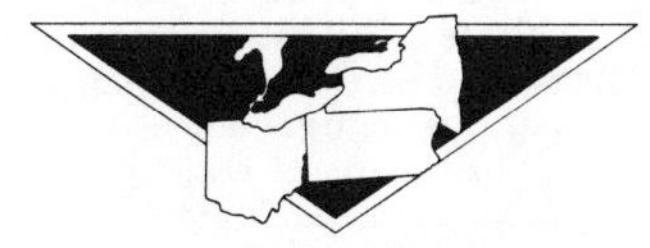

CAYUGA COUNTY

Cayuga County gets its name from the fourth tribe of the Iroquois League. Established in 1799 from Onondaga, the county was once the hunting grounds for the Cayugas. The first white settler, Roswell Franklin, settled here in 1789. The population in the area grew when the Cayuga Bridge was completed in 1800. Cayuga County was the childhood home of Millard Fillmore and William H. Seward, Secretary of State, who practiced law in Auburn.

Present-day Cayuga County offers visitors a wide range of water-related activities, appropriately, for the county either contains or borders on nine different bodies of water.

attractions

Fair Haven Beach State Park provides access to the best salmon fishing on Lake Ontario. The park has a wide variety of camping facilities from tent and trailer sites to cabins and camper recreation. Boating facilities include launching sites and a marina. Swimming is allowed from the beach and there is a bath house. Recreation programs, picnic facilities, and hiking and biking trails round out the park's attractions. Winter activities include ice skating, snowmobiling and cross-country skiing.

A 15-mile trail along an abandoned railroad bed from Fair Haven to Cato, is part of the **Cayuga County Trail**. A portion of the county trail, from Port Byron to Centerport, is also part of the state's canal park system. Activities include hiking, cross-country skiing and snowmobiling.

A scenic gorge area with unique rock formations, waterfalls, and a variety of summer activities are available at **Fillmore Glen State Park** in Moravia. Composed of shale, sandstone and limestone, Fillmore Glen was cut by Dry Creek into a narrow gorge. Visitors can see five waterfalls, including a three-story fall located on the north side of the gorge. Formations include a huge recess in the cliff wall and cliff section separated from the wall. The Gorge Trail is a 2 1/2 -mile trail that passes near waterfalls, rock formations and across eight bridges. The park offers cabins, tent and trailer sites, picnic facilities and swimming.

Long Point State Park, located on Cayuga Lake, is popular with boaters and campers. There are tent and trailer sites, launching sites and a marina. The lake contains both warm and cold water fish such as land-locked salmon, brown, rainbow and lake trout, northern pike, perch and bass.

The Montezuma National Wildlife Refuge is 6,432 acres of extensive marshes and other varied habitats. Wildlife species include waterfowl such as Canadian geese and mallards, and shore birds such as songbirds. White-tail deer and other mammals call the refuge home and bald eagles have been sighted . The visitor's center has maps of trails, the locations of observation towers, and there is a self-guided auto tour.

The **Howland Island Wildlife Management Area** protects waterfowl and 46 species of wildlife in an area over 3,600 acres. Hunting, fishing and trapping are subject to state law and special area requirements. There are hiking trails, an observation tower and boat access to the Barge Canal.

The **Bear Swamp** area provides 3,300 acres of wilderness preserve for a variety of wildlife. Hunting is allowed for deer, rabbit, squirrel and ruffled grouse, with wild turkey season in the spring. The area is also available for wilderness camping, cross-country skiing, snowmobiling and snowshoeing.

Pleasure Faire of the Renaissance is the ideal summer weekend getaway. Jousting, dancing, music, arts and crafts, and food are a few of the reasons why visitors flock to Pleasure Faire.

The **Cayuga Museum of History and Art** contains early Central New York artifacts and art as well as contemporary art. Exhibits include Indian artifacts, medicine, railroading and a research room.

Schweinfurth Memorial Art Center contains exhibits of photography, architecture, fine and folk arts. Concerts and lectures are also presented as well as workshops, special events and a museum shop.

The **Cayuga County Agricultural Museum** contains exhibits displaying the history of the county from the pre-Civil War era to the gasoline engine.

Located in Emerson Park, **Owasco Indian Village** carries exhibits depicting the culture and characteristics of pre-Iroquoian Owasco and Iroquois confederacy.

The **Seward House** is a National Historic Landmark and was the home of William Henry Seward, Presidents Lincoln and Johnson's Secretary of

State. The nation's history is vividly depicted in the home, in it's furnishings and the memorabilia throughout the house.

Harriet Tubman's House holds much memorabilia that once belonged to the woman who rescued hundreds of slaves by way of the Underground Railroad. Tubman once served in the Union Army, as well, as a spy and scout.

events

The Cayuga County Fair is held in mid-July at the Fairgrounds in Weedsport.

Sterling Renaissance Festival and Marketplace, held from July to August, is an open-air theme park that presents re-creations of a 16th Century English Village, arts and crafts, food and theater.

Weedsport

amusement

CAYUGA COUNTY FAIR SPEEDWAY, offers modified stocks from April through June, and trike racing and go-karts from June to August.

OSWEGO COUNTY

Oswego County was created in 1816 from Oneida and Onondaga Counties. Named after Oswego River, the county's origin has been traced to French Jesuits who set up missions for the Iroquois in the area in 1654.

It was the English who built trading posts in 1722. Fort Oswego was built five years later, and Fort Ontario over 25 years after that. Both forts were won and destroyed by French General Montcalm and rebuilt by Colonel Bradstreet a few years later.

great lakes coast

Lake Ontario and the area's canals brought much industry to Oswego County. Miller Brewing Company and Owens-Illinois Glass are two of many corporations that help boost Oswego's economy.

Another industry adding to Oswego County's financial health is fishing. The fantastic four seasons of fishing in Lake Ontario and Salmon River, among other bodies of water, attract tourists nationwide. The Pulaski area is called the "Great Salmon Capital of the Northeast."

attractions

Selkirk Shores State Park is a popular destination for a wide variety of activities. Campers will find tent and trailer sites, as well as cabins and camper recreation. The park offers launch access to the best fishing Lake Ontario has to offer. Picnicking facilities include shelters as well as concession stands. The recreation programs include performing arts. Playgrounds, hiking trails and swimming complete the park's attractions. Cross-country skiing is offered in the winter.

Fort Ontario features demonstrations of the activities of the troops from 1868-69 when the fort was strategic in guarding the water route from the Hudson and Mohawk Valleys to the Great Lakes. Exhibits, fully-furnished officers' quarters, and historical items from the French and Indian War through WWII are on display.

H. Lee White Marine Museum, on the port of Oswego, is open from Memorial Day to Labor Day and carries exhibits of artifacts, paintings and models of 300 years of marine heritage.

Constructed in 1934, **Oswego West Pierhead Lighthouse** is owned and operated by the U.S. Coast Guard. The original lighthouse, also built on the west pier, was built in 1822.

Flatrock Campgrounds has 124 camping sites, swimming and fishing facilities, boat rentals, a camp store, recreation building and area for children as well.

events

Harborfest takes place annually in July. A jazz fest and children's festival highlight the celebration's events.

accommodations

CANALS RESTAURANT, 156 West Villa Street, Oswego, New York 13126; Tel: (315) 343-3540. Italian-American Lunch and Dinner.

CAPTAINS LOUNGE, 27 East First Street, Oswego, New York 13126; Tel: (315) 342-0000. Breakfast, lunch, dinner, salad bar, private rooms.

THE CAPTAINS QUARTERS, 26 East First Street, Oswego, New York 13216; Tel: (315) 342-4040. Visa, MasterCard, American Express, Diners Club, Discover, and Carte Blanche are accepted.

restaurants

ADMIRAL WOOLSEYS, East First Street, Oswego, New York 13126; Tel: (315) 342-4433. Bank of Oswego River, view of harbor, fresh seafood and steaks.

FULTON

attractions

Observation and picnic areas, overnight dockage, and boat launching facilities are available at Canalview Marina in Fulton.

events

The annual Cracker Barrel Fair is held in the Fall.

accommodations

QUALITY INN RIVERSIDE, Jct 1-481 & SR 57, Fulton, New York; Tel: (315) 593-2444. Visa, MasterCard, American Express, Diners Club and Discover are accepted. It is located on the banks of the Oswego River.

SECTION FIVE: THE THOUSAND ISLANDS

JEFFERSON COUNTY

Jefferson County was named, appropriately, for Thomas Jefferson. Created in 1805 from Oneida County, it was included in the Macomb Purchase of 1791. Much of the purchase was sold to James D. LeRay de Chaumont, a French nobleman, who then settled much of the land along with Peter Chassanis, of Paris.

LeRay had livestock, artisans and progressive ideas imported to the area to help develop it. New Englanders, such as Henry Coffeen, established settlements in Watertown in 1800. Coffeen helped the county become recognized in 1805.

The St. Lawrence River, Thousand Islands and the county's many other water areas are brilliant examples of natural beauty and encourage fishing, touring, boating and other water-related activities.

attractions

Southwich Beach is located in the vicinity of the Lakeview Wildlife Management Area. The management area is a series of ponds, streams and marshes where hunting and canoeing are allowed. The park itself offers tent and trailer sites and camper recreation. Picnic facilities include concession stands and picnic tables. Swimming and boating are permitted on Lake Ontario as well as fishing for the best freshwater fish to be found anywhere. Hiking and nature trails are found throughout the park and recreation programs are offered. Cross-country skiing is the popular winter activity.

Westcott Beach State Park is known for its fishing, swimming beach, and boating. Other park attractions are camping for tents and trailers, picnic facilities and concession stands. Recreation programs are offered and there are hiking trails. Winter activities include cross-country skiing and snowmobiling.

The **Sackets Harbor National Historic District** is comprised of 156 historical buildings on 71 acres. This 19th century village is still active.

The **Sackets Harbor Battlefield** is the site of two battles fought during the War of 1812. The visitor center, located in the former Union Hotel, contains exhibits concerning the war, and offers self-guided tours.

Long Point State Park, located on Point Peninsula, offers tent and trailer sites, picnicking facilities, fishing and boating.

Burnham Point State Park offers tent and trailer sites, picnicking facilities, boating, playgrounds and fishing.

Cedar Point State Park is known for its fine boating and camping facilities. Other facilities include playgrounds, picnicking, swimming, fishing and recreation programs.

1000 Islands Zoo, where exotic wild animals are the specialty, also feature hoof stock, birds, carnivores and domestic farm animals. Picnic areas and refreshments are available.

Indian River Canoe Route, in Antwerp, has marked portages near the power plants in Philadelphia, New York. The river turns sharply, heads north toward Evans Mills to two portages in Theresa. Another portage around rapids and falls, and the canoe trip ends in Rossie.

Historical and agricultural items of the area, as well as craft classes, can be found at the **Historical Society of South Jefferson.**

events

Concerts-on-the-Waterfront, in Sackets Harbor, are held from June through September in Market Square. The public dock area is used as an outdoor auditorium for ethnic, folk, country and western, and children's music and performances.

The **Canadian-American War of 1812 Pageant** is held in mid-July in Sackets Harbor. A re-enactment of the attack, parades, food and fireworks round out the activities.

The longest-running fair in the county, the **Annual Jefferson County Fair** features hundreds of carnival rides, shows, agriculture and dairy displays, and clowns, among other things. The fair is held in July at Alex T. Duffy Fairgrounds.

Anniversary of Arbor Day Celebration is held in April and celebrates trees. A craft fair, lumbering demonstrations, tree-planting ceremonies and children's art contest are part of the excitement.

In June, Adams commemorates the yearly strawberry harvest with the **Annual South Jefferson Historical Society Strawberry Festival.** Craft-making, a craft fair, games and delicious fresh strawberry sundaes and shortcake highlight the "fruitful" event.

HENDERSON HARBOR/SACKETS HARBOR

accommodations

ASPINWALL HOUSE
Route 178 at Route 3
Henderson Harbor, New York 16351
Tel: (345) 938-5421
Hrs: Open May 1 to Thanksgiving.
Visa, MasterCard and American Express are accepted.

Although the Aspinwall House is only in its first year of operation as a motel, the charming homestead has a colorful history dating back to the late 1700s. Among the famous people who have frequented the House is Frederick Remington, one of history's most talented painters who often came to visit his grandfather, Rev. Seth Remington. What's incredible about the Aspinwall House is that it served as a rest stop for Stonewall Jackson as he took his daily walks in the 1850s, and as a hideaway station for escaped slaves as they traveled the Underground Railroad on their way to Canada. The overwhelming mystique doesn't stop there. Rumor has it that Edgar Allen Poe was also once a guest.

Only a few minutes from the famous fishing and boating facilities at Henderson Harbor, the Aspinwall House, with its 24 nicely furnished, spacious rooms, its hand-carved interior woodwork, and its comfortable colonial ambiance, seems to be beautifully trapped in time. Though this majestic homestead is approaching its bicentennial birthday, owners Lynn and Homer Trotter have done their best to provide guests with every modern convenience without losing the personal touches of hospitality and friendliness.

In addition to being close to many marinas and several state parks, the romantic Aspinwall House is adjacent to the Cherry Tree Restaurant, which offers American-Italian cuisine in a family setting. The easy access to Henderson Harbor's recreational facilities, the owners' warmth and hospitality, the motel's moderate prices, and the home's rich history make the Aspinwall House a welcome rest and recreation stop for everyone.

THE GILL HOUSE INN
Main Street
Henderson Harbor, New York 13651
Tel: (315) 938-5013
Hrs: Restaurant:
April - November:
Seven days 6:00 a.m. - 2:00 a.m.
Visa, MasterCard and American Express are accepted.

The Gill House Inn, located in Henderson Harbor, New York, has been described as one of the best kept secrets in the North County. Originally a boarding house that served as a stagecoach stop, it has evolved into a cozy country inn with a full service restaurant.

Glance over the guest book and discover the names of many famous people who have been in residence. The book is graced with accolades and artistic graphics from around the world: Argentina, Scotland, Switzerland, Holland, West Germany, Russia, China and Japan, to name a few.

The inn has 11 rooms, all with private baths, some with balcony views, and reasonable rates. This get-away-from-it-all accommodation takes care of each of its guest's comforts and needs and offers some of the finest fishing (perch, smallmouth bass, brown trout, coho, and chinook salmon) and sailing the northeast has to offer. A complete package can be arranged. The inn will arrange connections for small groups of six or corporate parties of 60, including meals, rooms, and charters. It is also known for its quaint lawn parties and weddings by the water.

The dining room is open for breakfast, lunch and dinner and offers a fine view of the harbor. For breakfast, it is suggested that visitors try the Bacon 'n Eggs Croissant with cheddar cheese sauce or Peaches 'n Cream French Toast (made with fresh peaches). The fresh blueberry pancakes and homemade cinnamon French toast are favorites here as well.

Lunch items include an unusual chicken and walnut salad and a tasty shrimp salad unlike any other. A Box Lunch or Shore Dinner is offered for charters. These are prepared by the guide in the same tradition, on a nearby island similar to what was done years ago.

The Gill House Inn is known for its fresh seafood and famous batter-dipped perch, caught fresh from Lake Ontario. When the dessert tray is presented, one finds it difficult to resist the Strawberry Amaretto Cake. After meals, many patrons head for the lounge, check out the inn's delightful gift shoppe, or retire to their personal rooms upstairs.

The Gill House Inn is a family affair in the warmest of American tradition, comparable to a New England inn.

bed & breakfast inns

THE DOBSON HOUSE
Harbor Road
Henderson, New York 13650
Tel: (315) 938-5901
Visa and MasterCard are accepted.

Mark and Barbara Boyle had their eye on the historic Dobson House for nearly 10 years before it finally became available. They thought this stone house that dates from the 1820s would make the perfect Bed and Breakfast, and they couldn't wait to share it with others. Since its opening on June 15, 1989, The Dobson House has indeed been the idyllic setting for guests in need of a break from the turmoil of everyday life. Much of the beauty that the house now radiates is due to the long hours of research and restoration that Mark and Barbara have done to bring it to near original condition.

The Dobson House is one of the older homes in Jefferson County. The land that the house sits on was purchased by Thomas Dobson, Jr. (of County Gwent, Whales) and his wife Fanny Whittier (cousin to the famous American poet John Greenleaf Whittier) on April 12, 1816. First, Mr. Dobson built a log cabin, then, after a few years, he replaced it with the stone house that is today's federal-style Dobson House. This two-story limestone building is situated on 20 acres of vast fields which are bordered by towering silver maples and American black walnut trees which date from the late 1800s.

Inside the house, guests are greeted by the Old English Sheepdog, Daisy, and a warm mixture of antiques and furnishings throughout the rooms. Four guest rooms are available with two of them featuring Cantored windows with window seats. Guests can take advantage of the parlor's fireplace, the rocking chairs on the back porch, and the comfortable peace of the sun room. Breakfast is an unbeatable combination of a main dish of blueberry pancakes or cinnamon glazed french toast along with fresh fruit, and Barbara's homemade blueberry and date-nut muffins served with homemade jams. The hospitality of Mark and Barbara and the serenity of their historic Dobson House make this a "Best Choice" for Bed and Breakfast fans traveling along New York's Seaway Trail in Jefferson County.

points of interest

MADISON BARRACKS--A HISTORIC RESORT COMMUNITY
85 Worth Road
Sackets Harbor, New York 13685
Tel: (315) 646-3385
Hrs: Open year-round.
Visa, MasterCard, American Express, Diners Club and Discover are accepted.

Madison Barracks--A Historic Resort Community, a joint venture by Mike Pontello, Sam Pompa and Tony Rodrigues, was started in 1988. Mike had the vision and Sam and Tony are responsible for the design and construction of the site.

Acclaimed as a living museum of military architecture, the Barracks have played a part in every war involving our nation from the War of 1812 to World War II. Nearby is the historic Sackets Harbor Battlefield and museum complex.

There is additional rich history in the Barracks. A typical vestige of the past is the graveside monument to General Zebulon Pike, discoverer of Pike's Peak and military hero who was killed while leading a successful attack on York--now Toronto, Canada.

There are 115 acres overlooking Lake Ontario in Sackets Harbor. Along with a rich history and wonderful view, Madison Barracks offers its residents and hotel guests an exceptional blend of recreational, social, educational, and other miscellaneous activities within its bounds. There is community shopping, a marina and yacht club, clubhouse and pool, tennis, performing arts, and paths for jogging, bicycling, and cross country skiing.

The new housing on this site is designed to offer architectural harmony with the existing historic stone and brick buildings. Madison Barracks is still growing and will boast a conference center, culinary school, bakery boutique, gift shops and much more in the near future.

There are condominiums, townhouses and single family homes available for rent. The emphasis here is on the total community.

The history, setting and the quality of life this community offers makes Madison Barracks a "Best Choice."

restaurants

THE BARRACKS INN
Madison Barracks
Sackets Harbor, New York 13601
Tel: (315) 646-2376
Hrs: Memorial Day- -to Labor Day:
Sunday - Thursday 11:00 a.m. - 11:00 p.m.
Friday - Saturday 11:00 a.m. - Midnight
Visa, MasterCard, American Express, Diners Club and Discover are accepted.

The Barracks Inn, located on Black River Bay at Lake Ontario, is one of the premier restaurants in the Great Lakes Region.

Owner Leo Coleman, Jr. opened the restaurant in 1981, but the building itself--one of the oldest in all of Sackets Harbor and Madison Barracks--dates back to the mid-1700s. The building is constructed of stone, brick, and wood, but Leo and Bobbi Jo have recently added lots of bayfront windows so that diners at nearly every table can enjoy the fantastic waterfront view.

The gorgeous view is not the only reason to visit the Barracks Inn. The Inn serves a wide variety of excellent cuisine. Leo has won several Restaurant Association awards for his delectible dishes. The steaks are hand-cut, properly aged, choice meat; the seafood is flown in fresh from New England.

Favorite appetizers include steamed New England clams and Leo's special-recipe French Onion soup. Some of the most popular entrees at the Inn are Shrimp Scampi, whole Main Lobster, Scallops, Seafood Fettucini, and slowly roasted Prime Rib. All of these connoiseur-quality dinners are served in hearty portions.

The Barracks Inn also offers unique gourmet sandwiches such as the Arabic Bread sandwich, which is stuffed with salami, provolone cheese, tomato, onions, and the Inn's special Italian dressing. Guests can also create their own sandwiches.

The restaurant has wonderful Italian dishes such as cut ziti, spaghetti, and rigatoni--each served with homemade Italian bread, a tossed salad and your choice of meatballs, sausage or both.

To complement any meal, the Barracks serves a wide variety of house winds--from Blue Nun Liebframilch to Robert Mondavi White Zinfandel.

Leo's recipe for making a top-notch restaurant is simple. Combine gourmet cuisine, hearty portion size and a moderate pricing scale, stir in an intriguing yet relaxing atmosphere, and add a healthy dash of friendly service. This recipe has made the Barracks Inn a "Best Choice"--Leo's numerous repeat customers are proof of that. While in Watertown, stop by Leo's two other restaurants, The Fairground Inn and Colemans Corner.

1812 STEAK AND SEAFOOD COMPANY
212 Main Street
Sackets Harbor, New York 13685
Tel: (315) 646-2041
Hrs: May 14 - Labor Day:
Seven days 5:00 p.m. - Close
Reduced hours during off season.
Visa, MasterCard and American Express are accepted.

A step back in time to the War of 1812 is a way one could describe the 1812 Steak and Seafood Company. Steve Sboro, owner of this historical restaurant in Sackets Harbor, thought that using the theme of the War of 1812 would add to the ambiance of the town. He thought that the restaurant, along with Sackets Harbor Battlefield, could help educate visitors about the war, as well as make it a lot of fun to learn about. He was right. Although the restaurant is relatively new, it has already acquired an outstanding reputation in the area.

Both Steve and Manager David Boucher have extensive experience in the restaurant field; it is quite visible from the surroundings and the dishes they create. Some of the specials featured are fresh steaks, seafood and lobster. Popular dishes include the seafood pasta with shrimp, scallops, fresh fish with a special scampi sauce, and the 1812 Lamb and Peppercorn Steak.

Many patrons of the 1812 Steak and Seafood Company rave about their tasty Bouillabaisse which is a shellfish, seafood combination with a rich sauce made from their seafood stock. The menu features nightly seafood specials--the freshest catch available. Many enjoy the delicious array of appetizers offered, such as the Fried Calamari or the special appetizer of the day, which could be clams, smoked salmon, mussels or snow crab. Also, save enough room for the assembly of scrumptious homemade desserts.

Sackets Harbor was the main staging area for the strategic campaigns by the United States into Canada. The only natural harbor (located behind the restaurant) made this an important naval area. The atmosphere of the 1812 Steak and Seafood Company reflects the history of the area's contributions to the war. Original prints on the walls, along with brief commentary, help explain the war better. Military uniforms and paraphernalia add to the restaurant's setting. Jacob Brown, a prominent U.S. General, spent some of his military career at Sackets Harbor and is prominently featured in the restaurant. "The General Guard," which is a re-enactment group from the area, often stands guard at the restaurant and share some of the history with visitors.

The outstanding food quality of the "North Country Cuisine," the use of local history and heritage, and the commitment of the community combine to make the 1812 Steak and Seafood Company a "Best Choice" along the Great Lakes.

WATERTOWN

Watertown, the county seat of Jefferson County, combines historical homes and museums with contemporary parks and zoos. A growing, vital community, it hosts many events and activities throughout the year.

attractions

A 19th century building that houses agricultural and wood-working tools, machinery portraits, clothing and photographs, is the **Jefferson County Historical Society Museum.** Victorian gardens and Tyler Coverlets are featured as well. The museum is open year-round, Tuesday through Saturday.

Watertown's Thompson Park provides a beautiful view of the area and features winding roads and paths great for bicycle riding. An open, beautifully-maintained lawn offers an excellent area for flying kites. A zoo, playground, swimming pools, tennis courts and picnic areas are added attractions to the lovely park.

events

Snowtown, USA is a festival, lasting for 10 days, that features over 60 events including hockey, snowmobiling and snow sculpture contests. The celebration honors the "Blizzard of '77," when Watertown received 224 inches of snow in two weeks. The event was named in 1984 when Watertown was declared "Snowtown, USA" by Mayor T. Urling Walker.

The **Festival of the Arts**, held in April, takes place at the Cultural Exchange Center. Local artists, crafts, an art show and sale, theater, music and painting demonstrations are available.

The largest Italian festival in Upstate New York, **Bravo Italiano** is held in September.

accommodations

DAYS INN WATERTOWN/1000 ISLANDS
1142 Arsenal Street
Watertown, New York 13601
Tel: (315) 782-2700
Hrs: Both Days Inn & Denny's are open 24 hours.
Visa, MasterCard, American Express, Diners Club, Discover and Carte Blanche are accepted.

The Days Inn of Watertown/1000 Islands is the newest hotel in Watertown and also stands as the first cooperative venture between Denny's Restaurant and Days Inn

Offering 135 guest rooms, this full-service hotel provides an indoor pool, room service, free HBO, meeting rooms and a covered walkway leading to Denny's Restaurant and Lounge, the first Denny's with a cocktail lounge.

Located just minutes from local shopping and downtown Watertown, this Days Inn is a step above what might be expected. Being ranked third out of 800 locations nationwide for Quality Assurance Points, a rating system based on service, cleanliness, corporate standards, and appearance, is a good indication that the Days Inns are now headed towards a more upscale image with the same moderate rates.

A classy, contemporary image is found throughout the establishment. The lobby and common areas are tastefully decorated with mauves and teal, crowned with brass accents. Elevators are also done in brass. Professionally designed furniture sets off the recessed lighting and appealing wallpaper completes the fine decor.

Rooms are available in a variety of configurations, from standard double rooms to king-size rooms and suites. Most rooms house a classy cherry wardrobe. Suites feature a microwave, refrigerator and other amenities. King rooms feature a sleeper sofa.

No matter what room is chosen, guests may become a member of any one of five Days Inn Clubs. This will make them eligible for many additional discounts as will as pay-per-view television and airport shuttle service.

The Days Inn of Watertown/1000 Islands offers the best in elegant and affordable accommodations.

RAMADA INN WATERTOWN
6300 Arsenal Street
Watertown, New York 13601
Tel: (315) 788-0700
Hrs: Casablanca Restaurant:
Seven days 7:00 a.m. - 10:00 p.m.
Rick's Cafe American:
Monday - Saturday 5:00 p.m. - 2:00 a.m.
Visa, MasterCard, American Express, Diners Club and Discover are accepted.

The Ramada Inn Watertown has it all, and is located near it all. Many of the area's attractions are only 30 minutes away from the well-equipped hotel. This means you can spend more time seeing the sights rather than wasting time to get to them.

The full service hotel offers a restaurant, two lounges, room service, and the best banquet facilities in the area which hold up to 400 people. The Casablanca Restaurant features a continental cuisine and has an outstanding reputation that has won the taste of the north country. The restaurant has received several awards for their desserts, preparation, and more. Some of the restaurant's specialties are fresh seafood, veal, poultry, and steaks, all served in large portions. A full time, in-house baker fills the dessert cart with a splendid array of desserts and pies. Fresh breads and desserts are made right on the premises, so be sure to save room for them, if you can.

The 145 rooms are tastefully appointed with fine furniture, color cable TV with HBO and pay-for-view movies, steam baths, jacuzzis, and heated pools. The Ramada Inn Watertown has several vacation packages available. One of the most popular is the fishing package to the Golden Crescent Fish area, where you can fish for trout, salmon, bass, and muskie. Another interesting package offered is white water rafting on the Black River.

Quality entertainment is what Rick's Cafe Lounge adds to the Ramada Inn Watertown. The best new and upcoming acts can be seen six nights a week.

So now you see, the Ramada Inn Watertown does "have it all". All the great cuisine you can eat, all the fun and entertainment anyone could want, and, most importantly, all the necessities and comforts of home.

rafting

ADIRONDACK RIVER OUTFITTERS, INC.
146 Newell Street
Watertown, New York 13420
Tel: (800) 525-RAFT
Hrs: Rafting Season (April - October):
Winter Camping available.
Reservations are required.
Visa and MasterCard are accepted.

Adirondack River Outfitters is one of the oldest and largest white water river rafting companies in New York. It was formed in 1981 by three friends who enjoyed the sport and decided to make a business out of it.

Bob Burke, Gary Staab, and Ron Smith pioneered river rafting on the Black and Moose Rivers and now provide river trips on five different rivers.

Each river features a different rafting adventure. There are calmer, easy waters for beginners and younger rafters such as the Salmon and Sacandaga Rivers. There are also rivers, such as the Moose River, which provide six hours and 14 miles of rugged wild water.

The trio has an unblemished safety record and licensed guides on staff. Instruction is available for all rafters, novice or experienced. Life jackets, wet suits and safety helmets are provided.

Accommodations nearby include campgrounds, elegant facilities, economy lodging, and first class hotels

Providing a safe, educational fun-filled experience for the outdoor enthusiast with rafting, camping and other activities is the goal of Adirondack River Outfitters, Inc., the "Best Choice" in the Great Lakes area.

restaurants

ART'S JUG
820 Huntington Street
Watertown, New York 13601
Tel: (315) 782-9764
Hrs: Tuesday - Sunday 4:00 p.m. - Close
Visa, MasterCard and American Express are accepted.

Art's Jug, a family-owned and operated restaurant since 1933, was originally named the "Stone Jug" because the building is constructed of limestone blocks made in Watertown. The word "Jug" refers to the bootlegging jugs used during the Prohibition.

Fifteen years after Mrs. Marie Attilio Sboro first opened the restaurant, her son, Arthur, returned from the war and she changed the name from the "Stone Jug" to "Art's Jug."

Art's son, Steve, and Steve's wife, Elizabeth, are the present owners. Steve and Elizabeth have seen to it that "Art's Jug" is synonymous with "Fine dining in northern New York." Aside from serving the Cadillac of Pizzas, Art's Jug serves other Italian specialties such as lasagne, manicotti, fresh seafood such as fresh lobster, crevettes sautees made of shrimp, scallops, shallots, wine, garlic and butter served over pasta, and juicy 14-ounce New York strip steaks.

The Jug still does things the old-fashioned way with Steve's grandmother's original recipes. The delicious entrees are served in large portions and are reasonably priced and the delicious house wines--white zinfandel, liebframilch, chablis, lambrusco, and burgundy--are served by the glass or the carafe.

Before Marie opened the Jug in 1933, her father had used the site as the first spaghetti factory in northern New York, but, because spaghetti was a relatively unknown dish at that time, the business failed. However, today, Art's Jug is well-known for its homemade spaghetti.

Steve loves to experiment with new menu items such as his mildly spiced Cajun-style cuisine.

At Art's Jug, the excitement doesn't stop with food. The warm decor is mostly original--from the stone wall behind the cash register to the natural oak bar. Don't be fooled by the outside of the restaurant--it hasn't changed much over the past 60 years, but the interior is wonderfully traditional and relaxed. Steve is happy to be the third generation of Sboros to offer fine cuisine and low pricing.

The sense of tradition, the quality of food, and the friendly atmosphere combine to made Art's Jug a "Best Choice" along the Great Lakes.

CLAYTON

The St. Lawrence River borders Clayton on three sides. Most activities, therefore, involve the water.

attractions

Thousand Islands Shipyard Museum, located adjacent to the St. Lawrence Seaway Channel, offers exhibits of crafted wooden boats, freshwater nautical history and a large collection of maps, books and other items. An exhibit devoted to the Prohibition Era and harness racing on ice are also available at the museum.

The **Textile Museum of the Thousand Island Craft School** displays handwoven fabric samples, tools and a library. Exhibits are on a rotating basis. Classes are held in basket making, pottery, carving, weaving and other handcrafts.

The **Thousand Island Museum Old Town Hall** contains a replica of Clayton's village square at the turn-of-the-century. Exhibits also include bird and decoy rooms and Indian artifacts.

events

The **Annual Decoy and Wildlife Show**, in July, is also held at the Clayton Recreation Park Arena. Over 200 exhibitors, national and international winners included, participate in the show each year.

The **Annual Antique Boat Show**, featuring a parade of boats on the waterfront and an awards ceremony, is held early in August at Thousand Islands Shipyard Museum and grounds, and the Municipal Dock.

Oktoberfest, a one-day festival in October, honors Germany's yearly "new beer" harvest. German food and beverages, along with music and live performances, are sure to bring out the German in everyone.

boat rentals

REMAR BOAT RENTALS
510 Theresa Street
Clayton, New York 13624
Tel: (315) 686-3579
Hrs: Monday - Saturday 8:00 a.m. - 5:00 p.m.
MasterCard and Visa accepted at the Gas Dock only.

Renting a boat from Remar Boat Rentals is a perfect way to explore the Thousand Islands. Audrey and Bob Lashomb, sole proprietors since 1978, are sure to provide a fun and friendly atmosphere for those who visit their establishment.

The rentals were originated by Audrey in 1971 on a part-time basis. The business expanded and was soon operating full time. Bob decided to change his position as a banker and learn more about the marina profession from the ground up. Audrey agreed and gave up her nursery school and focused all her attention on Remar Boat Rentals.

The Lashomb's dedication is definitely paying off as they have grown from three houseboats to a fleet of 12 ranging from 38 to 55 feet. They also have a fleet of 15 runabouts (supersports) powered by 70 horsepower Evinrude engines, which cater to fishing and sight-seeing only.

Private homes and quaint cottages can also be rented in the islands, many of which are only accessible by boat. These rentals range from estate homes (sleeping 10 or more) to cozy little cottages made for two. Several of these beautiful, fully-equipped private homes are located on their own island for a very private vacation spot. Homes are priced at $325 to $1250 per week and houseboat rates compare favorably when compared to hotels and boat rentals combined. Everything needed to know about how to run a houseboat is taught to all renters before they leave the dock.

Other facilities and services offered include a gas dock with full service, a service department with a travel-lift for boat repairs, a laundromat and a parts department.

A friendly home-like atmosphere, quality service, sincere concern and care from Audrey and Bob and a location in the heart of the Thousand Island vacation area combine to make Remar Boat Rentals an experience along the Thousand Islands no one would want to pass up.

gift shops

BOATEAK
Bluff Island
Clayton, New York 13624
Tel: (315) 686-3190
(315) 445-1520 (Mail Order)
Hrs: June 17 - Labor Day:
Seven days 10:00 a.m. - 5:00 p.m.
Mail orders are taken in the off season.
Visa and MasterCard are accepted.

The Boateak Gift Shop, only a two-mile shuttle-boat ride (by appointment) from Clayton, is beautifully situated on the breathtaking point of Bluff Island. This one-of-a-kind shop features a fantastic collection of items that can't be found elsewhere. Hand-crafted jewelry, brass lanterns, pewter, crystal, hand-sewn quilts and children's clothes, sweaters and antique lace nightgowns are only a handful of the Boateak's unique collectibles.

Located at the point of a protected lagoon, this secluded 3,000 square foot gift shop is actually a boathouse loft. Customers can spend hours exploring the varied selections of pottery, blown glass, stained-glass, and mint-condition antiques.

The Boateak also displays a collection of watercolor, acrylic, and oil paintings created by local artists. Twice each season, the Boateak features special art shows (call for information).

Discover more delightful surprises at the Boateak--a Christmas shop that displays hand-made ornaments and other decorations, a delicious assortment of Boateak's private-label jams, jellies, and relishes, and an original collection of hand-carved wooden toys and flower wagons.

The Boateak is an island paradise for those who love to shop for unique gifts or want to discover the many unique treasures that await them in every corner of the store. There are too many reasons why the Boateak shouldn't be missed. The beautifully-crafted gifts have been created by the best artisans in the country.

The Boateak is situated in a lovely pristine setting next to owners Cookie and Matt Tomaiuoli's gorgeous 1905 Victorian home, and the island atmosphere is thoroughly relaxing. Even Buddy and Bluffy, Cookie and Matt's friendly dogs, greet guests upon arrival to the island. The Boateak is a must-see on a trip to the Thousand Islands.

CAPTAIN SPICER'S GIFT SHOP
Route 12
Clayton, New York 13624
Tel: (315) 686-3419
Hrs: Seven day 10:00 a.m. - 5:00 p.m.
Closed only on major holidays.
Will ship merchandise.

Captain Spicer's Gift Shop carries items not found in other stores. As one enters the driveway, an anchor from 1830 makes an impressive greeting along with authentic channel markers from the Seaway Tower to the sky.

The shop opened in 1983 and carries items of a nautical nature. Custom hand painted stoneware featuring lighthouses and freighters that ply the river, and an ever increasing historical collection of Thousand Island scenes such as steamships, hotels, and mansions are but a few.

Included in the shop is an art gallery containing original art work and paintings by local and world renowned artists. Many ships, including The Edmund Fitzgerald, are on display.

Marine art is the specialty at Captain Spicer's Gift Shop.

resorts

C-WAY INN RESORT
Route 12 (Two miles south of Clayton)
Clayton, New York 13624
Tel: (315) 686-4214
Hrs: Seasonal - May to October
Visa, MasterCard and American Express are accepted.

Located two miles south of Clayton in the Thousand Islands area awaits the comfort and quality of the C-Way Inn Resort. The reasonably priced resort features 40 spacious double rooms and four apartments that are available for extended stays. Visitors of the inn can relax beside or go for a dip in the outdoor pool, however, if golfing is more your style, the complex has an 18-hole golf course directly across the street. This picturesque course offers beautiful scenery as well as many challenging holes.

A variety of fine food is what the Resort's restaurant offers. Open for breakfast, lunch, and dinner, it features delicious Italian cuisine, tender and juicy steaks, and fresh seafood dishes. The house specialty is their lean and tasty prime rib.

Steve and Mark Rzepechi are the owners of this comfortable resort located right off the Lawrence River. Even though it is located so close to the seaway, it is reasonably priced and the perfect place for families, groups, and seniors. The resort has a popular variety of vacation packages. Two examples are the family group package or the three days/two nights mini vacation.

Steve also operates Seaway Destination, a tour coach service in Buffalo. This service can be used with a single or multi-day package, complete with an informative guide. The tours are available for Montreal, Kingston, Lake Placid, Buffalo, Ottawa, Niagara Falls, and many other seaway traveler destinations.

The C-Way Inn Resort is very proud of their friendly, hospitable staff, and their reasonable prices bring them many returning customers. The owners of this family owned and operated Resort thrive on the enjoyment of their guests. The inn's comfortable air-conditioned rooms, color cable television viewing, and other modern conveniences help to add tio their enjoyment and comfort, and make the C-Way Inn Resort a definite "Best Choice" in the Upstate New York area.

restaurants

THE WILD GOOSE
413 Riverside Drive
Clayton, New York 13624
Tel: (315) 686-5004
Hrs: May 1 - September 30:
Lunch:
Monday - Saturday 11:30 a.m. - 3:00 p.m.
Dinner: 5:00 p.m. - 10:00 p.m.
Visa, MasterCard and American Express are accepted.

The Wild Goose Restaurant was started by Ellen Burr, who formerly taught baking at a local college. With ten years of experience in the restaurant business, Ellen's dream was to have her own place. Ellen opened her restaurant in a charming Victorian-style building overlooking the St. Lawrence river. Ellen was able to convert the building into a restaurant and still preserve the Victorian decor with wallpaper, light fixtures and other accessories. The Wild Goose is close to the public dock and makes it easy to combine a boat ride with a picnic lunch. It is accessible from Exit 50 off of Interstate 82.

Many tables offer a view of the St. Lawrence river where one can relax, converse, and listen to background music, all part of the perfect dining experience. The menu consists of only the freshest ingredients featuring six primary entrees which allow for individually prepared orders and dietary considerations. Choices include Sliced Tenderloin with Horseradish Mousseline, Breast of Chicken L'Orange, Veal Dijonnaise, Shrimp Stuffed with crabmeat and Pasta Carbonara. St. Lawrence Seafood chowder is available and made from the local catch. Other favorites are Veal Medallions with Apples, Creme and Brandy, and the Seafood and Fruit Brochettes, consisting of shrimp, scallops, fresh pineapple, strawberries, kiwi and melon basted with lime butter.

Although the Wild Goose has only been open for a short time, the reputation for gourmet dining has grown considerably throughout the region. It has received several awards in regional culinary competitions titled, Taste of the North Country. After experiencing a gourmet feast, it's easy to see why the Wild Goose is a great place to dine along the Great Lakes.

specialty shops

GOLD CUP FARMS
Riverside Drive
P.O. Box 116
Clayton, New York 13624
Tel: (315) 686-2480
Hrs: Summer:
Seven days 9:00 a.m. - 9:00 p.m.
January - April:
Thursday - Sunday 10:00 a.m. - 5:00 p.m.
Visa and MasterCard are accepted.

Gold Cup Farms dates from 1950 when Richard Brown started in Utica, New York as a retail outlet for his dairy. He made cheeses, ice cream and butter. He has been at this location in Clayton since 1979, when he closed the dairy and made Gold Cup Farms a wholesale and retail success.

Gold Cup Farms is a one-stop gourmet shop. From cheeses to nuts to coffees, this store has everything. Some specialty cheeses include: Peppercorn Cheddar, Hot Horseradish, Bacon Horseradish Cheddar, the world famous "Thousand Island River Rat Cheese", which is a New York Cheddar many say is the best, and many, many more. Gold Cup also has a fine selection of imported cheeses and sausages; favorites include Adirondack Sausage, and Croghan Bologna, which is a closely guarded family secret.

Some other items they carry are Fresh Cheese Curd, jams and jellies, New York Maple syrup, homemade fudge, ice cream, frozen yogurt, and Thousand Island honey. There are also dried fruits, nuts, imported baskets, gourmet coffee and teas, fine spices, and seafood.

The success of Gold Cup Farms is based on the quality of the products and the friendly helpful staff. The store itself is a bright, colorful inviting place and occupies over 2,000 square feet.

This shop is a must for the lover of cheeses and gourmet hard-to-find foods. A variety of gift boxes are available, ranging in price from $7.95 to $155, depending on the area or the country the recipient lives in.

There is truly something for every budget and every taste. Gift boxes are available from October though March, sent UPS. The rest of the year, most packages may be sent within two days with air service, for all different occasions. Order Christmas gifts early for assured arrival on time.

CAPE VINCENT

restaurants

HAFF-WAY CHALET
Route 12 East
Cape Vincent, New York 13624
Tel: (315) 686-2295

Hrs:	May - September:	
	Dinner:	
	Monday - Thursday	5:00 p.m. - 9:00 p.m.
	Friday - Saturday	5:00 p.m. - 10:00 p.m.
	October - April:	
	Dinner:	
	Thursday - Saturday	5:00 p.m. - 9:00 p.m.
	Sunday	Noon - 8:00 p.m.

Reservations are appreciated.
Visa and MasterCard are accepted.

Known for its outstanding food in a family-style atmosphere, the Haff-Way Chalet is a favorite of eaters of all ages. Located halfway between Cape Vincent and Clayton, the restaurant is owned by JoAnn Reed who once worked as a waitress at the Haff-Way and eventually bought it.

The restaurant boasts a spacious dining room and a full menu sure to please the pickiest eater. Chalet specials include BBQ Beef Ribs, Chicken or Veal Parmigiana with spaghetti, Shrimp Chalet, deepfried, and Stuffed Shrimp with Orange Sauce.

The Roast Duckling a L'Orange with homemade sage and onion dressing or Rice Pilaf is excellent if fowl is desired. Prime Rib of Beef is served in three different ways: House Specialty with Au Jus, Extra Large Cut or English Cut, thinly sliced with light mushroom gravy.

Of the seafood entrees offered at Haff-Way Chalet, Live Maine Lobster With Crabmeat Stuffing or Shrimp Scampi are sure to please. The Chef's Specialty is Chicken Cordon Bleu, served with the Chalet's own cheese sauce.

All dinners include soup, a salad bar that features 12 homemade salads, cheese, bread, a choice of potato, rice pilaf or an order of spaghetti, and dessert. Hot Fudge sundaes and Cheesecake with the choice of Blueberry, Cherry or Hot Fudge toppings meet any dessert connoisseur's highest standards.

The Haff-Way Chalet features a children's menu with favorites such as fried shrimp with french fries, spaghetti with homemade sauce, and others.

Trying to meet the needs of all customers is a priority with the staff of the Haff-Way. Recipes have been changed to provide for the health conscious.

JoAnn Reed is proud of the many returning customers the restaurant has due to the atmosphere and affordability.

Located on Route 12 East, eight miles west of Clayton and east of Cape Vincent, the restaurant is near two state parks and the lighthouse in

Cape Vincent. Family-style environment, moderate pricing, and the high quality of its food combine to make the Chalet a favorite in Jefferson County.

specialty shops

RIVER RAMS WOOL FARMS
River Road (Route 12E)
Cape Vincent, New York 13618
Tel: (315) 654-3673
Hrs: Seven days, year-round 1:00 p.m. - 6:00 p.m.

River Rams Wool Farms is a 135 acre working farm that dates back to the early 1800s. Stewart and VeVa Parkinson bought the farm in 1985 and opened a shop on the property in 1986 that features all sheepskin and wool products. The shop is a working processing area where one can observe the fascinating process that takes wool from the sheep to the shawl using cottage industry methods.

Stewart had worked for a large corporation, and VeVa had been a college professor before buying the farm. After their family was raised, the Parkinsons wanted to own a business and pursue other interests. This was their perfect opportunity. VeVa had an interest in animals and fiber and Stewart has always enjoyed the Thousand Islands while summering here as he grew up. The farm, with its rustic, country ambiance, seems to have satisfied their needs for a different lifestyle. Kordl, a Komodor guard dog, and Bear, the faithful host cat, are integral parts of the farm's charming atmosphere.

A trip to this farm is not only a learning experience but also a wise shopping move. Finished products here include yarns for knitting and weaving in various textures and colors, sheepskin slippers, hats, mittens, hand-crafted socks, scarfs, sweaters, fine woolen blankets, and novelty gift items that are sheep related. All are available at low farm prices. Items purchased are unique because most are created from wool taken from animals raised on the farm.

This farm is in a gorgeous area with a view of the St. Lawrence River and Canada. A favorite time of year is around Easter when adorable baby lambs make their debut. VeVa and Stewart are most proud of their breeding stock and the high quality wool fiber that they consistently produce. As a dealer for Ashford spinning wheels and accessories, VeVa teaches spinning to those looking for a fun and productive hobby. VeVa and Stewart are willing to help new shepherds get started. They can offer advice on breeding, fencing, husbandry, and many other areas. River Rams Wool Farms is a "Best Choice" for those looking for a fun day trip. It offers an interesting experience for animal lovers and bargain hunters alike. The Parkinsons give friendly, personalized attention to visitors and customers.

ALEXANDRIA BAY

Alexandria Bay was named for Alexander LeRay, son of James, who was one of the first settlers of Jefferson County. Alexandria Bay is now the center of tourist activities in the Thousand Islands area, featuring numerous restaurants, shops, museums, historic sites and night clubs.

attractions

Boldt Castle, located on Heart Island off shore from Alexandria Bay, features a beautiful castle, Alster Tower, and yacht house. All of this, plus the Italian garden and surrounding foliage, is a sight to behold. It is accessible by boat.

Grass Point State Park, located near Alexandria Bay, features camping, boating and fishing as its main attractions. Tent and trailer sites are available as well as a launch site and marina. Picnic tables and shelters, playgrounds and a swimming beach complete the amenities.

Canoe-Picnic Point State Park, located on Grindstone Island, offers campers a choice of tent and trailer sites or cabins. Also available are picnic facilities, playgrounds, fishing and boating. The park is only accessible by boat.

Wellesley Island contains two state parks. The **Wellesley Island State Park** is the region's largest and has been named as one of America's top 20 campgrounds. This 2,600-acre park offers 430 campsites, cabins, a beach, picnic facilities and concession stands. Fishing access, boat launches, a marina and a golf course are also available. **The Minna Anthony Common Nature Center**, located in the park, is a 600-acre wildlife sanctuary with eight miles of trails. The interpretive center contains a reference library and wildlife library and exhibits. **DeWolf Point State Park** offers trailer and tent sites, cabins, launching site, fishing and picnicking.

Keewaydin State Park , located near Alexandria Bay, offers a variety of facilities for fishing and boating. Tent and trailer sites, picnic tables, a swimming pool and hiking trails are also available. Winter activities include ice skating and cross-country skiing.

Mary Island State Park is only accessible by boat. Activities include camping, picnicking, fishing and, of course, boating.

King Point State Park offers campers a choice of tent and trailer sites or cabins. Other water activities include swimming, fishing and boating. Recreation programs, picnicking and playgrounds are also offered. Cross-country skiing is the popular winter activity.

Cornwall Brothers Store is located on the waterfront and offers museum-goers memorabilia dedicated to boats, hotels and river life. The museum has a gift shop which carries items made by local craftsmen.

WaterFun Village, located at the foot of Thousand Islands Bridge, offers a variety of activities: water slides, go-carts, miniature golf, mountain rafting, a petting zoo and much more.

The A. Graham Thomson Memorial Museum offers exhibits of period rooms depicting 19th century life. Local and Thousand Island memorabilia are also displayed.

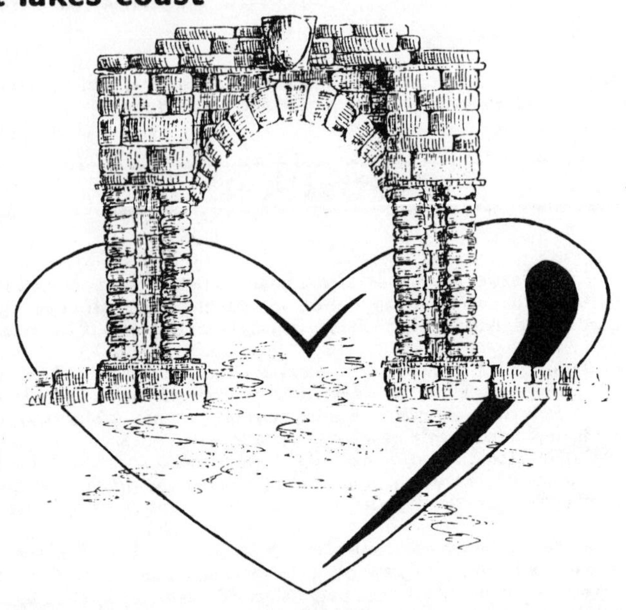

events

The Sportsman's Ice Fishing Derby, held the last week in January, is one of Alexandria's biggest winter events. The two-day event features a "weigh-in," prizes for the largest catch, an outdoor social gathering and plenty of hot beverages and food.

Each year, on the 4th of July, Alexandria Bay hosts the Gala Fireworks Display, set off from Boldt Castle on Heart Island.

accommodations

BONNIE CASTLE MANOR RESORT
Holland Street
Alexandria Bay, New York 13607
Tel: (315) 482-4511
1-800-521-5514
Hrs: Open year-round.
Visa, MasterCard and American Express are accepted.

Bonnie Castle Resort, originally built in 1877 by author Dr. Josiah Holland, was named after Captain Bonnicastle, a character from one of his books. Purchased in 1968 by Don Cole, the manor has undergone extensive remodeling and now, as "Showplace of the 1000 Islands," seems to be as much a fictional creation as the one it was named for.

Bonnie Castle is a paradise for vacationers; every comfort imaginable is accommodated in a grand fashion. One has a choice between deluxe rooms that feature two double beds, King-Jacuzzi rooms with king size beds and a jacuzzi in the bath, Royal Suites that include a King-Jacuzzi bedroom, living room, and kitchenette with a microwave and electric oven, full size refrigerator, and electric dishwasher, or Honeymoon Suites that have heart-shaped jacuzzis and mirrored ceilings. For fine dining, one doesn't have to go any further than the hotel's Crystal Dining Room. Tuxedoed waiters offer polite service and such specialties as Bermuda Triangle (Filet Mignon, Chicken a la Oscar, and Broiled Shrimp) and Roast Duckling with Red Raspberry Glaze. With piano music playing in the background, a meal here is sure to be a memorable event.

For relaxation, one can visit the Florida Room (a tropic setting that includes a gazebo surrounded by a heated pool and a bar) or the "Home of the Stars" night club. Seating for 700 is available and entertainment is provided by stars such as Chubby Checker and Wayne Newton. Other amenities offered at Bonnie Castle are tennis courts, a 36-hole miniature golf course, stables, a marina with 300 boat slips, a paddlewheel cruise boat available for sightseeing and special events, an air strip, ladies boutique, tanning salon, and childrens playground.

For those who enjoy pampering and luxury, Bonnie Castle is a "Best Choice" because "If it has everything...it has to be Bonnie Castle."

OTTER CREEK INN
2 Crossmon Street Extension
Alexandria Bay, New York 13607
Tel: (315) 482-5248
Hrs: Open year-round.
Visa and MasterCard are accepted.

The Otter Creek Inn, the newest motel in Alexandria Bay, is named after the creek which flows into the bay.

As previous owners of the Maple Crest Motel, Roger and Deborah Moyse have a wealth of experience in providing hospitality to guests. The Otter Creek Inn features 34 spacious rooms located on the upper bay on the St. Lawrence River. Fishing and docking facilities are close at hand, along with shopping, dining and entertainment. Rooms at the Inn have a classy elegance with contemporary furnishings in oak finish and inviting colors that are soft yet lively. Modern conveniences are available in each room.

Fishing packages can be arranged with some of the best fishing in the United States found here in Alexandria Bay. Bass, pike, and muskie fishing is available. Roger is a qualified fishing captain who can arrange fishing trips for groups of any size.

The climax to a chartered fishing trip may be a shore dinner. Prepared on an island with the fisherman's catch of the day, this shore dinner is a 100-year tradition in the Thousand Island area.

The perfect location on the river and the high level of hospitality, as evidenced by a number of repeat customers, account for the success of Roger and Deborah's Otter Creek Inn. It's the best of accommodations and fishing facilities in Alexandria Bay.

amusements

BONNIE CASTLE GREENS
Route 12
Alexandria Bay, New York 13607
Tel: (315) 482-5128
Hrs: Summer:
April - October:
Seven days 9:00 a.m. - 10:00 p.m.
Winter:
Closed November - March.
Visa and MasterCard are accepted.

Fun for the entire family is what Bonnie Castle Greens has to offer. Visitors can spend an eventful day playing "not so" miniature golf on 36 holes depicting U.S. and Canadian replicas and attractions. The course was designed and built by Jim and Shirley Kring who, before building the course, did extensive research of the best miniature courses throughout the United States.

The course is divided in half, featuring 18 holes with U.S. attractions and 18 holes for Canadian attractions. Cross the replica of the 1000 Island Bridge to start play for both of the courses. The Canadian side has a facsimile of Fort Henry complete with its cannons. It also has a likeness of a Great Lake fighter and historic Brockville.

A few sights on the American side include the Redwood Zoo and a walk under a waterfall. In addition, the course has three flowing streams, two fountains and a large body of water that represents the St. Lawrence Seaway. This family fun center offers a play area for tots, an all-weather driving range, roller racers and video games for those who do not wish to golf. They even have a complete snack bar to satisfy an appetite caused by a golfing work-out.

Event-filled birthday parties or family and friend outings can be held at the course's banquet room.

The Bonnie Castle Greens is adorned with original works of art, interesting and challenging rock formations, and lovely landscaping. It is a must-see in the Thousand Island area.

gift shops

THE CURIOUSITY SHOPPE
20 James Street
Alexandria Bay, New York 13607
Tel: (315) 482-9565
Hrs: Open seven days.
May - Mid October: 9:00 a.m. - 9:00 p.m.
June - Labor Day: 8:00 a.m. - 10:30 p.m.

Visa, MasterCard , American Express, Diners Club and Carte Blanche are accepted.

The Curiousity Shoppe, previously more of a discount store, is one of Alexandria Bay's most unique gift shops with over 1000 square feet of unique gifts. Since its opening in 1977, the shop has maintained a wide variety of merchandise that ranges from clothing to nautical memorabilia.

The store's owner, Paul Theoret, takes a great deal of pride in the cleanliness of his establishment, and even more so, the appealing colorful displays constructed by his staff. Included in those displays are over 50 different styles of T-shirts, sweatshirts and various other clothing items that carry the "1000 Island" insignia, undeniably one of the best selections in town.

Any gift shop is unworthy of its classification as such if it is short on souvenirs that uphold the theme of the area in which it was purchased. The Curiousity Shoppe has incurred very little trouble conforming to such requirements. It offers items like handcrafted wooden ships, especially the favorites that include seashells for sails, shell jewelry, wind socks, wind chimes and an entire selection for all ages and all price ranges.

In addition to the mugs, cups, postcards and hats that are inherent in a true gift shop, Paul Theoret is constantly in search of new and exciting merchandise to fill his shelves and interest his customers. The Curiousity Shoppe is something more than a dime store that offers inexpensive plastic. It is a place where the browser may find very simple and basic souvenirs as well as some of very high quality. As a sample, nautical brass lamps and handcarved "salty" captains offer fine workmanship as well as the classic ships in the bottle, a perennial favorite of all ages.

Located in the heart of Alexandria Bay's shopping district, the Curiousity Shoppe is within walking distance of all the hotels, resorts and boatlines, making it a convenient stop for all.

jewelers

TREASURE ISLAND
Alex Mosher
Silver and Goldsmith
27 Market
Alexandria Bay, New York 13607
Tel: (315) 482-2294
Hrs: Seven days 10:00 a.m. - 9:00 p.m.
Open Mother's Day and Thanksgiving.

In 1977, Alex and B.J. Mosher went to work restoring a 1500 square-foot shop which dates from the late 1800s. When they were satisfied with its appearance, Treasure Island was opened for business. With over 20 years in the jewelry business, Alex, a Syracuse native, decided on his present location. He once had a shop in Naples, Florida, but has always loved Alexandria Bay and its fundamental charm. It is here that this self-taught silver and goldsmith has established a shop that is well-known for the quality of its jewelry and finery.

In 1977, Alex and B.J. Mosher went to work restoring a 1500 square-foot shop which dates from the late 1800s. When they were satisfied with its appearance, Treasure Island was opened for business. With over 20 years in the jewelry business, Alex, a Syracuse native, decided on his present location. He once had a shop in Naples, Florida, but has always loved Alexandria Bay and its fundamental charm. It is here that this self-taught silver and goldsmith has established a shop that is well-known for the quality of its jewelry and finery.

Treasure Island, with its hardwood floors, pressed tin ceilings, and antique display cases, is the perfect showcase for Alex's creations which range from the traditional to the avante garde. The shop has over 400 styles of silver earrings. The gold items, priced by the gram, are the best price to be found anywhere. The work of other craftsmen is also available, made of such precious stones as diamonds, rubies, jade, natural turquoise and quality crystals.

In their off season, Alex and B.J. search the Eastern seaboard for truly unusual, creative and innovative jewelry and gift items, making their shop unique not only for Alexandria Bay but for the whole region as well. Additional treasures in their store include lead crystal and paperweights of Mt. St. Helen's ash, sculpted dragons and castles, brass lanterns, and Japanese porcelain masks. Exotic leather goods are also available made from eelskin, frogskin, anteater, and ostrich leg.

What does Alex enjoy most about running his own shop? Changing and displaying new merchandise each year to keep the store fresh to display commissioned pieces. B.J. and Alex have created a special place where visitors can search for treasures and make new discoveries. Alex's knowledge of the industry's changing fashions and the effort to find unique, high quality merchandise that can be moderately priced makes Treasure Island a "Best Choice" for jewelry collectors and treasure hunters alike.

points of interest

BOLDT CASTLE
Heart Island
Alexandria Bay New York 13607
Tel: (315) 482-2501
1-800-8ISLAND
Hrs: May 19 - October 7: 10:00 a.m. - 6:00 p.m.

In the middle of Heart Island rises a six-story structure that symbolizes a man's love for a woman. Boldt Castle was to be a precious gift from George C. Boldt to his wife Louise. In 1900, this proprietor of the Waldorf Astoria planned to build a full-sized replica of a Rhineland Castle to present to his wife. In January of 1904, Mrs. Boldt died suddenly, and with over $2.5 million invested in the castle, all construction was put to a halt. Three hundred workmen left the island never to return again. The 120 rooms were not to be finished or furnished. Visitors to the Thousand Islands are able to see the 11 buildings located here that were to be the summer home of Mr. Boldt and his family.

In 1977, The Thousand Islands Bridge Authority assumed ownership of the Island and Castle and has since been working to preserve it though revenues from the Castle operation. Now, many can enjoy this romantic island. Interpretational signs on the grounds guide visitors and give greater insight into George Boldt's dream. As one walks around the Castle, it is hard not to notice the hundreds of hearts that adorn it as a tribute to Louise. First floor exhibits tell the story of George and Louise and the development of 1000 Islands. For an island so small, there is quite a bit to see.

The castle itself is modeled after 16th century buildings. It is made of fireproof steel and concrete with granite walls that include decorative details of cast terra cotta. One portion of the island was turned into a level plateau to create the geometrically formal Italian Garden that is complete with marble statuary from Italy. The Arch, built at the water's edge, was to serve as the formal entry for visiting guests. The Underground Passage was to provide a way for goods to get from the servants dock to the castle foundation without having to go through the main floor. The Yacht House, the first of the buildings to be listed on the National Register of Historic Places, is located across the water on Wellesley Island. It was to accommodate the family's three yachts and houseboat. Aside from these structures, others to see include the Dove-Cote, the Alster Tower, and the Power House.

A visit to Heart Island and Boldt Castle is a must for architecture buffs, history lovers, and those romantics who love a great story.

resorts

THE EDGEWOOD RESORT
Edgewood Road off Route 12
P.O. Box 218
Alexandria Bay, New York 13607
Tel: (315) 482-9922
Hrs: Restaurant:

Breakfast:	7:00 a.m. - 11:00 a.m.
Lunch:	Noon - 2:00 p.m.
Dinner:	6:00 p.m. - 10:00 p.m.
Friday	5:30 p.m. - 11:00 p.m.
Schuttlebutt Saloon:	5:30 p.m. - Close
Gazebo Room:	Noon - 2:00 a.m.

Visa, MasterCard and American Express are accepted.

Food, fun, and hospitality since 1886 is exactly what the Edgewood Resort has to offer. The full service resort was originally founded in 1886 and has been owned and operated by the Hebert family for the past 40 years. The Edgewood has 160 rooms on 75 secluded acres, nestled on the St. Lawrence River shoreline. Complete meeting, banquet, and convention center facilities are offered. The rooms, which feature all of the latest conveniences (color, cable TV, and air conditioning) don't just overlook the water, they're on the water. Many rooms contain balconies that open out onto the bay for an exquisite view, and rooms can be reserved in various configurations and price ranges.

There are many things to do for fun and relaxation at the Edgewood Resort. For dining pleasure, Oscar's Harborside Restaurant has a breathtaking view as well as tantalizing cuisine. Featured are various steaks, a wide arrangement of chicken, lamb, veal, and fresh seafood. House favorites include the Surf and Turf, the Seafood Platter, and the Chicken Oscar with crabmeat and bernaise sauce. "The World's Largest Strawberry Shortcake" and "Fred's Fabulous Fudge Fantasia" are just two of many famous Oscar desserts. Oscar's restaurant offers a Seafood Buffet on Friday and brunch on Sunday. The mouth watering dishes are served with homemade bread that is out of this world with or without butter.

For outstanding entertainment, the resort has an array of Las Vegas-style shows at the Gazebo Room. The Schuttlebutt Saloon always has some fun and good times awaiting those staying at the resort. Other features include a heart-shaped pool complete with the "Chickee bar" for your poolside pleasures, hovercraft rides, boat tours, shuffleboard, volleyball, and jet ski rentals. Golf, tennis, and fishing are within minutes of the resort. Stop at the Yacht Club gift shop to search for interesting treasures for friends and family.

The fantastic setting, hard working staff, and the dedication of the Hebert family all combine to make the Edgewood Resort a "Best Choice" along the Great Lakes.

restaurants

CAVALLARIO'S RESTAURANT
24 Church Street
Alexandria Bay, New York 13607
Tel: (315) 482-9867
Hrs: April 15 - November 1:
Seven days 4:00 p.m. - 11:00 p.m.
Visa, MasterCard, American Express and Diners Club are accepted.

Located in the heart of Alexandria Bay, Cavallario's Restaurant has a charming Mediterranean atmosphere. The lovely, lush garden entices photographers to stop and snap. Featuring Italian-American cuisine, Cavallario's has an extensive menu with many favorites and a variety sure to please the most individual tastes.

Actually a converted garage which owner Frank Cavallario remodeled to accommodate his growing number of patrons, Cavallario's is one of the premiere restaurants in the region. One of the secrets to its success is owed to Frank's wife Concetta's own recipes. In this casual atmosphere, a super menu and perfect service are two more reasons for Cavallario's success.

Favorite appetizers include Clams Casino DiNatale and Shrimp Scampi a la Frankie. One may feast on live Maine lobsters from the Neptune Tank, ranging in weight from 1 1/4 to 5 pounds, several gourmet veal entrees, prime rib, aged hand-cut steaks, fresh North Atlantic seafood, lamb, duck and pork chops. All entrees include a relish tray, fresh baked bread, salad, potato or vegetable. After-dinner specialty coffees are the perfect end to a delicious meal. Be sure to save room for Concetta's own Key Lime Pie, a favorite with returning customers.

There is also limousine service from hotels and yachts. In the lounge there is live entertainment on weekends and a happy hour. Another element of their success is the friendly, prompt service and the willingness to please.

Cavallario's is a definite must for the lover of great food and a pleasing atmosphere.

ST. LAWRENCE GRANDE
9 Market Street
Alexandria Bay, New York 13607
Tel: (315) 482-6200
Hrs: May - October:
Seven days Serving breakfast, lunch and dinner.

The St. Lawrence Grande, located in downtown Alexandria, is a combination inn and restaurant which features wonderful dining and comfortable accommodations

Just a block from Boat Tours, the town docks, and a shopping area, the St. Lawrence Grande's building was constructed in the mid 1800s and has a flavor of early New England architecture.

The exterior features a large veranda that serves as an outdoor dining area, numerous plants, and finely-cut flowers in a relaxing atmosphere. High ceilings and a combination of modern and Early American decor, natural wood, fresh linen, and the original tin ceiling create an ambiance unequaled in the Thousand Island area.

The St. Lawrence Grande is owned by Jon and Cyndi Weisberg, who purchased the building and converted it into an inn and restaurant. There are 18 rooms available, all of which are meticulously maintained, one reason the Weisbergs feel they have so many repeat customers. Although it is one of the newer establishments in the area, the St. Lawrence Grande has quickly acquired a reputation as an impeccably clean inn and a fine dining restaurant.

Meals in the restaurant are prepared individually to order, and culminate in the freshest, most delectable mixture of flavors. The menu is heavily influenced by Northern Italian style cooking, using light, flavorful sauces.

As an excellent precuria to a meal, try the Grilled Seafood Skewer, consisting of marinated scallops, shrimp, and vegetables. Dinner favorites include Chicken Marsala, chicken and light Marsala wine sauce, sauteed to perfection; Jumbo Shrimp Parmigiana topped with freshly-grated parmesan and mozzarella cheeses and linguine, scallops, and mushrooms in white wine cream sauce. The tomatoes, herbs, and many more ingredients are grown on Jon's farm.

For dessert, one must save room for the Chocolate Mousse cake and creamy cheesecake, rumored to be the best in the area.

The St. Lawrence Grande offers a wonderful dining experience to all. A solo guitar player sets the mood for a relaxing evening in the newest restaurant and inn in Alexandria Bay: the St. Lawrence Grande.

tours

NORTH COUNTRY HELICOPTERS
Route 12 off I-81
Alexandria Bay, New York
127 West Flower Avenue
Watertown, New York 13601
Tel: (315) 782-6642
Hrs: May to Mid-June: Open weekends
Summer Season :
Seven days 10:00 a.m. - 7:00 p.m.
Closed Wednesday.
October : Open weekends
Off season available.
Mastercard and Visa are accepted.

Originally tourists themselves, Ken and Kathy Rucki translated their love and enthusiasm for the Alexandria Bay into a business.

Ken has been flying helicopters for over twenty years, and a helicopter tour is one of the best ways to experience all the interesting sights and picturesque views of the Thousand Islands. From this unique vantage point, the vast multitude of islands, their relation to each other, and the St. Lawrence Seaway can be seen.

Passengers will fly in a Hughes 500 which has a four passenger capacity. Extra time is taken with their first time and handicapped fliers.

North Country Helicopter offers a variety of different tours of the area. The two castle, two country tour includes a journey over the St. Lawrence River, a view of the bustle of downtown Alexandria Bay, a circle over the famous Boldt Castle, and a fly over the vast expanse of Cippewa Bay and Jorstandt Castle, situated mid-channel just inside the U.S. border.

Other popular tours take you over the Thousand Island Bridge System and into the Clayton tourist area. North Country Helicopter is a recognized member of the Helicopter Association International, and has won numerous awards for safety. The whole crew creates a relaxed atmosphere that the whole family can enjoy. Ken's piloting experience and informative, friendly commentary of the local color and flavor of the area has earned him a wonderful reputation and many repeat customers.

A helicopter tour is an excellent first or last stop in the Thousand Islands. Upon first arriving, visitors can get an overview look at the area and decide what interests them the most. The trip could be saved for last so that goodbyes can be said to the many sights enjoyed during the stay. Either way, it is definitely a "Best Choice" along the Great Lakes.

UNCLE SAM'S BOAT TOURS
1 James Street
Alexandria Bay, New York 13607
Tel: (315) 482-2611
Hrs: April 1 - end of November:
9:00 a.m. - 7:00 p.m.
Visa, MasterCard, American Express and Discover are accepted.

Uncle Sam's Boat Tours dates back to 1926, and is the oldest continuous tour operation on the river.

Originally started by Captain Thomson, who gave tours in a river skiff for a quarter a head, the tours have grown to have the largest fleet on the river, with several styles of boats and tours. In its third generation of family ownership, it is still a thriving business. Present owner Ronald G. Thomson is extremely proud of the number of people who come back year after year and frequent Uncle Sam's. He is equally proud of the instruction program, the staff and the way the yachts are maintained.

The nostalgic "Antique," boasting the original mahogany trim from 1926, and the brand new "Alexandria Belle," are capable of carrying 440 people and are both popular vessels. The "Alexandria Belle" also offers lunch and dinner cruises in air-conditioned comfort. She has a third deck, exposed for patrons who enjoy sun, surf, and a panoramic view of the Thousand Islands.

Uncle Sam's boats are specially designed for the Thousand Islands, with shallow drafts that enable the captains to get closer than other tours. A typical tour will take two and a quarter hours and will feature a stop at historic Boldt Castle. Other excursions include an Island Mansion tour, a Brockville, Canada shopping tour, a twilight tour and, of course, the lunch and dinner tours.

There are group tours available and special charters for wedding receptions and social or corporate gatherings. Fall is especially lovely, when the leaves put on their annual colorfest.

The professional, personalized narration by the guides and the special design of the boats combine to make Uncle Sam's Boat Tours the "Best Choice" along the Great Lakes.

WELLESLEY ISLAND

accommodations

THE WELLESLEY HOTEL & RESTAURANT
Rainbow Avenue
Thousand Island Park on Wellesley Island, New York 13692
Tel: (315) 482-9400 (Main)
(315) 482-7700 (Afterglow Pub)
Hrs: Mid-June to Mid-September:
Restaurant:

Tuesday - Thursday	11:00 a.m. - 9:00 p.m.
Friday - Saturday	11:00 a.m. - 10:00 p.m.
Sunday	11:00 a.m. - 5:00 p.m.

Pub Hrs:

Tuesday - Sunday	Open until Midnight

Visa, MasterCard, American Express and Diners Club are accepted.

The Wellesley Hotel and Restaurant, located on Wellesley Island in the heart of Thousand Island Park, offers outstanding cuisine, four nicely restored rooms for overnight lodging, a fun Afterglow Pub and an intriguing collection of exquisite boutiques.

The restaurant offers international cuisine, as well as nightly seafood specials. The restaurant serves a delicious variety of healthy menu items with very delicate sauces. Some favorite appetizers are the Bacon-Wrapped Shrimp with honey-dijon butter, the Carpaccio with herb mayonnaise on thin slices of marinated beef, and the Baked Brie in Puff Pastry with warmed fruit sauce.

One of the most popular entrees is the Veal Medallions with fresh basil pesto, provolone, and pinenuts in a cherry tomato Madeira sauce. The entrees include a vegetable and either rice pilaf or garlic-rosemary roasted baby potatoes. To bring any meal to a delicious finish, choose a dessert from a tray of delectible delights.

Try the Sunday Brunch, which features jam-filled French toast with honey-pecan sauce and seven Sunday croissants with filet mignon, poached egg, broccoli and Bernaise sauce.

After a relaxing dinner, visit the Afterglow Pub. The Pub has an extensive wine list including imported and domestic red, white, and dessert wines, and a healthy array of international beer.

The wonderful view of the St. Lawrence River is a perfect complement to Wellesley's fine food and drink. The inside view is equally gorgeous. The three-story Victorian-style building is decorated with a mixture of antique and reproduction furnishings--everything from Victorian antiques to original wicker items. Upstairs are the cozy Inn-like sleeping rooms and the exquisite gift shops that feature antiques, jewelry, Victorian nightgowns, specially crafted clocks, and original artwork by local artists.

Victorian ambiance, creatively healthy cuisine, intriguing gift shops, delicious drinks, and friendly service can be found at the Wellesley Hotel and Restaurant--owners Eileen and Windsor Price, Jr. will see to that.

golf

OAK RIDGE GOLF CLUB, INC.
Off County Road #100
Wellesley Island, New York 13607
Tel: (315) 482-5145
Hrs: Season: Mid-April - Mid-October
Visa and MasterCard are accepted.

Jack Webb owner/designer of the Oak Ridge Golf Club Inc. felt that there was a need for a challenging golf course in the 1000 Island area. He decided to fulfill that need by carving a demanding course out of the lush 1000 acre site once known as Bolt Farm.

The course was open in 1988, but the actual work began in 1986 so the course has aged already. Most people think the course is aged like a six or seven year course, therefore it doesn't play like a new course.

Oak Ridge has 19 holes, par 74 at 5020 yards. The course is short but still very challenging. It's a thinking man's course, designed to make the golfer use every club in his golf bag. Favorite holes on the course include the 6th hole where the tee off is on a cliff to a 2nd tier green. The #10 hole, par 5 tempts one to carry a 250 yard shot over water for a birdie. Other favorites are the 13th and 19th holes.

The setting of the course is beautiful. There is a 60 acre reserve in the middle of the course complete with nature trails, wild life and an array of beautiful flowers.

The course itself features Penn Cross Bent grass on the tees and greens, which are well watered and maintained. Thirteen of nineteen holes have water that comes into play or is in the field of vision. Lots are still available in the private development section, many are right on the course and future plans include rental units for a great golf vacation. Some other future facilities will include tennis courts,a swimming pool and raquetball courts. The marina is already complete and electric riding carts are also available.

A contemporary club house has a golf accessories shop and a dining room. The dining room offers its own ground meat, hand-cut french fries and delicious steak dinners. The club house also has a private room for meetings or golf outings which can accomodate 100 people.

John and Deborah Wacthl, recreation directors, are always on hand to help golfers in every way. The couples dedication, future plans for expansion, the club house, and the challenge of the course combine to make Oak Ridge Golf Club Course Inc. a great way to spend the day along the Great Lakes.

THOUSAND ISLANDS GOLF CLUB
Country Road #100
Wellesley Island, New York 13607
Tel: (315) 482-9454
Hrs: May 1 - November 1:
Seven days
Tee times are required.
Visa, Mastercard and American Express are accepted.

Thousand Islands Golf Club, one of the area's oldest golf courses, has quite a colorful history. After its completion in the early 1900s, the course was frequently played by tycoons such as Rockefeller, Boldt, and Pullman. Before the Depression, when the club was a private golf course, the initiation fee was $100,000.

The course has come a long way since then. Now it's an 18 hole, USGA, Scottish course with rolling Bluegrass fairways and tight greens. This challenging course features some interesting holes. Holes nine through 16 are in the woods, so golfers will encounter plenty of wildlife, such as seagulls, Canadian geese, deer, and raccoons.

Two of the most picturesque parts of the course are holes 11 and 12. The 11th hole is a Par 4, 330 yarder with an elevated tee overlooking the inland waterway to Canada; on the 12th hole, golfers must drive the ball across the water in to a blind second shot.

The Thousand Islands Golf Club also features a 2,000 square foot pro shop, a driving range, and a restaurant and lounge. Additional to these amenities, the club also provides golf club rentals, showers, 60 carts, and golf lessons.

Built in 1928, the clubhouse is a Mediterranean-style building that was converted into a 120-room hotel and a beautiful restaurant with a view of the St. Lawrence River. Other facilities include a conference center, tennis courts, and a gift shop.

Golf packages are available for guests who plan to stay two or more nights.

Check out the Thousand Islands Golf Club; it's any golfer's paradise; from the gorgeous greens to the lavish lodging, this club is way above par.

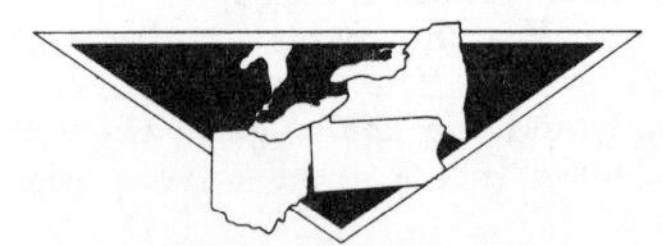

ST. LAWRENCE COUNTY

The largest county in New York State was named after the St. Lawrence River and established from Clinton and portions of Montgomery and Herkimer Counties in 1802.

A Frenchman, Francis Picquet, established an Indian mission at Oswegatchie River in 1749. The county's first white settlement was located in present-day Ogdensburg.

In Fowler, the first talc mill in the nation began operating in 1876. Lumbering and mining followed but were soon outdone by the booming dairy and hydropower industries. The St. Lawrence Seaway and Power Project began in the 1950s.

Today St. Lawrence County contains over 200 lakes and ponds and five major rivers. One-quarter of a million acres of public land are set aside for outdoor recreation. Whatever the season, St. Lawrence County has its share of indoor and outdoor recreation for young and old alike.

attractions

Accessible only by boat, **Cedar Island State Park** is primarily used for camping, picnicking, fishing and boating.

Higley Flow State Park offers tent and trailer sites, picnic facilities and playgrounds. There are recreation programs, hiking and nature trails. Water recreation includes swimming, fishing and boating.

Jacques Cartier State Park has facilities for camping, picnicking, swimming, fishing and boating.

St. Lawrence State Park is an undeveloped park offering concession stands, boating and a golf course. Winter activities include cross-country skiing, snowmobiling and sledding.

Eel Weir State Park, located south of Ogdensburg, offers recreational facilities such as tent and trailer sites, picnic facilities, fishing and boating.

Coles Creek State Park has a wide variety of facilities for camping, fishing and boating such as tent and trailer sites, camper recreation, boat launching, boat rental and a marina. Other facilities include concession stands, picnic facilities, a beach and playgrounds.

The **Frederic Remington Art Museum** contains the largest single collection of the artist's work. The collection contains watercolors, oils, bronzes, and pen and ink sketches. The museum, in the home of Remington's widow, includes a re-creation of the artist's studio as well as artifacts and memorabilia from the artist's travels. Original furnishings and the artist's personal art collection are also displayed.

Ogdensburg Harbor Lighthouse was constructed in 1900, 66 years after the original lighthouse was erected. The current lighthouse is located where the Oswegatchie and St. Lawrence Rivers meet. To the east, the **United States Customs House** stands, the oldest federal building in active use in the country and designated on the National Register of Historic Places.

Robert Moses State Park, on Barnhart Island, overlooks the dam on the St. Lawrence Seaway. This very popular park offers complete facilities for camping, fishing and boating. Other recreational facilities include picnicking, swimming and playgrounds. Recreational programs and hiking trails are also available. Winter activities include cross-country skiing and snowmobiling.

Dwight D. Eisenhower Lock, along the St. Lawrence Seaway, assists ocean-going ships in navigating by raising and lowering the ships, allowing them to pass from the Atlantic Ocean to the Great Lakes and return the same way.

great lakes coast

New York Power Authority's St. Lawrence-FDR Project Visitor Center offers visitors a spectacular view of the Moses-Saunders Power Dam. Exhibits of the electricity that is generated at the plant and Thomas Hart Benton murals, and a carved map of the discovery of St. Lawrence are on display at the center.

Wilson Hill Wildlife Refuge provides a nature trail and tower where individuals can observe waterfowl. Hunting for duck and geese in the Fall is a favorite here.

events

The Seaway Festival in July features arts and crafts, performing arts, music, rides, fishing derby, antique show and chicken barbecue.

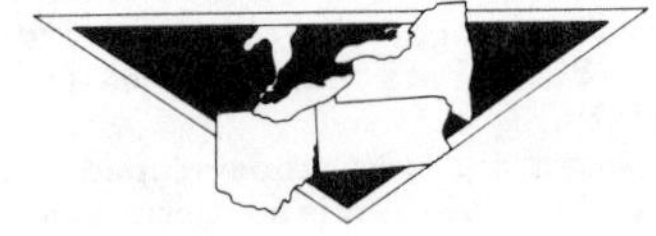

SECTION SIX: FRONTENAC AND LEEDS & GRENVILLE COUNTIES

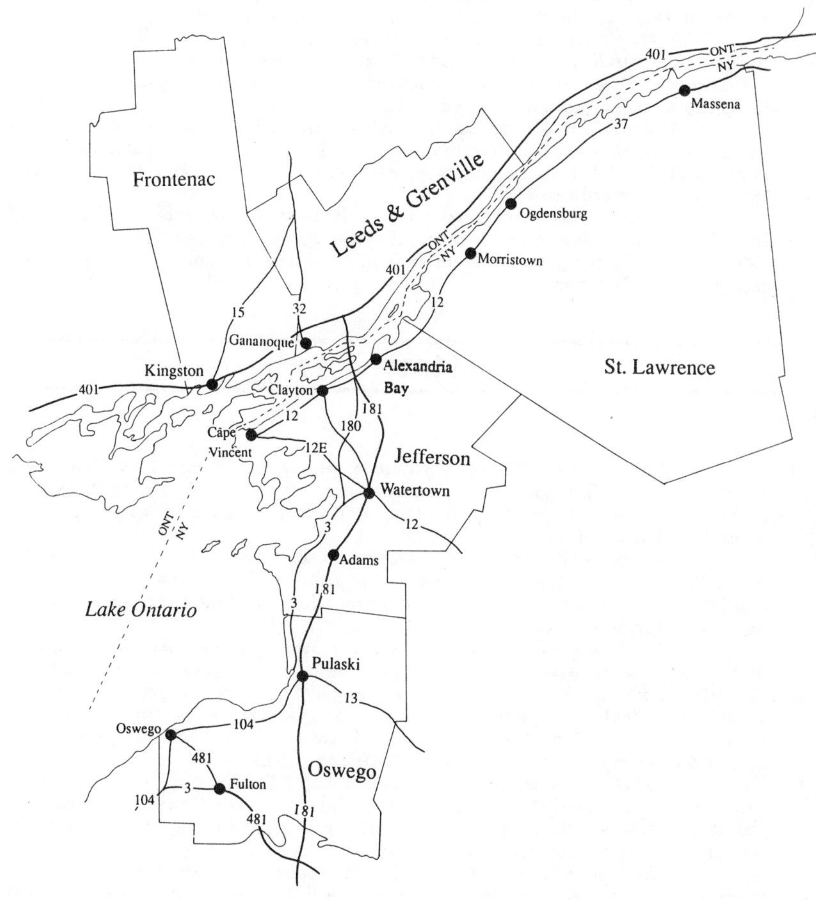

FRONTENAC COUNTY

KINGSTON

Ontario's oldest city is located at the point where Lake Ontario flows into the St. Lawrence River and at the southern end of Rideau Canal.

Kingston was first a meeting and trading place and later became a major military and shipping area during British colonial rule.

Today, Kingston is the home of many large manufacturing companies including Du Pont and Northern Telecom, a growing tourism industry and three universities, which collectively employ a great number of Kingston citizens and add to the city's economy.

Kingston is known as the "Limestone City" because of its great buildings, houses and churches, made of local grey stone. These structures are particularly popular spots, along with museums, other historical sites, race tracks and boat cruises.

Kingston is surrounded by the Rideau Lakes and the Thousand Islands and, therefore, offers wonderful water sports facilities. Boating, tours, fishing and swimming are convenient and fun-filled in "the freshwater sports capital of North America."

attractions

Built in the 1830s and restored a century later, **Old Fort Henry** is a historic site in Kingston. Live performances by the **Fort Henry Guard**, a guided tour, and displays of military uniforms, arms, and equipment are available at the fort.

Marine Museum of the Great Lakes at Kingston carries articles depicting shipping along the Great Lakes from 1679 to the present. New exhibits and galleries are also featured along with a gift shop, library, archives, and 3,000-ton icebreaker.

The **Agnes Etherington Art Centre** combines the 19th century home of the benefactor with six modern galleries and a studio facility. One of Canada's most attractive art museums, the permanent collection contains over 7,000 works including paintings, graphics and sculpture by major Canadian artists, European Old Master paintings, antique silver, heritage quilts, Inuit art, and the largest public collection of African art in Canada.

Bellevue House, the former residence of Sir John A. Macdonald, the first prime minister of Canada, is an early and important Canadian example of the Italian Villa-style architecture. Built around 1840, the house and park-like grounds have been restored.

The town's **City Hall** was built more than 100 years ago and remains, years later, as a classic representation of the limestone architecture prevalent in Upper Canada.

The **International Hockey Hall of Fame and Museum** features a memorable look back to the beginnings of hockey in 1885-86 up to the present through collections of equipment and pictures, among other memorabilia.

The **Rideau Canal** is a chain of lakes, rivers and canal cuts that stretches 198 kilometers from Kingston, Lake Ontario to Ottawa, Canada's capital city. Conceived in the wake of the War of 1812, the Rideau Canal was to be a war-time supply route to Kingston and the Great Lakes.

events

Folklore, scheduled in early June, offers visitors 19 pavilions featuring different cultures represented by dress, crafts, dance, and food.

In late July, Kingston holds its annual **Kingston Triathlon**. Participants run from City Hall, swim in Lake Ontario, and bicycle to Confederation Park.

accommodations

THE AMBASSADOR RESORT HOTEL
1550 Princess Street
Kingston, Ontario K7L 4X6
Tel: (613) 548-3605
1-800-267-7880
Hrs: Year-round, seven days
Visa, MasterCard, American Express and Diners Club are accepted.

The story behind The Ambassador Resort Hotel is a classic tale of the emigrant who begins a new life as a farmer in a foreign country and finds great success as an entrepreneur. Joseph Melo and his wife Maria, originally from Portugal, were not afraid to take a risk when they purchased the rundown 55-room Ambassador Motor Hotel in 1973. After 17 years of constant remodeling and an investment of millions of dollars, the Ambassador has more rooms and more banquet/meeting space than any other property in town.

The Ambassador is now a 250-room sprawling complex that provides guests with much more than just a place to sleep. The hotel's five-star rating has been awarded due to the luxurious rooms that are tastefully decorated with oak furnishings, and marble-topped bathroom counters with some offering in-room whirlpools. Active guests appreciate the indoor pool, water slide, professional squash and racquetball courts, putting green, exercise room, and shuffle board and table tennis facilities. The Children's Centre provides activities for younger guests and daycare is available.

The Ambassador Resort Hotel also houses a hair salon, gift shop, and a Garden Cafe. Dining room favorites include Prime Rib of Beef (au jus) and Chicken Supreme (baked with cheese, stuffed with three ounces of beef complemented with green pepper and mushroom sauce). For dessert, a rich

Chocolate Almond Surprise, completed with an after dinner drink such as Blueberry Tea (Amaretto and Grand Marnier) are favorites of the house. Having acquired the reputation as one of the finest banquet facilities in the area, the Ambassador is a superb choice for any banquet or meeting. Consultants are available to assist with all of the details.

Travelers in the Kingston area would do well to visit the Melo family at The Ambassador and discover for themselves how one hard-working family established a reputation for customer satisfaction that keeps visitors coming back. The Ambassador Resort Hotel is a "Best Choice" along the Great Lakes due to its excellent facilities and a family based staff that cares about every aspect of their operation.

FIRST CANADA INNS
1 First Canada Court
Kingston, Ontario K7K 6W2
Tel: (613) 541-1111
1-800-267-7889
Hrs: Lounge:
Seven days 4:00 p.m. - Midnight
Inn:
Seven days 24 hours
Visa, MasterCard, American Express and En Route are accepted.

Located on Route 41, First Canada Inns was opened in 1988 and quickly expanded into three other locations. All four inns are conveniently located near gas stations, 24 hour restaurants, and other major attractions such as Old Fort Henry, and Thousand Island Boat Tours.

The rooms are very comfortable, well decorated and affordable, with prices starting at $40 for a single. With oak furnishings, accented with a rose and beige color scheme, and amenities one would expect from a higher priced establishment, it's easy to see why First Canada Inns have increased in popularity. Each room has a touch-tone telephone and a color cable television with remote control. Manager Henry Schenk is very proud of the establishment and hopes that his guests will be comfortable. At First Canada Inns, try the Suite Life - an elite First Canada Suite, featuring a two person hot tub, color remote television, king-sized bed, a mini refrigerator and microwave. Beverages and snacks are available from the Limestone Lobby Bar.

A complementary newspaper and continental breakfast is provided for each guest. All First Canada Inns are within a short distance from a variety of restaurants.

The employees and staff at First Canada Inns provide a warm welcome with 75 rooms on two levels and an excellent track record of absolute customer satisfaction. The motto here is "treat the customer as you would want to be treated." This attitude, along with friendliness, initiative and hard work, are primary reasons for the success at First Canada Inns. An excellent location, affordable prices and tourist attractions located within minutes make First Canada Inns Kingston an attractive overnight stay for many.

HOLIDAY INN KINGSTON
1 Princess Street
Kingston, Ontraio K7L 1A1
Tel: (613) 549-8400

Overlooking Lake Ontario, Holiday Inn Kingston is within walking distance of the city's shopping and historical attractions. Historical points of interest include Kingston City Hall, which was built in 1843 as an expression of confidence in the future of Canada, Murney Tower, Bellevue House, the home of Canada's first Prime Minister, Old Fort Henry and the world-famous Fort Henry Guard.

Visitors to the Kingston area are pleased to find out what the Holiday Inn has to offer. The large and well-appointed guest rooms, of which there are 197, include singles, twins, suites and King Leisure rooms, all with balconies providing a serene lakeside view. Room service offers a wide variety of dishes to choose from or guests can try the sixth floor's Roof Garden Dining Room for a romantic dining experience.

The panoramic view from the Roof Garden is one that would enhance any visit to Kingston. The dining room offers a full a la carte menu plus breakfast, lunch, and dinner buffets which are the pride of Kingston. Complement the evening with an after dinner cocktail in the Slip Lounge. Dance the night away to live entertainment and enjoy Kingston's nightlife on the only patio situated right on Lake Ontario.

All ages will find something entertaining in the Holidome where an indoor pool, sauna, whirlpool, exercise area and children's play area are located. An outdoor pool is available in the summer months.

The Holiday Inn Kingston is the perfect location for convention groups from 10 to 350. Seven meeting rooms are available and they can be arranged to the coordinator's specifications. Pointers, flip charts, portable platforms, and public address systems can be provided by the banquet manager and items such as screens, projectors, closed circuit television and simultaneous translation equipment are available on a rental basis. The catering manager is pleased to assist with any food and beverage needs the group may have from coffee breaks to complete dinners.

The Holiday Inn Kingston, a fine resort hotel that offers many activities and is located near historic attractions, is a "Best Choice" for those on vacation or business in Ontario.

THE PRINCE GEORGE HOTEL
200 Ontario Road
Kingston, Ontario K7l 2Y9
Tel: (613) 549-5440
Hrs: Open year-round.

Located in the heart of Kingston is one of Canada's oldest operating hotels, The Prince George Hotel. Originally built in 1809, a 1978 renovation brought National Heritage recognition. This hotel/night spot successfully combines the classic style of the 19th century with the contemporary look of today. Currently with 26 beautifully appointed rooms, the Prince George Hotel is also known for its popular restaurant and night spots. The Prince George Hotel offers food, music, and accommodations to suit everyone's tastes.

The rooms of the Prince George Hotel offer the luxury one would expect from a nationally recognized hotel. Tastefully designed, each room has color cable television, air conditioning, and some have a gorgeous, balcony view of Lake Ontario. These accommodations help to make the Prince George the perfect place for business or vacations. Custom designed meeting packages are designed to suit business needs. The Canoe Club is the ideal spot after a long day of work or play. Seafood is the specialty at the Canoe Club. Guests can enjoy a variety of appetizers such as Cajun shrimp or scallops wrapped in bacon. The catch of the day, served several different ways, is always a favorite. The features of the Prince George don't end at the delicious dinners however, two of the area's most popular night spots are located there. The Shaky Landing is the perfect place to unwind with its combination of all types of music as well as delicious snacks and beverages including a long list of imported beers. The main attraction besides the famous P. G. Patio which seats over 150 patrons, is a club called Dollar Bill's. While Shaky Landing offers a more quiet and even classical ambiance, Dollar Bill's is contemporary all the way. Top forty music and videos will get visitors on their feet in Kingston's favorite nightclub. The young crowd and popular music make Dollar Bill's the area's best place to dance and mingle.

The Prince George Hotel is Kingston's ideal spot for business and pleasure. The luxury accommodations, popular night spots, and fine restaurant make the Prince George Hotel one of the elite four star hotels in Ontario.

RAMADA INN KINGSTON
Johnson Street
Kingston, Ontario K7L 5H7
Tel: (613) 549-8100
Hrs: Open year-round.
Restaurant:
Seven days 7:00 a.m. - 11:00 p.m.

Visa, Mastercard, American Express, Diners Club, Carte Blanche, Discover and JCB are accepted.

The Ramada Inn of Kingston, Ontario is run by Stel Hotels Limited, a firm started by Stephen Edwards while he was managing the Ramada. The primary focus of the Ramada, as well as all other hotels under Stel's eye, is good old-fashioned innkeeper's values. Those values are maintained by Stephen Edwards, but equally by the staff of excellent employees who are credited by Edwards for making the hotel what it is today.

There are 127 beautifully appointed guest rooms, each with a panoramic view of Lake Ontario and Kingston's historic waterfront. Some rooms are outfitted with small refrigerators, but every guest is afforded access to a variety of benefits. Enjoy the indoor swimming pool and sauna; sample the cuisine at Ollie's Restaurant; then finish it all off with a visit to the Harbor Shadow's Rooftop Lounge for a night of fine entertainment and dancing.

Guests will be able to take advantage of the indoor parking facilities, or request a non-smoking or handicapped room.

If sightseeing is desired, or if one wishes to simply get out for a bit, the Ramada Inn is in a very advantageous location. In addition to the benefits of next-door boat dockage and a train tour, all of downtown Kingston is within walking distance. The extremely popular Thousand Islands boat tour heads an extensive list of attractions that include Old Fort Henry, Queen's

University, the Pumphouse Steam Room, the Marine Museum and, of course, the downtown Tour Train.

The Ramada is famous for its Sunday Brunch, featuring omelettes to order, homemade breads, and magnificent crepes. Ollie's offers traditional Canadian cuisine with food that is fresh and made-to-order. The homemade breads and hand-cut steaks are excellent, and the semi-formal atmosphere gives way to the elegant dinner dishes. It would be unfair not to mention the quality of the seafood, but, no matter what the dining selection, the wise diner should complete a meal with the chef's Chocolate Mousse Cake.

The banquet facilities are more than adequate, with room for 110 in four separate rooms and seven parlor rooms. Whether utilizing the facilities for a large group, a family vacation, or a business trip, the Ramada Inn of Kingston is a "Best Choice".

air tours

CENTRAL AIRWAYS
Front Road (Norman Rodgers Airport)
Kingston, Ontario K7M 4M1
Tel: (613) 389-9300
Hrs: Dawn to Dusk
Call for reservations.
Visa, MasterCard and American Express are accepted.

Tourists everywhere, in order to maximize their vacation enjoyment, are always looking for new ways to "see it all and do it all." Central Airways, offering air tours in the Kingston and Thousand Island region, is providing sightseers with just this opportunity. Earthbound travelers experience the thrill of a lifetime as they are lifted from the ground and into the sky and are shown perspectives that can't be seen on foot, by car, or by boat.

A Cessna 172 aircraft is the means of transportation for these flights and an experienced fully-licensed pilot is the guide. Two flights are available at very reasonable rates; the 30-minute flight offers panoramic views of Kingston and one is able to appreciate many historical buildings and details that the terrestrial tourist may miss. The craft passes over the beautiful St. Lawrence Waterway on the way to Old Fort Henry. One can see the star-shaped battlements and trench-works in their entirety, a view that is only possible from this unique aerial vantage point. The 60-minute flight additionally provides a splendid vista of the Thousand Islands. The Cessna 172 comfortably seats three people and it is possible to arrange private charters.

Base Manager Glen Hyde is proud of the courteous and professional attitude of his staff. They show an interest in satisfying the customer's desires. In business since 1946, Central Airways also offers flight training for the novice and the experienced pilot. Aircraft rentals are available.

Located only six miles from downtown, one should take King St. West from downtown and then turn onto Front Road A snack bar is open for breakfast and lunch. Central Airways is a "Best Choice" for those who like to see new things in new ways.

bed and breakfast inns

CLARK'S BY THE BAY
4085 Bath Road (Highway 33)
Kingston, Ontario K7M 4Y8
Tel: (613) 384-3551
Hrs: Tuesday - Saturday 5:30 p.m. - Midnight
Closed Sunday and Monday.
Reservations are highly recommended.

Clark's By the Bay, located just seven miles from downtown Kingston, is not only a family-run Bed & Breakfast, but also a first-class gourmet restaurant. Opened in June 1987 by Clark and Laurie Day, the inn has quickly acquired a reputation for serving outstanding cuisine with an international flair.

All meals are prepared from scratch and are so unique that, for the most part, they defy categorization. Clark spends countless hours creating one of a kind delicacies such as the Cheese Springroll, a delightful mixture of Parmesan, Ricotta, Asiago and Romano cheese; surrounded by a light crispy Chinese pastry and an apple rosti.

The Table d'Hote is not to be missed. It is a complete gourmet experience of delicately prepared food, involving six courses and connoisseur quality wines and liqueurs.

Dinner favorites include the Agneau aux Noisettes, a whole rack of lamb coated with ground hazelnuts and dijon mustard, served with a garlic, port, and rosemary sauce; the Steak au Poivre, a choice of Filet Mignon or New York Strip Steak flambeed at the table; and the Salmon Feuillantine, Atlantic salmon filet, crab and chives, wrapped in sheets of phyllo pastry and baked until crisp and golden.

The scrumptious desserts are always a surprise. They vary daily, but they're always unique and exciting, as is everything else about Clark's By the Bay, including the decor.

Built in 1832, this three-story colonial house has a breathtaking view of the bay and rests on 14 acres of beautifully-landscaped property. The interior is equally gorgeous. The small, intimate rooms are decorated with colonial-period antiques and the perfectly set tables are laden with beautiful linens, exquisite china, silver place settings, and brightly colored flowers.

Clark's By the Bay is without a doubt one of the most impressive, inviting restaurants to visit in the entire Great Lakes Region.

doll shops

THE DOLL ATTIC & CO./THE ATTIC GALLERY
60 Brock Street
Kingston, Ontario K7L 1R9
Tel: (613) 545-1085

Hrs:	Monday - Saturday	10:00 a.m. - 5:30 p.m.
	July & August:	
	Thursday & Friday	Until 9:00 p.m.
	Closed Sundays.	
	Holiday hours (September - December):	
	Friday	Until 9:00 p.m.
	December:	
	Monday - Friday	Until 9:00 p.m.

Visa and MasterCard are accepted.

The Doll Attic & Co., located 100 yards from City Hall in Kingston's historic district, is both a delightful doll shop and a well respected art gallery.

The doll shop carries a range of international baby dolls, play dolls, and collector dolls by Madame Alexander, Effanbe, Gotz, Ann Parker, Robin Woods Bradley, World Doll, Lee Middleton, Dolfi, and Peggy Nisbit. The Doll Attic also stocks Inuit and Indian Dolls, antique dolls, doll books and magazines, Victorian style dollhouses, miniature furniture, and dollhouse accessories and kits.

The Doll Attic also offers teddy bear books and cuddly collector bears by Steift, Merrythought, Dakin, Polar Puff, and Gund.

Customers can choose from a wide variety of books, Victorian fans, linen and lace items, silk scarves, handmade candles, toys, wall hangings, and Inuit soapstone carvings.

The Attic Gallery is located in the back of the shop. It exhibits a colorful selection of original paintings by local Canadian artists. The artwork includes various styles of watercolor works, such as abstracts, florals, and Ontario landscape scenes. Art displays by Aquamedia, award-winning group of six highly regarded local artists (Helene Bowen, Sylvia Faray, Jean Monteith, Marjorie Mosher, Hazel Pidcock and Audrey Ross) are a major attraction at the gallery.

The Doll Attic/ Attic Gallery's extensive inventory of unique gifts makes the shop a premier specialty store, but the best part about shopping at the Doll Attic is the high level of service. If searching for a particular doll or other specialty item, Joan will go out of her way to find it. Joan is proud of her enormous inventory of dolls from all over the world. She has dolls from Germany, Hawaii, Czechoslovakia and many other countries. Send for the Doll Attic's national flyer, which lists hundreds of collector dolls. However, it is even more exciting to stop by the Doll Attic/Attic Gallery. The art exhibits will delight all visitors and Joan's beautifully detailed dolls will win almost any heart.

entertainment

THOUSAND ISLAND QUEEN SHOWBOAT
1 Brock Street
Kingston, Ontario K7L 1A2
Tel: (613) 549-5544
Hrs: Day May - October:
Three-hour 1000 Islands cruises
Departures daily
Evening June 25 - September 3
Sunday - Thursday
6:30 p.m. Dinner Cruise
Call for departure times.

The Island Queen Showboat is an opulent, 300-seat Mississippi-style paddlewheeler that offers vaudeville entertainment, catered buffets, snack bars, large immaculate restrooms, wheelchair accessibility, and sightseeing tours with live bilingual commentary.

This gorgeous vessel plies the St. Lawrence River from Kingston into the heart of the Thousand Islands. Sights include the Royal Military College of Canada, Navy Bay, Historic Old Fort Henry, Deadman's Bay, and the Martello Defense Towers. The incredible sights also include secluded island estates such as Nacomas Lodge, one owned by Jack Dempsey, Indian Island, Isle of View, Stones Throw Island, the Gingerbread House, Napoleon's Hat, and a score of other islands.

Sights may also include historic shipwrecks (over 300 in these waters), exotic fish (over 85 species), colorful sailboats, cruising yachts that belong to famous personalities, and antique speedboats.

A variety of cruises are scheduled: one and a half hour cruises with cold buffets; sunset cruises with a dinner buffet; general sightseeing tours; luncheon buffet cruises; one-day trips; party celebrations; and exclusive rentals. Custom tours are possible.

The Thousand Islands tours depart from Brock Street amid Kingston's first-class hotels, motels, restaurants, shops, and other attractions. The Thousand Islands cruises offer a glorious Mississippi riverboat ambiance, fascinating tours, great food, and live entertainment--all reminiscent of the Mark Twain days.

landmarks

FORT HENRY
Loyalist Parkway
Kingston, Ontario
Tel: (613) 542-7388
Hrs: May 20 - June 20: 10:00 a.m. - 5:00 p.m.
June 21 - Labor Day: 10:00 a.m. - 6:00 p.m.
Labor Day - October 7: 10:00 a.m. - 5:00 p.m.

Old Fort Henry, located where the St. Lawrence River and Lake Ontario meet, was originally built in the years following the War of 1812 as a bastion against further invasion from the south. Now the Fort is fully restored and thousands of visitors each year tour its ramparts, "reverse fires", dry ditches, magazines, barracks, parade square, kitchen, and officers' quarters learning what life was like for soldiers over a century ago. This "Citadel of Upper Canada" is also the home of the world-famous Fort Henry Guard; the 144 young Canadian students that make up the Guard have gained recognition in London, England and Washington, D.C. for the intricate maneuvers and split-second timing of their sunset Ceremonial Retreat.

The Ceremonial Retreat, a 1 1/2 hour long display consisting of drums, an infantry drill exhibition, and a mock battle with artillery support is now one of two shows offered by the Fort Henry Guard. Additionally, they hold an Officer of the Day's Parade which lasts for 45 minutes. The show will begin with the sounding of the bugle calling the Guard to assemble for an 1867 style inspection and will be followed by music, and artillery and infantry maneuvers. Visitors of all ages are thrilled to see battle tactics and drills performed by the Guard. David, mascot of the Fort Henry Guard, remains the favorite part of the show for children. David is a white saanen goat and is the sixth such mascot. It is his duty to lead the Guard when a formal parade takes place; on such occasions he will be freshly groomed, have his horns gilded, and wear a breast plate.

Fort Manager John Robertson says, "We intend increasingly to depict the life of the 1860s soldiers garrisoned at the Fort and the daily activities of their families." Fort Henry is a "Best Choice" for history buffs, with the Fort Henry Guard providing a fun way to see the past brought to life.

restaurants

DRAYTON'S RESTAURANT
271 Concession Street
Kingston, Ontario K7K 2B7
Tel: (613) 542-2777

Lunch:	
Monday - Friday	11:30 a.m. - 2:30 p.m.
Dinner:	
Monday - Thursday	5:00 p.m. - 9:30 p.m.
Friday & Saturday	5:00 p.m. - 10:00 p.m.
Closed Sunday.	

Reservations are recommended.
Visa, MasterCard and American Express are accepted.

Drayton's Restaurant has been serving delicious food since 1988 and, in that short period, has acquired many outstanding reviews and an excellent reputation. This very contemporary restaurant is tastefully done without the glitz associated with contemporary restaurants. The concept desired was a comfortable dining atmosphere, with high quality food and top-notch service. This concept has been achieved to perfection.

The menu defies classification and offers something for all tastes with a hint of sophistication. A dining experience can begin with one of the restaurant's favorite appetizers such as paper-thin Carpaccio with curry flavored mayonnaise or Fondue Parmesan with a raspberry puree. Drayton's salad has received acclaim by using warm chevre with fresh spinach, sauteed potatoes, bacon, and dijon to create a delight for most any palate. The salmon salad with poached salmon served warm on mixed leaves with lemon and avocado dressing speaks of the creativity found here. Heavenly dining continues with a choice of entrees which include Breast of Chicken baked with Brie and dijon, Atlantic Salmon poached with champagne and tarragon, Beef Tenderloin hand cut with red onions, and pommery mustard sauce and many other tantalizing dishes. All entrees have a flavor of creativity and style, a hint of delightful elegance and sophistication, all made with the freshest ingredients. Be sure to save room; dessert should not be passed up. Try the White Chocolate Mousse on a layer of chocolate truffle, so delightful it's beyond words. Also choose from Sweet-Tart Lemon and Raspberry Cheesecake or fine-textured Chocolate Hazelnut Torte.

The ambiance sets the tone for a wonderful dining experience. Tones of gray accented with peach, and subdued lighting create an aura of intimacy. One can tell that attention has been paid to the small details that add up to a great dining experience. The dedication and concern for atmosphere, food quality, and service makes Drayton's a must stop in the Kingston area.

ontario canada

specialty shops

CORNERSTONE ARTISAN CO-OP
255 Ontario
Kingston, Ontario K7L 2Z4
Tel: (613) 546-7967
Hrs: May - December: (Seven days)
Monday - Friday 9:30 a.m. - 6:00 p.m.
Saturday - Sunday 9:30 a.m. - 6:00 p.m.
July - August: (Seven days)
Monday - Friday 9:30 a.m. - 9:30 p.m.
Saturday - Sunday 9:30 a.m. - 6:00 p.m.
Rest of year:
Monday - Thursday & Saturday
10:00 a.m. - 6:00 p.m.
Friday
10:00 .m. - 9:30 p.m.
Closed Sunday.
Visa and MasterCard are accepted.

In the heart of Kingston, located at the intersection of Ontario and Princess Streets, in one of Kingston's historic limestone buildings, "a kaleidoscope of locally made crafts and fine arts," can be found. This designated Heritage Building provides 1200 square feet of space in which to display all sorts of items created by members of the Cornerstone Artisan Co-op. The Co-op was formed in 1981 by a group of 10 artists and craftspeople who shared a desire to bring to the public a wide selection of fine goods while holding down costs by sharing their workspace. The original group has grown to 14 with another 14 on consignment.

Soo Newberry, a professional weaver since 1978, offers a unique collection of scarves, handbags, skirts, jackets, rugs, and bedspreads. Leather crafter Richard Banister features soft and supple shoulder bags, clutches, wallets, and shoes. Warm Corner Sheepskin uses only the highest quality shearing for mitts, slippers and toys. Dunn Sohn, a professional woodworker, hand-carves bowls and vases in order to take advantage of particularly interesting formations. He also produces high-quality hardwood furniture. Other selections include pottery, designer clothing, silver jewelry, marquetry, stained, fused and blown glass, watercolors, batik, and much more.

A visit to the Cornerstone Artisan Co-op is a unique opportunity to view award-winning artists at work. The shop's relaxed atmosphere encourages patrons to touch the pieces and approach the artisans with any question they may have about their work. Patrons will find everything from an inexpensive gift to an item for the serious collector with prices ranging from $2 to $1,200. It is also possible to arrange commission and custom work. The Cornerstone Artisan Co-op, within easy walking distance of the waterfront hotels and the boatline, with its interesting array of crafts and fine arts is a "Best Choice" for anyone visiting along the Great Lakes.

DIVE QUEST
577 B. Division Street
Kingston, Ontario K7K 4B7
Tel: (613) 547-DIVE
Hrs: Monday - Saturday 9:00 a.m. - 6:00 p.m.
MasterCard is accepted.

Dive Quest is Kingston's only full service dive shop, supplying services for commercial, sport, and scientific divers in the area. David Baylis, owner and manager of the store, has been a diver for 20 years and an instructor for over 10 years. David's knowledge of diving, along with the ability he and his employees have to work with new divers, have made Dive Quest a success.

The shop is located on Division Street, a short distance from downtown Kingston. Its nautical ambiance is evident upon entering the store. David has acquired a fine reputation during the last three years after instructing hundreds of people in the Kingston area in this adventurous sport. He claims that "98 percent of people want to learn sport diving but don't know it yet."

Courses are run over two consecutive weekends to teach a diver all he needs to know. Rentals are available for those already certified and the newest in dive equipment can be purchased. Also available is the use of special equipment including Tekna Subs, underwater cameras (still and moving), as well as an abundance of literature. Diving trips are organized through the shop with group rates. Destinations are primarily in the Caribbean, but often include the eastern and western seaboards. But for something more immediate, climb aboard Dive Quest's 36-foot charter boat. This boat is available to divers for day and night dives as well as weekend charters.

Kingston is rapidly becoming the freshwater diving capital of North America due to the numerous shipwrecks in Lake Ontario not too far out of the historic city. For those that crave a taste of excitement or a new adventure, make Dive Quest a definite stop on a visit to the Kingston area. Who knows, maybe a rare coin or a historic shipwreck will be found.

FOREIGN CORRESPONDENCE
297 Princess Street
Kingston, Ontario K7L 1B4
Tel: (613) 541-1063

Hrs:	Monday & Saturday	8:00 a.m. - 7:00 p.m.
	Tuesday - Friday	8:00 a.m. - 10:00 p.m.
	Sunday	8:30 a.m. - 7:00 p.m.

Visa, MasterCard and American Express are accepted.

Many have heard the old adage that in order to create a successful business all that is necessary is that one find a need and fill it. This was an easy task for James E. Martin after he moved to Kingston in 1987 and had trouble finding out-of-town newspapers and his favorite magazines. A few short months later, James opened Foreign Correspondence, Kingston's most complete newsstand. Found only five blocks from the waterfront at Princess and Clergy, this shop seems to be ideally located for tourists and university students in the area. The 800 square feet of space and good lighting here make browsing through the 150 newspaper selections and 1500 magazine titles a pleasure rather than an inconvenience.

Magazines titles are arranged by categories so one can find a particular magazine by simply looking under headings such as travel, business, computers, fashion, current affairs, entertainment, sports, home improvement, and even cross-word puzzles or soap opera publications. Examples of widely read titles that James carries are The New Yorker, Time, Sports Illustrated, People, and Rolling Stone. More interesting than these however are the unique titles for sale here such as Russian History Review, Mothering, Commonwealth, National Interest, Canadian Geographic, Mother Earth News, Architectural Record, Skateboarding, Rugby World, Trains Illustrated, and British, Italian, and French issues of Vogue.

James has the only newsstand in the area which carries papers in foreign languages and the list of newspapers available is constantly growing. The New York Times, USA Today, The Wall Street Journal, and the New York Post are offered along with Ottawa Citizen, and Toronto Star and Sun as well as papers from England, Europe, Asia and the world over. If a customer can't find something, James will special order it. He also offers home delivery and mail orders. James is proud that his store is very successful in spite of the fact that he carries no pornography. He credits this success to the variety of selections his shop carries along with extended hours and the outstanding service given to customers. These qualities also make Foreign Correspondence a "Best Choice" for reading materials in Kingston.

ROB MCINTOSH CHINA & CRYSTAL
P. O. Box 338
Lancaster, Ontario K0C 1N0
Tel: (613) 347-2461
Hrs: Open year-round:
Seven days 9:30 a.m. - 9:00 p.m.

At Rob McIntosh's shop, customers will find savings of up to 80% on a wide variety of top name china and crystal crafted by Wedgwood, Noritake, Goebel, Waterford, Royal Doulton, and many more. The Lancaster Outlet, housed in a 120 year old restored school building and a 140 year old bank/post office, displays a unique gallery of fine china and prints. The Hill Island location features two displays of Eskimo Life that were once part of a government museum. The shop has two gift registries: for soon-to-be-brides, a bridal registry; and for customers who have always wished for a special piece or pattern of china, a wish registry.

In addition to selling specially crafted Hummels, collector plates, fine china, and crystal at warehouse prices, Rob McIntosh features special buys on Gund stuffed animals and flatware sets.

In the past 16 years since owners Rob and Barb McIntosh opened their first shop, the McIntosh chain has grown into an 11 store business. Other locations include Lancaster, Brockville at 1000 Island Mall, Belleville at Quinte Mall, Kingston at Kingston Centre, Cornwall at Brookdale Mall, Niagara Falls at Niagara Square, and Newmarket Upper Canada Mall.

It's obvious that Rob and Barb's "entrepreneurial spirit" has turned Rob McIntosh China & Crystal into one of the largest china retailers in Canada. They see to it that each store carries over 600 different stock patterns in dinnerware and over 100 different designs of crystal and flatware. The unique thing about these "big city stores," says Rob and Barb, is that they have "small-town values."

The top-quality merchandise, reasonable pricing, and friendly service make Rob McIntosh China & Crystal a "Best Choice" along the Great Lakes.

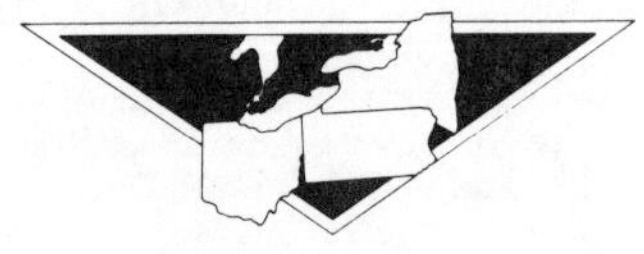

LEEDS COUNTY

GANANOQUE

Located in the heart of the Thousand Island tourist area, Gananoque is a popular resort and boarding place for tours to the islands.

Gananoque's name is derived from Iroquois Indian folklore. The first white settlers, however, date back to the arrival of the Empire Loyalists in the city.

A grist mill, built by a man named Johnson, was the first business set up in Gananoque. Joel Stone built the second business to arrive in the city, a saw mill. Stone provided much of the lumber used to build up the region and was therefore considered by many to be its founding father.

Present-day Gananoque does extremely well and is known for its boat tours. Its location, halfway between Toronto and Montreal, Canada's two largest cities, only adds to its popularity.

attractions

1000 Islands Wild Kingdom provides visitors with a close-up view of polar bears, owls and exotic animals, along with a petting zoo and youth roller coaster.

The **Gananoque Museum** is housed in the old Victorian Hotel built in 1840. With a concentration on local artifacts, the museum features furnishings of early Canadian pioneers, household utensils, and a variety of old photographs.

A fine example of new-classic architecture in the Ontario area can be found in a home built by Hon. John MacDonald in 1831. The home is part of the **Town Hall and Park** and was donated to Gananoque in 1911. Guided tours of the home are available.

The **Thousand Islands Gananoque Boat Line** offers tours of the Thousand Islands from the dock in Gananoque.

The **Thousand Island Playhouse** offers theatre productions from mid-May through mid-October. The renovated turn-of-the-century building is located on the banks of the St. Lawrence River.

The **Thousand Island Parkway** affords a scenic drive between Gananoque and Brockville. There are also 37 kilometres of paved cycling path along the St. Lawrence River.

events

Canada Day Celebrations in Gananoque are held on July 1 each year and feature a fishing derby, music, fireworks display, strawberry social, and showcase of talent in Gananoque's Town Park.

accommodations

THE ATHLONE INN
250 King Street West
Gananoque, Ontario K7G 2G6
Tel: (613) 382-2440
Hrs: Inn:
Open year-round.
Restaurant:
Seven days 5:00 p.m. - 10:00 p.m.

Outstanding food in a historic setting can be found at the Athlone Inn, a restaurant dating back to 1874 when it was named after the Earl of Athlone, a Governor General of Canada.

The inn is now owned by Gerald Schothuis, a Swiss-trained chef who bought the inn in 1966. Schothuis renovated the three-story, red brick Victorian house and built up its reputation to one of the finest restaurants in the region. The Athlone Inn has been listed in several books, including Where to Eat in Canada, and has received a four-star rating by Tourism Ontario.

There are 10 rooms available for overnight guests aside from the bar and restaurant, which seats 50. The dining room features Victorian decor with real linens and china done in pink, lace table settings and curtains, and marble fireplace which is over 100 years old. A second marble fireplace can be found in the bar.

The Athlone Inn's menu features French and Continental cuisine. Favorite dishes include the Supreme de Volaille "Kiev", chicken breast breaded lightly in garlic butter, Saumon Pochee, poached salmon with hollandaise sauce, and Escalopes de Veau "Oscar", milk fed veal with crabmeat, asparagus and hollandaise sauce. Bread is baked daily on the premises.

Located halfway between Toronto and Montreal, the Athlone Inn offers an exquisite dining experience in a setting which is comfortable yet elegant.

BEST WESTERN PROVINCIAL MOTEL
846 King Street East
Gananoque, Ontario K7G 1H3
Tel: (613) 382-2038
Hrs: April - November (Season):
Restaurant 7:30 a.m. - 9:00 p.m.
Visa, MasterCard, American Express and Diners Club are accepted.

The McCarney family history in the hospitality business dated back to 1865 when Great-Grandfather Neil McCarney operated the Provincial Hotel in Gananoque. The Best Western Provincial Motel, owned by Hal and Kally McCarney, is a full service motel with a fine local reputation. The motel has 72 rooms, a complete bar area, a restaurant that seats 250, a heated outdoor Olympic size pool, and gift shop. All units are on the ground floor with front door parking, cable television, air-conditioning and touch tone phones. The interior of the lobby and restaurant is composed of cedar, exposed brick, and glass--a contemporary look with a rustic flare. There are many antiques and collectibles on display throughout the lobby as well. The gift shop contains a wide variety of souvenirs, stuffed animals, T-shirts, collectibles, handmade crafts, hats, plates, mugs and more.

The restaurant specializes in steaks, seafood, chicken, pork chops and sandwiches. Other selections include Prime Rib, Rainbow Trout and Roast Turkey. They also have a children's menu. Guests have the added convenience of purchasing tickets at the motel for events at the Playhouse, Wild Kingdom, the Thousand Island Zoo and Boat Tours.

Maintaining the family tradition, concern for detail, and an accessible location are notable factors that contribute to the outstanding success of the Best Western Provincial Motel.

THE GANANOQUE INN LIMITED, INC.
550 Stone Street South
Gananoque, Ontario K7G 2A8
Tel: (613) 382-2165
1-800-257-3911 (Ontario only)
Hrs: May 15 - Labor Day:
Restaurant: 7:00 a.m. - 10:00 p.m.
Off season:
7:30 a.m. - 2:00 p.m.
5:00 p.m. - 9:00 p.m.
Visa, MasterCard and American Express are accepted.

Located on the banks of the St. Lawrence River, the Gananoque Inn is the only hotel in town situated at the water's edge.

Originally a Carriage Works built in 1870, the four-story building was made into a hotel in 1882. It maintains its French Provincial architectural overtones while its spacious rooms feature all the modern conveniences of a contemporary hotel.

The restaurant offers home-style cuisine and such favorites as Beef-ka-Bob, Fisherman's Platter for two, Stir Fry with either chicken, beef or shrimp, hot and cold sandwiches served in croissants and Phyllis's famous homemade carrot cake for dessert.

A large sports lounge serves favorite drinks while guests shoot pool, throw darts or watch spring events on a large screen television. Exposed brick and dark woods make this the area's favorite watering hole.

Chartered fishing trips can be arranged with Muskie Jake, a world famous fishing guide. Bass, pike and muskie fishing are within walking distance of the Gananoque Boat Line.

Landlubbers may enjoy the lovely courtyard which creates a serene atmosphere. Two outdoor patios are appropriate for sipping a beverage, eating a meal or simply admiring the sunset.

Its scenic location and historic charm make the Gananoque Inn a wonderful place to stay while visiting the Thousand Islands area.

TRINITY HOUSE
90 Stone Street South
Gananoque, Ontario K7G 1Z8
Tel: (613) 382-8383
Hrs: Seven days 10;00 a.m. - 6:00 p.m.
Visa and MasterCard are accepted.

Trinity House is a unique and award winning combination of a Historic Country Inn, fully licensed Cafe and Art Gallery. The 1859 structure boasts a Victorian style of architecture and was opened in 1989 by Jacques O'Shea and Brad Garside. Jacques and Brad are long-time sailing friends who often sailed the Thousand Island area and now offer personalized charters to their favorite islands for guests of the inn.

The newly restored building combines old-world charm with a casual yet elegant ambiance. The name Trinity is derived from the bricks, used in the construction, which were brought to Gananoque on ships from the district of Trinity in Scotland. There are six rooms to accommodate the guests, all with modern conveniences. Jacques and Brad are most proud of the way in which they have added amenities while maintaining the historical integrity of the house. The decor is a historic mixture of eclectic art and period furnishings that will make travelers feel at home. Across the driveway is Gananoque's first jail, circa 1840, which has been converted into a deluxe suite, "The Lock-Up," complete with a kitchen, that sleeps four.

The licensed Cafe on the first floor, with lounge and verandah, seats 40 in a cozy and relaxed setting. The menu offers an alternative to formal dining, featuring soups, salads, and appetizers with an emphasis on healthy, fresh foods. Creative entrees and exotic desserts grace the menu as well.

The art gallery offers displays by local artists and artisans including a varied theme of watercolors and oils, antique collectables, wood carvings, and a line of giftware. With moderately-priced items and a wide selection of styles from traditional to contemporary, Trinity House Art Gallery, Country Inn and Cafe is well worth a visit.

apparel

R.J. DEIR AND SONS
Gananoque, Ontario K7G 1G1
Tel: (613) 382-3823
Hrs: Year-round:
Monday - Thursday 9:00 a.m. - 5:30 p.m.
Friday 9:00 a.m. - 9:00 p.m.
Visa, MasterCard and American Express are accepted.

R.J. Deir and Sons has been a men's and women's clothier and merchant of British woolens since 1904. Located in Downtown Gananoque, the store is now owned by the third generation of the Deir family and remains in the same building that it began in 86 years ago.

The original building, constructed in 1847, is the oldest structure of its kind in Gananoque. The authentic facade and ceiling of the building are still visible while an interesting mural, hand-painted in 1949 depicts the Thousand Islands area and adds to the already colorful atmosphere.

R.J. Deir and Sons carries a unique collection of apparel from casual to classy. Among the more popular items are Hudson Bay blankets and coats, BurBerry's of London, London Fog, Tundra and Viyella shirts, and Woolen sport coats and blazers. Camel-hair jackets, Cottage Industry hand-knit sweaters from the East Coast, and Harris Tweeds rate high among customers as well. On the casual side, jeans, t-shirts and Canadian Marshland Sweatshirts, another popular item , are available.

The store carries private labels on several items, which are created exclusively for R.J. Deir & Sons. Other special services offered by the family-owned business are tailoring, gift certificates, alterations, local delivery, and mail orders.

The store has a friendly staff who are more than willing to help customers with their purchases. Owners Danny and John Deir are proud of the long-running business and are excited to be carrying on a tradition which their grandfather started 86 years ago.

A fine collection of men's and women's clothing by a well-established and experienced clothier can be found at R.J. Deir and Sons in Gananoque.

SIDNEY'S OF GANANOQUE
107 King Street East
Gananoque, Ontario K7G 2T7
Tel: (613) 382-8385
Hrs: Summer (July and August)

Monday - Friday	9:00 a.m.-9:00 p.m.
Saturday	9:00 a.m.- 5:00 p.m.
Sunday	Noon- 4:00 p.m.
Rest of the Year:	
Monday - Friday	9:00 a.m.- 6:00 p.m.
Saturday	9:00 a.m - 5:00 p.m.

Closed Sunday.
Also hours by appointment
Visa and MasterCard are accepted.

Sidney's is a warm, colorful store located in the heart of Gananoque's splendid shopping district. It is filled with exclusive gifts, men's and ladies' fashions, and elegant accessories.

Sidney's of Gananoque carries an extensive selection of impressive brand-name merchandise. Ralph Lauren, Boston Trader, Albert Nipon, Flora Kung, Jones New York, Alfred Sung, leathers by Jeno de Paris, Regatta Sports, London Fog, and Kasper suits are just a few of the famous designer labels found at this newly opened shop.

Owner's Anna and Roy Hicks are proud to offer beautiful men's and women's apparel designed with top-quality workmanship and very classy styling. The store carries only one or two items in each style in order to make the customers feel uniquely pampered.

Roy and Anna are wonderfully warm people who are happy to assist customers in any way. Warm hospitality is nothing new to the couple since they owned and operated the historic Gananoque Inn for 27 years before they opened Sidney's. The short time that Sidney's has been open, the shop has attracted tons of tourists and many regular customers.

Anna adds personal touches to everything at Sidney's from clothing selection to the shop's decor. The exterior combines a striking contrast of contemporary natural wood styling, forest green trim, and original exposed brick. The inside is just as interesting, filled with Roy's homemade shelves and racks, beautifully detailed display cases, and fascinating antiques which all contribute to the shop's delightful ambiance.

If the personal attention and premier quality of gorgeous merchandise weren't enough, Sidney's of Gananoque backs its merchandise with a full 100 percent guanantee.

So stop by Sidney's to choose from a fabulous range of gifts for someone special.

art galleries

TRINITY HOUSE, 90 Stone Street S., Gananoque, Ontario K7G 1Z8; Tel: (613) 382-8383. Also serving as a cafe and country inn, this art gallery features the works of local artists. Displayed works include watercolors, oils, prints, pen and ink, wood carvings, hand-painted porcelain, ceramics, stained glass, folk art, and sculptures. Items range from traditional to contemporary and are moderately priced.

bed & breakfast inns

THE BRITTON HOUSE
110 Clarence
Gananoque, Ontario K7G 2C7
Tel: (613) 382-4361
Hrs: Open year-round.
Calls accepted 8:00 a.m. - 10:00 p.m.
Visa and MasterCard are accepted.

For several years Nicole LaPrairie, a corrections officer, and Mark Bussieres, a chef and restaurateur, had been thinking about owning a bed and breakfast. In 1989 they decided to make this dream a reality and did so with the purchase of The Britton House. This historic Victorian home is the perfect setting for a comfortable stay while visiting the Thousand Islands. Originally built as a home, the house dates from 1906 and was occupied by the prominent Britton family for most of the century. In the 1930s it became a tourist home and was a private home onwards from the 1960s until its conversion into a bed and breakfast in 1987.

The Britton House has four guest rooms that will comfortably accommodate the corporate or leisure traveler. Mark and Nicole have restored the home and one now finds a comfortable mix of tasteful period furnishings along with modern conveniences. This 3-story structure has a red brick exterior that is accented with forest green and white colors. Six side porches offer guests a chance to take in a sunset or enjoy the river view. A classic yet comfortable ambiance is provided by 12' ceilings, original flooring and woodwork, numerous pocket doors, a stained leaded entryway, and ceiling medallions. All rooms are comfortably decorated and each has its own sink. Some rooms offer a private bath and one features its own veranda overlooking the gardens.

Evidence of the pleasure Mark and Nicole take in owning a bed and breakfast presents itself in the dining room. Scrumptious dishes include buckwheat waffles, limestone city eggs, blueberry pancakes, Nicole's homemade granola, and omelettes with cheddar and fresh herbs from the garden. The owners are pleased with the positive responses they receive from their guests. The Britton House, one block from the boat cruises and two blocks from downtown shopping and dining, is a "Best Choice" for explorers of the Thousand Islands and Gananoque.

entertainment

THOUSAND ISLANDS PLAYHOUSE
698 Charles Street
Gananoque, Ontario K7G 2T8
Tel: (613) 382-7020
Hrs: Mid-May - Mid-October:
Tuesday - Sunday Shows start at 8:30 p.m.

The Thousand Islands Playhouse provides live, professional theatre in a beautiful turn-of-the-century building that is perched on the banks of the scenic St. Lawrence River in Gananoque.

The playhouse has a reputation for providing the best live theatre found anywhere. The thrust or three-quarter surround stage creates an intimate relationship between the actors and the audience, who are part of each production in this dynamic setting. The recently-renovated stage is fully air conditioned for the comfort of both the audience and actors.

The playhouse provides a selection of plays that appeal to all tastes: comedies, musicals, and dramas. Previous shows that were popular include Man of La Mancha, Same Time Next Year, Sleuth, Private Lives, The Fantasticks, Noises Off, and The Importance of Being Earnest.

This summer theatre opens each spring in the middle of May and performances continue every Tuesday through Sunday at 8:30 p.m. until mid-October. Selected matinees are offered in July and August.

The Thousand Islands Playhouse is accessible by boat as well as car and is within walking distance of the Gananoque Boat Lines and some hotels. Discounts are available for students, senior citizens, and groups.

The talent both on stage and off, the lovely setting in the heart of the Thousand Islands, and the support of area residents are the primary factors contributing to the reputation of the Thousand Islands Playhouse, making it a "Best Choice" Along the Great Lakes.

marinas

GORDON MARINE
129 South Street
Gananoque, Ontario K7G 2T6
Tel: (613) 382-4315
Hrs: Open year-round 8:00 a.m. - 5:00 p.m.
Summer dock Open until 9:00 p.m.
Visa, MasterCard and Petro Canada are accepted.

Gordon Marine opened its doors in 1976 and has earned the reputation of being one of the most efficient marinas in Gananoque. The Gordon family owns and operates this full service marina located in the heart of the Thousand Island area on the St. Lawrence River. The marina is built on the site of an old coal dock which dates back to the 1800s.

The large showroom at Gordon's displays approximately 30 boats that are for sale, and the marine store has an extensive inventory of accessories, equipment, charts, apparel, hardware, and reference books to find any information for all boating needs. The transient dockage features electrical hook-ups and facilities for showering, pump-out service for the boats, gas and diesel fuel, and ice, all of which make Gordon's very popular among boaters. The service department at Gordon's has an outstanding reputation and Ross Gordon is a Mercury Master Mechanic. This is high praise since only two of these licenses are awarded each year in Canada. The parts department has one of the largest inventories in all of Southern Ontario and can fill almost any need when looking for parts.

Gordon Marine is a very clean facility within walking distance of downtown Gananoque. Boaters can reach the marina as easily as motorists by using the main Canadian Channel.

Its great location with easy access for all boaters, the outstanding reputation of their service department, and the full range of facilities offered make Gordon's one of the top marinas along the Great Lakes.

points of interest

THE HOUSE OF HAUNTS
280 Main Street
Gananoque, Ontario K7G 2M2
Tel: (613) 383-4154
Hrs: Mid-May - Mid-October:
July & August:
Seven days 9:00 a.m. - 9:00 p.m.
Rest of Season:
Seven days 9:00 a.m. - 6:00 p.m.
Visa and MasterCard are accepted.

The House of Haunts, located next to the Boat Line Dock on the Gananoque Waterfront, is the only haunted house of its kind in Canada. The frightful tour lasts roughly 15 minutes and includes the Exorcist Performance, the Grave of the Living Dead, and the Family Skeleton. There are also 20 fright filled rooms equipped with fully automated displays whose effects are bone-chilling. Not to worry, the ghost host will graciously guide guests through these haunting displays.

Once thoroughly thrilled and chilled by the House of Haunts, stay and enjoy a meal in the House of Haunt's dining room or on the outdoor patio lounge. The outdoor cafe serves excellent sandwiches, munchies, Italian style entrees, and special House of Haunts culinary dishes.

After getting a taste of the delicious cuisine at the House of Haunts, browse through the unique Souvenir and Gift Shop. The 4,000 square foot gift shop features hand-crafted figurines, and Quebec's famous wooden sculptures, as well as Austin collectibles, enamel jewelry, Dimu and Suku Eskimo carvings, copper, brass, jade, ivory, pewter items, t-shirts and Indian crafts.

The structure holding the House of Haunts dates back to 1883, but Phyllis and Charles McCauley bought it in 1974 and began to restore and remodel it to open a gift shop. When renovation began, Phyllis and Charles noticed the huge Victorian structure resembled a haunted house, and neither could resist turning the place into the House of Haunts, as well as the intended gift shop and restaurant.

The unique combination at The House of Haunts offers something for everyone. Adults and children alike will love the ghostly adventures and the after-tour attractions. Don't be ghoulish. Make the House of Haunts a part of a Thousand Island visit.

THOUSAND ISLANDS WILD KINGDOM
Stone Street (Highway 32)
Gananoque, Ontario K7G 2Y9
Tel: (613) 382-7141
Hrs: May - September:
Seven days 9:00 a.m. - 5:00 p.m.
July and August:
Seven days 9:00 a.m. - 7:00 p.m.
Handicapped access is available.

Open since 1982, Thousand Island Wild Kingdom (just off Highway 401) provides a 50-acre natural environment for exotic animals from all over the world and North American Native Wildlife. Visitors can see tigers, panthers, cougars, leopards and lions.

These big-game cats and other exotic animals are not the only intrigues that await visitors. Children and adults alike will enjoy hundreds of interesting creatures, including pygmy and angora goats, polar bears, Scottish four horn sheep, chinchillas, cockatiels, kinkajou and the black bellied barbados sheep.

The Wild Kingdom is more than a zoo. It also features a picnic area, restaurant, children's roller coaster, gift shop and a petting zoo where children can feed rabbits, goats, monkeys and unusual birds.

And that's not all the Thousand Island Wild Kingdom has to offer. From June 1 to Labor Day, the Kingdom also provides live shows featuring trained dogs and ducks and a monkey that roller skates and rides a bike.

Hal McCarney, founder of the Kingdom, and Dave and Anne Collis, directors of the establishment, are constantly on the lookout for more species to add to the Kingdom's already enormous array of fascinating animals.

At the Wild Kingdom, children can discover many animals they've never seen before, and adults can re-acquaint themselves with more than 250 intriguing species of birds and animals, some foreign and some native to the United States. This is a wonderful attraction for both adults and children with the beautiful and relaxing country-like setting and the many activities that are both entertaining and educational.

So save the safari for another time--there's plenty of exotic beauty and wildlife excitement at Thousand Islands Wild Kingdom.

---

rentals

HOUSEBOAT HOLIDAYS LTD.
R. R. #3
Gananoque, Ontario K7G 2V5
Tel: (613) 382-2845
Hrs: May 1 - Mid-October:
Office: 8:00 a.m. - 10:00 p.m. (By phone - seven days)

Located at Clarks Marina, only two miles west of Gananoque on Highway 2, in the heart of the Thousand Islands, Houseboat Holidays Ltd. rents houseboats for cruising, fishing, island picnicking, swimming, or simply relaxing on one of the most beautiful waterways in North America. Captained cruises are also available.

Dev and Joyce Nicholl-Carne, along with Frank and Shirley Latchmore, began Houseboat Holidays Ltd. in 1973 with only three boats and have since increased their fleet to 25. What's unique about this fleet is that the owners, with the help of a few family members, have built their own boats since 1974.

A houseboat is the perfect way to explore the Thousand Islands in comfort. The Deluxe and Special boats sleep six adults comfortably and are equipped with modern conveniences including refrigerators, ovens, stoves, water heaters, showers and cabin heaters. The linens and cooking utensils are also provided; guests need only bring food, drink, fishing gear, recreational supplies, soap, towels, and any other personal items.

The boats are designed so meticulously that it seems nothing has been forgotten. Boats feature front and rear decks as well as boat-top sundecks. All models are equipped with gas barbecue grills so fishers can broil that big one they've just caught. The boats are equipped with 50 horsepower mercury motors and hydraulic steering. Seasoned boaters and novices alike will find the houseboats easy and enjoyable to drive; full handling and docking instructions are provided. There's no need to worry about repairs. The owners attend to repairs immediately so that guests' vacations remain uninterrupted.

Rentals include free overnight dockage at all 23 Canadian National Park Islands. Access to the Rideau Waterway and canal system that boaters can take all the way to Ottawa is only a few miles away.

Points of interest include 50 scenic miles of waterways, islands, restaurants, shops, golf courses, museums, theaters and nature trails. Boaters can also visit Old Fort Henry at Kingston and Boldt Castle on Heart Island, (all in the Thousand Islands) as well as the Rideau Waterway.

The natural beauty of the Thousand Island Region, the well-built and maintained houseboats, the relaxation of touring the St Lawrence River by boat, and the reasonable prices combine to make Houseboat Holidays Ltd. a "Best Choice" in the Thousand Islands.

resorts

COUNTRY SQUIRE RESORT
715 King Street
Gananoque, Ontario K7G 1H4
Tel: (613) 382-3511
Hrs: Open year-round
Visa, MasterCard and American Express are accepted.

Completeness, strategic location and superb accommodations are just a sampling of the attributes of the Country Squire Resort. The name itself denotes stateliness. The resort was previously owned and operated by Warren, Rita and Wayne Gollogly until their retirement in 1979, at which time Rodger and Susan Gollogly took over the operation.

After 11 years of improvements, Country Squire Resort has become one of the best in the area. It is surrounded by lovely grounds and caters to families, tours, small conventions and seminars. Most of the recent additions were developed exclusively by Rodger and his wife Susan. The facilities now consist of 70 rooms (10 of which are suites), one indoor and outdoor pool, a restaurant and pub, a complete health club with weights and squash courts, and 10 cottages. Rodger is most proud of the completeness of the facilities.

Many of the rooms feature private screened patios and the luxurious suites are equipped with two-person whirlpools, handsome paintings, spot lighting, and fireplaces.

Local clientele frequent the Dickens Restaurant, a high-quality establishment that features Prime Rib, several steak selections, chicken, pasta, and seafood, as well as three popular buffets each day. The food is great and the prices are reasonable, with a tastefully appointed and comfortable atmosphere providing a touch of elegance.

Other amenities include basketball and tennis courts and a playground for children, all contributing to a well-balanced, family-oriented facility. The Golloglys have invested a tremendous amount of labor in creating a full-service resort, taking a great deal of pride in their ownership responsibility.

The Country Squire Resort has acquired a dazzling reputation for family fun and relaxation. It's an excellent choice for getaways with or without the kids.

restaurants

THE GOLDEN APPLE RESTAURANT
45 King Street East
Gananoque, Ontario K7G 2G1
Tel: (613) 382-3300
Hrs: April 15 - December 31:
Lunch:
Seven days 11:00 a.m. - 3:00 p.m.
Dinner:
Seven days 5:00 p.m. - 9:00 p.m.

A tradition in good food since 1928, the Golden Apple Restaurant combines colonial charm with fine dining.

The restaurant is located in a two-story building with a Flagstone walkway and colonial style architecture. Originally owned by Mefford Runyan, who operated it for 40 years, The Golden Apple has hosted famous individuals and visiting dignitaries through the years.

Present owners, Sel and Shirley Fernetech, acquired the restaurant in 1988. They feel it is a privilege to own and operate The Golden Apple and to serve their guests high-quality food with the hospitality they deserve.

The Ferneteches achieve this by providing a casual, comfortable atmosphere and a menu to please any taste. Food is prepared to order. Specials of the house include Prime Cut T-Bone Steak, Fillet of Sole with Bernaise, Veal Scaloppine Marsala, and Prime Rib, featuring special seasonings which make it a best seller. All entrees are served with traditional Sticky Buns, Tea Biscuits, and relish tray.

Dessert favorites are the Golden Apple Maple Nut Pie and the Golden Apple Pie.

Lunch and dinner are served in one of the three dining areas, each with a slightly different ambiance. From the second dining room, one can see the original outside stone "wall sculpture". A full service bar provides a more than adequate selection of drinks.

A bite of The "Golden Apple" Restaurant ensures fantastic food in a casual colonial atmosphere. It's a best bet along the lakes.

tours

GANANOQUE BOAT LINE
1 Water Street
Gananoque, Ontario K7G 2T7
Tel: (613) 382-2144
Hrs: May 1 - October 15
At least four cruises seven days a week
Times vary depending on the month
Mid-June - September 4:
Cruises every hour on the hour

The Gananoque Boat Lone, located on the waterfront in downtown Gananoque, offers one and a half hour and three hour tours through the St. Lawrence River, passing more than 1,500 of the 1,864 total islands surrounding Gananoque. The most intriguing part of each three hour tour is an unlimited stop at Boldt Castle on Heart Island.

The Boat Line features a fleet of four vessels, said to be the newest, largest, and best-equipped vessels in North America. Owners Hal McCarney, Harry Clarke and Robert Beckstead were so excited about acquiring the best-quality boats that they hired a local boatbuilder, Ted Larski, and a naval architect, John O'Neil. In what Hal describes as a " Background operation, " the men built the king of ships they wanted--riverboats with the elegance of the Queen Mary but the efficiency of a Boeing 747.

The boats feature complete facilities onboard: large, clean washrooms, a kitchen area for preparing meals and light snacks, heat for chilly spring and fall days, two enclosed lower decks, full, walk-around decks, and tour narrations in both French and English.

The vessels wind through scenic islands formed during the last Ice Age. Now the summer residences of Canadians and Americans alike, these magnificent islands were originally settled by Iroquois Indians and are rich in history.

In addition to seeing beautiful islands and Boldt Castle, tourists can view the famous Zavikin Island Bridge--the shortest international bridge in the world, which connects an American island and a Canadian island.

The Gananoque Boat Line provides guests with relaxing cruises and quality service. This is one tour not to miss no matter what time of the year. The scenery is gorgeous year-round.

THOUSAND ISLAND TOURS INC.
780 King Street West
Gananoque, Ontario K7G 2H5
Tel: (800) 267-9497

Hrs:	Colonial Resort	Open year-round
	Hill Island Resort	May - October
	Horse Drawn Trolley Tours	May - October
	Wentworth Lady 1000 Island Cruise	May - October

Call for times and tickets.
Visa and MasterCard are accepted.

Situated in Ontario's scenic Thousand Islands, Thousand Island Tours and Travel Inc. is the region's largest receptive tour operator.

For over a decade, motorcoach tours, conference delegates, school groups and family vacationers have enjoyed the comforts and hospitality of Thousand Island Tours' two owned/operated resort properties, the Colonial and Hill Island Resorts.

Two distinctively different but equally popular properties, the Colonial and Hill Island Resorts complement the area's natural beauty while including a wide range of amenities from large scenic patio decks to an indoor health club.

Boat cruises are a must for all visitors to the Thousand Islands area and the Wentworth Lady Tour boat provides passengers with the most intimate view of the islands available. The personal touch provided by the captain's live commentary and the vessel's ability to travel the swift waters and narrow channels allow visitors to see the islands at their best - up close.

A multi-service company, Thousand Island Tours has the required expertise and facilities to handle all vacation plans and is the "Best Choice" in the Thousand Islands area.

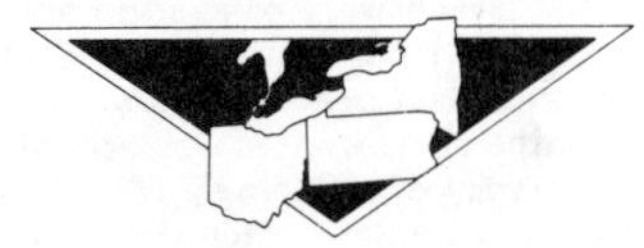

GREAT LAKES COAST BIBLIOGRAPHY

Condon, George E. *Stars in the Water: The Story of the Erie Canal.* New York: Doubleday & Company, Inc., 1974.

Flying the Colors: Ohio Facts by John Clements Research, Inc., Dallas, Texas.

Harlow, Alvin F. *Old Towpaths: The Story of the American Canal Era.* New York and London: D. Appleton and Company, 1926.

New York Atlas & Gazetteer. DeLorme Mapping Company, Freeport, Maine, 1987.

Ohio Atlas & Gazetteer. DeLorme Mapping Company, Freeport, Maine, 1987.

Pennsylvania Atlas & Gazetteer. DeLorme Mapping Company, Freeport, Maine, 1987.

Stover, John F. *The Life and Decline of the American Railroad.* New York: Oxford University Press, Inc., 1970.

TourBook - Illinois/Indiana/Ohio. American Automobile Association, Falls Church, Virginia, 1989.

TourBook - New Jersey/Pennsylvania. American Automobile Association, Falls Church, Virginia, 1989.

TourBook - New York. American Automobile Association, Falls Church, Virginia, 1989.

Willoughby, William R. *The St. Lawrence Waterway: A Study in Politics and Diplomacy.* Madison: The University of Wisconsin Press, 1961.

INDEX

notes

notes

notes

notes

notes

notes

notes

notes

notes

notes

notes